U.S. Master Estate and Gift Tax Guide

2013—2014 KEY TRANSFER TAX FIGURES

ANNUAL GIFT TAX EXCLUSIONS

	2013	2014
Per Donee	$14,000[1]	$14,000[1]
Split Gifts by Spouses	$28,000[1]	$28,000[1]
Gift to Noncitizen Spouse	$143,000[1]	$145,000[1]

ESTATE & GIFT TAX APPLICABLE CREDIT AND EXCLUSION AMOUNTS

Year	Applicable Credit	Applicable Exclusion
2000 and 2001	$220,550	$675,000
2002 and 2003	$345,800	$1,000,000
2004 and 2005	$555,800	$1,500,000
2006, 2007, and 2008	$780,800	$2,000,000
2009	$1,455,800	$3,500,000
2010*	$1,730,800	$5,000,000

Note: The gift tax applicable exclusion amount was $1 million for gifts made after 2001 and before 2011. For gifts made in 2010, the gift tax applicable credit amount was $330,800 because the maximum gift tax rate was 35%.

* Under the Tax Relief, Unemployment Insurance Reauthorization, and Job Creation Act of 2010 (Tax Relief Act of 2010), the estate of a decedent dying in 2010 could elect to have the estate tax not apply and instead have the basis of assets acquired from the decedent determined under the modified carryover basis rules.

ESTATE & GIFT APPLICABLE CREDIT AND BASIC EXCLUSION AMOUNTS

Year	Applicable Credit	Basic Exclusion
2011	$1,730,800	$5,000,000
2012	$1,772,800[1]	$5,120,000[1]
2013	$2,045,800[1]	$5,250,000[1]
2014	$2,081,800[1]	$5,340,000[1]

Note: The Tax Relief Act of 2010 added the concept of portability of a deceased spouse's unused exclusion amount, beginning in 2011. Accordingly, the term "applicable exclusion amount" is the sum of the "basic exclusion amount" and the "deceased spousal unused exclusion amount." The applicable credit amount shown is computed using the basic exclusion amount.

	Applicable Credit	Applicable Exclusion
Nonresidents Not Citizens (no treaty provision)	$13,000	$60,000

GENERATION-SKIPPING TRANSFER TAX

Year	GST Tax Exemption	Maximum GST Tax Rate
2000	$1,030,000	55%
2001	$1,060,000	55%
2002	$1,100,000	50%
2003	$1,120,000	49%
2004	$1,500,000	48%
2005	$1,500,000	47%
2006		46%
2007		45%
2008		45%
2009		45%
2010		0%
2011		35%
2012	$5,120,000	35%
2013	$5,250,000[1]	40%
2014	$5,340,000[1]	40%

QUICK TAX FACTS

Business Ref
336.24 C
S.O.
12/13
TS

UNIFIED RATE SCHEDULE — DECEDENTS DYING AND GIFTS MADE AFTER 2012

Column A	Column B	Column C	Column D
Taxable amount over	Taxable amount not over	Tax on amount in Column A	Rate of tax on excess over amount in Column A
$0	$10,000	$0	18%
$10,000	$20,000	$1,800	20%
$20,000	$40,000	$3,800	22%
$40,000	$60,000	$8,200	24%
$60,000	$80,000	$13,000	26%
$80,000	$100,000	$18,200	28%
$100,000	$150,000	$23,800	30%
$150,000	$250,000	$38,800	32%
$250,000	$500,000	$70,800	34%
$500,000	$750,000	$155,800	37%
$750,000	$1,000,000	$248,300	39%
$1,000,000	....	$345,800	40%

SPECIAL USE VALUATION

	2013	2014
Maximum reduction in value of special use property	$1,070,000[1]	$1,090,000[1]

CREDIT FOR ESTATE TAX ON PRIOR TRANSFERS

If the transferor predeceased the decedent by a period exceeding[2]	But not exceeding	Percent allowable
0 years	2 years	100
2 years	4 years	80
4 years	6 years	60
6 years	8 years	40
8 years	10 years	20
10 or more years		0

[1] Indexed for inflation.
[2] A credit of 100% is also allowed for transfers to a decedent within two years after the decedent's death.

QUICK TAX FACTS

2014
U.S. Master™
Estate and Gift
Tax Guide

CCH Editorial Staff Publication

Access the Latest Tax Legislative Developments

A special webpage created by CCH for the *U.S. Master™ Estate and Gift Tax Guide* will keep you up-to-date with late-breaking tax legislative developments occurring after publication of the 2014 edition. Visit *CCHGroup.com/TaxUpdates* to find the legislative information you'll need to keep *U.S. Master™ Estate and Gift Tax Guide* your first source for practical tax guidance.

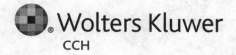
Wolters Kluwer
CCH

Editorial Staff

Editors . . . . Alicia C. Ernst, J.D.; Bruno Graziano, J.D., M.S.A.;
Caroline L. Hosman, J.D., LL.M; Thomas K. Lauletta, J.D.;
Michael G. Sem, J.D.; Laura A. Tierney, J.D.; James C. Walschlager, M.A.

Production . . . . Mohd. Lutfi b. Mohd. Khairuddin

ISBN: 978-0-8080-3641-8

4025 W. Peterson Ave.
Chicago, IL 60646-6085
800 248 3248
CCHGroup.com

Printed in the United States of America

SUSTAINABLE FORESTRY INITIATIVE

Certified Sourcing

www.sfiprogram.org

SFI-01042

Preface

The *2014 U.S. Master™ Estate and Gift Tax Guide* is designed as a reference for tax advisors, estate representatives, and estate owners involved in federal estate and gift tax return preparation and tax payment. The explanations and filled-in forms (compiled in the Appendix for easy use) reflect major federal estate, gift, and generation-skipping transfer (GST) tax developments occurring up to the date of publication. Generally, the law applicable to decedents dying, and gifts made, in 2013 is discussed.

This book reproduces filled-in samples of Form 706 (United States Estate (and Generation-Skipping Transfer) Tax Return) for decedents dying in 2013 (Rev. August 2013). This book includes filled-in samples of Form 709 (2013), the federal gift tax return for reporting gifts made in 2013. The book also includes filled-in samples of Form 706-NA (Rev. August 2013), the federal estate and GST tax return for nonresidents not U.S. citizens and the following GST forms: Form 706-GS(D) (Rev. August 2013), Form 706-GS(D-1) (Rev. October 2008), and Form 706-GS(T) (Rev. November 2013).

Filled-in samples of Form 706-A (Rev. September 2013), the return for reporting the additional tax owing on recapture of the benefits of a special use valuation election; Form 706-D (Rev. December 2008), to be used by qualified heirs to report and pay the additional estate tax due under Code Sec. 2057 when certain taxable events occur with respect to qualified family-owned business interests; and Form 706-QDT (Rev. August 2013), the estate tax return for qualified domestic trusts, are also reproduced herein.

An End to the Transfer Tax Law Uncertainty

The enactment of the American Taxpayer Relief Act (ATRA) on January 2, 2013, brought an end to more than 10 years of uncertainty regarding the transfer tax law that had begun with the passage of the Economic Growth and Tax Relief Reconciliation Act of 2001 (EGTRRA), and later, the Tax Relief, Unemployment Insurance Reauthorization, and Job Creation Act of 2010 (Tax Relief Act of 2010). Taken together, these three tax acts lowered the estate, gift, and GST tax rates, raised the transfer tax exclusions and exemptions, provided for a one-year repeal of the estate and GST taxes (in 2010) and, thereafter, permanently reinstated the estate and GST taxes (for 2011 and beyond).

With the exception of the early-year passage of ATRA, 2013 was largely devoid of legislative changes to the transfer tax law. However, the *2014 Guide* discusses significant regulatory and judicial changes that have occurred in 2013. Chief among these is the IRS's guidance on how the Internal Revenue Code and related tax rules will be implemented in light of the U.S. Supreme Court's landmark *Windsor* decision. In *Windsor*, the Court, on Constitutional grounds, invalidated section 3 of the federal Defense of Marriage Act, which had defined marriage as a legal union between one man and one woman. Interpreting the *Windsor* holding, the IRS has concluded that same-sex couples who are legally married in jurisdictions that recognize their marriages will now be treated as married for federal tax purposes, regardless of whether or not the jurisdiction of their residence recognizes same-sex marriages.

For latest legislative updates and changes to the Guide, see www.CCHGroup.com/Tax Updates.

November 2013

Table of Contents

UNIFIED ESTATE AND GIFT TRANSFER TAX

Chapter 1

OVERVIEW; RATES AND CREDITS

¶ 3 Transfer Tax Rules Made Permanent

On January 2, 2013, President Obama signed into law the American Taxpayer Relief Act of 2012 (P.L. 112-240) (ATRA). In so doing, the President ended the uncertainty that has swirled around the estate and gift taxes since passage of the Economic Growth and Tax Relief Reconciliation Act of 2001 (EGTRRA). When enacted in 2001, EGTRRA provided a wide range of changes to the estate, gift, and generation-skipping transfer (GST) taxes. Most of these provisions were favorable to donors and estates, including, most notably, phased-in reductions in tax rates and increases in exclusion amounts, culminating in 2009 with a maximum estate and GST tax rate of 45 percent and an applicable exclusion amount of $3,500,000. In 2010, the estate and GST taxes were to be repealed. However, because of the deep division in Congress at the time (and application of a Senate procedural rule), the repeal would only be effective for 2010; thereafter, a "sunset" provision would apply, and estate, gift, and GST rules that were applicable before EGTRRA would be reinstated, including a 55-percent maximum rate for most estates, and an exclusion amount of $1 million.

Although there were several efforts in Congress after passage of the 2001 Act to deal with the impending repeal (in 2010), and reinstatement (in 2011), nothing happened until the impasse was finally broken on December 17, 2010, with passage of the Tax Relief, Unemployment Insurance Reauthorization, and Job Creation Act of 2010 (P.L 111-312) (Tax Relief Act of 2010).

Some of the major provisions of the 2010 Act related to the federal transfer taxes are listed below. For the most part, the 2010 Act extended changes made by the 2001 Act for an additional two years. Thus, unless noted to the contrary, these changes (most of which were later made permanent by ATRA) were to apply to transfers from decedents dying, and lifetime transfers made, after December 31, 2009, and before January 1, 2013:

• Estate tax restored, at a maximum tax rate of 35 percent and an applicable exclusion amount of $5 million, for 2010 through 2012 (¶ 10).

• GST tax restored, but at a tax rate of zero for 2010, a 35-percent rate for 2011 and 2012, and a $5 million exemption for 2010 through 2012 (see ¶ 2455 and ¶ 2459).

- Gift tax rate remained at 35 percent for 2010 through 2012, but the applicable exclusion amount was $1 million in 2010, and $5 million in 2011 and 2012 (¶2005 and ¶2007).

- Applicable exclusion amount for estate and gift taxes, and exemption amount for the GST tax, indexed for inflation for estates of decedents dying, and gifts and GSTs made in 2011 and 2012.

- Stepped-up basis Code Sec. 1014 restored for 2010 and beyond, except that the estates of decedents dying in 2010 could elect out of the estate tax and apply the carryover basis rules (see ¶121).

- Carryover basis (Code Sec. 1022) repealed for 2010 (see ¶121), unless the estate executor made a special election for decedents dying in 2010 to apply pre-2010 Act law (carryover basis rules, but no estate tax liability).

- Beginning in 2011, the estate of a surviving spouse could qualify to utilize the unused portion of the estate tax applicable exclusion amount of his or her last predeceased spouse. An election on the part of the estate of the first spouse to die was required (see ¶16).

Changes that originated with the 2001 Act that continued to apply under the Tax Relief Act of 2010 included the following items.

- The estate tax deduction for state death taxes paid (Code Sec. 2058) continued to apply through 2012, but was to expire for estates of decedents dying after December 31, 2012 (see ¶1144). For decedents dying after that date, the state death tax credit (Code Sec. 2011) will apply (see ¶1145).

- The repeal of the distance requirements for the exclusion of a qualified conservation easement (Code Sec. 2031(c)) were to remain in effect through December 31, 2012 (see ¶253).

- Lifetime indirect skips under the GST tax rules qualified for a deemed (automatic) allocation of the GST exemption (Code Sec. 2632(c)(1)), through December 31, 2012 (see ¶2455).

- Retroactive allocations of unused GST tax exemptions in situations involving unnatural orders of deaths continued to be available through December 31, 2012 (Code Sec. 2632(d)(1))(see ¶2455).

- Qualified severance of trusts under the GST rules of Code Sec. 2642(a)(3) were to be available through December 31, 2012 (see ¶2455).

- GST relief provisions that allowed executors to file for extensions of time: (1) to correct an inadvertent failure to claim the transferor's GST exemption, or (2) to correct an allocation where the transferor did not fully comply with (but had substantially complied with) all GST allocations rules, were to remain in effect through December 31, 2012 (Code Sec. 2642(g)) (see ¶2455).

- For purposes of qualifying an estate for the installment payment of estate tax, the maximum number of partners or shareholders in a closely held business owned by a decedent at time of death was to remain at 45 for estates of decedents dying before January 1, 2013 (Code Sec. 6166(b)) (see ¶1672).

American Taxpayer Relief Act of 2012 (ATRA)

As a result of the elimination of the EGTRRA sunset provision by ATRA, the estates of decedents dying, gifts and GSTs made after December 31, 2012, will not be subject to a lower exclusion/exemption amount (Code Secs. 2010 and 2631).

The applicable tax rates and exclusion amounts are discussed separately at ¶10 and ¶15, respectively.

In addition to provisions relating to the transfer tax rates and exclusions (including annual inflation adjustments), ATRA made permanent most of the provisions that were effective under EGTRRA and the Tax Relief Act of 2010. Thus, the portability election of the deceased spousal unused exclusion (DSUE); the stepped-up basis of inherited property rules; the deduction for state death taxes paid; liberalized rules relating to the GST rules, qualification for installment payment of estate taxes and the estate tax exclusion for conservation easements; were made permanent. The application of the carryover basis at death rules continued to apply to one year only (2010), and only if an estate made the carryover basis election (see ¶121). Further, the qualified family-owned business interest (QFOBI) deduction was permanently repealed, and the five percent surtax on certain large estates was not reinstituted.

EGTRRA Sunset Provision

Until it was eliminated by ATRA, the sunset provision of EGTRRA (Act Sec. 901) stated that, for estates of decedents dying, gifts made, or generation-skipping transfers, after December 31, 2010, all changes made by EGTRRA ". . . shall be applied and administered to years, estates, gifts, and transfers . . . as if the provisions and amendments [of EGTRRA] had never been enacted." Thus, the estate, gift and generation-skipping transfer tax provisions were slated to revert to what they were before enactment of EGTRRA. The Tax Relief Act of 2010 extended the application of the EGTRRA provisions through December 31, 2013, by delaying the sunset until January 1, 2013. ATRA made most of the EGTRRA changes permanent by setting aside the EGTRRA sunset provision, effective January 1, 2013.

States Pass Beneficiary Protection Provisions

Until the matter was resolved by the Tax Relief Act of 2010 (P.L. 111-312), the year 2010, during which the estate and GST taxes did not apply, presented great uncertainty for estate planners and drafters of estate planning documents. While the uncertainty has been settled by the 2010 Tax Act, difficulty may remain with respect to formula bequests. Prior to passage of the 2010 Act, the estate of a wealthy decedent dying in 2010 would have the advantage of not having an estate tax or a GST tax at death. However, this might have been at the expense of unexpectedly excluding loved ones from receiving property under will and trust documents. Traditional estate planning has often employed mathematical formulas to determine the amount of marital and charitable bequests. These formulas often determined a bequest by reference to the amount of property that could be passed from the decedent without incurring an estate tax liability. Because no estate tax liability was to apply with respect to decedents dying in 2010, depending on the type of formula bequests and how they are used, a spousal or credit shelter bequest (in a marital bequest situation) or a bequest to charitable or noncharitable beneficiaries (in a charitable bequest situation) could unexpectedly be computed as zero, completely "cutting out" persons or organizations that the decedent wanted to support.

State Law Alert: Currently, the District of Columbia and the following 19 states have enacted legislation to avoid unintended disinheritances as noted above:

- Delaware
- District of Columbia

- Florida
- Georgia
- Idaho
- Indiana
- Maryland
- Michigan
- Minnesota
- Nebraska
- New York
- North Carolina
- Pennsylvania
- South Carolina
- South Dakota
- Tennessee
- Utah
- Virginia
- Washington
- Wisconsin

The majority of these state law provisions interpret certain formula clauses in testamentary documents for decedents dying in 2010 as though they refer to the federal estate tax law applicable in 2009. Personal representatives, trustees, and/or affected beneficiaries are given the right to have a determination made as to whether the decedent intended for the formula clause to be construed under the laws in effect after December 31, 2009. These laws do not apply to wills or trust documents amended after December 31, 2009, or wills or trusts that contain language as to what should occur if the decedent dies when there is no estate or GST tax in effect. These laws apply to decedents dying from January 1, 2010, through December 31, 2010.

Florida and South Carolina passed laws that differ from those passed in other states. Instead of automatically interpreting certain formula clauses in testamentary documents as though they refer to the federal estate tax laws effective in 2009, the Florida and South Carolina laws permit the trustees or beneficiaries of irrevocable trusts, or the personal representative or beneficiaries of wills, to go to court to request that certain formula clauses be interpreted according to the trustor's or decedent's likely intent.

Effect of state law "fix" provisions in light of the Tax Relief Act of 2010.—The state courts of each of the states listed above will ultimately decide the application of their state's beneficiary protection statutes, including the effect of the passage of the Tax Relief Act of 2010 on December 17, 2010, with retroactive application to estates of decedents dying after December 31, 2009. However, in light of this retroactive reinstatement, it would appear that most, if not all, of the state provisions listed above could be interpreted to mean that formula clauses would be deemed to reference the federal estate tax law as retroactively reinstated to the estates of decedents dying after December 31, 2009. If such an interpretation is made in a particular state, that state's beneficiary protection law seemingly would become moot.

¶3

States amend beneficiary protection laws.—Several states have taken further action intended to protect beneficiaries for unintended consequences of the federal estate tax repeal for 2010.

Idaho, Virginia, and **Washington** responded to the passage of the Tax Relief Act of 2010 by providing that a personal representative, trustee, or affected beneficiary may commence proceedings to determine whether the decedent intended that certain formula clauses in testamentary documents to be interpreted with respect to federal law after December 31, 2009, including the 2010 Act. These states (joined by **South Dakota**, which passed similar legislation), also enacted provisions whereby will and trust arrangements referencing or measuring a share of an estate or trust based on the amount that can pass free of federal estate and generation-skipping transfer (GST) taxes will be construed to refer to the federal and GST tax laws as they applied with respect to the estates of decedents dying and transfers made in 2010, unless the instrument indicates an intent that a contrary rule apply.

Under a change made by **New York**, a beneficiary designation, will, or trust of a decedent dying after December 31, 2009, and before January 1, 2011, which measures a share of an estate or trust based on an amount that can pass free of federal estate and generation-skipping transfer (GST) taxes is deemed to refer to the federal estate and GST tax laws as they applied with respect to the estates of decedents dying in 2010. This is done regardless of whether an election was made not to have the federal estate tax apply to a particular estate. Such construction would not apply if the beneficiary designation, will, or trust manifests a contrary intent. Any proceeding to determine the decedent's intent must be commenced within 24 months after the date or death, or by March 23, 2012, whichever is later. Similarly, the **Michigan** statutory provision concerning the construction and effect of wills and trusts has been amended to reflect the Tax Relief Act of 2010. Will and trust formulas referencing or measuring a share of an estate or trust based on the amount that can pass free of federal estate and GST taxes will be construed to refer to the federal estate and GST laws as they applied with respect to the estates of decedents dying and transfers made in 2010, regardless of whether the estate elects not to have the estate tax apply. Previously, the statute provided that such clauses be construed to refer to the federal transfer tax laws as they applied to the estates of decedents dying on December 31, 2009.

Florida also amended its probate law to permit courts to reform a decedent's will to achieve the decedent's tax objectives.

For more information regarding state beneficiary protection provisions, see CCH's STATE INHERITANCE, ESTATE AND GIFT TAX REPORTER.

¶ 5 Estate and Gift Taxes

An estate tax is an excise tax levied on the right to pass property at death. Estate taxes, such as the federal estate tax and the estate taxes used by several states, generally do not alter tax rates, exemptions, or deductions based on familial relationship. (The federal marital deduction is a notable exception to this general rule.) Aside from its utility as a revenue raiser, the estate tax has been championed by some as a mechanism to avoid undue accumulation of wealth in the hands of a relatively few families.

An estate tax is fundamentally different from an inheritance tax, which is the type of death tax that is used by several states. An inheritance tax is levied on the right to receive property from a deceased person (the decedent). Because of this, an inheritance tax usually provides different tax rates, exemptions, or deductions based on the relationship between the decedent and the recipient of the decedent's property (such as husband/wife, parent/child, brother/sister).

A gift tax is a tax levied on the giver (donor) of property to the recipient (donee), where the property has been transferred for less than adequate consideration. Unlike a gift determined under old English common law, or the rules applicable in many states, a gift for federal gift tax purposes does not have to be traceable to a "donative intent" (see ¶ 2155). The gift tax was enacted to stop an otherwise easy way to avoid the estate tax: without the gift tax, a wealthy individual could make "death bed" gifts of property to his heirs that would escape the federal estate tax.

If a federal gift tax liability is created, it is generally payable by the donor. Although the tax rates that applied to the gift tax previously were less than those that applied to the estate tax, the rates for both of these taxes were unified into one rate schedule in 1976. Changes made by the Economic Growth and Tax Relief Reconciliation Act of 2001 (EGTRRA) (P.L. 107-16) "de-coupled" these two taxes, providing separate exemption equivalents—and, therefore, separate effective tax rates—for each. The Tax Relief, Unemployment Insurance Reauthorization, and Job Creation Act of 2010 (P.L. 111-312) (Tax Relief Act of 2010) and the American Taxpayer Relief Act of 2012 (P.L. 112-240) (ATRA) generally "re-coupled" the estate and gift taxes.

The generation-skipping transfer (GST) tax is another federal tax that exists primarily to keep extremely wealthy individuals from avoiding the estate tax by using "generation-skipping transfers," that is, passing their property at death (or during lifetime) to their grandchildren (or great-grandchildren), rather than to their children. How this strategy worked, and the method used by Congress to combat it, are illustrated in the following examples.

> *Example 1:* At his death, Alex Able bequeaths $20,000,000 to his son, Baker. At his later death, Baker bequeaths his $20,000,000 estate to his son, Charlie.

> *Example 2:* At his death, Alex Able bequeaths $5,000,000 to his son, Baker, and $15,000,000 to his grandson, Charlie.

In Example 1, Alex Able's estate will have estate tax liability on the $20,000,000 transferred to his son, Baker, at Able's death. Likewise, Baker's estate will have an estate tax liability on the $20,000,000 transferred to his son, Charlie, at Baker's death. This is how Congress envisioned that the estate tax would work. Each generation was expected to pass its property to the next generation (parent to child, child to grandchild, and so on). In this way, property would be taxed once per generation.

However, the situation in Example 2 demonstrates how extremely wealthy individuals could avoid property being taxed once per generation. Because Able concluded that Baker did not need more than a $5,000,000 bequest (he may have had other sources of wealth), Able could bequeath $15,000,000 to his grandson, Charlie. Although Able's estate will pay federal estate tax on $20,000,000 under the facts of either Example 1 or Example 2, this is not the case for Baker's estate. Under Example 1, Baker's estate will be taxed on the full $20,000,000, while under Example 2, his estate will be taxed only on $5,000,000. Under this scenario, $15,000,000 has "skipped" taxation in Baker's generation. To combat this, Congress enacted the generation-skipping transfer tax, which in broad terms at-

¶5

tempts to approximate the tax result of property being taxed at each generation (see the discussion at ¶2430, and following).

Change has been the norm. For a variety of reasons, the federal transfer taxes have been changed frequently. First, as the economy and federal spending change from year to year, the government's need for the tax monies that the transfer tax generates becomes relatively more, or less, acute. This affects the feasibility of making changes to the transfer tax law. Second, changes to the transfer tax structure sometimes need to be made to close or rein in perceived tax "loopholes," like generation-skipping transfers (discussed above), or "estate freezes" (which resulted in enactment of Chapter 14 of the Internal Revenue Code—see ¶2500, and following). Finally, there are ideological differences (usually falling along political party lines) regarding the nature and utility of the transfer taxes—particularly the estate tax. Proponents of the estate tax see it as a valuable revenue raiser, and, most importantly, as a tool to avoid the concentration of great wealth in the hands of a very few people. Opponents of the estate tax see it as unfair: a person's wealth was taxed once when earned (as income), and will be taxed a second time at that person's death (as part of his or her taxable estate). Opponents also argue that the estate tax operates to cause the break up or sale of family owned businesses. (See ¶3 for a discussion of changes made by EGTRRA, the Tax Relief Act of 2010, and ATRA).

Dealing with the changes. Change may be the lifeblood of tax preparers and tax planners, but it certainly is not easy to deal with. Not only does Congress periodically make both dramatic and mundane changes to the law of estate, gift, and GST taxes, but the IRS and courts hand down rulings and decisions on an almost daily basis. Preparers and planners will need to devote time, effort, and resources to keep abreast of all these new developments in the tax law.

Tax Preparers. Congressional amendment of estate, gift, and GST tax provisions require the IRS to make changes to its tax forms. Important court decisions, and IRS regulations and rulings can also lead to such changes. Even minor nonsubstantive changes (such as requiring information formerly included on one line of a form to be listed on two lines, instead) can lead to preparation errors. Accordingly, the *2014 U.S. Master*™ *Estate and Gift Tax Guide* reproduces the most currently available estate, gift and generation-skipping transfer tax forms, and gives helpful line-by-line guidance and filled-in form examples. The *2014 Guide* is generally geared to decedents dying, and gifts made, in 2013. Accordingly, this edition of the *Guide* includes (at ¶2910 of the Appendix) a filled-in Form 706 (United States Estate (and Generation-Skipping Transfer) Tax Return (Rev. Aug. 2013) to be filed for the estates of decedents dying in 2013. A filled-in Form 709, U.S. Gift (and Generation-Skipping Transfer) Tax Return (2013), is reproduced in the *2014 Guide* at ¶3280.

Tax and Estate Planners. Although planners generally will be less concerned with changes to the IRS Forms than will tax preparers, planners have other challenges. Because tax and estate planning requires a forward-looking analysis of *future* conditions that may affect a client's financial well-being, the planner is put in the dubious position of having to be something of a seer. Some changes can be known, but may be "phased-in" or "phased-out" by way of a schedule of changes made by Congress (such as the phased-in increases in the estate tax applicable exclusion amount enacted by the EGTRRA). Other changes were scheduled to expire beyond a stated date (such as those slated to expire after 2012 pursuant to provisions in the Tax Relief Act of 2010, prior to passage of ATRA, which made most of EGTRRA's provisions permanent). Still other changes seemingly arise without warning, and are passed by Congress in response to political pressure or changed situations.

Regardless of how changes to federal tax law come about, planners will need to deal with them. This will mean not only keeping abreast of changes that have occurred, but also of those that are likely to occur. The *2014 Guide*, in either print or electronic version, can help with those changes that have occurred, but tracking impending changes will require a more planning-oriented product, such as CCH's *Financial and Estate Planning* (available in print and electronic versions), and the complete offering of CCH tax and estate planning products offered on-line on CCH's IntelliConnect®.

If the planner is also the drafter of documents implementing the tax or estate plan, existing documents (such as a will or trust) may be impacted by tax law changes. Assuming that these documents are not by their terms irrevocable (or made so because of the death of the grantor), the planner/drafter will want to consider amending the documents. Likewise, when drafting current documents, the drafter will want to consider the use of appropriate provisions that may give the executor or trustee the authority to exercise discretion when dealing with future law changes or other changed circumstances. Drafting document provisions that allow future fiduciary discretion, while not running afoul of state law or IRS attack is difficult and highly technical. CCH's IntelliConnect®, which contains such on-line products as *Drafting the Estate Plan: Law and Forms* by D.A. Handler and D.V. Dunn, and CCH *Financial and Estate Planning*, can be a valuable resource for the planner/drafter.

¶ 10   Unified Transfer Tax Rate Schedule and Unified Credit

The unified transfer tax that applies to estate and gift taxes is progressive and is based on cumulative lifetime and at-death transfers. The cumulated transfers to which the tentative tax applies are the sum of: (1) the amount of the taxable estate, and (2) the amount of taxable gifts made by the decedent after 1976, other than gifts includible in the gross estate. The tentative tax is then reduced by gift taxes payable on gifts made after December 31, 1976. For this purpose, the amount of the gift taxes paid by a decedent after 1976 is determined as if the rate schedule in effect in the year of death was in effect in the year of the gift. The result is the estate tax before credits.

The basic estate and gift tax rates with respect to which the tentative tax is computed are based on a rate schedule that, for decedents dying in 2010 through 2012, consisted of 10 graduated rates, beginning with an 18-percent tax rate for amounts not over $10,000 and increasing to a 35-percent tax rate for amounts in excess of $5.0 million. Despite there being 10 graduated rates, only the 35 percent rate applied with respect to the estate tax of decedents dying in 2010 through 2012. This is because the operation of the applicable credit amount (unified credit; see ¶ 15). For 2013 and beyond, changes made by the American Taxpayer Relief Act of 2012 (P.L. 112-240) (ATRA) (see the heading *"The 2012 Act"*, below), provides that there are 12 graduated rates, with the top rate of 40 percent being the only effective rate.

The 2001 Act. The enactment of the Economic Growth and Tax Relief Reconciliation Act of 2001 (P.L. 107-16) (EGTRRA) brought significant change to the transfer tax system, the most notable being the repeal of the estate and generation-skipping transfer (GST) taxes in 2010. Prior to repeal of the estate and the GST taxes, a number of modifications are made to the maximum estate tax rate and applicable exclusion amount (see below).

Under EGTRRA, the top marginal rate for estate, gift, and GST taxes was reduced to 45 percent for decedents dying, and gifts made, in 2007 through 2009. In 2009, when the applicable credit amount was $3,500,000 (¶15), the effective minimum tax rate for the estate and GST taxes is also 45 percent.

Sunset provision. In order to comply with the Congressional Budget Act of 1974, EGTRRA provided that all provisions of, and amendments made by, the 2001 Act will not apply (that is, they *sunset*) to estates of decedents dying, gifts made, or generation-skipping transfers, after December 31, 2010. This sunset was extended by two years by the Tax Relief Act of 2010 (see the heading *"The 2010 Act"*, below), and repealed altogether by ATRA (see the heading *"The 2012 Act"*, below).

The 2010 Act. The Tax Relief, Unemployment Insurance Reauthorization, and Job Creation Act of 2010 (P.L. 111-312) (the Tax Relief Act of 2010) reinstated the estate and GST tax for estates of decedents dying and GSTs made after December 31, 2009. The 2010 Act also made other substantial changes to the transfer tax system, including reducing the maximum unified rate to 35 percent effective for the estates of decedents dying and taxable transfers made after December 31, 2010 (see ¶11).

Election for decedents dying in 2010. The executors for estates of decedents dying after December 31, 2009, and before January 1, 2011, could elect to have the 2001 Act rules apply, with the result that such estates would be exempt from the estate tax, and the heirs would receive a carryover basis (rather than a stepped-up basis) in property received from the decedent (see ¶121).

Sunset extended, then repealed. The sunset of the transfer tax provisions pursuant to the EGTRRA, scheduled to apply to the estates of decedents dying, gifts made, or generation-skipping transfers made after December 31, 2010, was extended to apply to estates of decedents dying, gifts made, or generation-skipping transfers made after December 31, 2012 (Act Sec. 101(a)(1) of the 2010 Act). As a result, the amendments made EGTRRA and the new rules of the 2010 Act were scheduled to expire for estates of decedents dying, gifts made, or generation-skipping transfers made after December 31, 2012. However, ATRA repealed the sunset provision, with the result that most of the changes made by EGTRRA, and extended by the Tax Relief Act of 2010, were made permanent by ATRA (see the heading *"The 2012 Act"*, below).

The 2012 Act. The changes made to the estate, gift and generation-skipping transfer (GST) taxes made by EGTRRA (and extended through 2012 by the Tax Relief Act of 2010), have been made permanent by ATRA, effective for estates of decedents dying, gifts, and GSTs made after December 31, 2012. ATRA accomplished this by striking title IX (the sunset provision) of EGTRRA. Additionally, ATRA raised the maximum transfer tax rate to 40 percent (from 35 percent), and also made the portability of the deceased spousal unused exclusion (DSUE) amount election permanent, which had been enacted by the Tax Relief Act of 2010, but was scheduled to expire after December 31, 2012. The DSUE election is discussed at ¶16.

Transfer Tax Schedule: 1984–2001

Column A	Column B	Column C	Column D
			Rate of tax on
	Taxable	Tax on	excess over
Taxable	amount not	amount in	amount in
amount over	over	column A	column A
			Percent
$0	$10,000	$0	18
10,000	20,000	1,800	20
20,000	40,000	3,800	22
40,000	60,000	8,200	24
60,000	80,000	13,000	26
80,000	100,000	18,200	28
100,000	150,000	23,800	30
150,000	250,000	38,800	32
250,000	500,000	70,800	34
500,000	750,000	155,800	37
750,000	1,000,000	248,300	39
1,000,000	1,250,000	345,800	41
1,250,000	1,500,000	448,300	43
1,500,000	2,000,000	555,800	45
2,000,000	2,500,000	780,800	49
2,500,000	3,000,000	1,025,800	53
3,000,000	. . . . . .	1,290,800	55*

* The U.S. Court of Appeals for the Federal Circuit has upheld a provision of the Omnibus Budget Reconciliation Act of 1993 (P.L. 103-66) that on August 10, 1993, retroactively reinstated the 55-percent maximum transfer tax rate to transfers made after December 31, 1992. Prior to this change, the maximum transfer tax rate for post-December 31, 1992 transfers was 50 percent. *NationsBank of Texas, N.A.*, CA-FC, 2001-2 USTC ¶ 60,423, cert denied, Oct. 7, 2002.

• *Rate Schedule for 2002–2009*

The estate and gift tax rate schedule applicable to the estates of decedents dying and gifts made in 2002 through 2009 is as follows:

Transfer Tax Rate Schedule: 2002–2009*

(A) Amount subject to tax more than—	(B) Amount subject to tax equal to or less than—	(C) Tax on amount in column (A)	(D) Rate of tax on excess over amount in column (A) Percent
. . .	$10,000	. . .	18
$10,000	20,000	$1,800	20
20,000	40,000	3,800	22
40,000	60,000	8,200	24
60,000	80,000	13,000	26
80,000	100,000	18,200	28
100,000	150,000	23,800	30
150,000	250,000	38,800	32
250,000	500,000	70,800	34
500,000	750,000	155,800	37
750,000	1,000,000	248,300	39
1,000,000	1,250,000	345,800	41
1,250,000	1,500,000	448,300	43
1,500,000	2,000,000	555,800	45
2,000,000	2,500,000	780,800	49
2,500,000	. . . . . .	1,025,800	50*

* For years 2003 through 2009, the tentative tax is to be determined by using a table prescribed by the IRS, which will be the same as the rate schedule shown above except for the adjustments necessary to reflect the reductions in the maximum rate.

The 2001 Act reduces the top marginal rate for years after 2002, according to the following schedule:

- 49 percent for decedents dying, and gifts made, in 2003;

- 48 percent in 2004;

- 47 percent in 2005;

- 46 percent in 2006;

- 45 percent in 2007, 2008, and 2009.

For the gift tax rates for gifts made after December 31, 2009, see ¶2005.

• *Rate Schedule for 2010 - 2012*

A new rate structure applied to the estates of decedents dying after December 31, 2009, and before January 1, 2013, under the Tax Relief, Unemployment Insurance Reauthorization, and Job Creation Act of 2010 (P.L. 111-312) (the 2010 Act). Under that structure, the maximum estate tax rate was 35 percent (Code Sec. 2001(c)). Gifts continued to be taxed at a maximum rate of 35 percent, as they were in 2010. However, the related gift tax section of the Code no longer contained a separate rate structure, but instead referred to the corresponding estate tax provision as it did prior to passage of the Economic Growth and Tax Relief Reconciliation Act of 2001 (P.L. 107-16) (EGTRRA) (Code Sec. 2502(a)). Thus, the estate and gift taxes were again "unified."

The estate and gift tax rate schedule applicable to the estates of decedents dying and gifts made in 2010 through 2012 is as follows:

Transfer Tax Rate Schedule: 2010—2012

(A) Amount subject to tax more than—	(B) Amount subject to tax equal to or less than—	(C) Tax on amount in column (A)	(D) Rate of tax on excess over amount in column (A) Percent
...	$10,000	...	18
$10,000	20,000	$1,800	20
20,000	40,000	3,800	22
40,000	60,000	8,200	24
60,000	80,000	13,000	26
80,000	100,000	18,200	28
100,000	150,000	23,800	30
150,000	250,000	38,800	32
250,000	500,000	70,800	34
500,000	...	155,800	35

Sunset provision. See ¶3 regarding the "sunsetting" of this provision of the 2010 Act that was scheduled to occur after December 31, 2012, but was eliminated by ATRA.

- **Rate Schedule After December 31, 2012**

The basic rate structure that applied to decedents dying and gifts made during 2010 through 2012, will continue to apply to the estates of decedents dying and gifts made after December 31, 2012, with the exception of the rates applied to taxable estates in excess of $500,000. Accordingly, the maximum tax rate after December 31, 2012 will be 40 percent (Code Sec. 2001(c), as amended by the American Taxpayer Relief Act of 2012 (P.L. 112-240)).

The estate and gift tax rate schedule applicable to the estates of decedents dying and gifts made after December 31, 2012 is as follows:

Transfer Tax Rate Schedule: After December 31, 2012

(A) Amount subject to tax more than—	(B) Amount subject to tax equal to or less than—	(C) Tax on amount in column (A)	(D) Rate of tax on excess over amount in column (A) Percent
...	$10,000	...	18
$10,000	20,000	$1,800	20
20,000	40,000	3,800	22
40,000	60,000	8,200	24
60,000	80,000	13,000	26
80,000	100,000	18,200	28
100,000	150,000	23,800	30
150,000	250,000	38,800	32
250,000	500,000	70,800	34
500,000	750,000	155,800	37
750,000	1,000,000	248,300	39
1,000,000	...	345,800	40

- **Unified Credit**

The table below provides the unified credit amount for 1987-1997 and the applicable credit amount after 1997 and the applicable exemption/exclusion amount.

¶10

Year	Applicable Credit Amount	Applicable Exclusion Amount
1987–1997	$192,800	$600,000
1998	202,050	625,000
1999	211,300	650,000
2000 and 2001	220,550	675,000

As a result of changes made by the 2001 Act, different unified credit amounts apply to the estate tax and to the gift tax (see ¶ 15).

The estate tax unified credit (applicable credit amount) and the applicable exclusion amount for the years 2002 through 2014 are as follows:

Year	Applicable Credit Amount	Applicable Exclusion Amount
2002–2003	$345,800	$1,000,000
2004–2005	555,800	1,500,000
2006–2008	780,800	2,000,000
2009	1,455,800	3,500,000
2010*	1,730,800	5,000,000
2011	1,730,800	5,000,000
2012**	1,772,800	5,120,000
2013	2,045,800	5,250,000
2014	2,081,800	5,340,000

* The gift tax applicable exclusion amount remained at $1 million for gifts made in 2010 (see ¶ 2007). Beginning in 2011, the gift tax applicable exclusion is equal to the estate tax applicable exclusion (at $5 million) for the first time since 2003 (Code Sec. 2010(c)(2)(A) and 2505(a), as amended by the Tax Relief Act of 2010 (P.L. 111-312)).

** Beginning in 2012, the estate and gift tax, the applicable exclusion amounts and the GST exemption amount will be subject to an inflation adjustment (Code Sec. 2010(c)(2)(B), as amended by the Tax Relief Act of 2010 and ATRA (P.L. 112-240)).

¶ 11 Unified Rate Schedule

A single unified transfer tax rate schedule applies to estate, gift, and generation-skipping transfer (GST) taxes, effective for the estates of decedents dying, and gifts and GSTs, made after December 31, 1976.[1] The rates are progressive on the basis of cumulative lifetime transfers and those transfers occurring at death. For estates of decedents dying, and gifts made in 2011 through 2012, the unified transfer tax rates begin at 18 percent on cumulative transfers of $10,000 or less to a maximum rate of 35 percent, applicable to cumulative transfers over $5.0 million (see ¶ 10). For 2013, the minimum effective tax rate for purposes of the estate, gift, and generation-skipping transfer taxes is 40 percent.[2]

Special generation-skipping transfer tax rate for 2010. Effective only for GSTs made in 2010, the tax rate applicable for such transfers was 0 percent (the GST exemption was $5,000,000 for 2010).[3] GSTs made in 2011 were taxed at 35 percent on transfers exceeding the $5,000,000 exemption amount; GSTs made in

[1] Code Sec. 2001 and Code Sec. 2502; Reg. § 20.0-2 and Reg. § 25.2502-1.
[2] Code Sec. 2001(c)(1). See the Appendix at ¶ 2600 for the current unified transfer tax rate schedule, as well as the maximum rates that applied to pre-1984 decedents and transfers. See also ¶ 2640 and ¶ 2650 for the separate estate tax and gift tax rates that applied to pre-1977 decedents and transfers.
[3] Act Sec. 302(c), Tax Relief, Unemployment Insurance Reauthorization, and Job Creation Act of 2010 (P.L. 111-312).

2012 were taxed at 35 percent on transfers exceeding the $5,120,000 exemption amount; GSTs made in 2013 will be taxed at 40 percent on transfers exceeding $5,250,000, and in 2014 on transfers over $5,340,000.[4]

¶ 12   Application of Unified Rate Schedule

In computing the gift tax liability for any calendar year, the unified rate schedule is applied to the transferor's cumulative lifetime taxable gifts (see Chapter 34). The term "taxable gifts" means gross gifts, minus the annual exclusion (see Chapter 36) and any allowable charitable or marital deduction (see Chapter 37). Taxable gifts for the current period are aggregated with those for all prior periods (see ¶2355) and a tentative gift tax is computed. From this amount, a second tentative tax on the gifts from prior periods only is subtracted. In both cases, the current unified rate schedule is used to compute the tentative tax.[5] The applicable credit amount (see ¶15 and ¶2376) and the credit for foreign gift taxes, if any, are subtracted to arrive at the current year's gift tax liability.

In computing the estate tax liability under the unified transfer tax system, the unified rate schedule is applied to a decedent's cumulative transfers, both during life and at death. A tentative estate tax is computed on what is sometimes referred to as the "estate tax base," which is composed of the taxable estate (the gross estate minus allowable deductions (see Chapter 6 through Chapter 24)) plus all taxable gifts made after 1976, other than gifts includible in the gross estate (see Chapter 25).[6] The gross estate tax is then calculated by subtracting the gift tax payable on the post-1976 taxable gifts (using the current unified rate schedule).[7] The applicable credit amount (see ¶15) and additional allowable credits (see Chapters 26 and 27) are then applied against the gross estate tax liability to arrive at the net estate tax due.

Special phaseout rules applied with respect to both the gift tax and the estate tax for certain large transfers made before January 1, 2002 (see ¶18 and ¶2378).

The estate tax base does not include the value of lifetime transfers that are already included in the decedent's estate, such as transfers where the decedent retained certain interests, rights, or powers in the property (see ¶30). This precludes having the same lifetime transfers taken into account more than once for transfer tax purposes. The gift tax payable on these transfers is later subtracted in determining the correct estate tax.

Effective on and after June 17, 2008, a U.S. citizen or resident is subject to a special transfer tax upon receipt of property by gift or inheritance from an expatriate. This tax is equal to the value of the covered gift or estate multiplied by the highest rate in effect under Code Sec. 2001(c) (40 percent for 2013 and beyond) or, if greater, the highest rate in effect under Code Sec. 2502(a) (also 40 percent for 2013 and beyond) (Code Sec. 2801(a) and (b)), as added by the Heroes Earnings Assistance and Relief Tax Act of 2008 (P.L. 110-245). See ¶2593.

Special rules apply in the case of nonresidents not citizens (see ¶1635) and for certain split gifts (see ¶1426). See also ¶2350.

---

[4] Act Sec. 101(c)(1), American Taxpayer Relief Act of 2012 (P.L. 112-240), amending Code Sec. 2001(c).

[5] Code Sec. 2502(a).
[6] Code Sec. 2001(b).
[7] Code Sec. 2001(b)(2).

¶ 15   Unified Credit

The unified credit, now referred to as the "applicable credit amount" in Code Sec. 2010, is a one-time credit in life and at death against taxes payable on certain transfers.[8] Although the credit must be used to offset gift taxes on lifetime transfers, regardless of the amount so used, the full credit is allowed against the tentative estate tax. The rationale for such full application is that, under Code Sec. 2001(b)(2), the estate tax payable is calculated using the cumulative transfers at life and at death and is then reduced by the amount of gift tax paid by a decedent. If a portion of the unified credit was used to avoid the payment of gift taxes, the gift tax paid reflects the amount subtracted under Code Sec. 2001(b)(2). The estate tax payable is necessarily increased by the amount of the gift tax credit used. However, the credit for estate tax purposes cannot exceed the amount of the estate tax.

It should be noted that, because of the nature of the gift tax, the computation of the unified credit for gift tax purposes is different from that for estate tax purposes (see ¶ 2007 and ¶ 2376).

• *Impact of the 2001, 2010 and 2012 Tax Acts*

The enactment of the Economic Growth and Tax Relief Reconciliation Act of 2001 (P.L. 107-16) (EGTRRA), the Tax Relief, Unemployment Insurance Reauthorization, and Job Creation Act of 2010 (P.L. 111-312) (Tax Relief Act of 2010), and the American Taxpayer Relief Act of 2012 (P.L. 112-240) (ATRA), brought significant change to the transfer tax system, including a number of modifications are made to the maximum estate tax rate and the estate and gift tax applicable exclusion amounts. The *estate tax* applicable exclusion amount is determined according to the following schedule:

- For decedents dying in 2002 and 2003: $1 million;
- For decedents dying in 2004 and 2005: $1.5 million;
- For decedents dying in 2006, 2007, and 2008: $2 million;
- For decedents dying in 2009: $3.5 million;
- For decedents dying in 2010 and 2011: $5 million;
- For decedents dying in 2012: $5,120,000 (as adjusted for inflation); and
- For decedents dying in 2013: $5,250,000 (as adjusted for inflation).
- For decedents dying in 2014: $5,340,000 (as adjusted for inflation).

The Tax Relief Act of 2010 provides that, effective for deaths in 2011 and 2012, the estate of a surviving spouse may qualify to utilize the unused portion of the estate tax applicable exclusion amount of his or her last predeceased spouse (see ¶ 16.) This "portability" provision was made permanent by ATRA.

The *gift tax* applicable exclusion amount is $1 million for gifts made in 2002 through 2010. Thereafter, the gift tax and estate tax exclusion amounts are "re-unified," at $5 million for 2011. For 2012 and beyond, the unified credit amount is adjusted for inflation ($5,120,000 for 2012; $5,250,000 for 2013; $5,340,000 for 2014).

Computation of the credit. For years 2002 through 2010, the amount of the gift tax applicable credit amount is equal to (1) the applicable credit amount in

---

[8] Code Sec. 2010 and Code Sec. 2505. The unified credit replaced the pre-1977 $30,000 lifetime gift tax exemption and the $60,000 estate tax exemption.

effect under Code Sec. 2010(c) for such calendar year, determined as if the applicable exclusion amount were $1 million, reduced by (2) the sum of the amounts allowable as a credit under Code Sec. 2505 for all preceding calendar periods[9] (see ¶ 2007).

For years 2011 and 2012, the amount of the gift tax applicable credit amount is equal to (1) the applicable credit amount in effect under Code Sec. 2010(c) which would apply if the donor died as of the end of the calendar year, reduced by (2) the sum of the amounts allowable as a credit to the individual under Code Sec. 2505 for all preceding calendar periods[10] (see ¶ 2007).

• *Post-1997, Pre-2004 Unified Credit*

For the years 1998–2003, the unified credit was gradually increased to $345,800 and was determined by reference to the "applicable credit amount" and "the applicable exclusion amount" (formerly the exemption equivalent) ($1 million in 2002 and 2003). (See the table at ¶ 10.) For the years 2000 and 2001, the applicable exclusion amount was $675,000, resulting in an applicable credit amount of $220,550.

• *Pre-1998 Unified Credit*

The unified estate and gift tax credit was $192,800 for decedents dying after 1986 and before 1998. The exemption equivalent for these years was $600,000. The unified credit for previous years appears in the Appendix at ¶ 2600.

The estate tax and gift tax return filing requirements reflect the exemption equivalent (see ¶ 22 and ¶ 26).

A special transitional rule applies to gifts made between September 9, 1976, and December 31, 1976.[11]

¶ 16   Portability of Deceased Spousal Unused Exclusion (DSUE) Amount

Effective for deaths occurring after December 31, 2010, the unused portion of a decedent's applicable exclusion amount (as otherwise increased to $5 million under the Tax Relief, Unemployment Insurance Reauthorization, and Job Creation Act of 2010 (P.L. 111-312) (Tax Relief Act of 2010))[12] may be utilized by the estate of the decedent's surviving spouse at his or her later death. To take advantage of this provision, a special election must have been made by the predeceased spouse's estate (Code Sec. 2010(c)). This election is often referred to as the "portability," or "DSUE" election.

Computing exclusion amount of a surviving spouse. The applicable exclusion amount for a surviving spouse who dies after December 31, 2010 is the sum of:

---

[9] Code Sec. 2505(a), prior to amendment by the Tax Relief, Unemployment Insurance Reauthorizaiton, and Job Creation Act of 2010 (P.L. 111-312).

[10] Code Sec. 2505(a), as amended by the Tax Relief, Unemployment Insurance Reauthorization, and Job Creation Act of 2010 (P.L. 111-312); American Tax Relief Act of 2012 (P.L. 112-240), Sec. 101(a), striking title IX of the Economic Growth and Tax Relief Reconciliation Act of 2001 (P.L. 107-16)

and Sec. 304 of the Tax Relief, Unemployment Insurance Reauthorization, and Job Creation Act of 2010 (P.L. 111-312).

[11] Code Sec. 2010(b); Code Sec. 2505(b).

[12] Although the DSUE provisions enacted by the Tax Relief Act of 2010 were applicable for decedents dying in 2011 and 2012, the American Taxpayer Relief Act of 2012 (P.L. 112-240) made these provisions permanent for decedents dying after December 31, 2012.

- the basic exclusion amount ($5 million for 2011 and, as adjusted for inflation for deaths after December 31, 2011, $5,120,000 for 2012, $5,250,000 for 2013, and $5,340,000 for 2014); and

- the aggregate deceased spousal unused exclusion amount (discussed below).[13]

Any portion of the predeceased spouse's applicable exclusion amount that was used to reduce his or her estate tax liability may not be used to reduce the surviving spouse's estate tax liability under this new provision. The term "deceased spousal unused exclusion amount" (DSUE amount) is the lesser of:

- the basic exclusion amount, or

- the last deceased spouse's applicable exclusion amount, minus

- the amount with respect to which the tentative tax is determined under Code Sec. 2001(b)(1) on the estate of such deceased spouse.[14]

Example: Gina Parsons died in 2012 with a taxable estate of $3 million. An election is made on Gina's estate tax return to permit her husband, Henry, to use any of her unused exclusion amount. Henry, who had not made any lifetime taxable gifts, dies in 2013 with a taxable estate of $10 million. The executor of Henry's estate computes Henry's deceased spousal unused exclusion amount as the lesser of: (1) Henry's basic exclusion amount of $5 million or (2) Gina's basic exclusion amount ($5 million) minus (3) the amount of Gina's taxable estate ($3 million), or: $2 million. Accordingly, the total applicable exclusion amount available to Henry's estate at his death is $7 million: his basic exclusion amount of $5 million, plus $2 million in deceased spousal unused exclusion from Gina's estate.

Temporary Reg. § 20.2010-2T(c)(2) provides that amounts on which gift taxes were paid by a decedent are excluded from adjusted taxable gifts for purposes of computing that decedent's DSUE amount. This avoids the use of the exclusion on amounts if (1) gift tax was paid by the decedent on transfers that caused total taxable transfers to exceed the applicable exclusion amount at the time of the transfer and (2) the decedent's total adjusted taxable gifts are less than the applicable exclusion amount on the date of death.

Example: Assume the same facts as in the Example above, except that after Gina's death, Henry married a second spouse, Rita, who predeceased him leaving a taxable estate of $4 million. An election was made on Rita's estate tax return to permit Henry to use any of her unused exclusion amount. Although the combined unused applicable exclusion amounts of Gina and Rita is $3 million (Gina's $2 million and Rita's $1 million), only $1 million is available for use by Henry's estate because Henry's deceased spousal unused exclusion amount is the lesser of: (1) Henry's basic exclusion amount of $5 million or (2) Rita's basic exclusion amount ($5 million) minus (3) the amount of Rita's taxable estate ($4 million), or: $1 million. Accordingly, the total applicable exclusion amount available to Henry's estate at his death is $6 million, composed of his basic exclusion amount of $5 million, plus $1 million in deceased spousal unused exclusion from Rita's estate.

---

[13] Code Sec. 2010(c)(2), as amended by the Tax Relief Act of 2010.

[14] Code Sec. 2010(c)(4), as added by the Tax Relief Act of 2010.

Temporary Reg. §§ 20.2010-3T(a) and 25.2505-2T(a) explain that, if the decedent is the last deceased spouse of a surviving spouse on the date of a transfer by the surviving spouse that is subject to estate or gift tax, the surviving spouse (or the estate) may take into account the decedent's DSUE amount in determining the surviving spouse's applicable exclusion amount when computing the surviving spouse's estate or gift tax liability on that transfer. The portability election by the decedent's estate is effective as of the decedent's date of death. Accordingly, it is not possible for individuals who have been married multiple times to tack on multiple applicable exclusion amounts of their predeceased spouses.

Temporary Reg. §§ 20.2010-3T(a)(3) and 25.2505-2T(a)(3) clarify the scope of the "last deceased spouse" limitation. Remarriage does not affect the identity of the last deceased spouse and does not prevent the surviving spouse from including in the surviving spouse's applicable exclusion amount the DSUE amount of the deceased spouse who most recently preceded the surviving spouse in death. The identity of the last deceased spouse for purposes of portability is not affected by whether the executor of the decedent's estate elected portability of the deceased spouse's DSUE amount or the decedent had any DSUE amount available. For purposes of determining a surviving spouse's applicable exclusion amount when the surviving spouse makes a taxable gift, the last deceased spouse is identified as of the date of the taxable gift.

Generation-skipping transfer tax exemption. The JCT Report (Footnote 56, Committee on Taxation, Technical Explanation of the Revenue Provisions Contained in the "Tax Relief, Unemployment Insurance Reauthorization, and Job Creation Act of 2010" (JCX-55-10) (December 10, 2010) indicates that a surviving spouse is not allowed to use the unused GST tax exemption of a predeceased spouse.

Election of portability. In order for a decedent's estate to take advantage of the unused exclusion amount of the decedent's predeceased spouse, the executor of the predeceased spouse's estate must:

- file an estate tax return
- on which the amount of the deceased unused exclusion is computed, and
- elect on the return that such amount may be taken into account by the surviving spouse's estate (this election is deemed made if the decedent spouse's estate does not mark the checkbox denying portability on Part 6, Section A.—Opting Out of Portability, of Form 706 (Rev. August 2013)).

Preparation Tip: Once the above election is made, it is irrevocable. No such election will be allowed to be made if the deadline for filing the predeceased spouse's estate tax return (including extensions) had not been met.[15] In order for Form 706 to be considered timely filed, executors must file it nine months after a decedent's date of death. Executors may request an automatic six-month extension of time to file by filing Form 4768 before the due date of Form 706. Pursuant to Code Sec. 2010(c)(5)(B), the IRS may examine the estate tax return of a predeceased spouse to make a determination of the predeceased spouse's unused exclusion amount, even after the period of limitations under Code Sec. 6501 has closed.[16] A decedent's estate

---

[15] Code Sec. 2010(c)(5)(A), as added by the Tax Relief Act of 2010, and amended by ATRA.

[16] Notice 2011-82, IRB 2011-42, October 18, 2011.

¶16

wanting to opt out of the portability election should mark the checkbox in Form 706 (Rev. August 2013), Part 6, Section A.—Opting Out of Portability. Instructions for preparing Form 706, Part 6, Section A, appear at ¶1210. A filled-in Part 6, Section A, is reproduced at ¶2942.

Discussion of Form 709 (United States Gift (and Generation-Skipping Transfer) Tax Return (2013), Schedule C—Deceased Spousal Unused Exclusion (DSUE) Amount, appears at ¶2007. A filled-in Form 709, Schedule C is reproduced at ¶3280.

Portability filing extensions for certain decedents dying before July 1, 2012. The IRS has announced a six-month filing extension for purposes of the portability election for certain "qualifying estates" of married individuals who died during the first six months of 2011.[17] Thus, electing estates were given 15 months after the date of death, rather than the usual nine months. The first estate tax returns for estates that were eligible to make the portability election (which first applied to decedents dying after December 31, 2010) were due on April 2, 2012.

In order to be considered as a qualifying estate for purpose of the portability extension, the estate must relate to a decedent:

- whose date of death was after December 31, 2010 and before July 1, 2011,

- who is survived by a spouse, and

- whose gross estate does not exceed the $5,000,000 basic exclusion amount for 2011.

For purposes of Notice 2012-21, an estate will not be a qualifying estate if it had effectively requested an automatic six-month filing extension by timely filing a Form 4768 on or before the due date for filing Form 706. Also, if it is later determined that the estate does not meet the requirements for being a qualified estate, an extension under Notice 2012-21 will not be deemed granted, and therefore, the Form 706 will not be timely filed.

Even if an estate is a qualifying estate, in order to receive a six-month filing extension for the portability election, the decedent's executor must:

- file Form 4768 with the IRS office designated in the instructions to that form,

- file Form 4768 no later than 15 months from the decedent's date of death, and

- enter on the top of Form 4768 the notation "Notice 2012-21, Extension for Good Cause Shown" or otherwise sufficiently notify the IRS on or with Form 4768 that the form is being filed pursuant to the notice.

Compliance Pointer: By following the above three requirements the executor will be deemed to have shown good and sufficient cause and provided all explanations required under Reg. § 20.6081-1(c), without the need for the executor to include any further explanation on Form 4768.

Compliance Pointer: If, before issuance of Notice 2012-21, an executor of a qualifying estate filed a Form 706 after the due date for that return, but before 15 months from the decedent's date of death without having timely requested an automatic six-month extension to file, the executor who meets

---

[17] Notice 2012-21.

all the requirements of Notice 2012-21 still may file Form 4768, and the extension will relate back to the due date of Form 706.

The six-month extension granted under the rules of Notice 2012-21 may not be further extended, except in the case where an executor is abroad.[18]

Examination of prior returns. To ensure compliance, the IRS is granted the authority to examine estate and gift tax returns of a predeceased spouse in order make determinations regarding the surviving spouse's claim to the unused portion of the predeceased spouse's exclusion amount.[19] This authority extends even after the statutory period of limitations has expired under Code Sec. 6501. The 2010 Act also directs the IRS to issue "such regulations as may be necessary or appropriate" to implement the new rules regarding the use of deceased spousal unused exclusion amounts.[20]

> *Comment:* As noted at a hearing before the Senate Finance Committee on the future of the estate tax ("Outside the Box on Estate Tax Reform: Reviewing Ideas to Simplify Planning," Senate Finance Committee, April 3, 2008, testimony of Shirley L. Kovar, Esq.), the main impetus for the portability provision is undoubtedly simplicity. Although portability will not completely eliminate the need for trusts, for many couples, particularly those who have been married only once and who are in the lower echelons of exposure to the estate tax (e.g., estates of between $5 and $10 million under the new law), this change should prove to be beneficial. It was supported by, among others, the American College of Trust and Estate Counsel (AC-TEC). However, additional suggestions made by ACTEC, including (1) allowing portability with respect to the GST exemption and (2) instead of requiring an election, allowing for the possibility of attaching a special schedule to the deceased spouse's income tax return as a means of alerting the IRS to the portability issue, were not incorporated into the changes made by the Tax Relief Act of 2010.

EGTRRA sunset repealed and portability made permanent.—Under Act Sec. 101(a)(1) of the Tax Relief Act of 2010, the date that the tax provisions of EGTRRA were scheduled to sunset has been extended from December 31, 2010, to December 31, 2012. However, under Act Sec. 304 of the Tax Relief Act of 2010, the sunset provision of EGTRRA (Act Sec. 901), as amended by the Tax Relief Act of 2010, were to apply to the transfer tax provisions of the 2010 Act. In other words, on January 1, 2013, the portability election would sunset. However, the American Taxpayer Relief Act of 2012 (P.L. 112-240) (ATRA) repealed the EGT-RRA sunset provision, with the result that the DSUE provisions became permanent.

¶ 18　Benefits of Graduated Rates and Unified Credit Phased Out—Pre-1998 Transfers

The benefits of the graduated rates and the unified credit under the unified transfer tax system were phased out beginning with cumulative transfers above $10 million prior to 1998.[21] This was accomplished by adding five percent of the excess of any transfer over $10 million to the tentative tax computed in determining the ultimate transfer tax liability. This five-percent surtax was repealed by the Economic Growth and Tax Relief Reconciliation Act of 2001 (P.L. 107-16), effec-

---

[18] Code Sec. 6081.
[19] Code Sec. 2010(c)(5)(B), as added by the Tax Relief Act of 2010.

[20] Code Sec. 2010(c)(6), as added by the Tax Relief Act of 2010.
[21] Code Sec. 2001(c)(2).

tive for decedents dying, and gifts made, after December 31, 2001. (Although the repeal of the surtax was scheduled to sunset after December 31, 2012, the repeal was made permanent by the American Taxpayer Relief Act of 2012 (P.L. 112-240) (ATRA).)

For estates of decedents dying, and gifts made, after 1987 and before 1998, the tax was levied on amounts transferred in excess of $10 million but not exceeding $21,040,000 in order to recapture the benefit of any transfer tax rate below 55 percent and the unified credit. Due to mistakes in the wording of the amendment to Code Sec. 2001(c)(2) by the Taxpayer Relief Act of 1997 (P.L. 105-34), the five-percent additional tax phased out the benefits of graduated rates, but not the benefits of the unified credit (applicable credit amount), for estates of decedents dying, and gifts made, after 1997, but before 2002. Therefore, the additional tax was levied on amounts transferred in excess of $10 million, but not exceeding $17,184,000, for decedents dying after 1997. The benefit of the applicable credit amount was not recaptured.

¶ 20   Unified Rates and Credit for Nonresidents Not Citizens

Effective for the estates of decedents dying after November 10, 1988, the estate and gift tax rates applicable to U.S. citizens are also applicable to the estates of nonresident aliens.[22] With respect to the unified credit, where permitted by treaty, the estate of a nonresident alien is allowed the same unified credit as a U.S. citizen multiplied by the percentage of the total gross estate situated in the United States. In other cases, the estate of a nonresident alien is allowed a unified credit of $13,000 (which exempts the first $60,000 of the estate from estate tax) or, for residents of U.S. possessions, the greater of $13,000 or a pro rata share of $46,800 based on the percentage of property located in the United States.[23] Consistent with the repeal of the five-percent surtax applicable to U.S. citizens dying after December 31, 2001, the five-percent surtax applicable to nonresidents not citizens is also repealed with respect to such post-2001 transfers.[24]

With respect to transfers made before 2002, in order to reflect the fact that in some cases the estate of a nonresident noncitizen did not receive the same unified credit available to U.S. citizens, the additional Code Sec. 2001(c)(2) five-percent recapture rate was adjusted.[25] Accordingly, the additional five-percent rate applied to the taxable transfers of nonresident noncitizens in excess of $10 million only to the extent that it was necessary to phase out the benefit of the graduated rates and unified credit actually allowed by statute or treaty.

See ¶1615 for a list of countries that have death tax conventions in effect with the United States.

---

[22] Code Sec. 2101(a).
[23] Code Sec. 2102(c).

[24] Code Sec. 2101(b), as amended by the Job Creation and Worker Assistance Act of 2002 (P.L. 107-147).
[25] Code Sec. 2101(b).

Chapter 2
FILING REQUIREMENTS

¶ 22   Estate Tax Returns for U.S. Citizens and Residents

An estate tax return (Form 706, United States Estate (and Generation-Skipping Transfer) Tax Return) generally is due within nine months after the date of a decedent's death.[1] Extensions of time to file may be granted in certain circumstances, and an automatic six-month extension may be available for estate tax returns (see ¶ 66).

> *Comment:* Due to the shutdown of the federal government from October 1, 2013, through October 16, 2013, the release of Form 706 (Rev. Aug. 2013) was delayed until October 28, 2013. However, the estate tax returns of decedents dying in January 2013, would be due as early as October 1, 2013. Accordingly, any decedent estates in this situation (other than those that had elected a six month filing extension) seemingly would be in a predicament: they would be required to file a Form 706, but the revised form was not yet available. The last time a similar situation arose, in 1990, the IRS advised practitioners to file the existing form and make adjustments for any law changes.[2] As we went to press, the IRS had not issued guidance about how to deal with the estate tax filing deadlines occurring 2013 prior to the release of Form 706 (Rev. Aug. 2013).

Filing requirements. For estates of U.S. citizens and residents dying after 1976, the filing requirements are triggered for estates that exceed the applicable exclusion amount—that is, the amount of property sheltered from tax by the unified credit. For decedents dying in 2011, the applicable exclusion amount is $5 million. For 2012 and beyond, the unified credit amount is adjusted for inflation ($5,120,000 for 2012; $5,250,000 for 2013; $5,340,000 for 2014). The filing threshold is equal to the applicable exclusion amount.[3] However, if lifetime gifts are made and the applicable credit amount is offset against the gift tax, this amount is reduced accordingly (see the unified credit table at ¶ 10).[4]

Filing thresholds applicable to decedents dying before 2010 are reproduced in the Appendix at ¶ 2600.

Filing extension under 2010 Tax Act. For decedents dying after December 31, 2009 and before December 17, 2010, the Tax Relief Act of 2010 set the due date for filing Form 706, the United States Estate (and Generation-Skipping Transfer) Tax Return (Rev. July 2011) as September 19, 2011.[5] However, responding to

---

[1] Code Sec. 6075(a); Reg. § 20.6075-1.
[2] Ann. 90-98, 1990-2 CB 71.
[3] Code Sec. 2010(c).
[4] Code Sec. 6018(a)(3).
[5] Instructions for Form 706 (Rev. July 2011), p. 1. The due date under Act Sec.

301(d)(1) of the Tax Relief Act of 2010 was extended to no later than nine months after the date of enactment of the Act, which would have been September 17, 2011. But because this date was a Saturday, the extended due date was September 19, 2011.

concerns that executors may not have had sufficient time to make an informed decision as to whether to make the Code Sec. 1022 election and complete the required filings, the IRS provided additional filing relief for the estates of 2010 decedents.[6] Executors representing decedents who died in 2010 had until January 17, 2012, to file the carryover basis information return (Form 8939; see ¶121) or until March 2012 to file Form 706 (see ¶66). Deadlines for income and gift tax returns were not extended.

According to the IRS, executors filing Form 706 for decedents dying in 2010 were required to file Form 4768 (see ¶66) on or before the due date of the estate tax return in order to receive an automatic six-month extension to both file and pay the estate tax. Executors were not required to substantiate the reason for requesting the extension. Additional extensions of time to file were not to be granted, except in the case of an executor who was abroad, but executors could request additional time to pay tax pursuant to Code Sec. 6161. No late filing or late payment penalties were to be imposed if Form 4768 was timely filed. However, the IRS clarified that interest would accrue on any unpaid estate tax liability from the due date of the return, excluding extensions.[7]

¶ 24   Estate Tax Returns for Nonresidents Not Citizens

For estates of nonresidents not citizens of the United States, the estate representative must file a return if the value of that part of the gross estate that is located in the United States exceeds $60,000 (see ¶1600 et seq.).[8]

¶ 26   Gift Tax Return Filing Requirements

A gift tax return (Form 709, United States Gift (and Generation-Skipping Transfer) Tax Return) is to be filed, and any gift tax is to be paid, on an annual basis. Generally, the due date for filing the gift tax return is April 15 following the close of the calendar year in which gifts are made (see ¶2052).[9]

> *Example:* Joan Ellis makes a taxable gift on January 1, 2013. The gift tax return is due on April 15, 2014.

However, for a calendar year in which a donor dies, the gift tax return must be filed no later than the due date for the donor's estate tax return, including extensions.[10] These rules apply to U.S. citizens, residents, and nonresident aliens alike.

A gift tax return must be filed if the donor (1) gave gifts to any donee other than the donor's spouse that are not fully excludable from gift tax under one or a combination of the annual, educational, or medical exclusions (see ¶2250), (2) gave gifts to charity unless the donor transfers his or her entire interest in the property transferred and no noncharitable donee receives an interest in the property, (3) gave gifts of terminable interests (other than a life estate with a general power of appointment) to his or her spouse (see ¶2318), or (4) gave gifts of any amount that are split with his or her spouse (see ¶2200).[11]

---

[6] IRS News Release IR-2011-91, September 13, 2011; Notice 2011-76, IRB 2011-40, October 3, 2011.

[7] Notice 2011-76 , IRB 2011-40, October 3, 2011.

[8] Code Sec. 6018(a)(2).

[9] Code Sec. 6075(b)(1).

[10] Code Sec. 6075(b)(3).

[11] Code Sec. 6019.

¶ 27 Generation-Skipping Transfer Tax Return Filing Requirements

IRS regulations detail the filing requirements for generation-skipping transfer (GST) tax returns.[12] The return requirements depend on the type of generation-skipping transfer involved. In general, in the case of a direct skip (other than from a trust), a return must be filed on or before the date on which an estate[13] or gift tax return is required to be filed with respect to the transfer.[14] In all other cases, the due date for the return is on or before the 15th day of the fourth month after the close of the tax year of the person required to file such a return. Exceptions to these general rules are set forth in Reg. § 26.2662-1 (see ¶ 2471).

As noted below, the type of generation-skipping transfer involved determines which return is to be used in reporting the tax.

• Taxable Distributions

In the case of a taxable distribution (defined at ¶ 2433), the transferee must report the generation-skipping transfer on Form 706-GS(D) (Generation-Skipping Transfer Tax Return For Distributions) (Rev. August 2013), and the trust involved in such a transfer must file Form 706-GS(D-1) (Notification of Distribution From a Generation-Skipping Trust) (Rev. October 2008) and send a copy to each distributee.[15]

• Taxable Terminations

The trustee in the case of a taxable termination (defined at ¶ 2433) is required to report the GST tax on Form 706-GS(T) (Generation-Skipping Transfer Tax Return For Terminations) (Rev. November 2013).[16]

• Direct Skips

In specifying the form of return to be used for reporting the GST tax on direct skips (defined at ¶ 2433), Reg. § 26.2662-1 distinguishes between *inter vivos* direct skips and direct skips occurring at death. For any direct skip that is subject to the federal gift tax and that occurs during the life of the transferor, Form 709 (United States Gift (and Generation-Skipping Transfer) Tax Return) must be filed.[17]

The GST tax that is imposed on direct skips that are subject to the estate tax and occur at the death of a decedent is reported on Form 706 (United States Estate (and Generation-Skipping Transfer) Tax Return). Schedule R-1 (Generation-Skipping Transfer Tax) of Form 706 must be filed for any direct skip from a trust if such a direct skip is subject to the estate tax.[18]

---

[12] Reg. § 26.2662-1.

[13] Effective for any GSTs made after December 31, 2009, and before December 17, 2010 (the date of enactment of the Tax Relief Act of 2010 (P.L. 111-312)), the due date for filing any returns due under Code Sec. 2662 (including any election required to be made on such a return) was set at no earlier than September 19, 2011 (Tax Relief Act of 2010, Act Sec. 301(d)(2)). However, the IRS provided filing relief whereby executors for decedents dying in 2010 who file Form 4768 by the due date of the estate tax return may obtain an automatic six-month extension to both file and pay tax. See ¶ 22.

[14] Code Sec. 2662(a)(2).

[15] Reg. § 26.2662-1(b)(1). See ¶ 2479 for instructions for reporting taxable distributions on Forms 706-GS(D) and 706-GS(D-1).

[16] Reg. § 26.2662-1(b)(2). See ¶ 2487 for instructions for reporting taxable terminations on Form 706-GS(T).

[17] Reg. § 26.2662-1(b)(3)(i).

[18] Reg. § 26.2662-1(b)(3)(ii).

Comment: Certain *inter vivos* transfers may be subject to both gift and GST taxes. A generation-skipping transfer is subject to the gift tax if it is required to be reported on Schedule A (Computation of Taxable Gifts) of Form 709 under the rules contained in the gift tax portion of its instructions, including the split gift rules.

For a more detailed discussion of the GST tax return requirements, see Chapter 39, beginning at ¶ 2430.

ESTATE TAX
Chapter 3
NATURE OF TAX

¶ 28   Description of Tax

The federal estate tax is an excise tax levied on the transfer of a person's property at the time of that person's death.[1] It is neither a tax on the property itself nor a tax on the privilege of an heir to receive the property.

The amount of the tax is determined by applying the relevant tax rates to the tax base or the taxable estate (see ¶ 12 and ¶ 29). With only one exception (noted below), the tax is not affected by the relationship of the beneficiaries to the decedent as is the case under inheritance tax laws in effect in many states.

A special deduction for amounts transferred to a surviving spouse reduces the size of the taxable estate of a U.S. citizen or resident if the transferred amounts meet the conditions of such deduction (see ¶ 1000).[2]

¶ 29   Taxable Estate

The taxable estate is determined by subtracting certain deductions (see ¶ 780 through ¶ 1175) from the gross estate (see ¶ 150).[3] A tentative tax applies to the amount of the taxable estate and the amount of taxable gifts made after 1976, using the unified rate schedule (see ¶ 10). The estate tax is computed by determining the amount of the tentative tax and subtracting gift taxes paid on gifts made after 1976.[4] To the extent that the applicable credit amount was not used to offset gift taxes, the amount of estate tax is reduced.[5]

¶ 30   Gross Estate

The value of the gross estate of a decedent is the total value of the interests described in Code Sec. 2033 through Code Sec. 2044, whether real or personal, tangible or intangible, wherever situated.[6] Generally, the gross estate of a decedent is composed of the value of:

> (1) all property to the extent of the decedent's interest in it at the time of the decedent's death (see ¶ 150);

> (2) any interest of the surviving spouse existing as dower or curtesy, or similar interest (see ¶ 175);

---

[1] Code Sec. 2001(a); Reg. § 20.0-2(a).

[2] Code Sec. 2056(a).

[3] Code Sec. 2051.

[4] Code Sec. 2001(b).

[5] Code Sec. 2010.

[6] Code Sec. 2031 and Reg. § 20.2031-1, detailing certain exceptions to Code Sec. 2033 through Code Sec. 2044.

(3) property transferred by the decedent during life, if: (a) the transfer was made within three years before death and the transfer involved life insurance (see ¶430) or certain other property that would have been includible in the decedent's gross estate for the reasons described in (b), (c), or (d) (see ¶555); (b) the decedent had retained the income or enjoyment for life or for a period not determinable without reference to the decedent's death (see ¶570); (c) the transfer was not intended to take effect until the decedent's death and the decedent retained a reversionary interest in the property transferred (see ¶565); (d) the decedent possessed a power to change the enjoyment through a power to alter, amend, or revoke (see ¶580 and ¶585); or (e) the decedent had relinquished a right of the type referred to in (b), (c), or (d) within three years before the decedent's death (see ¶595); and

(4) certain other types of property interests, including: (a) one-half of the value of qualified joint interests (see ¶502); (b) jointly held property interests that are not qualified joint interests (the interest being based on the decedent's contribution to the purchase of joint interests) (see ¶500); (c) life insurance proceeds, if the decedent or the decedent's estate had any interest in the proceeds or held any incidents of ownership in the policy at the time of death (see ¶400); (d) property over which the decedent had a general power of appointment received from another; (e) certain annuities (see ¶700); or (f) qualified terminable interest property (see ¶773).[7]

The above summary is not all-inclusive and is subject to various qualifications. These qualifications are discussed in more detail at the paragraphs noted above.

¶ 32   Deductions

The items listed below are deductible from the amount of the gross estate in determining the taxable estate of U.S. citizens and residents:

(1) funeral expenses (see ¶785);

(2) various expenses incidental to the administration of the estate (see ¶790);

(3) losses incurred due to casualty or theft, etc., during administration (see ¶900);

(4) debts of the decedent and enforceable claims against the estate, including taxes (see ¶800);

(5) mortgages and liens (see ¶850);

(6) a marital deduction for qualifying property passing to the decedent's spouse (see ¶1000);

(7) the value of property transferred to, or for the use of, charitable, educational, religious, or public institutions, or the government (see ¶1100); and

(8) state death taxes paid, effective for estates of decedents dying, and generation-skipping transfers made after December 31, 2004.[8]

---

[7] Code Sec. 2031 and Code Sec. 2033 through Code Sec. 2044.

[8] Code Sec. 2051 and Code Sec. 2053 through Code Sec. 2058.

¶ 35   Rates

The maximum transfer tax rate on cumulative lifetime and at-death transfers is 35 percent for estates of decedents dying in 2011 and 2012.[9] Because of the operation of the estate tax applicable credit amount of $5 million in 2011 and $5,120,000 (indexed) in 2012, the minimum effective estate tax rate was also 35 percent. The American Taxpayer Relief Act of 2012 (P.L. 112-240) raised the maximum transfer tax rate to 40 percent, effective for decedents dying after December 31, 2012. Because of the $5,250,000 (indexed) applicable credit amount for 2013, the 40 percent rate was also the maximum effective rate for 2013. The transfer tax may be further reduced by other credits (see ¶ 36).

¶ 36   Credits

A unified credit (applicable credit amount) is subtracted from the amount of tentative estate tax liability (see ¶ 15) for estates of decedents dying after 1976. Additionally, the unused applicable exclusion amount of a decedent's prede-ceased spouse, who died after December 31, 2010, may also be available to reduce a decedent's estate tax liability (see ¶ 16).[10]

In addition to the unified credit, credits are allowed to reduce federal estate taxes for taxes paid on prior transfers to the decedent by or from a person who died within 10 years before or two years after the decedent (see ¶ 1300); federal gift taxes paid by the decedent on pre-1977 transfers made by the decedent during his lifetime (see ¶ 1382); and foreign death duties paid (see ¶ 1401).[11] The credit allowed against the estate tax for gift tax paid on property included in a decedent's gross estate is eliminated for post-1976 gifts. The credit for state death taxes paid that was scheduled to be available for the estates of decedents dying after December 31, 2012, has been permanently repealed by the American Tax-payer Relief Act of 2012 (P.L. 112-240) (see ¶ 1145).

In computing the net estate tax, these credits, the sum of all gift taxes payable on gifts made after 1976, and the allowable unified credit are subtracted (see ¶ 1426) from the tentative tax.[12]

¶ 37   Effect of State Law

The question of whether, and the extent to which, particular property interests are owned by a decedent at death and, thus, are includible in the decedent's gross estate generally is determined on the basis of the law of the state where the decedent resided or where the property was located.[13] The federal courts will follow state law in deciding whether something is a property interest. State law, for this purpose, includes both statutes and state court decisions interpreting statutes. Therefore, it is necessary, in many cases, to refer both to the statutes and to state court decisions in determining whether a decedent owns a property interest that is includible in the gross estate. Although state law classi-fies a property interest as a certain type, it is federal law that determines whether that type of interest is includible in the gross estate.

Where the type and character of property interests held and transferred by a decedent is determined with respect to state court decisions, the decisions of the highest court of a state have binding effect for federal estate tax purposes. The decision of the state's highest court can involve the actual interest to be reported

---

[9] Code Sec. 2001(c)(1).

[10] Code Sec. 2010.

[11] Code Sec. 2010 through Code Sec. 2015.

[12] Code Sec. 2001(b).

[13] *J. Morgan, Exr.*, SCt, 40-1 USTC ¶ 9210, 309 US 78.

on the decedent's estate tax return or it can involve the estate of another decedent under the same general factual situation. However, in a National Office Technical Advice Memorandum, the IRS refused to follow, for federal estate tax purposes, a decision of the Georgia Supreme Court that a decedent's power of appointment was limited by an ascertainable standard (see ¶ 653).[14] The lawsuit giving rise to the Georgia court's decision was a will construction proceeding filed by a bank as executor of the decedent's estate, and only the IRS, which was notified but declined to intervene, had an interest adverse to that of the estate. In the IRS's view, the decisions of a state's highest court are binding for estate tax purposes only if the underlying lawsuit was adversarial and affected the property rights of the litigants. In a separate National Office Technical Advice Memorandum, involving a Georgia decedent in a factual situation similar to that resulting in the Georgia Supreme Court's decision, the IRS also refused to accept the Georgia court's decision as controlling for estate tax purposes.[15]

Lower state court decisions are not binding for estate tax purposes, and their effect is not clear. The U.S. Supreme Court has held that, in the absence of a decision by a state's highest court, a federal court must apply what it finds the state law to be after giving "proper regard" to decisions of other courts of the state.[16] Intermediate state court decisions may be disregarded if the federal court is convinced that the highest state court would decide otherwise. A state trial court decision must also be given "proper regard" by a federal court; however, such a decision cannot have a binding effect for federal estate tax purposes.[17]

> *Comment:* The allowance of estate tax deductions for funeral expenses, the expenses of administering a decedent's estate, claims against a decedent's estate, and mortgages on a decedent's property are all governed by the laws of the jurisdiction where the estate is being administered. Otherwise, the allowance of estate tax deductions is generally determined by the Internal Revenue Code.

¶ 38   Decedents Whose Estates Are Subject to Tax

The estate tax applies to the estate of any person who dies leaving property having a taxable situs within the United States. Its application varies in detail, however, between persons who are considered either residents or citizens of the United States and those who are considered nonresidents not citizens. The term "resident," as used with reference to any person for federal estate tax purposes, relates to the person's domicile, regardless of citizenship. Under the general rules of domicile, length of residency and amount of assets held in the location of domicile are not determinative. Rather, a person can acquire a domicile in a place by living there, even for a brief period of time, if he or she had no definite present intention of removing from that location. Residence in the U.S. without this requisite intention to remain indefinitely is not sufficient to confer domicile, nor will intention to change domicile effect such a change unless accompanied by an actual removal (see Reg. § 20.0-1). Contrast this general rule with the recently-enacted rule regarding estate tax liability for individuals who voluntarily relinquish their status as citizens or long-term residents (see ¶ 1635).

---

[14] IRS Technical Advice Memorandum 8339004 (June 14, 1983).

[15] IRS Technical Advice Memorandum 8346008 (Aug. 4, 1983).

[16] *H.J. Bosch Est.*, SCt, 67-2 USTC ¶ 12,472, 387 US 456, consolidated with *Second Nat'l Bank of New Haven, Ex'r (Will of F.F. Brewster).*

See also *D.L. Hastings, Pers. Rep.*, DC Md., 86-1 USTC ¶ 13,662.

[17] *H.J. Bosch Est.*, SCt, 67-2 USTC ¶ 12,472, 387 US 456, consolidated with *Second Nat'l Bank of New Haven, Ex'r (Will of F.F. Brewster).* See also *D.L. Hastings, Pers. Rep.*, DC Md., 86-1 USTC ¶ 13,662.

Generally, the *U.S. Master*™ *Estate and Gift Tax Guide* deals with the status of estates of U.S. residents and citizens. The variations applicable to the estates of decedents considered nonresidents not citizens are discussed at ¶1600 and following.

Chapter 4
RETURNS—FORMS REQUIRED

¶ 50 Forms Required

The estate tax return, Form 706 (United States Estate (and Generation-Skipping Transfer) Tax Return) (Rev. August 2013), is used to report and pay the estate tax in the case of the estates of decedents dying in 2013 who were U.S. citizens or residents. Form 706-NA (United States Estate (and Generation-Skipping Transfer) Tax Return—Estate of nonresident not a citizen of the United States) (Rev. August 2013) is filed for nonresident aliens (see ¶ 85). Form 706-A (United States Additional Estate Tax Return) (Rev. August 2013) is to be used to report the recapture of tax benefits previously enjoyed under an election to have farm or closely held business real property valued under the special use valuation provisions of Code Sec. 2032A (see ¶ 80).

The estate tax return generally must be filed within nine months after a decedent's death unless otherwise extended.[1] Payment of the tax is also due at this time unless one of the provisions for extension of time to pay tax applies (see ¶ 1685).[2] Special extended due dates apply to decedents dying in 2010 (see ¶ 66).

> *Practice Tip:* If the tax cannot be finally computed within the filing period, arrangement may be made with the IRS for an extension of time for filing and payment. In order to reduce interest liability, the return may be filed with whatever necessary information is available before expiration of the filing period and with a payment of taxes based on an estimate. If the return is not filed within one year after it is due (including extensions), the right to use the alternate valuation method is lost (see ¶ 105).

¶ 65 Estate Tax Return

An estate tax return must be filed for the estate of every U.S. citizen or resident whose gross estate exceeds the amount of the applicable exclusion amount (based on the applicable credit amount) on the date of death.[3] The value of the gross estate at the date of the decedent's death is used to determine

---

[1] Code Sec. 6075(a); Reg. § 20.6075-1 and Reg. § 20.6081-1.

[2] Code Sec. 6151(a); Reg. § 20.6151-1, Reg. § 20.6161-1, and Reg. § 20.6163-1.

[3] Code Sec. 6018(a)(1) and Code Sec. 6018(a)(3).

whether a return must be filed, even though the executor may elect to have the gross estate valued as of the alternate valuation date (see ¶ 107).[4]

The amount of the unified credit and, therefore, the applicable exclusion amount (termed the "exemption equivalent" before 1998) that a decedent's gross estate must exceed before a return is required depends on the date of the decedent's death (see ¶ 15). For decedents dying in 2011, the decedent's representative must file a federal estate tax return only if the gross estate of the decedent exceeds the applicable exclusion amount of $5 million. Because of an adjustment for inflation, the applicable exclusion amount rises to $5,120,000 for estates of decedents dying in 2012, $5,250,000 for estates of decedents dying in 2013, and $5,340,000 for estates of decedents dying in 2014 (see 2600 for applicable exclusion amounts for 1977 through 2010). However, the applicable exclusion amount is reduced to reflect the amount of adjusted taxable gifts made by the decedent after 1976, plus the aggregate amount allowed as a specific exemption under former Code Sec. 2521 for gifts made by the decedent after September 8, 1976.[5]

An estate tax return must also be filed by the estate of a nonresident alien if the part of his or her estate situated in the United States exceeds $60,000 (after certain adjustments) at the date of death (see ¶ 85).

¶ 66   Time for Filing Return

Estate tax return Form 706 (United States Estate (and Generation-Skipping Transfer) Tax Return (Estate of a citizen or resident of the United States) (Rev. August 2013)) or Form 706-NA (United States Estate (and Generation-Skipping Transfer) Tax Return (Estate of nonresident not a citizen of the United States) (Rev. August 2013)) generally must be filed within nine months after the date of a decedent's death, unless the estate applies for a six-month extension to file the return.[6] The due date is the day of the ninth calendar month after the decedent's death numerically corresponding to the date of the calendar month on which death occurred. For example, if the decedent died on February 3, 2013, the federal estate tax return must be filed on or before November 3, 2013. If there is no numerically corresponding day in the ninth month, the last day of the ninth month is the due date. Thus, if the decedent died on July 31, 2013, the due date is April 30, 2014.

Form 706-A (United States Additional Estate Tax Return) (Rev. September 2013) must be filed within six months after an early disposition or cessation of qualified use of a specially valued property, that is, real property for which the special use valuation under Code Sec. 2032A is elected (see ¶ 80).

Preparation Tip: When the due date for the filing of an estate tax return falls on a Saturday, a Sunday, or a legal holiday, the due date for filing the return is the next succeeding day that is not a Saturday, a Sunday, or a legal holiday.[7] The term "legal holiday" means a legal holiday in the District of Columbia and, in the case of any document required to be filed or any other act required to be performed at any office of the United States outside the District of Columbia, but within an internal revenue district, the term also means a statewide legal holiday in the state where the office is located.[8]

Comment: Due to the shutdown of the federal government from October 1, 2013, through October 16, 2013, the release of Form 706 (Rev.

---

[4] Reg. § 20.6018-1.
[5] Code Sec. 6018(a)(3).
[6] Reg. § 20.6081-1(b).

[7] Reg. § 301.7503-1.
[8] Reg. § 301.7503-1.

August. 2013) was delayed until October 28, 2013. However, the estate tax returns of decedents dying in January 2013, would be due as early as October 1, 2013. Accordingly, any decedent estates in this situation (other than those that had elected a six month filing extension) seemingly would be in a predicament: they would be required to file a Form 706, but the revised form was not yet available. The last time a similar situation arose, in 1990, the IRS advised practitioners to file the existing form and make adjustments for any law changes.[9] As we went to press, the IRS had not issued guidance about how to deal with the estate tax filing deadlines occurring 2013 prior to the release of Form 706 (Rev. August 2013).

Filing extended under 2010 Tax Act. For decedents dying after December 31, 2009 and before December 17, 2010, the Tax Relief Act of 2010 set the due date for filing Form 706, the United States Estate (and Generation-Skipping Transfer) Tax Return (Rev. July 2011) as September 19, 2011.[10] However, responding to concerns that executors may not have had sufficient time to make an informed decision as to whether to make the Code Sec. 1022 election and complete the required filings, the IRS provided additional filing relief for the estates of 2010 decedents.[11] Executors representing decedents who died in 2010 had until January 17, 2012, to file the carryover basis information return (Form 8939; see ¶121) or until March 2012 to file Form 706. More specifically, for the estates of decedents dying after December 31, 2009, and before December 17, 2010, the due date for filing Form 706 (or Form 706-NA) was March 19, 2012. For estates of decedents dying after December 16, 2010 and before January 1, 2011, the due date for filing Form 706 (or Form 706-NA) was the date 15 months after the decedent's date of death. Deadlines for income and gift tax returns were not extended.

According to the IRS, executors filing Form 706 for decedents dying in 2010 must filed Form 4768 on or before the due date of the estate tax return in order to receive an automatic six-month extension to both file and pay the estate tax. Executors are not required to substantiate the reason for requesting the extension. Additional extensions of time to file cannot be granted, except in the case of an executor who is abroad, but executors may request additional time to pay tax pursuant to Code Sec. 6161. No late filing or late payment penalties will be imposed if Form 4768 is timely filed. However, the IRS has clarified that interest will accrue on any unpaid estate tax liability from the due date of the return, excluding extensions.

• *Returns Mailed from Foreign Country*

The IRS will accept, as timely filed, a federal tax return, claim for refund, statement, or other document that is mailed from and officially postmarked in a foreign country on or before the last date prescribed for filing (including any extensions of time for filing). In addition, a return, refund claim, statement, or other document filed with the IRS or the Tax Court that is given to a designated international delivery service in a foreign country and recorded as described in Code Sec. 7502 before midnight on the prescribed due date will be deemed timely filed. If the last date for filing falls on a Saturday, Sunday, or legal holiday, the return or other document will be considered timely filed if it is postmarked,

---

[9] Ann. 90-98, 1990-2 CB 71.

[10] Instructions for Form 706 (Rev. July 2011), p. 1. The due date under Act Sec. 301(d)(1) of the Tax Relief Act of 2010 was extended to no later than nine months after the date of enactment of the Act, which would be September 17, 2011. But because this date was a Saturday, the extended due date was September 19, 2011.

[11] Notice 2011-76, IRB 2011-40, October 3, 2011.

or given to the delivery service, on the next succeeding day that is not a Saturday, Sunday, or legal holiday. The term "legal holiday" does not include legal holidays in foreign countries, unless such holidays are also legal holidays in the District of Columbia or the state where the return or other document is required to be filed.[12]

> *Comment:* The estate tax return cannot be amended after the expiration of the extension period granted for filing. However, the estate representative may subsequently file supplemental information that may result in a finally determined tax different from the amount indicated on the return.[13]

• *Filing Extensions*

An estate will be allowed an automatic six-month extension if (1) the application (Form 4768, Application for Extension of Time to File a Return and/or Pay U.S. Estate (and Generation-Skipping Transfer) Taxes (Rev. August 2012)) is filed on or before the due date prescribed in Code Sec. 6075(a); (2) the application is filed with the IRS office designated in the application's instructions (excepting hand-carried documents); and (3) the application includes an estimate of the amount of estate and generation-skipping transfer tax liability for the estate.[14] A six-month extension of time for filing the return generally does not operate to extend the time for payment of the estate tax (but see the above heading "Filing extended under 2010 Tax Act" with respect to estates of decedents dying in 2010, and see, also, ¶1685). Form 4768 includes a checkbox for requesting the automatic extension. A separate checkbox is provided by which an executor who is abroad may request an extension in excess of six months. The instructions state that the executor should apply for an automatic six-month extension and then apply for any additional extension and that applications for automatic and additional extensions cannot be combined on the same Form 4768. Form 4768 should be used to apply for automatic extensions of time to file Forms 706, 706-A, 706-D, 706-NA, and 706 QDT.

> *Comment:* Unless the Form 706 filing falls under the rules discussed under the heading "Filing extended under 2010 Tax Act" (above), an executor who fails to timely apply for an automatic extension is still permitted to apply for an extension by demonstrating good and sufficient cause.[15] To support the extension for cause, the executor must attach a written statement to the Form 4768 explaining in detail why the executor was unable to request an automatic extension, why it was impossible or impractical to file the Form 706 by the due date, and why the executor should be granted an extension at the present time. Unless the executor is out of the country, an extension will not be granted for more than six months beyond the original due date of the estate tax return.[16] The latest revision of Form 4768 (Rev. August 2012) includes *Part V—Notice to Applicant*, which is used by the IRS to notify the executor whether his or her request for extension to pay has been approved, denied, or requires other action.

> *Preparation Tip:* Executors filing for an extension should take great care to correctly fill in all required Parts, Checkboxes and information fields contained in Form 4768. A failure to do so may mean that the estate has not

---

[12] Rev. Rul. 2002-23, 2002-1 CB 811.

[13] Reg. § 20.6081-1(c).

[14] Reg. § 20.6081-1(b).

[15] Demonstration of cause for the extension is not required if the estate falls within

the rules discussed under the heading "Filing extended under 2010 Tax Act" (above).

[16] Instructions for Form 4768 (Rev. August 2012), p. 2.

formally requested the extension. In this situation, the IRS can be expected not to grant the extension, and to impose a failure to file/failure to pay penalty. See *R. Baccei*, CA-9, 2011-1 USTC ¶60,612, where the Court of Appeals for the Ninth Circuit further held that because the Code and Regulations set forth strict guidelines for the payment of tax, the doctrine of substantial compliance did not apply, and an extension of time was not available to the estate.

• *Victims of Natural Disasters, Terrorist Attacks*

Deadlines for certain tax-related acts, such as the filing of returns and the payment of tax, may be suspended by the IRS for up to one year in response to a presidentially declared disaster (such as a major hurricane), or terrorist or military attacks (see ¶1650). Additionally, a special toll-free telephone number has been created by the IRS for individuals with tax issues related to recently declared federal disasters, or related to participation in a combat zone, as designated by the Department of Defense. The number (1-866-562-5227) is operated by the IRS Monday through Friday, 7:00 a.m. to 10:00 p.m., local time.[17]

Taxpayers whose situations do not fall within these categories should seek IRS answers to their tax questions at 1-800-829-1040.

¶ 67   Penalties

The willful failure to make and file the estate tax return, to pay the tax, or to keep any records or supply any information at the time or times required by law or regulation constitutes a misdemeanor.[18] These offenses are punishable by a fine of not more than $25,000 or imprisonment of not more than one year, or both, with costs of prosecution.

If the estate tax return is not filed within the prescribed time (see ¶66), the IRS will impose a penalty of five percent of the estate tax liability per month or part of a month, up to a maximum of 25 percent, until the return is filed, unless the estate representative can show that the failure to file is due to reasonable cause and not to willful neglect.[19] In addition, if the failure to file is shown to be due to fraud, the penalties range from 15 percent to a maximum of 75 percent.[20]

• *Reliance on Accountant or Attorney*

The question of whether an executor's reliance on an attorney, accountant, or other tax professional to timely file the estate tax return constitutes reasonable cause for late filing of the return has frequently been the subject of litigation. In resolving this issue, the Tax Court and several U.S. courts of appeal have utilized different approaches and arrived at conflicting results.[21] The U.S. Supreme Court, in an attempt to establish a "bright line rule" with respect to this issue, has stated that the delegation of an executor's duty to comply with unambiguous and fixed filing requirements does not relieve the executor of his or her burden to ascertain the relevant filing deadlines and to ensure that they are met.[22] Accordingly, the Court held that where an executor relies on an attorney, accountant, or tax

---

[17] IRS News Release IR-2001-84, Sept. 24, 2001.

[18] Code Sec. 7203.

[19] Code Sec. 6651(a)(1).

[20] Code Sec. 6651(f).

[21] *S.E. Young Est.*, 46 TCM 324, CCH Dec. 40,605(M), TC Memo. 1983-686; *M. Ferrando*, CA-9, 57-2 USTC ¶11,702, 245 F2d 582; *C.I.*

Lillehei Est., CA-3, 81-1 USTC ¶13,389, 638 F2d 65; and *A. Geraci Est.*, CA-6, 74-2 USTC ¶13,024, 502 F2d 1148, cert. denied, 420 US 992, have adopted a *per se* rule that reliance on counsel is not "reasonable cause."

[22] *R. Boyle, Exr.*, SCt, 85-1 USTC ¶13,602, 469 US 241, rev'g CA-7, 83-2 USTC ¶13,530, 710 F2d 1251.

advisor to comply with these filing requirements, the executor's reliance will not constitute reasonable cause for a late filing of the estate tax return.

The Court did recognize that where an executor relies on the erroneous advice of counsel regarding a substantive question of law (e.g., as to whether or not a tax liability exists), such reliance may constitute reasonable cause for a late filing. However, the Court chose not to define the circumstances in which this would be true. The Tax Court has explored this issue and held that a donor's reliance on the advice of her accountant regarding the necessity for filing gift tax returns was reasonable cause for her failure to file the returns. Although the donor's estate eventually conceded gift tax liability for stock and cash advances she had made to her son and that were never repaid, the Tax Court stated that the donor had justifiably relied on her accountant's advice that no gift tax returns were necessary because the advances were intended to be loans at the time of their making.[23] In a similar case, the Tax Court held that an executrix's reliance on her attorney's advice that no estate tax return was due because the estate was too small constituted reasonable cause that excused the executrix's failure to file.[24] The Tax Court has also held that a personal representative's reliance on the erroneous advice of her attorney that an estate was entitled to a second automatic extension of time to file the estate tax return constituted reasonable cause for the untimely filing of the return.[25]

Additionally, an estate administrator's reliance on his attorney was found by a U.S. district court in Tennessee to be reasonable cause for his failure to timely file an estate tax return. The court held that because of his age (78), poor health, and lack of experience in estate administration, the administrator was unable to deal with the "emergency situation" created by the unexpected illness of his attorney shortly before the return was due. The district court noted that the Supreme Court had expressly left open the issue of whether an executor's reliance on his attorney would be reasonable cause for delay when that reliance was due to the executor's incapacity. The court found that the administrator was incapable of exercising ordinary business care and prudence by hiring another attorney to file the return or by obtaining an extension of time in which to file and, therefore, the delay in filing was due to reasonable cause.[26]

> *Comment:* The unusual factual circumstances in the Tennessee case limit the application of its holding. Later decisions on this issue have uniformly held that reliance on an attorney or accountant will not excuse late filing.[27] However, another Tennessee court has held that reliance on a qualified professional's erroneous advice as to when the estate tax return was due was reasonable cause.[28]

---

[23] *S.S. Buring Est.*, 51 TCM 113, CCH Dec. 42,539(M), TC Memo. 1985-610. See also *H.J. Knott*, 55 TCM 424, CCH Dec. 44,653(M), TC Memo. 1988-120.

[24] *F.G. Paxton Est.*, 86 TC 785, CCH Dec. 43,021; *L. Chagra Est.*, 60 TCM 104, CCH Dec. 46,713(M), TC Memo. 1990-352; see also, *C.J. Autin*, 102 TC 760, CCH Dec. 41,906, regarding the gift tax.

[25] *E.E. La Meres*, 98 TC 294, CCH Dec. 48,085.

[26] *C. Brown*, DC Tenn., 86-1 USTC ¶ 13,656.

[27] See *L.F. Blumberg Est.*, DC Cal., 86-1 USTC ¶ 13,658; *G.M. Brandon Est.*, 86 TC 327, CCH Dec. 42,911, rev'd and rem'd on another issue, CA-8, 87-2 USTC ¶ 13,733; *R. Cox Est.*, DC Fla., 86-2 USTC ¶ 13,681; *S.B. Gardner Est.*, 52 TCM 202, CCH Dec. 43,285(M), TC Memo. 1986-380; and *H.E. Rothpletz Est.*, 53 TCM 1214, CCH Dec. 43,998(M), TC Memo. 1987-310; *J.K. Fleming Est.*, CA-7, 92-2 USTC ¶ 60,113, 974 F2d 894; *F.S. Newton Est.*, 59 TCM 469, CCH Dec. 46,546(M), TC Memo. 1990-208; *K.S. Wilbanks Est.*, 61 TCM 1779, CCH Dec. 47,153(M), TC Memo. 1991-45, aff'd, CA-11 (unpublished opinion 1-22-92); *J. Nemerov Est.*, 75 TCM 2344, CCH Dec. 52,709(M), TC Memo. 1998-186; *J.G. Maltaman Est.*, 73 TCM 2163, CCH Dec. 51,917(M), TC Memo. 1997-110.

[28] *W.F. Sharp, Jr. Est.*, DC Tenn., 97-1 USTC ¶ 60,268.

¶67

¶ 68   Place for Filing Return

All estate tax returns filed for decedents dying in 2013 must be filed at the following address: Department of the Treasury, Internal Revenue Service Center, Cincinnati, OH 45999.[29] This is true, regardless of whether the decedent was a U.S. citizen residing in the U.S., a U.S. citizen residing outside the U.S., a resident alien, or a nonresident alien. Returns for pre-2006 decedents with a foreign, APO, or FPO address were to be filed at the Philadelphia Service Center, Philadelphia, PA 19255. Returns of nonresidents (whether citizens or not) dying before 2006 were to be filed with the IRS Service Center, Philadelphia, PA 19255.

¶ 69   Payment of Tax

The estate tax is due and payable at the same time and place the return is due. In other words, the payment must be made with the return.[30] Thus, the estate tax is due nine months after a decedent's death, without regard to extensions of time to file (see ¶ 66, generally, and the heading thereunder "Filing extended under 2010 Tax Act," regarding the special deadlines, extension, and payment rules apply for decedents dying in 2010).

Failure to pay the tax with the return may result in the imposition of a penalty of one-half of one percent of the estate tax liability for each month or part of a month that the tax remains unpaid, up to a maximum of 25 percent.[31] This penalty is in addition to the late-filing penalty discussed at ¶ 67. Code Sec. 6651(d) provides that in cases where a taxpayer fails to pay the tax due on notice and demand thereof by the IRS, the penalty is further increased each month. If an addition to tax applies both for failure to file a return on the due date and for failure to pay the tax on the due date, the addition for failure to file is reduced by the amount of the addition for failure to pay for any month or part of a month to which both additions apply.[32] See ¶ 1685 for details concerning extensions of time for paying the tax.

¶ 70   Persons Required to File Return

The duly qualified executor or administrator of a decedent's estate is required to file the estate tax return. If there is more than one executor or administrator qualifying, all listed fiduciaries are responsible for the return. It is sufficient, however, for only one of the co-fiduciaries to sign the return.[33]

If there is no executor or administrator appointed, qualified, and acting in the United States, every person in actual or constructive possession of any property of a decedent situated in the United States is considered an "executor" for estate tax purposes and is required to make and file a return.[34]

Where two or more persons are liable for the filing of the return, it is preferable for all to join in the filing of one complete return.[35] If all of them are unable to do so, each person is required to file a return disclosing all the information each has with respect to the return (including the name of every person holding a legal or beneficial interest in the property and a full description of the property). Similarly, in the event the appointed, qualified, and acting executor or administrator is unable to make a complete return, every person

---

[29] Instructions for Form 706 (Rev. August 2013), p. 3.

[30] Reg. § 20.6151-1.

[31] Code Sec. 6651.

[32] Code Sec. 6651(c)(1).

[33] Instructions for Form 706 (Rev. August 2013), p. 3.

[34] Reg. § 20.6018-2.

[35] Instructions for Form 706 (Rev. August 2013), p. 3.

holding an interest in property comprising the decedent's estate must make a return, on receipt of notice from the district director, as to the interest held by that person.[36]

The person or persons filing the estate tax return must sign, under penalty of perjury, the first declaration on page 1 of the return. If the return is prepared by an attorney or an agent for the person or persons filing the return, the attorney or agent must also sign the second declaration on page 1 under penalty of perjury.

PTINs required for return preparers. The IRS has issued final regulations, providing guidance to tax return preparers regarding furnishing an identifying number on tax returns and claims for refund.[37] Under the final regulations, for estate, gift, and generation-skipping transfer tax returns or refund claims filed after December 31, 2010, tax return preparers must obtain and exclusively use a preparer tax identification number (PTIN), rather than a Social Security number, as the identifying number to be included with the preparer's signature on a tax return or claim for refund. The term "tax return preparer" is defined as any individual who is compensated for preparing, or assisting in the preparation of, all, or substantially all of, a tax return or claim for refund of tax. The term does not include an individual who is not otherwise a tax return preparer as that term is defined in Reg. § 301.7701-15(b)(2) or who is an individual described in Reg. § 301.7701-15(f). Beginning after December 31, 2010, in order to obtain a PTIN an individual must be an attorney, certified public accountant, enrolled agent, or registered tax return preparer authorized to practice before the IRS (Reg. § 6109-2(d)).

Practice by a registered tax return preparer is generally limited to preparing and signing tax returns and claims for refunds and other documents submitted to the IRS and limited representation of the taxpayer before the IRS. To qualify as a registered tax return preparer, an individual must: (1) be at least 18 years of age; (2) complete a minimum competency exam; (3) not have engaged in disreputable conduct that results in suspension or disbarment under Circular 230; and (4) have a valid PIN (Circular 230 § 10.8, T.D. 9527, May 31, 2011).

Effective November 25, 2011, the IRS has issued Final regulations establishing a user fee of $27 for registered tax return preparers taking the competency test.[38] Tax return preparers who currently have valid PTINs are required to take a competency test in order to be designated as registered tax return preparers. Enrolled agents, certified public accountants and attorneys are exempt from the new testing and educational requirements because they already meet more stringent guidelines to obtain their professional credentials.

The IRS has provided special procedures to obtain PTINs for tax return preparers who are foreign persons or U.S. citizens without Social Security numbers due to conscientious religious objections (Rev. Proc. 2010-41, IRB 2010-48, November 29, 2010).

> *Practice Tip:* The IRS has also announced in IRS News Release IR-2010-99, that an online application system to obtain a PTIN is now available through the Tax Professionals page of the IRS's website. Individuals who currently possess a PTIN will need to reapply under the new system but generally will be reassigned the same number.[39] Return preparers will receive a PTIN immediately after successfully registering

---

[36] Reg. § 20.6018-2.

[37] T.D. 9501, filed with the Federal Register on September 28, 2010.

[38] T.D. 9559, filed with the Federal Register on November 22, 2011.

[39] IRS News Release IR-2010-99.

online. Alternatively, return preparers can submit a paper application on Form W-12, IRS Paid Preparer Tax Identification Number Application, and receive a response in four to six weeks. Regulations that impose a $50 user fee on individuals who apply for or renew a PTIN have also been finalized by the IRS. The $50 user fee is based on an annual PTIN renewal period and is nonrefundable regardless of whether the applicant receives a PTIN. An additional $14.25 will be charged by the third-party vendor to cover the cost of administering the application and renewal process. The regulations are effective after September 30, 2010.[40]

¶ 71   Missing Person's Return

A duty to file an estate tax return for a missing person's estate rests on any person who would be an executor or administrator of the estate in the event of the missing person's actual death. The executor or administrator must ascertain from existing facts whether the missing person is a "decedent" for purposes of filing the estate tax return.[41]

Facts establishing a missing person's death for estate tax return purposes include the following:

(1) administration of the absentee's property pursuant to adjudication by a court of competent jurisdiction;

(2) transfer to or vesting of the absentee's assets in a beneficiary pursuant to state law;

(3) taking of or receipt of the absentee's property by any person without court order or statutory authority; or

(4) circumstances indicating that the absentee's property has been disposed of as if he or she were dead.[42]

The mere appointment of a receiver for the missing person's property does not indicate that person's death for estate tax purposes in the absence of any transfer of title or assets. In any event, if the value of the missing person's estate is such as to otherwise require that an estate tax return be filed (see ¶ 22), such a return must be filed within nine months following the period of continuous and unexplained absence after which the person may be declared legally dead under applicable state law.

In a National Office Technical Advice Memorandum, the IRS has ruled that, where there is a court adjudication of death based on a presumption of death and no fixed date thereof, the date of death for federal estate tax purposes is the ending date of the state presumptive period and not the date of adjudication. In the IRS's view, any other rule would leave the determination of the date of death, for federal estate tax purposes, to the discretion of the interested party filing the petition in state court.[43]

¶ 72   Supplemental Documents

If the decedent was a U.S. resident and died testate, a certified copy of the decedent's will must be filed with the estate tax return. The executor may also

---

[40] T.D. 9503, filed with the Federal Register on September 28, 2010.

[41] Rev. Rul. 66-286, 1966-2 CB 485, as clarified and modified by Rev. Rul. 80-347, 1980-2 CB 342, and by Rev. Rul. 82-189, 1982-2 CB 189.

[42] Rev. Rul. 66-286, 1966-2 CB 485, as clarified and modified by Rev. Rul. 80-347, 1980-2 CB 342, and by Rev. Rul. 82-189, 1982-2 CB 189.

[43] IRS Technical Advice Memorandum 8526007 (March 14, 1985).

file copies of any documents that the executor desires to submit in explanation of the return. Various other supplemental documents, required for the several property schedules of the return, are discussed in the following chapters.

If the decedent was a nonresident citizen, the following documents must also be filed with the return:

(1) a copy of any inventory of property and any schedule of liabilities, claims against the estate, and expenses of administration filed with the foreign court of probate jurisdiction and certified by a proper official of such court; and

(2) a copy of any return filed under a foreign inheritance, estate, legacy, succession, or other death tax act and certified by a proper official of the foreign tax department, if the estate is subject to such a foreign tax.[44]

Comment: Form 2848 (Power of Attorney and Declaration of Representative) (Rev. March 2012) must be filed in order to grant authority to an individual to represent a taxpayer before the IRS and to receive tax information (see ¶79). Form 8821 (Tax Information Authorization) (Rev. October 2012) is to be used to authorize any designated individual, corporation, firm, organization, or partnership to inspect and/or receive confidential information in any office of the IRS for the type of tax and years or periods listed on the form (see ¶79).

See also the material discussing the following: alternate valuation, ¶115; real estate, ¶262; stocks and bonds, ¶313; life insurance, ¶481; business interests, ¶527; miscellaneous properties, ¶535; transfers during life, ¶615; powers of appointment, ¶670; attorneys' fees, ¶792; marital deduction, ¶1075; charitable deduction, ¶1140 and ¶1141.

¶73   Execution of the Return

Form 706 (United States Estate (and Generation-Skipping Transfer) Tax Return) is used to report the estate tax liability of estates of decedents dying in 2013. Form 706 (Rev. August 2013)[45] is arranged in the following sequence:

• Page 1 contains questions dealing with general information pertaining to the decedent, a "Tax Computation" section (Part 2), and a section for signing the return by the executor. (For purposes of Form 706, the term "executor" means an executor, personal representative, administrator, or person in actual possession of the decedent's property.) Lines 9a through 9d are used to calculate the applicable exclusion amount, factoring in any Deceased Spousal Unused Exclusion (DSUE) amount received from a predeceased spouse. The allowable unified credit (applicable credit amount) is subtracted on line 11 of the "Tax Computation" section. The credit for foreign death taxes, and the credit for tax on prior transfers, are claimed on Lines 13, and 14, respectively, of the "Tax Computation" section where applicable.

• Page 2 of Form 706 includes an "Elections by the Executor" section (Part 3) in which the executor can make elections to use the alternate valuation date (see ¶107), to specially value property (see ¶280 through ¶296), and to pay tax in installments under Code Sec. 6166 or to postpone taxes under Code Sec. 6163 (see ¶1650 through ¶1685). Page 2 also contains "General Information" questions (Part 4), which continue onto page 3.

---

[44] Reg. §20.6018-4.

[45] Form 706 (Rev. July 2011), is used for reporting the estate tax liability of estates of decedents dying in 2010.

• Page 3 of Form 706 contains a "Recapitulation" (Part 5) that has two sections. The decedent's gross estate (from Schedules A through I) is reported in the first section of the Recapitulation, and, after subtracting any qualified conservation easement exclusion (from Schedule U), the "Total gross estate less exclusion" for this section is then reported on line 1 of the "Tax Computation" section (Part 2) on page 1 of Form 706. The second section of the Recapitulation is used to record the deductions (from Schedules J through M and O), and the "Tentative total allowable deductions" (line 24) are then carried over and deducted on line 2 of the "Tax Computation" section on page 1.

The Recapitulation (Part 5) of Form 706 (Rev. August 2013) contains two lines (line 10 and line 23) that relate to executors of estates that are not required to file a Form 706 under Code Sec. 6018, but must estimate the value of certain property eligible for a marital or charitable deduction.

Part 6 of Form 706 is used to compute Deceased Spousal Unused Exclusion (DSUE) (see ¶16).

Form 706 also includes the following schedules:

• Schedules A through I, which are used to report a decedent's gross estate.

• Schedule A-1 (Section 2032A Valuation), which is used to report information required to support the election to value certain farm and closely held business property at its special use value. Schedule A-1 includes the Notice of Election (part 2) and the Agreement to Special Valuation Under Section 2032A (part 3).

• Schedules J through M and O, which are used to report deductions.

• Schedule P (Credit for Foreign Death Taxes) and Schedule Q (Credit for Tax on Prior Transfers), which are used to report tax credits. Note that IRS Form 706-CE (Certificate of Payment of Foreign Death Tax) (Rev. October 2013) must also be filed in order to claim a credit for foreign death tax.

• Schedule R (Generation-Skipping Transfer Tax), which is used to compute the generation-skipping transfer (GST) tax payable by an estate, and Schedule R-1 (Generation-Skipping Transfer Tax—Direct Skips From a Trust—Payment Voucher), which is used for the computation of the tax payable by certain trusts that are includible in the gross estate. Only GST tax imposed as a result of a direct skip occurring at death is reported using Form 706. See Chapter 41 (¶2471 through ¶2487) for a discussion of the other forms used for reporting the GST tax.

• Schedule U (Qualified Conservation Easement Exclusion) is used to report information required to support the election to exclude a portion of the value of land that is included in the decedent's gross estate and is subject to a qualified conservation easement. The amount of the exclusion is entered on Form 706, part 5, item 12, page 3.

Schedule PC (Protective Claims for Refund) can be used by executors to preserve the estate's right to an estate tax refund when a claim or expense that is a subject of an unresolved controversy at the time of filing later becomes deductible under Code Sec. 2053.

• A Continuation Schedule is to be used for listing additional assets from Schedules A, B, C, D, E, F, G, H, and I and additional deductions from Schedules J, K, L, M, and O if there is no more room on the particular schedule. Totals on a Continuation Schedule should be carried over to the appropriate line of the main

¶73

schedule. A separate Continuation Schedule must be used for each main schedule being continued.

Money items may be shown on the return as whole-dollar amounts. The rounding off of amounts to whole-dollar figures requires the elimination of any amount less than 50 cents and an increase of any amount in the range of 50 cents to 99 cents to the next higher dollar amount.[46]

The final computation of the tax must be shown in detail. The estate tax return does not provide a detailed schedule for the purposes of this computation, however. If the executor determines that no estate tax is owed by the decedent's estate, he or she should enter a zero on line 20—"Balance due" under "Tax Computation" (Part 2) on page 1 of the return. Executors must provide documentation proving their status as such. Documentation will vary, but may include documents such as a certified copy of the will or a court order designating the executor(s). A statement by the executor(s) attesting to their status is insufficient.[47]

- *Total Gross Estate Exceeding the Applicable Exclusion Amount*

In the case of a decedent whose total gross estate exceeds the applicable exclusion amount ($5.0 million for 2010 and 2011; $5,120,000 for 2012; $5,250,000 for 2013; and $5,340,000 for 2014), the first three pages of Form 706 and all required supporting schedules must be filed, in accordance with the following rules:

(1) If the gross estate does not include assets reportable on Schedule A (Real Estate), Schedule B (Stocks and Bonds), Schedule C (Mortgages, Notes, and Cash), Schedule D (Insurance on the Decedent's Life), or Schedule E (Jointly Owned Property), it is not necessary to file these schedules, and a zero should be entered on the applicable line of the Recapitulation on page 3 of Form 706. However, Schedule D must be filed if it is indicated in the "General Information" portion of Form 706 (Part 4, Question 9a) that there was insurance on the decedent's life that was not included on the return as part of the gross estate.

(2) Schedule F (Other Miscellaneous Property Not Reportable Under Any Other Schedule) must be filed with every return.

(3) Schedule G (Transfers During Decedent's Life) must be filed if, as indicated in the General Information portion of Form 706 (Part 4, Questions 11a, 11b and 12a), the decedent made certain types of transfers during life or if there existed at the date of death any trusts created by the decedent during his or her lifetime (Question 13a). Schedule H (Powers of Appointment) must be filed if it is indicated in the General Information portion of Form 706 (Part 4, Question 14) that the decedent ever possessed, exercised, or released any general power of appointment. Schedule I (Annuities) must be filed if it is indicated in the General Information portion of Form 706 (Part 4, Question 16) that the decedent, immediately before death, was receiving an annuity.

(4) Schedule J (Funeral Expenses and Expenses Incurred in Administering Property Subject to Claims), Schedule K (Debts of the Decedent, and Mortgages and Liens), Schedule L (Net Losses During Administration and Expenses Incurred in Administering Property Not Subject to Claims),

---

[46] Instructions for Form 706 (Rev. August 2013), p. 4.

[47] Instructions for Form 706 (Rev. August 2013), p. 3.

Schedule M (Bequests, etc., to Surviving Spouse), and Schedule O (Charitable, Public, and Similar Gifts and Bequests) must be filed only if a deduction is claimed for a particular item. For Schedule M, which is used to list the assets for which a marital deduction has been taken, the QTIP election is deemed to have been made if property qualifying for QTIP treatment is listed on Schedule M.

(5) Schedule P (Credit for Foreign Death Taxes) and Schedule Q (Credit for Tax on Prior Transfers) must be filed only if the particular credit is claimed.

(6) Schedule U (Qualified Conservation Easement Exclusion) must be filed if the exclusion is claimed on part 5, item 12.

(7) Schedule PC (Protective Claim for Refund) must be filed (two copies for each pending claim or expense) if a protective claim was indicated on Part 4, Question 6.

¶ 74   Estate Beneficiaries

Individuals, trusts, or estates receiving benefits of $5,000 or more from the decedent's estate (other than charitable beneficiaries) are to be listed on page 2 of the Form 706 (United States Estate (and Generation-Skipping Transfer) Tax Return) (Rev. August 2013) estate tax return, together with their taxpayer identification numbers (Social Security numbers in the case of individuals, and employer identification numbers for trusts and other estates), relationship to the decedent, and the approximate dollar value of property received from the estate. The total of these distributions should approximate the amount of the gross estate, reduced by funeral and administration expenses, debts and mortgages, bequests to the surviving spouse, charitable bequests, and any federal and state estate and generation-skipping transfer taxes paid relating to the benefits received by the beneficiaries.

¶ 75   Beneficiaries Receiving Specially Valued Property

Individuals who received an interest in specially valued property (see ¶ 280 through ¶ 296) must be listed on Schedule A-1 (Section 2032A Valuation) of the estate tax return, along with their taxpayer identification numbers, relationship to the decedent, and addresses. In the case of an individual beneficiary, the identification number is the Social Security number; for trusts and estates, the employer identification number should be used.

¶ 78   Entering Principal and Income on Schedules

For every item of principal, any income accrued thereon at the date of the decedent's death must be separately entered on the appropriate schedule under the column headed "Value at date of death." If the alternate valuation method is elected, any includible income with respect to each item of principal must be separately entered under the column headed "Alternate value."

The information indicated by the columns headed "Alternate valuation date" and "Alternate value" should not be shown unless the executor elects the alternate valuation method. "Alternate value" information should be omitted in the space provided in the Recapitulation, Part 5, Form 706 (United States Estate (and Generation-Skipping Transfer) Tax Return) (Rev. August 2013), if the alternate valuation method is not elected.

The items must be numbered under every schedule. The total of the items on each schedule should be shown at the bottom of the schedule, but the totals should not be carried forward from one schedule to another. The total for each schedule, however, should be entered under the Recapitulation section.

¶ 79   Representation by Lawyer or Agent

If the executor is to be represented before the IRS by someone else, by correspondence or otherwise, in refund claims and other matters, a power of attorney must be filed on Form 2848 (Power of Attorney and Declaration of Representative) (Rev. March 2012) and signed by the fiduciary.

Form 2848 authorizes a person or persons to represent an estate in a proceeding before the IRS and to receive confidential information. It also authorizes the person or persons named as a representative to perform one or more of the three following acts: (1) execute waivers (including offers of waivers) of restrictions on assessment or collection of deficiencies; (2) execute consents extending the statutory period for assessment or collection of taxes; and (3) execute closing agreements. In order to grant additional powers, such as the power to delegate authority, to substitute another representative, or to sign the return, specific language designating the additional power must be inserted. Form 8821 (Tax Information Authorization) (Rev. October 2012) is to be used to authorize any designated individual, corporation, firm, organization, or partnership to inspect and/or receive confidential information in any office of the IRS for the type of tax and years or periods listed on the form. It will not authorize an individual to represent a taxpayer and/or perform other acts on the taxpayer's behalf such as executing waivers, consents, or closing agreements. Form 2848 must be used for that purpose. A properly executed declaration on page 2 (Part 4) of Form 706 (United States Estate (and Generation-Skipping Transfer) Tax Return) (Rev. August 2013) will also authorize an attorney, certified public accountant, or enrolled agent to represent the estate and receive confidential tax information, such as a copy of the closing letter.

Generally, only one power of attorney to represent the estate may be in effect in an IRS office in any one matter. Therefore, the names and addresses of all lawyers or agents to whom the executor has delegated authority to represent the estate in the matter should be included in the power of attorney. The power of attorney should be filed with the IRS District Director in whose office the estate tax return has been, or will be, filed.

> *Practice Tip:* Attorneys and certified public accountants are not required to be enrolled to practice before the IRS. However, they must file as evidence of recognition a written declaration stating that they are qualified and are authorized to represent the particular parties on whose behalf they are acting.[48] Attorneys are qualified if they are members in good standing of the bar of the highest court of any state, possession, territory, commonwealth, or the District of Columbia and are not currently under suspension or disbarment from practice before the IRS. Similarly, certified public accountants are qualified if they are authorized to practice as certified public accountants in any state, possession, territory, commonwealth, or the District of Columbia and are not currently under suspension or disbarment from practice before the IRS.

In both instances noted above, the declarants must be authorized to act on behalf of their clients. If the representative has a CAF number, it is to be entered on Line 2 or Form 2848. Otherwise, "None" should be entered, and the IRS will

---

[48] Statement of Procedural Rules § 601.502.

assign one to the representative.[49] A CAF number is a unique nine-digit number that the IRS assigns to representatives.

Form 2848 contains a declaration to be completed, which contains the following information:

(1) A statement that the representative is authorized to represent the taxpayer as a certified public accountant, attorney, enrolled agent, enrolled actuary, unenrolled return preparer, member of the taxpayer's immediate family, officer, full-time employee, etc. An actuary enrolled by the Joint Board for the Enrollment of Actuaries may represent a taxpayer before the IRS. However, the actuary's representation is limited to certain areas of the Internal Revenue Code. See § 10.3(d)(1) of Treasury Department Circular No. 230 for a list of the Code sections involved and the areas covered by them.

(2) The jurisdiction recognizing the representative. For an attorney or certified public accountant: Enter in the "Jurisdiction" column the state, District of Columbia, possession, or commonwealth that has granted the declared professional recognition. For an enrolled agent or actuary: Enter in the "Jurisdiction" column the enrollment card number.

(3) The signature of the representative, and the date signed.

If the estate is to be represented before the IRS by an agent, the agent must be enrolled to practice in accordance with the regulations contained in the Rules on Administrative Procedure. The requirements for enrollment of agents are contained in Treasury Department Circular No. 230 (Title 31, part 10, Code of Federal Regulations), which may be obtained from the Director of Practice, U.S. Treasury Department, Washington, D.C. 20009. Unenrolled agents may represent taxpayers only under limited circumstances.[50]

Any person qualified under § 10.5(c) (relating to temporary recognition of an applicant for enrollment) or § 10.7 (relating to limited practice without enrollment in the case of a full-time employee, or a bona fide officer of a corporation, trust, estate, association, or organized group, and certain others) of Circular No. 230 will also be recognized to practice before the IRS.[51] Effective September 26, 2007, practice before the IRS is defined to include rendering written advice with respect to any entity, transaction, plan, or arrangement, or arrangement having a potential for tax avoidance or evasion.[52]

¶ 80 Special Use Valuation Additional Tax—Form 706-A

Where the election to have farm or closely held business real property valued under the special use valuation provisions is made under Code Sec. 2032A, the tax benefits gained as a result are recaptured as an additional estate tax if the property is disposed of to nonfamily members or ceases to be used for farming or closely held business purposes within 10 years after the death of the decedent. Form 706-A (United States Additional Estate Tax Return) (Rev. September 2013) is used to report the recapture of these tax benefits. For a discussion of the Code Sec. 2032A election, see ¶ 280 through ¶ 296.

The basic Form 706-A computation of the additional estate tax due under Code Sec. 2032A is made on Part II, lines 1–15. Lines 16–18 incorporate informa-

---

[49] Instructions for Form 2848 (Rev. March 2012), p. 3.
[50] Statement of Procedural Rules § 601.502.

[51] Statement of Procedural Rules § 601.502.
[52] Circular 230, § 10.2(a)(4), T.D. 9359.

tion relating to involuntary conversions or exchanges reported on Schedule B before arriving at the additional estate tax amount on line 19. If an individual is using Form 706-A to report an exchange or involuntary conversion, he or she should not use the same Form 706-A to report any cessations of qualified use or dispositions of specially valued property that are not exchanges or involuntary conversions.[53] A separate Form 706-A should be used for the cessations or other dispositions. However, involuntary conversions and exchanges may be reported together on the same form. A separate Form 706-A must be used for each qualified heir.

It should be noted that Form 706-A also includes a Schedule C for purposes of reporting dispositions to family members of the qualified heir.

Form 706-A should be completed in the following order:

(1) Part I,

(2) Schedules A and B,

(3) Part II, and

(4) Schedule C.

Form 706-A must be filed with the IRS office where the decedent's estate tax return was filed. Unless an extension for filing is obtained, Form 706-A must be filed within six months after the taxable disposition or cessation of qualified use of the property.

A filled-in Form 706-A appears in the Appendix at ¶3200.

¶ 85   Nonresidents Not Citizens

An estate tax return must be filed for the estate of a nonresident not a citizen if the part of the decedent's gross estate having a situs in the United States exceeded a value of $60,000, after reduction for (1) taxable gifts made after 1976, and (2) the aggregate amount that was allowable as a specific exemption under Code Sec. 2521, as it existed prior to its repeal by the Tax Reform Act of 1976, for gifts made between September 9, 1976, and December 31, 1976.[54] Form 706-NA (United States Estate (and Generation-Skipping Transfer) Tax Return (Estate of nonresident not a citizen of the United States) (Rev. August 2013)) is used for the estates of nonresidents not citizens dying in 2013 (see ¶3260). This return must be filed and the estate tax paid (in U.S. currency at par) within nine months after a decedent's death. The estates of nonresidents who are not citizens are entitled to the same filing and payment extensions that are available to U.S. citizens and residents. Returns of nonresident, not citizens who died in 2013 must be filed with the Internal Revenue Service Center, Cincinnati, OH 45999. If the decedent died testate, a certified copy of the will must be attached to the return. Executors must provide documentation of their status.[55]

Caution: 706-NA (Rev. July 2011) is to be used to report the estate tax liability of the estates nonresidents not citizens dying in 2011 or 2012, as well as estates of nonresidents not citizens dying in 2010. However, preparers should note that when preparing a Form 706-NA for the estate of a decedent dying in 2011 or 2012, the Form 706-NA Instructions dated Rev. August 2011 must be used. When a Form 706-NA is prepared for the estate

---

[53] Instructions for Form 706-A (Rev. September 2013), p. 3.
[54] Code Sec. 6018(a)(3).

[55] Instructions for Form 706-NA (Rev. August 2013), p.1.

of a decedent dying in 2010, the Form 706-NA Instructions dated Rev. July 2011 must be used.[56]

Schedule A of Form 706-NA (Rev. August 2013) is used to report that portion of the nonresident alien's gross estate that is situated in the United States. See ¶ 1617 and ¶ 1620 for further details. Property reported on this schedule must be valued in U.S. dollars, and the "alternate valuation method," discussed at ¶ 105, can be elected. All property must be separately listed on Schedule A (page 2) and must be described in such a manner that it can be readily identified. The total value of property listed in Schedule A is reported on line 1 of Schedule B (page 2) of Form 706-NA.

Schedule E of Form 706 must be attached to Form 706-NA if, at the time of death, the decedent owned any property located in the United States in joint tenancy with the right of survivorship, as a tenant by the entirety, or with a surviving spouse as community property.

Schedule G of Form 706 must be attached to Form 706-NA if the decedent made certain lifetime transfers (described in detail in the Instructions for Form 706, Schedule G) of property that was located in the United States either at the time of the transfer or at the time of the decedent's death. A Form 706 Schedule G must also be filed with Form 706-NA if the decedent created any trusts during his lifetime that were in existence at the time of transfer or at the time of the decedent's death.

Schedule H of Form 706 must be attached to Form 706-NA if the decedent, at the time of his or her death, possessed a general power of appointment over property located in the United States and/or if the decedent exercised or released such a power at any time.

If the gross estate in the United States includes any interests in property transferred to a "skip person" as defined in the Instructions to Form 706, Schedule R (Generation-Skipping Transfer Tax) and/or Schedule R-1 (Generation-Skipping Transfer Tax—Direct Skips From a Trust) must be attached.

Schedule B of Form 706-NA is used to compute the taxable estate of a nonresident alien. This schedule is filled out as follows:

(1) The decedent's gross estate located in the United States, as reported on Schedule A, is entered on line 1 of Schedule B. The decedent's gross estate located outside the United States is then reported on line 2 of Schedule B. The total of lines 1 and 2, or the decedent's entire gross estate wherever situated, is entered on line 3.

(2) The deduction for administration expenses, claims, etc., is determined and claimed on lines 4 and 5 of Schedule B. A deduction for mortgages will be allowed only if the full value of the mortgaged property was included in the total gross estate reported on line 3.

(3) The charitable deduction is claimed on line 6. Line 6 of Schedule B indicates that Schedule O of Form 706 must be attached to support this deduction. However, the Form 706-NA instructions indicate that, if a charitable deduction is claimed under a treaty, the applicable treaty must be specified and the computation of the charitable deduction must be at-

[56] Unless noted to the contrary, the discussions in *2014 U.S. Master™ Estate and Gift Tax* *Guide* generally pertain to the estates of decedents dying in 2013.

tached.[57] The marital deduction that is available to the estates of decedents only under certain treaties is also claimed on line 6. Estates of decedents claiming this deduction must attach Schedule M of Form 706 and a sheet showing the computation of the amount of the deduction.

(4) The state death tax deduction for death taxes (estate, inheritance, legacy, or succession taxes) paid to any state or the District of Columbia on property listed in Schedule A is claimed on line 7. This deduction must generally be claimed within four years of filing the return. A certificate signed by the appropriate official of the taxing state must be filed to substantiate the deduction. The certificate must show (a) the total tax charged, (b) any discount allowed, (c) any penalties and interest imposed, (d) the tax actually paid, and (e) each payment date.[58]

(5) The total deductions (i.e., the total of lines 5, 6, and 7) are entered on line 8.

(6) The taxable estate is computed on line 9 by subtracting line 8 from line 1. (See ¶1625 and ¶1630 for further details concerning the allowance of deductions for the estates of nonresident aliens.)

After Schedules A and B of Form 706-NA have been completed, the "Tax Computation" section (part II) on page 1 can be completed. The taxable estate, from line 9, Schedule B, is entered on line 1 of this Tax Computation section. The sum of the taxable estate (line 1) and the decedent's adjusted taxable gifts of tangible or intangible property located in the United States (line 2) is entered on line 3. Prior gifts made by the decedent must be calculated at the rate in effect on the date of the decedent's death (see ¶2008). The tentative tax on the total of the taxable estate and the total taxable gifts (line 3) and the tentative tax on the total taxable gifts alone (line 2) are then entered on lines 4 and 5, respectively. The amount on line 5 is then subtracted from the amount on line 4, and the resulting amount—the gross estate tax—is entered on line 6.[59]

The estate and gift tax rates applicable to the estates of U.S. citizens are also applicable to the estates of nonresident aliens.[60]

The allowable unified credit against estate taxes is entered on line 7. "Other credits" (including the Canadian marital credit and the credit for federal gift taxes) are entered on line 9, the credit for tax on prior transfers on line 10 and the total of these two credits is entered on line 11. The net estate tax liability is entered on line 12 after subtracting the line 11 amount from the amount on line 8. The generation-skipping transfer tax (see instructions to Schedule R of Form 706) imposed on transfers of interests in property that is part of the gross estate in the United States is entered on line 13. The addition of lines 12 and 13 results in the amount of total transfer taxes entered on line 14. The total reductions for prior payments is entered on line 15. The balance of estate tax due (computed as the amount on line 15 subtracted from the amount on line 14) is entered on line 16.

> *Comment:* It should be noted that, where permitted by treaty, the estate of a nonresident alien is allowed the same unified credit as that of a U.S. citizen, multiplied by the proportion of the total gross estate situated in the United States. In other cases, the estate of a nonresident alien who is not a resident of a U.S. possession is allowed a unified credit of $13,000 (which exempts the first $60,000 of the estate from estate tax).[61]

---

[57] Instructions for Form 706-NA (Rev. August 2013), p. 5.

[58] Instructions for Form 706-NA (Rev. August 2013), p. 5.

[59] Form 706-NA (Rev. August 2013).

[60] Code Sec. 2101(b).

[61] Code Sec. 2102(c).

Chapter 5

VALUATION—DATE AND METHODS

¶ 100   Election Available

The representative of an estate has an election with respect to the time property included in the gross estate is to be valued. The representative may elect to value property as of the date of the decedent's death or as of an "alternate valuation date." The alternate valuation date is, generally, a date six months after the date of the decedent's death. See ¶ 107 for further details. Even property that was transferred some time before death, but that is included in the gross estate because of the retention of certain rights or for other reasons, is valued as of the date of death or as of a date six months after death.

¶ 101   Rules Applicable to Various Types of Property

Even though all property included in the gross estate is valued as of the same date—that is, the date of death or the alternate valuation date—special problems arise in valuing particular types of property. For this reason, special rules apply in valuing the various kinds of property or interests in property that might be included in the gross estate, such as: real estate; stocks and bonds; mutual funds; interests in business; notes, secured and unsecured; cash on hand or on deposit; household and personal effects; annuities, life estates, remainders, and reversions; and certain other property.

¶ 102   Request for IRS Valuation Basis

The IRS may be required to furnish a written statement explaining any determination or proposed determination of the value of an item of property in a decedent's estate. The statement must be furnished no later than 45 days after a written request by the executor or donor or 45 days after the determination or proposed determination, whichever is later.[1]

The statement must (1) explain the basis of the valuation, (2) set forth any computation, and (3) include a copy of any expert appraisal. The method used by the IRS in arriving at the valuation is not binding on the IRS.

A request for such a statement must be filed with the District Director's office that has jurisdiction over the estate tax return by the deadline for claiming a refund of the tax that is dependent on the valuation.[2]

[1] Code Sec. 7517.   [2] Reg. § 301.7517-1.

¶ 105   Alternate Valuation Method

The alternate valuation method for determining the value of a decedent's estate is authorized by Code Sec. 2032. The use of this method is limited to situations in which the election would reduce both the value of the decedent's gross estate and the federal estate and generation-skipping transfer (GST) tax liability of the estate.[3] In evaluating an estate's eligibility to make the alternate valuation election, the regulations clarify that the determination of whether there has been a decease in the estate tax and GST tax liability is made with reference to the estate and GST tax payable by reason of the decedent's death.[4] The regulations also provide that a protective election may be made on the decedent's estate tax return if it is subsequently determined that the estate meets the Code Sec. 2032(c) eligibility requirements. A protective election is irrevocable as of the due date of the return (including extensions of time actually granted).

The alternate valuation date may be elected on an estate tax return that is filed no more than one year late.[5] Once elected, the use of the alternate valuation date is irrevocable.[6] Further, the alternate valuation method must be elected on the first return filed or on a subsequent return if filed by the due date of the original return. The regulations provide that estates that fail to make the alternate valuation election on the last estate tax return filed before the due date, or the first return filed after the due date, will still be able to request an extension of time to make the election. However, a one-year filing deadline applies: No request for an extension of time to make the election will be granted if the request is submitted to the IRS more than one year after the due date of the return (including extensions of time to file that were actually granted).[7]

> *Election:* The alternate valuation method is not automatic. It must be expressly elected on the estate tax return by checking the box at line 1 of Part 3 (Elections by the Executor) of Form 706 (United States Estate (and Generation-Skipping Transfer) Tax Return) (Rev. August 2013). However, the mere failure to designate the election on the return will not necessarily preclude the use of alternate valuation. A determination of whether an election has been made must be reached by looking at all of the facts on the return.[8]

¶ 107   Applicable Alternate Valuation Dates

If the estate representative chooses the alternate valuation method, all property included in the gross estate is valued as of six months after the decedent's death, except that property sold, distributed, exchanged, or otherwise disposed of during the six months is to be valued as of the date of disposition.[9] If there is no day in the sixth month following the decedent's death that corresponds numerically to the date of death, the alternate valuation date is the last day of the sixth month.[10] The actual selling price of securities sold in arm's-length transactions during the alternate valuation period must be used in valuing such securities by a person electing the alternate valuation method.[11]

The phrase "distributed, sold, exchanged, or otherwise disposed of" includes all possible ways by which property may cease to form a part of the gross

---

[3] Code Sec. 2032(c).
[4] Reg. § 20.2032-1(b).
[5] Code Sec. 2032(d).
[6] Code Sec. 2032(d).
[7] Reg. § 301.9100-1 and Reg. § 301.9100-3.

[8] Rev. Rul. 61-128, 1961-2 CB 150.
[9] Code Sec. 2032(a).
[10] Rev. Rul. 74-260, 1974-1 CB 275.
[11] Rev. Rul. 68-272, 1968-1 CB 394; Rev. Rul. 70-512, 1970-2 CB 192.

estate. Property is considered "distributed," either by the estate representative or by a trustee of property included in the gross estate, on the date on which the first of the following events occurs:

> (1) entry of an order or decree of distribution (if the order or decree subsequently becomes final);

> (2) separation of the property from the estate or trust so that it is completely available to the distributee; or

> (3) actual distribution of the property to the beneficiary or other distributee.

In order to eliminate changes in value due only to lapse of time, Code Sec. 2032 provides that any interest or estate "affected by mere lapse of time" is to be included in the gross estate under the alternate valuation method at its value as of the date of the decedent's death. Adjustments for any difference in value as of the alternate valuation date not due to mere lapse of time are allowed. Property "affected by mere lapse of time" includes patents, estates for the life of a person other than the decedent, remainders, and reversions.[12]

> **Comment:** The IRS takes the position that the use of the alternate valuation date election is limited to circumstances where market conditions, not voluntary conditions, have caused a decrease in the fair market value of an estate's property.[13] Thus, it has announced that it will not follow a Tax Court decision[14] holding that an estate's closely held stock was appropriately valued on the alternate valuation date, and accordingly, discounts were properly claimed for transfer restrictions and a purchase option to which the new stock was subject. The IRS, in Action on Decision, AOD-2008-01, noted that the valuation discounts were the result of a tax-free reorganization that occurred two months after the decedent's death. Its position is that the transfer restrictions should have been disregarded in valuing the stock because the legislative history to the predecessor to Code Sec. 2032 indicated that Congress intended to provide relief for post-death decreases in value due to market forces, not voluntary changes. The Tax Court allowed the estate in *Kohler* to elect alternate valuation because it concluded that the reorganization was not a "disposition" for purposes of Code Sec. 2032(a)(1) or Reg. § 20.2032-1(c)(1).

Proposed regulations[15] would clarify that the election to use alternate valuation is only available to estates that experience a reduction in the value of the gross estate within six months of the decedent's death due to market conditions and not any other post-death events. Market conditions are defined by the proposed regulations as events outside the control of the decedent, the decedent's estate, or other persons whose property is being valued that affect the fair market value of the property of the estate. Examples are provided of post-death events that are not considered changes as a result of market conditions. These include, but are not limited to, the reorganization of an entity in which the estate holds an interest, a distribution to the estate from such an entity, or distributions by the estate of a fractional interest in such an entity. Once finalized, the proposed regulations will be applicable to decedents dying on or after April 25, 2008.

---

[12] Reg. § 20.2032-1(f).

[13] *A. Flanders*, DC Calif., 72-1 USTC ¶ 12,881, 347 FSupp 95.

[14] *H. Kohler*, 92 TCM 48, CCH Dec. 56,573(M), TC Memo. 2006-152.

[15] Prop. Reg. § 20.2032-1, NPRM-REG 112196-07.

¶ 109   Property to Be Valued

The property to be valued as of the alternate valuation date is the property included in the gross estate on the date of the decedent's death. Property interests remain "included property" for the purpose of valuing the gross estate under the alternate valuation method even though they change in form during the alternate valuation period by being actually received or disposed of by the estate.[16] Consequently, it is necessary in every case to determine what property comprised the gross estate at the decedent's death.

The alternate valuation election applies to *all* the property included in the gross estate on the date of a decedent's death. The election cannot be applied to only a portion of such property.[17] However, the IRS has ruled that a decedent's estate could elect both to value the decedent's assets on the alternate valuation date and to value the decedent's qualifying farm property under the special use valuation provisions of Code Sec. 2032A.[18] In addition, an estate electing both the alternate valuation date and special use valuation was required to use the alternate valuation date to determine the special use value of farmland owned by the decedent. For purposes of applying the limit on the aggregate reduction in the value of qualified real property, the alternate valuation date was also to be used to compute the difference between fair market value and special use value.[19]

¶ 110   Income After Death

Rents, dividends, and interest received during the six months following the decedent's death are not includible in a decedent's gross estate by reason of the executor's election to adopt the alternate valuation method. If the right to such income has accrued at the date of death, such income is includible.

Any partial payment of the principal of interest-bearing obligations, such as notes and bonds, made between the date of death and the subsequent valuation date is includible in the gross estate at its value on the date of payment. Similarly, any advance payment of interest for a period after the subsequent valuation date made during the alternate valuation period that has the effect of reducing the value of the principal obligation as of the subsequent valuation date will be included in the gross estate at its value on the date of payment.[20] The principle applicable to interest paid in advance also applies to advance payments of rent.

Ordinary dividends out of earnings and profits declared to stockholders of record after the decedent's death are to be excluded from the alternate valuation method. However, if the effect of the declaration of dividends is that the decedent's shares of stock on the alternate valuation date do not reasonably represent the same property existing at the date of death, such dividends are includible in determining the alternate valuation to the extent paid from earnings of the corporation prior to the date of the decedent's death. For example, a stock dividend received during the alternate valuation period affects the value of the decedent's total shares so that, at the alternate valuation date, his total shares "do not reasonably represent the same property existing at the date of his death." The stock dividend is therefore includible in determining the alternate valuation of the gross estate.[21]

---

[16] Reg. § 20.2032-1(d); *N.S. Johnston Est.*, CA-5, 86-1 USTC ¶ 13,655, 779 F2d 1123, cert. denied, 6-23-86.

[17] Reg. § 20.2032-1(b)(2).

[18] Rev. Rul. 83-31, 1983-1 CB 225.

[19] Rev. Rul. 88-89, 1988-2 CB 333.

[20] Reg. § 20.2032-1(d).

[21] Rev. Rul. 58-576, 1958-2 CB 625.

The IRS National Office has ruled that, under Reg. § 20.2032-1(d), post-death corporate earnings must have been declared as a dividend or otherwise distributed during the alternate valuation period for such earnings to be considered excluded property. In determining that corporate earnings were not excluded property, the IRS concluded that no distinction was to be made between the situation where the corporation was controlled by a decedent's estate, and one that was not so controlled.[22]

A mutual fund capital gains dividend declared and paid between the time of death and the alternate valuation date is not includible in the gross estate of a decedent, even though the payment reduces the value of the shares outstanding (and the asset value on the alternate valuation date), because the value of a mutual fund share is equal to a pro rata share of the fund's net assets.[23]

¶ 112   Life Insurance Policies

With respect to policies of insurance on the life of a person other than the decedent, a distinction is made, for alternate valuation purposes, as to the cause of the value increase. When the value of a policy of insurance that had been owned by the decedent on the life of another increases following the date of the decedent's death, and such increase is attributable to the payment of premiums or to interest earned, the increase is excluded from the value of the insurance as determined under the alternate valuation method.[24] However, the appreciation in the value of insurance policies caused by the *death of the insured* during the alternate valuation period after the policy owner's death is not considered property earned or accrued during that period. Therefore, the entire value of the proceeds is includible in the deceased policy owner's gross estate.[25]

¶ 115   Return Information Under Alternate Valuation Method

If the alternate valuation election is exercised, the estate tax return (Form 706, United States Estate (and Generation-Skipping Transfer) Tax Return) (Rev. August 2013) must include:

> (1) an itemized description of all property included in the gross estate on the date of the decedent's death, together with the value of each item as of that date;

> (2) an itemized disclosure of all distributions, sales, exchanges, and other dispositions during the six-month period after the decedent's death, together with the dates of such dispositions; and

> (3) the value of each item of property on the appropriate alternate valuation date.[26]

This information must be reflected under the appropriate columns on *each applicable* property schedule of the return.[27]

Under the column headed "Description" on the applicable schedule, a brief statement explaining the status or disposition governing the alternate valuation date must be shown for each item. For example, the statement could be one of the following: "Not disposed of within six months following death," "Distributed," "Sold," or "Bond paid on maturity." A description of each item of

---

[22] IRS Technical Advice Memorandum 200343002, June 11, 2003.

[23] *R.W. Bartram*, DC Conn., 75-1 USTC ¶ 13,041. See also Rev. Rul. 76-234, 1976-1 CB 271.

[24] Rev. Rul. 55-379, 1955-1 CB 449.

[25] Rev. Rul. 63-52, 1963-1 CB 173.

[26] Reg. § 20.6018-3(c)(6).

[27] Instructions for Form 706 (Rev. August 2013), p. 9.

principal and includible income must be separately entered in the same column. The applicable date for each separate entry must be shown in the adjacent column headed "Alternate valuation date."

The amount of principal and includible income must also be shown under the heading "Alternate value." In the case of any interest or estate having a value "affected by mere lapse of time," the value shown under the heading "Alternate value" must be the adjusted value. Under the heading "Value at date of death," the amounts of the principal and includible income must again be entered separately.

¶ 120   Supplemental Documents

Statements as to distributions, sales, exchanges, and other dispositions of a decedent's property within the six-month period after the decedent's death must be supported by evidence. If a court issues an order of distribution during that period, a certified copy of the order of distribution must be submitted with the return. The Director of an IRS Service Center or the District Director may require the submission of any additional evidence deemed necessary.[28]

¶ 121   Income Tax Basis of Inherited Property

Generally, the income tax basis of property acquired from a decedent by bequest, devise, or inheritance receives a "stepped-up" basis equal to its fair market value on the date of the decedent's death. Although the Economic Growth and Tax Relief Reconciliation Act of 2001 (P.L. 107-16) (EGTRRA) provided for the replacement of the stepped-up basis rules with a modified carryover basis regime for property acquired from a decedent dying after December 31, 2009, this change was retroactively repealed by the Tax Relief, Unemployment Insurance Reauthorization, and Jobs Creation Act of 2010 (P.L. 111-312) (Tax Relief Act of 2010).[29] However, executors of the estates of decedents dying in 2010 had the option of electing the application of the carryover basis rules (see the discussion under the heading "Elective Carryover Basis Rules for Decedents Dying in 2010," below).

If the alternate valuation date has been elected, the basis is the fair market value of the property on the alternate valuation date.[30] If the property was sold, distributed, or disposed of within six months of death, its basis is the fair market value at the date of sale, distribution, or disposition. See ¶ 296 for rules on the basis of special use valuation property acquired from a decedent.

A special rule applies to appreciated property acquired by a decedent as a gift within one year of death if such property passes from the decedent to the original donor or to the donor's spouse.[31] The basis of such property in the hands of the original donor or his or her spouse is its basis to the decedent immediately prior to death, rather than its fair market value on the date of death. This provision is intended to prevent individuals from transferring property in anticipation of a donee's death merely to obtain a tax-free step up in basis upon receipt of the property from the donee's estate.

---

[28] Reg. § 20.6018-4(e).
[29] The American Taxpayer Relief Act (P.L. 112-240) left the EGTRRA repeal of the carryover basis rules intact. Therefore, the carryover basis rules continue to apply only for

one year (2010), and only if the decedent's estate elected application of carryover basis.
[30] Code Sec. 1014.
[31] Code Sec. 1014(e).

• *Elective Carryover Basis Rules for Decedents Dying in 2010*

The Economic Growth and Tax Relief Reconciliation Act of 2001 (P.L. 107-16) (EGTRRA) repealed the estate tax with respect to the estates of decedents dying after December 31, 2009, but the Tax Relief, Unemployment Insurance Reauthorization, and Job Creation Act of 2010 (P.L. 111-312) (Tax Relief Act of 2010) retroactively reinstated the estate tax for decedents dying after December 31, 2009. Only with respect to decedents dying in 2010, the Tax Relief Act of 2010 gave executors the power to elect not to have the estate tax apply, However, if this election was made, the property acquired from the decedent received a carryover basis under Code Sec. 1022, rather than a stepped-up basis under Code Sec. 1014(f). As a result, if the carryover basis election was made, effective for property acquired from a decedent dying after December 31, 2009, and before January 1, 2011, the income tax basis of property acquired from a decedent would generally be carried over from the decedent. More specifically, the recipient of the property would receive a basis equal *to the lesser of* the adjusted basis of the property in the hands of the decedent, or the fair market value of the property on the date of the decedent's death.

Under the carryover basis at death rules, executors could elect to increase the basis of estate property by up to $1.3 million, and possibly an additional $3 million, in the case of property passing to a surviving spouse.[32]

Carryover Basis Form Due Date; Safe Harbor Election Rules. The IRS released guidance regarding the time and manner in which the executor of the estate of a decedent who died in 2010 could opt out of the estate tax and elect to apply the carryover basis rules under Code Sec. 1022.[33] Additionally, the IRS set the due for filing Form 8939, (Allocation of Increase in Basis for Property Acquired From a Decedent), as November 15, 2011, but this due date was later pushed back (see the heading "IRS Filing Relief: Carryover Basis Election Due Date," below).

The election to apply the carryover basis rules was to be made on a timely filed Form 8939. If the IRS received both a Form 706 or 706-NA and Form 8939 for the same decedent, the IRS would issue a letter to each person who filed the forms, explaining that each person who filed such a form on behalf of the decedent must collectively sign and file a restated Form 706, 706-NA, or 8939 within 90 days. If a restated Form 706 or 8939 was not filed within the 90-day period, the IRS would determine whether the carryover basis election was made or whether the estate tax rules were to apply to the estate.

According to Form 8939, the executor was required to name each individual, trust, estate or entity that receives property from the estate and supply that party's tax identification number. The executor must also report the built-in loss, capital loss carryforward, the general basis increase, and the spousal basis increase. In addition, the executor must supply the following information on property acquired from the decedent's estate on Schedule A: a description of the property; the date the decedent acquired the property; the adjusted basis at death; the fair market value; any basis increase allocated to the property; and the amount of gain that would be ordinary.

Within 30 days after the date that a Form 8939 was filed, the executor was required to furnish each beneficiary, trustee, trust, or other entity acquiring property from the decedent a separate copy of Schedule A. Each property or interest required to be disclosed on Form 8939 must be included on Schedule A,

---

[32] Code Sec. 1022(b).   [33] Notice 2011-66, I.R.B. 2011-35, 184.

regardless of whether the executor allocated basis increase to the property. Updated statements were to be provided within 30 days of any adjustments made to the information on Form 8939.

If no executor had been appointed for an estate, any person in possession of property acquired from the decedent could file a Form 8939. Amendments to Form 8939 could be made but only on a subsequent Form 8939 filed on or before the due date. Subject to certain exceptions, the IRS would not grant extensions of time to file Form 8939 or accept a late-filed return.

The IRS provided safe harbor procedures applicable to executors of the estates of decedents who died in 2010 and recipients of property acquired from a 2010 decedent if the carryover basis election under Code Sec. 1022 was made. If the executor of the estate of a 2010 decedent made the election and followed the provisions of section 4 (Application) of Rev. Proc. 2011-41,[34] and took no return position contrary to the provisions of section 4, the IRS would not challenge the taxpayer's reliance on section 4 on either Form 8939 or any other tax return. Rev. Proc. 2011-41 because effective August 29, 2011, but taxpayers may rely on the safe harbor procedures for prior periods.

Additionally, Rev. Proc. 2011-41 provided clarifications to the application of Code Sec. 1022 not directly addressed by statutory language with respect to:

- Recipient's basis of assets acquired from a decedent that are later sold or distributed;
- Items of income in respect of a decedent;
- Decedent's interest in a qualified terminable interest property (QTIP) trust;
- Trusts created by the decedent during lifetime;
- Carryovers and unrealized losses;
- Allocation of spousal basis increase in event of sale;
- Allocation of spousal property basis increase to a testamentary charitable remainder trust;
- Determination of fair market value;
- Community property rules; and
- Charitable remainder trusts.

IRS Filing Relief: Carryover Basis Election Date Set. The IRS provided filing relief for the estates of 2010 decedents,[35] stating that executors may not have had sufficient time to make an informed decision as to whether to make the Code Sec. 1022 election and complete the required filings. Executors representing decedents who died in 2010 had until January 17, 2012, to file the carryover basis information return (Form 8939) or until March 2012 to file the estate tax return (Form 706). Deadlines for income and gift tax returns were not extended.

The due date for Form 8939 was changed by the IRS from November 15, 2011, to January 17, 2012. Because this was a change in the specified due date rather than an extension, no statement or form needed to be filed with the IRS to have this new due date apply. Accordingly, executors had until January 17, 2012, to decide whether to make the Code Sec. 1022 election. The IRS stated it would not grant any extensions of time to file, except as discussed in Notice 2011-66,

---

[34] Rev. Proc. 2011-41, I.R.B. 2011-35, 188.　　　[35] Notice 2011-76, IRB 2011-40, October 3, 2011.

IRB 2011-35. In addition, executors were not to be subjected to penalties under Code Sec. 6716 solely because Form 8939 was not filed until January 17, 2012, and the required statements to beneficiaries were not provided until February 17, 2012.

The IRS also provided relief for the recipients of assets from the estates of 2010 decedents. When filing their income tax returns, such recipients might not have known whether the executor would make a Code Sec. 1022 election. Likewise, they may not have been informed of the basis, character, or holding period of the assets. Thus, when filing their income tax returns, such recipients had to make good faith estimates based on the available facts and circumstances. As relief for these recipients, the IRS has stated that to the extent that a recipient's tax liability was increased by the application of Code Sec. 1022, the recipient's reasonable cause and good faith would be presumed. Accordingly, penalties under Code Sec. 6651(a)(2) and Code Sec. 6662(a) will not be imposed on the recipients.

Executor's power to allocate basis adjustments. EGTRRA granted the executor of a decedent's estate the authority to increase—subject to stated maximums—the basis of assets passing from the decedent from their carryover value to a stepped-up, date-of-death, value. Once made, the allocation could only be changed pursuant to rules to be provided by the IRS.[36]

Two separate basis increase provisions were generally available for property passing from decedents, although special rules applied to property passing from nonresident decedents who were not U.S. citizens. First, the executor generally could step up the basis of assets of the executor's choosing by a total of $1.3 million. (For purposes of this discussion, this basis increase will be referred to as the "general basis increase.") This step-up available under the general basis increase provision[37] could be allocated to assets passing to any property recipient. Second, for properties that passed to the decedent's surviving spouse, an additional $3 million in basis step-up was available.[38] (This basis increase will be referred to as the "spousal property basis increase" for purposes of this discussion.) In order for the spousal property basis increase to have been available, the property transferred must have been "qualified spousal property" (discussed below).

> *Comment:* Both the $1.3 million general basis increase and the $3 million spousal property basis increase could be applied to property passing to the surviving spouse. Thus, up to $4.3 million in date-of-death basis step up could be allocated to property received by a surviving spouse.

> *Example:* Frank Kenilworth died in 2010, leaving an estate that consisted entirely of 100,000 shares of Global Warming, Inc., having an aggregate date of death value of $7.5 million and an aggregate basis (determined under the carryover basis rules) of $2.2 million. Assuming that Kenilworth had a surviving spouse to whom he bequeathed all of this stock, his executor could increase the total basis of the stock to $6.5 million ($2.2 million carryover basis + $1.3 million general basis increase + $3 million spousal property basis increase). Had Kenilworth's spouse not survived him (or had he not bequeathed any stock to his surviving spouse), his executor could have only increased the basis of the stock to a maximum of $3.5 million ($2.2 million + $1.3 million).

---

[36] Code Sec. 1022(d)(3).
[37] Code Sec. 1022(b)(2)(B).

[38] Code Sec. 1022(c).

Basis increase limited to fair market value. Basis increases made under any of the basis increase provisions of the carryover basis rules could not be used to increase the basis of any property above its fair market value in the hands of the decedent on the date of his or her death.[39]

    Example: Assume the same facts as in Example 1, except that the aggregate date-of-death value of the stock going to Kenilworth's surviving spouse was $6 million. This $6 million amount limited the amount to which the stock could be stepped up; the potential additional $500,000 in basis step up would have gone unused.

    Adjustments to $1.3 million amount. The $1.3 million general basis increase amount could be increased by:

> • the sum of any capital loss carryover under Code Sec. 1212(b), and the amount of any net operating loss carryover under Code Sec. 172 that would have been carried over from the decedent's last tax year to a later tax year, but for the decedent's death, plus

> • the sum of any losses that would have been allowable under Code Sec. 165, if the property acquired from the decedent had been sold at fair market value immediately before the decedent's death.[40]

Nonresident, U.S. citizens. In place of the $1.3 million general basis increase amount that was available to the estates of U.S. citizens and residents, the estates of nonresidents who were not U.S. citizens were allowed an aggregate step up of only $60,000.[41] Although the estates of nonresident, non-U.S. citizens were allowed the $3 million spousal property basis increase, they were not allowed adjustments for carryover basis under Code Sec. 1212(b), net operating loss carryovers under Code Sec. 172, or losses that would have been allowable under Code Sec. 165.[42]

Spousal property basis increase. In order for the $3 million spousal property basis increase to be available, the property transferred to the surviving spouse must be "qualified spousal property".[43] To be classified as qualified spousal property, the transferred property must be either "outright transfer property," or "qualified terminable interest property" (QTIP property).

Ownership by decedent. In order for property to have been eligible for either the $1.3 million general basis increase or the $3 million spousal property basis increase, the property must have been owned by the decedent at the time of his or her death.[44] Specific rules determine this ownership question for jointly held property, revocable trusts, property subject to a power of appointment, and community property.

Property acquired within three years of death. The basis increase provisions of the modified carryover basis at death rules do not apply to property acquired by the decedent by gift or lifetime transfer for less than adequate and full consideration in money or money's worth during the three-year period ending on the date of the decedent's death.[45] However, this prohibition does not apply to property received by the decedent from his or her spouse during the three-year period, provided that the spouse did not acquire the property in whole or in part by gift or by lifetime transfer for less than adequate and full consideration.[46]

---

[39] Code Sec. 1022(d).
[40] Code Sec. 1022(b)(2)(C).
[41] Code Sec. 1022(b)(3)(A).
[42] Code Sec. 1022(b)(3)(B).
[43] Code Sec. 1022(c)(3).
[44] Code Sec. 1022(d)(1)(A).
[45] Code Sec. 1022(d)(1)(C)(i).
[46] Code Sec. 1022(d)(1)(C)(ii).

Stock of certain entities. The provisions of the modified carryover basis at death rules that allow basis increases generally do not apply to the stock of certain foreign entities, or to the stock of a DISC (Domestic International Sales Corporation).[47]

Property acquired from a decedent. In order for the carryover basis rules at death rules to apply, the property in question must be "acquired from the decedent."

> **Comment:** The above three categories were evidently designed to incorporate within the definition of "property acquired from the decedent," all property transfers not supported by consideration that cannot fairly be characterized as gifts.

Income in respect of a decedent. The carryover basis at death rules do not apply to property that constitutes an item of income in respect of a decedent under Code Sec. 691.[48] (Income in respect of a decedent is income that the decedent had an enforceable right to during life, but was not received until after death, and thus, was not reportable on the decedent's final income tax return.)

Liabilities in excess of basis generally disregarded. For purposes of computing basis in property acquired from a decedent, and in determining whether gain is recognized on an acquisition of property, an asset's liabilities in excess of basis are generally disregarded.[49]

Reporting provisions. If an executor elects application of the carryover basis with respect an estate of a decedent dying in 2010, the estate is also bound by carryover basis reporting and penalty provisions.

Information returns required. Effective for estates of decedents dying after December 31, 2009, and before January 1, 2011, an executor of a decedent's estate must file an information return (Form 8939), with the IRS for the following property transfers:

- property acquired from a decedent in a "large transfer;" that is, property with a fair market value that exceeds the Code Sec. 1022(b)(2)(B) dollar amount ($1.3 million), without regard to any increase for built-in losses or loss carryovers.

- appreciated property acquired from a decedent that was acquired by the decedent by gift or other lifetime transfer for less than adequate consideration during the three-year period ending on the date of the decedent's death, and for which the filing of a gift tax return was required.[50]

Special rules apply in the case of nonresident alien decedents[51] and with respect to incomplete returns.[52]

Information required to be furnished. Executors must provide the following information:

- the name and taxpayer identification number (TIN) of the recipient of the property,

- an accurate description of the property,

- the adjusted basis in the hands of the decedent, and its fair market value on the date of the decedent's death,

---

[47] Code Sec. 1022(d)(1)(D).
[48] Code Sec. 1022(f).
[49] Code Sec. 1022(g).

[50] Code Sec. 6018(b)(4).
[51] Code Sec. 6018(b)(3).
[52] Code Sec. 6018(b)(4).

- the decedent's holding period for the property,

- sufficient information to determine if gain on any sale of the property would be ordinary income,

- the amount of basis increase allocated to the property: the portion of the $1.3 million general basis increase ($60,000 for nonresidents not citizens) under Code Sec. 1022(b) and the $3 million spousal property basis increase under Code Sec. 1022(c), and

- any additional information as may be prescribed by regulations issued by the IRS.[53]

Statements to property recipients. In addition to Form 8939 (Allocation of Increase in Basis for Property Acquired From a Decedent) that is required to be filed with the IRS, executor or other person required to file that return was required to provide a written statement to each person listed as a property recipient on the return. The statement must include:

- the name, address, and telephone number of the executor or other person required to make the return, and

- the decedent's adjusted basis in the property and its fair market value of the date of the decedent's death.[54]

The written statement must be furnished no later than 30 days after the date that the Form 8939 was filed. The due date for filing Form 8939 was January 17, 2012. A copy of the completed Schedule A of Form 8939 could be used to meet this requirement.

Donor's written statement to lifetime gift recipients. A donor who is required to file a gift tax return (Form 709) with respect to gifts made within a calendar year was also required to send the following written information to the donees listed on the return:

- the name, address, and telephone numbers of the person required to file the gift tax return, and

- the information specified in the gift tax return regarding the property the donee received.

> **Comment:** Generally, such information would include the donor's adjusted basis in the gifted property, the date of the gift, value of the property at the date of gift, whether the gift was a split gift between spouses, the description of the gift, and the CUSIP number, if the gifted property was stock (Schedule A, Form 709).

The above written statement was to be furnished to the donee no later than 30 days after the gift tax return due date, which is generally April 15 following the calendar year in which the gifts were made.[55]

Penalty provisions. Penalty provisions were enacted to encourage compliance with the carryover basis reporting requirements. These penalties applied both to failures to provide information required for property received from a decedent, and property received from a living donor who was required to file a gift tax return relating to the transfer.

---

[53] Code Sec. 6075.
[54] Code Sec. 6018(e).

[55] Code Sec. 6019(b).

GROSS ESTATE

Chapter 6

PROPERTY INTEREST AT TIME OF DEATH

¶ 150   What Is Included

All property owned in whole or in part by a citizen or a resident at the time of his or her death is included in the decedent's gross estate to the extent of the value of the decedent's interest in the property.[1] Foreign realty involves special rules, discussed at ¶ 251.

In the estate tax return (Form 706, United States Estate (and Generation-Skipping Transfer) Tax Return) (Rev. August 2013), four schedules are concerned solely with property and interests in property that are owned by the decedent at the time of death and which pass to others either under the terms of the decedent's will or by intestacy. The four schedules are: (1) Schedule A (Real Estate); (2) Schedule B (Stocks and Bonds); (3) Schedule C (Mortgages, Notes, and Cash); and (4) Schedule F (Other Miscellaneous Property Not Reportable Under Any Other Schedule).

¶ 155   Tests for Includibility

Although the types of property reported on each of the four schedules (Schedule A (Real Estate); Schedule B (Stocks and Bonds); Schedule C (Mortgages, Notes, and Cash); and Schedule F (Other Miscellaneous Property Not Reportable Under Any Other Schedule) of Form 706 (United States Estate (and Generation-Skipping Transfer) Tax Return) vary, the tests for determining whether particular property interests are includible in the gross estate are the same for all. Three questions arise in determining whether property should be reported in one of the above four schedules as part of the gross estate. They are:

(1) What types of property are includible in the decedent's estate?

(2) Did the decedent have an interest in such property sufficient to warrant inclusion in the decedent's gross estate of the value of the interest involved?

(3) If the decedent had an interest, did the decedent still possess it at the time of death, and to what extent?

The answers to these questions, which determine the character of property interests held and transferred by a decedent, are determined under state law. See ¶ 37 for further details as to the application of state law.

---

[1] Code Sec. 2033; Reg. § 20.2033-1.

Questions concerning valuation are peculiar to the specific type of property involved. They are discussed, therefore, in connection with the individual schedules dealing with the particular type of property. Similarly, the taxability of interests and transfers not governed by the general taxing statute, Code Sec. 2033, is also discussed in connection with the schedule on which such interests or transfers are reportable.

¶ 156　First Question: Type of Property

As to the first question regarding type of taxable property, there is little for the courts to decide. Usually, because the terms of Code Sec. 2033 are so general, it is conceded that all property of the decedent is taxable, unless a state law, the peculiar nature of the interest, or some other external factor suggests a means for excluding the property from the gross estate. Except where the question involves property subject to a power of appointment, it is almost a certainty that any property in which a decedent has a valuable interest at the time of death will be includible in the decedent's gross estate. Not even property set aside for the surviving spouse by state law escapes inclusion in the decedent's gross estate if it has been established that the decedent had an interest in the property.

Lump-sum Social Security death benefits payable to the decedent's surviving spouse or to any person equitably entitled to such payments are not includible in the gross estate of the decedent. Such amounts are not considered property of the decedent.[2] Uncashed Social Security benefit checks that are payable to the decedent and his or her surviving spouse are also not includible.[3] State and municipal bonds that are exempt from federal income taxation are includible in a decedent's gross estate[4] (see ¶ 329). An exclusion applies to Indian trust lands, royalties, and funds held by the United States as trustee under the General Allotment Act of 1887, where the decedent dies before receiving a patent in fee simple.[5] Provisions of death tax treaties with other countries also have some exclusionary effects.

¶ 157　Second Question: Sufficient Interest

The issue involved in the second question, that of the sufficiency of the decedent's interest, has almost always been a question of property law. The cases turn largely on common-law and statutory rights. Most of the cases are decided by the application of property law to the facts.

If the decedent held the property in trust for someone else, it is generally not includible. If the property is in the decedent's name for convenience, but the property belongs to another, it is not includible. Conversely, property held in the name of another for convenience, but belonging to the decedent, is includible in the decedent's gross estate.

¶ 158　Third Question: Possession at Death

The third question, regarding possession of property interest at time of death, presents most of the estate tax difficulties. This question is concerned basically with the duration of the decedent's interest and with interests that have begun to accrue or that have come into existence about the time of the decedent's death, but that have not yet come into the decedent's possession.

---

[2] Rev. Rul. 67-277, 1967-2 CB 322; Rev. Rul. 55-87, 1955-1 CB 112.

[3] Rev. Rul. 75-145, 1975-1 CB 298.

[4] Rev. Rul. 81-63, 1981-1 CB 455.

[5] Rev. Rul. 69-164, 1969-1 CB 220.

Certain general conclusions may be drawn from the decisions involving this question. If the interest came into existence prior to the decedent's death and was not defeated by death, its value at the time of death is includible in the gross estate. Thus, vested remainders are includible, but contingent remainders, defeated by the decedent's death, are not includible. Similarly, where the decedent has only a life interest under a transfer by another, nothing is left to tax at the time of the decedent's death.

If the property interest was accruing to the decedent at the time of death, and was enforceable by the decedent's estate, so much of it as had accrued at the time of death is includible in the decedent's gross estate. Therefore, accrued salary, commissions, and income are includible. But, where these items are not *required* to be paid into the decedent's estate, they are not includible, even though actually paid to the executor.

¶ 165   Community Property

Property in which a decedent had an interest at the time of death is includible in the decedent's gross estate for estate tax purposes to the extent of the value of the decedent's interest in such property. Laws in community property states, however, generally limit the extent of a person's interest in community property to one-half of the value of the property.[6]

The federal estate tax law recognizes these state limitations by purposely failing to provide a distinct, specific method of treating community property. This failure causes the application of the estate tax to be governed by state law. Consequently, only one-half of the value of each item of community property held by a decedent and the decedent's spouse may be included in the gross estate of the decedent. The IRS has ruled, in a National Office Technical Advice Memorandum, that this is true even though the decedent's estate actually received selected community assets with an aggregate date-of-death value equal to the decedent's portion of the total amount of community property.[7]

> *Comment:* This limitation applies not only to property in which the decedent still had an interest at the time of death but also to life insurance purchased with community funds and to property which was the subject of certain lifetime transfers. However, one-half of the proceeds of life insurance policies purchased with community funds is not includible in the gross estate of the decedent if, under the facts of a particular case or the applicable state law, it can be shown that such policies were the separate property of another.[8]

¶ 170   Reciprocal Transfers

Reciprocal trusts receive special consideration. Under a reciprocal trust arrangement, each grantor (usually related to the other grantor) transfers property to a trust, at about the same time, and gives the other grantor the lifetime right to enjoy the property as beneficiary. The trust created for the beneficiary is includible in the beneficiary's gross estate when the trusts are found to be interrelated and leave the grantors in the same economic position they would

---

[6] See, for example, IRS Technical Advice Memorandum 9018002 (Jan. 17, 1990).

[7] IRS Technical Advice Memorandum 8505006 (Oct. 19, 1984).

[8] *A.M. Kroloff*, CA-9, 73-2 USTC ¶ 12,959, 487 F2d 334; *A.G. Kern*, CA-9, 74-1 USTC ¶ 12,979, 491 F2d 436; *V.F. Saia Est.*, 61 TC 515, CCH Dec. 32,428 (CA-5, appeal dismissed pursuant to stipulation, 1-27-75); *E.W. Marks, Jr., Est.*, 94 TC 720, CCH Dec. 46,594.

have been in had they created the trusts and named themselves as beneficiaries.[9] In essence, inclusion will result when (1) the two trusts are substantially identical in terms, (2) the trusts were created at about the same time under some sort of arrangement, and (3) each grantor gives the other grantor approximately the same economic rights.[10]

In at least one case (*B. Bischoff Est.*[11]), the reciprocal trust doctrine has been applied, even though the trust powers exchanged did not have substantial economic value. The existence of the crossed powers in *B. Bischoff Est.* was held sufficient to cause inclusion of the corpora of two trusts in the estates of a husband and wife, each of whom had created identical trusts for the grandchildren wherein each spouse named the other as trustee. Similarly, the value of stock that a decedent transferred to his wife to hold in custody for their children under a Uniform Gifts to Minors Act was includible in his gross estate under the reciprocal trust doctrine because his wife made identical transfers of stock to him to hold in custody for the children.[12] However, in one case, the Tax Court refused to apply the doctrine to reciprocal transfers and held that the value of stock transferred by a decedent's wife to a trust that she had created with the decedent as trustee was not includible in the decedent's gross estate even though he transferred the same amount of stock to a trust that he had created with his wife as trustee. Although the decedent granted a special power of appointment to his wife over the corpus of the trust he had created, he received no such power over the trust created by his wife; however, in all other respects the terms of the trusts were identical. In the court's view, the doctrine was inapplicable because the special power of appointment held by the decedent's wife put her in an economic position different from that of the decedent.[13]

¶ 175   Dower and Curtesy

The gross estate includes the value of dower, curtesy, and all interests created by statute in lieu of dower or curtesy.[14] This is true even though the statutory interest may differ in character from dower or curtesy. Therefore, the full value of the property is required to be included, without deduction of the value of the interest of the surviving spouse, and without regard to the time when the right to such an interest arose.[15]

> *Comment:* Arguments that dower and curtesy are not transfers by the decedent have been unsuccessful. The right of the surviving spouse to use or enjoy the property during the surviving spouse's lifetime becomes consummate by reason of the decedent's death, and this fact is sufficient support for applying a death tax.

¶ 180   Dower or Curtesy Transferred for Consideration

Transfers of property in which the decedent retains an interest, for consideration of money or money's worth, are included in the gross estate to the extent that the fair market value of the transferred property at the time of death exceeds the value of the consideration received in exchange by the decedent. The relin-

[9] *J.P. Grace Est.*, SCt, 69-1 USTC ¶ 12,609, 395 US 316.

[10] IRS Letter Ruling 8019041 (Feb. 12, 1980).

[11] *B. Bischoff Est.*, 69 TC 32, CCH Dec. 34,702.

[12] *Exchange Bank and Trust Co. of Florida, Exr.*, CA-FC, 82-2 USTC ¶ 13,505, 694 F2d 1261.

[13] *H. Levy Est.*, 46 TCM 910, CCH Dec. 40,323(M), TC Memo. 1983-453.

[14] Code Sec. 2034.

[15] Reg. § 20.2034-1.

quishment of dower or curtesy, or a statutory estate created in lieu of dower or curtesy, is not considered the giving of consideration and may not be used in determining the reduction from the transferred property.[16] See ¶610 for further details.

---

[16] Code Sec. 2043(b); Reg. § 20.2043-1.

Chapter 7
REAL ESTATE

¶ 250   Real Property

The value of all real property owned by a U.S. citizen on the date of death is includible in the decedent's gross estate under Code Sec. 2033. For this purpose, it is immaterial whether the decedent was a resident or a nonresident, or whether the property came into the possession and control of the executor or administrator or passed directly to the heirs or devisees. Real property includes certain types of loans classified as real property under local law, as well as mineral rights and royalties. Real estate owned by a decedent is reported on Schedule A (Real Estate) of Form 706 (United States Estate (and Generation-Skipping Transfer) Tax Return) (Rev. August. 2013),[1] unless such property is owned by a sole proprietorship. In that case, the real estate should be reported on Form 706, Schedule F (Other Miscellaneous Property Not Reportable Under Any Other Schedule) (see ¶ 525). Schedule A does not have to be filed with the estate tax return if the decedent did not own reportable real estate.

¶ 251   Real Property Outside the United States

The value of interests in foreign real estate, regardless of when acquired, must be included in the gross estates of property owners. In addition, the value of foreign real property acquired by a decedent after January 31, 1962, is also includible unless it was acquired by *gift, devise, inheritance, or survivorship* and the donor or prior decedent had acquired the interest in the foreign realty (or a power of appointment with respect to it) before February 1, 1962.

Capital additions or improvements to foreign real estate, to the extent they materially increase the value of the property and to the extent they are attributable to construction after January 31, 1962, must be treated in the same manner as real property acquired after that date.[2]

¶ 253   Qualified Conservation Easement Exclusion

The executor of the estate of a decedent dying after 1997 may elect to exclude from the gross estate up to 40 percent (the "applicable percentage") of the value of land that is subject to a qualified conservation easement. The amount that may be excluded from the gross estate is limited to $500,000 in 2002 or thereafter. In addition, the exclusion applicable in any year is reduced by the amount of any charitable deduction that was taken with respect to the land under Code Sec. 2055(f).[3]

---

[1] A filled-in example of Form 706, Schedule A, for a decedent dying in 2013, is reproduced at ¶ 2950.

[2] Reg. § 20.2031-1(c).
[3] Code Sec. 2031(c).

The election is made by filing Form 706 (United States Estate (and Genera-tion-Skipping Transfer) Tax Return) (Rev. August. 2013), Schedule U (Qualified Conservation Easement Exclusion), and claiming the exclusion on Page 3, Part 5, line 12. Once made, the election is irrevocable.[4]

Special use valuation property. The granting of a conservation easement does not affect specially valued property under Code Sec. 2032A. Thus, the granting of such an easement is not treated as a disposition and does not trigger the additional estate tax. In addition, the existence of a qualified conservation easement does not prevent the property from subsequently qualifying for special use valuation.

Partnerships, corporations, and trusts. An interest in a partnership, corpo-ration, or trust will qualify for the qualified conservation easement exclusion provided that at least 30 percent of the entity is owned, directly or indirectly, by the decedent, as determined under the rules applicable to the qualified family-owned business interest (QFOBI) deduction under Code Sec. 2057 (prior to its repeal by the Economic Growth and Tax Relief Act of 2001 (EGTRRA) (P.L. 107-16), and the American Taxpayer Relief Act of 2012 (P.L. 112-240)); see ¶1150.[5]

• Land Subject to a Qualified Conservation Easement

In order to qualify for the exclusion, the land must be located in the United States or in a U.S. possession,[6] and must have been owned by the decedent or a member of the decedent's family during the three-year period ending on the date of the decedent's death. Further, the land must be subject to a qualified conserva-tion easement granted by the decedent or a member of the decedent's family. In addition, a post-mortem conservation easement may be placed on the property, provided the easement has been made no later than the date of the election.[7]

Members of the family. The Code Sec. 2032A(e)(2) definition of "member of the family" applies to the qualified conservation easement exclusion. Thus, with respect to any decedent, a member of the family is (1) an ancestor of the decedent, (2) the spouse of the decedent, (3) a lineal descendant of the decedent, of the decedent's spouse, or of a parent of the decedent, or (4) the spouse of any individual described in (3).

Debt-financed property. The exclusion does not apply to the extent that the land is debt-financed property. Thus, debt-financed property is eligible for the exclusion only to the extent of the net equity in the property. Debt-financed property means property with respect to which there is an acquisition indebted-ness on the date of the decedent's death. Acquisition indebtedness includes the unpaid amount of (1) indebtedness incurred by the donor in acquiring the property, (2) indebtedness incurred before the acquisition of the property if such indebtedness would not have been incurred but for such acquisition, (3) indebt-edness incurred after the acquisition of the property if such indebtedness would not have been incurred but for such acquisition and the incurrence of the indebtedness was reasonably foreseeable at the time of acquisition, and (4) the extension, renewal, or refinancing of an acquisition indebtedness.[8]

[4] Code Sec. 2031(c)(6).
[5] Code Sec. 2031(c)(10).
[6] Code Sec. 2031(c)(8)(A)(i).
[7] Code Sec. 2031(c)(8)(A).
[8] Code Sec. 2031(c)(4).

• *Qualified Conservation Easement Defined*

A qualified conservation easement is a qualified conservation contribution, defined in Code Sec. 170(h)(1) as a contribution of a qualified real property interest to a qualified organization exclusively for conservation purposes.

A qualified real property interest means a restriction, granted in perpetuity, on the use that may be made of the real property. Conservation purposes are defined in Code Sec. 170(h)(4)(A) and include such things as the preservation of land areas for outdoor recreation or the education of the general public, the protection of natural habitat for fish, wildlife, or plants, and the preservation of open space. However, for purposes of the qualified conservation easement exclusion, the preservation of an historically important land area or an historic structure does not qualify as a conservation purpose. In addition, a *de minimis* commercial recreational activity that is consistent with the conservation purpose, such as the granting of hunting and fishing licenses, will not cause the property to fail to qualify for the exclusion.[9]

For estates of decedents dying after December 31, 2012, the exclusion for a qualified conservation easement had been scheduled to be restricted to real property within 25 miles of a metropolitan area (as defined by the Office of Management and Budget), a national park, or a wilderness area (unless the land is not under significant development pressure as determined by the IRS) or 10 miles of an Urban National Forest (as designated by the Forest Service of the U.S. Department of Agriculture). However, these distance requirements were repealed by the American Taxpayer Relief Act of 2012 (P.L. 112-240).

• *Exclusion Amount*

The exclusion amount is calculated based on the value of the property after the conservation easement has been placed on the property. However, the exclusion amount does not extend to the value of any development rights retained by the decedent or the donor. Development rights are defined as any rights retained to use the land for any commercial purpose that are not subordinate to and directly supportive of the land as a farm or for farming purposes within the meaning of Code Sec. 2032A(e)(5). However, if every person in being who has an interest in the land executes an agreement to extinguish permanently some or all of any development rights retained by the donor, on or before the date the estate tax return is due, the estate tax may be reduced accordingly. If the agreement is not implemented by the earlier of the date that is two years after the decedent's death or the date of the sale of the land, an additional tax is imposed in the amount of the estate tax that would have been due on the retained development rights subject to the agreement.[10]

Applicable percentage. If the executor makes the election, there is excluded from the gross estate the lesser of the applicable percentage of the value of the land subject to the qualified conservation easement or the exclusion limitation. The applicable percentage means 40 percent reduced, but not below zero, by two percentage points for each percentage point (or fraction thereof) by which the value of the qualified conservation easement is less than 30 percent of the value of the land.[11] For this purpose, the value of the land is determined without regard to the value of the easement and reduced by the value of any retained development rights. As a result, if the value of the easement is 10 percent or less

---

[9] Code Sec. 2031(c)(8)(B).

[10] Code Sec. 2031(c)(5).

[11] Code Sec. 2031(c)(2).

of the value of the land before the easement, less the value of any retained development rights, the applicable percentage will be zero.

Effective for the estates of decedents dying after December 31, 2000, the values to be taken into account in calculating the applicable percentage are such values as of the date of the contribution of the qualified conservation easement.[12]

"Development rights" means any right to use land that is subject to a qualified conservation easement for any commercial purpose that is not subordinate to and directly supportive of the use of the land as a farm for farming purposes (within the meaning of Code Sec. 2032A(e)(5)).[13]

> *Example:* Dolores Jones died owning land subject to a qualified conservation easement. She did not retain any development rights in the property. The fair market value of the real property on the date of her death was $500,000 without the conservation easement and $400,000 with the easement. Thus, the value of the conservation easement is $100,000, or 20% of the value of real property without the easement. The applicable percentage for the estate is 20% (40% reduced by twice the difference between 30% and 20%). Therefore, the exclusion amount is $80,000 (20% of $400,000).

¶ 262   Reporting Real Property on Return

In reporting real estate that is taxable under Code Sec. 2033, the property should be described and identified in a manner that permits the IRS to locate it readily for inspection and valuation. The area of each parcel of real estate should be given. If the parcel is improved, a short statement of the character of the improvements should be included. For urban property, the following information should also be given: street and number, ward, subdivision, block, and lot. For rural property, the description should include the township, range, and any landmarks.[14]

If an item of real estate is subject to a mortgage for which the decedent's estate is liable, the full value of such property must be reflected in the relevant value column of Schedule A (Real Estate) of Form 706, (alternate or date-of-death value). In other words, if the indebtedness is enforceable against other property of the estate not subject to such mortgage, or if the decedent was personally liable for such mortgage, the full value of the property must be shown.[15] The amount of the mortgage is to be noted in the "Description" column, and it should be deducted on Schedule K (Debts of the Decedent, and Mortgages and Liens) of Form 706.

If, however, the decedent's estate is not liable for the amount of the mortgage, only the value of the equity of redemption (or value of the property less the indebtedness) need be included in the "Value" column as part of the gross estate, and no deduction as a mortgage or lien for the indebtedness is allowable.[16] Similarly, "points" that a decedent has agreed to pay to a mortgage lender are not includible in the value of the property for estate tax purposes unless the decedent's estate is liable for payment.[17]

---

[12] Code Sec. 2031(c)(2), as amended by the Economic Growth and Tax Relief Reconciliation Act of 2001 (P.L. 107-16) (EGTRRA), extended to estates of decedents dying before January 1, 2013, by the Tax Relief, Unemployment Insurance Reauthorization, and Job Creation Act of 2010 (P.L. 111-312), and made permanent by the American Taxpayer Relief Act of 2012 (P.L. 112-240).

[13] Code Sec. 2031(c)(5)(D).
[14] Instructions for Form 706, Schedule A (Rev. August 2013), p. 18.
[15] Reg. § 20.2053-7.
[16] Reg. § 20.2053-7.
[17] Rev. Rul. 80-319, 1980-2 CB 252.

Preparation Tip: Real property that the decedent has contracted to purchase should be listed in Schedule A. The full value of the property and not the equity must be reflected in the value column of the schedule. The unpaid portion of the purchase price should be deducted under Schedule K. If the land is subject to a valid contract to sell entered into by the decedent, the contract, rather than the land, is reportable. It is reportable on Schedule C (Mortgages, Notes, and Cash) of Form 706.

¶ 265 Dower and Curtesy

The value of dower and curtesy (or a statutory estate created in lieu thereof) is taxable (see ¶175 and ¶180). The extent of the decedent's interest in real property may not be reduced on account of such interest or on account of homestead or other exemptions in reporting real property on the return.

¶ 270 Valuation

The value of real property, each parcel being unique in the eyes of the law, can never be determined by a set formula. Each valuation must be fixed individually in accordance with the requirements and circumstances of the particular situation.

Expert testimony is desirable in most cases, not only to apply a local or general market situation to the parcel of land involved, but often to provide the primary means of establishing value for purposes of the tax. Generally, expert testimony, market activity, and local sales, rentals, and recent mortgages are important in establishing value, if the same valuation can be obtained by the use of two or more of such factors. The local tax assessment values, or only one of the above factors, will frequently not carry sufficient weight to establish valuation contrary to that set by the IRS.

The value is determined as of the date of the decedent's death unless the executor elects to use the alternate valuation date. Whatever the method of valuation employed, the method should be stated on the return. If based on an appraisal, a copy of the appraisal, together with an explanation of the basis of the appraisal, should be attached to the return.

See ¶280 through ¶296 for special use valuation of real estate of a farm or other closely held business.

¶ 275 Community Property

If community property is involved, only one-half of the value of each item of community property is to be reported on the decedent's Form 706 (United States Estate (and Generation-Skipping Transfer) Tax Return) (see ¶165), with an appropriate explanation. For example, the value of a decedent's one-half interest in a house and lot in Tucson, Arizona (valued at $300,000), would be reported as $150,000 on the date of death and the description would be followed by the following statement:

> One-half only of value reported because the house and lot were held in community with the surviving spouse.

Likewise, only one-half of the value of any rental income from the property would be listed.

Chapter 8

FARMS AND CLOSELY HELD BUSINESSES

¶ 280   Special Use Valuation

Real property used as a family farm or in a closely held business may be valued on the basis of its "current" use rather than on the basis of "highest and best" use.

The maximum amount by which the value of qualifying real property can be reduced under the special use valuation provision[1] is $1,000,000 for 2010; $1,020,000 for 2011, $1,040,000 for 2012; $1,070,000 for 2013; and $1,090,000 for 2014.[2]

> *Example:* If the estate of Madison Carver, dying in 2013 consists of qualifying real property valued at $1,475,000 on the basis of its "highest and best" use, and the property's value under the special use valuation provision is $350,000, the gross estate will be reduced by only $1,070,000 (although the difference in value is $1,125,000, the maximum reduction allowed is $1,070,000).[3]

The IRS has ruled that an estate electing both the alternate valuation date and special use valuation was required to use the alternate valuation date to determine the special use value of farmland owned by the decedent at death. Additionally, in applying the applicable limit on the aggregate reduction in the value of qualified real property as a result of valuing the property for a qualified use, the difference between the fair market value and the special use value was to be determined as of the alternate valuation date.[4]

Real property may qualify for special use valuation if it is located in the United States and if it is devoted to either (1) use as a farm for farming purposes

---

[1] Code Sec. 2032A(a); Reg. § 20.2032A-8.

[2] Rev. Proc. 2009-50, IRB 2009-45, 617; Rev. Proc. 2010-40, IRB 2010-46, 663; Rev. Proc. 2011-52, IRB 2011-45, 701; Rev. Proc. 2012-41, IRB 2012-45, 539; Rev. Proc. 2013-35, IRB 2013-47, October 31, 2013..

[3] The maximum reductions based on the special use valuation provision for previous years are as follows: $1,000,000 for 2009; $960,000 for 2008; and $940,000 for 2007. Code Sec. 2032A(a)(3); Rev. Proc. 2008-66, 2008-2 CB 1107; Rev. Proc. 2007-66, 2007-2 CB 970; and Rev. Proc. 2006-53, 2006-2 CB 996.

[4] Rev. Rul. 88-89, 1988-2 CB 333.

or (2) use in a closely held trade or business other than farming. In either case, there must be a trade or business use.

¶ 281   Qualifying Conditions

In order to qualify for the special use valuation procedure, the following conditions must be satisfied:

(1) the decedent must have been a resident or a citizen of the United States and the property must be located in the United States;

(2) the property must pass to a qualified heir (see ¶ 282) and a requisite agreement must be filed (see ¶ 289);

(3) the property must be devoted to a qualified use (see ¶ 291) on the date of the decedent's death;

(4) the decedent or a member of the decedent's family must have owned the qualifying property and have materially participated in the operation of the farm or other business for the required period (see ¶ 291 and ¶ 292);

(5) the adjusted value of the real and personal property used in the farm or closely held business must comprise at least 50 percent of the adjusted value of the decedent's gross estate; and

(6) at least 25 percent of the adjusted value of the gross estate must be qualified real property.[5]

For purposes of the 50-percent and 25-percent tests, the special use value is not used in determining the value of property included in the gross estate. With respect to requirement (5), the value of any transfer made within three years of death (see ¶ 555) is includible in the decedent's gross estate for the limited purpose of determining the estate's qualification for special use valuation.[6]

The IRS has allowed an estate to combine the adjusted values of personal property used for farming, farm property, and a building used in a business other than farming in order to meet the 50-percent test for special use valuation. The personal property was used in connection with the qualifying farm property, and the real estate was otherwise eligible for special use valuation.[7]

The IRS distinguished its result from a Tax Court decision in which a decedent's estate was not entitled to elect special use valuation for farmland owned by the decedent because personal property owned and used by him in a business unrelated to farming could not be aggregated with the farmland to meet the 50-percent requirement. In the court's view, Congress enacted the special use valuation rules in order to lessen the estate tax burden that might result from valuation of real property used in the family farm or business at its highest and best use rather than at its value to the farm or business. Because the rules were designed to protect family farms and businesses, the court reasoned that personal property should be considered in meeting the percentage requirements only if it is used in the family business together with the real property that is to be specially valued.[8]

---

[5] Code Sec. 2032A(a) and Code Sec. 2032A(b).

[6] Code Sec. 2035(d)(3). See IRS Letter Ruling 8514032 (Jan. 8, 1985); Rev. Rul. 87-122, 1987-2 CB 221.

[7] Rev. Rul. 85-168, 1985-2 CB 197.

[8] W.H. *Geiger Est.*, 80 TC 484, CCH Dec. 39,936.

¶ 282 Qualified Heir

The term "qualified heir" (to whom special use valuation property must pass) refers to a member of the decedent's family who acquired the real property from the decedent or to whom the property has passed.[9] Where there is a further disposition of any interest in the property from a qualified heir to a member of the heir's family, the family member is to be treated as a qualified heir.[10] However, the IRS has ruled that the post-1981 disposition of specially valued farm property by a qualified heir to his cousin within the recapture period resulted in imposition of the recapture tax (see ¶ 284). For purposes of this exception, the cousin was not considered a member of the qualified heir's family.[11]

An individual's family members are (1) the individual's ancestors, (2) the individual's spouse, (3) lineal descendants of the individual, of the individual's spouse, or of the individual's parents, and (4) the spouse of any descendant mentioned in (3).[12] In interpreting this provision, the Tax Court has held that the nephew of a decedent's predeceased spouse was not a qualified heir because he was not a lineal descendant of the decedent's parents but, rather, was a lineal descendant of the decedent's husband's parents.[13]

For purposes of the preceding discussion, a legally adopted child of an individual is treated as the individual's child by blood.

All interests in the property to be specially valued must pass to qualified heirs. Thus, if successive interests are created in the property such as, for example, a life estate followed by a remainder interest, qualified heirs must receive all interests.[14] The IRS has ruled that an estate could elect special use valuation for farm property in which a qualified heir received a life estate under the decedent's will, even though the heir also received the power to appoint the remainder interest in the property to a nonqualified heir. The election was allowed because the heir executed a qualified disclaimer (see ¶ 2009) of the power of appointment, thus causing the remainder interest to vest in another qualified heir.[15] However, the IRS has also disallowed special use valuation elections because not all successive interests in otherwise qualifying real property passed to qualified heirs.[16]

Two Tax Court cases have held that Reg. § 20.2032A-8(a)(2) is invalid to the extent that *all* successive interests are required to go to qualified heirs.[17] In the *Davis* case, the court held that *de minimis* successive interests that do not go to qualified heirs will not prevent special use valuation for otherwise qualified property. Similarly, the *Clinard* case limited Reg. § 20.2032A-8(a)(2) by holding that special use valuation is permitted where a qualified heir possesses a life estate with a special power of appointment. In other words, the fact that a qualified heir could direct that an unqualified heir receive a remainder interest would not preclude the use of special use valuation for the interest in question. Both cases recognize that where unqualified heirs are in a position to receive an interest, special use valuation will not be precluded if those interests are exceedingly remote. This principle has also been followed by the U.S. Court of Appeals

---

[9] Code Sec. 2032A(e)(1).

[10] Code Sec. 2032A(e)(1).

[11] Rev. Rul. 89-22, 1989-1 CB 276.

[12] Code Sec. 2032A(e)(2).

[13] *I.M. Cone Est.*, 60 TCM 137, CCH Dec. 46,722(M), TC Memo. 1990-359.

[14] Reg. § 20.2032A-8(a)(2).

[15] Rev. Rul. 82-140, 1982-2 CB 208.

[16] IRS Letter Rulings 8337015 (June 7, 1983), and 8346006 (July 29, 1983).

[17] See *D. Davis IV, Est.*, 86 TC 1156, CCH Dec. 43,105, and *C.M. Clinard Est.*, 86 TC 1180, CCH Dec. 43,106.

for the Seventh Circuit in affirming a decision of a U.S. district court in Illinois that allowed special use valuation despite a remote possibility that the contingent remainder interest in the property could pass to nonqualified heirs.[18]

A U.S District Court,[19] has also declared Reg. § 20.2032A-8(a)(2) invalid to the extent that it stated that an estate could not elect special use valuation for less than 25 percent of the adjusted gross estate. This requirement was a substantive addition to Code Sec. 2032A(b), which required that at least 25 percent of the adjusted gross estate must be real property that was passed from a qualified decedent to a qualified heir. The Court stated that Code Sec. 2032A(b) does not require that the special use valuation be made for all or a certain percentage of the qualified property.

¶ 283   Valuation Methods

Two valuation methods are used for farms or closely held businesses that qualify for the special use valuation.

• Farm Method

If a farm qualifies for special use valuation, it may be valued on the basis of a formula of cash rentals, real estate taxes, and effective interest rates. Under the formula, the value of a farm is determined as follows:

> (1) the average annual gross cash rental for comparable land used for farming purposes and located in the same region as such farm, less the average annual state and local real estate taxes for such comparable land, divided by

> (2) the average annual effective interest rate for all new Farm Credit Bank loans.

Each average annual computation described in the formula is to be made on the basis of the five most recent calendar years ending before the date of the decedent's death.[20] "Net-share" rentals (i.e., crop-share rentals) may be used in the formula valuation method if cash rentals for comparable land in the same locality are not available. The amount of a net share is equal to the value of the produce received by the lessor of the comparable land on which such produce is grown minus the cash operation expenses (other than real property taxes) of growing the produce paid by the lessor.[21]

For an aid to computing a special use valuation under the Farm Valuation Method, see the special use valuation calculator in CCH's on-line product, IntelliConnect® (Financial and Estate Planning/Financial and Estate Planning Practice Tools/Special Use Valuation Calculator.)

• Multiple Factor Method for Closely Held Businesses

If a closely held business or a farm that does not use the farm method described above qualifies for special use valuation, its valuation generally is determined by the following factors:

> (1) capitalization of income;

> (2) capitalization of fair rental values;

---

[18] *L. Smoot, Exr.*, CA-7, 90-1 USTC ¶ 60,002, aff'g DC Ill., 88-1 USTC ¶ 13,748.

[19] *D. Finfrock-Ware Est.*, DC Ill., 2012-1 USTC ¶ 60,641, following *M.S. Miller*, DC Ill, 88-1 USTC ¶ 13,757, 680 FSupp 1269.

[20] Code Sec. 2032A(e)(7)(A).
[21] Code Sec. 2032A(e)(7)(B).

(3) assessed land values in a state that provides a differential or use value assessment law;

(4) comparable sales of other farm or closely held business land where nonagricultural use is not a significant factor in the sales price; and

(5) any other factor that fairly values the farm or closely held business value of the property.[22]

However, in applying special use valuation to farm property, the IRS has ruled that a fiduciary could not select only one of the factors enumerated in Code Sec. 2032A(e)(8) as the exclusive basis of valuation. Each factor that was relevant to the respective valuation was to be applied, although, depending on the circumstances, certain factors could be weighed more heavily than others.[23]

The Tax Court has held that if an estate that has elected special use valuation has not provided all of the necessary documentation to utilize the farm method, it is deemed to have, by default, elected to use the multiple factor method.[24]

• *Change in Method*

The IRS has ruled that an estate that had made a valid special use valuation election with respect to farmland included in the decedent's gross estate could amend the election in order to substitute the farm method of valuation for the multiple factor method that was originally applied. The executor valued the decedent's farm under the multiple factor method because he was unable to obtain the information (rentals for comparable farmland) necessary for computing value under the formula method until after the return was filed. Although the special use valuation election is irrevocable, the IRS did not bar the estate from changing the method of valuation once the election was made. In addition, the IRS noted that a change from the multiple factor method is allowable even where information regarding comparable farmland was available but the executor nevertheless originally applied the multiple factor method.[25]

¶ 284   Recapture of Taxes

Tax benefits realized by an estate that elects special use valuation may be fully or partially recaptured if the qualified real property passes out of the family or ceases to be used as a farm or closely held business within a 10-year "recapture period" measured from the decedent's death (but before the death of the qualified heir).[26] Tax liability incurred as a result of such a disposition or cessation of qualified use is to be reported on Form 706-A (United States Additional Estate Tax Return) (Rev. September 2013) (see the Appendix at ¶ 3200).

A second disposition of the property or cessation will not trigger a second tax on the same qualified interest.[27] Thus, where a qualified heir ceases to use the property for its qualified purpose and later sells the property within the recapture period, a recapture tax will be imposed as to the first event that triggers recapture (cessation of use), but not as to the second event (sale of the property).

The amount of the tax benefit potentially subject to recapture is the excess of the estate tax liability that would have been incurred had the special use valuation procedure not been used over the actual estate tax liability based on

---

[22] Code Sec. 2032A(e)(8).

[23] Rev. Rul. 89-30, 1989-1 CB 274.

[24] *R. Wineman*, 79 TCM 2189, CCH Dec. 53,925(M), TC Memo. 2000-193.

[25] Rev. Rul. 83-115, 1983-2 CB 155.

[26] Code Sec. 2032A(c)(1).

[27] Code Sec. 2032A(c)(3).

the special use valuation. In other words, the maximum additional or "recapture" tax is the amount that the special use valuation has saved the estate. This is called the "adjusted tax difference."[28]

The tax will be less than the maximum if the excess of the fair market value of the interest or the proceeds of an arm's-length sale over the value of the interest determined with the special use valuation is less than the "adjusted tax difference."

• *Qualified Use*

As noted above, the tax recapture provision applies if the property ceases to be used for the qualified use (see ¶291) under which the property qualified for the special use valuation. However, a qualified heir may begin qualified use of the property at any time within two years of the decedent's death without triggering recapture tax; the recapture period does not begin until the qualified use begins.[29] For tax recapture purposes, a qualified use may cease even if the property continues to be used for its qualifying purpose. A cessation occurs if within the recapture period, during any eight-year period ending after the decedent's death and before the qualified heir's death, there have been periods aggregating more than three years during which there has been no "material participation" (see ¶292) by the decedent or family member in the case of property held by the decedent. In the case of property held by a qualified heir, like periods of nonparticipation by the qualified heir or a family member will result in a cessation of qualified use.[30] However, "active management" (see ¶293) will constitute material participation in the case of "eligible qualified heirs." Such heirs are the decedent's spouse or a qualified heir who is under the age of 21, a full-time student, or disabled.[31]

The decedent's surviving spouse and lineal descendants may rent special use property to a family member on a cash rental basis without triggering the recapture tax.[32] Similarly, a family trust's lease of farmland to a family farming corporation for fixed cash payments did not trigger the special use valuation recapture tax for a decedent's children, who were trust beneficiaries. They necessarily retained the financial risks of farming, as owners of the farmland and of the family farming corporation.[33] The rule allowing net cash rental to a family member was extended to lineal descendants by the Taxpayer Relief Act of 1997 (P.L. 105-34) and applies retroactively to leases executed after December 31, 1976.

Under Code Sec. 2032A(c)(8), a qualified conservation contribution by "gift or otherwise" is not a disposition under Code Sec. 2032A(c)(1)(A), and is not subject to the recapture tax. However, the IRS has privately ruled that a *sale* of a qualified conservation easement on farmland for which special use valuation had been elected triggered the recapture tax.[34]

Applying the rationale of Rev. Rul. 88-78,[35] which discussed subsurface oil and gas interests, the IRS has ruled that a conveyance of subterranean water rights with respect to a property specially valued under Code Sec. 2032A was a separate asset from the specially valued property. Accordingly, the conveyance of water rights and the granting of an easement would not constitute a disposi-

---

[28] Code Sec. 2032A(c)(2).

[29] Code Sec. 2032A(c)(7).

[30] Code Sec. 2032A(c)(6). See also IRS Letter Ruling 8939031 (June 30, 1989).

[31] Code Sec. 2032A(c)(7).

[32] Code Sec. 2032A(b)(5).

[33] *M. Minter*, CA-8, 94-1 USTC ¶60,160, 19 F3d 426, rev'g unpublished DC N.D. decision.

[34] IRS Letter Ruling 200840018 (May 13, 2008).

[35] 1988-2 CB 330.

tion or cessation of the qualified use of the properties under Code Sec. 2032A(c)(1).[36]

The additional tax on recaptured property is due on the day that is six months after the recapture event (premature disposition of the property or cessation of qualified use).[37] As noted at ¶ 288, each heir remains expressly liable for the recapture tax with respect to his or her interest in the property.

The three-year statute of limitations for assessing the recapture tax does not begin to run until the IRS is notified of the disposition or cessation.[38] In one case decided prior to the enactment of the Taxpayer Relief Act of 1997, a qualified heir's cash rental of qualified farm property to her brother constituted a cessation of qualified use resulting in liability for additional estate tax. The heir's alleged participation in the farming operations with her brother was insufficient to change the substance of the arrangement between the parties from that of a landlord-tenant relationship. However, the disclosure of the cash rental arrangement in response to a questionnaire provided by the IRS served as notification to the IRS of the cessation of qualified use and commenced the Code Sec. 2032A(f) three-year statute of limitations on assessment and collection. Accordingly, notices of deficiency that were issued more than three years after the IRS received notification of cessation of qualified use precluded the IRS from assessing and collecting the additional tax.[39]

¶ 285   Pecuniary Bequests and Purchases

Normally, property qualifying for special use valuation is acquired by a qualified heir from a decedent by bequest, devise, or inheritance. However, a special use valuation election may also be allowed where property is acquired by either:

(1) a distribution of qualified property by an estate or trust in satisfaction of a pecuniary bequest; or

(2) a purchase of qualified property by a qualified heir from a decedent's estate or trust.[40]

An estate recognizes gain on such a distribution or sale only to the extent of the post-death appreciation of the property. This appreciation is equal to the difference between the property's fair market value on the date of the distribution or sale and its estate tax value as determined *without* regard to Code Sec. 2032A. In computing the gain on distribution or sale, therefore, the estate tax value will be the property's fair market value on the date of the decedent's death or the alternate valuation date.[41]

Specially valued property that is transferred to a qualified heir in satisfaction of a pecuniary bequest or that is purchased from the decedent's estate by a qualified heir is deemed to meet the holding period requirement for long-term capital gain treatment on a subsequent sale of the property to another qualified heir.[42]

---

[36] IRS Letter Ruling 200608012 (Nov. 3, 2005).

[37] Code Sec. 2032A(c)(4).

[38] Code Sec. 2032A(f).

[39] *M.E. Stovall*, 101 TC 140, CCH Dec. 49,183.

[40] Code Sec. 2032A(e)(9); Rev. Proc. 82-9, 1982-1 CB 413.

[41] Code Sec. 1040(a).

[42] Code Sec. 1223(12).

¶ 286   Involuntary Conversions and Tax-Free Exchanges

No recapture tax (see ¶ 284) will be imposed where farm or closely held business property that has been specially valued is involuntarily converted. However, the proceeds from the involuntary conversion must be reinvested in real property that is used for the same qualified use as was the involuntarily converted property.[43]

No recapture tax will be imposed on an exchange of specially valued real property to the extent that the exchange qualifies as tax free under Code Sec. 1031 so long as the property received is employed in the same qualified use as was the property exchanged. Real property received in an exchange that is employed in the qualified use is known as "qualified exchange property." If both qualified exchange property and other property are received, the recapture tax is reduced by an amount bearing the same ratio to the recapture tax as the fair market value of the qualified exchange property bears to the fair market value of the property that was exchanged[44] (see ¶ 80 and the Appendix at ¶ 3200).

The special use valuation provision permits the aggregation ("tacking") of ownership, qualified use, and material participation periods in the case of replacement property acquired pursuant to like-kind exchanges under Code Sec. 1031 or involuntary conversions under Code Sec. 1033.[45] This tacking is available only if the replacement property is employed in the same qualified use as was the original property, and only for that portion of the replacement property equal in value to the original property.

¶ 287   Special Lien on Qualified Property

A government lien is imposed on all qualified property for which an election to use the special use valuation procedure has been made. The lien applies to the extent of the adjusted tax difference attributable to the qualified real property. The lien arises at the time an election is filed and is to continue until the tax benefit is recaptured, until the time limit for collecting the potential liability ceases (that is, the qualified heir dies or the recapture period (see ¶ 284) lapses) or until it can be established to the satisfaction of the IRS that no further liability will arise. In addition, if qualified replacement property is purchased following an involuntary conversion of special use valuation property (see ¶ 286), the lien that was applicable to the original special use valuation property attaches to the qualified replacement property. Similarly, if specially valued property is exchanged for qualified exchange property (see ¶ 286), the lien attaches to the qualified exchange property.[46]

> *Practice Pointer:* The IRS can issue a certificate of subordination of the government's lien that arose on any part of the qualified property for which the special use valuation election was made if it determines that the interests of the United States are adequately protected thereafter.[47]

¶ 288   Personal Liability for Recapture Tax

A qualified heir is personally liable for the portion of recapture tax that is imposed with respect to his or her interest in specially valued property. A qualified heir's liability is extinguished in two instances: (1) where the recapture period lapses; and (2) where the heir dies without converting or disposing of the

[43] Code Sec. 2032A(h)(1)(A).
[44] Code Sec. 2032A(i)(1).
[45] Code Sec. 2032A(e)(14)(A).

[46] Code Sec. 6324B; Reg. § 20.6324B-1.
[47] Code Sec. 6325(d)(3).

property.[48] Additionally, a sale or other disposition by one qualified heir to another of specially valued property is not considered a recapture event and the second heir is treated as if he or she received the property from the decedent, rather than from the first heir. The second heir then becomes liable for the recapture tax and the other qualified heir (the seller) is released from further recapture tax liability.[49] Even if the second heir has paid full consideration for the property, the special estate tax lien (see ¶ 287) remains on the property.

• Discharge from Liability

An heir may be discharged from personal liability for future potential recapture taxes imposed on the heir's interest in the qualified property by furnishing a bond for the maximum additional tax that could be imposed on the interest.[50]

The qualified heir must make written application to the IRS for determination of the maximum additional tax that could be imposed. The IRS is then required to notify the heir within one year of the date of the application of such maximum amount.[51]

¶ 289 Election and Agreement

An election to use special use valuation is to be made on Form 706 (United States Estate (and Generation-Skipping Transfer) Tax Return) (Rev. Aug. 2012) by checking the box marked "Yes" on line 2 of Part 3, the "Elections by the Executor" section on page 2 of the return. Such an election may be made on a late-filed return so long as it is the first return filed.[52]

In order to make a valid election, an estate must file Schedule A-1 (Section 2032A Valuation) of Form 706 and attach all of the required statements and appraisals.[53] Schedule A-1 contains the Notice of Election and the Agreement to Special Valuation Under Section 2032A.[54] The Notice of Election provides information such as the fair market value of the property to be specially valued, its special use valuation, and the method used in computing special use valuation.[55]

An estate may elect special use valuation for less than all of the qualified property included in the gross estate. However, property for which an election is made must have an adjusted value of at least 25 percent of the adjusted value of the gross estate.[56]

• Agreement

An estate executor making the election must also complete and file with the return Schedule A-1, part 3 (Agreement to Special Valuation Under Section 2032A), signed by each person having an interest in the qualified real property for which the election is made.[57] It is immaterial whether such person is in possession of the property. In the case of a qualified heir, the agreement ex-

[48] Code Sec. 2032A(c)(1).

[49] IRS Letter Ruling 8115085 (Jan. 16, 1981).

[50] Code Sec. 2032A(c)(5) and Code Sec. 2032A(e)(11).

[51] Code Sec. 2032A(e)(11).

[52] Code Sec. 2032A(d)(1).

[53] Form 706 (Rev. August 2013), p. 6.

[54] A filled in example of Form 706, Schedule A-1, for a decedent dying in 2013, is reproduced at ¶ 3150.

[55] Reg. § 20.2032A-8(a)(3).

[56] Reg. § 20.2032A-8(a)(2). But see *M.S. Miller, Exr.*, DC Ill., 88-1 USTC ¶ 13,757, holding Reg. § 20.2032A-8(a)(2) invalid insofar as it imposed an additional substantive requirement to the statutory rules governing qualification for special use valuation.

[57] Reg. § 20.2032A-8(c). Also see *R.H. Lucas, Pers. Rep.*, CA-11, 96-2 USTC ¶ 60,247, barring an estate from electing under Code Sec. 2032A because the estate failed to file the recapture agreement.

presses consent to personal liability in the event of recapture of additional estate tax due to premature cessation of qualified use or disposition of the property. Signatories other than qualified heirs must express consent to collection of any such additional estate tax from the qualified property.

The IRS National Office has ruled that farmland owned by a decedent in his capacity as shareholder of a corporation could not be valued under the special use valuation provisions because the agreement filed with the election did not contain a signature that bound the corporation. The decedent had bequeathed his estate assets, including stock of the corporation, to his children. Rather than signing the agreement as representatives of the corporation, the children, who were also corporate officers, had signed it in their individual capacities.[58]

Similarly, the IRS ruled that a decedent's interest in farmland that was to pass to a testamentary trust created for the benefit of her two minor grandchildren was not eligible for special use valuation because the beneficiaries did not consent to be personally liable for the recapture tax. Although the recapture agreement was signed by the decedent's daughter in her capacity as trustee, she did not have the right to execute a lien in favor of the government and lacked the capacity to legally bind the two minor beneficiaries of the trust. Thus, the agreement failed to include the required signatures of qualified heirs.[59]

The Tax Court has held, however, that Reg. § 20.2032A-8(c)(2) is invalid insofar as it requires that individuals having tenancy in common interests in property that is subject to a special use election sign the required recapture agreement.[60] The court noted that, although all persons having an interest in property to be specially valued must sign the recapture agreement, the surviving tenants in the instant case did not have such an interest since only the decedent's tenancy in common interests were includible in his gross estate and subject to the election.

• Protective Election

Where it is not certain that property meets the requirements for special use valuation, an estate may make a protective election to specially value qualified real property, contingent on the property values as finally determined meeting the requirements of Code Sec. 2032A.[61] This election is made by filing a notice of protective election with a timely estate tax return. If it is finally determined that the property qualifies for special use valuation, the estate must file an additional notice of election within 60 days of such determination. The IRS National Office has ruled that an estate could make a protective election with respect to a decedent's farmland even though, at the time the estate tax return was filed, the estate met the percentage requirements for special use valuation.[62] However, in another National Office ruling, the IRS has pointed out that neither Code Sec. 2032A nor the regulations thereunder sanction the use of a protective election as a substitute for a timely special use valuation election.[63]

---

[58] IRS Technical Advice Memorandum 8602007 (Sept. 7, 1985).

[59] IRS Technical Advice Memorandum 8802005 (Sept. 29, 1987).

[60] M.F. Pullin Est., 84 TC 789, CCH Dec. 42,060; W.C. Bettenhausen Est., 51 TCM 488, CCH Dec. 42,887(M), TC Memo. 1986-73.

[61] Reg. § 20.2032A-8(b).

[62] IRS Technical Advice Memorandum 8407005 (Nov. 8, 1983).

[63] IRS Technical Advice Memorandum 9013001 (date not given).

• *Cure of Technically Defective Elections*

For elections made prior to August 6, 1997, if a timely special use valuation election was made and the estate tax return, as filed, evidenced substantial compliance with the requirements of the regulations relating to special use valuation, the executor of the decedent's estate had a reasonable period of time (not exceeding 90 days) in which to cure any technical defects or flaws in the form of the election that would prevent it from being valid otherwise.[64] The 90-day period commenced following the IRS's notification to the estate that a defect existed. Examples of technical defects or flaws in the election include the failure to include all required information in the notice of election and the failure to include the signatures of all persons having an interest in the qualifying property.

The Taxpayer Relief Act of 1997 (P.L. 105-34) expanded the ability of the executor to correct omissions. For elections made after August 5, 1997, the executor must file a timely notice of election and a recapture agreement, but need not have substantially complied with the regulations in order to be entitled to submit missing information or signatures.[65] On filing, if the election or agreement fails to include all the required information or signatures, the executor may cure the omission by providing the missing information or signatures within 90 days after receiving written notice from the IRS.

There has been much litigation with respect to whether an estate is entitled to perfect a defective special use valuation election under the substantial compliance provisions of Code Sec. 2032A(d)(3) (prior to its amendment by P.L. 105-34) and whether an executor has provided substantially all of the information required on the estate tax return for a valid special use election. The U.S. Court of Appeals for the Seventh Circuit has held that an estate was entitled to special use valuation, even though no recapture agreement was filed with the federal estate tax return. In this case, substantially all the information required for making the election was provided with the estate tax return, and the executed agreement was filed four months later.[66] However, the U.S. Court of Appeals for the Seventh Circuit later ruled that an estate's failure to submit a recapture agreement with the estate tax return could not be corrected subsequent to the due date of the return by operation of the substantial compliance doctrine, because relief under that doctrine is limited to correcting minor errors in a recapture agreement.[67]

The U.S. Court of Appeals for the Fifth Circuit has held that where an election and recapture agreement were signed by the executrix of an estate but not by any of the beneficiaries of a testamentary trust, the lack of the beneficiaries' signatures could be perfected on an amended recapture agreement filed within 90 days of the IRS's notification to the estate's representative of the defect.[68] Similarly, the U.S. Court of Appeals for the Tenth Circuit has held that an executor's failure to attach to the decedent's federal estate tax return a previously obtained appraisal of the fair market value of certain property for which a special use value election was made was not an incurable defect.[69]

---

[64] Code Sec. 2032A(d)(3), prior to amendment by P.L. 105-34.

[65] Code Sec. 2032A(d)(3), as amended by P.L. 105-34.

[66] *L. Prussner, Exrx.*, CA-7, 90-1 USTC ¶ 60,007.

[67] *C. Grimes Est.*, CA-7, 91-2 USTC ¶ 60,078.

[68] *M. McAlpine, Jr., Est.*, CA-5, 92-2 USTC ¶ 60,109, 968 F2d 459.

[69] *L. Doherty Est.*, CA-10, 93-1 USTC ¶ 60,125, 982 F2d 450.

In contrast, however, the U.S. Court of Appeals for the Eighth Circuit has held that a recapture agreement that failed to include the signatures of the decedent's children (who received an interest as a result of the surviving spouse's disclaimer) did not constitute substantial compliance with the requirements for special use valuation.[70] This was also found to be the case, according to the Tax Court, where the estate failed to attach any notice of election or a signed recapture agreement to a decedent's estate tax return.[71]

¶ 290   Qualified Real Property

Real property may be eligible for special use valuation if it is located in the United States and used as a farm for farming purposes or in a trade or business other than farming. Additionally, the property must satisfy the qualified use (see ¶ 291) and material participation (see ¶ 292) requirements.

A "farm," for purposes of the special valuation procedure, includes stock, dairy, poultry, fruit, fur-bearing animal, and truck farms, plantations, ranches, nurseries, greenhouses or other similar structures used primarily for the raising of agricultural or horticultural commodities, and orchards and woodlands.[72] The term "farming purposes" includes cultivation of the soil, raising agricultural or horticultural commodities and preparing such commodities for market, as well as the planting, cultivating, caring for, cutting down, and preparing for market of trees.[73]

Qualified property includes residences and related improvements located on the qualifying real property and occupied on a regular basis by the owner, the owner's lessee, or the owner's employees for occupational or maintenance purposes. Also considered qualified real property are roads, buildings, and other structures and improvements functionally related to the qualified use of the property.[74]

• *Qualified Woodlands*

An executor may elect special use valuation for standing timber as part of "qualified woodlands," which are identifiable areas of real property (for which business records are normally maintained) used for growing and harvesting timber.[75] A recapture tax will be imposed when the qualified heir severs or otherwise disposes of the timber during the recapture period.[76]

¶ 291   Qualified Use Requirement

Real property for which a special use valuation election is made must be devoted to a qualified farm or business use for five of the eight years prior to the decedent's death. This requirement is satisfied if either the decedent or a member of the decedent's family is utilizing the property for the qualified use.[77] The IRS National Office has interpreted the qualified use requirement to mean that the decedent or a family member must bear some of the financial risk associated with an active farm or other business.[78] In another example of this concept, the U.S. Court of Appeals for the Seventh Circuit has held that a cash lease of farm

---

[70] *G.L. McDonald*, CA-8, 88-2 USTC ¶ 13,778, cert. denied, 4-3-89.

[71] *G. Merwin Est.*, 95 TC 168, CCH Dec. 46,817.

[72] Code Sec. 2032A(e)(4).

[73] Code Sec. 2032A(e)(5).

[74] Reg. § 20.2032A-3(b)(2).

[75] Code Sec. 2032A(e)(13).

[76] Code Sec. 2032A(c)(2)(E).

[77] Code Sec. 2032A(b)(1)(A)(i).

[78] IRS Technical Advice Memorandum 8201016 (Sept. 22, 1981).

property to a nonrelative did not constitute a qualified use.[79] However, for all leases entered into after December 31, 1976, a qualified heir may enter into a cash lease of farm property with a member of the heir's family without triggering recapture.[80]

¶ 292 Determination of "Material Participation"

In order for a property to qualify for special use valuation, the decedent or a member of the decedent's family must materially participate in the farm or business operations for five of the eight years prior to the decedent's death.[81] This eight-year period is measured from the earliest of (1) the date of the decedent's death, (2) the date that the decedent became disabled, or (3) the date that the decedent retired.[82] Whether there has been "material participation" by the decedent or family members in a farm or other closely held business is determined in a manner similar to that set forth in the income tax provisions relating to whether income is subject to self-employment taxes.[83] However, regulations adopted under Code Sec. 2032A[84] provide additional factors to be considered in making this determination for estate tax purposes. The standards for material participation under Code Sec. 469, governing passive activity losses, are similar to the material participation standards under Code Sec. 2032A. Consequently, the estate of a decedent who reported her losses from a ranch as passive activity losses, rather than as losses from an active trade or business, could not elect special use valuation for ranch property because the decedent had not materially participated in ranching during her lifetime.[85]

• *Employment and Management*

Although no single factor determines whether a decedent or family member has materially participated in a farm or closely held business, physical work and participation in management decisions are the principal factors to be considered. The involvement of such an individual on a full-time basis, or to any lesser extent necessary to allow the individual to manage fully the farm or business, is considered material participation. Payment of self-employment taxes on income derived from the farm or closely held business is also an indicator of material participation. Although payment of such taxes is not conclusive evidence of material participation, if no such taxes have been paid, material participation is presumed not to have occurred unless the executor demonstrates otherwise and explains why no self-employment tax was paid. In addition, all such tax determined to be due must be paid before an effective special use valuation election may be made. For this purpose, "tax determined to be due" does not include tax assessments that are barred by the statute of limitations on collection or assessment.[86]

At a minimum, an individual must regularly advise or consult with the other managing party with respect to the operation of the business and participate in making a substantial number of management decisions.[87] According to

---

[79] *T.S. Heffley, Exrx. (O. Heffley Est.)*, CA-7, 89-2 USTC ¶ 13,812; *M.L. Brockman, Admr. (S. Donahoe Est.)*, CA-7, 90-1 USTC ¶ 60,026.

[80] Code Sec. 2032A(c)(7)(E), as added by the Tax Relief Act of 1997 (P.L. 105-34).

[81] Code Sec. 2032A(b)(1)(C).

[82] Code Sec. 2032A(b)(4).

[83] Code Sec. 2032A(e)(6), referring to Code Sec. 1402(a)(1).

[84] Reg. § 20.2032A-3.

[85] IRS Technical Advice Memorandum 9428002 (Mar. 29, 1994).

[86] Reg. § 20.2032A-3(e); Rev. Rul. 83-32, 1983-1 CB 226.

[87] Reg. § 20.2032A-3(e). See also *C.E. Coon Est.*, 81 TC 602, CCH Dec. 40,478.

the regulations, passive collection of rents, salaries, draws, dividends, or other income does not constitute material participation, nor does the mere advancement of capital and review of crop plans or other business proposals.[88] Thus, for farmland to qualify for special use valuation when all or a portion of it is leased to nonqualified heirs, a decedent's financial stake or other involvement must be more than that of a landlord passively collecting a fixed rental from an unrelated tenant.[89]

The U.S. Court of Appeals for the Seventh Circuit has held that farmland rented pursuant to a cash lease containing a rent adjustment clause providing for a 20-percent downward adjustment of the annual rent if gross income from farm production fell below a specified amount qualified for special use valuation. The appellate court stated that the adjustment clause allocated a portion of the risk of poor yield or low crop prices to the decedent and, therefore, the income derived from the lease of the farmland was substantially based on production. However, the court noted that, as the owner of only moderately productive farmland, the decedent was subject to a higher degree of risk than would be the owner of very productive farmland because it was more likely that the rent adjustment clause would be triggered.[90]

• *Financial Risk*

Another factor considered in the determination of material participation is the extent to which an individual has assumed financial responsibility for the farm or other business. This includes the advancement of funds, and, in the case of a farm, the provision of a substantial portion of machinery, livestock, and implements used in production.

• *Residence*

For farms, hotels, or apartment buildings operated as a trade or business, an individual's maintenance of the individual's principal place of residence on the premises is a factor to be considered in determining material participation.

• *Other Considerations*

The activities of at least one family member must amount to material participation at a given time because the activities of a number of family members cannot be considered in the aggregate as material participation. Finally, if nonfamily members participate in the farm or other business, part-time activities by the decedent or family members must be pursuant to a provable oral or written arrangement providing for actual participation by the decedent or family members. For example, the hiring of a professional farm manager will not prevent satisfaction of the material participation requirement if the decedent or family member materially participates under the terms of such an arrangement.[91]

¶ 293   Active Management by Surviving Spouse

A special rule applies to liberalize the material participation requirement with respect to a surviving spouse who receives qualifying property from a decedent in whose estate the property was eligible for special use valuation

---

[88] Reg. § 20.2032A-3(a).

[89] *H.F. Sherrod Est.*, 82 TC 523, CCH Dec. 41,084, rev'd, CA-11, 85-2 USTC ¶ 13,644, 774 F2d 1057, cert. denied, 10-6-86. See *M.J. Martin et al.*, 84 TC 620, CCH Dec. 41,998, aff'd, CA-7, 86-1 USTC ¶ 13,659, 783 F2d 81.

[90] *M. Schuneman*, CA-7, 86-1 USTC ¶ 13,660, 783 F2d 694, rev'g DC Ill., 83-2 USTC ¶ 13,540, 570 FSupp. 1327.

[91] Reg. § 20.2032A-3(e).

Farms and Closely Held Businesses

(whether such valuation was actually elected). "Active management" by the surviving spouse will satisfy the material participation requirement for purposes of electing special use valuation in the surviving spouse's gross estate. The Internal Revenue Code defines active management as the making of management decisions of a business (other than daily operation decisions).[92] Combinations of activities such as inspection of crops, review of crop plans, and marketing decisions constitute active management in farming operations.[93]

The "tacking" of active management by a surviving spouse with material participation by a retired or disabled spouse is allowed in order to qualify the property for special use valuation in the spouse's estate.[94] This provision is applicable only if the spouse died within eight years of the retired or disabled spouse.[95]

¶ 294 Qualifying Property Passing in Trust

The rules for the special use valuation procedure apply to qualifying property that passes in trust. However, future interests in trust property will not qualify for the special use valuation. Trust property will be considered to have passed from the decedent to a qualified heir only to the extent that the qualified heir has a present interest in that trust property. Real property otherwise qualifying for special use valuation and passing to a trust may be specially valued even if the trustee has the discretionary power to fix the amounts receivable by any individual beneficiary, so long as all potential beneficiaries are qualified heirs.[96] If the decedent created successive interests in the trust property that is to be specially valued, all of those interests must be received by qualified heirs (see ¶282).

¶ 295 Community Property

Community-owned property may be valued under the special valuation rules. For purposes of determining whether community-owned real property meets the two percentage tests necessary to qualify real property for special use valuation (see ¶281), the entire value of the property must be taken into account.[97] This ensures equal treatment of community and individually owned property under the special valuation rules.

¶ 296 Basis of Special Use Valuation Property

The basis of specially valued property in the hands of the qualified heir is its value as determined under the special use valuation provisions.[98] In the case of a pecuniary bequest or purchase (see ¶285), the basis of the property to the qualified heir is the estate's basis in the property immediately before the distribution or sale (generally, the property's special use value) plus the amount of post-death appreciation recognized as gain by the estate.[99]

See ¶121 for a discussion of the stepped-up basis rules, as well as the special election of the carryover basis rules available for estates of decedents dying in 2010.

---

[92] Code Sec. 2032A(b)(5) and Code Sec. 2032A(e)(12).

[93] General Explanation of the Economic Recovery Tax Act of 1981, Staff of the Joint Committee on Taxation, p. 246.

[94] Code Sec. 2032A(b)(5); IRS Technical Advice Memorandum 200911009, November 24, 2008.

[95] House Committee Report on the Technical Corrections Act of 1982 (P.L. 97-448).

[96] Code Sec. 2032A(g).

[97] Code Sec. 2032A(e)(10); Rev. Rul. 83-96, 1983-2 CB 156.

[98] Code Sec. 1014(a)(3).

[99] Code Sec. 1040(c).

• *Basis Increase on Recapture*

A qualified heir may make an irrevocable election to increase the income tax basis of special use valuation property to its fair market value on the date of the decedent's death (or on the alternate valuation date, if the estate so elected) if recapture tax is paid.[100]

---

[100] Code Sec. 1016(c).

Chapter 9
STOCKS AND BONDS

¶ 310   Inclusion of Stocks and Bonds

Stocks and bonds owned by a decedent at the date of death are includible in the decedent's gross estate under Code Sec. 2033. They are listed on Schedule B (Stocks and Bonds) of Form 706 (United States Estate (and Generation-Skipping Transfer) Tax Return) (Rev. August 2013), which does not have to be filed if the decedent did not own stocks or bonds.

¶ 311   Dividends and Interest

Dividends and interest on stocks and bonds are included in the gross estate along with the securities on which they are paid. They are usually reflected separately in the same schedule used for reporting stocks and bonds.

Dividends payable to the decedent or to the decedent's estate because, on or before the date of death, the decedent was a shareholder of record must be included in the gross estate and listed on the return as separate items.[1] If dividends have merely been declared and are payable to stockholders of record on a date after the decedent's death, they are not includible in the gross estate.[2] However, they are undoubtedly reflected in the value of the stock.

On the other hand, if the stock is traded on an exchange and the stock is selling "ex-dividend" on the date of the decedent's death, the amount of the dividend must be added to the ex-dividend stock price quotation in fixing the value of the stock.[3] It should not be reported as a separate item in the return schedule. Similarly, if the stock is not traded on an exchange, the dividends must be reported when the record date for determining to whom the dividends are to be paid has passed.

Interest on bonds is includible in the bond owner's gross estate if it has accrued at the owner's date of death.[4] In the case of certain government bonds, however, interest cannot accrue between interest payment dates. With respect to these government bonds, no interest should be included for the period between the last interest payment date and the date of death.

---

[1] Reg. § 20.2033-1(b).
[2] Rev. Rul. 54-399, 1954-2 CB 279.
[3] Reg. § 20.2031-2(i).
[4] Reg. § 20.2033-1(b).

¶ 313   Reporting Stocks and Bonds on Return

A decedent's stocks and bonds are to be reported on Schedule B (Stocks and Bonds) of the estate tax return (Form 706, United States Estate (and Generation-Skipping Transfer) Tax Return) (Rev. August 2013). The description of the stock should indicate (1) the number of shares, (2) whether the stock is common or preferred, (3) the issue, (4) the par value, (5) the price per share, (6) the exact name of the corporation, and (7) the stock CUSIP number. The CUSIP number is a nine-digit number assigned to traded securities by the American Banking Association. If the stocks are listed on a stock exchange, and the principal exchange on which the stock is sold, should be included in the description. If the stock is not listed on an exchange, the description should include the company's principal business office.

A description of bonds should include (1) quantity, (2) denomination, (3) name of the obligor, (4) kind of bond, (5) date of maturity, (6) rate of interest payable, (7) interest due dates, and (8) the bond CUSIP number. The exchange on which the bond is listed should be given. If the bond is not listed on an exchange, the principal business office of the company must be supplied.

¶ 315   Stocks and Bonds Subject to Foreign Death Duties

If an estate, inheritance, legacy, or succession tax has been paid to a foreign country on any stocks or bonds included in the gross estate, the stocks and bonds subjected to the foreign death tax should be grouped separately on Schedule B (Stocks and Bonds) of Form 706 (United States Estate (and Generation-Skipping Transfer) Tax Return) (Rev. August 2013) with a heading "Subjected to Foreign Death Taxes."[5]

¶ 318   Valuation

Stocks and bonds included in the gross estate are to be reported at their value on the date of death or on an alternate valuation date (generally, six months after death) if the estate representative so elects.

When the alternate valuation method is elected, the selling price of any securities sold during the six-month period will control their valuation, if the sale is an arm's-length transaction.[6] In reporting securities under the alternate valuation method, their value at the date of death, as well as that on the alternate date, should be shown on the return.

If the alternate valuation method has been elected, stock includible in the gross estate and selling "ex-dividend" must be valued at its "ex-dividend" quoted selling price as of the alternate valuation date, increased by the amount of dividends declared during the alternate valuation period and payable to stock-holders of record after the alternate valuation date.[7] Although the dividends themselves are not includible in the gross estate of a decedent in such case, the value of such stock on the alternate valuation date includes the value of the right to the declared dividends.[8]

If a taxpayer and the IRS cannot agree on the proper valuation of corporate stock, the taxpayer can challenge the IRS's valuation in the Tax Court, or pay the tax and sue for a refund in a federal district court or the Claims Court. In either case, the burden of proof is on the taxpayer to show that the IRS valuation is

---

[5] See Instructions for Form 706 (Rev. August 2013), p. 22.

[6] Rev. Rul. 70-512, 1970-2 CB 192.

[7] Rev. Rul. 60-124, 1960-1 CB 368.

[8] *C.D. Fleming Est.*, 33 TCM 1414, CCH Dec. 32,873(M), TC Memo. 1974-307.

incorrect. However, if the IRS's valuation is shown to be invalid, the burden of persuasion shifts from the taxpayer to the IRS to prove whether a deficiency actually exists, and if so, how much.[9]

• *Stock Held in Retirement Account*

In a case of first impression, a U.S. district court in Texas[10] has held that the value of a decedent's retirement accounts was not discounted to reflect the income tax liability to be incurred by the beneficiaries upon distribution of the accounts. The estate included two employer-sponsored retirement accounts, both comprised of marketable securities. In valuing the retirement accounts, the court concluded that at the time of death the accounts were equivalent to the securities contained within them and applied the willing buyer/willing seller tests of Reg. § 20.2031-1(b). According to the court, a hypothetical willing buyer of the accounts would not take the income tax liability of the beneficiaries into consideration. The court concluded that Congress had chosen to address the issue of double taxation through Code Sec. 691(c) and that permitting a valuation discount would provide the beneficiaries with "undue relief."

The U.S Court of Appeals for the Fifth Circuit upheld the lower court decision in *Smith*.[11] The appellate court observed that the willing buyer/willing seller valuation standard of Reg. § 20.2031-1(b) was an objective test involving hypothetical parties. Consequently, in applying the test, it was incorrect to treat the sale as one between the decedent's estate and the actual beneficiaries of the accounts. According to the court, considering the income tax that would be paid by the particular account beneficiaries inappropriately altered the test from a hypothetical sale into an actual sale. A hypothetical buyer would not consider the income tax liability because he was not the beneficiary, and therefore, would not be paying the tax on income in respect of a decedent. Rather, the court concluded, the hypothetical buyer would pay the value of the securities held in the accounts. Other cases where potential tax liability was a factor in valuation were distinguishable because they involved a different kind of asset (closely held stock) and the tax involved (capital gains) transferred to the hypothetical buyer. The Tax Court has followed the reasoning in *Smith*, holding that the value of IRA accounts in a decedent's gross estate would not be reduced by anticipated income tax liability that would be incurred by the beneficiaries on distribution of the IRAs.[12]

¶ 319   Separate Appraisal of Tangible and Intangible Assets

If the value of stocks and bonds is determined by the value of the underlying assets, and these assets are both tangible and intangible ones that do not permit a separate appraisal, no general rule is applicable for valuing such assets. Each case will vary and the value of such assets must be determined on the factors present in that particular case.[13]

---

[9] *P. Mitchell Est.*, CA-9, 2001-1 USTC ¶ 60,403, 250 F.3d 696. The IRS has announced that it will not follow this decision: Nonacquiescence Announcement, I.R.B. 2005-23, June 6, 2005, and Action on Decision 2005-01, June 7, 2005.

[10] *L. Smith, Est*, DC Tex., 2004-1 USTC ¶ 60,476.

[11] *L. Smith Est.*, CA-5, 2004-2 USTC ¶ 60,493, aff'g DC Tex., 2004-1 USTC ¶ 60,476.

[12] *D. Kahn Est.*, CCH Dec. 56,195, 125 TC 227.

[13] Rev. Rul. 65-193, 1965-2 CB 370.

¶ 320   Restricted Stock

Certain shares of unregistered stock are "restricted" under federal securities law and may not be sold to the general public but may only be sold to certain types of investors and only in limited amounts. Because of these restrictions, such stock is typically discounted when valued for estate tax purposes. In determining the amount of the discount, the following factors are relevant:

(1) the earnings, net assets, and net sales of the corporation;

(2) the resale provisions found in the restriction agreements;

(3) the relative negotiating strengths of the buyer and the seller; and

(4) the market experience of freely traded securities of the same class as the restricted securities.

All relevant facts and circumstances bearing on the value of the restricted stock must be considered in arriving at the estate tax value of the stock.[14]

> *Comment:* The IRS may contend that no discount should be allowed because the corporation could register the stock and, thus, remove the restrictions on its sale. Whether the corporation would register the stock must be resolved on the facts of each case.[15]

Restricted management accounts. A restricted management account (RMA) is an investment account where the account holder gives a bank or other investment manager management responsibilities over the account, to be exercised over the term of the agreement without withdrawal or investment interference by the account holder. The idea of an RMA is to maximize the portfolio's long-term performance without risk of withdrawal of the assets before the close of the term. Thus, unlike the situation of unregistered stock, where the restriction on sale is based on federal securities law, RMA restrictions are self-imposed by the account holder.

In a ruling dealing with restricted management accounts, the IRS has concluded that the fair market value of an RMA (which held cash and marketable securities) for estate and gift tax purposes was the actual value of the assets in the account without any reduction or discounts.[16] The RMA's value was based on the value of the underlying assets because the RMA agreement had no effect on the ownership, the nature, or the value of the RMA assets and the restrictions imposed by the RMA agreement related primarily to the investment purpose stated in the agreement. (RMAs have been suggested as planning alternatives to family limited partnerships; see ¶ 2545.)

¶ 321   Selling Prices

The estate tax value of stocks and bonds is the fair market value per share or bond on the applicable valuation date. If there is a market for stocks or bonds on a stock exchange or in an over-the-counter market, through a broker or otherwise, the mean between the highest and lowest quoted selling prices on the valuation date is the fair market value of each share or bond.

---

[14] Rev. Rul. 77-287, 1977-2 CB 319, amplifying Rev. Rul. 59-60, 1959-1 CB 237. See also *E.O. Sullivan Est.*, 45 TCM 1199, CCH Dec. 40,015(M), TC Memo. 1983-185, and *C. McClatchy Est.*, CA-9, 98-2 USTC ¶ 60,315, rev'g TC, 106 TC 206, CCH Dec. 51,277.

[15] See, e.g., *S. Brownell Est.*, 44 TCM 1550, CCH Dec. 39,459(M), TC Memo. 1982-632, and *F. Stratton Est.*, 45 TCM 432, CCH Dec. 39,597(M), TC Memo. 1982-744, both holding that a discount was allowable.

[16] Rev. Rul. 2008-35, 2008-2 CB, 116.

If there were no sales on the valuation date, but there were sales on trading dates within a reasonable period both before and after the valuation date, the fair market value is determined by (1) taking the mean between the highest and lowest sales on the nearest trading date before and nearest trading date after the valuation date, (2) prorating the difference between such mean prices to the valuation date, and (3) adding or subtracting, as the case may be, the prorated portion of the difference to or from the mean price on the nearest trading date *before* the valuation date.[17]

Example: Assume that sales of stock nearest the valuation date (Wednesday, June 20) occurred two trading days before (Monday, June 18) and three trading days after (Monday, June 25). Assume further that on these days the mean sale prices per share were $10 and $15, respectively. The price of $12 would be taken as representing the fair market value of a share of stock as of the valuation date:

$$\frac{(3 \times 10) + (2 \times 15)}{5}$$

If, instead, the mean sale prices per share on June 18 and June 25 were reversed—$15 and $10, respectively—the price of $13 would be taken as representing the fair market value.

When a decedent dies on a weekend, the stock included in the decedent's gross estate is valued at the average of the mean sale prices for Friday and Monday.[18] Where the stock begins to sell ex-dividend on the following Monday, the amount of the dividend is added to Monday's quotations to determine the mean sales price.[19]

An alternate method is provided for valuing listed bonds if the highest and lowest selling prices for such bonds are not generally available in a listing or publication on the valuation date. Generally, in such case, the fair market value of a bond at the valuation date is the mean price between the closing selling price on the valuation date and the closing selling price on the trading day before the valuation date.

Special rules are provided for cases where (1) there were no sales on the trading day before the valuation date but there were sales on a date within a reasonable period before the valuation date, (2) there were no sales within a reasonable period before the valuation date but there were sales on the valuation date, or (3) there were no sales on the valuation date but there were sales on dates within a reasonable period both before and after the valuation date.[20]

Stocks and bonds (other than Treasury bonds) that are usually traded in dollars and dollar fractions not smaller than one-eighth are to be reported in dollars and fractions smaller than eighths, for federal estate and gift tax purposes, when the mean of the high and the low quoted selling prices results in a fraction smaller than an eighth on the applicable valuation date. Treasury bonds that are normally traded in dollars and dollar fractions of thirty-seconds are to be valued and reported in dollars and fractions smaller than thirty-seconds, for estate and gift tax purposes, when the mean between the high and low selling prices results in a fraction smaller than a thirty-second.[21] Although this rule will retain its validity, it seemingly will become less important in light of several

---

[17] Reg. § 20.2031-2(b).
[18] Reg. § 20.2031-2(b).
[19] Rev. Rul. 68-610, 1968-2 CB 405.

[20] Reg. § 20.2031-2(b)(2).
[21] Rev. Rul. 68-272, 1968-1 CB 394.

major stock exchanges (including the New York Stock Exchange and NASDAQ) replacing fractional dollars with decimal reporting of stock values.

In valuing listed stocks and bonds, the executor should be careful to consult accurate records to obtain values on the applicable valuation date. If stocks or bonds are listed on more than one exchange, the records of the exchange where the stocks or bonds are principally traded should be used.

> *Preparation Tip:* If quotations of securities are obtained from brokers, copies of the letters furnishing the quotations should be attached to the estate tax return. Similarly, if evidence as to the sale of securities is obtained from officers of the issuing companies, copies of the letters furnishing the evidence should be attached to the return.[22]

¶ 322   Large Blocks of Stock

An exception to the usual procedures for valuing listed securities can sometimes be sustained if the decedent owned a large block of stock in a single company. For example, if the executor can show that the block of stock to be valued is so large in relation to the actual sales on the existing market that it could not be liquidated in a reasonable time without depressing the market, the price at which the block could be sold outside the usual market—such as through an underwriter—may be a more accurate determination of value than market quotations or a mean between the high and low on the valuation date. On the other hand, if the block of stock to be valued represents a controlling interest, either actual or effective, in a going business, the price at which other lots change hands may have little relation to its true value.[23]

The IRS has ruled that underwriters' fees incurred by an estate in selling a large block of a decedent's stock were not to be considered in determining the allowable blockage discount. The IRS noted that the estate tax value of the block of stock was the price at which it could be sold to the general public even though the estate would receive less than this price because it paid the underwriters' fees. However, because it was necessary to sell the stock in order to pay debts, expenses and taxes of the estate, the fees were a deductible administration expense.[24]

> *Comment:* Expert testimony, together with evidence that the stock must be specially handled by one who will discount its value, is usually necessary to establish a valid "blockage" discount.

¶ 323   Lack of Sales

If stock is sold on an exchange or over the counter and there are no sales during a reasonable period beginning before and ending after the valuation date, the valuation may be based on the bid and asked prices. The fair market value is then determined by taking the mean between the bona fide bid and asked prices on the valuation date.

If there are no bid and asked prices on the valuation date, the value may be determined by (1) taking the mean between the bona fide bid and asked prices on the nearest date before and the nearest date after the valuation date, (2) prorating the difference between the mean prices to the valuation date, and (3)

---

[22] See Instructions for Form 706 (Rev. August 2013), p. 23.

[23] Reg. § 20.2031-2(e).
[24] Rev. Rul. 83-30, 1983-1 CB 224.

adding or subtracting, as the case may be, the prorated portion of the difference to or from the mean price on the nearest date before the valuation date.[25]

¶ 324   Incomplete Prices

If actual sale prices or quoted bona fide bid and asked prices are available on a date within a reasonable period *before* the valuation date, but are not available on a date within a reasonable period *after* the valuation date, then the mean between such highest and lowest sales or bid and asked prices may be taken as the fair market value. Similarly, if prices are available within a reasonable period after, but not before, the valuation date, the mean between the highest and lowest available sales or bid and asked prices may be accepted as the value.[26]

¶ 325   Inactive and Unlisted Securities

When stock and other securities are not listed on an exchange and their value cannot be determined on the basis of sales or bid and asked prices because of the absence of sales, the value of the unlisted stock and securities is determined by taking into consideration, in addition to all other factors, the value of stock or securities of corporations engaged in the same or similar line of business that are listed on an exchange.[27] If no active market exists, consideration is also usually given (1) in the case of bonds, to the soundness of the security, the interest yield, the date of maturity, and other relevant factors, and (2) in the case of stocks, to the company's net worth, earning power, dividend-paying capacity, and other relevant factors.[28]

> *Preparation Tip:* Complete financial and other data on which the estate bases its valuation should be submitted with the return. This information must include balance sheets (particularly the one nearest to the valuation date), and statements of the net earnings or operating results and dividends paid for each of the five years immediately preceding the valuation date.

¶ 326   Close Corporation Stock

The term "close corporation" does not appear in the regulations, which establish only general valuation rules in the absence of sales or bona fide bid and asked prices. However, a ruling by the IRS defines closely held corporations as "those corporations the shares of which are owned by a relatively limited number of stockholders." Often the entire stock issue is held by one family. The result of this situation is that little, if any, trading in the shares takes place. There is, therefore, no established market for the stock and such sales as occur at irregular intervals seldom reflect all of the elements of a representative transaction as defined by the term "fair market value."[29]

• *Valuation Factors*

The factors to be considered in determining the value of closely held stock, and of unlisted securities generally, vary with the particular facts involved. The weight to be given any one factor in any given case depends on the circumstances. Sometimes, earnings are given the greatest weight. At other times, assets of the corporation provide the best test. The existence of special conditions in the industry at the time of valuation may also have some effect.

---

[25] Reg. § 20.2031-2(c).
[26] Reg. § 20.2031-2(d).
[27] Code Sec. 2031(b).
[28] Reg. § 20.2031-2(f).

[29] Rev. Rul. 59-60, 1959-1 CB 237, modified by Rev. Rul. 65-193, 1965-2 CB 370, and amplified by Rev. Rul. 77-287, 1977-2 CB 319, and Rev. Rul. 83-120, 1983-2 CB 170.

Although no formula can be devised for the determination of the fair market value of closely held corporations or stock of corporations where market quotations are either lacking or too scarce to be recognized, all available financial data, as well as all relevant factors affecting the fair market value, should be considered.[30] These factors include:

(1) the nature of the business and the history of the enterprise from its inception;

(2) the economic outlook in general and the condition and outcome of the specific industry in particular;

(3) the book value of the stock and the financial condition of the business;

(4) the earning capacity of the company;

(5) the dividend-paying capacity of the company;

(6) goodwill or other intangible value of the company;

(7) sales of the stock and the size of the block to be valued;

(8) the market price of stocks of corporations engaged in the same or a similar line of business having their stocks actively traded in a free and open market, either on an exchange or over the counter; and

(9) the life insurance proceeds received by a corporate beneficiary on a policy covering the sole or controlling stockholder.

Under (9), above, the incidents of ownership in a policy of insurance on the life of a sole surviving shareholder held by the corporation will not be attributed to the insured decedent (the sole or controlling stockholder) through the decedent's stock ownership under Reg. § 20.2042-1(c) because it will be considered a nonoperating asset of the corporation in determining the stock value included in the decedent's gross estate under Reg. § 20.2031-2(f). Thus, life insurance proceeds excluded from the decedent's gross estate are considered a nonoperating asset of the corporation for purposes of valuing the stock of the decedent that is includible in his estate. However, the incidents of ownership will be attributed to the insured decedent who is the sole or controlling stockholder under Reg. § 20.2042-1(c) if such proceeds are not payable to the corporation or a third party for a valid business purpose.[31]

The degree of control of the business represented by the block of stock being valued must also be considered.[32] Thus, if the decedent held control over the corporation, the IRS may contend that a control premium should be added to the stock's value to determine its estate tax value. In the Tax Court's view, "a premium for control is generally expressed as the percentage by which the amount paid for a controlling block of shares exceeds the amount that would have otherwise been paid for the shares if sold as minority interests . . . ."[33] The IRS National Office has ruled that the majority voting power of shares of preferred stock in a closely held corporation owned by a decedent at death was to be considered in valuing the stock for estate tax purposes even though the voting rights expired at the owner's death.[34] With respect to the control issue, the Tax Court has held that the possibility of protracted litigation over the relative

---

[30] Rev. Rul. 77-287, 1977-2 CB 319; Rev. Rul. 59-60, 1959-1 CB 237.

[31] Reg. § 20.2031-2(f) and Reg. § 20.2042-1(c), respectively.

[32] Reg. § 20.2031-2(f).

[33] *J.E. Salsbury Est.*, 34 TCM 1441, CCH Dec. 33,503(M), TC Memo. 1975-333, at 1451.

[34] IRS Technical Advice Memorandum 8401006 (Sept. 28, 1983).

rights of different classes of stock served to limit the date-of-death value of a decedent's interest in a closely held corporation. In addition, the fact that a decedent held the largest block of shares in the company did not necessarily warrant a control premium where the power to unilaterally direct and change the direction of the company was not present.[35]

A determination of the value of stock in an S corporation transferred by parents to their children did not have to be reduced to reflect "tax affecting," a process whereby a discounted future cash flow of a company is adjusted downward to reflect hypothetical income tax on future corporate earnings. In upholding the Tax Court's holding, the U.S. Court of Appeals for the Sixth Circuit noted that there was a difference within the appraisal profession regarding the propriety of the "tax affecting" procedure. Further, there was no evidence that the corporation would lose its subchapter S status and be subject to taxation at the corporate level.[36]

- *Aggregation of Stock Holdings*

The IRS National Office has ruled that two blocks of stock includible in a decedent's gross estate under two different Code sections (Code Sec. 2033 and Code Sec. 2038) can be aggregated to determine the fair market value of the stock for estate tax purposes.[37] A control premium could then be applied if the aggregated stock constituted a controlling interest in a closely held corporation. Similarly, the Tax Court has held that stock held in trust over which a decedent possessed a general power of appointment was to be aggregated for valuation purposes with stock in the same company that was owned outright by the decedent.[38]

In another Technical Advice Memorandum[39], the IRS National Office treated a decedent's voting preferred stock and voting common stock as a single controlling interest in determining the value of a decedent's gross estate under Code Sec. 2033. A control premium was applied, even though the stock passed to two different beneficiaries. However, when it came to determining the amount of the estate tax marital deduction, the block of stock that passed to the decedent's surviving spouse was valued as a separate minority interest.

A block of publicly traded stock held in a revocable trust that was includible in a decedent's gross estate under Code Sec. 2033 was not merged for valuation purposes with additional shares of the same stock in a qualified terminable interest property (QTIP) trust that was includible in her gross estate under Code Sec. 2044, the Tax Court has ruled. The IRS argued that the decedent should be considered the outright owner of a majority block of stock for purposes of valuation and that the shares should be valued at a premium rather than at a discount. In rejecting this argument, the court relied on the fact that neither Code Sec. 2044 nor the legislative history of that section indicates that the decedent should be treated as the owner of QTIP property for purposes of aggregation. The court stated that QTIP property is merely treated as passing from the surviving spouse for estate tax purposes and does not actually pass to or from the surviving spouse. Moreover, the surviving spouse could not exercise any

---

[35] *S. Newhouse Est.*, 94 TC 193, CCH Dec. 46,411 (Nonacq.).

[36] *W. Gross, Jr.*, CA-6, 2001-2 USTC ¶60,425 (cert. den. Oct. 7, 2002), aff'g TC, 78 TCM 201, CCH Dec. 53,481(M), TC Memo. 1999-254 (gift tax decision).

[37] IRS Technical Advice Memorandum 9403002 (Sept. 17, 1993).

[38] *A. Fontana Est.*, 118 TC 318, CCH Dec. 54,693.

[39] IRS Technical Advice Memorandum 9403005 (Oct. 14, 1993).

control over the stock. Therefore, the decedent was not considered the owner of the stock in the QTIP trust for estate tax valuation purposes.[40]

• Buy-Sell Agreements

Another element may also be important, however, and may limit or nullify the weight to be given to the above factors in determining the value of close corporation stock. This element is the restrictive sales agreement, primarily the mutual buy-sell type of agreement. Mutual buy-sell agreements are those whereby a corporation or individual (usually a co-stockholder) promises to buy stock, and the stockholder promises to sell, on the happening of a certain contingency, usually the stockholder's death.

The rules to determine if a buy-sell agreement will be deemed to set the estate tax value for the corporate stock to be transferred will depend on whether such agreement is between related or unrelated parties, and if related parties are involved, whether it was entered into or substantially modified after October 8, 1990.

If the parties to the agreement are not related, the regulations and case law[41] state that to establish the estate tax value of the stock to be transferred, the following four requirements must be met:

(1) the price of the stock must be fixed or determinable by a formula within the agreement;

(2) the estate must be obligated to sell the stock at the fixed price;

(3) if the decedent shareholder chooses to sell the shares during life, he or she must sell them at the price fixed by the agreement; and

(4) the agreement must represent a bona fide business arrangement, rather than a device to pass the decedent's shares to the natural objects of his or her bounty at less than full and adequate consideration.

A buy-sell agreement between family members that was created or substantially modified after October 8, 1990, will not be effective in setting the estate tax value of a closely held business unless the decedent's estate can show that the agreement:

(1) is a bona fide business arrangement;

(2) is not a device to transfer property to family members for less than full and adequate consideration; and

(3) is comparable to similar arrangements entered into by persons in arm's-length transactions.[42]

Additionally, the post-October 8, 1990, buy-sell agreement would also have to meet the requirements stated above with respect to agreements between unrelated parties.

See, also, ¶2500 for a discussion of the special valuation rules for estate freezes.

---

[40] H. Mellinger Est., 112 TC 26, CCH Dec. 53,218 (Acq.).

[41] Reg. §20.2031-2(h); M. Caplan Est., 33 TCM 189, CCH Dec. 32,461(M), TC Memo. 1974-39; O.B. Littick Est., 31 TC 181, CCH Dec. 23,331 (Acq.); M.G. Seltzer Est., 50 TCM 1250, CCH Dec. 42,423(M), TC Memo. 1985-519.

[42] Reg. §25.2703-1(b)(1). If more than 50 percent of the value of the property subject to the buy-sell agreement is owned by persons who are not members of the transferor's family, these three requirements are deemed satisfied, thus effectively removing them with regard to buy-sell arrangements between unrelated parties.

• Minority Discounts

For several years, the IRS maintained that no minority discount should apply when shares in a closely held corporation were transferred from a decedent to other family members, if the corporation remained under family control after the decedent's death. Unless there was evidence of hostility among family members or other indications that the family would not cooperate in corporate matters, the IRS generally challenged the application of a minority discount in these circumstances. However, several courts disagreed with the IRS, finding it appropriate, instead, to consider *only* the decedent's shares of stock in valuing the decedent's interest in the corporation for estate tax purposes.[43] The IRS finally reversed its earlier position and announced that it would no longer disallow a minority discount solely because the transferred interest, when aggregated with interest held by other family members, was a controlling interest.[44]

> **Comment:** Although the IRS's position is seemingly consistent with Tax Court decisions[45] that have allowed a minority discount with respect to minority family members' interests in a family corporation for purposes of both the estate tax and the gift tax, it remains uncertain how the policy announced in Rev. Rul. 93-12 will develop.

For example, the IRS, in a Technical Advice Memorandum[46] involving a donor's gift of three 30-percent blocks of stock to his three children, concluded that the "swing vote" characteristic of each 30-percent block could properly be taken into consideration for determining the fair market value of the stock for gift tax purposes. Any of the three 30-percent owners could combine with any other to control the corporation, whether the 30-percent owners were family members or outsiders. The IRS also concluded that the swing vote attribute enhanced the value of each block of stock. If the three transfers had not been made simultaneously, the second transfer of a 30-percent block would not only have possessed swing-vote value, according to the IRS, but would also have enhanced the value of the first transferee's interest. Moreover, the IRS viewed this enhancement of value as an indirect gift to the first transferee. However, the U.S. Court of Appeals for the Fifth Circuit has ruled that aggregation is not required for the valuation of fractional interests.[47]

• Discount for Lack of Marketability

A substantial discount may be available on the basis that the closely held stock lacks marketability, that is, that there is an absence of a ready or existing market for the sale of the securities being valued.[48] In its *Valuation Training for Appeals Officers Coursebook,* the IRS recognizes that if owners of closely held stock should try to list a block of securities on a stock exchange for sale to the public, they probably would have to make the offerings through underwriters, incurring costs for registration, distribution, and underwriters' commissions. The use of such costs to determine lack of marketability has been upheld by the courts. In

---

[43] *M. Bright Est.,* CA-5, 81-2 USTC ¶13,436, 658 F2d 999; *J.A. Propstra,* CA-9, 82-2 USTC ¶13,475, 680 F2d 1248; *W. Andrews Est.,* 79 TC 938, CCH Dec. 39,523; and *E. Lee Est.,* 69 TC 860, CCH Dec. 35,017.

[44] Rev. Rul. 93-12, 93-1 CB 202, revoking Rev. Rul. 81-253, 1981-2 CB 187, and substituting acquiescence for the nonacquiescence (1980-2 CB 2) in *E. Lee Est.,* 69 TC 860, CCH Dec. 35,017.

[45] *W. Andrews Est.,* 79 TC 938, CCH Dec. 39,523, and *E. Lee Est.,* 69 TC 860, CCH Dec. 35,017 (estate tax decisions); and *C. Ward,* 87 TC 78, CCH Dec. 43,178 (gift tax decision).

[46] IRS Technical Advice Memorandum 9436005 (May 26, 1994).

[47] *L. Bonner, Sr. Est.,* CA-5, 96-2 USTC ¶60,237, 84 F3d 196.

[48] *M. Gallo Est.,* 50 TCM 470, CCH Dec. 42,241(M), TC Memo. 1985-363.

addition, even though securities law restrictions on unregistered stock owned by a decedent terminated on his death, the date-of-death value of the stock was reduced to reflect the restrictions that existed at the time of death.[49]

• Built-in Capital Gains

A lack of marketability discount has been allowed with respect to gifts made from a father to his two sons of stock in a holding company containing built-in capital gains. Although no sale or liquidation of the stock was planned, the estate argued that, as a result of the repeal of the *General Utilities* doctrine by the Tax Reform Act of 1986 (P.L. 99-514), if the holding company were liquidated, gain would be recognized and the estate should be given a discount for the potential capital gains tax. It also argued that any potential buyer would take this tax into account in fixing a purchase price. Despite the absence of plans to sell or liquidate the stock, the Tax Court allowed the discount because it found that a hypothetical willing buyer and seller would have taken the potential tax into account under the circumstances.[50] A full discount in the estate tax value of stock in a personal holding company to reflect built-in capital gains based on a liquidation of the company was allowed, rather than a lesser amount computed to estimate the capital gains liability of the company if it continued to operate as a going concern following the decedent's death. In so holding, the U.S. Court of Appeals for the Fifth Circuit[51] concluded that the Tax Court had erred in assuming that a hypothetical buyer would continue the underlying business as a going concern where the rate of return of the business was substantially lower than the rate of return that an investor would require. Allowing a reduction for the full amount of built-in capital gains based on an assumed liquidation was necessary to reflect the economic reality surrounding the decedent's stock holdings.

• Stock Issued Pursuant to an Estate "Freeze"

The gross estate of the owner of a closely held corporation may include preferred stock in the corporation issued pursuant to a recapitalization designed to "freeze" the value of the individual's interest in the corporation for estate tax purposes. Such a recapitalization is intended to transfer the potential appreciation of the individual's common stock to others active in operating the corporation, often younger members of the individual's family. Typically, this involves the exchange of the individual's common stock for preferred stock that has a stated par value equal to nearly all of the value of the common stock.[52] The individual also receives new common stock having only a low fair market value, and this new stock is then transferred to the younger family members.

The Revenue Act of 1987 (P.L. 100-203) added Code Sec. 2036(c), which was intended to reduce the benefits available from such an "estate freeze." Code Sec. 2036(c) was repealed retroactively by the Revenue Reconciliation Act of 1990

---

[49] *C. McClatchy,* CA-9, 98-2 USTC ¶60,315, 147 F3d 1089, rev'g 106 TC 206, CCH Dec. 51,277.

[50] *A. Davis Est.,* 110 TC 530, CCH Dec. 52,764. Followed, *I. Eisenberg,* CA-2, 98-2 USTC ¶60,322, 155 F3d 50 (Acq.), rev'g and rem'g 74 TCM 1046, CCH Dec. 52,321(M), TC Memo. 1997-483; *P. Welch,* CA-6, 2000-1 USTC ¶60,372, 208 F3d 213, rev'g and rem'g 75 TCM 2252, CCH Dec. 52,689(M), TC Memo. 1998-167. *B. Dunn,* CA-5, 2002-2 USTC

¶60,442, rev'g and rem'g 79 TCM 1337, CCH Dec. 53,713(M), TC Memo. 2000-12; *F. Jelke III,* CA-11, 2007-2 USTC ¶60,552, rev'g and rem'g 89 TCM 1397, CCH Dec. 56,048(M), TC Memo. 2005-131.

[51] *H. Jameson Est.,* CA-5, 2001-2 USTC ¶60,420, vac'g and rem'g 77 TCM 1383, CCH Dec. 53,247(M), TC Memo. 1999-43.

[52] The recapitalization is often structured as a tax-free reorganization under Code Sec. 368(a)(1)(E).

¶326

(P.L. 101-508) and was replaced by a series of rules intended to curb perceived valuation abuses by valuing certain interests at the time of transfer rather than by including previously transferred property in the transferor's gross estate.[53] See ¶2500 for a further description of the limitations on valuation freezes resulting from the Chapter 14 special valuation rules.

The value of the common stock issued in such a recapitalization, according to the IRS, is largely dependent on the corporation's past growth experience, the economic condition of the industry in which the corporation operates, and general economic conditions. However, under certain circumstances, voting rights of the preferred stock could increase the value of the preferred stock and reduce the value of the common stock, especially if the preferred stock has voting control of the corporation.

¶ 327   Worthless Securities

Securities reported on the estate tax return as without value, with nominal value, or obsolete should be listed last on Schedule B (Stocks and Bonds) of Form 706 (United States Estate (and Generation-Skipping Transfer) Tax Return) (Rev. August 2013). The address of the company, the state in which it is incorporated, and the date of incorporation should be stated. Copies of correspondence or statements used as the basis for determining that the stock is without value should be attached.

¶ 328   Mutual Fund Shares

The fair market value of shares in open-end investment companies (mutual funds) is to be set at the "bid" or public redemption price of such shares at the date of death or on the alternate valuation date if the alternate valuation method is elected.[54] In the absence of an affirmative showing of the public redemption price in effect at the time of death, the last public redemption price quoted by the company for the date of death is presumed to be the applicable public redemption price. If there is no public redemption price quoted by the company for the applicable valuation date (for example, where the valuation date is a Saturday, Sunday, or holiday), the mutual fund shares are valued by using the last public redemption price quoted by the company for the first day preceding the applicable valuation date for which there is a quotation.[55]

¶ 329   Tax-Exempt Bonds

With respect to securities of privately owned corporations, the question of taxability does not arise. If the securities were held by the decedent at the time of death (see ¶310), or if the decedent transferred them during life in a manner coming within the definitions of taxable transfers (see ¶550), the value of the securities is includible in the decedent's estate. However, where the securities involved are securities of government-created public corporations or entities, another question arises: What is the effect of provisions stating that the securities shall be exempt from tax? The courts almost invariably answer this question by stating that the federal estate tax is a tax on the transfer of property and not on the property itself—that the exemption granted the securities is an exemption from taxes on the property itself and not an exemption from excise taxes.

---

[53] Code Sec. 2701 through Code Sec. 2704.

[54] Reg. §20.2031-8(b); *D.B. Cartwright*, SCt, 73-1 USTC ¶12,926, 411 US 546.

[55] Reg. §20.2031-8(b).

The various statutory provisions that exempt bonds, bills, notes, and certificates of indebtedness of the federal government or its agencies (and the interest thereon) from taxation are not applicable to estate and gift taxes. U.S. government bonds, U.S. Treasury bonds, and U.S. savings bonds are all subject to federal estate and gift taxation. Similarly, despite state statutory exemptions, state and municipal bonds are subject to estate and gift taxation. However, such bonds issued prior to March 1, 1941, and beneficially owned by a nonresident who is not a U.S. citizen and is not engaged in business in the United States at the time of death are exempt from tax because they are considered "situated outside the United States."[56]

• Anti-Haffner Provision

The Tax Reform Act of 1984 (P.L. 98-369) provided that nothing in any provision of law exempting any property from taxation will exempt the transfer of such property (or interest therein) from federal estate, gift, and generation-skipping transfer taxes.[57] This provision, in effect, reverses the decision of a U.S. district court in Illinois (later affirmed by the U.S. Court of Appeals for the Seventh Circuit) that public housing agency bonds owned by a decedent were exempt from estate taxes under a provision of the Federal Housing Act of 1937.[58] This rule, also referred to as the "anti-Haffner provision," is effective with respect to the estates of decedents dying, and gifts and transfers made, on or after June 19, 1984.[59]

Although the anti-Haffner provision was ruled unconstitutional by a U.S. district court, that decision has been reversed by the U.S. Supreme Court in Wells Fargo Bank.[60] The district court had held that the provision was unconstitutional because the amended legislation amounted to the imposition of a wholly new tax and the retroactive application of that tax would constitute a constitutional violation of due process and equal protection. The Supreme Court, however, held that the language of Section 5(e) of the Housing Act of 1937 exempting property from all taxation applied only to direct taxes, such as the federal income tax, but not to excise taxes, such as the federal estate tax. Because it concluded that the Housing Act did not create an estate tax exemption, the Court found it unnecessary to rule on the constitutionality of the 1984 Tax Reform Act provision.

Basing its reasoning on the principle that a tax exemption cannot be implied, the Tax Court has also refused to infer an exemption from the estate tax for public housing agency bonds. The Tax Court has concluded that because public housing agency bonds had never expressly been exempted from the federal estate tax, their value was includible in the decedent's gross estate.[61] According to the Tax Court, the exemption contained in the Housing Act applied to direct taxes (such as the income tax) and not to the federal estate tax on transfers of property.

The 1984 Act also provides that any provision of law enacted on or after June 19, 1984, will not be construed as exempting the transfer of property from federal estate, gift, and generation-skipping transfer taxes, unless the provision refers to an appropriate rule under the Internal Revenue Code.[62] The rule denying exemp-

---

[56] Reg. § 20.2105-1.

[57] Act Sec. 641(a), P.L. 98-369.

[58] C.C. Haffner III, Exr., 84-1 USTC ¶ 13,571, 585 FSupp. 354, aff'd, CA-7, 85-1 USTC ¶ 13,611.

[59] Act Sec. 641(b)(1), P.L. 98-369.

[60] Wells Fargo Bank et al., SCt, 88-1 USTC ¶ 13,759 (consolidated with H. Rosenberg), rev'g DC Cal., 86-2 USTC ¶ 13,703.

[61] L.G. Egger Est., 89 TC 726, CCH Dec. 44,251.

[62] Act Sec. 641(a), P.L. 98-369.

tion from estate and gift taxes also applies with respect to any property that was reported on an estate or gift tax return as subject to estate or gift tax.[63] Finally, with respect to a transfer of property (or interest therein) made before June 19, 1984, the Act provides that no inference is to arise that such transfer is exempt from federal estate and gift taxation.[64]

• *Reporting Requirements*

Taxpayers are required to provide the IRS with relevant information regarding the transfer of public housing bonds of a type that the district court in *Haffner* held were exempt from estate taxes. This provision is effective with respect to transfers of public housing bonds occurring after 1983 and before June 19, 1984.[65]

¶ 330   U.S. Treasury Bonds

U.S. savings bonds purchased by a decedent with the decedent's own funds are includible in the decedent's gross estate if (1) the bonds are registered in the decedent's own name, (2) the bonds are registered in the decedent's own name, but are payable to another person on the purchaser's death, or (3) the bonds are registered in the names of the decedent and another person as co-owners. Bonds purchased with the separate funds of two persons and registered in their names as co-owners are includible in the estate of the first co-owner to die, to the extent of the percentage of the purchase price that the decedent provided.[66] However, the "consideration-furnished" test does not apply to qualified joint interests (see ¶ 502).

Where the purchaser registers bonds in the purchaser's own name and in the name of another person as co-owners, the bonds must be surrendered to the Treasury Department and be reissued solely in the name of this other person in order to remove them from the purchaser's estate as joint property. The mere physical delivery of such jointly owned bonds to the other person, with the intent to make a gift, will not be recognized so as to remove the bonds from a purchaser's estate.[67]

In determining the value of U.S. savings bonds, a decedent's estate was not entitled to apply a discount for lack of marketability to reflect the income tax due on interest that had accrued on the bonds.[68] In so ruling, the IRS distinguished court holdings in *A. Davis Est.*[69] and *I. Eisenberg*[70] (see ¶ 326, under the heading "Liquidation Discount"), in which liquidation discounts on close corporation stock were allowed based on the conclusion that a hypothetical willing buyer would negotiate a discounted purchase price for the acquisition of stock because the corporation owned appreciated assets with built-in capital gains. This rationale did not apply to the U.S. savings bonds, the IRS reasoned, because the U.S. government was the only buyer, and the sales price was fixed by contractual agreement at the time of original purchase.

---

[63] Act Sec. 641(b)(2), P.L. 98-369.

[64] Act Sec. 641(b)(3), P.L. 98-369.

[65] Act Sec. 642(a), P.L. 98-369.

[66] Rev. Rul. 68-269, 1968-1 CB 399.

[67] *E.G. Chandler, Exr. (M.E. Baum Will),* SCt, 73-1 USTC ¶ 12,902, 410 US 257.

[68] IRS Technical Advice Memorandum 200303010 (Sept. 19, 2002).

[69] *A. Davis Est.,* 110 TC 530, CCH Dec. 52,764.

[70] *I. Eisenberg,* CA-2, 98-2 USTC ¶ 60,322, 155 F3d 50 (Acq.), rev'g and rem'g 74 TCM 1046, CCH Dec. 52,321(M), TC Memo. 1997-483.

¶ 331   Nonresidents Not Citizens

Except as indicated below, only property located in the United States is includible in the gross estate of a nonresident alien decedent.[71] The notable exception to this general situs rule is the stock of domestic corporations, which is includible in a decedent's gross estate, regardless of where it is located. Likewise, except as mentioned below, debt obligations (bonds, etc.) that are owned and held by a nonresident alien are considered property located within the United States if the primary obligor is a domestic corporation or other U.S. person, the United States, a state, a political subdivision of a state, or the District of Columbia.[72] For this purpose, it is immaterial whether the written evidence of the debt obligation is treated as being the property itself. Currency, however, is not to be considered a debt obligation.

Short-term original issue discount obligations will not be treated as U.S. situs property. For this purpose, a short-term obligation means an obligation payable 183 days or less from the date of the obligation's issue.[73] Additionally, debts of a domestic corporation deriving less than 20 percent of its gross income from U.S. sources for the three-year period prior to the nonresident's death are not considered as having a situs in the United States. Other debt obligations are not, according to the House Ways & Means Committee Report to the Foreign Investors Tax Act of 1966 (P.L. 89-809), to be considered property within the United States even if written evidence of the obligation that is considered as the property itself is located in the United States.[74]

The situs rules may, however, be modified by a death tax treaty with the country of domicile of the decedent (see also ¶ 1615).

---

[71] Code Sec. 2103.
[72] Code Sec. 2104.
[73] Code Sec. 2105(b)(4).

[74] House Ways & Means Committee Report to the Foreign Investors Tax Act of 1966 (P.L. 89-809).

Chapter 10

MORTGAGES, NOTES, CONTRACTS TO SELL LAND, AND CASH

¶ 350   Inclusion in Gross Estate

As with property interests reportable in schedules concerned with real property and stocks and bonds, the taxability of mortgages, notes, contracts to sell land, and cash is generally determined under Code Sec. 2033. These items must be valued as of the date of decedent's death unless the executor elects to have them valued as of the alternate valuation date. They are reported on Schedule C (Mortgages, Notes, and Cash) of Form 706 (United States Estate (and Generation-Skipping Transfer) Tax Return) (Rev. August 2013).[1] This schedule does not have to be filed if the decedent did not own property reportable on it.

¶ 355   Mortgages and Notes

In describing mortgages on the estate tax return (Form 706, United States Estate (and Generation-Skipping Transfer) Tax Return) (Rev. August 2013), the following information should be set out:

(1) face value and unpaid balance;

(2) date of mortgage;

(3) date of maturity;

(4) name of maker;

(5) property subject to mortgage; and

(6) interest dates and rate of interest.

Similar data should be shown when reporting notes.

The value of notes, whether secured or unsecured, is the amount of unpaid principal, together with accrued interest, unless the estate representative establishes a lower value or proves them worthless. If included on the return at less than face value, plus interest, the lower value must be established by satisfactory evidence. A lower value may be justified because of the interest rate or date of maturity. For example, the IRS National Office has ruled that the estate tax value of an installment note payable to a decedent was less than its face value because the note provided for payment of interest at a rate below the prevailing interest rate on the date of the decedent's death.[2] If a note is wholly or partially uncollectible because of insolvency of the debtors or any collateral for the loan is insufficient to satisfy the debt, a lower valuation is permitted.[3]

If an estate contends that the actual value of mortgages or mortgage participation certificates is less than their face value, the controlling valuation factors include (1) the valuation of real estate and any collateral covered by the mort-

---

[1] A filled-in example of Form 706, Schedule C, for a decedent dying in 2013, is reproduced at ¶ 2970.

[2] IRS Technical Advice Memorandum 8229001 (Feb. 1, 1982).

[3] Reg. § 20.2031-4.

gages, (2) arrearages in taxes and interest, (3) gross and net rentals, (4) foreclosure proceedings, (5) assignment of rents, (6) prior liens or encumbrances, (7) present interest yield, (8) over-the-counter sales, and (9) bid and asked quotations. The existence of an over-the-counter market for mortgage notes and certificates and the quotations and opinions furnished by brokers and real estate appraisers will not be accepted by the IRS as conclusive evidence of their value. Where the mortgage is amply secured, the value will be the mortgage's face value plus accrued interest to date of death. Where the security is insufficient, the mortgage will be valued on the basis of the fair market value of the property less back taxes, estimated foreclosure expenses, and, where justified, the expense of rehabilitation. The estate must prove the lesser value.[4]

• Self-Canceling Notes

Promissory notes that by their terms are deemed canceled on the death of the payee may escape estate taxation at the payee's death, provided that the cancellation provision is part of a bargained-for exchange supported by full and adequate consideration. In so ruling, the Tax Court distinguished the situation where a decedent tries to avoid estate taxation on promissory notes held at death by canceling the indebtedness by a will provision or separate writing.[5] With regard to the income tax consequences of a cancellation of an installment obligation at death, the U.S. Court of Appeals for the Eighth Circuit agreed with the IRS[6] that the payee's estate would have to recognize, as income in respect of a decedent, deferred installment gain on the notes. Although not part of the formal holding of the case, the appellate court noted, consistent with taxing gain to the estate, that the obligor of a self-canceling installment note would have a basis in the purchased property equal to the note's face value, not just the amount of principal actually paid.[7]

¶ 360   Contracts to Sell Land

In reporting a contract to sell land on the estate tax return, it is necessary to provide the following information:

    (1) name of purchaser;

    (2) date of contract;

    (3) description of property to be sold;

    (4) sale price;

    (5) initial payment;

    (6) amounts of installment payments;

    (7) unpaid balance of principal; and

    (8) interest rate.

The listing of contracts to sell realty is a listing in lieu of the realty. If the decedent has an unpaid mortgage or other indebtedness on the property being sold under the contract and the decedent's estate is liable for it, the full value of the contract must be included as part of the gross estate. The mortgage or indebtedness is allowed as a deduction in such a case. If the decedent's estate is not liable, only the value of the redemption equity (or the value of the contract, less the mortgage or indebtedness) need be reported as part of the value in the

[4] Rev. Rul. 67-276, 1967-2 CB 321.

[5] *J.A. Moss*, 74 TC 1239, CCH Dec. 37,230 (Acq.).

[6] Rev. Rul. 86-72, 1986-1 CB 253.

[7] *J. Frane Est.*, CA-8, 93-2 USTC ¶ 50,386, 998 F2d 567.

gross estate. In no case may the deduction on account of the mortgage exceed the liability actually contracted for. Only interest accrued to the date of the decedent's death is deductible even though the alternative valuation method is elected.[8]

¶ 365   Cash

In reporting cash on the estate tax return, cash in the decedent's possession should be listed separately from cash deposited in banks or other financial organizations.

In reporting cash deposited in financial organizations, the return should show:

> (1) name and address of each organization;
>
> (2) amount in each account;
>
> (3) serial number or account number;
>
> (4) nature of accounts (checking, savings, time deposit, etc.); and
>
> (5) unpaid interest accrued from date of last interest payment to the date of death.

If statements are obtained from the financial organizations, they should be retained for inspection by the IRS.

Cash that belongs to the decedent at the time of death must be reported in full, whether in the decedent's or another's possession and whether it is on deposit in a bank. Checks outstanding at the time of death may be subtracted from the total if they are subsequently honored and charged against the decedent's account, but only if the obligation is not claimed as a deduction.[9] The amount of any check that was given under circumstances indicating a taxable lifetime transfer cannot be claimed as a deduction.

If interest on a particular savings bank account does not accrue between interest payment dates, no interest between the last interest payment date and the date of decedent's death should be included in the valuation.[10] However, if certificates of deposit can be redeemed without forfeiture of interest on the death of the owner, the interest accrued but unpaid at death is includible in the value of the certificates for estate tax purposes even if the interest would have been forfeited had the decedent redeemed the certificates prior to death.[11]

U.S. silver coins (or paper currency) that are held by a decedent at the time of death and that are worth more than their face value must be valued at their fair market value for estate tax purposes, even if the decedent had never been a coin collector.[12] If the cash consists of foreign currency or foreign bank accounts, the value should be stated in terms of the official rate of exchange.[13] Restrictions or difficulties concerning convertibility can justify a lower value.

> *Preparation Tip:* If the decedent had an interest in, or a signature or other authority over, a financial account in a foreign country, such as a bank account or securities account, this must be indicated in the "Yes" checkbox in Question 15, Part 4, Form 706 (Rev. August 2013).

---

[8] Reg. § 20.2053-7.
[9] Reg. § 20.2031-5.
[10] Rev. Rul. 55-301, 1955-1 CB 442.

[11] Rev. Rul. 79-340, 1979-2 CB 320.
[12] Rev. Rul. 78-360, 1978-2 CB 228.
[13] *A. Fry Est.*, 9 TC 503, CCH Dec. 16,030 (Acq.).

Chapter 11

LIFE INSURANCE

¶ 400 Inclusion of Life Insurance

Life insurance, for estate tax purposes, includes not only the common forms of insurance taken out by an individual on the individual's own life, but also the proceeds of certain other types of insurance policies. Proceeds of accident insurance policies, including flight insurance of the type commonly purchased at air terminals, are proceeds of life insurance for estate tax purposes.[1] Similarly included are proceeds of War Risk insurance and of National Service Life insurance. Amounts paid under group insurance and under double indemnity clauses by reason of the accidental death of an insured are also treated as the proceeds of life insurance.

The more common forms of insurance that are regarded as life insurance are ordinary life, universal life, variable life, limited payment life, endowment, term insurance, survivor life policies, split-dollar arrangements, and retired lives reserves insurance.

Insurance that a decedent may have taken out on the life of another individual is not taxed under the insurance provision of Code Sec. 2042, but, rather, under the general taxing rules of Code Sec. 2033.

> *Comment:* The fact that a contract is called an insurance contract does not automatically entitle it to treatment as insurance for estate tax purposes if it is not, in fact, a contract of insurance. To be an insurance contract, an element of risk must be involved. The risk must be an actuarial one under which the premium cost is based on the likelihood that the insured will live for a certain period of time and under which the insurer stands to suffer a loss if the insured does not, in fact, live for the expected period.

---

[1] *M.L. Noel Est.*, SCt, 65-1 USTC ¶ 12,311, 380 US 678.

The IRS has ruled that the value of no-fault death benefits payable to the estates of a driver and a passenger who were killed in an automobile accident was includible in their gross estates as the proceeds of life insurance policies. This was so because, under applicable state law, payment of the death benefits did not preclude the decedents' estates or heirs from bringing wrongful death actions. Accordingly, because the insurer was unconditionally bound to make payment in the event of the insureds' deaths, the no-fault insurance policy had the necessary risk-shifting and risk-distributing elements necessary to be considered life insurance for purposes of Code Sec. 2042.[2]

> *Preparation Tip:* Insurance on the decedent's life is reported on Schedule D (Insurance on the Decedent's Life) of Form 706 (United States Estate (and Generation-Skipping Transfer) Tax Return) (Rev. August 2013). Schedule D does not have to be filed with the return where there is no insurance on the decedent's life. Insurance on another person's life, which is includible in the decedent's gross estate, is not reportable on Schedule D. Rather, it must be reported on Schedule F (Other Miscellaneous Property Not Reportable Under Any Other Schedule).

¶ 403   Group Insurance

Proceeds of group life insurance are treated the same as the proceeds of any other insurance. Generally, they are includible in the estate of the insured because the insured has incidents of ownership, or is regarded as having them, at the time of death.

• Assignability

A group-term life insurance policy, the cost of which is paid by the employer, is excludable from the estate of a deceased employee if the decedent has irrevocably assigned all interest in the policy and did not die within three years of making the assignment.[3] The assignment, in order to be valid, must not be prohibited by state law or by the terms of the policy. Most states now have specific laws permitting assignments of group life insurance policies by insured employees. However, where state law fails to affirmatively provide for assignment, but does not expressly prohibit it, it may be possible to assign the policy and to remove it from the employee's estate.[4]

The IRS will recognize assignments made by employees in those cases where the master policy permits assignments and the individual policy certificates issued to employees do not.[5] On the other hand, where the master policy did not permit assignments, an attempted assignment was held to be invalid, and the proceeds of the policy were includible in an insured-employee's gross estate.[6]

Estates of stockholder-employees of closely held corporations may face difficulty if they attempt to exclude previously assigned group life insurance from the decedent's gross estate.[7] The government has argued that a controlling stockholder had incidents of ownership over a group policy because of his right to surrender or cancel the policy while acting as a corporate officer. The U.S. Court of Claims rejected this argument in a situation involving a corporation

---

[2] Rev. Rul. 83-44, 1983-1 CB 228.

[3] Code Sec. 2035.

[4] *M.J. Gorby Est.*, 53 TC 80, CCH Dec. 29,801 (Acq.); *L. Landorf, Exr.*, CtCls, 69-1 USTC ¶ 12,593, 408 F2d 461.

[5] *M.J. Gorby Est.*, 53 TC 80, CCH Dec. 29,801 (Acq.).

[6] *S.F. Bartlett Est.*, 54 TC 1590, CCH Dec. 30,278 (Acq.).

[7] *L. Landorf, Exr.*, CtCls, 69-1 USTC ¶ 12,593, 408 F2d 461.

jointly owned by two unrelated officers. However, the court indicated that this power might exist where the decedent was the sole stockholder or, in effect, had control over minority stockholder-officers. Presently, this question remains unresolved. For corporate-owned group-term life insurance where the decedent is the sole or controlling stockholder, the power to surrender or cancel a policy held by the corporation will not be attributed to the decedent through the decedent's stock ownership to the extent the proceeds of the policy are payable to the corporation.[8] Also, the IRS has privately ruled that the sole shareholder of a closely held corporation did not possess incidents of ownership in a life insurance policy on his own life, despite his ability to terminate the policy beneficiary's employment contract, causing the distribution of insurance proceeds to a trust for the benefit of the shareholder's family.[9]

A post-1976 assignment of a group policy made by an employee within three years of death evidently will be automatically includible in the employee's estate. However, an assignment of a group-term policy within three years of death will not result in inclusion of the policy in the transferor's gross estate if the assignment was necessitated by the employer's change of insurance carrier and was made pursuant to an "anticipatory assignment" of all present and future employer-provided policies executed more than three years before the transferor's death (see ¶ 555).[10]

• *Conversion Privilege*

A group-term life insurance policy can be excluded from the estate of a deceased employee even though neither the policy nor state law gives the employee the right to convert the group-term coverage to individual life insurance on termination of employment, provided the employee has irrevocably assigned all interests in such policy, and such assignment is not prohibited by state law or the policy.[11] This is true because the power to cancel the group-term policy solely by terminating employment is not considered to be an incident of insurance ownership.

In addition, the Tax Court has held, and the IRS has agreed, that a decedent's right to convert an employer-owned group policy of insurance on his life to individual insurance on termination of employment is not an incident of ownership in the policy.[12] In the view of the court and the IRS, termination of employment by an employer is not within a decedent's control, and voluntary termination would be so detrimental to an employee's economic position that a conversion privilege should not be considered an incident of ownership. Therefore, if a decedent transfers all incidents of ownership in the policy, but retains the right to convert the group coverage to an individual policy on termination of employment, the proceeds of the group policy are not includible in the decedent's gross estate.

• *Settlement Options*

It is an open question whether the proceeds of a noncontributory group-term life insurance policy are includible in an employee's gross estate where the employee has the right to vary the time and manner in which the proceeds are payable to the beneficiaries even though, under the policy, the employee cannot

---

[8] Reg. § 20.2042-1(c).
[9] IRS Letter Ruling 9421037 (Feb. 28, 1994).
[10] Rev. Rul. 80-289, 1980-2 CB 270.

[11] Rev. Rul. 72-307, 1972-1 CB 307.
[12] *J. Smead Est.*, 78 TC 43, CCH Dec. 38,722 (Acq.); Rev. Rul. 84-130, 1984-2 CB 194.

benefit himself or his estate.[13] The IRS maintains that the right to elect optional modes of settlement for the proceeds of life insurance on a decedent's life is an incident of ownership within the meaning of Code Sec. 2042. In addition, the IRS has announced that it will not follow the decision of the U.S. Court of Appeals for the Third Circuit in *Connelly*, which holds that the right to select such optional settlement modes is not an incident of ownership within the meaning of Code Sec. 2042 if the option merely allows the decedent to alter the time of enjoyment of the insurance proceeds.[14]

¶ 405   Death Benefits

Death benefits, payable other than under a life insurance contract, do not ordinarily qualify as proceeds of insurance. Benefits paid by employers, for example, voluntarily or otherwise, usually are lacking in some of the elements essential for qualification as insurance (see ¶ 420 and ¶ 733 for further details).

¶ 410   Insurance on the Life of Another

If a person, at the time of death, owns policies of insurance on the life of another individual, the value of such insurance is includible in the decedent's gross estate, but not as proceeds of insurance. It is included in the decedent's estate under Code Sec. 2033 as property in which the decedent had an interest at the time of death. It must be reported on Schedule F (Other Miscellaneous Property Not Reportable Under Any Other Schedule) of Form 706 (United States Estate (and Generation-Skipping Transfer) Tax Return) (Rev. August 2013).

The value of such insurance is the cost of replacement and not the cash surrender value. Replacement cost is the cost of buying another policy of the same value and same status on the life of the same insured. This cost can only be obtained from the insurer. If the policy has been in force for some time at the decedent's death and further premiums are to be paid, the value may be approximated by adding to the interpolated terminal reserve at the date of the decedent's death the proportionate part of the gross premium last paid before the decedent's death that covers the period extending beyond death.[15]

> *Comment:* Conflict exists in those cases where a beneficiary-owner and the insured person die simultaneously. The IRS takes the position that the entire proceeds of a policy are to be included in the owner-beneficiary's gross estate. The courts have almost uniformly rejected this view and have held that the policy is to be valued under the interpolated terminal reserve method in accordance with Reg. § 20.2031-8.[16]

If, however, a policy is sold to the insured within six months following the death of the person who owned the policy, and the estate is valued as of a date six months after the death, the amount received on the sale of the policy will govern its value for estate tax purposes. Likewise, if the policy is actually surrendered for cash during the alternate valuation period after death, the amount received should be the acceptable value. If premiums are paid by the

[13] See *J.H. Lumpkin, Jr., Est.,* CA-5, 73-1 USTC ¶ 12,909, 474 F2d 1092; *J.J. Connelly, Sr., Est.,* CA-3, 77-1 USTC ¶ 13,179, 551 F2d 545.

[14] Rev. Rul. 81-128, 1981-1 CB 469.

[15] Reg. § 20.2031-8(a)(2).

[16] *N. Meltzer Est.,* CA-4, 71-1 USTC ¶ 12,754, rev'g TC, 29 TCM 265, CCH Dec. 30,004(M),

TC Memo. 1970-62; *Old Kent Bank,* CA-6, 70-2 USTC ¶ 12,703, 430 F2d 392; *R.M. Chown Est.,* CA-9, 70-2 USTC ¶ 12,702, 428 F2d 1395, rev'g TC, 51 TC 140, CCH Dec. 29,202; *E.M. Wien Est.,* CA-5, 71-1 USTC ¶ 12,764, 441 F2d 32, rev'g TC, 51 TC 287, CCH Dec. 29,238; *E.W. Marks, Jr., Est.,* 94 TC 720, CCH Dec. 46,594.

estate preceding the sale, it is likely that the value will be the total proceeds reduced by the portion attributable to the premiums paid after death.

See also ¶112 as to appreciation in value of insurance policies during the alternate valuation period.

¶ 415   Life Insurance and Annuity Combination

Persons who cannot pass the physical examination on which the issuance of the usual type of life insurance contract is predicated may purchase a special type of insurance and annuity combination. The insurance portion of such a combination cannot be purchased separately. It is issued on the assumption that, if the purchaser does not live long enough to receive full benefits from the annuity portion of the combination, the amount left over from the cost of that portion will make up the difference between the price paid for the insurance portion and the total amount of the death benefit. If the person does live to receive full benefits from the annuity portion, the money paid for the insurance portion will have gathered interest for a period long enough to build up the full amount of the death benefit. The insurance company actually takes no risk.

Formerly, it was generally believed that the insurance portion of such a combination was excludable from an insured decedent's estate where the decedent had irrevocably assigned all rights in the policy to the named beneficiaries.[17] However, this tax-saving technique was apparently eliminated by a 1972 case.[18] In this case, the IRS claimed, and the Tax Court and the U.S. Court of Appeals for the Fifth Circuit agreed, that the insurance and annuity contracts were part of one transaction and, therefore, the insurance portion was includible in the decedent's estate as an annuity under Code Sec. 2039. Both courts held that the *Fidelity-Philadelphia Trust Co.* case was not controlling because it was decided before Code Sec. 2039 was enacted.

¶ 420   Death Benefits Under Retirement Plans

Life insurance proceeds paid under a qualified pension or profit-sharing plan are includible in the gross estate under Code Sec. 2042 (dealing with insurance), rather than Code Sec. 2039 (dealing with annuities).[19] Thus, it may be possible to have the insurance proceeds excluded from the employee's gross estate by having the employee-plan participant transfer all incidents of ownership in the policy to someone else. To be effective, this transfer would have to take place more than three years before the participant's death.

The inclusion of payments from a nonqualified employees' plan or contract depends on whether the payment is, in fact, the payment of proceeds of insurance under a policy on the life of the employee or whether the payment, in fact, represents an annuity payment.[20] (Typically, such plans provide for pension payments and for the payment of a death benefit where the employee dies before retirement.) If the payment represents insurance proceeds, the inclusion of the payment depends on whether the decedent-employee has retained "incidents of ownership" over the policy (see ¶430). If the payment is an annuity, the estate tax treatment of the payment is based on the annuity rules discussed beginning at ¶700.

---

[17] *Fidelity-Philadelphia Trust Co., Exr. (M. Haines Est.),* SCt, 58-1 USTC ¶11,761, 356 US 274.

[18] *L. Montgomery Est.,* 56 TC 489, CCH Dec. 30,822, aff'd per curiam, CA-5, 72-1 USTC ¶12,840, cert. denied, 409 US 849; *I.T. Sussman, Exr. (J. Sussman Will),* DC N.Y., 76-1 USTC ¶13,126.

[19] Reg. §20.2039-1(d).

[20] Reg. §20.2039-1(d).

¶ 425   Refunds in Case of Suicide

If an insured commits suicide before a policy becomes incontestable, the beneficiary will receive only a refund of premiums instead of the face amount. This refund does not constitute a payment of insurance proceeds.[21]

¶ 430   Proceeds Payable to Named Beneficiaries

Life insurance payable to named beneficiaries is subject to special rules. If the insured merely names the beneficiary, but disposes of none, or only some, of the rights that the insured normally receives under the terms of a policy, the proceeds will be includible in the decedent-insured's gross estate just like any other property. On the other hand, if the insured disposes of all rights over the policy (incidents of ownership), the entire amount of the proceeds may be kept out of the decedent's gross estate.[22]

Insurance is considered payable to a "named beneficiary" (one other than the estate) when the recipient is not required to use any of the proceeds for the benefit of the estate. Therefore, it may be paid to an executor if the executor may keep the proceeds for the executor's own benefit. It may be paid to a trustee if the trustee is not charged with a duty to apply the proceeds in payment of taxes or other estate charges. Likewise, it may be paid to a corporation, a partnership, or a profit-sharing plan.

The term "incidents of ownership" is not limited in its meaning to ownership of the policy in the technical, legal sense. The term refers to the right of the insured or the insured's estate to the economic benefits of the policy. The retention of any of the following will result in inclusion of the insurance proceeds in the gross estate:[23]

(1) the right to change beneficiaries or their shares;

(2) the right to surrender the policy for cash or to cancel it;

(3) the right to borrow against the policy reserve;

(4) the right to pledge the policy as collateral;

(5) the right to assign the policy or to revoke an assignment;

(6) the right to prevent cancellation of an insurance policy owned by an employer by purchasing the policy for its cash surrender value;[24] and

(7) a reversionary interest by which the insured or the estate of the insured may regain one or more of the above rights in the event a beneficiary should predecease the insured or if certain other contingencies should occur. (The chances that the right or rights will return to the insured must exceed five percent of the value of the policy immediately before the death of the insured.)

The possession of any of the above rights will result in inclusion of the proceeds in the insured's gross estate even if the consent of some other person is necessary for the exercise of the right. Estate tax liability depends on a general,

---

[21] *W.D. Chew, Jr., Est.,* CA-5, 45-1 USTC ¶ 10,181, 148 F2d 76, aff'g TC, 3 TC 940, CCH Dec. 13,953, cert. denied, 325 US 882.

[22] Code Sec. 2042; Reg. § 20.2042-1(c).

[23] Code Sec. 2042; Reg. § 20.2042-1(c).

[24] Rev. Rul. 79-46, 1979-1 CB 303. The Tax Court, however, has indicated that such a right is too contingent to warrant inclusion of policy proceeds in the gross estate; see, e.g., *J.C. Morrow Est.,* 19 TC 1068, CCH Dec. 19,510, and *J. Smith Est.,* 73 TC 307, CCH Dec. 36,443.

legal power to exercise ownership, without regard to actual ability to exercise it at a particular moment (as on a trans-Atlantic flight).

• Right to Receive Dividends

A right to receive the dividends of a life insurance policy is not a right to the income of that policy. Instead, it is a reduction in the amount of premiums paid.[25] Accordingly, the right to receive dividends, on its own, is not an incident of ownership.[26]

• Insured Decedent as Trustee

Powers held by a decedent as fiduciary with respect to an insurance policy on his or her life will not constitute incidents of ownership in the policy so long as (1) the powers are not exercisable for the decedent's personal benefit, (2) the decedent did not directly transfer the policy or any of the consideration for purchasing or maintaining the policy to the trust, and (3) the decedent did not retain the powers as settlor of the trust.[27] Where all of the above conditions are met, a decedent-trustee will not be deemed to have incidents of ownership in the policy even if the decedent held, at the time of death, such broad discretionary powers over the policy as the right to elect to have the proceeds made payable according to various plans, to use the loan value to pay the premiums, to borrow on the policy, to assign or pledge the policy, or to elect to receive annual dividends.[28] This IRS position is consistent with the decisions of several appellate courts.[29]

• Transfers Within Three Years of Death

The gross estate of a decedent who transferred all rights over an insurance policy on the decedent's life within three years of death and after 1976 includes the entire proceeds of the policy.[30] However, the proceeds are not reported on Schedule D (Insurance on the Decedent's Life) of Form 706 (United States Estate (and Generation-Skipping Transfer) Tax Return) (Rev. August 2013); rather, they are reported on Schedule G (Transfers During Decedent's Life).[31]

Some courts have held that, if a policy of insurance on the life of a decedent is issued within three years of death and the decedent pays the premiums, the policy proceeds are includible in the decedent's gross estate even if the decedent did not own the policy.[32] In the view of these courts, the decedent in each case effectively transferred the policy within three years of death by having it issued in the name of some other person (usually a family member) and paying the premiums. Although these cases were decided prior to the amendment of Code Sec. 2035 by the Economic Recovery Tax Act of 1981 (P.L. 97-34), the IRS National Office has adopted the reasoning of these courts and ruled that the proceeds of a policy of insurance on a decedent's life purchased within three years of the

---

[25] C. Bowers Est., 23 TC 911, Dec. 20,878, Acq. 1955-2 CB 4.

[26] Chief Counsel Advice 201328030, March 18, 2013.

[27] Rev. Rul. 84-179, 1984-2 CB 195, revoking Rev. Rul. 76-261, 1976-2 CB 276.

[28] Rev. Rul. 84-179, 1984-2 CB 195, revoking Rev. Rul. 76-261, 1976-2 CB 276.

[29] H.R. Fruehauf Est., CA-6, 70-1 USTC ¶12,688, 427 F2d 80, aff'g TC, 50 TC 915, CCH Dec. 29,146; H.R. Skifter Est., CA-2, 72-2 USTC ¶12,893, 468 F2d 699; and S.A. Hunter et al., CA-8, 80-2 USTC ¶13,362, 624 F2d 833; but see C.M. Rose, CA-5, 75-1 USTC ¶13,063, 511 F2d 259; and N.C. Terriberry, CA-5, 75-2 USTC ¶13,088, 517 F2d 286, cert. denied, 424 US 977.

[30] Code Sec. 2035.

[31] Instructions to Form 706 (Rev. August 2013), p. 27.

[32] D.M. Bel, Exr. (J.A. Bel Will), CA-5, 72-1 USTC ¶12,818, 452 F2d 683, cert. denied, 406 US 919; and First National Bank of Oregon, Exr. (F.M. Slade Est.), CA-9, 74-1 USTC ¶12,966, 488 F2d 575.

decedent's death in 1983 were includible in the decedent's gross estate even though the decedent never actually possessed any incidents of ownership in the policy.[33]

However, the U.S. Court of Appeals for the Tenth Circuit has held that the rule requiring inclusion of transfers within three years of death applies only to a gift of life insurance where the decedent retained incidents of ownership in the insurance policy under the rules of Code Sec. 2042.[34] Even though the decedent's wholly owned corporation paid the premiums on the policy, only his spouse and children, as owners and beneficiaries of the policy, held incidents of ownership. Thus, the proceeds of the life insurance policy purchased within three years of the decedent's death in 1983 were not includible in his gross estate. Other Tax Court decisions with similar fact situations have been affirmed by the U.S. Courts of Appeal for the Fifth and Sixth Circuits as well.[35] In fact, the U.S. Court of Appeals for the Fifth Circuit held that, following the amendment of Code Sec. 2035, the IRS's position was no longer substantially justified.[36]

On the other hand, the Tax Court has also held that an insurance policy on a decedent's life that was purchased by his spouse within three years of his death was includible in his gross estate in proportion to the decedent's interest in the community funds used to pay the policy premium.[37] The court stated that the payment of the policy premiums out of community property funds effected a "transfer" by the decedent of his interest in those funds, and that the ultimate effect of the transaction was similar to that which would have occurred had the decedent purchased the policy himself and then transferred all incidents of ownership to his wife.

A variation of this reasoning has been applied by some courts to require inclusion of proceeds in the gross estate where the decedent transferred funds to a trust within three years of death and the trustee purchased the policy. Two courts have held the proceeds to be includible in such a situation on the ground that the trustee acted as the decedent's agent in purchasing the policy.[38] Another court held that the proceeds would be includible in the decedent's gross estate if it could be shown that a trustee acted as her agent in purchasing a policy within three years of her death, and remanded the case to a lower court for a factual determination of the agency issue.[39] However, the Tax Court has held that even though a decedent created an irrevocable trust that purchased an insurance policy on her life within three years of her death, and she paid the policy premiums, the insurance proceeds were not includible in her gross estate because she did not possess any of the incidents of ownership in the policy.[40]

The Tax Court has held that when a wife purchased a life insurance policy on the life of her husband within three years of his death and paid for the policy

---

[33] IRS Technical Advice Memorandum 8509005 (Nov. 28, 1984).

[34] *J. Leder Est.*, CA-10, 90-1 USTC ¶60,001, aff'g TC, 89 TC 235, CCH Dec. 44,093.

[35] *F.M. Perry, Sr., Est.*, CA-5, 91-1 USTC ¶60,064, aff'g TC, 59 TCM 65, CCH Dec. 46,442(M); *E.L. Headrick Est.*, CA-6, 90-2 USTC ¶60,049, aff'g TC, 93 TC 171, CCH Dec. 45,914.

[36] *F.M. Perry Est.*, CA-5, 91-1 USTC ¶60,073.

[37] *R.W. Hass Est.*, 51 TCM 453, CCH Dec. 42,874(M), TC Memo. 1986-63. See *M. Baratta-Lorton Est.*, 49 TCM 770, CCH Dec.

41,890(M), TC Memo. 1985-72, aff'd by CA-9, in unpublished opinion, 3-24-86.

[38] *Detroit Bank & Trust Co., Exr. (F.W. Ritter Est.)*, CA-6, 72-2 USTC ¶12,883, 467 F2d 964, cert. denied, 410 US 929; and *T. Kurihara Est.*, 82 TC 51, CCH Dec. 40,914. See also *J. Schnack*, CA-9, 88-1 USTC ¶13,768, 848 F2d 933, rev'g TC, 52 TCM 1107, CCH Dec. 43,518(M), TC Memo. 1986-570.

[39] *G.H. Hope, Exr.*, CA-5, 82-2 USTC ¶13,504, 691 F2d 786.

[40] *M.F. Richins Est.*, 61 TCM 1706, CCH Dec. 47,125(M), TC Memo. 1991-23.

out of a joint checking account, no portion of the policy proceeds was includible in the decedent's estate because no agency relationship existed between the decedent and his wife. Therefore, the decedent did not have a transferable interest in the policy that would warrant the inclusion of the insurance proceeds in his gross estate in proportion to his contributions to the joint checking account.[41] In addition, in affirming a decision of the Tax Court, the U.S. Court of Appeals for the Sixth Circuit has held that life insurance proceeds were not includible in a decedent's gross estate where an *inter vivos* trust purchased the policy and paid the premiums pursuant to a trust agreement that permitted, but did not require, the purchase of the policy. Although the decedent contributed to the trust funds that were used to purchase the policy and pay premiums, this was not considered a sufficient nexus to establish that the decedent was indirectly paying the premiums while the trustee acted as his agent.[42]

Where the decedent-insured transfers a life insurance policy to a transferee within three years of his death and, after the assignment, the transferee pays the insurance premiums, the amount includible in the decedent's gross estate is that portion of the face value equaling the ratio of premiums paid by the decedent to the total premiums paid.[43]

¶ 435   Proceeds Payable for the Benefit of the Estate

Life insurance payable to one's estate, or to an executor or other person for the benefit of the estate, is always includible in the gross estate for estate tax purposes. It is includible even though it may have been purchased by another who retains complete control over the policy during the lifetime of the insured.[44] It is even taxable when made payable to a trustee if the trustee is required to apply the proceeds to the payment of taxes, claims, or administration expenses. If the trustee is merely *permitted* to pay such charges, however, the insurance is subject to the same rules as insurance paid to named beneficiaries.[45]

If the proceeds of an insurance policy made payable to the decedent's estate are community assets under state community property law and, as a result, one-half of the proceeds belong to the decedent's spouse, then only one-half of the proceeds are deemed to be receivable by or for the benefit of the decedent's estate.[46] Where the decedent's spouse dies before the decedent and the community property interest is not partitioned at the time of the spouse's death, the community status of the policy is retained up to the time of maturity, and a tenancy in common is created as of the spouse's date of death.[47]

Where a Louisiana decedent purchased a life insurance policy on the decedent's life during marriage, named the decedent as the policy owner, and did not transfer ownership of the policy, the policy is presumed to be community property under Louisiana law. Accordingly, one-half of the policy proceeds is includible in the decedent's gross estate under Code Sec. 2042 and Reg. §20.2042-1(c)(5). In the event that the decedent's spouse had predeceased the

[41] *L.J. Clay Est.*, 86 TC 1266, CCH Dec. 43,128. Cf. *J. Schnack*, CA-9, 88-1 USTC ¶13,768, 848 F2d 933, rev'g TC, 52 TCM 1107, CCH Dec. 43,518(M), TC Memo. 1986-570.

[42] *E.L. Headrick Est.*, CA-6, 90-2 USTC ¶60,049, aff'g TC, 93 TC 171, CCH Dec. 45,914.

[43] *S. Friedberg Est.*, 63 TCM 3080, CCH Dec. 48,254(M), TC Memo. 1992-310.

[44] Reg. §20.2042-1(b).

[45] *Old Colony Tr. Co., Exr. (Est. of L.E. Flye)*, 39 BTA 871, CCH Dec. 10,687 (Acq. and Nonacq.).

[46] Reg. §20.2042-1(b).

[47] *H.R. Cavenaugh Est.*, CA-5, 95-1 USTC ¶60,195, aff'g in part and rev'g in part TC, 100 TC 407, CCH Dec. 49,030.

decedent, one-half of the value of the policy would have been includible in the spouse's gross estate under Code Sec. 2033 and Reg. §20.2031-8(a)(2).[48] This result is distinguishable where, under Louisiana law, a decedent used community funds to purchase a policy of insurance on the decedent's life and designated the decedent's spouse as the sole owner of the policy. In this case, no portion of the policy proceeds is includible in the decedent's gross estate at death.[49] But the U.S. Court of Appeals for the Fifth Circuit has held that the entire proceeds of community property life insurance policies on a decedent's life that were designated as payable to his estate were includible in the gross estate.[50] Although premiums were paid with community funds, under Texas law, the entire proceeds of policies made payable to a decedent's estate are includible in the gross estate if designation of the estate as beneficiary was not made in fraud of the decedent's spouse (as found by the Tax Court). The appellate court noted that the insurance proceeds were (1) payable to the decedent's estate, (2) paid to the estate, and (3) allowed to remain in the estate's possession following the surviving spouse's state court challenge regarding her community property interest and, thus, could not be characterized as not "receivable by the executor" as required under Code Sec. 2042(1).

The proceeds of an insurance policy purchased by a decedent in favor of another person or a corporation as collateral security for a loan or other accommodation are also considered to be receivable for the benefit of the estate. However, the amount of the loan outstanding at the date of the decedent's death, with interest accrued thereon to that date, will be deductible in determining the taxable estate.[51]

¶ 440   Proceeds to Pay Estate Taxes

Although attempts have frequently been made to provide an estate tax exemption for the proceeds of insurance that are used to pay estate taxes, none of the attempts in Congress have been successful. If the recipient of the proceeds is required to use them to pay taxes, the proceeds are includible in the gross estate as insurance receivable by the executor. If a person who receives the proceeds would otherwise receive them free of tax, they do not become taxable by that person's election to apply them toward payment of the estate taxes in order to prevent liquidation of other assets.

¶ 445   Marital Deduction

If an insured's spouse is named as the beneficiary under a policy of life insurance and the insured retains no incidents of ownership in the policy, the proceeds will not be included in the insured decedent's gross estate. Consequently, the Code Sec. 2056 marital deduction will not apply.

Insurance proceeds payable to the spouse or to the spouse's estate—either in a lump sum or in installments—on the condition that the spouse survive the insured by as much as six months will qualify for the marital deduction.[52] The proceeds will also qualify if they are left at interest during the life of the

---

[48] W. Burris Est., 82 TCM 400, CCH Dec. 54,444(M), TC Memo. 2001-210; Rev. Rul. 2003-40, 2003-1 CB 813.

[49] Rev. Rul. 94-69, 1994-2 CB 241, revoking Rev. Rul. 48, 1953-1 CB 392, and Rev. Rul. 232, 1953-2 CB 268.

[50] W. Street Est., CA-5, 98-2 USTC ¶60,327, aff'g TC, 73 TCM 1787, CCH Dec. 51,834(M), TC Memo. 1997-32.

[51] Reg. §20.2042-1(b).

[52] Reg. §20.2056(b)-3.

surviving spouse, but are to be paid to the spouse's estate or to persons the spouse may appoint following his or her death.[53]

If the insurance proceeds are to be paid to persons that the spouse may appoint, the proceeds will qualify even if provision is made for payment to contingent beneficiaries in the event the spouse fails to exercise the power. If the proceeds are to be paid in installments for at least a certain specified period of time, or if there is to be a refund of a part of principal in the event that the spouse fails to recover a specified amount in installments, the proceeds will still qualify if any payments following the death of the surviving spouse are to be made to the spouse's estate or to persons he or she may appoint.

¶ 450 Business Insurance

Life insurance is frequently used in connection with various types of business transactions, including the funding of agreements for purchase of an insured's business interest. It may also be purchased to protect a business against loss that might occur on the death of a key employee of the business.

In these situations, the treatment of the insurance for estate tax purposes depends on the terms of the agreement, if any is involved, and on the terms of the insurance contract. In addition to affecting the treatment of the insurance for tax purposes, agreements for the purchase of a business interest can also affect the treatment of the interest itself.

Special problems arise where a closely held corporation owns insurance on the life of a stockholder-employee. The incidents of ownership held by a corporation on a corporate-owned life insurance policy covering a sole or controlling stockholder will not be attributed to the insured stockholder through his stock ownership under Code Sec. 2042 where the proceeds of such policy are received by the corporation or a third party for a valid business purpose.[54] Such proceeds are considered a nonoperating asset of the corporation in determining the stock value includible in the decedent's estate under Reg. § 20.2031-2(f). The Tax Court has ruled that the regulations do not permit the shareholder's stock to be valued by first finding the value of the stock without the insurance proceeds and then adding the proceeds.[55] Rather, the proceeds must be taken into consideration as corporate assets in determining the value of the stock.

Except for group-term life insurance, the incidents of ownership will be attributed to the insured decedent who is the sole or controlling stockholder if such proceeds are not payable to the corporation or a third party for a valid business purpose. For this purpose, a decedent is considered to be the controlling stockholder of a corporation if he owned stock possessing more than 50 percent of the total combined voting power of the corporation at the time of his death. In this regard, the IRS has ruled that life insurance proceeds were includible in a controlling shareholder's gross estate where, within three years of his death, the corporation assigned the policy for less than adequate consideration and the shareholder then disposed of his controlling interest in the corporation. Under similar circumstances, the proceeds were includible where, instead of the corporation assigning the policy, the controlling shareholder disposed of his interest in the corporation for less than adequate consideration.[56] However, in a private ruling, the IRS did not attribute incidents of ownership to the sole shareholder of

---

[53] Reg. § 20.2056(b)-6.
[54] Reg. § 20.2042-1(c)(6).

[55] *J.L. Huntsman Est.*, 66 TC 861, CCH Dec. 33,976 (Acq.).
[56] Rev. Rul. 90-21, 1990-1 CB 172, amplifying Rev. Rul. 82-141, 1982-2 CB 209.

a corporation who could terminate the employment contract of the beneficiary of a life insurance policy on the shareholder's life, even though the termination would cause the insurance proceeds to be distributed to a trust for the benefit of the shareholder's family.[57]

Even if the insured person is not the sole stockholder, the value of the policy may be includible if the insured retains incidents of ownership in the policy and the policy is not used to purchase stockholdings. Inclusion resulted in such a case where an insured stockholder had rights of ownership through the policy terms, even though the premiums were paid by the corporation, the policy was assigned by the corporation as collateral for corporate loans, and the cash surrender value was reflected on the corporate books.[58] The terms of the policy should be examined to make sure that the insured has not retained ownership through them. At least one court has ruled that terms of policies could not be rebutted by external evidence that showed that the decedent-insured intended to transfer all ownership rights to a corporation.[59]

## ¶ 455	Insurance on Stockholder

Life insurance often is used to fund agreements for the purchase and sale of stock in a close corporation following the death of a stockholder. The life insurance proceeds are used to provide part or all of the price for which the stock is to be sold.

The insurance under such an agreement may be purchased by the corporation, by the insured, or by other stockholders. The proceeds may be payable to the corporation, to a trustee, to the insured's estate, or to a person or persons designated by the insured. The agreement may give one or both parties an option, or it may require that the insured's stock be sold by the insured's estate and purchased by the corporation or other stockholders.

If the agreement requires the purchase and sale of the stock following the death of the insured, there will be included in the insured's estate either the value of the stock that is to be sold or the proceeds of the sale of the stock. If the insured has no rights in the insurance policy that would have required inclusion of the proceeds in the insured's estate had no stock transaction been involved, only the value of the stock will be included in the insured's gross estate. Only the value of the stock is includible even if a beneficiary or beneficiaries should actually receive insurance proceeds in excess of the value of the stock. Such a situation, however, is very unlikely. Usually, the insurance proceeds are less than the amount for which the stock is to be sold.

When the agreement for the purchase and sale of the stock is a mandatory one, the agreement normally will serve to limit the amount actually to be included in the estate (but see also ¶ 326, relating to buy-sell agreements for close corporation stock). The estate tax value is limited to the amount for which the stock is actually sold. This assumes that some fair method of valuation is used to arrive at the selling price and that all elements, including goodwill, are accounted for in fixing the value. Thus, if book value is to be the basis for fixing the price, there should be no litigation concerning some other method of valuation.

---

[57] IRS Letter Ruling 9421037 (Feb. 28, 1994).

[58] *G.H. Piggot Est.*, CA-6, 65-1 USTC ¶ 12,290, 340 F2d 829, aff'g TC, 22 TCM 241, CCH Dec. 25,985(M), TC Memo. 1963-61.

[59] *H.B. Cockrill, Exr.*, DC Tenn., 69-2 USTC ¶ 12,610, 302 FSupp. 1365.

Planning Pointer: In situations where the various stockholders themselves purchase the stock (known as cross-purchase arrangements), the one who dies is likely to own insurance on one or more of the other stockholders. This insurance is not treated as life insurance for tax purposes. It is treated as any ordinary estate asset. Its value is the cost of replacement rather than the cash or loan value, unless it is disposed of within six months after death and the estate is valued as of six months after death (see ¶ 410).

The stockholders whose lives are covered by the policies are the most likely purchasers of such insurance. Sometimes the purchase agreement requires that the insureds be given an opportunity to purchase the insurance on their own lives. The purchase opportunity is retained because they may no longer be otherwise insurable. In addition, state law may provide that the estate no longer has an insurable interest.

¶ 460   Partnership Insurance

The estate tax treatment of the proceeds of insurance and the value of the partnership interest is the same as under the stock purchase agreement. It is less likely, however, that the partnership, as opposed to the individual partners, will be the purchaser of the insurance, since premiums have to be paid out of net income after individual taxes regardless of whether the partnership or the partners purchase the insurance.

Partners who purchase life insurance on the lives of each other to fund partnership purchase agreements should make sure (1) that they are named as owner-beneficiaries of a policy on the life of an insured partner, and (2) that policy terms do not give an insured partner incidents of ownership over the policy. In such cases, the IRS has attempted to include the face amount of the policy in the insured partner's gross estate, where the face value exceeded the value of the decedent's partnership interest as agreed on. In two such cases, the IRS's attempt was unsuccessful because the Tax Court ruled that the partnership agreement controlled over the policy terms. Because the partnership agreements provided that proceeds were to be used to pay for the insured partners' interest, the court concluded that the partners could not exercise any incident of ownership that directly affected the economic benefits arising from the policies.[60]

The IRS has ruled that the proceeds of a policy of insurance on the life of a partner, which policy was owned by the partnership, were includible in the partner's gross estate because they were not payable to, or for the benefit of, the partnership.[61] The IRS concluded that the insured partner, by virtue of his one-third interest in the partnership, held an incident of ownership in the policy at death. This was so because the insured partner in his capacity as partner had the right (exercisable in conjunction with the other partners) to direct the economic benefits of the policy. However, where insurance proceeds were payable to a partnership, the Tax Court has ruled that a deceased partner's estate did not include insurance proceeds under the predecessor to Code Sec. 2042(2), despite the partner's incidents of ownership.[62] The IRS acquiesced in this result based on the fact that the value of the decedent's partnership interest reflected the payment of insurance proceeds to the partnership.

---

[60] *B.L. Fuchs Est.*, 47 TC 199, CCH Dec. 28,186 (Acq.); *H.F. Infante Est.*, 29 TCM 903, CCH Dec. 30,250(M), TC Memo. 1970-206, CA-7, appeal dism'd, 6-2-71.

[61] Rev. Rul. 83-147, 1983-2 CB 158.

[62] *F. Knipp Est.*, 25 TC 153, CCH Dec. 21,311 (Acq.), aff'd on another issue, CA-4, 57-1 USTC ¶ 11,693, 244 F2d 436.

The IRS has also ruled that the proceeds of a partnership group-term insurance policy were not includible in the gross estate of an insured partner who, more than three years before his death, assigned all of the incidents of ownership in the policy to his children.[63] This was true even though the partnership retained the power to surrender or cancel the policy—a power that is an incident of policy ownership under Reg. § 20.2042-1(c)(2). Applying the rationale of regulations promulgated under Code Sec. 79 that deal with attribution of incidents of ownership in group-term policies held by controlled corporations, the IRS ruled that the partnership's power to surrender or cancel the policy was not to be attributed to the partner.

¶ 465   Insurance on Sole Proprietor

Insurance taken out by a sole proprietor on the proprietor's own life has the same status for estate tax purposes as insurance taken out by any individual on the individual's own life. The presence or absence of rights of ownership determines whether the proceeds are includible in the insured's estate.

The insurance may have been taken out by the employees or other persons with an insurable interest as a means of providing funds for the purchase of all or a part of the business of the sole proprietor. The status of the insurance and the interest to be sold is the same as in the case of the corporation or partnership. Either the value of the business or the proceeds of its sale will be included in the sole proprietor's gross estate. If the agreement to sell to the employees is a mandatory one, the agreement will serve to limit the amount at which the value of the interest will be fixed.

¶ 470   Key-Employee Insurance

Sometimes a corporation will purchase insurance on the life of an officer or stockholder, not to implement a purchase agreement, but to protect the corporation against the loss that it feels would result from the untimely death of the insured. This insurance is usually referred to as "key-employee insurance."

In key-employee insurance policies, the insured individuals are personally responsible for a substantial share of the company's success, so that their death may result in a loss of a certain amount of business. The insurance taken out on their lives is calculated to make up for the loss the company expects to incur. The proceeds are made payable to the corporation rather than to any individual.

A person insured under such an arrangement usually has no interest in the insurance. None of its proceeds will be included in the insured's gross estate. Its presence will, however, be felt in fixing a value for any stock that the insured may have owned in the company. The insurance is includible among corporate assets in determining the value of the insured's stock for estate tax purposes.

> *Comment:* If, at the time of death, it does appear likely that the key employee's absence will have an adverse effect on the conduct of the business, that factor can be taken into account in fixing the value of the stock. The estate is also protected against loss resulting from the death by its right to elect to value the estate as of six months after the insured's death. Insurance of this type is sometimes purchased by partnerships or sole proprietorships, with similar results.

---

[63] Rev. Rul. 83-148, 1983-2 CB 157.

¶ 472   Split-Dollar Life Insurance

Split-dollar life insurance is permanent insurance acquired under an arrangement by which the company and an employee (usually a company executive) split the premium cost and the company and the executive's beneficiaries split the proceeds on an agreed basis, on the executive's death.[64] In the typical split-dollar arrangement, the executive will have the right to name the beneficiary of his or her portion of the policy (usually the term insurance component), and the employer will pay the current premiums and retain the right to the cash values that accumulate under the policy.

> *Planning Pointer:* For the employer, split-dollar plans are a cost-effective benefit aimed at retaining executives, without the administrative difficulties of a qualified plan. The executive benefits from the receipt of insurance coverage at a lower out-of-pocket cost than would otherwise be possible.

The estate tax treatment of split-dollar life insurance proceeds closely follows the general rules relating to life insurance on the life of a decedent. Such proceeds will be included in the deceased executive's gross estate if (1) the policy proceeds were paid to, of for the benefit of, his or her estate, or (2) the decedent owned incidents of ownership in the policy at his or her death. Where such proceeds are includible in the executive's gross estate, they are reportable on Form 706 (United States Estate (and Generation-Skipping Transfer) Tax Return), Schedule D (Insurance on the Decedent's Life) (Rev. August 2013). However, in the typical situation, the executive with an interest in a split-dollar policy will seek to avoid estate tax inclusion by a lifetime assignment of all his or her incidents of ownership in the policy to another (usually a family member). See ¶ 2109 for the valuation, for gift tax purposes, of an assignment of a split-dollar insurance policy.

The IRS has issued an explanation of the standards it will use in valuing current life insurance protection under what it has termed abusive split-dollar arrangements. More specifically, the IRS is targeting arrangements where a party pays inappropriately high current term insurance premiums, prepays premiums, or uses other techniques in order to understate the value of the taxable policy benefits.[65] Under such a scenario, it appears that the IRS intends to disregard policy arrangements that use two different insurance rates (one for the amount of coverage, and another one for purposes of the gift tax).[66] Under IRS Notice 2002-59, a party participating in a split-dollar life insurance arrangement may use the premium rates in Table 2001 (see Notice 2002-8), or the insurer's lower published premium rates only for the purposes of valuing current life insurance protection and when such protection confers an economic benefit by one party on another party, disregarding the premiums actually paid by this other party. However, if one party has any right to current life insurance protection under the split-dollar arrangement, neither the premium rates in Table 2001 nor the insurer's lower published rates may be used to value such party's current life insurance protection for purposes of determining the value of any policy benefits to which another party may be entitled.

---

[64] See Notice 2002-8, 2002-1 CB 420, for the income tax treatment of split-dollar life insurance.

[65] Notice 2002-59, 2002-2 CB 481.

[66] Notice 2002-8, 2002-1 CB 420.

¶ 473   Survivor Life Insurance

A survivor life insurance policy (also known as a "second-to-die policy") is a single policy covering two named insureds. On the death of the first insured, no benefit is paid. The benefit is paid only on the death of the survivor. Such policies offer the practical economy of being less costly than a separate policy for each insured since there is only one death benefit.

Survivor life policies are typically used by married couples who foresee the likelihood that the surviving spouse will die with a large enough estate to face an estate tax liability. With the unlimited marital deduction, the first spouse to die usually can arrange his or her plan of disposition so that there will be no estate tax liability. However, there will be an increased estate on the death of the second spouse because of the deferral of estate tax on the assets that passed to the survivor at the death of the first spouse. The use of a survivor life policy may provide the needed liquidity for the estate of the second spouse to die.

¶ 475   Valuation

The amount to be reported if insurance proceeds are payable to or for the benefit of the estate is the amount receivable. If the proceeds are payable to a named beneficiary, the amount receivable is again the amount reportable (although not necessarily taxable). Where the proceeds are to be paid in the form of an annuity, for life or for a certain number of years, the amount to be reported is the one sum payable at death under the lump-sum option. If no lump-sum option exists, the amount to be reported is the sum used to determine the amount of the annuity.[67] As to the valuation of reversionary interests in determining taxability, see ¶ 530.

If the estate must sue the insurance company in order to collect policy proceeds, the amount includible with respect to the policy may be less than the face amount of the proceeds. The IRS National Office has ruled that the amount includible in a decedent's gross estate with respect to two policies of insurance on the decedent's life is the fair market value, on the date of the decedent's death, of claims resulting from lawsuits that the decedent's estate filed to obtain the proceeds payable under the policies. Neither the amount of the proceeds nor the amount received by the estate in settlement of the claims was the correct amount includible. Although Code Sec. 2042 controls the includibility of policies in the estate, it does not control the valuation of the policies which, accordingly, must be valued on the basis of all facts and circumstances existing on the date of death.[68]

¶ 477   Life Insurance Trusts

Like almost any other type of property, life insurance policies are suitable for ownership by a trust. In fact, a special type of trust optimized to hold life insurance policies—the insurance trust—is often used to accomplish tax and nontax objectives. A revocable lifetime insurance trust can provide some significant nontax advantages, such as avoidance of probate, ability to tailor distributions to the estate owner's personal wishes (rather than be tied to the insurance company's settlement options), and availability of professional management. However, to obtain the significant estate tax advantages that are available, the insurance trust must be irrevocable.

---

[67] Reg. § 20.2042-1(a)(3).

[68] IRS Technical Advice Memorandum 8308001 (Jan. 21, 1982).

• *Estate and Gift Tax Issues*

In order for policy proceeds received by an irrevocable insurance trust to avoid being brought back into the deceased insured's gross estate, the trustee—not the insured—must hold all incidents of ownership in the policies. Also, any insurance policies transferred into the trust must have been so transferred more than three years before the decedent's death[69] (see ¶ 430).

> *Planning Pointer:* A transfer from the insured to his or her insurance trust will constitute a taxable gift. One way to avoid this potential problem would be to transfer either term policies (which would have little or no current value) or cash value policies from which nearly all of the cash value has been removed by policy loans. Another way to minimize possible gift tax liability would be for the trust to purchase a new policy on the life of the donor from cash initially transferred to the trust. This would also avoid the "three-years-of-death rule" since the trust's purchase of the policy will not be attributed to the donor.[70]

To the extent that a transfer to the trust is a taxable gift, the trust beneficiaries, rather than the trustee, are regarded as the donees. However, in order for the transfers to the donees to be considered gifts of present, rather than future, interests (and thus qualify for gift tax annual exclusions), the donees will have to have present powers to withdraw trust property (see ¶ 2265).

In the typical estate planning use of an irrevocable life insurance trust, it is not contemplated—and is normally not desired—for the beneficiaries to actually exercise their yearly withdrawal powers (which are usually limited to a noncumulative right to withdraw $10,000 per year, as adjusted for inflation ($11,000 for 2002 through 2005; $12,000 for 2006 through 2008;[71] $13,000 for 2009 through 2012[72] and $14,000 for 2013 and 2014[73]), the amount of the gift tax annual exclusion). The fact that the beneficiaries do not choose to exercise their withdrawal power (sometimes called a "*Crummey* power"[74] after the name of the court decision that validated use of such a power) does not put the annual gift tax exclusions for transfers into the trust in jeopardy, provided that the beneficiaries have a reasonable opportunity to make such withdrawals during the calendar year in which the gift tax exclusion is claimed[75] and have not entered into an agreement with the donor that they would not exercise their powers.[76] Rev. Proc. 2013-35

> *Comment:* Unless the insured-transferor also initially transfers cash or cash-generating property into the trust to pay future policy premiums, he or she will have to make additional payments to or on behalf of the trust to keep the policies in force. These payments will also constitute taxable gifts to the beneficiaries, unless shielded by gift tax annual exclusions.

---

[69] Code Sec. 2035.

[70] *E. Headrick Est.*, CA-6, 90-2 USTC ¶ 60,049; *J. Leder Est.*, CA-10, 90-1 USTC ¶ 60,001. In order to ensure this result, the amount of the initial trust funding should exceed the amount of the first year's policy premium, and should not be earmarked for payment of premiums (*T. Kurihara Est.*, 82 TC 51, CCH Dec. 40,914).

[71] Rev. Proc. 2007-66, 2007-45, 2007-2 CB 2007; Rev. Proc. 2006-53, 2006-48, 2006-2 CB 996; Rev. Proc. 2005-70, 2005-2 CB 979.

[72] Rev. Proc. 2008-66, 2008-2 CB 1107; Rev. Proc. 2009-50, IRB 2009-45, 617; Rev. Proc. 2010-40, IRB 2010-46, 663; Rev. Proc. 2011-52, IRB 2011-45, 701.

[73] Rev. Proc. 2012-41, IRB 2012-45, IRB 2012-45, 539; Rev. Proc. 2013-35, IRB 2013-47, October 31, 2013

[74] *D.C. Crummey*, CA-9, 68-2 USTC ¶ 12,541, 397 F2d 82.

[75] Rev. Rul. 73-405, 1973-2 CB 321; Rev. Rul. 81-7, 1981-1 CB 474.

[76] See *M. Cristofani*, 97 TC 74, Dec. 47,491 (Acq. in result only), 1992-1 CB 1.

As noted above, irrevocable trusts (including insurance trusts) may contain a *Crummey* power in order to obtain gift tax annual exclusions for yearly transfers into the trust. However, there is another type of beneficiary withdrawal power— the "five by five" power—that may be used instead. This power gives trust beneficiaries a yearly noncumulative right to withdraw from the trust the greater of $5,000 or five percent of the trust principal. This power is used so as to shield the beneficiaries from being hit with gift tax if they do not exercise their yearly withdrawal rights under the trust.

Depending on the size of the principal of the insurance trust in question, a donor may be able to obtain both the full amount of the gift tax annual exclusion for yearly amounts transferred into the trust ($11,000 for 2002 through 2005; $12,000 for 2006 through 2008;[77] $13,000 for 2009 through 2012;[78] and $14,000 for 2013 and 2014[79]) per donee, and also make sure that the beneficiaries will not be deemed to make taxable gifts by failing to exercise their withdrawal powers (the "five by five" provision). However, in 2013, the donor will have to choose to forgo a portion of his or her gift tax annual exclusion, or subject the donee-beneficiaries to gift tax themselves, if the trust does not exceed $280,000.

> *Example (1):* Ralph Law sets up an irrevocable life insurance trust for his two children, Mary and John. Each child has a noncumulative withdrawal power limited to the amount of the gift tax annual exclusion in effect in the year the withdrawal right is available (in 2013, this amount is $14,000). If in 2013 the corpus of the trust is $280,000, each child could forgo the exercise of the yearly power without incurring a gift tax liability, since the amount deemed lapsed would qualify under the "five by five" provision of the Code ($280,000 × 5% = $14,000).
>
> However, a different result will occur if the trust corpus were only $175,000. Although Law's transfer of $14,000 to the trust would qualify for the $14,000 annual gift tax exclusion (so he would not be hit with a gift tax liability), on nonexercise of the yearly power, each of the children would be deemed to make a taxable gift of $5,250 to the trust remaindermen:
>
> $14,000 (Annual exclusion limitation in 2013)
> − 8,750 (Five by five limit: the greater of $5,000 or 5% of trust corpus: $175,000 × 5% = $8,750)
> ———
> $ 5,250 Taxable gift by each beneficiary to trust remaindermen

If the insurance trust donor is faced with the problem noted in Example (1), he or she can choose between the following two broad strategies (although there are additional variations):

> (1) Structure the withdrawal right, by its terms, so that it would be limited to the amount that will qualify as a five by five power. (In Example 1, such a provision would limit the beneficiaries' withdrawal rights to $8,750.) This would solve the beneficiaries' potential gift tax problem, at the cost of limiting the donor's contribution to the trust that year to $8,750. (Or, if a larger gift is made, it would be a taxable gift of a future interest by the donor.)
>
> Or

---

[77] Rev. Proc. 2007-66, 2007-2 CB 970; Rev. Proc. 2006-53, 2006-2 CB 996; Rev. Proc. 2005-70, 2005-2 CB 979.

[78] Rev. Proc. 2008-66, 2008-2 CB 1107; Rev. Proc. 2009-50, IRB 2009-45, 617; Rev. Proc. 2010-40, IRB 2010-46, 663; Rev. Proc. 2011-52, IRB 2011-45, 701.

[79] Rev. Proc. 2012-41, IRB 2012-45, 539; Rev. Proc. 2013-35, IRB 2013-47, October 31, 2013.

(2) Give each of the beneficiaries a yearly withdrawal right of $14,000 (in 2013) under the trust. This would allow the donor to transfer up to this amount during the year without incurring a gift tax liability, but it would mean that each beneficiary, upon failure to exercise the right, would be deemed to make a taxable gift to the remaindermen equal to the amount that exceeds the five by five limit.

Which alternative is chosen will largely be determined by the facts of the individual situation, including the size of the trust subject to the power, and the respective gift tax liabilities to be faced by the donor and donees.

• *Trust Substitution Power*

A grantor's retention of the power, exercisable in a nonfiduciary capacity, to acquire an insurance policy held in trust by substituting other assets of equivalent value would not, by itself, cause the value of the insurance policy to be includible in the grantor's gross estate under Code Sec. 2042, the IRS has ruled.[80] Under the terms of the trust, the grantor was prohibited from serving as trustee. The IRS noted that the substitution power would not result in inclusion in the grantor's gross estate, provided that the trustee had a fiduciary obligation to ensure the grantor's compliance with the terms of the substitution power by satisfying itself that the properties acquired and substituted by the grantor were of equal value. Furthermore, the substitution power could not be exercised in a manner that shifted benefits among the trust beneficiaries. If a trustee had the power to reinvest the trust corpus and a duty of impartiality with regards to the beneficiaries, or if the trustee's investment or the income produced by the investments did not impact the respective interests of the beneficiaries, a substitution power could not be exercised in a manner that shifted benefits.

• *Income Tax Issues*

Although judicious use of a "five by five" beneficiary withdrawal power can avoid gift tax liability for both the trust grantor and beneficiaries, the beneficiaries may face an income tax problem if they let their withdrawal rights lapse each year. This is because, under the grantor trust provisions of the Code,[81] since the beneficiaries will retain a power in the trust after such a lapse, they will be deemed, for income tax purposes, to be the owner of the portion of the trust property attributable to such lapse.[82] Even though these powers are noncumulative, the income tax will be exacerbated with each additional year the withdrawal power lapses.

> *Example (2):* Sally Fisher has a yearly, noncumulative "five by five" power over a trust principal of $1 million. After she allows her power to lapse at the end of year one, she will be deemed to be the owner of $50,000 of the trust property, or 5%.
>
> In year two, she would be deemed the owner of the $50,000, plus an increasing portion of the trust (assuming that the value of the trust corpus does not appreciate), calculated as followed:
>
> $50,000 × $950,000/$1,000,000 = $47,500
>
> Thus, at the end of year two, Sally would be the owner of $97,500 (or 9.75%) of the trust.

---

[80] Rev. Rul. 2011-28, IRB 2011-49, December 5, 2011.

[81] Code Sec. 671 through Code Sec. 677.
[82] Rev. Rul. 67-241, 1967-2 CB 225.

Gross Estate

How severe the income tax consequences will be to the beneficiaries as a result of a yearly lapse of withdrawal powers will depend on such factors as how much income (if any) the trust is generating and the respective income tax brackets of the trust and the beneficiaries.

¶ 480   Description of Insurance on Return

All insurance on a decedent's life is reportable on Schedule D (Insurance on the Decedent's Life) of Form 706 (United States Estate (and Generation-Skipping Transfer) Tax Return) (Rev. August 2013). Every policy of insurance on the life of a decedent must be listed, whether or not it is included in the gross estate. The name of the insurance company and the policy number should be listed under "Description." For every policy listed, the decedent's estate should request a statement from the company that issued the policy on Form 712 (Life Insurance Statement) (Rev. April 2006) (see ¶ 481).

If the policy proceeds are paid in one sum, the value to be entered in the valuation column is the net proceeds received, from Form 712, line 24. However, if the policy proceeds are not paid in one sum, the value to be entered is the value of the proceeds as of the date of the decedent's death, from Form 712, line 25. If part or all of the policy proceeds are not included in the gross estate, an explanation of the reason for their exclusion must accompany the policy description.

In the case of an estate of a nonresident not a citizen, the proceeds of insurance on the nonresident's life are not taxable and need not be included in the schedule.[83]

¶ 481   Life Insurance Statement

The executor of a decedent's estate must file a Form 712 (Life Insurance Statement) (Rev. April 2006) with the estate tax return for every policy of life insurance on the decedent's life that is listed on the schedule and that constitutes a part of the gross estate.[84] It is also the duty of the executor to obtain the statement from the insurance company that issued the policy.

An executor should file Form 712 in order to facilitate valuation of insurance owned by the decedent on the life of another person.

¶ 485   Community Property

Special rules apply when insurance is paid for out of community funds. See ¶ 165 and ¶ 435 for a discussion of the status of community property.

---

[83] Code Sec. 2105(a).

[84] Reg. § 20.6018-4; Schedule D, Instructions for Form 706 (Rev. August 2013), p. 24.

Chapter 12

JOINTLY OWNED PROPERTY

¶ 500   Interest of Joint Owners

Property in which the decedent at the time of death held an interest either as a joint tenant or as a tenant by the entirety, with right of survivorship, is the subject of special treatment under the estate tax law. Such joint interests are removed from the scope of Code Sec. 2033, which provides for inclusion of property in which the decedent had an interest at death, and are taxed under the even broader concepts of Code Sec. 2040.

Ordinarily, under property law, each participant in a joint tenancy or tenancy by the entirety is regarded as owning an undivided equal share. The estate tax law follows this concept only with respect to property held jointly with right of survivorship and only if acquired by gift, devise, bequest, or inheritance.[1]

However, special rules apply to certain joint interests held by spouses, in which each spouse will be considered as owning a one-half interest in the joint property for estate tax purposes (see ¶502). Therefore, in the case of property acquired by a spouse by inheritance as a tenant by the entirety or a joint tenant with right of survivorship, one-half of the value of the property would be included in the gross estate of the first spouse to die. Similarly, in the case of three tenants of property acquired by gift as a joint tenancy, each tenant is regarded as owning one-third of the property.

For a discussion of the special rules that apply when a taxable transfer is deemed to be made with respect to jointly held property, see ¶2162.

¶ 501   Property Acquired by Purchase

The estate tax law provides a general rule in the case of property acquired by purchase and held in joint tenancy or by the entirety. The portion to be included in the deceased tenant's gross estate is based on the percentage of the decedent's contribution to the total cost. This percentage is multiplied by the fair market value of the entire property on the date of the decedent's death (or on the alternate valuation date, if so elected).[2] (Different rules apply to property acquired by married joint tenants; see ¶502.)

The value of the entire property will be included in the gross estate unless the amount contributed by the survivor is proven. In determining the amount of the survivor's contribution, any part of the contribution that was originally received from the decedent by gift cannot be included.

Example: Amy Cooper and her daughter, Julie, buy a residence for $100,000 as joint tenants. Amy contributed $80,000 to the cost and Julie contributed $20,000. Amy will be regarded as having an 80% interest in the

[1] Reg. § 20.2040-1(a)(1).

[2] Reg. § 20.2040-1(a)(2).

property. If she dies first and if, on her death, the property is worth $200,000, 80%, or $160,000, will be included in her gross estate.

This provision also covers joint bank accounts and jointly held bonds, stocks, or other instruments, but has no application to property held by the decedent and any other person as tenants in common.[3]

Where property held in joint tenancy was purchased with community property funds in which the spouses had equal vested interests, one-half of the value of the jointly held property is excluded from the decedent's gross estate.[4]

> **Preparation Tip:** A decedent's interest as a tenant in common is not reportable on Form 706 (United States Estate (and Generation-Skipping Transfer) Tax Return) (Rev. August 2013), Schedule E (Jointly Owned Property), as jointly owned property. The proper schedule for reporting the property interest is dictated by the nature of the property—realty on Form 706, Schedule A (Real Estate), stocks and bonds on Form 706, Schedule B (Stocks and Bonds), etc.

In all instances where the executor or administrator seeks to exclude a part of the value of the jointly held property from the gross estate, the executor has the burden of proving a right to include the reduced value and, therefore, should be prepared to prove the extent, origin, and nature of each joint owner's interest.[5]

¶ 502　Spousal Joint Tenancies

The estate of the first spouse to die includes only one-half of the value of a "qualified joint interest" in property regardless of which spouse furnished the consideration for the property. For purposes of this provision, "qualified joint interest" is defined as any interest in property held solely by spouses as joint tenants with the right of survivorship or as tenants by the entirety.[6]

However, the U.S. Court of Appeals for the Sixth Circuit has held that a surviving spouse was entitled to a stepped-up basis for jointly held property created prior to 1977 where her husband had provided all of the consideration for the property. Because the effective date of the Economic Recovery Tax Act of 1981 (P.L. 97-34) (ERTA) (generally applicable to estates of decedents dying after December 31, 1981) did not expressly or by implication repeal the effective date of the Tax Reform Act of 1976 (P.L. 94-455), the contribution test as it existed prior to 1977 was applicable in determining the amount of jointly held property includible in the gross estate of the decedent who died after the effective date of ERTA. Accordingly, because 100 percent of the value of the jointly held property was includible in the decedent's gross estate, his surviving spouse was entitled to a stepped-up date-of-death basis for the entire property.[7] (See, also, ¶2107 for treatment of pre-1982 lifetime gifts of spousal joint interests.)

• *Special Rule Where Spouse Is Noncitizen*

The creation of a joint tenancy in property is generally treated as a completed gift. Before July 14, 1988, such a gift between spouses qualified for the marital deduction for estate and gift tax purposes, and only one-half of the jointly held property was included in the gross estate of the first spouse to die

---

[3] Reg. § 20.2040-1(b).

[4] *J.A. Kammerdiner*, CA-9, 44-1 USTC ¶10,084, 140 F2d 569; Rev. Rul. 78-418, 1978-2 CB 236.

[5] Reg. § 20.2040-1(a)(2).

[6] Code Sec. 2040(b).

[7] *M.L. Gallenstein*, CA-6, 92-2 USTC ¶60,114, aff'g DC Ky., 91-2 USTC ¶60,088; *J. Patten*, CA-4, 97-2 USTC ¶60,279; *E.M. Baszto*, DC Fla., 98-1 USTC ¶60,305; and *T. Hahn*, 110 TC 140, CCH Dec. 52,606 (Acq.).

under the "qualified joint interest" rule described above. However, the gift tax marital deduction (see ¶ 1000) for gifts made to noncitizen spouses on or after July 14, 1988 is repealed, and the entire value of jointly held property is includible in the deceased spouse's estate, reduced by the portion of the property for which consideration was received.

In determining the federal estate tax, the value of gifts includible in the gross estate is effectively reduced by the value of taxable gifts when made. Thus, for joint tenancies created on or after July 14, 1988, where the donee spouse is a noncitizen, the amount included in the gross estate of the first spouse to die is effectively reduced by the amount transferred when the tenancy was created. In the case of joint tenancies created prior to July 14, 1988, no such reduction occurred because the gift qualified for the marital deduction and was not taxable. For purposes of determining the amount of joint tenancy property includible in a decedent's gross estate, a gift made by creating a joint tenancy in property prior to July 14, 1988, is treated as consideration belonging to the surviving spouse if the transfer would have constituted a gift had the donor been a U.S. citizen. Thus, the amount of joint tenancy property included in the gross estate of the first spouse to die is reduced proportionately by the amount of the gift.[8]

¶ 510 Valuation of Jointly Owned Property

If the decedent and any person with whom the decedent held property jointly transferred that property to others during the decedent's lifetime, the transfer is reportable as a transfer made during the decedent's lifetime, rather than as jointly held property.

The principles governing valuation of jointly held property are the same as those governing other types of property. Therefore, reference should be made to the instructions preceding the various schedules for information concerning the valuation of the specific kinds of property held jointly. However, the Tax Court has ruled that fractional interest discounts and lack of marketability discounts do not apply in the valuation of joint tenancy property.[9]

¶ 515 Description on Return

Property owned at the time of death by a decedent in joint tenancy with the right of survivorship or in a tenancy by the entirety is to be reported on Schedule E (Jointly Owned Property) of Form 706 (United States Estate (and Generation-Skipping Transfer) Tax Return) (Rev. August 2013). If the decedent's spouse was the only other co-tenant, the tenancy constitutes a qualified joint interest (see ¶ 502) and is to be reported in part I of Schedule E. All other joint tenancy property must be reported in part II of Schedule E, including the names and addresses of the surviving joint owners.

In reporting jointly owned property on Schedule E, a statement under the column headed "Description" must disclose whether the whole or only a part of the property is included in the gross estate. If only a part of the property is included in the gross estate, the fair market value of the whole must nevertheless be shown under "Description."

Property in which the decedent held an interest as a tenant in common should not be listed on Schedule E. The value of the decedent's interest as a tenant in common should be returned under the schedule for real estate, or, if

---

[8] Act Sec. 11701(l), P.L. 101-508, amending Act Sec. 7815(d)(16), P.L. 101-239.

[9] *Wayne-Chi Young Est.*, 110 TC 297, CCH Dec. 52,691.

personal property, under such other appropriate schedule. Similarly, community property held by the decedent and spouse should be returned under appropriate other schedules. The decedent's interest in a partnership should be shown on Schedule F (Other Miscellaneous Property Not Reportable Under Any Other Schedule) of Form 706.

Chapter 13
MISCELLANEOUS PROPERTY

¶ 525   Items Termed "Miscellaneous"

The classification "Other Miscellaneous Property" on the estate tax return, Form 706 (United States Estate (and Generation-Skipping Transfer) Tax Return) (Rev. August 2013), relates to property that is includible in the gross estate under Code Sec. 2033, but that does not fall within any of the preceding property-schedule classifications. It includes such items as:

(1) debts due the decedent (other than notes and mortgages included on Schedule C (Mortgages, Notes, and Cash) of Form 706);

(2) interests in business;

(3) insurance on the life of another;

(4) claims (including the value of the decedent's interest in a claim for refund of income taxes, or the amount of the refund actually received);

(5) rights;

(6) royalties;

(7) leaseholds;

(8) judgments;

(9) shares in trust funds;

(10) household goods and personal effects, including wearing apparel;

(11) farm products and growing crops;

(12) livestock;

(13) farm machinery;

(14) automobiles;

(15) reversionary or remainder interests; and

(16) Code Sec. 2044 property (property for which the marital deduction was previously allowed).

¶ 526   Reporting Property Interests

The various property interests that are described at ¶525 as being reportable on Form 706 (United States Estate (and Generation-Skipping Transfer) Tax Return) (Rev. August 2013), Schedule F (Other Miscellaneous Property Not Reportable Under Any Other Schedule),[1] are taxable under Code Sec. 2033 as property in which the decedent had an interest at the time of death. Schedule F must be filed with Form 706.

If any of the property reportable under this category was transferred by the decedent during the decedent's life, that property should not be listed with the "miscellaneous" property. It should be reported on Schedule G (Transfers During Decedent's Life) of Form 706 for transfers during the decedent's lifetime. The method of valuing such property, however, is the same, no matter which schedule is applicable. If the transfer, by trust or otherwise, was made by a written instrument, a copy of such document should be submitted with the return.

¶ 527   Interests in Business

Business interests, other than corporate, are reported on Form 706 (United States Estate (and Generation-Skipping Transfer) Tax Return), Schedule F (Other Miscellaneous Property Not Reportable Under Any Other Schedule) as "Other Miscellaneous Property." In determining the fair market value of any business interest or intangible asset for estate tax purposes, the general approach, methods, and factors in Rev. Rul. 59-60,[2] pertaining to valuation of stock in closely held corporations, are applicable, but will not control when better evidence of value is available.

> *Planning Pointer:* The valuation of interests in business requires great care. A fair appraisal should be made of all of the assets of the business, including goodwill. The business should be given a net value equal to the amount that a willing purchaser would pay to a willing seller in view of asset value and earning capacity. Where the decedent's interest in a partnership, for instance, is subject to an agreement to sell to survivors at a price determined by some equitable means, that price normally will determine the value. In the absence of a purchase agreement, special attention should be given to fixing an adequate figure for the value of the goodwill.

• *Discounts*

In determining the fair market value of an interest in an entity such as a family limited partnership (FLP) or a family limited liability company (FLLC), it may be appropriate to apply valuation discounts. The valuation determination, including application of discounts, is normally fact-specific and heavily dependent on the particular characteristics of the interest being valued. As a result, each decision stands alone to a considerable degree; precedent is a less meaningful concept it this area of the law. The determinative factor in valuation cases typically will be the quality of the evidence presented, usually through the reports and testimony offered by expert witnesses.

Two of the most commonly applied discounts are those for lack of marketability and minority interest. In some instances the Tax Court has allowed sizable discounts, including: a combined 47-percent discount to reflect both lack of marketability and minority interest in valuing a 27.5-percent partnership inter-

---

[1] An example of a filled-in Form 706, Schedule F, for a decedent dying in 2013, is reproduced at ¶ 3000.

[2] Rev. Rul. 59-60, 1959-1 CB 237. Additional valuation information is contained in Reg. § 20.2031-3; Rev. Rul. 65-193, 1965-2 CB 370; Rev. Rul. 77-287, 1977-2 CB 319, corrected by Ann. 77-168, IRB 1977-51, 22; and Rev. Rul. 83-120, 1983-2 CB 170, which modified and amplified Rev. Rul. 59-60.

est;[3] a combined marketability and minority discount of 40 percent for a 40-percent limited partnership interest;[4] and a 20-percent minority discount, and a 35-percent lack of marketability discount, *coupled with* a 10-percent portfolio discount.[5]

The IRS has posted on its website *Appeals Settlement Guidelines: Family Limited Partnerships and Family Limited Liability Corporations,* relating to valuation discounts for FLP and FLLC interests. The *Settlement Guidelines,* which are effective October 20, 2006, include discussion of whether the fair market value of transfers of FLP or FLLC interests by death or gift is properly discounted from the pro rata value of the underlying assets. The IRS takes the position that, under certain circumstances, there should be minimal or no discount from the pro rata value of the entity's underlying asset. The IRS supports this position by citing current case law, certain studies that conclude that there should be minimal discounts for minority interest and lack of marketability, and certain alternative valuation methods. In analyzing the issue, the IRS cities several recent Tax Court decisions where minority interest and lack of marketability discounts were applied in valuing FLP interests. The IRS noted that the combined discount in these cases ranged from 27 to 32 percent. The recent case of *W. Kelley Est.*[6] was cited with disapproval. In *Kelley,* the Tax Court allowed a 12-percent minority discount and a 23-percent lack of marketability discount for a FLP that consisted solely of cash and certificates of deposit. The *Settlement Guidelines* is available at www.irs.gov on the "Appeals Coordinated Issues (ACI)" page.

• *Documentation*

All evidence bearing on the valuation of an interest in a business should be submitted with the return. This includes copies of reports in any case in which examinations of the business have been made by accountants, engineers, or any technical experts as of or near the applicable valuation date. If the decedent owned any interest in a partnership or unincorporated business, a statement of assets and liabilities as of the valuation date and for the preceding five years, along with statements of the net earnings for the same five years, should be submitted with the return. In general, the same information should be furnished and the same methods followed as in valuing interests in close corporations.

¶ 528 Limited Interests

Annuities, interests for life or for a term of years, and remainder and reversionary interests present special valuation problems. For a commercial annuity or insurance policy on the life of a person other than the decedent that is payable under a contract with an insurance or other company regularly engaged in selling such contracts, the value is the price of a comparable contract on the applicable valuation date (see ¶ 760). In all other instances, the value is determined by discounting future payments.

The valuation date for such interests is the date of death regardless of whether the alternate valuation date is used. When the alternate valuation date has been elected, the value at death is then adjusted for any difference in value

---

[3] *M. Hoffman Est.,* 81 TCM 1588, Dec. 54,330(M), TC Memo. 2001-109.

[4] *E. Dailey Est.,* 82 TCM 710, Dec. 54,506(M), TCM Memo. 2001-263.

[5] *P. Adams, et al.,* DC Tex., 2001-2 USTC ¶ 60,418, on remand from CA-5, 2000-2 USTC ¶ 60,379.

[6] 90 TCM 369, Dec. 56,163(M), TC Memo. 2005-235.

between the date of death and the applicable valuation date that is due to causes other than the mere lapse of time.[7]

Special tables are used to determine the present value of a private annuity, an interest for life or for a term of years, and a remainder or reversionary interest (see ¶530).

¶ 530   Valuation of Limited Interests

The appropriate authority for determining the estate tax value of limited interests in property such as annuities, interests for life or a term of years, and remainder and reversionary interests depends on the date of the decedent's death. Limited property interests valued with respect to decedents dying after April 30, 2009, are governed by Reg. §20.2031-7.[8] In general, the fair market value of a limited interest is determined by using an actuarial factor prescribed by the Secretary of the Treasury in conjunction with the appropriate Code Sec. 7520 interest rate. The Code Sec. 7520 interest rate is computed as 120 percent of the applicable federal midterm rate (rounded to the nearest two-tenths of one percent) and is published monthly by the IRS.

For decedents dying before May 1, 2009, Reg. §20.2031-7A provides the applicable rules for valuing limited property interests, depending on whether the decedent died before 1952 (Reg. §20.2031-7A(a)), after 1951 and before 1971 (Reg. §20.2031-7A(b)), after 1970 and before December 1, 1983 (Reg. §20.2031-7A(c)), after November 30, 1983, and before May 1, 1989 (Reg. §20.2031-7A(d)), after April 30, 1989, and before May 1, 1999 (Reg. §20.2031-7A(e)), for after April 30, 1999 and before May 1, 2009 (Reg. §20.2031-7(f)).

IRS Publication No. 1457, "Actuarial Valuations, Version 3A," contains many standard actuarial factors not included in the regulations, including last-to-die factors for valuing limited property interests dependent on more than one life (Table R(2)). It also includes examples that illustrate how to compute special factors for more unusual situations. The factors set forth in IRS Publication 1457 involving life contingencies reflect the most recent mortality data contained in the mortality component table (Table 2000CM) located in Temp. Reg. §20.2031-7T(d)(7). While the publication includes examples, it does not contain the tables of actuarial factors used in the examples. The actuarial tables cited in the examples can be found on the IRS website (http://www.irs.gov/retirement/article/0,,id=206601,00.html).

The valuation of commercial annuity contracts and insurance policies on the lives of persons other than the decedent must be determined under Reg. §20.2031-8.

See ¶2800 for a table of the applicable Code Sec. 7520 interest rates for valuation dates after 2002.

A person's age at his or her nearest birthday is to be used for computation purposes.

Decedents Dying After April 30, 2009

For decedents dying after April 30, 2009, the present value of a remainder or reversionary interest postponed for a term certain is determined by multiplying the fair market value of the property by the appropriate remainder interest factor

---

[7] Reg. §20.2032-1(f).

[8] Reg. §20.2031-7, as amended by T.D. 9540, August 9, 2011.

from Table B in Reg. § 20.2031-7(d)(6). If the interest is postponed until after the death of one individual, the appropriate remainder interest factor from Table S in Reg. § 20.2031-7(d)(7) is used. The appropriate remainder interest factor is that factor that corresponds to the applicable Code Sec. 7520 interest rate and either the Table B term certain or the Table S current age of the individual who is the measuring life. The interest rate component is based on a rate that is 120 percent of the applicable federal midterm rate compounded annually for the month in which the valuation date falls.

Ordinary term-of-years and life interest. The present value of a right to receive the income of property, or to use nonincome-producing property, for a term of years or for the life of one individual is determined by multiplying the fair market value of the property by the appropriate term-of-years or life interest factor that corresponds to the applicable Code Sec. 7520 interest rate. Although the term-of-years and life interest factors are not included in Table B or Table S in Reg. § 20.2031-7(d)(6) and Temp. Reg. § 20.2031-7T(d)(7), they may be derived mathematically. The term-of-years (income interest) factor is derived by subtracting the correlative Table B term certain remainder factor that corresponds to the applicable Code Sec. 7520 interest rate from 1.000000. Similarly, the factor for the life of one individual (life estate) is derived by subtracting the correlative Table S single life remainder factor that corresponds to the applicable Code Sec. 7520 interest rate from 1.000000. These actuarial factors for income interests and life estates are included in Table B and Table S, respectively, in IRS Publication 1457, "Actuarial Valuations, Version 3A", which is available on the IRS website (see Temp. Reg. § 20.2031-T(d)(4)).

Annuities. The present value of an annuity that is payable at the end of each year for a term certain or for the life of one individual is determined by multiplying the aggregate amount payable annually by the appropriate annuity factor that corresponds to the applicable Code Sec. 7520 interest rate. These actuarial factors are included in Table B and Table S in IRS Publication 1457, "Actuarial Valuations, Version 3A," available on the IRS website. Although the annuity factors are not included in Table B or Table S in Reg. § 20.2031-7(d)(6) and Temp. Reg. § 20.2031-7T(d)(7), they may be derived mathematically. The term certain annuity factor is derived by subtracting the correlative Table B term certain remainder factor that corresponds to the applicable Code Sec. 7520 interest rate from 1.000000 and then dividing the result by the applicable Code Sec. 7520 interest rate expressed as a decimal number. Similarly, the single life annuity factor is derived by subtracting the correlative Table S single life remainder factor that corresponds to the applicable Code Sec. 7520 interest rate from 1.000000 and then dividing the result by the applicable Code Sec. 7520 interest rate expressed as a decimal number.

Example: George Miller died in November 2013 and was entitled to receive an annuity of $24,000 a year for six years, payable at the end of each year. The Code Sec. 7520 interest rate for November 2013 is 2.0%. The Table B term certain remainder factor at 2.0% is .887971. The term certain annuity factor is 5.6014 ((1.000000 − .887971 ÷ .020). The present value of the annuity interest at the date of the decedent's death is $134,434 ($24,000 × 5.6014). (Calculations made using CCH® IRS Actuarial Factors™.)

Comment: Certain adjustment factors must be applied to the valuations determined above if the annuity is payable at any time other than the end of each year. Table J (Reg. § 20.2031-7(d)(6)) contains the adjustment factors applicable for term certain annuities if the annuity is payable at the beginning of annual, semiannual, quarterly, monthly, or weekly periods. Table K

(Reg. §20.2031-7(d)(6)) contains the adjustment factors applicable if the annuity is payable at the end of semiannual, quarterly, monthly, or weekly periods. Regardless of which table applies, the product obtained by multiplying the aggregate amount payable annually by the applicable annuity factor is then multiplied by the applicable adjustment factor to obtain the present value of the annuity.

The present value of an annuity or unitrust interest that is payable for a term of years or until the prior death of an individual may be computed by following the examples set forth in Temp. Reg. §25.2512-T(d)(2)(v).

Split-interest trusts. Reg. §20.2031-7 and Temp. Reg. §20.2031-7T(d)(7) are used to determine the present value, after April 30, 2009, of a remainder interest in a charitable remainder annuity trust (CRAT), as defined and valued in Reg. §1.664-2(a) and (c). The fair market value of a CRAT is the net fair market value of the property placed in trust less the present value of the annuity, which can be computed by using Table B or Table S in Reg. §20.2031-7(d)(7) and Temp. Reg. §20.2031-7T(d)(7).

The present value of a remainder interest in a pooled income fund as defined in Reg. §1.642(c)-5 is valued pursuant to Reg. §1.642(c)-6.

The present value of a remainder interest in a charitable remainder unitrust (CRUT) as defined in Reg. §1.664-3 is valued pursuant to Reg. §1.664-4. These calculations can also be performed by using CCH® FinEst Calcs™.

Exceptions to the use of standard factors. The IRS has set forth several situations under Reg. §20.7520-3(b)(2) and (3) in which the standard actuarial factors may not be used. These include (1) transfers to high payout annuities if the annuity is expected to exhaust the fund before the last possible annuity payment is made in full, (2) transfers to split-interest trusts in which a grantor retains an income interest in a trust funded with unproductive or underproductive property, (3) transfers with a retained life interest for which the person who is the measuring life has a terminal illness, and (4) situations where the decedent, and the individual who is the measuring life, die in a common accident. Thus, the standard factors may not be used if the governing instrument fails to provide an income beneficiary with that degree of beneficial enjoyment of the property that the principles of the law of trusts accord to a person who is unqualifiedly designated as the income beneficiary of a trust. In addition, an individual is deemed to be terminally ill if such individual is known to have an incurable illness or other deteriorating physical condition such that there is at least a 50-percent probability that the individual will die within one year. If the individual survives for at least 18 months after the date the gift is completed, however, the presumption is made that there was no terminal illness at the time of the transfer, unless there is clear and convincing evidence to the contrary.

Transitional rules. If the date for valuing a life estate or an annuity, remainder, or reversion that is based on one or more measuring lives is after April 30, 2009, and before July 1, 2009, the present value of the interest may be determined under the tables based on either Life Table 90CM under Reg. §20.2031-7A(f)(4) or Table 2000CM under Temp. Reg. §20.2031-7T(d)(7), at the option of the executor. However, the Code Sec. 7520 interest rate will be the appropriate rate for the month in which the valuation date occurs. See Reg. §20.2031-7(d)(3) and Reg. §25.2512-5(d)(3).

In cases involving a charitable deduction, if the valuation date occurs after April 30, 2009, and before July 1, 2009, and an election is made under Code Sec.

7520(a) to use the Code Sec. 7520 interest rate for March 2009 or April 2009, then the tables based on the mortality experience contained in Life Table 90CM must be used. If the Code Sec. 7520 interest rate for May 2009 or June 2009 is used, the tables based on either Table 90CM or Table 2000CM may be used. However, if the valuation date occurs after June 30, 2009, the tables based on the mortality experience contained in Table 2000CM must be used, even if a prior month interest rate election under Code Sec. 7520(a) is made. See Reg. § 1.642(c)-6(e)(2), Reg. § 1.664-2(c), and Reg. § 1.664-4(e)(2).

A transitional rule is also provided if a decedent was mentally incompetent on May 1, 2009, and dies without having regained competency or dies within 90 days of the date on which the decedent first regained competency. Under the rule, the fair market value of an annuity, interest for life, or a term of years, or a remainder or reversionary interest includible in the gross estate may be determined under either Temp. Reg. § 20.2031-7T(d) or the corresponding applicable section at the time the decedent became incompetent.

Valuation Tables Prescribed by Code Sec. 7520

The tables containing actuarial factors to be used in determining the present value of certain limited interests of decedents dying after April 30, 2009, and to gifts of such interests made after that date, are listed below:[9]

Table 2000CM	Life Table
Table S	Single Life
Table R(2)	Interest
Table B	Term Certain Factors
Table H	Commutation Factors
Table K	Adjustment Factors
Table D	Term Certain Unitrust
Table U(1)	Single Life Factors
Table U(2)	Adjusted Payout Rates
Table D	Term Certain Factors
Table F	Payout Rate Adjustment Factors
Table Z	Commutation Factors

The tables containing actuarial factors to be used in determining the present value of certain limited interests of decedents dying after April 30, 1999, and before May 1, 2009, and to gifts of such interests made after that date, are arranged in the following order:[10]

Table 90CM	Life Table
Table S	Single Life
Table J	Adjustment Factors
Table K	Adjustment Factors
Table B	Term Certain
Table U(1)	Single Life Unitrust
Table D	Term Certain Unitrust
Table F	Payout Factors

---

[9] Reg. § 20.2031-7 and Temp. Reg. § 20.2031-7T(d)(7); T.D. 9448, filed with the *Federal Register* on May 1, 2009. Also see IRS Publications 1457 (pertaining to remainder, income, and annuity calculations) and 1458 (pertaining to unitrust remainder and life estate calculations). The lowest rate available these regulations and IRS Publications was 2.2 percent. However, Notice 2009-18, IRB 2009-10, 648, provides extensions to the ta-

bles for interest rates from 0.2 percent to 2.0 percent.

[10] Reg. § 20.2031-7 and Reg. § 1.664-4; T.D. 8886, 2002-2 CB 3, filed with the *Federal Register* on June 9, 2000. Also see IRS Publications 1457 and 1458. The lowest rate available under these regulations and IRS Publications was 2.2 percent. However, Notice 2009-18, IRB 2009-10, 648, provides extensions to the tables for interest rates from 0.2 percent to 2.0 percent.

The following tables applicable to decedents dying, and gifts made, after April 30, 1989, and before May 1, 1999, are also reproduced. Tables S, J, K, B, D, and F, above, also apply to decedents dying, and gifts made, after April 30, 1989, and before May 1, 1999.

Table 80CNSMT . . . . Life Table
Table S . . . . Single Life
Table U(1) . . . . Single Life Unitrust

Software to Calculate Actuarial Factors

CCH has several products available that help practitioners calculate the various actuarial factors contained in IRS Publications 1457 "Actuarial Valuations, Version 3A" (5-2009), and 1458 "Actuarial Valuations, Version 3B" (5-2009).

CCH IRS Actuarial Factors™, is a finding device that enables practitioners to input the applicable Table (e.g., Table S, U(1), U(2)), interest rate, term of years, age, etc., that is needed and automatically calculates the factor. Users can choose factors based on Table 2000CM, Table 90CM, or Table 80CNSMT. This valuable Practice Aid is included as an enhancement to the federal tax products on CCH Internet tax research product IntelliConnect™.

In addition to IRS Actuarial Factors, CCH® FinEst Calcs™ will calculate the remainder factors for various split-interest trusts. This software program provides for what-if scenarios and allows for the graphing of results for presentation to clients. CCH®FinEstCalcs™ is now available on the CCH® IntelliConnect™.

To subscribe to CCH IntelliConnect, or to order CCH® FinEst Calcs™ call 1-888-CCH-REPS or visit our Internet site: http://tax.cchgroup.com.

Decedents Dying Before May 1, 2009

For decedents dying after April 30, 1999, but before May 1, 2009, the present value of a remainder or reversionary interest postponed for a term certain is determined by multiplying the fair market value of the property by the appropriate remainder interest factor from Table B in Reg. § 20.2031-7(d)(6). If the interest is postponed until after the death of one individual, the appropriate remainder interest factor from Table S in Reg. § 20.2031-7(d)(7) is used. The appropriate remainder interest factor is that factor that corresponds to the applicable Code Sec. 7520 interest rate and either the Table B term certain or the Table S current age of the individual who is the measuring life. The interest rate component is based on a rate that is 120 percent of the applicable federal midterm rate compounded annually for the month in which the valuation date falls.

Ordinary term-of-years and life interest. The present value of a right to receive the income of property, or to use nonincome-producing property, for a term of years or for the life of one individual is determined by multiplying the fair market value of the property by the appropriate term-of-years or life interest factor that corresponds to the applicable Code Sec. 7520 interest rate. Although the term-of-years and life interest factors are not included in Table B or Table S in Reg. § 20.2031-7(d)(6) and Reg. § 20.2031-7(d)(7), they may be derived mathematically. The term-of-years (income interest) factor is derived by subtracting the correlative Table B term certain remainder factor that corresponds to the applicable Code Sec. 7520 interest rate from 1.000000. Similarly, the factor for the life of one individual (life estate) is derived by subtracting the correlative Table S single life remainder factor that corresponds to the applicable Code Sec. 7520 interest rate from 1.000000. These actuarial factors for income interests and life estates are included in Table B and Table S, respectively, in IRS Publication 1457, "Actuarial Values, Book Aleph" (7-1999) (see Reg. § 20.2031-7(d)(4)).

Annuities. The present value of an annuity that is payable at the end of each year for a term certain or for the life of one individual is determined by multiplying the aggregate amount payable annually by the appropriate annuity factor that corresponds to the applicable Code Sec. 7520 interest rate. These actuarial factors are included in Table B and Table S in IRS Publication 1457, "Actuarial Values, Book Aleph." Although the annuity factors are not included in Table B or Table S in Reg. § 20.2031-7(d)(6) and Reg. § 20.2031-7(d)(7), they may be derived mathematically. The term certain annuity factor is derived by subtracting the correlative Table B term certain remainder factor that corresponds to the applicable Code Sec. 7520 interest rate from 1.000000 and then dividing the result by the applicable Code Sec. 7520 interest rate expressed as a decimal number. Similarly, the single life annuity factor is derived by subtracting the correlative Table S single life remainder factor that corresponds to the applicable Code Sec. 7520 interest rate from 1.000000 and then dividing the result by the applicable Code Sec. 7520 interest rate expressed as a decimal number.

> *Example:* Miller Burke died in January 2009 and was entitled to receive an annuity of $24,000 a year for six years, payable at the end of each year. The Code Sec. 7520 interest rate for January is 2.4%. The Table B term certain remainder factor at 2.4% is .867362 The term certain annuity factor is 5.5266 ((1.000000 − .867362) ÷ .024). The present value of the annuity interest at the date of the decedent's death is $132,638 ($24,000 × 5.5266). (Calculations made using CCH® IRS Actuarial Factors™.)

> *Comment:* Certain adjustment factors must be applied to the valuations determined above if the annuity is payable at any time other than the end of each year. Table J (Reg. § 20.2031-7(d)(6)) contains the adjustment factors applicable for term certain annuities if the annuity is payable at the beginning of annual, semiannual, quarterly, monthly, or weekly periods. Table K (Reg. § 20.2031-7(d)(6)) contains the adjustment factors applicable if the annuity is payable at the end of semiannual, quarterly, monthly, or weekly periods. Regardless of which table applies, the product obtained by multiplying the aggregate amount payable annually by the applicable annuity factor is then multiplied by the applicable adjustment factor to obtain the present value of the annuity.

The present value of an annuity or unitrust interest that is payable for a term of years or until the prior death of an individual may be computed by following the examples set forth in Reg. § 25.2512-5(d)(2)(v).

Split-interest trusts. The fair market value of a remainder interest in a charitable remainder annuity trust (CRAT) is the net fair market value of the property placed in trust less the present value of the annuity, which can be computed by using Table S or Table B under Reg. § 20.2031-7(d).[11] The present value of an annuity interest that is payable until the earlier to occur of the lapse of a specific number of years or the death of an individual may be computed using Tables B, K, S, and 90CM. Reg. § 25.2512-5(d)(2)(v)(A) provides an example for computing the value of such an annuity interest using these tables.

The present value of a remainder interest in a pooled income fund as defined in Reg. § 1.642(c)-5 is valued pursuant to Reg. § 1.642(c)-6.

---

[11] Reg. § 1.664-2(c).

The present value of a remainder interest in a charitable remainder unitrust (CRUT) as defined in Reg. § 1.664-3 is valued pursuant to Reg. § 1.664-4 using Tables F and D or U(1). The present value of a unitrust interest that is payable until the earlier to occur of the lapse of a specific number of years or the death of an individual may be computed using Tables D, F, U(1), and 90CM pursuant to the example provided in Reg. § 25.2512-5(d)(2)(v)(B).

Exceptions to the use of standard factors. The IRS has set forth three situations under Reg. § 20.7520-3(b)(2) and (3) in which the standard actuarial factors may not be used. These include (1) transfers to high payout annuities if the annuity is expected to exhaust the fund before the last possible annuity payment is made in full, (2) transfers to split-interest trusts in which a grantor retains an income interest in a trust funded with unproductive or underproductive property, and (3) transfers with a retained life interest for which the person who is the measuring life has a terminal illness. Thus, the standard factors may not be used if the governing instrument fails to provide an income beneficiary with that degree of beneficial enjoyment of the property that the principles of the law of trusts accord to a person who is unqualifiedly designated as the income beneficiary of a trust. In addition, an individual is deemed to be terminally ill if such individual is known to have an incurable illness or other deteriorating physical condition such that there is at least a 50-percent probability that the individual will die within one year. If the individual survives for at least 18 months after the date the gift is completed, however, the presumption is made that there was no terminal illness at the time of the transfer, unless there is clear and convincing evidence to the contrary.

Transitional rules. If the date for valuing a life estate or an annuity, remainder, or reversion that is based on one or more measuring lives is after April 30, 1999, and before July 1, 1999, the present value of the interest may be determined under the tables based on either Life Table 80CNSMT under Reg. § 20.2031-7A(e)(4) or Table 90CM under Reg. § 20.2031-7(d)(7). However, the Code Sec. 7520 interest rate will be the appropriate rate for the month in which the valuation date occurs. See Reg. § 20.2031-7(d)(3) and Reg. § 25.2512-5(d)(3).

In cases involving a charitable deduction, if the valuation date occurs after April 30, 1999, and before July 1, 1999, and an election is made under Code Sec. 7520(a) to use the Code Sec. 7520 interest rate for March 1999 or April 1999, then the tables based on the mortality experience contained in Life Table 80CNSMT must be used. If the Code Sec. 7520 interest rate for May 1999 or June 1999 is used, the tables based on either Table 80CNSMT or Table 90CM may be used. However, if the valuation date occurs after June 30, 1999, the tables based on the mortality experience contained in Table 90CM must be used, even if a prior month interest rate election under Code Sec. 7520(a) is made. See Reg. § 1.642(c)-6(e)(2), Reg. § 1.664-2(c), and Reg. § 1.664-4(e)(2).

A transitional rule is also provided if a decedent was mentally incompetent on May 1, 1999, and dies without having regained competency or dies within 90 days of the date on which the decedent first regained competency. Under the rule, the fair market value of an annuity, interest for life or a term of years, or a remainder or reversionary interest includible in the gross estate may be determined under either Reg. § 20.2031-7(d)(3) or the corresponding applicable section at the time the decedent became incompetent.

Decedents Dying Before May 1, 1999

Different rules apply in the case of decedents dying before May 1, 1999.

¶530

Valuation of gross estate before January 1, 1952. In the case of a decedent dying before 1952, the present value of limited interests that are dependent upon the continuation or termination of one or more lives, or upon a term certain concurrent with one or more lives, is computed on the basis of interest at the rate of four percent a year, compounded annually, and life contingencies as to each life involved from values that are based on the Actuaries' or Combined Experience Table of Mortality, as extended.[12] This table and related factors are contained in 26 CFR Part 81 edition revised as of April 1, 1958. The present value of an interest measured by a term of years is also computed on the basis of interest at the rate of four percent a year.

Valuation of gross estate after December 31, 1951, and before January 1, 1971. In the case of a decedent dying after 1951 and before 1971, the present value of limited interests that are dependent upon the continuation or termination of one or more lives, or upon a term certain concurrent with one or more lives, is computed on the basis of interest at the rate of 3.5 percent a year, compounded annually, and life contingencies as to each life involved are taken from U.S. Life Table 38.[13] This table and related factors are contained in 26 CFR Part 20 edition revised as of April 1, 1984. The present value of an interest measured by a term of years is also computed on the basis of interest at the rate of 3.5 percent a year.

Valuation of gross estate after December 31, 1970, and before December 1, 1983. In the case of a decedent dying after 1970 and before December 1, 1983, the present value of limited interests that are dependent upon the continuation or termination of one or more lives, or upon a term certain concurrent with one or more lives, is computed on the basis of interest at the rate of six percent a year, compounded annually, and life contingencies as to each male and female life involved are taken from Table LN of former Reg. §20.2031-10.[14] This table and related factors are contained in 26 CFR Part 20 edition revised as of April 1, 1994. The present value of an interest measured by a term of years is also computed on the basis of interest at the rate of six percent a year.

It should be noted that, with respect to interests that are dependent on the continuation or termination of one or more lives, the six-percent tables make a distinction between an interest that is based on the life of a male (Table A(1)) and one that is based on the life of a female (Table A(2)). This is true because the tables use one set of actuarial assumptions for men and a different set for women. Table B is used if the interest is dependent on a term of years.

IRS Publication No. 723, "Actuarial Values I: Valuation of Last Survivor Charitable Remainders," and IRS Publication No. 723A, "Actuarial Values II: Factors at 6 Percent Involving One and Two Lives," contain many special factors involving one or two lives. Although no longer available from the Superintendent of Documents, a copy of each may be obtained from: Internal Revenue Service, CC:DOM:CORP:T:R (IRS Publication No. 723 or 723A), Room 5228, POB 7604, Ben Franklin Station, Washington, D.C. 20044.[15]

Valuation of gross estate after November 30, 1983, and before May 1, 1989. In the case of a decedent dying after November 30, 1983, and before May 1, 1989, the present value of an annuity, interest for life, or a remainder or reversionary interest that is dependent upon the continuation or termination of a single life is computed using Table A contained in Reg. §20.2031-7A(d)(6). An annuity, interest for a term of years, or a remainder or reversionary interest that is dependent

---

[12] Reg. §20.2031-7A(a).
[13] Reg. §20.2031-7A(b).

[14] Reg. §20.2031-7A(c).
[15] Reg. §20.2031-7A(c).

upon a term certain is valued using Table B of the regulation. These tables are based on a 10-percent interest factor and are actuarially gender-neutral.

If the valuation of the interest involved is dependent upon more than one life or on a term certain that is concurrent with one or more lives, a special factor must be used. The factor is to be computed on the basis of interest at the rate of 10 percent a year, compounded annually, and life contingencies determined, as to each person involved, from the values of 1(x) that are set forth in column 2 of Table LN, contained in Reg. § 20.2031-7A(d)(6). Table LN contains values of 1(x) taken from the life table for the total population appearing as Table 1 of United States Life Tables: 1969-1971, published by the Department of Health and Human Services.[16]

IRS Publication No. 723E, "Actuarial Values II: Factors at 10 Percent Involving One and Two Lives," contains special factors involving one or two lives. Although no longer available from the Superintendent of Documents, a copy of the publication may be obtained from: Internal Revenue Service, CC:DOM:CORP:T:R (IRS Publication No. 723E), Room 5228, POB 7604, Ben Franklin Station, Washington, D.C. 20044. If a special factor is required in the case of an actual decedent, the IRS will furnish the factor to the executor on request. The request must be accompanied by a statement setting forth the date of birth of each person whose life may affect the value of the interest and copies of the relevant instruments.[17]

If an annuity is payable at the end of each year for the life of an individual, its value is determined by multiplying the amount payable by the applicable factor in column 2 of Table A, taking into consideration the age of the individual whose life measures the duration of the annuity. Similarly, if the annuity is payable annually at the end of each year for a definite number of years, the amount payable is multiplied by the figure in column 2 of Table B corresponding to the number of years for which the annuity is payable.[18]

Certain adjustment factors must be applied to the valuations determined above if the annuity is payable at the end of semiannual, quarterly, monthly, or weekly periods.[19] The product of the Table A or B factors and the aggregate amount to be paid within a year is multiplied by the applicable factor below, depending upon when the payments are made. The factors for the various periods are as follows:

Semiannual payments	1.0244
Quarterly payments	1.0368
Monthly payments	1.0450
Weekly payments	1.0482

If an annuity for the life of an individual is payable at the beginning of annual, semiannual, quarterly, monthly or weekly periods, the general valuation procedure is slightly different. The value of that annuity is the sum of the first payment *plus* the present value of a similar annuity that would not be payable until the *end* of each payment period (determined as above).

If the first payment of an annuity for a definite number of years is payable at the beginning of the annual or other payment period, the *applicable factor* is the *product* of the factor shown in Table B multiplied by the following additional factor, as appropriate:[20]

---

[16] Reg. § 20.2031-7A(d)(5).
[17] Reg. § 20.2031-7A(d)(5).
[18] Reg. § 20.2031-7A(d)(2).

[19] Reg. § 20.2031-7A(d)(2)(ii).
[20] Reg. § 20.2031-7A(d)(2)(iii).

Annual payments	1.1000
Semiannual payments	1.0744
Quarterly payments	1.0618
Monthly payments	1.0534
Weekly payments	1.0502

The estate of a decedent dying after November 30, 1983, but before August 9, 1984, can use either the 10-percent tables of Reg. § 20.2031-7A(d)(6) or the six-percent tables pursuant to Reg. § 20.2031-7A(c), whichever is more advantageous, to value an annuity, an interest for life or for a term of years, or a remainder or reversionary interest that is includible in the decedent's gross estate. The estate of a decedent dying on or after August 9, 1984, must use the 10-percent tables unless the estate is subject to a special rule relating to the incompetency of the decedent. Under this rule, where the valuation date is before May 1, 1989, and the decedent was subject to a mental disability on December 1, 1983, such that the disposition of his or her property could not be changed, and the decedent either dies without regaining competency or within 90 days after doing so, the decedent's estate may use either the six- or 10-percent tables.[21]

Valuation of gross estate after April 30, 1989, and before May 1, 1999. In the case of a decedent dying after April 30, 1989, and before May 1, 1999, the present value of an annuity, interest for life or a term of years, or a remainder or reversionary interest is governed by Reg. § 20.2031-7A(e). Generally, the same methodologies for valuing limited property interests for decedents dying after April 30, 1999, are also applicable for decedents dying after April 30, 1989, with one major exception. The single life Table S, based on Life Table 80CNSMT, and Table 80CNSMT in Reg. § 20.2031-7A(e)(4) apply. Because the Table B term certain remainder factors and the Table J and Table K annuities adjustment factors at Reg. § 20.2031-7(d)(6) are not based on mortality experience, those tables also apply to decedents dying after April 30, 1989.

Although no longer available for purchase, IRS Publication No. 1457, "Actuarial Values, Alpha Volume," includes many actuarial factors and examples not contained in the regulations. Pertinent factors contained in this publication may be obtained from: CC:DOM:CORP:R (IRS Publication 1457) Room 5226, IRS, POB 7604, Ben Franklin Station, Washington, D.C. 20044.

Transitional rules. If a decedent was incompetent on May 1, 1989, such that the disposition of his or her property could not be changed, and the decedent dies either without regaining competency or within 90 days after regaining competency, the decedent's executor has an option with respect to valuation methodologies. Under such circumstances, the fair market value of an annuity, life estate, term of years, remainder and reversion included in the decedent's gross estate may be calculated under Reg. § 20.2031-7A(e)(4) or under the appropriate section of the regulation that was applicable when the decedent became mentally incompetent.

¶ 534   Actuarial Factors vs. Actual Health

For estate tax purposes, the value of life and remainder interests must be determined from facts available at the time of the decedent's death. The fact that the life tenant may in fact survive the decedent by only a short period of time is not controlling. The IRS actuarial tables reflect the deaths of those who die prematurely as well as those who enjoy lives of greater longevity.

---

[21] Reg. § 20.2031-7A(d)(1).

Nonetheless, for the estates of decedents dying, and gifts made, after December 13, 1995, IRS regulations provide that the actuarial tables may not be used to determine the present value of a limited interest if it is known at the time of the decedent's death, or at the time the gift is completed, that the individual who is a measuring life of the interest is terminally ill.[22] An individual who is known to have an incurable illness or other deteriorating physical condition is considered terminally ill if there is at least a 50-percent probability that the individual will die within one year. Under the regulations, a special actuarial factor must be computed that takes into account the projection of the actual life expectancy. However, if the individual survives for 18 months or longer after the date of the decedent's death, the individual shall be presumed to have not been terminally ill at the date of death unless the contrary is established by clear and convincing evidence. For purposes of the credit allowable to the transferee's estate for tax on a prior transfer, the value of the property shall be the value determined previously in the transferor's estate.

Prior to December 14, 1995, if it was known on the valuation date that a life tenant was afflicted with a fatal and incurable disease in its advanced stages such that death was clearly imminent, a departure from the actuarial tables could be made and the value of a life or remainder interest determined by reference to known facts based on the expert testimony of a physician.[23] Generally, cases indicate a reluctance to depart from valuations determined through the use of actuarial tables unless an incurable or fatal disease exists *and* there is evidence indicating imminent death or a life expectancy so brief as to require a departure from such tables.[24] In the majority of cases permitting departures from such tables, the life tenant's maximum actual life expectancy was one year or less.[25] These principles apply in the valuation of interests for charitable and marital deduction purposes as well. They are also applicable for purposes of computing the allowable credit for tax on prior transfers. However, the Tax Court rejected the use of valuation tables for purposes of computing the credit in valuing a husband's usufruct interest in his wife's share of community property after their simultaneous deaths.[26]

¶ 535   Other Property Interests

The various other items reportable on Form 706 (United States Estate (and Generation-Skipping Transfer) Tax Return) (Rev. August 2013), Schedule F (Other Miscellaneous Property Not Reportable Under Any Other Schedule), as "Other Miscellaneous Property" are valued as indicated below.

• Debts Owed Decedent

Debts owed to the decedent should be reported in the amount of the principal plus accrued interest. The executor possibly can establish a lower valuation.

---

[22] Reg. § 20.7520-3(b)(3) and Reg. § 25.7520-3(b)(3).

[23] *N.H. Jennings*, 10 TC 323, CCH Dec. 16,263 (Acq.). See *M.P. Fabric Est.*, 83 TC 932, CCH Dec. 41,667; *C. McDowell Est.*, 51 TCM 319, CCH Dec. 42,831(M), TC Memo. 1986-27.

[24] *Cont. Ill. Nat'l Bk. & Tr. Co. of Chicago*, CA-7, 74-2 USTC ¶ 13,034; *Mercantile-Safe De-*

posit & Trust Co., DC Md., 74-1 USTC ¶ 12,985, 368 FSupp. 742.

[25] *Cont. Ill. Nat'l Bk. & Tr. Co. of Chicago*, CA-7, 74-2 USTC ¶ 13,034.

[26] *E.W. Marks Est.*, 94 TC 720, CCH Dec. 46,594. See also *A.P. Carter Est.*, CA-5, 91-1 USTC ¶ 60,054, 921 F2d 63, cert. denied.

• *Leasehold Interests*

The renewal value of leases is an important factor in valuing leaseholds.

• *Household Goods and Personal Effects*

Household goods and personal effects should be reported at the price that a willing buyer would pay a willing seller. A room-by-room itemization is desirable. All articles should be named separately. Items in the same room with individual values of not more than $100 may be grouped. A separate value should be given for each article named.[27]

The executor may furnish a sworn statement in lieu of the itemized list, however. This statement may set forth the aggregate value of the property as appraised by a competent appraiser or appraisers, or dealers in the kind of property involved (see ¶540).

If the estate includes articles of marked artistic or intrinsic value, such as jewelry, furs, silverware, works of art, oriental rugs, or stamp collections, and any one article is valued in excess of $3,000 or any collection of articles is valued at more than $10,000, the appraisal of an expert or experts, under oath, must be filed with the return.[28]

• *Farm Products and Automobiles*

Farm products, growing crops (other than timber for which special use valuation is elected, see ¶290), livestock, farm machinery, and automobiles are valued at the price at which such items would change hands between a willing buyer and a willing seller. The fair market value is not to be determined by a forced sale price. All relevant facts and elements of value as of the applicable valuation date must be considered[29] (see ¶540).

Feed on hand at the date of the decedent's death, but consumed by livestock during the elected alternate valuation period is includible in the gross estate at its value on the date of disposition—the date on which it was fed to the livestock.[30] The disposition price is to be used for any farm asset that is sold or disposed of during the alternate valuation period.[31]

• *Deferred Compensation Payments*

Many employees enter into contracts or agreements with their employers that provide for the payment of deferred compensation to the employee, usually on the employee's retirement. These contracts also usually provide for the payment of specified sums to a named beneficiary (commonly the employee's spouse) if the employee dies before retirement.

Comment: The IRS has attempted to include the commuted value of the latter payments (commonly called "death benefits") in the estates of deceased employees as property owned at death. However, most courts have held that these payments are not includible in a deceased employee's estate because the employee's interest in the employment contract is deemed to terminate at death.

Comment: The IRS also has attempted to include death benefits of this type in decedents' estates under pre-1977 Code Sec. 2035 (as transfers in

---

[27] Reg. §20.2031-6.

[28] Reg. §20.2031-6.

[29] Reg. §20.2031-1(b).

[30] Rev. Rul. 58-436, 1958-2 CB 366, modified by Rev. Rul. 64-289, 1964-2 CB 173 (income tax conclusions only).

[31] Rev. Rul. 68-154, 1968-1 CB 395.

contemplation of death for gifts made prior to 1977) and under Code Sec. 2036 (transfers with retained life estate), Code Sec. 2037 (transfers taking effect at death), Code Sec. 2038 (revocable transfers), and Code Sec. 2039 (annuities) (see ¶733 for further details).

¶ 540 Retail Price and Auction Price

In general, the fair market value of property includible in a decedent's estate is the price at which it would change hands between a willing buyer and a willing seller, both having reasonable knowledge of relevant facts. However, if an item is generally available to the public in a particular market, the fair market value of the property is the price obtainable on the market in which it is most commonly sold to the public. If the item of property is generally obtainable by the public on the retail market, the fair market value of the item is the price at which that item or a comparable one will sell at retail in a particular geographical market.[32]

> *Example:* The fair market value of a car (property generally obtained by the public on the retail market) is the price at which a car of the same make, model, age, and condition could be purchased by members of the public. Fair market value is *not* the price that a used-car dealer would pay for the decedent's car.

The price paid for an item in a decedent's gross estate at a public auction or in answer to a classified newspaper advertisement will also be considered its retail price.[33] There are two conditions, however. The sale must be made within a reasonable period after the applicable valuation date, and there must not be a substantial change in market conditions during that period.

---

[32] Reg. §20.2031-1(b).

[33] Rev. Proc. 65-19, 1965-2 CB 1002.

Chapter 14

TRANSFERS DURING LIFETIME

¶ 550   Scope of Estate Tax

If the estate tax law applied only to property in which the decedent had an interest at the time of death, the application of the estate tax to any estate could easily be prevented by lifetime transactions. State laws relating to trusts and other property rights make it easy to divest oneself of title to property. At the same time, one could retain either control or beneficial ownership for life. Likewise, when persons realized that they did not have long to live, they could dispose of any remaining property by outright gift, thereby removing such property from their gross estates.

In recognition of these possibilities, Congress included within the scope of the estate tax law various types of lifetime transfers that would otherwise permit complete escape from estate taxes. In prescribing that the value of certain lifetime property transfers are includible in the gross estate, Congress provided for almost every type of lifetime gift in which the decedent did not dispose of every consequential right. These transfers normally involve transfers to trusts.

¶ 555   Transfers Within Three Years of Death

Generally, the value of outright transfers (other than transfers of life insurance) made by a decedent within three years of death is not includible in a decedent's gross estate. However, the value of property is includible in a decedent's gross estate if, within three years of death, the decedent transferred an interest in or power over the property that, if retained by the decedent, would have caused the property to be includible in the decedent's gross estate under Code Sec. 2036 (transfers with retained life estate), Code Sec. 2037 (transfers taking effect at death), Code Sec. 2038 (revocable transfers), or Code Sec. 2042 (life insurance proceeds).[1] The exercise of a general power of appointment, as defined in Code Sec. 2041 (see ¶ 650), within three years of death does not require inclusion of the property subject to the power in the decedent's gross estate under Code Sec. 2035. In addition, for decedents dying after August 5, 1997, annual exclusion gifts made from a decedent's revocable trust within three years of the decedent's death are not includible in the decedent's gross estate.[2]

---

[1] Code Sec. 2035(a).　　　　[2] Code Sec. 2035(e).

The value of any transfer made within three years of death is includible in the decedent's gross estate for the limited purpose of determining the estate's qualification for special use valuation (see ¶280), deferral of estate taxes (see ¶1672), and stock redemptions under Code Sec. 303. Additionally, the value of such a transfer is includible in the gross estate for purposes of determining property that is subject to estate tax liens.[3] This provision is designed to preclude deathbed transfers intended to qualify the estate for such favorable treatment by reducing the amount of nonqualifying property.[4] This provision also applies to transfers to a spouse within three years of death, even though an unlimited gift tax marital deduction is available for gifts made after 1981 (see ¶2311). Note that transfers within three years of death, as well as certain transfers within 10 years of death, are also includible for purposes of the qualified family-owned business deduction (see ¶1150).

- *Gifts for Which Gift Tax Return Not Required*

The value of transfers made within three years of death that are includible in the gross estate under exceptions to the general noninclusion rule of Code Sec. 2035 is includible even if no gift tax return was required to be filed with respect to the transfer.[5] In the case of a gift to a spouse within three years of death for which no gift tax return is required because of the unlimited gift tax marital deduction, the value of the gift is includible in the decedent's gross estate for the limited purposes of determining the estate's qualification for special use valuation, deferral of estate taxes, stock redemptions under Code Sec. 303, and for purposes of determining property that is subject to estate tax liens.

- *"Gross-Up" for Gift Tax Paid on Transfers Within Three Years of Death*

Gift taxes paid on transfers made within three years of a transferor's death are includible in the decedent's gross estate.[6] The amount subject to this rule includes the tax paid by the decedent or the decedent's estate on any gift made by the decedent or his or her spouse within the three-year period ending on the date of the decedent's death. In contrast with the general rule that a period of limitations begins the day after the triggering event (here, the date of death), the triggering event is included when determining the period of limitations for Code Sec. 2035(b).[7]

> *Example:* Mel Frankerlain died on December 31, 2013, and had made a gift on December 31, 2010, for which he had paid gift tax of $5,000. Because the three-year limitation period that ends on December 31, 2013, includes December 31, 2013, this limitation period began on January 1, 2011. Thus, the $5,000 gift tax paid with respect to the December 31, 2010 transfer did not occur within three years of Frankerlain's death, and this amount is not included in his gross estate.

Within the context of computing the estate tax liability due for the amount of gift taxes "grossed up," the Tax Court has rejected an estate's argument that Code Sec. 2043(a) permitted the estate to reduce the amount of includible gift taxes by "consideration" allegedly received by the decedent for his payment of gift taxes. The court held that no reduction was allowed because (1) the plain language of Code Sec. 2035(c) (the predecessor of current Code Sec. 2035(b))

---

[3] Code Sec. 2035(c)(1)(C).

[4] *General Explanation of the Economic Recovery Tax Act of 1981*, Staff of the Joint Committee on Taxation, p. 262.

[5] Code Sec. 2035(c)(3).

[6] Code Sec. 2035(b).

[7] IRS Technical Advice Memorandum 200432016 (March 10, 2004).

made no provision for the netting of consideration received, (2) the Code Sec. 2035(c) "gross-up" rule was not a "transfer" within the meaning of Code Sec. 2043(a), and (3) the decedent's obligation to pay the gift taxes arose by operation of law and not as a result of any agreement he may have made with another party.[8] The value of this decision as precedent seems questionable in light of a recent decision by the Court of Appeals for the Fifth Circuit (*C. McCord, Jr.*).[9] See ¶ 2117.

Another court decision demonstrates that the IRS may be able to use the "step-transaction" doctrine to successfully fight a transferor's attempt to avoid the "gross-up" rule by having a spouse pay the transferor's gift tax liability. In *B. Brown*, the transferor funded, with a $3.1 million payment, an insurance trust holding a policy on his wife's life. He also transferred $1.4 million to his wife's personal checking account, from which she paid her husband's $1.4 million gift tax liability arising from the funding of the insurance trust. The court held that the transferor's death within three years of the transfer triggered application of the "gross-up" provision of Code Sec. 2035 with respect to the transferor's gross estate. In so ruling, the court disregarded the wife's payment of her husband's gift tax liability as merely a conduit to facilitate a prearranged, tax-avoidance, step transaction that did not reflect the reality of the underlying situation.[10]

> *Comment:* The "gross-up" rule does not apply to the gift tax paid by a spouse on a gift made by the decedent within three years of death that is treated as made one-half by the spouse under the gift-splitting provisions of Code Sec. 2513.

• *Transfer for Adequate Consideration*

Even though transferred within three years of the decedent's death, the value of property for which the decedent received a full and adequate consideration in money or money's worth is not includible in the gross estate.

¶ 565   Transfers Intended to Take Effect at Death

The estate tax law requires the inclusion in the gross estate of the value of lifetime transfers intended to take effect at death.[11]

A transfer made by the decedent and taking effect at the decedent's death is one under which possession or enjoyment of the property can be obtained only by surviving the decedent. However, such a transfer is not treated as a transfer taking effect at death unless the decedent retained a reversionary interest in the property that immediately before the decedent's death had a value in excess of five percent of the value of the transferred property.[12] In determining whether or not a reversionary interest exceeds five percent of the value of the transferred property, the value of the reversionary interest is compared with the value of the transferred property, including interests therein that are not dependent upon survivorship of the decedent. For this purpose, a reversionary interest includes a possibility that property transferred by the decedent:

(1) may return to the decedent or to the decedent's estate; or

(2) may become subject to a power of disposition by the decedent.

---

[8] *F. Armstrong, Jr. Est.*, TC, 119 TC 220, CCH Dec. 54,921.

[9] *C. McCord, Jr.*, CA-5, 2006-2 USTC ¶ 60,530, 461 F3d 614.

[10] *B. Brown*, CA-9, 2003-1 USTC ¶ 60,462, 329 F3d 664, cert. denied, 10/6/2003.

[11] Code Sec. 2037.

[12] Reg. § 20.2037-1(a).

If the interest is in income only, a decedent does not have a reversionary interest.[13]

This reversionary interest of the decedent may be expressly written into the instrument or it may arise by way of state law.[14] In other words, it may be explicit: "To A for life, remainder to B, but if B should predecease me, then the remainder to me or my heirs." It also may be implicit: "To A for life, remainder to B if B doesn't predecease me." In the second example, the entire fee interest has not been disposed of by the decedent. There is a possibility that B will not be eligible to take after A's life estate. Since the property is not otherwise disposed of, it will revert to the decedent by operation of law.

If, in either of these cases, the reversionary interest could be valued in excess of five percent of the value of the property, the value of the property (less the value of any outstanding, preceding interests in persons other than the transferor) would be included in the decedent's gross estate. Such a valuation in excess of five percent is quite possible if only one remainderman is named. The value of such an interest is to be determined by the usual methods of valuation, including the use of mortality tables and actuarial principles (see ¶ 530).

A transfer intended to take effect at death will not be included in the decedent's estate if possession or enjoyment of the property could have been obtained by any beneficiary during the decedent's lifetime through the exercise of a general power of appointment that was exercisable immediately before the decedent's death.[15]

• *Transfers Made Prior to October 8, 1949*

All transfers made prior to October 8, 1949, and intended to take effect at death, require the same estate tax consequences as those made after that date, with one exception. The reversionary interest must be expressly included in the instrument of transfer. If it arises by operation of law, the property is not included in the decedent's gross estate.[16]

¶ 570   Transfers with Possession or Enjoyment Retained

The gross estate includes the value of property or property interests transferred by a decedent, in trust or otherwise, if the decedent reserved or retained for life, or for any period not ascertainable without reference to the decedent's death, or for a period that does not in fact end before the decedent's death:

    (1) the use, possession, right to the income, or other enjoyment of the transferred property; or

    (2) the right, either alone or in conjunction with any other person, to designate the person or persons who will possess or enjoy the transferred property or the income therefrom.[17]

A reservation by the decedent for a period not ascertainable without reference to the decedent's death may be illustrated by the following Example.

    Example: Larry Collins reserved the right to receive the income from transferred property in quarterly payments on the condition that no part of the income between the last quarterly payment and the date of his death was to be received by him or his estate.

---

[13] Reg. § 20.2037-1(c).

[14] Reg. § 20.2037-1(c); Rev. Rul. 82-24, 1982-1 CB 134.

[15] Reg. § 20.2037-1(b).

[16] Reg. § 20.2037-1(f).

[17] Code Sec. 2036.

If the decedent retained or reserved one or more of these rights or interests as to all of the property he transferred, the amount includible in the gross estate is the value of the entire property transferred, less the value of any outstanding income interest that is not subject to the decedent's interest or right and that is actually being enjoyed by another person at the time of the decedent's death. If the decedent during life retained or reserved an interest or right as to only a part of the property transferred, the amount includible in the decedent's gross estate is only a corresponding portion of the entire value of the property.[18]

Effective for decedents estates having a gross estate valuation date on or after July 14, 2008,[19] if a grantor transfers property to a trust and retains the right to use the property or the right to an annuity, unitrust, or other income payments for the grantor's life, for any period not ascertainable without reference to the grantor's death, or for any period that does not in fact end before the grantor's death, the grantor has retained the right to income from all or a specific portion of the trust property. The portion of the trust includible in the grantor's gross estate is equal to the portion of the trust corpus, valued as of the decedent's date of death, necessary to generate the annual payment (or use) using the applicable Code Sec. 7520 interest rate.

The use, possession, right to the income, or other enjoyment of the transferred property is considered as having been retained by or reserved to the decedent to the extent that it is to be applied toward the discharge of a legal obligation of the decedent or otherwise for the decedent's pecuniary benefit. The term "legal obligation" includes a legal obligation by the decedent during the decedent's lifetime to support a dependent.[20]

If the rights are retained for life, however, or for a period not ascertainable without reference to the decedent's death, the property will in all cases be includible unless one of the special exceptions noted below is applicable. With respect to their right to designate the person or persons who shall possess or enjoy the transferred property or income therefrom, the manner of making the transfer is immaterial. If these rights are retained, they are taxable whether made in trust or otherwise.[21] However, the Tax Court has held that the concept of a transfer with a retained life estate was not applicable to transfers that were deemed to have been made by a decedent under the Uniform Simultaneous Death Act. Thus, in a situation where a decedent and her husband died in a common accident, the proceeds of two policies of insurance on the husband's life that were payable to a trust in which the decedent had a life income interest were not includible in her gross estate, even though she owned the policies and was deemed to have survived her husband under the Uniform Simultaneous Death Act. In the court's view, the Act is intended solely to provide rules for passage of property of both decedents to their beneficiaries.[22]

If the retained use is a natural one, however, such as the use with a spouse of a home that the decedent purchased for the spouse, rather than a use that has been reserved in the instrument of transfer or by a withholding of the property from the transferee, the transfer is not taxable in the absence of an understanding or agreement, expressed or implied. Continued occupancy in a residence, where the donor and donee are husband and wife, does not itself support an inference

---

[18] Reg. § 20.2036-1(a).

[19] Reg. § 20.2036-1(a)(2), amended by T.D. 9414, July 11, 2008.

[20] Reg. § 20.2036-1(b); see *E.E. German Est.*, CtCls, 85-1 USTC ¶ 13,610.

[21] Reg. § 20.2036-1(b)(3).

[22] *L. Goldstone Est.*, 78 TC 1143, CCH Dec. 39,138.

of an agreement or understanding as to retained possession or enjoyment by the donor.[23] Where the donor and donee are persons other than husband and wife, for example, a parent and child, the IRS has ruled that the continued occupancy of the transferred realty itself implies the existence of an agreement of retained enjoyment by the donor.[24] This IRS position has been sustained by an appellate court.[25]

Where the retention of a right to income was one that did not take effect until after the death of a primary life tenant and the decedent died before the primary life tenant, the entire value of the trust, less only the value of the outstanding life estate, is includible.[26] Unrequested income amounts that were irrevocably added to trust principal were includible in the gross estate of a life income beneficiary as a transfer with a retained life estate where the beneficiary had the right to income from the augmented trust principal.[27]

• Effect of Consideration

If the transfer was made for a consideration, the value of the consideration is deductible from the value of the property in determining the taxable value. As in the case of other transfers, the consideration is considered purely from the standpoint of monetary value. Sentimental attachments and sufficiency of consideration from a purely legal standpoint do not enter into the picture. If the value of the transferred property exceeds the value of the consideration, the difference is included in the decedent's gross estate.[28] Dispositions of life estates and remainder interests, discussed below, may not cause inclusion of the property if a seller receives the actuarial value of the interest.

• Transfers of Stock in Closely Held Corporations

The retention of the right to vote (either *directly or indirectly*) shares of stock in what is called "a controlled corporation," by a person who has irrevocably transferred the stock for other than full consideration after June 22, 1976, is treated as the retention of the enjoyment of the transferred shares; thus, retention of the right causes the transferred shares to be includible in such a donor's estate at death.[29] A corporation is a "controlled corporation" for purposes of this rule if, at any time after the transfer of the stock and during the three-year period ending on the date of the decedent's death, the decedent *owned* (ownership being determined by applying the "constructive ownership" rules of income tax Code Sec. 318), or *had the right* (either alone or in conjunction with any person) to vote stock possessing at least 20 percent of the total combined voting power of all classes of stock.[30] If the stock is not in a "controlled corporation," the stock is not includible in the gross estate of a decedent even if the decedent directly held the power to vote the transferred shares.

In determining whether a transferor owns at least 20 percent of the stock in a corporation, the indirect or constructive ownership rules are applied.[31] Under these rules, stock owned by the members of a transferor's family (spouse,

---

[23] Rev. Rul. 70-155, 1970-1 CB 189.

[24] Rev. Rul. 78-409, 1978-2 CB 234.

[25] *J.C. Guynn*, CA-4, 71-1 USTC ¶ 12,742, 437 F2d 1148, rev'g and rem'g DC, 70-1 USTC ¶ 12,661, 309 FSupp. 233. But see *Est. of S.H. Roemer*, 46 TCM 1176, CCH Dec. 40,384(M), TC Memo. 1983-509 (no implied agreement between mother and daughter).

[26] Reg. § 20.2036-1(b).

[27] *S. Horner, Exr.*, CtCls, 73-2 USTC ¶ 12,956, 485 F2d 596.

[28] Reg. § 20.2043-1.

[29] Code Sec. 2036(b)(1). For an example of indirect retention of voting rights, see Rev. Rul. 80-346, 1980-2 CB 271.

[30] Code Sec. 2036(b)(2).

[31] Code Sec. 318.

children, grandchildren, and parents) is treated as being owned by the transferor. These rules can also apply to stock that is owned by (1) partnerships and estates, (2) trusts, and (3) corporations in which the transferor has an interest.

These rules preclude the use of a formerly popular planning device sanctioned by a 1972 U.S. Supreme Court decision that a decedent who made this type of transfer did not retain the right to enjoy the transferred stock by reason of his voting control over it, and that he did not retain the right to designate the persons who would enjoy the income from the stock (see ¶ 580) by reason of his ability to control corporate dividends.[32] The decedent retained the power to (1) vote the stock held by a trust, (2) veto the transfer by the trustee of any of the stock, and (3) remove the trustee and appoint another corporate trustee.

• *Transfers to Family Limited Partnerships*

A transfer to a family limited partnership may also be seen by the IRS as a means of retaining control over the transferred property sufficient to cause inclusion of its value in the transferor's gross estate. Court decisions that analyze the application of Code Sec. 2036 to family limited partnership (FLP) situations usually involve a highly fact-specific investigation of the FLP agreement, the rights and discretionary powers of the decedent under it, whether the formalities of the FLP agreement actually are being followed in the FLP's operation, and the extent to which the creation of the FLP was supported by consideration. Although properly structured and implemented FLP arrangements may allow a transferor to avoid estate tax liability on the value of the assets transferred to the FLP, the weight of recent judicial authority suggests that this result is increasingly difficult to obtain.

The decision of the Court of Appeals for the Fifth Circuit affirmed a Tax Court decision (*A. Strangi Est.*[33]), holding that the value of property transferred by a decedent to a family limited partnership (FLP) and to the FLP's corporate general partner (the corporation) was includible in the decedent's gross estate. Two months before his death, the decedent, assisted by his attorney in fact (who was also his son-in-law), created a FLP. The decedent transferred about $10 million to the FLP (mostly in cash and securities) in exchange for a 99-percent LP interest. Concurrent with the creation of the FLP, a corporation was formed to act as the FLP's managing general partner, with the decedent purchasing a 47-percent interest in the corporation for approximately $50,000. The decedent's attorney in fact was subsequently hired to manage the day-to-day business of the corporation. The Tax Court held that the decedent had retained a right to the income from the transferred property for purposes of Code Sec. 2036(a)(1) because the documents governing the operation of the FLP and the corporation did not preclude the decedent himself, acting through his attorney in fact, from being designated as a recipient of income from those entities. Moreover, the court concluded, the decedent retained the possession or enjoyment of the transferred property because of an implied agreement among the parties that the decedent would retain the economic benefit of the transferred property. The existence of this implied agreement was supported by the transfer of the majority of the decedent's assets, the decedent's continued occupation of his residence following

---

[32] *M.A. Byrum, Exrx. (M.C. Byrum Will)*, SCt, 72-2 USTC ¶ 12,859, 408 US 125.

[33] *A. Strangi Est.*, CA-5, 2005-2 USTC ¶ 60,506, 417 F3d 468, aff'g TC, 85 TCM 1331,

CCH Dec. 55,160(M), TC Memo. 2003-145, on remand from CA-5, 2002-2 USTC ¶ 60,441, 293 F3d 279. See, also, *M. Harper Est.*, 83 TCM 1641, CCH Dec. 54,745(M), TC Memo. 2002-21.

its transfer to the FLP, the use of entity funds to pay for the needs of the decedent and his estate, and the testamentary nature of the arrangements.

Additionally, the *Strangi* court held that the transferred property was includible in the decedent's gross estate because the decedent retained the right to designate the persons who would enjoy the transferred property.[34] The court noted that, under the FLP agreement and the corporation's shareholder agreement, the decedent could act with other shareholders to essentially revoke the FLP arrangement and thereby bring about the present enjoyment of the FLP assets. These, and other rights conferred under the FLP/corporation arrangement, were not constrained in any meaningful way by the fiduciary duties held by directors and shareholders. The Tax Court rejected the estate's argument that the creation and funding of the FLP were supported by consideration, viewing the arrangement as a mere "recycling" of value through the use of the FLP and corporate forms.

In another case, the Court of Appeals for the Third Circuit upheld a Tax Court decision holding that assets transferred by a decedent to two family limited partnerships (FLPs) were includible in the decedent's gross estate because the decedent retained the enjoyment of the property during lifetime.[35] The Tax Court had concluded that the decedent's failure to retain sufficient assets to support himself for the expected duration of his life, cash distributions from the FLPs to the decedent exceeding $170,000 over two years, and the general testamentary nature of the FLP arrangements were all factors pointing to an implied agreement that the decedent would retain the benefit of the transferred property. The appellate court agreed that the decedent's relationship with the transferred assets remained the same both before and after the contribution of the assets to the FLPs.

The appellate court in *Thompson* further held that the Code Sec. 2036(a) exception for adequate and full consideration did not apply. There was no transfer for consideration because neither FLP engaged in a functioning business enterprise that provided the decedent with a substantive, non-tax benefit for transferring the assets (mainly securities) to the FLPs. Instead, the only potential benefit to the decedent for holding the assets in partnership form was the estate tax savings to be garnered from valuation discounts. The Court distinguished the result reached in *Kimbell* (discussed below), where the FLP arrangement provided the transferor with centralized management and protection from personal liability.

An opinion of the Court of Appeals for the First Circuit in *I. Abraham Est.*, illustrates the fact that the IRS may successfully rely on surrounding facts and circumstances (rather than a written agreement) to establish that a decedent had retained rights in transferred FLP assets. Although the decedent in this case did not have a legally enforceable right to income from the FLPs in question, trial testimony, documentary evidence, and the understanding of the decedent's children and her legal representative established that the decedent was entitled to all of the FLP income required to satisfy her needs. Accordingly, the decedent retained the right to enjoy and use the property transferred to the FLPs within the meaning of Code Sec. 2036. Rejecting the estate's contention that the children had purchased remainder interests in the FLPs in bona fide sales, the appellate

[34] Code Sec. 2036(a)(2).

[35] *T. Thompson Est. (B. Turner, Exrx.)*, CA-3, 2004-2 USTC ¶60,489, 382 F3d 367, aff'g TC,

CCH Dec. 54,890(M), 84 TCM 374, TC Memo. 2002-346. Similarly, *Korby Est.*, CA-8, 2006-2 USTC ¶60,534, 471 F3d 848, and *V. Bigelow Est.*, 2007-2 USTC ¶60,548.

court pointed out evidence contradicting this characterization: (1) the estate had attempted to show at trial that the children purchased present fee interests; (2) the documents memorializing the transfers did not identify the sales as sales of remainder interests; and (3) the purchase price was calculated in reliance on minority and lack of marketability discounts and not the actuarial value of the remainder interests.[36]

The Tax Court decision in *W. Bongard Est.*[37] handed the IRS both a defeat and a victory. This decision is not only significant because it is a reviewed-by-the court decision, but also for its demonstration that there exists within the Tax Court considerable difference of opinion concerning the application of the legal standards of Code Sec. 2036 to the facts of an FLP situation. In *Bongard*, the court held that closely held company stock transferred by a decedent to a limited liability company (LLC) was not includible in his gross estate under Code Sec. 2036(a) because the transfer was a bona fide sale for adequate and full consideration. However, the LLC membership units transferred by the decedent to an FLP were includible in his gross estate because he retained the enjoyment of the property held by the FLP under an implied agreement between the parties involved.

The court concluded that the transfer of stock in the decedent's plastics manufacturing company to the LLC was part of an effort to raise capital necessary for the corporation to maintain competitive in its market. Thus, the acquisition of capital was a legitimate and significant nontax reason for creating the LLC. In other words, there was a legitimate business purpose for the transaction. There was no evidence that unrelated parties would have reached a different result with respect to the terms and conditions of the LLC agreement. The court concluded that the creation of the LLC was the result of an arm's length transaction, and the decedent and a trust that held shares in the family corporation each received an LLC interest that represented adequate and full consideration and their respective capital accounts were properly credited. Accordingly, the court held that the stock transferred to the LLC was not includible in the decedent's gross estate because the bona fide sale exception of Code Sec. 2036(a) was satisfied.

On the second issue, the Tax Court decided in *Bongard* that the value of the LLC units transferred to the FLP was includible in the decedent's gross estate. On this issue, the court determined that the estate had failed to establish that the transfer of the LLC units was motivated by a significant nontax reason. The court observed that the FLP never invested or diversified its assets following the decedent's contribution of the LLC units. Because the only benefit that the decedent received was in the form of transfer tax savings, the transfer to the FLP was not a bona fide sale for adequate and full consideration. The court further ruled that the decedent's practical control over the FLP evidenced an understanding among the parties involved that the decedent retained the right to control the LLC units transferred to the FLP.

Comment: Although nine Tax Court judges joined in the majority opinion in *Bongard*, the fact that seven other judges filed (or agreed with) separate opinions concurring or dissenting in part suggests that there is considerable differences in the court regarding how the relevant Code Sec. 2036 rules are to be applied to FLP factual situations. Judge Laro, in a concur-

---

[36] *I. Abraham Est.*, CA-1, 2005-1 USTC ¶60,502, aff'g TC, T.C. Memo. 2004-68, CCH Dec. 55,546(M).

[37] 124 TC 95, CCH Dec. 55,955.

ring opinion, rejected the majority opinion's "legitimate and significant business purpose" test, and stated that the adequate and full consideration exception should apply "only where the transferor's receipt of consideration is of a sufficient value to prevent the transfer from depleting the transferor's gross estate." Also writing a separate opinion, Judge Halpern believed that the majority had incorporated an "inappropriate motive test" into the bona fide sale exception. Dissenting in part, Judge Chiechi argued that the majority was wrong to hold that there was an implied agreement that allowed the decedent to retain enjoyment of the property in the FLP, citing the text of Code Sec. 2036(a)(1) and the Supreme Court's decision in *M. Byrum*.[38]

In *D. Kimbell, Sr., Exr.*, the Court of Appeals for the Fifth Circuit reached the opposite result, holding that assets transferred to a FLP were made pursuant to a bona fide sale for adequate and full consideration.[39] In *Kimbell*, the decedent created a revocable trust, with herself and her son designated as co-trustees. Several years later, but less than three months before her death, the decedent, her son and her daughter-in-law formed an LLC. The decedent's revocable trust contributed $20,000 to the LLC in exchange for a 50-percent interest. The decedent's son was the sole manager of the LLC. Later that month, the revocable trust and the LLC formed the FLP under Texas law. The revocable trust contributed approximately $2.5 million in various assets (including oil and gas working and royalty interests) to the FLP in exchange for a 99-percent LP interest. The LLC received a one-percent general partner interest in exchange for its $25,000 cash contribution. The appellate court vacated the district court's grant of summary judgment[40] for the government that the formation of the FLP was not the result of an arm's-length transaction and that the decedent's receipt of the LP interest was nothing more than a "circuitous recycling of value." Citing the Fifth Circuit's decision in *J. Wheeler*[41] as the only case on point, the court concluded that the transfer to the FLP was made for adequate and full consideration because: (1) the decedent received a partnership interest that was proportionate to the assets contributed; (2) the decedent's capital account was properly credited with the assets that she contributed; and (3) the decedent was entitled to a distribution commensurate with her capital account balance upon termination or dissolution of the FLP. The fact that the estate claimed a 49-percent discount in valuing the decedent's LP interest did not preclude a finding that the interest was adequate consideration for the transferred assets. This was so because the "willing buyer/ willing seller" test could not be equated with the full consideration test under Code Sec. 2036. The court further ruled that the estate had shown that the transfer of the FLP was a bona fide sale and not a disguised gift or sham transaction. This conclusion was supported by several objective facts, including: (1) the decedent retained sufficient assets outside of the FLP for her own support and did not commingle FLP and personal assets; (2) partnership formalities were observed and the contributed assets were actually assigned to the FLP; and (3) there were credible non-tax business reasons for the formation of the FLP, including centralized management and protection from personal liability.

In a Tax Court Memorandum decision (*E. Stone, III Est.*), none of the assets transferred to five family limited partnerships by a husband and wife was held

---

[38] 72-2 USTC ¶12,859, 408 U.S. 125.

[39] *D. Kimbell, Sr., Exr.*, CA-5, 2004-1 USTC ¶60,486.

[40] *D. Kimbell, Sr., Exr.*, DC Tex., 2003-1 USTC ¶60,455, rev'd by CA-5, 2004-1 USTC ¶60,486, 371 F3d 257.

[41] *J. Wheeler*, CA-5, 97-2 USTC ¶60,278, 116 F3d 749.

¶570

includible in their respective gross estates because the transfers were bona fide sales for adequate and full consideration under Code Sec. 2036(a).[42] The transfers did not constitute a mere "recycling of value," because the FLPs had economic substance and operated as joint enterprises for profit through the management of the couple's children. The transfers were motivated primarily by investment and business concerns relating to the management of the couple's assets. In addition, the couple retained assets outside of the FLPs sufficient to maintain their accustomed standard of living. Moreover, all of the partners in each of the FLPs received partnership interests proportionate to the value of the assets transferred to the FLPs and the transferred assets were properly credited to the partners' respective capital accounts.

The law concerning the includibility of FLP assets in a transferor's gross estate under Code Sec. 2036(a) will, undoubtedly, continue to develop in future judicial decisions. However, based on the court rulings above, a taxpayer contemplating the formation of a FLP that may be vulnerable to a Code Sec. 2036 attack should consider the following:

(1) Prior to a transfer of assets to the FLP, the transferor's advisors should do a careful cash flow analysis regarding the amount of assets that will be needed to maintain the transferor's lifestyle throughout his or her expected life span.

(2) Significant non-tax reasons for the transaction should be identified and closely documented.

(3) If avoidance of estate tax liability with respect to the arrangement depends on a finding of adequate and full consideration, competent independent valuation appraisals of all exchanged property and property interests should be obtained.

(4) The transferor's house should probably not be placed in a FLP.

(5) Estate taxes should not be paid from FLP assets, unless these assets are includible in the gross estate.

(6) All formalities of the partnership form should be respected. The partnership should be conducted as if it were a commercial entity.

(7) Probably not all of the assets in the FLP should be financial assets; at least some of the assets should require active management.

The IRS has ruled[43] that the fair market value of assets held at death in a decedent's restricted management account (RMA) were included in the decedent's gross estate under Code Sec. 2036(a). Such accounts have been marketed as alternatives to FLPs (see also ¶320).

• *Estate Freezes*

In 1987, Code Sec. 2036(c) was enacted in an attempt to prevent perceived valuation abuses involving a strategy known as an "estate freeze."[44] The "estate freeze" was an estate planning device whereby an older owner of a closely held business would retain an income interest in the company, usually preferred stock and certain liquidation rights, and transfer to younger members of the family an interest in the company, usually common stock, that was likely to appreciate in value. The value of the retained interests (for example, liquidation rights) could

---

[42] *E. Stone, III Est.*, 86 TCM 551, CCH Dec. 55,341(M), TC Memo. 2003-309.

[43] Rev. Rul. 2008-35, 2008-2 CB 116.

[44] Revenue Act of 1987 (P.L. 100-203), Act Sec. 10402, repealing Code Sec. 2036.

easily be inflated, thus lowering the value of the interest transferred and reducing the amount of the taxable gift. Under the provisions of Code Sec. 2036(c), the post-transfer appreciation in value of certain transferred property interests was includible in the transferor's gross estate.

Later, in 1990, Congress repealed Code Sec. 2036(c)[45] retroactive to its original effective date (December 17, 1987) and enacted the Chapter 14 special valuation rules, effective for transfers after October 8, 1990 (see ¶2500). The special valuation rules (Code Sec. 2701—2704) take a more direct approach by providing rules for valuing the transferred interest for gift tax purposes rather than focusing on the transferor's estate.

• *Dispositions of Life Estates and Remainder Interests*

On the theory that estate tax liability for a transfer with a retained life estate arises at the time of the transfer, the U.S. Court of Appeals for the Tenth Circuit has held that the subsequent sale of the retained life interest at its fair market value reduced only the value of the taxable property.[46] There still would be included in the gross estate of the transferor the value of the property less the purchase money paid for the life estate. Accordingly, under this reasoning, to remove the transferred property from her gross estate, the transferor must have received full and adequate consideration for the interest that would otherwise be included in her gross estate.

The U.S. Court of Appeals for the Tenth Circuit later limited this theory to transfers of property solely owned by the decedent.[47] Following the decision of the U.S. Court of Appeals for the Seventh Circuit,[48] the Tenth Circuit held that the transfer with retained life estates of jointly held property for which the decedent furnished the entire consideration (and which, therefore, would have been includible in his gross estate to the extent of its entire value if held at his death) required only the inclusion in decedent's gross estate of the value of his one-half interest in the property transferred. See ¶502 for tax treatment of "qualified joint interests" created or recreated after 1976.

With respect to the issue of valuing an interest for purposes of the bona fide sale exception, the U.S. Court of Appeals for the Federal Circuit has held that where a decedent sold a remainder interest in property and retained a life interest, the payment of the actuarial value of the remainder interest did not satisfy the exception. Thus, the value of the transferred interest was includible in the decedent's gross estate (offset by the amount of consideration received, as provided under Code Sec. 2043).[49] However, both the U.S. Court of Appeals for the Third Circuit[50] and the Court of Appeals for the Ninth Circuit[51] have held that the value of the transferred remainder interest is to be the measure of whether adequate and full consideration has been received. Thus, where it is

---

[45] Revenue Reconciliation Act of 1990 (P.L. 101-508), Act Secs. 11601 and 11602, repealing Code Sec. 2036(c) and adding Code Secs 2701-2704.

[46] C. Allen, Exr. (Allen Est.), CA-10, 61-2 USTC ¶12,032, 293 F2d 916, cert. denied, 368 US 944.

[47] E. Heasty, Exr. (King Est.), CA-10, 67-1 USTC ¶12,442, 370 F2d 525, aff'g DC Kan., 65-1 USTC ¶12,304, 239 FSupp. 345.

[48] H. Glaser, Jr., Admr., CA-7, 62-2 USTC ¶12,094, 306 F2d 57, aff'g and rev'g DC Ind., 61-2 USTC ¶12,031, 196 FSupp. 47.

[49] G.S. Gradow, CA-FC, 90-1 USTC ¶60,010, 897 F2d 516, aff'g ClsCt, 87-1 USTC ¶13,711, 11 ClsCt 808.

[50] R. D'Ambrosio Est., CA-3, 96-2 USTC ¶60,252, rev'g and rem'g TC, 105 TC 252, CCH Dec. 50,903, cert. denied 5/19/97. See also, J.M. Wheeler, CA-5, 97-2 USTC ¶60,278, 116 F3d 749, which noted that selling a remainder interest for its actuarial value does not deplete a seller's estate.

[51] C. Magnin Est., CA-9, 99-2 USTC ¶60,347, 184 F3d 1074, rev'g TC, 71 TCM 1856, CCH Dec. 51,127(M), TC Memo. 1996-92.

demonstrated that full price was paid for the remainder interest, no part of the value of the transferred property will be included in the transferor's gross estate because of his or her retained income interest.

• *Trust Reimbursement of Grantor's Income Tax Liability*

Where a grantor of a trust is deemed to be its owner under the rules of Code Secs. 671–679, trust income is taxed to the grantor, rather than to the trust. The IRS has issued estate tax guidance with respect to three factual situations where a grantor trust reimbursed the grantor for tax liability assessed on trust income. In the first situation ("Scenario One"), neither applicable state law nor the trust instrument contained any provision requiring or permitting the trustee to reimburse the grantor's income tax liability. Here, because the grantor did not retain the right to have trust property used to discharge the grantor's legal obligation to pay the income tax on trust income, no portion of the trust was includible in the grantor's gross estate under Code Sec. 2036. Under Scenario Two, the trust instrument required the trustee to reimburse the grantor for income tax incurred on trust income. Here, the IRS ruled, such a retained right caused the full value of the trust's assets to be includible in the grantor's gross estate. The result would be the same if state law required the trustee to reimburse the grantor, unless the trust instrument provided otherwise. The IRS will not apply the rule announced in Scenario Two to any decedent's estate with respect to any trust that was created prior to October 4, 2004. Under Scenario Three, the trust instrument gave the trustee the discretion to reimburse the grantor. The IRS concluded that this discretionary power (whether granted by the trust instrument or by state law), did not cause estate tax inclusion of the trust's assets, even if the trustee actually did reimburse the grantor for the income tax incurred. However, the trustee's discretionary power, coupled with other facts, such as an understanding between the grantor and the trustee regarding the trustee's exercise of the discretionary power, could cause inclusion of the trust assets in the grantor's gross estate under Code Sec. 2036.[52]

• *Pre-1931 and Pre-1932 Transfers*

Special exceptions exist in the case of transfers made before March 4, 1931. The exceptions concern any of the rights described above that were retained for life or for any period that does not in fact end before the decedent's death. Similar exceptions exist with respect to transfers made before June 7, 1932, under which the rights were retained for a period not ascertainable without reference to the decedent's death. Such pre-1931 and pre-1932 transfers are not includible in the estate of a decedent unless there is some other basis for taxability, such as the retention of other rights as well.

¶ 580   Right Retained to Designate Who Shall Possess or Enjoy

The retention of income, possession, use, or enjoyment of property requires inclusion of the value of the transferred property in the gross estate under Code Sec. 2036. A transfer also will be taxed under Code Sec. 2036 if a decedent reserved or retained the right, either alone or in conjunction with any other person or persons, to designate the persons who shall possess or enjoy the property or the income therefrom. The requirements as to the period for which such designated person retains such rights are the same as if the decedent retained those rights.[53]

---

[52] Rev. Rul. 2004-64, 2004-2 CB 7.   [53] Reg. § 20.2036-1(b).

If a grantor creates an irrevocable trust for the benefit of other persons and acts as trustee or co-trustee, and the trustees have the power to accumulate or distribute and add trust income to trust principal, the Supreme Court has held that the value of the trust property and the accumulated trust income will be included in the decedent's gross estate.[54] Each accumulation of income represents a taxable transfer. The grantor-trustee's power to deny the beneficiaries the immediate enjoyment of that income is a retention of the power to designate the persons who would enjoy the income.

The IRS has attempted to apply the rationale of this case to situations where the grantor-trustee has not directly retained the power to accumulate or distribute income but, instead, has retained only certain administrative and managerial powers over the trust. Frequently, these administrative powers are called "boiler-plate" powers. The two most common of the types of such powers causing trouble for estates are (1) the right to allocate receipts and disbursements between trust income and principal, and (2) the right to invest in "non-legal" investments. Most courts have held that the existence of these powers does not give the decedent the right to designate the persons who shall possess or enjoy the transferred property.[55] The common denominator that has led the courts to exclude these trusts has been the existence of state laws governing the duties of trustees toward income beneficiaries and remaindermen.

The IRS will include the value of irrevocable trusts in a grantor's gross estate where the trustee is given the power to accumulate or distribute income to beneficiaries and the grantor retains the right to appoint a successor trustee that includes himself.[56] The Tax Court has agreed in at least one case.[57] However, the Tax Court has refused to follow this rule in the case of a trust set up by a Texas resident who was legally incompetent at death.[58] The IRS will not include the value of the assets of such a trust in the grantor's gross estate where the grantor merely retains the right to appoint a successor corporate trustee that was not related or subordinate to the grantor after the original trustee has resigned or been removed by judicial process.[59]

The Tax Court has held that a corporate trustee's power to distribute income and principal was not attributable to the grantor simply because of the grantor's ability to remove and replace one corporate trustee with another corporate trustee, without cause. Noting that a trustee has a duty to display complete loyalty to the interests of the beneficiary, the court would not include the trust property in the grantor's estate without evidence of fraudulent collusion.[60] In another case, the U.S. Court of Appeals for the Eighth Circuit concluded that a decedent had not retained dominion and control over property that the decedent transferred to a trust by reason of his right to remove and replace trustees with successor trustees who were not related or subordinate to the decedent.[61] In view of these decisions, the IRS ruled that a grantor's reservation of an unqualified power to change corporate trustees will not result in the inclusion of the trust corpus in the grantor's gross estate.[62] The IRS has also privately ruled that an

---

[54] *C.E. O'Malley*, SCt, 66-1 USTC ¶ 12,388, 383 US 627.

[55] For example, see *R. Budd Est.*, 49 TC 468, CCH Dec. 28,841 (Acq.).

[56] Rev. Rul. 73-21, 1973-1 CB 405.

[57] *J.A. Alexander Est.*, 81 TC 757, CCH Dec. 40,554.

[58] *R.T. Reid Est.*, 71 TC 816, CCH Dec. 35,883.

[59] Rev. Rul. 77-182, 1977-1 CB 273, modified by Rev. Rul. 95-58, 1995-2 CB 191.

[60] *H.S. Wall Est.*, 101 TC 300, CCH Dec. 49,330.

[61] *J. Vak Est.*, CA-8, 92-2 USTC ¶ 60,110, rev'g and rem'g TC, 62 TCM 942, CCH Dec. 47,674(M), TC Memo. 1991-503.

[62] Rev. Rul. 95-58, 1995-2 CB 191.

income beneficiary's power to remove and replace a current trustee with a corporate trustee will not cause inclusion of the value of the trust in the beneficiary's gross estate.[63]

• *Pre-1931 and Pre-1932 Transfers*

Similarly, the same exceptions as to pre-1931 and pre-1932 transfers and the same means of escaping the tax by relinquishing rights exist (see ¶570). In addition, transfers made before June 7, 1932, are excepted if the decedent's right to govern enjoyment was reserved to the decedent in conjunction with any other person or persons. The courts, however, are not in agreement as to whether the transfer contemplated by the statute is limited to irrevocable transfers made prior to the above dates.

¶ 585 Revocable Transfers

Property transferred during lifetime is includible in the decedent's gross estate if, at the time of the decedent's death, the enjoyment of the property is subject to change through the exercise of a power to alter, amend, revoke, or terminate by the decedent alone or by the decedent in conjunction with another person. The retention of a power in conjunction with "any person" is not limited to nonbeneficiaries.

Taxation will result even though the only effect of the exercise of the decedent's power to revoke would have been to accelerate the enjoyment of principal by the beneficiaries.[64] No tax will result, however, if the power can be exercised only with the consent of all parties having an interest, vested or contingent, in the transferred property.[65]

• *Powers Resulting in Taxability*

The courts often have had to determine what is a power to alter, amend, revoke, or terminate. They have decided that the following powers result in taxability:

(1) power to revoke or terminate the trust, whether such power results in a return of corpus to the settlor or acceleration of enjoyment by the remaindermen;

(2) power to control and manage the corpus (except where such power is concerned only with mechanics or details—the designation of funds as income or principal, investment policy, the issuance of voting proxies, or other matters that do not alter the rights or interests of the beneficiaries);

(3) power to change beneficiaries or to vary the amounts distributable (except where the transfer was made prior to March 3, 1931, and the power is applicable only to income during the decedent's lifetime);

(4) power to appoint by will or to change shares by will;

(5) power to revoke that exists by virtue of state law;[66] and

(6) power to invade the corpus of a trust created by another for whose benefit the decedent created a similar trust.

---

[63] IRS Letter Ruling 9746007 (Aug. 11, 1997).

[64] *City Bank Farmers Trust Co.*, SCt, 36-1 USTC ¶9001, 296 US 85.

[65] Reg. §20.2038-1(a)(2).

[66] *S. Swanson Est.*, FedCl, 2000-1 USTC ¶60,371, 46 FedCl 388; aff'd, CA-FC, in an unpublished opinion, 2001-1 USTC ¶60,408; *O. Casey Est.*, CA-4, 91-2 USTC ¶60,091, 948 F2d 895, rev'g TC, 58 TCM 176, CCH Dec. 46,035(M), TC Memo. 1989-511.

If the powers involved are applicable only to a part of the trust, only that part is taxable.[67]

> *Comment:* The fact that the transferor will not benefit by exercise of the power is not important so long as the transferor can affect the interests of beneficiaries. This includes the power to distribute or accumulate trust income. Capital gains by the trust and additions to it traceable to the decedent have the same status as original corpus. Additions by a decedent to trusts created by others are governed by the decedent's right over the trusts even though the original corpus may not be taxable in his estate.

The IRS maintains that when a donor transfers property to a minor under a state Uniform Gifts to Minors Act, a Model Gifts of Securities to Minors Act, or a Uniform Transfers to Minors Act, and is acting as custodian of the custodial property at the date of death, the custodial property is includible in the custodian's gross estate.[68] This position has been uniformly sustained by the courts because a custodian has the right, under most uniform acts, to terminate the custodianship by paying over the income and principal to the minor beneficiaries at any time. If a parent transfers property and serves as custodian, the custodial property is also includible in the parent's gross estate, under Code Sec. 2036, because the parent can apply custodial funds in satisfaction of the legal obligation of support.[69] This rule has also been applied where the decedent and the decedent's spouse made reciprocal transfers to each other in custodianship for their parents.[70]

• Powers Not Resulting in Taxability

The courts have decided that the following do not constitute powers sufficient to cause taxability under Code Sec. 2038:

> (1) power in other than the grantor to revoke the transfer or to return part of it to the grantor (but such transfers may be taxed as transfers intended to take effect at death; see ¶ 565);

> (2) certain powers contingent on the happening of a certain event;

> (3) powers as to mechanics or details only, such as powers to direct issuance of voting proxies, to help determine investment policies, and to direct investment and reinvestment of funds;

> (4) power to add to corpus; and

> (5) power over trusts created by others with funds not derived from the decedent and not supported by similar trusts created by others.

If the decedent-transferor was unable to relinquish a power because of the existence of a mental disability for a continuous period beginning before October 1, 1947, and ending with death after August 16, 1954, the retained power to revoke or amend will not result in tax.

• Power to Substitute Assets

The IRS has ruled that if certain requirements are met a grantor retained power to acquire property from an irrevocable trust by substituting other prop-

---

[67] Reg. § 20.2038-1.

[68] Rev. Rul. 57-366, 1957-2 CB 618, and Rev. Rul. 70-348, 1970-2 CB 193.

[69] *H. Prudowsky Est.*, 55 TC 890, CCH Dec. 30,671, aff'd per curiam, CA-7, 72-2 USTC ¶ 12,870, 465 F2d 62.

[70] *Exchange Bank and Trust Co. of Florida*, CA-FC, 82-2 USTC ¶ 13,505, aff'g ClsCt, 82-1 USTC ¶ 13,444, 694 F2d 1261.

erty of equivalent value will not cause the inclusion of the trust corpus in the grantor's gross estate under Code Sec. 2036 or Code Sec. 2038. In Rev. Rul. 2008-22,[71] the grantor established and funded an inter vivos irrevocable trust for the benefit of his descendants and retained a non-fiduciary power to substitute trust assets. The trust documents required the grantor to substitute property of equivalent value to the trust property and also prohibited the grantor from serving as trustee.

The IRS contrasted the result in Rev. Rul. 2008-22 to that of the Tax Court decision in *A. Jordahl Est.*,[72] where the grantor retained the power to substitute trust assets but also served as a trustee. The Tax Court held that the grantor's fiduciary duties prevented him from exercising the substitution power to deplete the trust or shift benefits among beneficiaries. The IRS determined in Rev. Rul. 2008-22 that a nonfiduciary substitution power alone would not cause the trust corpus to be includible in the grantor's gross estate, provided that certain limitations and requirements are placed on the trustee through local law or the trust instrument. The IRS concluded that a trustee must have a fiduciary obligation to ensure that the properties acquired through substitution are equal in value. In addition, the IRS stated that either: (1) the trustee must have the power to reinvest the trust corpus and a duty of impartiality that would ensure that the substitution power is not being used to shift benefits among beneficiaries; or (2) it must be apparent that the nature of the trust's investments or the level of income produced by the trust does not impact the respective interests of the beneficiaries. In this example, local law imposed a fiduciary duty of the trustee that would ensure that the exchanged property was equal in value. Further, local law gave the trustee the ability to reinvest assets and required a duty of impartiality with regard to the beneficiaries.

• *Split-Gift Election*

Code Sec. 2038 contemplates a transfer by the decedent of the decedent's own property before death. Thus, individually owned securities transferred by the husband of a decedent to himself as custodian for his minor daughter under the Uniform Gifts to Minors Act and held by the decedent as successor custodian at the time of her death were not includible in the decedent's gross estate for estate tax purposes even though a split-gift election was made under Code Sec. 2513 and the decedent was considered a donor of half the value of the securities for gift tax purposes.[73]

¶ 590   Exercisability of Power

If the retained power comes within the scope of Code Sec. 2038, it is taxable whether exercisable by the decedent as trustee or as transferor, alone,[74] or in conjunction with trustees or outsiders. The transfer is taxable so long as any beneficiary, vested or contingent, is excluded from the group that, with the transferor, can exercise any of the powers.[75]

If the transfer was made on or before June 22, 1936, the value of an interest in property is not includible in the transferor's gross estate unless the power to

---

[71] Rev. Rul. 2008-22, IRB 2008-16, 796.

[72] CCH Dec. 33,462, 65 TC 92.

[73] Rev. Rul. 74-556, 1974-2 CB 300.

[74] See *S.A. Levin Est.*, 90 TC 723, CCH Dec. 44,706, holding that the retained power need

not be exercisable by the decedent in his individual capacity; the ability to exercise it as a member of the board of directors of a company in which he held the controlling interest made it taxable.

[75] Reg. § 20.2038-1(a)(2).

alter, amend, revoke, or terminate was reserved at the time of transfer.[76] A power that is acquired by the decedent from the trustees by being appointed as a trustee some time after the transfer and not under provisions in the instrument of transfer will not result in taxability.

¶ 595   Relinquishment of Powers Within Three Years of Death

A retained power to alter, amend, revoke, or terminate a property interest that is relinquished after 1976 and within three years of the death of the holder of the power will require that the value of the property be included in the holder's gross estate.[77] However, effective for decedents dying after August 5, 1997, a transfer of property from a revocable trust within three years of the transfer of such property to the trust will not be included in the decedent's gross estate.[78] Under prior law, the U.S. Court of Appeals for the Eighth Circuit had held that irrevocable fractional interests in the corpus of a revocable trust that were assigned by a decedent to her children within three years of death were not includible in the decedent's gross estate. The fractional interests portions of the trust functioned in the same way as if the decedent had withdrawn the fractions from the initial revocable trust and transferred them to a new irrevocable trust.[79]

¶ 600   Reciprocal Transfers

Estate taxation cannot be avoided through the use of reciprocal transfers whereby two taxpayers make transfers in trust to each other of similar economic rights under substantially identical terms. Thus, two persons cannot escape the estate tax by giving the other a right that would have resulted in an estate tax if the transferor had retained it for himself[80] (see ¶ 170). The U.S. Court of Appeals for the Sixth Circuit has held, however, that if the fiduciary powers provided to each transferee do not rise to the level of a retained economic benefit, then the value of the trusts is not included in the transferors' gross estates.[81]

¶ 605   Valuation Date

Property transferred by the decedent during life but included in the decedent's gross estate must be valued as of the date of the decedent's death or, if the alternate valuation date is chosen, in accordance with Code Sec. 2032 rules (see ¶ 105). If only a portion of the property is so transferred as to come within the terms of the statute, a corresponding proportion of the value of the property is included in the value of the gross estate. Because Code Sec. 2036 and Code Sec. 2038 overlap, the IRS will apply the Code section that results in the greatest amount being included in the gross estate.[82]

> *Preparation Tip:* If the transferee makes additions or enhancements to the property, the enhanced value of the property at the valuation date due to such additions or enhancements is not includible in the transferor's gross estate. Because the additions were not made by the decedent, they are not deemed to be part of the transferred property. When only a portion of the value of the property is includible, the value of the whole must still be

---

[76] Reg. § 20.2038-1(c).

[77] Code Sec. 2035.

[78] Code Sec. 2035(e), as amended by P.L. 105-34.

[79] *E. Kisling Est.,* CA-8, 94-2 USTC ¶ 60,176, rev'g and rem'g TC, 65 TCM 2956, CCH Dec. 49,097(M), TC Memo. 1993-262 (Acq.) (*H. McNeely,* CA-8, 94-1 USTC ¶ 60,155, followed).

[80] *J.P. Grace Est.,* SCt, 69-1 USTC ¶ 12,609, 395 US 316.

[81] *J. Green Est.,* CA-6, 95-2 USTC ¶ 60,216, 68 F3d 151, aff'g unreported decision.

[82] *H.B. Joy, Jr., Exr.,* CA-6, 69-1 USTC ¶ 12,570, 403 F2d 419, aff'g DC Mich., 67-2 USTC ¶ 12,482, 272 FSupp. 544.

disclosed on Schedule G (Transfers During Decedent's Life) of Form 706 (United States Estate (and Generation-Skipping Transfer) Tax Return) (Rev. August 2013) under the column headed "Description," together with an explanation of the proportionate inclusion.[83]

¶ 610   Transfers for Consideration

The value of property transferred by a decedent during life for adequate and full consideration is not includible in the decedent's gross estate. To constitute an exchange or sale for adequate and full consideration in money or money's worth, the exchange or sale must have been made in good faith. The price must have been an adequate and full equivalent and reducible to a money value. Transfers of property during lifetime made within three years of death (in the case of a decedent dying before 1982) or with rights retained (Code Sec. 2035 through Code Sec. 2038) and otherwise taxable powers of appointment (Code Sec. 2041) for less than full and adequate consideration are includible in the transferor's gross estate to the extent of the excess of the fair market value of the property (as of the valuation date) over the price or value of consideration received by the decedent.[84] The adequacy of the consideration received for a transfer is determined as of the date of the transfer and not at a later date, such as the date of the transferor's death.

For estate tax purposes (except for determining deductibility of claims against the estate (see ¶ 800), the relinquishment or promised relinquishment of dower, curtesy, a statutory estate created in lieu of dower or curtesy, or other marital rights in the decedent's property or estate is not consideration in money or money's worth.[85]

A release of support rights, pursuant to a divorce decree, is consideration to the extent of the value of the rights as determined on a case-by-case basis.[86] The IRS has ruled, in a National Office Technical Advice Memorandum, that a decedent's gross estate included the value of farmland transferred by him to his children pursuant to a property settlement agreement because the decedent had retained a life estate in the property and the transfer was not made for adequate consideration. The transfer of the remainder interest in the property to the children was deemed not to have been a part of the release of the decedent's obligation to support his minor children since the divorce decree already provided for child support payments that adequately satisfied the children's need for support. Accordingly, the IRS concluded that the transfer was not made for consideration, but, rather, was based on the decedent's donative intent.[87]

Whether the consideration paid by a decedent to his father in conjunction with the father's transfer of stock into a trust naming the decedent as life beneficiary constituted a transfer with a retained life estate was decided by the U.S. Court of Appeals for the Sixth Circuit.[88] A payment made by a son in 1941 to his father in exchange for shares of stock, which were, thereafter, used to fund a trust for the benefit of the son for life and his wife and children after his death, constituted a purchase by the son of an undivided interest in approximately 11

---

[83] Instructions for Form 706 (Rev. August 2013), p. 28.

[84] Code Sec. 2043.

[85] Code Sec. 2043(b).

[86] Rev. Rul. 68-379, 1968-2 CB 414, Rev. Rul. 60-160, 1960-1 CB 374, and Rev. Rul.

80-82, 1980-1 CB 209; *J.H. Scholl Est.*, 88 TC 1265, CCH Dec. 43,918.

[87] IRS Technical Advice Memorandum 8526003 (no date given).

[88] *D.J. Mahoney, Jr., Exr.*, CA-6, 87-2 USTC ¶ 13,737, 831 F2d 641, rev'g DC Ohio, 86-1 USTC ¶ 13,653, cert. denied, 6-13-88.

percent of the value of the trust assets. Accordingly, the appellate court concluded that 11 percent of the value of the trust assets on the date of the son's death was includible in his gross estate as property transferred by him during his life subject to his retained life estate.

In determining, for estate tax purposes, whether the decedent received, in exchange for property transferred, property approximately equal to it in value, the transactions he made in the years just before his death are particularly subject to scrutiny. Agreements whereby the decedent has transferred property to another in return for a promise to support and care for the decedent have been found to be supported by adequate and full consideration.[89]

¶ 615   Valuation and Description on Return

Reportable lifetime transfers are, for the most part, listed on one special schedule, Schedule G (Transfers During Decedent's Life) of Form 706 (United States Estate (and Generation-Skipping Transfer) Tax Return) (Rev. August 2013), without regard to the kind of property transferred. Lifetime transfers of real property and certain lifetime transfers of insurance are reportable under this schedule, even though there are other schedules that are specifically concerned with the kind of property transferred. The other schedules are largely confined to property interests owned by the decedent at the time of death. Although various lifetime transfers are all reportable on Schedule G, the principles governing valuation and description of the transferred property are the same as those of the other schedules.

Copies of Form 709 (United States Gift (and Generation-Skipping Transfer) Tax Return) relating to the lifetime transfers should be attached to Schedule G of Form 706. In addition, gift taxes paid on transfers made within three years of death are to be reported on the schedule (see ¶ 555).

¶ 625   Instruments Evidencing Transfers

If a transfer, by trust or otherwise, was made by a written instrument, a copy must be filed with the return. If the instrument is of public record, the copy should be certified; if not of record, the copy should be verified. The name of the transferee, date and form of the transfer, and a complete description of the property should be set forth in this schedule. Rents and other income must be included.

---

[89] *S.A. Bergan Est.*, 1 TC 543, CCH Dec. 12,954 (Acq.).

Chapter 15

POWERS OF APPOINTMENT

¶ 650   Powers of Appointment

The value of all property over which a decedent possessed a general power of appointment at death is includible in the decedent's gross estate.[1] The term "power of appointment" refers to a power given to the possessor by another, rather than to a power that has been created and retained by the same person. It authorizes the possessor of the power to control, with certain limitations, the ultimate disposition of the property subject to the power. The person who receives the power is usually referred to as the donee of the power.

Under some kinds of powers, the donee has almost as much authority over property as an owner of such property would have. Therefore, the creation of such a power of appointment could, in the absence of special tax treatment, afford an easy means of preventing the application of estate taxes to the estate of the donee—taxes that would be fully applicable if the property were the donee's own or had been given to the donee in fee. Code Sec. 2041 provides specifically for the taxing of property subject to powers of appointment, the provisions being based largely on how nearly the power given to the donee resembles complete ownership of the property.

Only powers defined as "general powers of appointment" result in taxability, except in certain very special cases. Basically, for tax purposes, a "general power of appointment" is one that can be exercised by the donee in favor of the donee, the donee's estate, or the creditors of the donee or the donee's estate.[2] State law is applied in determining whether the decedent has a "general power of appointment."

"Power of appointment" is defined, for estate tax purposes, to include all powers that are in substance and effect powers of appointment, regardless of the wording used in creating the power and regardless of local property law connotations. Thus, a power in a life tenant to appropriate or consume the principal of a trust may be a power of appointment.

Preparation Tip: All property over which a decedent possessed a power of appointment must be reported on Schedule H (Powers of Appointment) of Form 706 (United States Estate (and Generation-Skipping Transfer) Tax Return) (Rev. August 2013). If Schedule H is filed, certified or verified copies of the instrument granting the power and of any instrument by which the power was exercised or released must be attached to the schedule. All powers of appointment must be reported even if the estate

---

[1] Code Sec. 2041.   [2] Reg. § 20.2041-1(c).

contends that property subject to a particular power is not includible in the gross estate.[3]

¶ 652   General Powers of Appointment

Only powers defined as *general* powers of appointment can result in estate or gift tax liability. A "general power of appointment" is defined as "a power which is exercisable in favor of the decedent, his estate, his creditors, or the creditors of his estate."[4] However, there are exceptions, and a general power of appointment does *not* include:

(1) a power to consume, invade, or appropriate property for the benefit of the decedent, which is limited by an ascertainable standard relating to the health, education, support, or maintenance of the decedent;

(2) a power created on or before October 21, 1942, which is exercisable by the decedent only in conjunction with another person; and

(3) a power created after October 21, 1942, which is exercisable by the decedent only in conjunction with the creator of the power, or with a person having a substantial interest in the property, subject to the power, where this interest is adverse to the exercise of the power in the decedent's favor. If the power may be exercised both in favor of the decedent and of the persons whose consent the decedent must have, the power is general to the extent of the decedent's fractional interest in it.

A power of appointment created by will is, in general, considered as created on the date of the testator's death.[5] A power created by an instrument effective during the life of the creator is considered as created on the date the instrument takes effect. This is so even though at that time the power may not be exercisable, may be revocable, or the identity of the holder may not be ascertainable. If the holder of a power exercises it by creating a second power, the second power is considered as created at the time of the exercise of the first. Generally, property subject to a general power of appointment is includible in a decedent's gross estate even if at the time of death the decedent was an adjudicated incompetent, at least in the absence of a showing that the adjudication of incompetency barred exercise of the power by any person in any capacity.[6] Similarly, it has been held that property subject to a general power of appointment was includible in the decedent's gross estate even though the decedent, as a minor, was precluded by state law from exercising the power.[7]

Even if a power of appointment is not limited by an ascertainable standard (see ¶ 653), the power will not be a general power for estate tax purposes unless it is in existence at the death of the decedent. Thus, a decedent's power to invade trust corpus for her "comfort and happiness" (which does not qualify as an ascertainable standard) was determined to be not in existence at her death where the power would become effective only if a spendthrift clause of the trust were triggered, an event that did not occur.[8]

---

[3] Instructions for Form 706 (Rev. August 2013), p. 29.

[4] Reg. § 20.2041-1(c).

[5] Reg. § 20.2041-1(e).

[6] Rev. Rul. 75-350, 1975-2 CB 366; *W.R. Boeving*, CA-8, 81-2 USTC ¶ 13,415; *A.L. Gilchrist Est.*, CA-5, 80-2 USTC ¶ 13,378, 630 F2d 340; *F. Alperstein Est.*, CA-2, 80-1 USTC

¶ 13,326, 613 F2d 1213, cert. denied, 446 US 918; *Pennsylvania Bank and Trust Co., Exr.*, CA-3, 79-1 USTC ¶ 13,299, 597 F2d 382, cert. denied, 444 US 980; and IRS Technical Advice Memorandum 9344004 (July 13, 1993).

[7] *N.E. Rosenblatt Est.*, CA-10, 80-2 USTC ¶ 13,374, 633 F2d 176.

[8] IRS Technical Advice Memorandum 200847015, July 30, 2008.

It should be noted that the general power of appointment under Code Sec. 2041 is not necessarily equivalent to a power of appointment often given to a decedent's surviving spouse in connection with a life estate. The IRS has ruled that property that passed to a trust for the benefit of a decedent's surviving spouse did not qualify for a marital deduction, even though the spouse received a life estate in the trust corpus and a power to appoint the trust corpus to herself or her creditors, because the trustee could prevent the spouse from exercising the power. Thus, for marital deduction purposes, the power was not exercisable "alone and in all events." However, because the trustee did not have a substantial interest in the trust adverse to that of the spouse, the value of the trust corpus was includible in the spouse's gross estate as property subject to a general power of appointment.[9]

¶ 653   Powers Limited by Ascertainable Standard

A power to consume, invade, or appropriate income and corpus for the donee's benefit is not a taxable general power if the power is limited by an ascertainable standard relating to the health, education, support, or maintenance of the decedent.[10] In short, the holder's duty regarding use of the power must be reasonably measurable in terms of the holder's needs for health, education, or support—or any combination of them.

The words "support" and "maintenance" are considered synonymous. Their meaning is not limited to the bare necessities of life. For example, a power of appointment will be regarded as limited by the necessary standard if it is exercisable for the holder's (1) support, (2) support in reasonable comfort, (3) maintenance in health and reasonable comfort, (4) support in the holder's accustomed manner of living, (5) education, including college and professional education, (6) health, or (7) medical, dental, hospital, and nursing expenses.

However, a power to use property for the comfort, welfare, or happiness of the holder of the power generally will not meet the required ascertainable standard for invasion. However, under Illinois law, the word "comfort" was deemed to be an ascertainable standard that refers to maintaining someone in the station of life to which the person has become accustomed.[11] In determining the existence of an ascertainable standard, it is immaterial that the trust agreement may or may not require the beneficiary first to exhaust other income.[12]

Generally, the extent of a decedent's interest is governed by state law.[13] The U.S. Court of Appeals for the Tenth Circuit has held that a decedent's power to invade the corpus of a trust for her benefit "in case of emergency or illness" was not a general power of appointment, under New Mexico law, because its exercise was limited by an ascertainable standard. Accordingly, the court held that the value of the trust corpus was not includible in the decedent's gross estate.[14] The IRS has ruled in a National Office Technical Advice Memorandum that the power of a co-trustee and life beneficiary to invade trust corpus if the trust income was not sufficient for the comfort, support, and education of the beneficiary and her children was not a general power under state law. Because the Missouri statute

---

[9] Rev. Rul. 82-156, 1982-2 CB 216.

[10] Reg. § 20.2041-1(c)(2).

[11] *V.J. Strauss Est.*, 69 TCM 2825, CCH Dec. 50,680(M), TC Memo. 1995-248.

[12] Reg. § 20.2041-1(c).

[13] But see IRS Technical Advice Memorandum 8339004 (June 14, 1983) (state supreme court decision not followed because the state court proceeding was not adversarial and, based on applicable case law and an analysis of the words used in the invasion clause, the decedent's power of appointment was general).

[14] *I.M. Sowell Est.*, CA-10, 83-1 USTC ¶ 13,526, 708 F2d 1564.

prohibited the trustee from exercising any power to distribute corpus to herself, regardless of whether or not the power was limited by an ascertainable standard, the power was not a general power.[15]

The U.S. Court of Appeals for the Sixth Circuit has held similarly that a decedent who was trustee and life beneficiary of a trust did not have a general power of appointment over the trust because her "right to encroach" on the corpus was limited by an ascertainable standard under Tennessee law.[16] However, the U.S. Court of Appeals for the Seventh Circuit has held that a decedent who was the trustee and one of the beneficiaries of a trust established under the terms of her predeceased husband's will held a general power of appointment over the trust corpus because she was authorized to use so much of the principal as she deemed appropriate for her maintenance and support. Language giving the decedent the right to use the property "for whatever purpose she desires" was found by the court to negate any ascertainable standard under Wisconsin law.[17]

¶ 655　Taxable Powers Created After October 21, 1942

A general power created after October 21, 1942, and held by the donee will result in taxability of the subject property in the donee's gross estate, if the power is held until death, whether or not the donee exercises it by will. The exercise or release of the power during the donee's lifetime will be deemed a transfer for gift tax purposes.[18]

Estate tax liability will also result if the exercise or release was effected under circumstances that would have resulted in tax under Code Sec. 2035 through Code Sec. 2038 if the property had been the decedent's own.[19]

• *Release, Lapse, and Disclaimer of Powers*

Release of a power of appointment created after October 21, 1942, will result in taxation just as completely as would an exercise of the power by will or possession at death of an unexercised power. A release of a power need not be formal or express in character. Failure to exercise a power of appointment within a specified time, so that the power lapses, is considered a release of the power.[20]

However, a lapse of the power in any calendar year during the decedent's life is considered a release for estate tax purposes only to the extent that the property over which the power existed exceeded the greater of $5,000 or five percent of the value, at the time of the lapse, of the assets out of which the exercise could have been satisfied.

Example: In 2013, Jim Dorsey transferred $200,000 worth of securities in trust with provision for payment of income to his son, George, for life and the remainder to George's issue. George was also given a right to withdraw $15,000 a year from the trust fund (which neither increased nor decreased in value prior to George's death). The right is noncumulative, so that George can never withdraw more than $15,000 in any one year, even if he fails to withdraw the full amount in a preceding year.

[15] IRS Technical Advice Memorandum 200014002 (Nov. 29, 1999).

[16] *P.W. Finlay, Exr.*, CA-6, 85-1 USTC ¶ 13,604, 752 F2d 246.

[17] *Independence Bank Waukesha, N.A.*, CA-7, 85-1 USTC ¶ 13,613, 761 F2d 442. See also IRS Technical Advice Memorandum 8601003

(Sept. 20, 1985) (decedent's right to invade the trust corpus for "any special need" that might arise was a general power of appointment).

[18] Code Sec. 2514(b).

[19] Code Sec. 2041(a)(2).

[20] Code Sec. 2041(b)(2).

The failure to exercise his power of withdrawal in any single calendar year is considered a release to the extent that $15,000 exceeds 5% of the trust fund. Assuming that George fails to exercise his power of withdrawal for 2013, $5,000 ($15,000 – $10,000) is deemed to be a taxable transfer to the trust from George with a retained right to income. (The $5,000 stays in the trust fund of which George is life income beneficiary.) The remaining $10,000 is not considered a release because it falls within the 5% rule. The taxable proportion created by the release in 2013 at death is $1/40$ ($5,000 ÷ $200,000) of the value of the trust corpus on the date of death (or alternate valuation date). If the value of the trust principal remained at $200,000 at George's death, $5,000 ($1/40 × $200,000) would be included in his gross estate.

If the failure to exercise a power, such as a right of withdrawal, occurs in more than a single year, the proportion of the property over which the power lapsed, which is to be treated as a taxable disposition, must be determined separately for each year. Thus, in the Example above, if George had failed to exercise the power of withdrawal in three separate calendar years, $15,000 would be included in his gross estate, assuming the value of the corpus subject to the power remained at $200,000. The aggregate of the taxable proportions for all years is includible in the holder's gross estate, limited only by the aggregate value of the assets out of which an exercise of the power could have been satisfied on the applicable valuation date.[21] In addition, if in the year of death, the power has not been exercised and has not lapsed, the entire amount for which the power may be exercised is includible in the decedent's gross estate.

A widow's unexercised right, during the statutory period, to take against her husband's estate does not constitute an unexercised general power of appointment within the meaning of Code Sec. 2041 because the failure to assert the inchoate right constitutes a complete and effective disclaimer or renunciation of a power of appointment by operation of law.[22]

A restriction of a trustee-beneficiary's fiduciary power by operation of state law will not be deemed to cause a lapse of a general power under Code Sec. 2514.[23]

• Post-1976 Disclaimers

A post-1976 "qualified disclaimer" of a general power of appointment is not a release of the power and does not constitute a taxable gift. A "qualified disclaimer" is based on federal, rather than state, requirements[24] (see ¶2009 for details).

• Pre-1977 Disclaimers

A pre-1977 disclaimer or renunciation of a general power of appointment is not considered to be a release of the power.[25] In the absence of facts to the contrary, the failure to renounce or disclaim a power within a reasonable time after learning of its existence will be presumed to constitute an acceptance of the power. A disclaimer or renunciation of a power that is unequivocal and meets the requirements of local law will not result in a taxable gift.

---

[21] Reg. § 20.2041-3(d)(5).
[22] Rev. Rul. 74-492, 1974-2 CB 298.
[23] Rev. Proc. 94-44, 1994-2 CB 683.

[24] Code Sec. 2046 and Code Sec. 2518.
[25] Reg. § 20.2041-3(d)(6).

• *Creation of New Power*

If a donee by will or by a lifetime transfer exercises a power of appointment (general or special) created after October 21, 1942, by creating another power, taxability will result. The property subject to the power will be included in the original donee's estate if, under local law, the power can be exercised to postpone the vesting of any estate or interest in such property, or suspend the absolute ownership or power of alienation of such property, for a period ascertainable without regard to the date of the creation of the first power.[26]

• *Avoidance of Tax*

A donee of a power of appointment does have some measure of control over whether the property subject to a general power will be included in the donee's gross estate at death. The donee may renounce or disclaim the power when it first comes to the donee's attention. If the donee follows either of these courses, the action will not create either estate or gift tax liability. The requirements for a federal "qualified disclaimer" are described at ¶ 2009.

A donee may escape estate tax liability by releasing or by exercising the power during life, only if the donee does not reserve rights that would cause a transfer of the donee's own property during life to be included in the gross estate. Generally, a release or exercise within three years of death will not result in inclusion of the property subject to the power in the decedent's gross estate in the case of decedents dying after 1981. When the donee seeks to keep the property out of the donee's own estate other than by a renunciation or disclaimer, the donee must consider the application of the gift tax law (see ¶ 2163) to his or her actions.[27]

¶ 665   Powers Created Before October 22, 1942

As to powers created on or before October 21, 1942, only general powers that are exercised can result in tax.[28] Under no circumstances is it necessary for the donee of the power to release it to keep it out of the estate.

If the donee does not exercise a pre-October 22, 1942 general power, and whether the donee exercises a limited or special power, no tax will result, except in one special case discussed below. Under a corresponding provision of the gift tax law (Code Sec. 2514), a complete release of a pre-October 22, 1942, general power will not result in gift tax liability or generation-skipping transfer tax consequences.[29]

If a general power of appointment created on or before October 21, 1942, is partially released so that it no longer is a general power of appointment, under certain circumstances the subsequent exercise of the power is not deemed to be the exercise of a general power of appointment. However, such partial release must have been made:

(1) before November 1, 1951; or

(2) if, on October 21, 1942, the donee of such power was under a legal disability to release the power, then within six months after the termination of such legal disability.[30]

---

[26] Reg. § 20.2041-3(e).

[27] Code Sec. 2514.

[28] Code Sec. 2041(a).

[29] IRS Letter Ruling 9732034 (May 15, 1997).

[30] Code Sec. 2041(a).

¶ 670   Instruments Granting Power

If the decedent at any time possessed a power of appointment, a certified or verified copy of the instrument granting the power, together with a certified or verified copy of any instrument by which the power was exercised or released, must be filed with the return. These copies must be filed even though the executor feels that the power is not a general power of appointment or that the property is not otherwise includible in the gross estate.[31]

---

[31] Instructions for Form 706 (Rev. August 2013), p. 29.

Chapter 16
ANNUITIES

¶ 700   General Requirements

Subject to certain limited exceptions (see ¶735, ¶737, and ¶739), all or a portion of an annuity or other payment receivable by any beneficiary by reason of surviving the decedent is includible in a decedent's gross estate.[1] The annuity or other payment is not taxable under the annuity rules unless it is payable under a contract or agreement and the following four factors exist:

(1) The contract or agreement is not a policy of insurance on the life of the decedent.

(2) The contract or agreement was entered into after March 3, 1931.

(3) The annuity or other payment is receivable by the beneficiary by reason of the beneficiary's having survived the decedent.

(4) Under the contract or agreement—

(a) an annuity or other payment was payable to the decedent, either alone or in conjunction with another, for the decedent's life or for any period not ascertainable without reference to the decedent's death or for any period that did not in fact end before the decedent's death, *or*

(b) the decedent possessed the right to receive the annuity or other payment, either alone or in conjunction with another, for the decedent's life or for any period not ascertainable without reference to the decedent's death or for any period that did not in fact end before the decedent's death.

The amount to be included in the gross estate is the value at the decedent's death of the annuity or other payment receivable by the survivor. It is immaterial whether the annuity or other payment to the survivor is payable in a lump sum or in installments. If payable in installments, it is immaterial whether the installments are in the same amount as, or in a greater or lesser amount than, the annuity or payments to the decedent.

---

[1] Code Sec. 2039(a); Reg. § 20.2039-1.

Annuities may be includible under other provisions of the Internal Revenue Code. For example, if an annuitant retained the right to have any payments due after the annuitant's death paid to the annuitant's estate or to persons whom the annuitant might subsequently designate, the amounts payable could be included as property in which the annuitant had an interest at the time of death.[2] They could also be treated as transfers in which the annuitant had reserved the power to alter, amend, or revoke.[3] The relinquishment of an annuitant's additional rights within three years of death would cause inclusion in the annuitant's gross estate.

¶ 710   "Annuity" Defined

The term "annuity" includes periodic payments for a specified period of time. The following are examples of contracts (but not necessarily the only forms of contracts) for payments that constitute annuities or other payments for the purpose of inclusion in Schedule I (Annuities) of Form 706 (United States Estate (and Generation-Skipping Transfer) Tax Return) (Rev. August 2013):[4]

(1) A contract under which the decedent immediately before death was receiving or was entitled to receive, for the duration of the decedent's life, an annuity, or other stipulated payments that were to continue after the decedent's death to a designated, surviving beneficiary.

(2) A contract under which the decedent immediately before death was receiving or was entitled to receive, together with another person for their joint lives, an annuity or other stipulated payment to continue to the survivor following the death of either.

(3) A contract or agreement entered into by the decedent and the decedent's employer. Under the contract the decedent immediately before death and following retirement was receiving, or was entitled to receive, an annuity or other stipulated payment. Payments to the decedent were for the duration of the decedent's life. Thereafter, payments were to a designated beneficiary, if the beneficiary survived the decedent. (It is immaterial whether the payments after the decedent's death are fixed by the contract or subject to an option or election exercised or exercisable by the decedent.)

(4) A contract or agreement entered into by the decedent and the decedent's employer. At the decedent's death, prior to retirement or prior to the expiration of a stated period of time, an annuity or other payment was payable to a designated surviving beneficiary.

(5) A contract or agreement under which the decedent immediately before death was receiving or was entitled to receive an annuity or other payment for a stated period of time, with the annuity or other payment to continue to a designated, surviving beneficiary on the decedent's death prior to the expiration of such period.

¶ 715   Types of Payments Involved

In determining whether amounts payable under an annuity contract following the death of a primary annuitant are taxable under Code Sec. 2039, the exact method of payment following death is seldom important. It does not matter whether the payments that accrue following death are to be in the nature of:

(1) a continuing annuity to another person or persons;

---

[2] Code Sec. 2033.   [4] Reg. § 20.2039-1(b).
[3] Code Sec. 2038.

(2) a periodic payment (whether fixed in number, duration, or total amount);

(3) a lump sum based on the difference between the cost of the annuity and the total payments to the primary beneficiary; or

(4) a lump sum fixed in amount without regard to how much the primary annuitant received during the annuitant's lifetime.

The tests for includibility revolve around the rights of the primary annuitant. In addition to the annuitant's right to an annuity, the question of who paid for the annuity is important. The value of the benefits payable after the death of the primary annuitant will, however, vary with the nature of the payments.

Preparation Tip: Sometimes there are payments due that accrued to the primary annuitant before the annuitant's death. These payments generally become payable to the decedent's estate and are automatically included in the gross estate as property in which the decedent had an interest at the time of death. They are reported as miscellaneous property on Schedule F (Other Miscellaneous Property Not Reportable Under Any Other Schedule) of Form 706 (United States Estate (and Generation-Skipping Transfer) Tax Return) (Rev. August 2013).

¶720 Primary Annuities Purchased by Decedent as Annuitant

Proceeds of an annuity contract payable after the death of the purchaser and primary annuitant are includible in the annuitant's gross estate for estate tax purposes. They are includible whether they are paid to the estate or to a named beneficiary. It is immaterial whether they represent payments due to the primary annuitant or payments due only after the annuitant's death. An annuity purchased by a deceased primary annuitant before March 4, 1931, is excludable from a decedent's gross estate under Code Sec. 2039.

• Partial Payments by Others

If the primary annuitant did not pay the entire purchase price of the annuity, that part of the value of amounts payable after the primary annuitant's death that is attributable to the part of the price paid by persons other than the primary annuitant may be excluded from the primary annuitant's gross estate.[5]

• Death Before First Payment

Even if the primary annuitant did not receive any payments under the annuity contract because of death prior to the date when the first payment was to be made, the payments after the annuitant's death are taxable. They are taxable to the same extent as if the annuitant had lived to receive the first payment. The amount payable after the annuitant's death is includible in the gross estate in the proportion in which the annuitant provided the purchase price for the annuities.

• Partial Payment by Employer

The portion (if any) of the purchase price paid by an employer or former employer, under a "nonqualified" benefit plan, is deemed to have been paid by the primary annuitant if made by reason of employment.[6] This results whether the employer made the payment directly or through an employee's trust or fund forming part of a pension, annuity, retirement, bonus, or profit-sharing plan. Totally voluntary payments made by a company to its employee's widow were

---

[5] Reg. § 20.2039-1(c).

[6] Reg. § 20.2039-1(c).

not taxable as annuities because they were not payable to the employee during the employee's lifetime[7] (see ¶733).

See ¶735 and ¶737 for a discussion of the includibility of annuities payable under a qualified plan or trust, Keogh plan, or an individual retirement account.

¶725   Annuities Not Purchased by Decedent

The annuity provisions of Code Sec. 2039 do not apply to annuities treated as having been purchased by someone other than the primary annuitant. Nor do they apply to portions of annuities purchased by another where the decedent, as primary annuitant, did pay a part of the purchase price. Such annuities, or parts of annuities, are governed by other provisions in the estate tax law.[8]

The taxability of any after-death payments under annuities, or portions of annuities, deemed purchased by persons other than the decedent depends on the rights that the primary annuitant possesses (in addition to the right to receive an annuity for life). If the primary annuitant has no rights beyond the mere right to receive an annuity, any interest in the annuity contract or other property from which the payments stemmed ceases with the annuitant's death. Nothing remains to be taxed in the gross estate.

If any payments are to be made to the annuitant's estate after the annuitant's death, or to persons whom the annuitant names, these payments may be included in the annuitant's gross estate as property in which the annuitant had an interest at the time of death,[9] or as property over which the annuitant had a power of appointment.[10]

¶730   Service Members Survivorship Annuities

Effective for decedents dying after December 31, 1984, the exclusion for the value of annuities receivable by a surviving spouse or certain child beneficiaries under the Retired Serviceman's Family Protection Plan or the Survivor Benefit Plan is repealed.[11] However, the repeal does not affect a decedent whose benefit was in pay status on December 31, 1984, and who, prior to July 18, 1984, made an irrevocable election to designate the form of the benefit distribution.[12]

¶733   Employees' Death Benefits

Many employers pay surviving spouses of employees sums of money that are commonly called death benefits. Such death benefits may be paid by reason of a contract with the employee or they may be paid by reason of a formal or informal company policy or plan, often on a case-by-case basis. The following comments apply to payments under "nonqualified" plans.

The inclusion of death benefits in the estates of deceased employees, as annuities, is dependent upon the terms of the particular employment contract or plan. Therefore, it is difficult to distill any general rules of law from court cases, which often seem contradictory despite the existence of common provisions in these plans or agreements. Here are a few examples of how the courts have ruled in these cases:

(1) Death benefits paid to a surviving spouse of an active employee were not includible in the employee's gross estate, as an annuity, where the

---

[7] *W.E. Barr Est.,* 40 TC 227, CCH Dec. 26,103 (Acq.).

[8] Reg. § 20.2039-1(a).

[9] Code Sec. 2033.

[10] Code Sec. 2041.

[11] Code Sec. 2039(c), prior to repeal by the Tax Reform Act of 1984 (P.L. 98-369).

[12] Act Sec. 525(a), P.L. 98-369.

employment contract provided for the payment of a salary and the death benefit, but did not provide for any retirement benefits.[13]

(2) Where the employment contract provided for annual payments for a period of 15 years starting with the employee's retirement or termination of employment and for the payment of these benefits to named beneficiaries if the employee died, the payments made to the beneficiaries were includible in the employee's gross estate where he died while employed by the company.[14] The payments were to continue so long as the decedent did not engage in certain acts that were detrimental to the operations of the company—a standard feature in many such contracts.

(3) Two courts have reached opposite conclusions concerning the inclusion of death benefits that were paid under employment contracts that provided for (a) the employment of the decedent at a fixed salary, (b) the payment of a salary to a decedent who had become disabled or ill, and (c) payments to the employees' surviving spouses after their death. (The terms of the contracts were slightly different, but both contained essentially the same standard provisions that are included in contracts of this type.) The U.S. Court of Claims (now, U.S. Court of Federal Claims) held that the "death benefit" paid to the surviving spouse was not included in the employee's gross estate because he had died before retirement.[15] A U.S. district court, on the other hand, held that the death benefit was includible in an active employee's gross estate.[16]

(4) Payments made under nonqualified employees' plans have been included in the gross estates of deceased employees where the death benefits were vested or automatically payable to the beneficiaries at the employee's death. This rule has been applied in the case of a retired employee receiving a pension[17] and in the case of an employee who was not retired.[18] If the employee has more than one type of plan, the provisions of all the plans have been examined to determine whether an annuity is payable to a beneficiary at the decedent's death.[19] The U.S. Court of Appeals for the Second Circuit has held that a survivorship annuity payable to beneficiaries only if the decedent became totally disabled during employment was too dissimilar from a true annuity and too contingent to be aggregated with other plans covering the decedent for purposes of determining whether an annuity was payable to a beneficiary at death.[20] However, a U.S. district court in Georgia construed the same plans considered by the Second Circuit and concluded that the annuity payable to a decedent's beneficiaries was includible in the decedent's gross estate because the decedent had the right during his life to receive an annuity in the event that he became totally disabled.[21]

[13] *F.D. Fusz Est.*, 46 TC 214, CCH Dec. 27,944 (Acq.).

[14] *E.H. Wadewitz Est.*, CA-7, 65-1 USTC ¶12,277, 339 F2d 980, aff'g TC, 39 TC 925, CCH Dec. 26,015.

[15] *C. Kramer, Exrx.*, CtCls, 69-1 USTC ¶12,585, 406 F2d 1363.

[16] *J.C. Silberman, Exr.*, DC Pa., 71-2 USTC ¶12,814, 333 FSupp. 1120.

[17] *H.C. Beal Est.*, 47 TC 269, CCH Dec. 28,204 (Acq.).

[18] *J.W. Bahen Est.*, CtCls, 62-2 USTC ¶12,091, 305 F2d 827.

[19] *J.W. Bahen Est.*, CtCls, 62-2 USTC ¶12,091, 305 F2d 827; *J. Gray, Exr.*, CA-3, 69-1 USTC ¶12,604, 410 F2d 1094.

[20] *W.V. Schelberg Est.*, CA-2, 79-2 USTC ¶13,321, 612 F2d 25. See also *G.J. Van Wye Est.*, CA-6, 82-2 USTC ¶13,485, 686 F2d 425.

[21] *J.B. Looney, Admrx.*, DC Ga., 83-2 USTC ¶13,538, 569 FSupp. 1569. Although the government prevailed in *Looney*, it moved to vacate the judgment of the district court when the estate appealed to CA-11, and this motion was granted on Jan. 24, 1984.

(5) Death benefits that were paid to the surviving spouse of an active employee were excludable from the employee's gross estate where the benefits were paid only after a company investigation into the circumstances of the employee's family and only with the approval of the board of directors.[22]

(6) The payment of death benefit annuities to the spouses (or other dependents) of police officers and firefighters who died in the line of duty were not includible in the decedents' gross estates as annuities under Code Sec. 2039 because such payments were made under New York State and New York City Municipal codes to provide for the dependents of such decedents, rather than being made pursuant to a contract or agreement arising from the decedents' employment. Moreover, the decedents possessed no right to receive any annuity payments during life. In addition, according to the IRS, such annuities were not includible under Code Sec. 2033 because decedents possessed no property or ownership rights in these death benefits. (However, any amounts paid to a deceased police officer or firefighter that represented a return of his or her contributions to a New York City qualified pension plan were includible as property owned at death under the general tests for inclusion discussed at ¶155.)[23]

The IRS also has attempted to include death benefits under nonqualified plans or agreements as property owned at death under Code Sec. 2033 (see ¶535), as transfers with the right to govern enjoyment under Code Sec. 2036, as transfers taking effect at death under Code Sec. 2037, and as revocable transfers under Code Sec. 2038. The Tax Court and the U.S. Court of Appeals for the Second Circuit sustained the inclusion of death benefits as a transfer taking effect at death.[24] Three courts have ruled that death benefits paid pursuant to employment contracts are not includible in the gross estates of deceased employees as a revocable transfer or a transfer with the right to govern enjoyment.[25] However, the Tax Court has ruled that a post-mortem annuity payable to the surviving spouse of a decedent, the chairman of the board of directors and controlling shareholder of a closely held corporation, was includible in his gross estate as a revocable transfer.[26]

The amount includible in a deceased employee's estate is usually the present value of the payments to the beneficiary.

¶735   Annuities from Qualified Employees' Benefit Plans

Effective with respect to decedents dying after December 31, 1984, to the extent that retirement benefits payable under qualified plans fall within the annuity inclusion rules discussed at ¶700, such benefits are generally includible in a decedent's gross estate. For decedents dying before this date, a $100,000 estate tax exclusion had been available for certain retirement benefits payable under qualified plans, tax-sheltered annuities, individual retirement arrangements (¶737), and certain military retirement plans (see ¶730).[27]

---

[22] *W.E. Barr Est.*, 40 TC 227, CCH Dec. 26,103 (Acq.).

[23] Rev. Rul. 2002-39, 2002-2 CB 33.

[24] *H. Fried Est.*, CA-2, 71-2 USTC ¶12,796, 445 F2d 979, aff'g TC, 54 TC 805, CCH Dec. 30,065, cert. denied, 404 US 1016.

[25] *C. Kramer, Exrx.*, CtCls, 69-1 USTC ¶12,585, 406 F2d 1363; *L.D. Hinze*, DC Cal., 72-1 USTC ¶12,842; *J.N. Harris*, DC Cal., 72-1 USTC ¶12,845.

[26] *S.A. Levin Est.*, 90 TC 723, CCH Dec. 44,706.

[27] Code Sec. 2039(c), prior to repeal by P.L. 98-369.

The rights that can bring about inclusion of all or a portion of the fund from which the annuity stems are the same rights that would result in taxability of other interests. For example, a tax will result if the decedent is found to have a power of appointment that would require inclusion in the estate of any other property. The fact that the decedent had an annuity rather than some other type of interest does not influence the result.

If the decedent created the trust, the retention of an annuity from the trust will result in the inclusion of the value of the balance of the trust in the decedent's gross estate. Exceptions exist for certain instances if the trust was created before March 4, 1931 (see ¶570).

If a person creates an annuity interest in a trust that is to continue after the person's death, the fact that an annuity is created is of concern only if the remainder of the trust is deductible as a charitable interest or if the remainder, but not the annuity, is includible in the gross estate. In such instances, the value of the annuity must be determined before the amount of either the charitable deduction or the taxable remainder may be established (see ¶1122).

¶760 Valuation

The value of benefits under an annuity contract is determined as of the date of death of the primary annuitant. If the estate is valued under the alternate valuation method (see ¶105), the value of these benefits is little affected. Any lower value six months after the date of death is attributable to mere lapse of time.[36] The benefits paid out during the six months cannot be excluded from the evaluation.

Only that part of the value of the annuity or other payment receivable by the surviving beneficiary that the decedent's contribution to the purchase price of the contract or agreement bears to the total purchase price is actually includible in the gross estate.[37]

• Lump-Sum Payments

If the benefits are payable in a lump sum, the amount payable is the value.

• Installment Payments

When the benefits are payable in installments—whether payable for a fixed period, payable in a fixed number, or payable for the life of the beneficiary—the valuation must be made on a commuted basis.

• Insurance Company Contract

If the payments are made under a contract issued by an insurance company, the value of a continuing annuity to the survivor is to be based on the cost of an annuity of a similar amount at the time of the decedent's death.

• Fixed Payments

If the payments to the survivor are fixed in duration or amount, it is likely that they will be valued as an annuity for a term certain under the tables provided pursuant to Code Sec. 7520 (IRS Publications 1457 and 1458; see ¶530).

---

[36] *J.A. Hance Est.,* 18 TC 499, CCH Dec. 19,025 (Acq.).

[37] Reg. §20.2039-1(c).

• *Comparable Contract Method*

If the annuity is purchased by the decedent solely for the benefit of another but is includible in the decedent's gross estate, the value will be based strictly on the cost of a comparable contract at the time of the decedent's death. If the annuity is payable from a trust or from any other source, except under a commercial annuity contract, the value is determined by applying factors obtained from tables in Publications 1457 and 1458.

• *Lottery Payments*

The value of a decedent's interests in lottery payments will be includible in the gross estate for estate tax purposes. However, the method by which the interests would be valued is subject to debate and there is now a split at the appellate court level on the question. According to a district court in California and the U.S. Court of Appeals for the Ninth Circuit, the decedent's interest would not be valued as a commercial annuity under Reg. § 20.2031-8, and departure from the private annuity Reg. § 20.2031-7 tables would be warranted if the tables produced substantially unrealistic and unreasonable results.[38] Similarly, applying the rationale of the *Shackleford* decision, the U.S. Court of Appeals for the Second Circuit reversed the Tax Court and held that, although future lottery payments constituted an annuity within the meaning of Code Sec. 7520, departure from the valuation tables provided thereunder was justified in order to account for transferability restrictions placed on the winnings under applicable state (Connecticut) law.[39]

The U.S. Court of Appeals for the Fifth Circuit specifically declined to apply the holdings in *Shackleford* and *Gribauskas* to a recent case involving the valuation of a decedent's right to receive 19 annual payments of lottery winnings. In *Cook*,[40] the Fifth Circuit held that the annuity tables of Code Sec. 7520 provided the proper method for valuing the payments because the lottery prize fell within the definition of a private annuity. The court ruled that the use of the tables did not create an unrealistic or unreasonable valuation result because a marketability discount (which the decedent's estate had claimed) was not properly applied to lottery winnings. According to the court, the nonmarketability of a private annuity was an assumption underlying the annuity tables. It would be unreasonable to apply a marketability discount to the winnings, the court added, because the interest being valued was not a capital asset, but a right, independent of market forces, to receive a stated sum of money annually for a specified term. The court noted that other kinds of private annuities, such as survivor annuities payable under qualified plans and charitable remainder annuity trusts, were valued under the tables despite being nonmarketable. A dissent in *Cook* would have applied the holdings of the *Shackleford* and *Gribauskas* decisions.

Following the decision in *G. Cook Est.*, the U.S. Court of Appeals for the Sixth Circuit also concluded that the estate tax valuation of future lottery payment by the use of the IRS annuity tables did not produce an "unrealistic and unreasonable result".[41]

---

[38] *T. Shackleford Est.*, DC Cal., 98-2 USTC ¶ 60,320; 99-2 USTC ¶ 60,356, aff'd CA-9, 2001-2 USTC ¶ 60,417, 262 F3d 1028.

[39] *P. Gribauskas Est.*, CA-2, 2003-2 USTC ¶ 60,466, 343 F3d 85, rev'g and rem'g TC, 116 TC 142, CCH Dec. 54,267.

[40] *G. Cook Est.*, CA-5, 2003-2 USTC ¶ 60,471, 349 F3d 850.

[41] *C. Negron, Exrx.*, CA-6, 2009-1 USTC ¶ 60,571, Rev'g, DC Ohio, 2007-1 USTC ¶ 60,541, 502 FSupp 2d 682.

Adopting the rationale of *G. Cook Est.*, above, U.S. district courts in Massachusetts[42] and New Hampshire[43] held that lottery payments were to be valued by using the annuity tables.

• *Structured Settlements*

A decedent's right to receive payments from nontransferable private annuities obtained in settlement of an injury claim was valued for estate tax purposes using the Code Sec. 7520 annuity tables. Relying on the *G. Cook Est.* decision (2003-2 USTC ¶60,471) and Reg. §20.7520-3(b)(1)(ii), the U.S. Court of Appeals for the Fifth Circuit held that the annuities were appropriately valued using the annuity tables because the annuities' nonmarketability did not disprove a fundamental assumption underlying the tables.[44]

¶ 770   Description on Return

The description of an annuity on Schedule I (Annuities) of Form 706 (United States Estate (and Generation-Skipping Transfer) Tax Return) (Rev. August 2013) must include the name and address of the grantor. If the annuity was payable out of a trust or other fund, the description of the annuity must identify the payment and the trust. A description of an annuity payable for a term of years must include the duration of the term and the date on which it began. If the annuity is payable for the life of a person other than the decedent, the date of birth of that person should be given.

If the annuity is under a qualified plan, the ratio of the decedent's contribution to the total purchase price of the annuity must be reported. Similarly, the ratio of the amount paid for an annuity under an individual retirement account, annuity, or bond that was not allowable as an income tax deduction under Code Sec. 219 (other than a rollover contribution) to the total amount paid for such account, annuity or bond must also be given.[45]

---

[42] *J. Donovan, Jr. Est.*, DC Mass., 2005-1 USTC ¶60,500.

[43] *M. Davis, Exrx*, DC N.H., 2007-1 USTC ¶60,542, 491 FSupp2d 192.

[44] *T. Anthony, Admx.*, CA-5, 2008-1 USTC ¶60,558, 349 F3d 850.

[45] Instructions for Form 706 (Rev. August. 2013), p. 30.

Chapter 17

QTIP PROPERTY FROM PRIOR ESTATE

¶773   Property Received Under Marital Deduction Rules

Property for which a marital deduction was allowed in the estate of a decedent dying after 1981 is includible in the surviving spouse's gross estate if the property is qualified terminable interest property (QTIP) (discussed at ¶1002)[1] and if the surviving spouse does not transfer the property during lifetime. The amount included in the gross estate of the surviving spouse is its fair market value on the date of death or alternate valuation date, if elected.

The main focus of litigation involving Code Sec. 2044 has been whether a particular interest is QTIP. The U.S. Court of Appeals for the Fifth Circuit, for example, has held that certain property interests the decedent received from his predeceased wife for which he elected QTIP treatment were includible in his gross estate despite the fact that neither the will nor state law expressly prohibited income accumulation. The court determined that the manifest intent of the will was not to accumulate income and, thus, the interest was QTIP.[2] In addition, the U.S. Court of Appeals for the Eleventh Circuit has held that a testamentary QTIP trust that did not entitle the surviving spouse to receive or appoint the trust income accumulating between the date of last distribution and the date of the surviving spouse's death (so-called stub income) was nonetheless QTIP. As such, the value of the interest at death was included in the surviving spouse's gross estate pursuant to Code Sec. 2044.[3]

QTIP property includible in a spouse's gross estate is considered as property passing from the spouse for estate and generation-skipping transfer tax purposes. Accordingly, such property may qualify for a marital deduction if it passes to the decedent's spouse, assuming that the spouse has remarried. Additionally, such property may qualify for a charitable deduction if it passes to a charitable organization. The basis of QTIP property acquired from a deceased spouse is its fair market value on the date of the spouse's death.[4]

In construing Code Sec. 2044, the courts will apply a duty of consistency. Thus, for example, the Tax Court has held that the value of QTIP property that passed to a decedent from her predeceased husband was includible in her estate, even though the predeceased husband's estate had not made a QTIP election for the property but had claimed a marital deduction for it.[5] According to the court, the duty of consistency required inclusion in the decedent's estate because (1) the husband's estate made a factual representation in one year, (2) the IRS relied on that fact in that year, and (3) the earlier year was closed by the statute of

---

[1] Code Sec. 2044; Reg. §20.2044-1.

[2] *H.R. Cavenaugh Est.,* CA-5, 95-1 USTC ¶60,195, aff'g in part and rev'g in part TC, 100 TC 407, CCH Dec. 49,030; IRS Letter Ruling 8028765 (Sept. 18, 1980).

[3] *L.P. Shelfer Est.,* CA-11, 96-2 USTC ¶60,238, rev'g TC, 103 TC 10, CCH Dec. 49,967.

[4] Code Sec. 2044(c).

[5] *M. Letts Est.,* 109 TC 290, CCH Dec. 52,368, aff'd, CA-11, 2000-1 USTC ¶60,374, in an unpublished per curiam opinion.

limitations and the decedent's estate attempted to change the earlier factual representations.

• Right of Recovery for Estate Tax

Additional estate tax liability attributable to taxation of the QTIP in the recipient spouse's gross estate is to be borne by the person or persons receiving the property unless the recipient spouse indicates in a will or revocable trust an intent to waive any right of recovery by specifically referring to Code Sec. 2044, Code Sec. 2207A, the QTIP, or the QTIP trust.[6]

• Successive QTIP Elections

A donor's transfer of property to an irrevocable trust that established a qualified income interest for the donor's spouse and a successive qualified income interest for the donor if she survived the donee spouse, for which a qualified terminal interest property (QTIP) election was made for gift tax purposes, qualified for the gift tax marital deduction. Under such circumstances, the trust property would not be included in the estate of the donor if she predeceased the donee, but would be included in the donee's gross estate. However, if the donee predeceased the donor and the donee's executor elected QTIP treatment for all or a part of the trust property, such property would qualify for the QTIP marital deduction in the donee's estate and would be includible in the gross estate of the donor upon the donor's subsequent death. If the donee died first and no QTIP election was made by the donee's estate, the trust property would be includible in the estate of the donee, and excluded from the estate of the donor.[7]

• Unnecessary QTIP Elections

The IRS has issued a procedure (Rev. Proc. 2001-38) under which it will treat unnecessary QTIP elections as null and void for purposes of Code Sec. 2044. A QTIP election will be deemed to be unnecessary if it is not needed to reduce the estate tax liability to zero. For example, this rule will apply where a QTIP election was made, even though the taxable estate (before the allowance of the marital deduction) was less than the applicable exclusion amount. It will also apply to a situation where QTIP elections were made for both the marital and the "credit shelter" trusts created by a decedent's estate plan where no estate tax would have been imposed regardless of whether an election was made for the credit shelter trust.[8]

A taxpayer will be required to produce sufficient evidence to establish that a particular QTIP election comes within the scope of this IRS procedure. For example, a taxpayer may produce a copy of the predeceased spouse's estate tax return to show that the election was not necessary to reduce the estate tax liability to zero. The rule is effective as of June 4, 2001, and applies to elections qualifying under the procedure, regardless of when made.

The IRS has privately ruled that the relief provisions of Rev. Proc. 2001-38 are not available where the trustee of a decedent's trust was attempting to revoke in part (rather than to totally revoke) a QTIP election that had previously been made. (A total revocation of the election would not have served the interests of

---

[6] Code Sec. 2207A.

[7] IRS Letter Ruling 9437032, June 20, 1994.

[8] Rev. Proc. 2001-38, 2001-1 CB 1335.

the trust because it would not have reduced the decedent's estate tax liability to zero.)[9]

> *Preparation Tip:* If QTIP property from a prior estate (Code Sec. 2044 property) is includible in a decedent's gross estate, this fact is to be indicated by answering "yes" to question 7, Part 4, on page 2 of Form 706 (United States Estate (and Generation-Skipping Transfer) Tax Return) (Rev. August 2013). The property is to be reported on Schedule F (Other Miscellaneous Property Not Reportable Under Any Other Schedule).[10] Question 17 on page 3 of Form 706, part 4, requires the executor to identify whether the decedent was the beneficiary of a QTIP trust for which a deduction was claimed by the predeceased spouse's estate and that is not otherwise reported on the decedent's Form 706.

---

[9] IRS Letter Ruling 200219003 (Feb. 5, 2002).

[10] Form 706 (Rev. August 2013), Schedule F, p. 14. An example of a filled-in Form 706, Schedule F, for a decedent dying in 2013, is reproduced at ¶3000.

DEDUCTIONS

Chapter 18

FUNERAL AND ADMINISTRATION EXPENSES

¶ 780 Deductions Allowed

A deduction from the value of the gross estate is allowed for funeral and administration expenses allowable under the laws of the jurisdiction in which the estate is being administered. The deduction is allowable even if the jurisdiction is outside the United States.[1]

Deductions are allowable both for expenses incurred in administering property subject to claims and for expenses incurred in administering property *not* subject to claims. See ¶ 805 for the allowance of deductions where the amount of deductions exceeds the value of property subject to claims. Property not subject to claims must be included in the gross estate of the decedent, and the expenses must be paid within three years after the estate tax return is filed.

> *Preparation Tip:* In the estate tax return, funeral expenses and the expenses incurred in administering property subject to claims are reported on Schedule J (Funeral Expenses and Expenses Incurred in Administering Property Subject to Claims) of Form 706 (United States Estate (and Generation-Skipping Transfer) Tax Return) (Rev. August 2013). Expenses incurred in administering property not subject to claims are deducted on Schedule L (Net Losses During Administration and Expenses Incurred in Administering Property Not Subject to Claims) of Form 706.

If expenses are not currently deductible because they are subject to an unresolved controversy at the time when the estate tax return is due, Schedule PC (Protective Claim for Refund) should be filed (see ¶ 804).

Amounts allowable as expenses under Code Sec. 2053 or as losses under Code Sec. 2054 for federal estate tax purposes may not again be allowed as deductions in computing the taxable income of the decedent's estate. This rule also applies to trusts or any other person who might benefit from the expense, claim, or loss item incurred. To secure a deduction for income tax purposes, a waiver of the right to claim the deductions for estate tax purposes must be filed (see ¶ 797).[2]

¶ 783 Trustees' Commissions

Trustees' commissions, if deductible, generally should be considered with expenses incurred in administering property not subject to claims. This is proper

---

[1] Code Sec. 2053(a); Reg. § 20.2053-1(a)(1)(i).

[2] Code Sec. 642(g); Reg. § 20.2053-1(e).

tax treatment whether the commissions are received by the executor acting as trustee or by a separate trustee.[3]

¶ 785   Funeral Expenses

Deductible funeral expenses are those amounts actually expended by the executor or administrator. Under the laws of the local jurisdiction, expenses must be payable out of the decedent's estate.[4]

Included among the expenses deductible under this classification are reasonable expenditures for a tombstone, monument, or mausoleum, or for a burial lot (whether for the decedent or the decedent's family). These expenses must be allowable under local law. Also included as a funeral expense is the cost of transportation incurred by a person who brings the decedent's body to the place of burial. Amounts paid for perpetual care of a cemetery lot or mausoleum are deductible if allowable under local law.

If a decedent dies a resident of a state in which the spouse is responsible for the payment of funeral expenses, in the absence of contrary instructions in the decedent's will, funeral expenses are not deductible.[5] The deduction must be reduced by Social Security and Veterans Administration death benefits.[6] The funeral expense deduction must be reduced by any reimbursement that is received for such expenses under a state's wrongful death statute or by the reasonable value of such a claim filed for such expenses.[7]

> *Preparation Tip:* In community property states, the extent of deductibility depends on whether the funeral expenses are deemed to be an expense of the community estate or of the decedent's estate. If they are an expense of the community estate, only one-half the amount expended is deductible. If the expenses are allowable against the estate of the decedent, they are deductible to the extent so allowable (see ¶ 795).

¶ 790   Administration Expenses

To be deductible, administration expenses must be actually and necessarily incurred in the administration of the estate. They include those expenses incurred in (1) collection of assets, (2) payment of debt, and (3) distribution among the persons entitled to share in the estate. These expenses, in turn, include executor's commissions, attorneys' fees, and miscellaneous expenses.[8]

Administration expenses incurred for the individual benefit of the heirs, legatees, or devisees are never deductible. To be deductible, expenses must be incurred in connection with the transfer of estate property to the beneficiaries or to a trustee. Therefore, the expenses incurred in obtaining from the probate court the award of a support allowance for the widow during administration of the estate are not deductible.[9]

See ¶ 803 for a discussion of protective claims for administrative expenses.

As to community property estates, see ¶ 795.

---

[3] Reg. § 20.2053-3(b).
[4] Reg. § 20.2053-2.
[5] Rev. Rul. 76-369, 1976-2 CB 281.
[6] Rev. Rul. 66-234, 1966-2 CB 436.
[7] Rev. Rul. 77-274, 1977-2 CB 326.
[8] Reg. § 20.2053-3(a).
[9] *W.A. Landers Est.*, 38 TC 828, CCH Dec. 25,650.

¶785

¶791   Executors' Commissions

Executors' and administrators' commissions are deductible in the amount actually paid or in an amount that, at the time the return is filed, is reasonably expected to be paid.[10] It is best that the fee be fixed by decree of the proper court. In the event that it has not been so fixed, the deduction will be allowed on the final audit of the return if:

(1) the District Director is reasonably satisfied that the commissions claimed actually will be paid;

(2) the amount claimed as a deduction is within the amount allowable by the laws of the jurisdiction in which the estate is being administered; and

(3) it is customary in that jurisdiction to allow such an amount in estates of similar size and character.

If the executors' commissions have not been paid at the time of the final audit of the return, the amount claimed as a deduction must be supported with an affidavit or statement signed under the penalty of perjury that the amount has been agreed on and will be paid. If the deduction is not allowed in full at the time of the final audit, the amount disallowed may be later modified on the basis of subsequent events. If the deduction is allowed in full but actual commissions are less than the amount allowed, the difference should be reported. Any resulting increase in the tax should be paid, together with interest.

See ¶803 for a discussion of protective claims for executors' commissions.

If the decedent, by will, fixes the compensation payable to the estate representative, that amount is deductible. It must not exceed the compensation allowable by local law or practice, however. If the will provides that the executor should receive a bequest or devise in lieu of commissions, no deduction is available for the amount of the bequest or devise.

Although the term "executors' commissions" may be taken to include administrators' commissions, it does not include trustees' commissions, even if received by an executor or administrator as trustee. Principal commissions paid with respect to trust property included in the gross estate are deductible as expenses in connection with property not subject to claims.

As to community property estates, see ¶795.

¶792   Attorneys' Fees

Attorneys' fees are deductible, at the time the return is filed, to the extent that they have been actually paid or to the extent that it is reasonably expected that they will be paid. If, when the return is finally audited, the fees claimed have not been awarded by the proper courts and paid, they still may be allowed. It must be shown to the satisfaction of the IRS that the amount claimed will be paid and that it is reasonable for the services rendered.[11] Where circumstances warrant, a protective claim for unpaid attorneys' fees may be filed (see ¶803).

If the fees claimed have not been paid at the time of the final audit of the return, the amount deducted must be supported by an affidavit, or statement signed under penalties of perjury, of the executor or the attorney stating that such amount has been agreed on and will be paid. Even if part of the amount claimed is disallowed on final audit, subsequent adjustment may be made if

---

[10] Reg. § 20.2053-3(b). [11] Reg. § 20.2053-3(c).

warranted by the facts.[12] Deductible fees are those incurred for services that benefit the estate. Fees incurred by beneficiaries incident to litigation with regard to their interest are not deductible unless the litigation is essential to the proper settlement of the estate.[13]

The return, itself, can reflect only fees of which there is some knowledge at the time of preparation and filing. If there should later be litigation or other action requiring services of attorneys in finally establishing the amount of tax due, deductions on account of such fees should be claimed at the time of the contest. The IRS will not allow deductions for legal fees that are incurred in litigation and that are paid after a Tax Court decision becomes final and more than three years after the filing of the estate tax return.[14] The IRS will allow a deduction and refund in such cases only where the final decision of the Tax Court allows attorneys' fees as an additional deduction. The Tax Court has held that even where the estate tax was assessed against the transferees of the estate, thereby extending the statutory period for assessing the tax one year beyond the initial three-year period, a deduction will not be allowed for legal fees paid after such three-year period.[15]

Expenses incurred in contesting the inclusion of trust property in the gross estate are deductible as expenses incurred with respect to property not subject to claims. These expenses must be paid within three years after the final date for filing the return.

As to community property estates, see ¶ 795.

¶ 793 Miscellaneous Expenses

Deductible miscellaneous administration expenses are sufficiently broad in scope to include court costs, surrogate's fees, appraisers' fees, and clerk hire. They also include the cost of storing or maintaining estate property and other expenses necessary to the preservation and distribution of the estate. Brokers' and auctioneers' fees are also deductible if the sale of the property is necessary to pay debts or administration expenses, or to effect distribution.[16]

• Selling Expenses

Pursuant to IRS regulations, selling expenses (such as broker fees, survey fees, or transfer stamps) are deductible if the sale is necessary in order to pay the decedent's debts, expenses of administration or taxes, to preserve the estate, or to effect distribution.[17]

> *Example:* Because, following Robert Smith's death, his estate did not have sufficient assets to pay his debts and taxes, the estate sold his residence to raise funds to do so. The selling expenses incurred in selling the residence are a deductible expense.

The Internal Revenue Code, however, allows a deduction for administration expenses that are allowable under local law.[18] The IRS has stated, and the courts have agreed,[19] that the expense must be both allowable under local law and necessary for the preservation and distribution of the decedent's estate.

---

[12] Reg. § 20.2053-3(c).
[13] *P.W. Reilly Est.*, 76 TC 369, CCH Dec. 37,691 (Acq.).
[14] Rev. Rul. 78-323, 1978-2 CB 240.
[15] *D.A. Gillum*, 49 TCM 240, CCH Dec. 41,654(M), TC Memo. 1984-631.

[16] Reg. § 20.2053-3(d).
[17] Reg. § 20.2053-3(d)(2).
[18] Code Sec. 2053(a).
[19] *C. Swayne*, 43 TC 190, CCH Dec. 27,054; *D. Smith*, CA-2, 75-1 USTC ¶ 13,046, 510 F2d 479; *S. Marcus*, CA-11, 83-1 USTC ¶ 13,521, 704

• Interest

Interest on loans that were incurred by estates to pay estate and inheritance taxes are deductible as an administration expense where the loans are incurred to avoid "forced" sales of estate assets and are permitted by state probate laws.[20] However, the interest is deductible only as it accrues and, therefore, no deduction may be computed based on an estimation of the interest expense.[21] Similarly, interest on deferred federal estate taxes (see ¶1672) is deductible only when accrued.[22] In addition, interest on deferred state death taxes is a deductible administration expense.[23] However, interest paid with respect to recapture tax was not deductible as an administration expense because it is separately imposed on the qualified heir(s) rather than the estate.[24]

Interest on a federal estate,[25] gift,[26] or income[27] tax deficiency is a deductible administration expense to the extent the expense is allowable under local law. This is true even for interest accruing after the decedent's death.[28]

However, penalties for late filing of an estate tax return and late payment of estate taxes are not deductible on an estate tax return as administration expenses even if allowable under state law, the IRS has ruled.[29] The executor's willful failure to file the return was a breach of his fiduciary duty and, therefore, the resulting penalties were not necessary to the administration of the estate.

Interest payable on the installment payment of the estate tax is not deductible.[30]

¶794 Support of Dependents

No deduction is allowed for payments to support dependents. This does not prevent deduction of a spousal allowance in all cases. When the allowance to the surviving spouse under state law constitutes a vested right that will survive as an asset of the surviving spouse's estate in the event of remarriage or death, it will qualify for the marital deduction.

¶795 Community Property States

In community property states, the extent to which the administration expenses are deductible depends on their treatment under state law. If they are deemed to be an expense of the entire community estate under state law, only one-half of the expenses are deductible, even if the decedent directs that his estate bear all the expenses.[31] If they are regarded as expenses of the decedent

---

(Footnote Continued)

F2d 1227; *S.L. Payne, Exr.*, DC Fla., 75-1 USTC ¶13,059; *M.F. Park*, CA-6, 73-1 USTC ¶12,913, 475 F2d 673.

[20] *J.S. Todd Est.*, 57 TC 288, CCH Dec. 31,087 (Acq.); *F.M. Hipp, Admr.*, DC S.C., 72-1 USTC ¶12,824.

[21] Rev. Rul. 84-75, 1984-1 CB 193. See IRS Technical Advice Memorandum 8450003 (Aug. 22, 1984) (timely filing of a claim for refund of estate taxes protected estate's right to a refund based upon interest paid on a long-term loan after the expiration of the limitations period); *M. Milliken Est.*, CA-6, 97-2 USTC ¶60,287.

[22] Rev. Rul. 80-250, 1980-2 CB 278.

[23] Rev. Rul. 81-256, 1981-2 CB 183.

[24] Rev. Rul. 90-8, 1990-1 CB 173. Also see IRS Technical Advice Memorandum 8902002 (Sept. 26, 1988).

[25] Rev. Rul. 79-252, 1979-2 CB 333.

[26] *J. DeP. Webster*, 65 TC 968, CCH Dec. 33,661.

[27] *R. Maehling*, DC Ind., 67-2 USTC ¶12,486.

[28] *J. DeP. Webster*, 65 TC 968, CCH Dec. 33,661; *R. Maehling*, DC Ind., 67-2 USTC ¶12,486; *B. Turner, Exrx.*, DC Tex., 2004-1 USTC ¶60,478, 306 FSupp 668.

[29] Rev. Rul. 81-154, 1981-1 CB 470.

[30] Code Sec. 2053(c)(1)(D).

[31] *D.A. Stapf*, 63-2 USTC ¶12,192, 375 US 118.

alone, the entire amount may be deducted. The usual limitations on deductions generally are applicable.

¶ 796   Execution of Schedule

Funeral expenses and expenses incurred in administering property subject to claims are itemized on Schedule J (Funeral Expenses and Expenses Incurred in Administering Property Subject to Claims) of Form 706 (United States Estate (and Generation-Skipping Transfer) Tax Return) (Rev. August 2013)[32]. Funeral expenses less any amounts that were reimbursed, such as death benefits payable by the Social Security Administration and the Veterans Administration, are listed on Part A. Administration expenses are to be included in the four categories under Part B. The total deduction for executors' commissions should be entered at item 1, attorneys' fees should be entered at item 2, accountant fees should be entered at item 3, and miscellaneous administration expenses should be itemized under item 4 of the schedule. Schedule J must be filed only if the estate claims a deduction on item 14 of the Recapitulation (see ¶73).

An item may be entered for deduction, even though the exact amount is not known at the time the return is filed. The item must be ascertainable with reasonable certainty and be expected to be paid. No deduction may be taken on the basis of a vague or uncertain estimate. All vouchers and receipts should be retained for possible inspection by the IRS.

¶ 797   Estate Tax vs. Income Tax Deduction

The executor or administrator of an estate has the choice of claiming administration expenses and casualty losses, under Code Sec. 2053 and Code Sec. 2054, as deductions on either the decedent's estate tax return or the fiduciary income tax return, but not on both.[33] This so-called double deduction prohibition also applies to such expenses or losses that are paid or incurred by trusts or other persons, instead of the estate. In addition, the rule against double deductions applies with respect to items that would be deductible in determining the taxable amount for taxable distributions and taxable terminations under the generation-skipping transfer tax.[34]

Administration expenses that are subject to the above double deduction prohibition include executors' commissions, attorneys' fees, and other expenses that are incurred in managing, maintaining, and conserving estate assets, such as court costs, appraisal fees, custodial fees, investment counsel services, accountants' fees, etc. In addition, selling expenses may not be used to offset the sales price on a sale of property by an estate or trust in determining gain or loss on a fiduciary income tax return, if they have also been deducted as an administration expense for federal estate tax purposes.[35]

The rule against double deductions does not apply to deductions for taxes, interest, business expenses, and other items that are accrued at the date of a decedent's death, and that, therefore, are claims against his or her estate. These expenses can be claimed as an estate tax deduction and as a deduction in respect of a decedent for income tax purposes under Code Sec. 691.

The total amount of one deduction or of all deductions does not have to be treated in the same way. One deduction or portion of a deduction may be

---

[32] An example of a filled-in Form 706, Schedule J, for a decedent dying in 2013, is reproduced at ¶3050.

[33] Reg. §1.642(g)-1 and Reg. §20.2053-1(d).
[34] Code Sec. 642(g).
[35] Code Sec. 642(g).

allowed for income tax purposes if the waiver is filed, while another deduction or portion is allowed for estate tax purposes. The election to treat administration expenses as income or estate tax deductions may be made on a year-to-year basis, if the required waiver is filed.[36]

Preparation Tip: If the executor decides to claim administration expenses and casualty losses as estate tax deductions, the deductions are claimed on the estate tax return. On the other hand, if the executor decides on claiming such expenses and losses as income tax deductions, the estate must file a statement, in duplicate, with the IRS indicating that the amount has not already been claimed as an estate tax deduction and that it is waiving its right to claim them as estate tax deductions.[37] A waiver of the right to the estate deduction cannot be revoked, even though it is later discovered that only a portion of the deducted expenses was of any income tax benefit.

Comment: Although Reg. § 1.642(g)-1 indicates that failure to file the waiver statement precludes the allowance of an income tax deduction, the Tax Court has held that items previously deducted on a federal income tax return (where no waiver was filed) can be deducted as claims against the estate so long as they were personal obligations of the decedent at death.[38] An executor's decision to claim administration expenses or casualty losses as either income tax or estate tax deductions should be based on the course of action that will produce the greatest overall tax savings, after considering the beneficiaries and the provisions of the will.

---

[36] Rev. Rul. 70-361, 1970-2 CB 133.
[37] Reg. § 1.642(g)-1 and Reg. § 1.642(g)-2.

[38] *M. Love Est.,* 57 TCM 1479, CCH Dec. 45,987(M), TC Memo. 1989-470.

Chapter 19
DEBTS OF DECEDENTS

¶ 800   Claims Against the Estate

Claims against the estate that are allowable by the laws of the jurisdiction under which the estate is being administered are deductible.[1] Such claims, when founded on a promise or agreement, are deductible to the extent that they are contracted in good faith and for adequate and full consideration. To the extent that they require the making of a contribution or gift to any charitable donee, they are deductible if similar transfers by will would qualify for deduction as a charitable transfer.

The amounts that are deductible as claims against a decedent's estate are those that represent personal obligations of the decedent existing at the time of his death. Interest that has accrued to the obligations at the time of death may be added. Only interest accrued to the date of decedent's death is deductible, even though the executor elects the alternate valuation method.[2]

If the claims represent personal obligations of the decedent at the time of his death, they are deductible whether or not they are then matured. Only claims enforceable against the estate are deductible, however. Interest accruing after a decedent's death on a claim is deductible as an administration expense if payment of the debt is postponed to benefit the estate and is allowable under state law.

Generally, a claim that becomes unenforceable (and that will not be paid) because of a creditor's failure to file as required under state law is not deductible.[3] However, the U.S. Court of Appeals for the Seventh Circuit has held that an amount owed to a creditor under a compromise agreement entered into with the decedent's estate was an enforceable and, therefore, deductible, claim against the estate even though the creditor did not file a claim within the time period prescribed by state law.[4] Similarly, a U.S. district court in Illinois has allowed a deduction for late-filed claims because the enforceability of the claims at the time of death, rather than at the time of filing, was controlling.[5] However, the court denied a deduction for loans made to the decedent, the collection of which was barred by the state statute of limitations. A U.S. district court in Ohio held that a promissory note received by the executor of a decedent's estate from the decedent and payable at the decedent's death was valid and enforceable on the date

---

[1] Code Sec. 2053(a); Reg. § 20.2053-1(a)(1)(iii).

[2] Reg. § 20.2053-4.

[3] Rev. Rul. 60-247, 1960-2 CB 272; *F.G. Hagmann Est.*, CA-5, 74-1 USTC ¶ 12,996, 492 F2d 796.

[4] *B.L. Thompson*, CA-7, 84-1 USTC ¶ 13,568, 730 F2d 1071.

[5] *B. Greene, Exr. (A. Greene Est.)*, DC Ill., 78-1 USTC ¶ 13,240, 447 FSupp. 885. See also *First Interstate Bank of Arizona, Pers. Rep.*, DC Ariz., 86-1 USTC ¶ 13,665.

of death and, therefore, was deductible even though the executor failed to present the claim to the probate court for allowance as required under state law.[6] The Tax Court has held that the value of a decedent's obligation to pay an annuity was deductible as a claim against the estate even though the annuitant did not present a claim to the estate as required under state law.[7]

The U.S. Court of Appeals for the Tenth Circuit has held that an estate's settlement payment of a claim of tortious interference with an inheritance that was made by the decedent's descendants was not deductible as a claim against the estate. According to the court, the payment obligation did not arise out of a tort liability that was a personal obligation of the decedent that existed as the time of his death. Instead, the payment was in the nature of a nondeductible settlement of an inheritance claim.[8]

A claim that is enforceable against multiple sources of payment, but that is not asserted against the estate, is also not deductible.[9] A valid and enforceable claim that is informally presented to the executor within the period for presenting claims under state law and paid with the approval of the beneficiaries (in order to relieve the executor of personal liability) is deductible,[10] as is an informal claim that may be deemed to have been paid through the payment of a legacy to the sole beneficiary of the estate in an amount at least equal to that of the claim.[11] Life insurance proceeds paid to the decedent's former wife under a property settlement agreement incorporated in a divorce decree are deductible, even though the insurance company made such payment directly to the beneficiary and no claim was filed against the estate, where the executor would have been obligated to pay over such proceeds to the former wife if he had received such proceeds.[12]

The amount of the deduction is the value of the claim. This has led to some dispute as to whether events occurring after the decedent's death should be considered in determining the value of a claim. In the IRS view, post-death events should be considered in valuing claims against the estate,[13] and the deduction is limited to the amount actually paid in settlement of claims against the estate.[14] However, the IRS position has been rejected in several circuit courts of appeal, which were decided before amendment of the estate tax regulations under Code Sec. 2053 (effective for estates of decedents dying after October 20, 2009). The U.S. Court of Appeals for the Ninth Circuit has held that the amount of deduction allowable with respect to a lien on a parcel of real property was the amount of the claim that was due and owing on the date of the decedent's death, rather than a lower amount that was later paid in settlement of the claim.[15] Similarly, the Ninth Circuit has held that the executor of a decedent's estate properly determined, under actuarial tables, the amount of the allowable federal estate tax deduction for a claim consisting of an annuity payable to the decedent's ex-husband, even though the total value of the annuity payments actually

---

[6] *R.C. Wilder, Exr. (C.H. Manley Est.),* DC Ohio, 83-2 USTC ¶13,546, 581 FSupp. 86.

[7] *C. McDowell Est.,* 51 TCM 319, CCH Dec. 42,831(M), TC Memo. 1986-27.

[8] *J. Lindberg,* CA-10, 99-1 USTC ¶60,334, 164 F3d 1312.

[9] *Q.P. Courtney Est.,* 62 TC 317, CCH Dec. 32,639.

[10] Rev. Rul. 75-24, 1975-1 CB 306.

[11] Rev. Rul. 60-247, 1960-2 CB 272.

[12] *W.P. Gray, Exr. (Will of W.G. Robertson),* DC Cal., 74-2 USTC ¶13,019, 391 FSupp. 693, and 78-1 USTC ¶13,244, 440 FSupp. 684.

[13] Reg. §20.2053-1(d)(2), as amended by T.D. 9468, October 16, 2009; Rev. Rul. 60-247, 1960-2 CB 272.

[14] Reg. §20.2053-4, as amended by T.D. 9468, October 16, 2009; adopting the rule of *J. Jacobs, Exrs.,* CA-1, 1 USTC ¶420, 34 F2d 233.

[15] *J.A. Propstra, Pers. Rep.,* CA-9, 82-2 USTC ¶13,475.

made was far less than the annuity's actuarial value because the ex-husband died seven months after the decedent's death.[16]

A decedent's estate was permitted to claim an estate tax deduction for federal and state income tax owed at the time of the decedent's death, even though the decedent later became entitled to a refund for the tax year at issue, the U.S. Court of Appeals for the Tenth Circuit has held.[17] The appellate court, reversing the decision of the Tax Court,[18] held that events occurring after death are not to be considered in valuing a claim taken as an estate tax deduction under Code Sec. 2053(a)(3). The appellate court determined that it would adopt the date-of-death valuation rule of *Ithaca Trust Co.*,[19] which provides that post-mortem events are not to be considered in valuing an estate tax charitable deduction, and extend it to the estate's tax debt claim.

Also relying on *Ithaca Trust Co.*, the Court of Appeals for the Eleventh Circuit held that a deduction claimed by a decedent's estate, relating to the estate's reimbursement of gift tax liability paid by the decedent's heirs, was to be valued as of the date of death, without consideration of any post-death events.[20] However, where the value of the claim was not "ascertainable with reasonable certainty, and will be paid," deduction was limited to the amount paid during the administration of the estate under the rules of Reg. § 20.2053-1(b)(3).[21]

•*Claims and Counterclaims in a Related Matter*

Even though payment has not yet been made, an executor may take an estate tax deduction for the current value of a claim or claims against the estate if the decedent's estate includes: (1) one or more claims or causes of actions and there are one or more claims against the estate in the same or substantially related matter, or (2) a particular asset and there are one or more claims against the decedent's estate that are integrally related to that particular asset. Additionally, all of the following must be true:

(1) each claim must otherwise satisfy the requirements of Reg. § 20.2053-1;

(2) each claim was a personal obligation of the decedent existing at the decedent's death;

(3) each claim is enforceable against the decedent's estate (and is not unenforceable when paid);

(4) the value of each claim is determined from a "qualified appraisal" performed by a "qualified appraiser" (within the meaning of Code Sec. 170 and corresponding regulations);

(5) the value of the claim is subject to adjustment for post-death events; and

(6) the aggregate value of the related claims or assets included in the decedent's estate exceeds 10 percent of the decedent's gross estate.

The deduction allowed under the special rule for claims and counterclaims in a related matter is effective for estates of decedents dying after October 19,

---

[16] *A.E. Van Horne Est.*, CA-9, 83-2 USTC ¶13,548, 720 F2d 1114, cert. denied, May 14, 1984.

[17] *E. McMorris Est.*, CA-10, 2001-1 USTC ¶60,396.

[18] *E. McMorris Est.*, 77 TCM 1552, CCH Dec. 53,291(M), TC Memo. 1999-82.

[19] *Ithaca Trust Co.*, SCt, 1 USTC ¶386, 279 US 151.

[20] *E. O'Neal Est.*, CA-11, 2001-2 USTC ¶60,412, aff'g in part and vac'g and rem'g in part, DC Ala., 99-2 USTC ¶60,365.

[21] *G. Saunders Est.*, TC, Dec. 58,610, 136 TC 406.

2009, and is limited to the value of the related claims or particular assets included in the decedent's gross estate.[22]

• *Claims Totaling Not More Than $500,000*

Effective for estates of decedents dying after October 19, 2009, an executor may claim an estate tax deduction for the current value of one or more claims against the estate, even though payment has not been made on the claims, provided that:

(1) each claim must otherwise satisfy the requirements of Reg. § 20.2053-1;

(2) each claim was a personal obligation of the decedent existing at the decedent's death;

(3) each claim is enforceable against the decedent's estate (and is not unenforceable when paid);

(4) the value of each claim is determined from a "qualified appraisal" performed by a "qualified appraiser" (within the meaning of Code Sec. 170 and corresponding regulations);

(5) the value of the claim is subject to adjustment for post-death events);

(6) the total value of the amount deducted by the estate under this special provision does not exceed $500,000; and

(7) the full value of each claim, rather than just a portion of that amount, must be deductible under this special provision, and for this purpose, the full value of each such claim is deemed to be the unpaid amount of the claim that is not deductible after application of Reg. § 20.2053-1 and Reg. § 20.2053-4(b).[23]

See, also, ¶ 803 for discussion of protective claims for refunds.

¶ 803   Protective Claims for Refunds

Effective for estates of decedents dying after October 19, 2009, a protective claim for refund may be filed before expiration of the Code Sec. 6511(a) limitation period to preserve the estate's right to claim a refund relating to claims against the estate or expenses that have not been paid or do not otherwise meet the requirements for deductibility under Code Sec. 2053 (or the regulations thereunder). Such protective claims must be filed before the close of the limitations period under Code Sec. 6511(a). It is not necessary that the protective claim state a dollar amount or demand an immediate refund.

Although it is not necessary that the protective claim state a dollar amount or demand an immediate relief, under guidance issued by the IRS in Rev. Proc. 2011-48,[24] the claim must identify in detail the Code Sec. 2053 expense claimed and include documentary evidence to establish the authority of the individual filing the protective claim to act on behalf of the estate. A separate protective claim for refund must be filed for each claim or expense. For protective claims involving contested claims against the estate, the contested matter and the potential liability must be identified, as well as the name or names of the claimants, the basis of the claim, the extent or amount of the liabilities claimed,

---

[22] Reg. § 20.2053-4(b), as amended by T.D. 9468, October 16, 2009.

[23] Reg. § 20.2053-4(c), as amended by T.D. 9468, October 16, 2009.

[24] IRB 2011-42, October 14, 2011.

and the status of the contested matter. No separate identification is required for ancillary expenses. However, ancillary expenses must still meet the requirements of Code Sec. 2053 in order to be deductible.

Preparation Tip: Depending on the circumstances, protective claims for refund filed for decedents dying after December 31, 2011, may be filed by attaching a completed Schedule PC (see ¶804) to Form 706 or by filing Form 843 and writing, "Protective Claim for Refund under Section 2053," across the top. Protective claims for refund filed for decedents dying after October 19, 2009, and before January 1, 2012, must be made by filing Form 843. Protective claims filed for decedents dying after December 31, 2011 should be filed by executing Form 706 Schedule PC (Protective Claim for Refund) (Rev. August 2013), indicating that it is the initial notice of protective claim for refund. However, if the estate's initial claim is submitted after it has filed Form 706, the estate should file Form 843.[25] Each protective claim for refund should indicate whether additional Code Sec. 2053 protective claims for refund have or will be filed.

Filing for a protective claim under Schedule PC will not suspend the IRS's examination of an estate tax return, nor will it delay issuance of a closing letter for the estate.[26]

The IRS may reject claims that are not timely filed, do not include a properly executed perjury statement, or do not adequately describe the claim. The failure to properly execute a perjury statement may only be cured before the close of the limitations period under Code Sec. 6511(a). The failure to satisfy the identification requirement may be cured after the close of the limitations period as long as the original claim was timely filed with a properly executed perjury statement.

When the Code Sec. 2053 claim or expense that was subject to a protective claim for refund meets the requirements for deductibility under Reg. §20.2053-1, the estate must notify the IRS that the claim is ready for consideration. Generally, the notification must be provided within 90 days after payment or 90 days after the amount of the claim becomes certain and is no longer subject to contingency. Notification of consideration of a protective claim for refund filed for decedents dying after December 31, 2011, may be submitted by filing an updated Form 706, including all schedules affected by the allowance of the deduction and an updated Schedule PC for each claim, or by filing an updated Form 843. Notification of consideration of a protective claim for refund filed for decedents dying after October 19, 2009, but before January 1, 2012, must be submitted by filing an updated Form 843. The updated forms should also include any necessary adjustments to the charitable and marital deductions.[27]

The IRS will act on protective claims within a reasonable time after being notified by the executor that the contingency has been resolved and that the amount deductible under Reg. §20.2053-1 has been established.[28]

Generally, whenever a claim for refund is issued, the IRS reexamines the estate tax return to determine if there has been an overpayment of tax. However, with regard to protective refund claims made to preserve an estate's right to a refund for a deduction for a claim or an expense made pursuant to Reg. §20.2053-1(d)(5), the IRS has provided a limited administrative exception to its

---

[25] Instructions for Form 706 (Rev. August 2013), p. 48.
[26] Instructions for Form 706 (Rev. August 2013), p. 48.
[27] Rev. Proc. 2011-48, IRB 2011-42, October 14, 2011.
[28] Reg. §20.2053-1(d)(5), as amended by T.D. 9468, October 16, 2009.

normal estate tax return examination procedures. Under guidance announced in Notice 2009-84,[29] if a timely filed protective claim for refund becomes ready for consideration after the period for assessment has expired, the IRS will not examine each item on the estate tax return. Instead, the IRS will limit its examination to the deduction under Code Sec. 2053 that is related to the protective claim. After the IRS establishes whether the deduction is allowable, it will recalculate the estate tax based on that determination. Notice 2009-84 is applicable to protective claims filed by estates of decedents dying after October 19, 2009.

¶ 804   Execution of Schedule PC

Schedule PC (Protective Claim for Refund) of Form 706 (U.S. Estate (and Generation-Skipping Transfer) Tax Return) (Rev. August, 2013) is to be used by the estates of decedents dying after December 31, 2011, to preserve the estate's right to file for a claim for refund relating to assets that have been included in the gross estate where an amount would be deductible under the rules of Code Sec. 2053 except for the fact that the amount has not been paid, or would not otherwise meet the deductibility requirements of Code Sec. 2053, until after the limitations period for filing the claim has passed. Schedule PC can only be filed with the estate's Form 706. Because each separate claim or expense requires the filing of a separate Schedule PC, more than one Schedule PC may be included with a Form 706. Two copies of each Schedule PC must be included with the Form 706 filed.

If the initial protective claim for refund is not filed on the Form 706, it estate must use Form 843 (Claim for Refund and Request for Abatement). Form 843 will also be use to inform the IRS when the contingency leading to the protective claim has been resolved and the refund due the estate is finalized.

Schedule PC is to be used in three situations related to protective claims for refund:

- For initial protective claims for refunds;
- For partial refunds claimed: partial resolution or satisfaction relating to a protective claim previously filed; and
- For notice to the IRS of the final resolution of the claim.

Initial notice of claim

Once the estate has filed a Schedule PC for an initial claim for refund, the IRS will send the estate a written acknowledgement of receipt of the claim. Because a certified mail receipt or other evidence of delivery is not sufficient to confirm receipt and processing of the Schedule PC, if the estate does not receive IRS's written acknowledgement within 180 days of filing the Schedule PC, the estate fiduciary should contact the IRS at (888) 699-4043.

The claims entered on the Schedule PC generally will not be substantively reviewed by the IRS until the amount of the claim has been established. However, the Schedule PC claim can be rejected for reasons such as:

- The claim was not timely filed;
- The claim was not filed by a fiduciary having authority to act on behalf of the estate;
- The required acknowledgment of penalties of perjury statement on page 1 of Form 706 was not signed; or

---

[29] IRB 2009-44, 592.

- The claim was not adequately described.

If the IRS does not reject the Schedule PC claim when filed based on an above noted defect, it can still do so on a later substantive review.

The IRS may allow an estate to cure defects in the Schedule PC claim if the estate files the corrected claim before expiration of the limitations period of Code Sec. 6511(a), or within 45 days of the IRS notice of the defect, whichever is later.

Related Ancillary Expenses. If a claim has been adequately identified on Schedule PC, the IRS will presume that the claim includes certain expenses related to resolving, defending or satisfying the claim. These expenses may include attorney's fees, court costs, appraisal fees, and accounting costs. The estate does not have to separately identify or substantiate these ancillary expenses.

Notice of final resolution of claim

Once an expense listed on Schedule PC is finally determined, the estate must notify the IRS that the claim for refund is ready for consideration. A separate notice of final resolution must be filed for each Schedule PC claim that has been resolved. The estate should send this notification to the IRS within 90 days of the date that the claim or expense becomes certain, and no longer subject to contingency, whichever is later. Separate notifications must be submitted for each claim that was listed on Schedule PC. If the final claim or expense involves multiple or recurring payments, the 90-day period begins on the date of the last payment.

In order to qualify for a partial refund, the estate may also notify the IRS (no more frequently that yearly) as payments are being made.

There are two methods by which an estate can notify the IRS of a final resolution of a claim: (1) by filing a supplemental Form 706 with an updated Schedule PC, or (2) by filing an updated Form 843.

Notification by Schedule PC requires submission of:

- An updated Schedule PC;

- Each Form 706 Schedule affected by allowance of the deduction for the protective claim;

- Page 1 of Form 706, which should contain the notation: "Supplemental Information—Notification of Consideration of Section 2053 Protective Claim(s) for Refund." The filing date of the initial notice of protective claim should also be noted on page 1 of Form 706; and

- A copy of the initial notice of claim.

Notification by Form 843 requires submission of:

- A copy of the updated Form 843, page 1, containing the notation: "Notification of Consideration of Section 2053 Protective Claim(s) for Refund." The filing date of the initial notice of protective claim should also be noted on page 1 of Form 843; and

- A copy of the initial notice of claim.

Schedule PC line-by-line instructions

Part 1, General Information

Lines 1—6 relate to general information concerning the decedent and the decedent's fiduciary, including the fiduciary's address and daytime telephone number.

Line 7: The number of Schedules PC being filed with the Form 706 are entered on line 7.

Line 8: If the fiduciary filing the Schedule PC is the same fiduciary who filed the original Form 706, this is indicated in the line 8 checkbox. If a different fiduciary is filing the Schedule PC, that fiduciary should attach to Schedule PC documentary evidence of the fiduciary's authority to file the Schedule PC (such as letters testamentary, letters of administration, or similar documentation).

Part 2: Claim Information

The fiduciary must check one of the following checkboxes that applies:

a. Protective claim for refund made for unresolved claim or expense. The amount in contest is to be included on the line provided.

b. Partial refund claim: partial resolution and/or satisfaction of the protected claim or expense. The date of the protective claim, and the amount of the claim or expense partially resolved/satisfied, are to be included on the lines provided.

c. Full and final refund claimed for the claim or expense. The date of the protective claim, and the amount of the claim or expense final resolved/satisfied and presently claimed as a deduction under Code Sec. 2053, are to be included on the lines provided,

The second page requires the following information for each claim, included under Columns A through F:

Column A: The Form 706 Schedule and Item number relating to the claim.

Column B: The following identification information for the claim: (1) Name/names of the claimant(s); (2) Basis of the claim, or description of the pending claim or expense; (3) Reasons and contingencies delaying resolution; (4) Status of contested matters; and attachments relating to relevant pleadings or other documents.

Column C: Any amount deducted under Reg. § 20.2053-1(d)(4)or Reg. § § 20.2053-4(b) or (c) for the identified claim.

Column D: Amount presently claimed as a deduction under Code Sec. 2053 for the identified claim.

Column E: Ancillary expenses estimated/agreed upon/paid. One alternative should be indicated.

Column F. Amount of the tax to be refunded.

Part 3. Other Schedules PC and Forms 843 Filed by Estate

Part 3 is used to identify each claim for refund previously reported on a Form 706, Schedule PC, or a Form 843.

The following information for each claim is to be entered under Columns A through E:

Column A: Date of the decedent's death.

Column B: Internal Revenue office where Schedule PC or Form 843 was filed.

Column C: Date filed.

Column D: The fiduciary is to indicate one of the following: (1) Protective Claim for Refund; (2) Partial Claim for Refund; or (3) Full and Final Claim for Refund.

Column E: Amount in contest.

An example of a filled-in Form 706, Schedule PC, for a decedent dying in 2013, is reproduced at ¶3135.

¶ 805   Claims Exceeding Assets Available for Payment

In the event that the claims against the estate exceed the value of property subject to the payment of claims, special rules apply. Deductions of such claims (together with funeral expenses, certain administration expenses, mortgages and liens) are disallowed to the extent they exceed the value of the property subject to the claims. Deductions for such amounts nevertheless will be allowed if they are actually paid before the date prescribed for filing the estate tax return.

"Property subject to claims" is the property out of which the deductible amounts would be paid under applicable law upon the settlement of the estate. The value of such property must be reduced by any administration expenses deducted against such property.[30]

The IRS takes the position that the total amount deducted as claims against the estate cannot exceed the decedent's probate estate, citing the holding in a decision of the Court of Appeals for the Third Circuit.[31] The Federal Claims Court has rejected this limitation, stating that, where local law (Ohio) subjected nonprobate trust assets, as well as probate assets, to payment of an EPA superfund liability of $750,000, the deduction as a claim against the estate was not limited to the amount of the probate assets. The Claims Court concluded that a plain reading of the statutory language of Code Sec. 2053(c)(2) did not impose the "probate estate" limitation argued by the IRS.[32]

¶ 810   Deductible Claims

The following items are among those that have been held to be deductible as claims against the estate:

(1) alimony decreed by a court but past due (if payments are to continue periodically after the decedent's death, the commuted value of such payments is also deductible[33]);

(2) commissions owed to trustee for services during decedent's lifetime;[34]

(3) the commuted value of support payments due a decedent's wife for her release of her support and maintenance rights under a valid separation agreement;[35]

(4) amounts due on judgments against the decedent, including tort liabilities;[36]

(5) amounts due under guarantees executed by the decedent and not collectible from primary obligor; and[37]

(6) amounts due on notes.[38]

---

[30] Code Sec. 2053(c)(2).

[31] *S. Wilson v. U.S.,* CA-3, 67-1 USTC ¶12,451, 372 F2d 232.

[32] *R. Snyder Est.,* FedCl, 99-2 USTC ¶60,357.

[33] Rev. Rul. 67-304, 1967-2 CB 224.

[34] *F.E. Baldwin Est.,* 44 BTA 900, CCH Dec. 11,878 (Acq.).

[35] Rev. Rul. 71-67, 1971-1 CB 271.

[36] *E.C. Moore, Exr.,* 21 BTA 279, CCH Dec. 6467 (Acq.).

[37] *E.L. Benz, Exr.,* CA-1, 37-2 USTC ¶9337, 90 F2d 747.

[38] *Security Tr. Co., Exr.,* 4 BTA 983, CCH Dec. 1647 (Acq.).

Although, as noted at (4), above, amounts paid to satisfy judgments against the decedent are deductible, the IRS has ruled that a decedent's estate could not deduct amounts paid in satisfaction of a collusive lawsuit filed against the decedent by his son.[39] In so ruling, the IRS noted that the decedent's child filed the suit pursuant to a plan to reduce federal estate taxes that was devised by a financial planner. Even though the decedent did not contest the lawsuit and a judgment was awarded to the child under a consent decree, the amounts paid in satisfaction of the claim were not deductible because the lawsuit was without merit and was merely a device to allow the transfer of property free of estate and gift taxes.

¶ 813   Medical Expenses

The medical expenses resulting from a decedent's last illness are a deductible claim against the estate. In lieu of deducting these expenses on the estate tax return, the executor may deduct these expenses on the decedent's last income tax return. However, it may be preferable for the estate to deduct these expenses on the estate tax return because the tax rate schedule for estate tax is significantly higher than the tax rate schedule for income tax. Moreover, for estate tax purposes, the medical expenses are fully deductible. The medical expenses for income tax purposes are deductible only to the extent that such expenses exceed 7.5 percent of the decedent's adjusted gross income. However, if the decision is made to deduct medical expenses on the decedent's last income tax return, a statement that such amount has not been claimed as a deduction on the estate's Form 706 (United States Estate (and Generation-Skipping Transfer) Tax Return) (Rev. August 2013) and that the estate waives any right to do so in the future must be filed.[40]

In community property states, the deductibility of a decedent's medical expenses for estate tax purposes is dependent on whether such costs are treated as an expense of the community estate or of the decedent's estate.[41] If such costs are a community expense, only one-half of the costs are deductible for estate tax purposes. If such costs are allowable against the decedent's estate, they are deductible to the extent so allowed.

¶ 815   Claims Founded on Promise or Agreement

A claim against the estate based on a promise or agreement by the decedent to pay over certain property or a specified amount of money is subject to special treatment. It will be denied as a deduction except to the extent that it was contracted in good faith and for an adequate and full consideration in money or money's worth.[42]

Generally, the requirements as to consideration here are the same as those that apply in determining whether a lifetime transfer should escape inclusion in the gross estate. A special exception is provided with respect to claims made by charitable organizations. The consideration requirements are waived if the claimant is one to whom a testamentary transfer would be deductible as a charitable transfer.

---

[39] Rev. Rul. 83-54, 1983-1 CB 229.

[40] Code Sec. 213(c); Reg. § 1.213-1(d).

[41] Rev. Rul. 78-242, 1978-1 CB 292.

[42] Code Sec. 2053(c)(1). Also see *M. Wedum Est.*, 57 TCM 219, CCH Dec.

45,637(M), TC Memo. 1989-184. See, also, *A. Shapiro Est.*, CA-9, 2011-1 ustc ¶ 60,614, where an estate was allowed to deduct a portion of a palimony.

• Claims Under a Divorce Decree

The consideration requirement applies to claims "founded on a promise or agreement." However, claims founded on a divorce decree are not founded on an agreement and, as such, are deductible without regard to the consideration requirement so long as they meet the general requirements for deduction.[43]

The obligation to transfer property to a former spouse of the decedent is deductible as a claim against the estate if the transfer is pursuant to an agreement satisfying the conditions for the gift tax exemption under Code Sec. 2516 (see ¶2165).[44] Thus, the deduction will be available if the transfer is pursuant to a written agreement between the spouses and if divorce occurred within the three-year period beginning one year before execution of the agreement. In the event the decedent dies before the divorce, the transfer would be eligible for the marital deduction (see ¶1000).

With respect to estates of decedents dying prior to July 18, 1984, the Tax Court has held that a decedent's estate could not deduct as a claim against the estate amounts paid to the decedent's ex-wife in settlement of her right to be named beneficiary of certain life insurance policies pursuant to a separation agreement. Although the parties were divorced and the separation agreement made part of the divorce decree, the court noted that because, under applicable state law (Missouri), the divorce court had no power to award the insurance policies to the ex-wife, the amounts were paid pursuant to the separation agreement rather than pursuant to the divorce decree. Because the estate could not show that support rights relinquished by the ex-wife and the couple's children were consideration for the insurance provision in the agreement, the court denied the deduction.[45]

The U.S. Court of Appeals for the Second Circuit, in a case involving a separation agreement under a Mexican divorce decree, has indicated its disagreement with the Tax Court's position as stated above.[46] In that case, the Second Circuit held that a decedent's estate could deduct as a claim against the estate an amount paid to the decedent's ex-wife pursuant to a separation agreement because the Mexican court had incorporated the agreement (which was executed in New York) into the divorce decree, as it was empowered to do by Mexican law. However, the Second Circuit noted that the payment would have been deductible, even if it had been made pursuant to the agreement rather than to the divorce decree because the agreement was deemed made for full and adequate consideration under Code Sec. 2516, prior to amendment by the Tax Reform Act of 1984 (P.L. 98-369).[47] In the Second Circuit's view, such a holding was necessary in view of the U.S. Supreme Court's rulings that the estate and gift tax statutes are to be construed in a similar manner.[48]

¶ 820   Taxes

As a general rule, neither inheritance nor estate taxes payable on a decedent's estate are deductible, whether payable to the state, to the U.S. federal, or

---

[43] *W.E. Robinson Est.*, 63 TC 717, CCH Dec. 33,099 (Acq.), and *M.C. Watson Est.*, CA-2, 54-2 USTC ¶10,973, 216 FSupp. 941.

[44] Code Sec. 2043(b).

[45] *E. Satz Est.*, 78 TC 1172, CCH Dec. 39,151.

[46] *D.E. Natchez and P. Natchez, Exrs.*, CA-2, 83-1 USTC ¶13,519, 705 F2d 671.

[47] The decedent and his wife were divorced within two years after executing the separation agreement, as required under Code Sec. 2516.

[48] See, e.g., *C. Harris*, SCt, 50-2 USTC ¶10,786, 340 US 106, and *Merrill v. Fahs*, SCt, 45-1 USTC ¶10,180, 324 US 308.

foreign governments. However, a deduction is available for state death taxes paid by estates of decedents dying after 2004 (see ¶1144).[49] Further, an executor may elect to deduct foreign death taxes paid on charitable transfers, rather than take the Code Sec. 2015 credit for foreign death taxes, if the decease in the estate tax will inure solely to the benefit of the charitable transferee.[50]

Gift taxes due and payable on all post-1976 gifts made by a decedent dying after 1976 are subtracted from the estate tax.[51]

Property taxes are deductible only if they accrued under state law prior to the decedent's death.[52]

Excise taxes incurred in selling property of a decedent are deductible as expenses of administration if the sale is necessary to (1) pay the decedent's debts, taxes, or expenses of administration, (2) preserve the estate, or (3) effect distribution.

Unpaid income taxes are deductible if they are on income properly includible in an income tax return of the decedent for a period prior to his death. If a joint income tax return was filed, the portion of the joint liability (although entirely paid by the estate) that is deductible is the amount for which the estate would be liable under local law after enforcement of any effective right of reimbursement or contribution.[53]

Interest accruing after a decedent's death on his federal and state income tax deficiencies, which are contested by an executor or administrator, is deductible as an administration expense to the extent permitted by state law.[54] For decedents dying prior to 1998, interest payable by an estate on the unpaid balance of a decedent's federal estate tax, which the estate had elected to pay in installments pursuant to Code Sec. 6166 is also deductible as an administration expense,[55] although only as the interest liability accrues.[56] However, an estate was entitled to an immediate administration expense deduction for excess Code Sec. 6166 interest that it had paid pursuant to a deficiency assessment of the IRS that was later overturned in court. On reconsideration of its prior ruling in *Succ. of B. Helis*,[57] the U.S. Court of Federal Claims has held that an estate was not entitled to an immediate administration expense deduction for excess Code Sec. 6166 interest that it had paid pursuant to an IRS deficiency assessment that was later judicially overturned. According to the court, the estate was not considered to have "actually and necessarily" incurred the disputed interest expense for purposes of Reg. § 20.2053-3(a) because, prior to closing, the estate was to recover the interest overpayment, along with statutory interest on that overpayment. Therefore, from an economic standpoint, the estate would be left no worse off than if its valuation figure had been accepted without litigation. Accordingly, the estate was not entitled to deduct the excess interest payments that were later refunded as part of the final judgment in the estate tax litigation.

---

[49] Code Sec. 2058, as added by the Economic Growth and Tax Relief Reconciliation Act of 2001 (P.L. 107-16), extended by the Tax Relief, Unemployment Insurance Reauthorization, and Job Creation Act of 2010 (P.L. 111-312), and made permanent by the American Taxpayer Relief Act of 2012 (P.L. 112-240).

[50] Code Sec. 2053(d), as amended by P.L. 107-16.

[51] Code Sec. 2001.

[52] Reg. § 20.2053-6.

[53] Reg. § 20.2053-6.

[54] Rev. Rul. 69-402, 1969-2 CB 176.

[55] Rev. Rul. 78-125, 1978-1 CB 292.

[56] Rev. Rul. 80-250, 1980-2 CB 278; *Est. of E.H. Hoover*, 49 TCM 1239, CCH Dec. 42,031(M), TC Memo. 1985-183.

[57] *Succ. of B. Helis*, FedCl, 2003-1 USTC ¶60,454, vacating, in part, the court's opinion at 2002-2 USTC ¶60,445.

¶820

For decedents dying after 1997, no deduction is allowable for interest payable pursuant to Code Sec. 6166.[58] Post-death interest on a decedent's gift tax liability is deductible while the gift tax liability is being contested along with the questions of whether such interest is an allowable expense under state law.[59]

¶ 825   Execution of Schedule K

In claiming a deduction for claims against the estate, the claims should be itemized on Schedule K (Debts of the Decedent, and Mortgages and Liens) of Form 706 (United States Estate (and Generation-Skipping Transfer) Tax Return) (Rev. August 2013).[60] Notes unsecured by a mortgage or other lien should be listed. Any indebtedness secured by a mortgage or other lien upon property of the gross estate should be listed separately under "Mortgages and Liens." Schedule K has to be filed only if the decedent had debts that are deductible on this schedule (see ¶ 73).

If the amount of the debt is disputed or is the subject of litigation, only the amount that the estate representative concedes to be a valid claim is deductible. If the claim is contested, that fact must be stated on the schedule. If a debt is not currently deductible because it is subject to an unresolved controversy at the time when the estate tax return is due, Schedule PC (Protective Claim for Refund) should be filed (see ¶ 804).

Full details must be included in the description of unsecured notes, including (1) the name and address of the payee, (2) the face amount of the note, (3) the unpaid balance, (4) the date and term of the note, (5) the interest rate, and (6) the date to which interest was paid prior to death. Care must be taken to state the exact nature of the claim as well as the name of the creditor. If the claim is for services rendered over a period of time, the period covered by the claim should be stated. For example: Edison Electric Illuminating Co., for electric service during April 2012, $150.

If the amount of the claim is the unpaid balance due on a contract for the purchase of any property included in the gross estate, the schedule and item number at which the property is reported must be identified. If the claim represents a joint and several liability, the facts must be fully stated and the financial responsibility of the co-obligor explained. All vouchers or original records should be preserved for inspection by the IRS.

If the executor elects to take a deduction, rather than a credit, for foreign death taxes on certain charitable transfers, these taxes should be listed as a debt on the "Debts of the Decedent" portion of Schedule K. Executors who have difficulty computing this deduction can request IRS help. They should send a request within a reasonable time before the due date to the Commissioner of Internal Revenue, Washington, D.C. 20224. Attached to the request should be a copy of the will and relevant documents, a statement showing the distribution of the estate under the decedent's will, and a computation of the state or foreign death tax showing any amount payable by a charitable organization.[61]

¶ 830   Community Property

If debts to be listed in the return are community debts, only one-half of the amount of such community debts should be listed. An appropriate explanation should be made.

---

[58] Code Sec. 2053(c)(1)(D).

[59] *J. DeP. Webster*, 65 TC 968, CCH Dec. 33,661 (Acq.).

[60] An example of a filled-in Form 706, Schedule K, for a decedent dying in 2013, is reproduced at ¶ 3060.

[61] Instructions for Form 706 (Rev. August 2013), p. 32.

Chapter 20

MORTGAGES, LOSSES, AND PROPERTY NOT SUBJECT TO CLAIMS

¶ 850 Excluding Mortgages and Liens

The amounts of any mortgages and liens that are charges against the estate of the decedent or against any specific property in the estate and that date from before decedent's death are excluded from the taxable estate. If the charges are collectible against specific property only, they are excluded by including in the gross estate only the net value of the subject property. In other instances, the value of the property is first included in the gross estate in full. Then the mortgage or lien is taken as a deduction.[1]

¶ 855 Reporting Mortgage and Lien Deductions

Only obligations secured by mortgages or other liens upon property included in the gross estate at its full value (undiminished by the amount of the mortgage or lien) are to be itemized as "Mortgages and Liens" on Schedule K (Debts of the Decedent, and Mortgages and Liens) of Form 706 (United States Estate (and Generation-Skipping Transfer) Tax Return) (Rev. August 2013).[2] If the decedent's estate is liable for the amount of the indebtedness secured by such mortgage or lien, the full value of the property subject to the mortgage or lien must be included in the gross estate under the appropriate schedule. The estate is considered liable for the indebtedness if it is enforceable against other property of the estate not subject to the mortgage or lien, or if the decedent was personally liable.[3] Schedule K need only be filed if the decedent has mortgages and/or liens that are deductible on this schedule.

> *Comment:* If mortgages and liens are not currently deductible because they are subject to unresolved controversies at the time when the estate tax return is due, Schedule PC (Protective Claim for Refund) should be filed (see ¶ 804).

There are instances where the decedent's estate is not liable for the amount of a debt secured by a mortgage or lien and the amount of the debt is greater than the value of the property subject to such mortgage or lien. In these

---

[1] Code Sec. 2053(a)(4); Reg. § 20.2053-1(a)(1)(iv).

[2] An example of a filled-in Form 706, Schedule K, for a decedent dying in 2013, is reproduced at ¶ 3060.

[3] Reg. § 20.2053-7.

situations, it is not possible to obtain a deduction for the full amount of the debt by entering the full value of the property as a part of the gross estate and then deducting the full amount of the debt under this schedule. Where the estate is not liable, only the redemption value (or the value of the property, less the mortgage or indebtedness) is reported as part of the gross estate.

Generally, the amount of mortgage liability on a decedent's property is available either as a deduction from the gross estate or as a reduction in the value of the property includible in the gross estate. However, the U.S. Court of Appeals for the Eleventh Circuit disallowed a deduction for the unpaid principal balances of mortgages on two parcels of real estate that were includible in the estates of a husband and wife because the decedents were mere accommodation parties to the mortgages and notes and, thus, were not primarily liable for the indebtedness.[4]

Notes and other obligations secured by the deposit of collateral, such as stocks and bonds, should also be listed under "Mortgages and Liens" on Schedule K. Each mortgage and lien should be identified by indicating in the "Description" column the particular schedule and item number at which the property subject to the mortgage or lien is reported. The description of the obligation should show (1) the name and address of the mortgagee, payee, or obligee, (2) the date and term of the mortgage, note, or other agreement under which the indebtedness is established, (3) the face amount, (4) the unpaid balance, (5) the rate of interest, and (6) the date to which interest was paid prior to the decedent's death.

¶ 860   Limitations as to Amount

Mortgages on, or any indebtedness with respect to, property included in the gross estate are deductible only to the extent that the liability was contracted in good faith and for an adequate and full consideration in money or money's worth.[5] Only interest accrued to the date of the decedent's death is deductible, even though the estate representative elects the alternate valuation method.[6]

The IRS has ruled that a decedent's estate could claim a deduction for the full amount of a mortgage on the decedent's farmland, even though the farmland was included in the gross estate at its special use value (see ¶ 280 through ¶ 296).[7] The IRS noted that all of the property subject to the mortgage was included in the gross estate and that the estate was liable for payment of the mortgage. Generally, the amount of a mortgage for which a decedent's estate is liable is deductible from the gross estate if the full value of the property subject to the mortgage is included in the gross estate. Under the facts of the ruling, the full value of the decedent's farmland was included in the gross estate because, for estate tax purposes, the special use value of property is equivalent to its full value.

¶ 870   Community Property Subject to Mortgage or Lien

If mortgages to be listed in the return are community obligations, such status should be made clear. Only one-half of the amount should be listed as an obligation of the estate.

---

[4] *C.F. Theis Est.*, CA-11, 85-2 USTC ¶ 13,639, 770 F2d 981.
[5] Reg. § 20.2053-7.
[6] Reg. § 20.2053-7.
[7] Rev. Rul. 83-81, 1983-1 CB 230.

¶ 900   Claiming Net Losses During Administration

Casualty and theft losses that occur during settlement of the estate are deductible to the extent they are not compensated by insurance.[8] Losses with respect to an estate asset are not deductible if they occur after distribution of the asset to the beneficiary. The term "casualty losses" encompasses losses resulting from fire, storm, shipwreck, and war. The loss contemplated is a loss with respect to tangible property.[9]

Depreciation in value of intangibles, even though occasioned by destruction, damage, or theft of underlying physical assets, is not deductible under Code Sec. 2054. Losses in value of intangibles can serve to reduce the taxable estate, but only if they occur within six months after death so that the intangibles may be included in the estate at their value as of a date six months after death.

Casualty and theft losses are not deductible for estate tax purposes if, at the time the return is filed, they had been claimed as an income tax deduction.[10]

¶ 910   Alternate Valuation

When the estate representative elects to value the estate as of a date six months after death, losses during this period are reflected in the value or absence of value of the damaged or lost property. Losses are shown in the values of the specific property rather than as a deductible item, except in unusual situations. The loss or theft cannot be reflected both as a deduction and in the valuation of the affected items of property.[11]

¶ 925   Reporting Net Losses

Full details of the amount and cause of loss must be reported under "Net losses during administration" on Schedule L (Net Losses During Administration and Expenses Incurred in Administering Property Not Subject to Claims) of Form 706 (United States Estate (and Generation-Skipping Transfer) Tax Return) (Rev. August 2013). This schedule must be filed if the estate has deductible losses. In instances where insurance payments or other compensation is received on account of loss or theft, the amount received should be stated. The property on which loss is claimed should be identified by indicating the particular schedule and item number at which the property is reported.

> *Comment:* If losses are not currently deductible because they are subject to unresolved controversies at the time when the estate tax return is due, Schedule PC (Protective Claim for Refund) should be filed (see ¶ 804).

¶ 935   Community Property Losses

If losses have been incurred with respect to property that had been held as community property, only one-half of the amount of such losses may be listed. Such losses should be accompanied by an appropriate explanation.

¶ 950   Expenses of Property Not Subject to Claims

Expenses of administering property that is included in the decedent's gross estate, but is not subject to claims against it, are deductible under certain circumstances. Such expenses are deductible if (1) they would be allowed as deductions if the property being administered were subject to claims (see ¶ 780),

---

[8] Code Sec. 2054.
[9] Reg. § 20.2054-1.

[10] Reg. § 20.2054-1.
[11] Reg. § 20.2032-1(g).

and (2) they are paid before the expiration of the period of limitation for assessment (three years after the return was filed or at any time after such tax became due and before the expiration of three years after the date on which any part of such tax was paid).[12] Usually, such expenses include principal commissions paid with respect to trust property included in the gross estate and attorneys' fees incurred to contest the inclusion of trust property in the decedent's gross estate. However, they may also be incurred in connection with the collection of other assets, or the transfer or clearance of title to other property included in the decedent's gross estate but not included in the probate estate.

¶ 955   Reporting Expense Deductions

Amounts representing expenses incurred in administering property included in the gross estate but not subject to claims should be itemized under "Expenses incurred in administering property not subject to claims" on the lower portion of Schedule L (Net Losses During Administration and Expenses Incurred in Administering Property Not Subject to Claims) of Form 706 (United States Estate (and Generation-Skipping Transfer) Tax Return) (Rev. August 2013).[13]

The names and addresses of persons to whom the expenses are payable and the exact nature of the particular expense should be stated. The property with respect to which the expense was incurred should be identified by indicating the schedule and item number at which the property is reported.

An item may be entered for deduction, even though the exact amount is not known at that time. It must be ascertainable with reasonable certainty and expected to be paid before the expiration of the period of limitation for assessment (three years after the estate tax return is filed). No deduction may be taken on the basis of a vague or uncertain estimate. All vouchers and receipts should be retained for inspection by the IRS.

---

[12] Code Sec. 2053; Reg. § 20.2053-8(a), as amended by T.D. 9468, October 16, 2009.

[13] An example of a filled-in Form 706, Schedule L, for a decedent dying in 2013, is reproduced at ¶ 3070.

Chapter 21
MARITAL DEDUCTION

¶ 1000   Transfers to Surviving Spouse

An unlimited marital deduction is available for computing the taxable estate of an individual where any part of the deceased person's estate passes or has passed to the surviving spouse. The property so passing is deductible in computing the taxable estate to the extent that it is includible in the gross estate.[1] The amount of the allowable marital deduction depends on the year of death. For estates of decedents dying after 1981, the amount of the deduction is generally unlimited. However, for estates of decedents dying after 1976 and before 1982, the deduction was limited to the greater of one-half of the adjusted gross estate or $250,000. The post-1981 rules are discussed at ¶1001. The pre-1982 rules are explained at ¶1005.

• *Requirements for Marital Deduction*

An estate tax marital deduction is available if the following general rules are met:

---

[1] Code Sec. 2056(a); Reg. § 20.2056(a)-1.

(1) the decedent was married at the time of his or her death (see ¶1015);

(2) the decedent was survived by his or her spouse (see ¶1030);

(3) the surviving spouse was a U.S. citizen, or the property interest transferred passed through a qualified domestic trust (see ¶1004);

(4) the property interest was included in the decedent's gross estate (see ¶1001);

(5) the property interest passed from the decedent to the surviving spouse (see ¶1045); and

(6) the property interest is not a nondeductible terminable interest (see ¶1020; see also, ¶1002, relating to qualified terminable interest property).

Special rules apply with respect to a claim of a marital deduction with respect to bequests to a surviving spouse who is not a U.S. citizen[2] (see ¶1004).

Property qualifying for the martial deduction is listed on Schedule M (Bequests, etc., to Surviving Spouse) of Form 706 (United States Estate (and Generation-Skipping Transfer) Tax Return) (Rev. Aug. 2012) (see ¶1065).

¶1001   Amount of Deduction

In general, an unlimited marital deduction is allowed the estates of decedents dying after 1981. However, estates of decedents who died after 1981, but who had executed a will or trust before 1982 containing a maximum marital deduction formula are subject to the law as in effect prior to amendment by the Economic Recovery Tax Act of 1981 (P.L. 97-34) (see ¶1005). Under prior law, the maximum estate tax marital deduction for property passing from the decedent to the surviving spouse was the greater of one-half of the decedent's gross estate or $250,000.

The marital deduction is allowed only with respect to property, the value of which is included in determining the gross estate.[3] Thus, if the surviving spouse acquired property of the decedent during the decedent's life for full consideration in money or money's worth, no deduction will be available in the decedent's estate for such transferred property.

• *Formula Marital Bequests*

Estate planners use formula marital bequests in order to limit the marital deduction to the smallest possible amount that will minimize federal estate taxes on the estate of the first spouse to die. Since the marital deduction should be treated as merely a deferral of estate tax until the surviving spouse's death, using the unlimited marital deduction for an estate owner's entire estate could squander the estate owner's available unified credit. However, if the unified credit and the martial deduction are coordinated, estate tax at the surviving spouse's death can be reduced because fewer assets will be subject to estate tax at such time.

Decedents dying in 2010. Until the matter was resolved by the Tax Relief, Unemployment Insurance Reauthorization, and Job Creation Act of 2010 (P.L. 111-312), the year 2010, during which the estate and GST taxes did not apply, presented difficulty and uncertainty for estate planners and drafters of estate planning documents. Prior to passage of P.L. 111-312, the estate of a wealthy decedent dying in 2010 would have the advantage of not having an estate or GST tax at death. However, this might have been at the expense of unexpectedly

---

[2] Code Sec. 2056(d).   [3] Reg. §20.2056(a)-2(b)(1).

excluding loved ones from receiving property under will and trust documents. Traditional estate planning has often employed mathematical formulas to determine the amount of marital and charitable bequests. These formulas often determined a bequest by reference to the amount of property that could be passed from the decedent without incurring an estate tax liability. Because no estate tax liability was to be generated with respect to decedents dying in 2010, depending on the type of formula bequests and how they were used, a spousal or credit shelter bequest (in a marital bequest situation) (or a bequest to charitable or noncharitable beneficiaries (in a charitable bequest situation)) could unexpectedly be computed as zero, completely "cutting out" persons or organizations that the decedent wanted to support.

In response to this situation, the District of Columbia and several states enacted legislation to avoid unintended disinheritances for estates of decedents dying in 2010 (see the discussion under the heading "States Pass Beneficiary Protection Provisions," at ¶ 3).

¶ 1002 Qualified Terminable Interest Property

An estate or gift tax marital deduction is allowed for the value of qualified terminable interest property (QTIP) if the donor or decedent's executor so elects. Qualified terminable interest property is property passing from the decedent to a spouse who is entitled to all income from the property (or a portion thereof) for life, payable at least annually. This income interest is known as a "qualifying income interest." The QTIP rule is an exception to the general rule that transfers of terminable interests (such as life estates, terms for years, annuities, etc.) do not qualify for the marital deduction (see ¶ 1020 through ¶ 1029 for a detailed discussion of the terminable interest rule).[4] Under the QTIP exception, if all requirements are met, a life interest granted to a surviving spouse will not be treated as a terminable interest. The entire property subject to such an interest will be treated as passing to the spouse and, accordingly, the entire value of the transferred property will qualify for a martial deduction.[5]

The issue of whether an income interest for life fails to qualify when accumulated income for the period between the last distribution date and the date of the surviving spouse's death ("stub" income) is not distributed to the surviving spouse's estate or subject to the spouse's general power of appointment has been a subject of dispute. The Tax Court held that such an interest was not a qualifying interest,[6] but this decision was reversed by the U.S. Court of Appeals for the Ninth Circuit.[7] Later, the IRS issued final regulations that agreed with the position taken by the Ninth Circuit.[8] In a case decided after issuance of the final regulations, but arising prior to their effective date, the Tax Court reasserted the position it took in *Howard*, but again was reversed, this time by the U.S. Court of Appeals for the Eleventh Circuit.[9]

A recent decision by the Court of Appeals for the Ninth Circuit[10] demonstrates that a bequest may fail to meet the qualifying income interest requirement if trust language in any way restricts a surviving spouse/trustee's right to all of the annual income from the trust. In *Davis*, the surviving spouse, as trustee of her deceased husband's trust, was given the discretion to pay herself (as beneficiary)

---

[4] Code Sec. 2056(b)(1).

[5] Code Sec. 2056(b)(7).

[6] *R. Howard Est.*, 91 TC 329, CCH Dec. 45,002.

[7] *R. Howard Est.*, CA-9, 90-2 USTC ¶ 60,033.

[8] Reg. § 20.2056(b)-7(d)(4).

[9] *L. Shelfer Est.*, CA-11, 96-2 USTC ¶ 60,238, rev'g TC, 103 TC 10, CCH Dec. 49,967.

[10] *R. Davis Est.*, CA-9, 2005-1 USTC ¶ 60,497, 394 F3d 1294.

income for her "health, education, or support, maintenance, comfort and welfare" in accordance with her "accustomed standard of living." The court interpreted the trust language as showing the deceased husband's intent to leave the surviving spouse with an interest in trust that was restricted by the above language. Because there was no language to suggest that the decedent intended the surviving spouse's interest to qualify for the marital deduction, applicable state law (California) did not operate to reform the terms of the trust.

In community property states, a nonparticipant spouse may be treated as having a vested community property interest in his or her spouse's qualified plan, IRA, or simplified employee pension plan. Upon the death of a nonparticipant spouse, the nonparticipant spouse's survivorship interest in such a plan that is attributable to community property laws may be treated as QTIP.[11]

No person, including the spouse, can have the power to appoint any part of the property subject to the qualified income interest to any person other than the spouse during the spouse's life. However, creation or retention of any powers over all or a portion of the corpus is allowed, provided that all such powers are exercisable only on or after the spouse's death. Further, income interests granted for a term of years or a life interest subject to termination upon occurrence of a condition (such as remarriage) are not qualifying income interests.

• *Specific Portion*

The marital deduction is available when the spouse is entitled to all the income from the entire interest in the property or to the income from a specific portion of the property. For example, the right to receive 60 percent (or $3/5$) of the income of a trust for life or the right to receive the income for life from 60 percent of a trust would qualify for QTIP treatment if all other requirements for QTIP treatment are satisfied.[12]

For most decedents dying after October 24, 1992, the term "specific portion" includes only amounts determined on a fractional or percentage basis, and not pecuniary amounts.

> *Example:* Alice Green's 2009 will provided for creation of a trust funded with $3 million and providing for a benefit of $70,000 per year payable to her surviving spouse for life. Assume the trust assets are producing income of 7% per year. This is not a qualifying interest on $1 million of the property despite the fact that $70,000 of income (given the 7% income level) could be translated into all of the income on $1 million of property.

Under transitional rules, a pecuniary amount can still be a specific portion under certain circumstances for decedents dying after October 24, 1992.[13]

• *Annuities*

A survivor annuity includible in a decedent's gross estate under Code Sec. 2039 where only the surviving spouse has the right to receive payments before his or her death is treated as a qualifying income interest for life.[14] There is a presumption under the Code that a QTIP election is desired. Thus, an executor who does not intend QTIP treatment must elect out of the QTIP provision.[15]

---

[11] Code Sec. 2056(b)(7)(C).

[12] Reg. §20.2056(b)-5(c), as made applicable by Reg. §20.2056(b)-7(b)(1)(ii).

[13] Reg. §20.2056(b)-5(c)(3) and Reg. §20.2056(b)-7(e).

[14] Code Sec. 2056(b)(7)(C).

[15] Code Sec. 2056(b)(7)(C)(ii).

Special rules apply in the case of a decedent dying with a will or trust executed on or before October 24, 1992, that provides the surviving spouse with a lifetime annuity interest payable from the trust or other assets passing from the decedent. In such cases, the surviving spouse's annuity interest is treated as a qualifying income interest for life if the decedent was under a mental disability to change the disposition of his property on October 24, 1992, and the decedent did not regain competence before death. The annuity interest will not be treated as a qualifying income interest for life if any person other than the surviving spouse may receive, during the surviving spouse's lifetime, any distribution of the property or its income from which the annuity is payable. For purposes of the marital deduction, the deductible interest is that *specific portion* of the property that, assuming the interest rate generally applicable for the valuation of annuities under Code Sec. 2031 and Code Sec. 7520, would produce income equal to the minimum amount payable annually to the surviving spouse.[16]

A usufruct interest for life under Louisiana law constitutes a qualifying income interest for QTIP purposes.[17] The QTIP election will be available for both consumable and nonconsumable property; however, in the case of consumable property, the value of the usufruct will be includible in the surviving spouse's gross estate under Code Sec. 2044 (see ¶ 773) rather than under Code Sec. 2033.

• IRA and Qualified Retirement Plans

The IRS has described three circumstances where a surviving spouse would have a qualifying income interest in an IRA or other qualified retirement plan and in a marital trust that is the beneficiary of the IRA for purposes of the election to treat both the IRA and the trust as QTIP property.

In the ruling,[18] the trust provided the payment of all income to the decedent's surviving spouse. The spouse also would have the power, exercisable annually, to compel the trustee to withdraw from the IRA an amount equal to all of the IRA's income for the year and distribute the income to the spouse. In *Situation 1*, the trust was governed by applicable state law that provided that the trustee would be authorized to make adjustments between income and principal to fulfill the trustee's duty of impartiality between income and remainder beneficiaries. In *Situation 2*, the trust was administered pursuant to a state law providing that the trust income would be a certain unitrust amount of the fair market value of the trust assets determined annually. In *Situation 3*, the trustee would apply the applicable state law regarding the allocation of receipts and disbursements to income and principal, with no power to allocate between the two, to determine the amount of income that the spouse could compel the trustee to withdraw.

The IRS concluded that, in *Situation 1*, the allocation of the total return of the trust and the IRA in a manner that would fulfill the trustee's duty of impartiality would constitute a reasonable apportionment of the total return of the IRA and the trust between the income and remainder beneficiaries in accordance with Reg. § 20.2056(b)-5(f)(1) and Reg. § 1.643(b)-1. Under the circumstances of *Situation 2*, the IRS ruled that the determination of trust income and IRA income pursuant to the unitrust statute would meet the requirements of those same regulations. Therefore, in *Situations 1* and *2*, the IRA and trust would meet the requirements of Code Sec. 2056(b)(7)(B)(ii) and the surviving spouse would have a qualifying income interest for life in the IRA and the trust because the spouse

---

[16] Reg. § 20.2056(b)-7(e).
[17] Code Sec. 2056(b)(7)(B)(ii).

[18] Rev. Rul. 2006-26, 2006-1 CB 939.

would have the power to access all of the IRA income. In *Situation 3*, the IRS determined that the IRA and the trust would meet the requirements of Code Sec. 2056(b)(7)(B)(ii) and the spouse would have a qualifying income interest for life because the spouse would receive the trust income (excluding the IRA) annually and would have the power to access all of the IRA income determined pursuant to Reg. § 20.2056(b)-5(f)(1).

The principles described in *Situations 1* and 2 will not be applied adversely to taxpayers for tax years beginning before May 20, 2006, in which the trust was administered pursuant to a state statute described in Reg. § 1.643(b)-1, Reg. § 20.2056(b)-5(f)(1), and Reg. § 20.2056(b)-7(d)(1), granting the trustee the power to adjust between income and principal or authorizing a unitrust payment.[19]

• QTIP Election

The election to treat property as QTIP property is made on Schedule M (Bequests, etc., to Surviving Spouse) of Form 706 (United States Estate (and Generation-Skipping Transfer) Tax Return) (Rev. Aug. 2012) by the estate's executor.[20] Once made, an election or failure to make an election is irrevocable.[21] A QTIP election is made on Form 706 by simply listing the qualified terminable interest property on Schedule M and deducting its value.

The election may be made for a portion of property that meets the QTIP requirements, provided that the election relates to a fractional or percentile share of the property. This fraction may be defined by means of a formula.[22]

• Unnecessary QTIP Elections

The IRS has issued a procedure (Rev. Proc. 2001-38) under which it will treat unnecessary QTIP elections as null and void for purposes of Code Sec. 2056. A QTIP election will be deemed to be unnecessary if is not needed to reduce the estate tax liability to zero. For example, this new rule will apply where a QTIP election was made, even though the taxable estate (before the allowance of the marital deduction) was less than the applicable exclusion amount. It will also apply to a situation where QTIP elections were made for both the marital and the "credit shelter" trusts created by a decedent's estate plan where no estate tax would have been imposed regardless of whether an election was made for the credit shelter trust.[23]

A taxpayer will be required to produce sufficient evidence to establish that a particular QTIP election comes within the scope of this IRS procedure. For example, a taxpayer may produce a copy of the predeceased spouse's estate tax return to show that the election was not necessary to reduce the estate tax liability to zero. The new rule is effective as of June 4, 2001, and applies to elections qualifying under the procedure, regardless of when made.

The IRS has privately ruled that the relief provisions of Rev. Proc. 2001-38 are not available where the trustee of a decedent's trust was attempting to revoke in part (rather than to totally revoke) a QTIP election that had previously been made with respect to the entire corpus of the decedent's marital trust. (A total revocation of the election would not have served the interests of the trust because it would not have reduced the decedent's estate tax liability to zero.)[24]

---

[19] Rev. Rul. 2006-26, 2006-1 CB 939; modifying and superseding Rev. Rul. 2000-2, 2001-1 CB 305.

[20] Reg. § 20.2056(b)-7(b)(3).

[21] Code Sec. 2056(b)(7)(B)(v).

[22] Reg. § 20.2056(b)-7(b)(2)(ii).

[23] Rev. Proc. 2001-38, 2001-1 CB 1335.

[24] IRS Letter Ruling 200219003 (Feb. 5, 2002); IRS Letter Ruling 200422050 (Feb. 20, 2004).

A different result was allowed, however, where a decedent's estate had *underfunded* a marital trust due to a miscalculation of the value of property passing to that trust, and had made an unnecessary QTIP election with respect to the decedent's credit shelter trust. If this error in calculating the value of the property in the marital trust had not been made, the QTIP election with respect to the marital trust would have yielded a marital deduction sufficient to reduce the estate's estate tax liability to zero. The IRS concluded that the rationale of Rev. Proc. 2001-38 would void the QTIP election for the property in the credit shelter trust. Because the estate's QTIP election for the marital trust was timely and elected in a valid manner, the marital deduction for the full value of the property actually passing to the marital trust was available, provided the estate subsequently filed a supplemental return correcting the error prior to the Code Sec. 6511 deadline for claiming a credit or refund.[25]

• Contingent Income Interests

Generally, an income interest will not qualify for QTIP treatment if it is contingent on the happening of some event. One exception to this rule is making the interest contingent on the election of QTIP treatment by the executor. Effective for estates whose returns are due after February 18, 1997, Reg. § 20.2056(b)-7(d)(3)(i) permits QTIP treatment to be contingent on the executor making a QTIP election. Prior to that time, the IRS successfully challenged several such contingent QTIP elections at the Tax Court,[26] only to be reversed each time.[27] The IRS finally acquiesced to this issue upon the Tax Court's abandonment of its position.[28] Certain estates of decedents whose estate tax returns were due on or before January 18, 1997, that did not make a QTIP election because the surviving spouse's interest was contingent on the executor making the election are granted an extension of time to make the election. To be eligible, the Code Sec. 6511(a) period of limitations for filing a claim for credit or refund must not have expired.[29]

• Protective QTIP Election

Executors may make a protective election in certain limited circumstances. Such an election is allowed only if, at the time the estate tax return is filed, the executor of the estate reasonably believes there is a bona fide issue as to whether an asset is includible in the gross estate or as to the nature of the property the surviving spouse is entitled to receive.[30]

• Tax on Transfer of Interest

Property for which a QTIP election is made will be subject to transfer taxes at the earlier of (1) the date on which the spouse disposes (by gift, sale or otherwise) of all or part of the qualifying income interest, or (2) the date of the spouse's death. If a spouse transfers the qualifying income interest during life, the entire value of the property, reduced by any amount received by the spouse upon disposition, is a taxable gift (see ¶ 2313).[31] Otherwise, the entire value of the property subject to the qualified income interest will be included in the spouse's

---

[25] IRS Letter Ruling 200323010 (Feb. 19, 2003).

[26] *A. Clayton Est.*, 97 TC 327, CCH Dec. 47,612; *W. Robertson Est.*, 98 TC 678, CCH Dec. 48,310; *J. Spencer Est.*, 64 TCM 937, CCH Dec. 48,546(M), TC Memo. 1992-579.

[27] *A. Clayton Est.*, CA-5, 92-2 USTC ¶ 60,121, 976 F2d 1486; *W. Robertson Est.*, CA-8, 94-1

USTC ¶ 60,153; *J. Spencer Est.*, CA-6, 95-1 USTC ¶ 60,188.

[28] *W. Clack Est.*, 106 TC 131, CCH Dec. 51,193 (Acq.).

[29] Reg. § 20.2056(b)-7(d)(3)(ii).

[30] Reg. § 20.2056(b)-7(c).

[31] Code Sec. 2519.

gross estate at its fair market value on the date of death or on the alternate valuation date, if elected (see ¶ 773).[32]

The spouse or the spouse's estate may recover from the recipient of the property the gift tax paid on the remainder interest as a result of a lifetime transfer of the income interest, or the estate tax paid as a result of the inclusion of the value of the property in the spouse's gross estate, as well as any penalties or interest attributable to the additional estate or gift tax.[33]

¶ 1003   Split Gifts to Spouse and Charity

There is a special rule for transfers of interests in the same property to a spouse and a qualifying charitable organization. If an individual creates a qualified charitable remainder annuity trust or unitrust and the donor and his or her spouse are the only beneficiaries who are not a charitable beneficiary or an employee stock ownership plan beneficiary, the prohibition on deduction of terminable interests (see ¶ 1020) does not apply. The individual (or his or her estate) receives a charitable deduction for the value of the remainder interest and a marital deduction for the value of the annuity or unitrust interest, and no transfer tax is imposed.[34]

If the individual transfers a qualified income interest to his or her spouse with a remainder to charity, the entire value of the property will be considered as passing to the surviving spouse, and will qualify for a marital deduction and no part of the value of the property qualifies for the charitable deduction.[35] Although, upon the spouse's death, the entire value of the property will be included in the spouse's gross estate, any property passing outright to charity may qualify for a charitable deduction.

¶ 1004   Qualified Domestic Trusts

Effective for estates of decedents dying after November 10, 1988, property passing to a surviving spouse who is not a U.S. citizen is not eligible for the estate tax marital deduction unless the property passes through a qualified domestic trust (QDOT). However, in the case of a nonresident alien whose spouse is a U.S. citizen, the marital deduction will be allowed for estate tax purposes without the need for a QDOT.

In order to be considered a QDOT, the trust instrument must provide that at least one of the trustees be a U.S. citizen or domestic corporation and that any corpus distribution be subject to the U.S. trustee's right to withhold the estate tax imposed on such distribution. For trust instruments of decedents dying after November 10, 1988, if the instrument provides that all the trustees must be either U.S. citizens or domestic corporations, then the withholding requirement is deemed satisfied regardless of whether the withholding requirement is explicitly stated in the trust instrument.[36] The trust must also meet security requirements designed to ensure collection of the estate tax imposed on the trust. The trust instrument must require that at least one of the trustees be an individual citizen of the United States or a domestic corporation.[37] In addition, if the trust assets, as of the date of the decedent's death or, if applicable, the alternate valuation date, exceed $2 million, the trust's governing instrument must require that either:

---

[32] Code Sec. 2044.
[33] Code Sec. 2207A.
[34] Code Sec. 2056(b)(8).

[35] Reg. § 20.2056(b)-9.
[36] Act Sec.1303, Taxpayer Relief Act of 1997 (P.L. 105-34).
[37] Code Sec. 2056A(a)(1).

    (1) during the entire term of the QDOT, at least one U.S. trustee be a bank; or

    (2) the U.S. trustee furnish a bond in favor of the IRS in an amount equal to at least 65 percent of the fair market value of the trust assets; or

    (3) the U.S. trustee furnish an irrevocable letter of credit issued by a U.S. branch of a foreign bank or by a foreign bank and confirmed by a U.S. bank, in an amount equal to 65 percent of the trust assets.[38]

If the fair market value of the trust assets as finally determined for federal estate tax purposes is less than $2 million, the QDOT need not meet any of the three requirements listed above if the trust instrument expressly provides that no more than 35 percent of the fair market value of the trust assets, determined annually, may be invested in real property located outside of the United States.[39]

In addition, the executor must make an irrevocable QDOT election on the estate tax return with respect to the trust. This election is made by listing the QDOT on Schedule M (Bequests, etc., to Surviving Spouse) of Form 706 (United States Estate (and Generation-Skipping Transfer) Tax Return) and taking the marital deduction therefor.[40] However, no election may be made on a return filed more than one year after the due date of such return, including extensions.[41]

Property passing directly to the surviving spouse may qualify for the marital deduction if, before the estate tax return is filed and while the QDOT election can still be timely made, the property is transferred or irrevocably assigned to the QDOT.[42]

An estate tax is imposed on corpus distributions from the trust that are made prior to the date of the surviving spouse's death and on the value of the property remaining in a QDOT on the date of death of the surviving spouse. However, the estate tax will no longer be imposed on a QDOT after the surviving spouse becomes a U.S. citizen if (1) the spouse was a U.S. resident at the time of the decedent's death and at all times thereafter, (2) no tax was imposed on a QDOT distribution before the spouse became a U.S. citizen, or (3) the spouse elected to treat any distribution on which tax had been imposed as a taxable gift made by the spouse (thereby reducing the unified credit available to the spouse) for the purpose of determining the spouse's future estate and gift tax liability.[43] In addition, the estate tax on distributions is itself a distribution subject to the estate tax.[44] Further, a distribution of corpus from a QDOT to a surviving spouse is excluded from the estate tax if the distribution is made "on account of hardship."[45] If no property other than the property passing to the surviving spouse is transferred to the QDOT, the trust need not otherwise qualify for the marital deduction. If the trust is funded with other property passing from the decedent, however, then all of the assets in the QDOT must qualify for the marital deduction.[46]

A special rule applies if more than one QDOT exists with respect to a decedent.[47] In such cases, the amount of estate tax imposed on the trusts is determined using the highest rate of tax in effect at the time of the decedent's

---

[38] Reg. § 20.2056A-2(d)(1)(i).

[39] Reg. § 20.2056A-2(d)(1)(ii).

[40] Instructions for Form 706, Schedule M, p. 36 (Rev. August 2013).

[41] Code Sec. 2056A(d).

[42] Reg. § 20.2056A-4(b)(1).

[43] Code Sec. 2056A(b)(12).

[44] Code Sec. 2056A(b)(11).

[45] Code Sec. 2056A(b)(3)(B).

[46] Reg. § 20.2056A-4(b)(1).

[47] Code Sec. 2056A(b)(2)(C).

death, unless a U.S. citizen or domestic corporation is responsible for filing all estate tax returns for such QDOTs and meets IRS regulatory requirements.

Another special rule states that estate tax is not imposed on distributions defined as income. However, the IRS is authorized to prescribe such regulations as necessary to determine when payments under an annuity would be treated as income for purposes of the estate tax on distributions. The IRS is also empowered to prescribe regulations under which an annuity or other payment, includible in a decedent's gross estate and payable for life or a term of years, may be treated as a QDOT.[48] Such interests would include property interests that cannot be transferred to a QDOT under federal law, such as an interest in an IRA or qualified plan.[49]

Certain estate tax benefits, such as charitable and marital deductions, special use valuation, and extensions of time to pay estate tax, are allowed against the estate tax on QDOT distributions if such benefits would be allowable with respect to the estate of the surviving spouse.[50] In addition, property distributed from a QDOT during the surviving spouse's lifetime would receive a carryover basis. However, the carryover basis would be increased by an amount equal to the proportion of any QDOT estate tax paid that the net appreciation in the property bears to the distribution.[51]

• *Returns*

Form 706-QDT (U.S. Estate Tax Return for Qualified Domestic Trusts) (Rev. August 2013) is used to report the estate tax due with respect to taxable distributions from a QDOT, the death of the noncitizen surviving spouse, the trust's ceasing to qualify as a QDOT, and hardship distributions from the trust. Form 706-QDT must be filed within nine months following the date of the surviving spouse's death or the date that the trust ceases to qualify as a QDOT. The return is due by April 15 of the year following the year in which the taxable event or hardship distribution occurs.[52]

If the estate tax for the decedent spouse's estate has not been finally determined (such as in the case where a judicial determination of the tax is pending), a tentative tax is imposed using the highest estate tax rate in effect as of the date of the decedent's death. When a final determination is made, any amount of the tentative tax that is in excess of the additional estate tax that would have been imposed had the property been included in the decedent's estate is refundable if a claim is filed not later than one year after the date of final determination. A refund of tentative tax imposed pending final resolution of estate tax liability bears interest.[53]

A trustee is personally liable for the tax, but may be discharged from such liability.[54] The tax imposed on a QDOT is treated as an estate tax with respect to the decedent spouse's estate. Therefore, it qualifies as a previously paid tax for purposes of the Code Sec. 2103 credit for tax on prior transfers, determined without regard to the date of the decedent spouse's death.[55] In addition, there is a lien against the property giving rise to such tax for 10 years after the taxable event.

---

[48] Code Sec. 2056A(e).

[49] Conference Committee Report to the Revenue Reconciliation Act of 1989 (P.L. 1001-239); Reg. § 20.2056A-4(b)(7) and Reg. § 20.2056A-4(c).

[50] Reg. § 20.2056A-6(b).

[51] Reg. § 20.2056A-12.

[52] Code Sec. 2056A(b)(5).

[53] Code Sec. 2056A(b)(2)(B).

[54] Code Sec. 2204.

[55] Reg. § 20.2056A-7.

¶ 1005   Pre-1982 Marital Deduction Rules

For estates of decedents dying before 1982, the maximum estate tax marital deduction for property passing from the decedent to the surviving spouse was equal to the greater of one-half of the decedent's adjusted gross estate, or $250,000.[56]

• *Transitional Rule for Pre-1982 Marital Deduction Formula Clauses*

An unlimited marital deduction is allowed for estates of decedents dying after 1981 (see ¶ 1001). However, many wills and trusts that were executed prior to 1982 included maximum marital deduction formula clauses under which the amount of property transferred to the surviving spouse was to be determined by reference to the maximum allowable marital deduction. Because, with respect to estates of decedents dying before 1982, the maximum estate tax deduction was the greater of $250,000 or one-half of the adjusted gross estate, many individuals may not have intended any greater amount to pass to their surviving spouses as might be the case if the unlimited marital deduction were used in the computation of the marital deduction under the formula clause.

Under a transitional rule, the unlimited marital deduction is not applicable to transfers resulting from a will or trust executed before September 12, 1981, that contains a maximum marital deduction formula clause. The transitional rule applies provided that (1) the decedent died after 1981, (2) the formula clause was not amended at any time after September 12, 1981, and before the death of the decedent to refer specifically to the unlimited marital deduction, and (3) there is no state law that would construe the formula clause as referring to the unlimited marital deduction.[57]

Whether a particular will or trust contains a maximum marital deduction formula has been a frequently litigated question. The mere appearance of a marital deduction formula clause in a will or trust will not satisfy the requirements of the transitional rule. Rather, the will or trust must contain a formula *expressly* providing that the surviving spouse is to receive the maximum amount of property qualifying for the marital deduction. Any additions to the formula that might further reduce the amount received by the spouse to ensure that the unified credit or other credits of the estate are fully utilized will not be a formula clause for purposes of the transitional rule.[58]

¶ 1010   Same-Sex Marriages

In a 5 to 4 decision relating to the allowance of a marital deduction for the surviving spouse of a same-sex marriage, the U.S. Supreme Court[59] held that section 3 of the Defense of Marriage Act (DOMA), which defined marriage as only a legal union between one man and one woman as husband and wife, is unconstitutional because it violates the Fifth Amendment's Equal Protection Clause as applied to persons of the same sex who are legally married under the laws of a state that recognizes same-sex marriage. In implementing this decision, the IRS will take a "state-of-celebration" approach.[60] Thus, same-sex couples who

---

[56] Code Sec. 2056(c), prior to its repeal by P.L. 97-34. For the estates of decedents dying before 1977, the marital deduction was limited to 50 percent of the value of the adjusted gross estate.

[57] Act Sec. 403(e), P.L. 97-34.

[58] *L. Neisen Est.*, CA-8, 89-1 USTC ¶ 13,790, 865 F2d 162; *F.L. Bruning Est.*, CA-10, 89-2

USTC ¶ 13,821; *S.I. Levitt Est.*, 95 TC 289, CCH Dec. 46,873; IRS Technical Advice Memorandum 9206001 (December 7, 1991).

[59] *E. Windsor*, SCt, 2013-2 USTC ¶ 60,667, aff'g CA-2, 2012-2 USTC ¶ 60,654.

[60] Rev. Rul. 2013-17, IRB 2013-38, 201.

are legally married in jurisdictions that recognize their marriages will be treated as married for federal tax purposes, regardless of whether or not the jurisdiction of their residence recognizes same-sex marriage. As of November 20, 2013, 16 states (California, Connecticut, Delaware, Hawaii, Illinois, Iowa, Maine, Massachusetts, Maryland, Minnesota, New Hampshire, New Jersey, New York, Rhode Island, Vermont, and Washington) and the District of Columbia recognized same-sex marriages. Additionally, several counties in New Mexico are issuing marriage licenses to same-sex couples.

Over 200 Internal Revenue Code provisions and regulations include the terms "spouse" or "marriage", or derivatives thereof. According to the IRS, those terms, along with, "husband" and "wife" now include same-sex married individuals, if the marriage was lawful. This gender-neutral reading of the code follows the Supreme Court's decision in *Windsor*. However, those terms do not include individuals in a registered domestic partnership, civil union, or other similar formal arrangement. These individuals will still be considered to be unmarried for purposes of the Internal Revenue Code.

In explaining its reliance on the state-of-celebration approach to implement the *Windsor* decision, the IRS noted that it previously used this approach regarding common-law marriages.[61] The IRS concluded that dealing with same-sex marriages (which, like common-law marriages, are not recognized in every state), would be extremely difficult and expensive for administrative purposes if a couple's marital status changed simply by moving to a different state. Furthermore, because spouses are treated as related parties, property may be attributed to the other spouse under a number of code provisions. Thus, if the couple moved, and the IRS did not adopt a uniform rule of recognition, the attribution of a property interest could change. This could potentially impact other parties involved in the transaction, as well as entities created.

> *Election:* Same-sex couples may, but are not required to, file amended returns for prior tax years that remain open under the Code Sec. 6511 statute of limitations, which is generally the later of three years from the date the return was filed or two years from the date the tax was paid. Individuals who wish to file a refund claim for gift or estate tax should file Form 843, Claim for Refund and Request for Abatement. Rev. Rul. 2013-17 is effective as of September 16, 2013, but may be relied upon for earlier periods, subject to the statute of limitations.

¶ 1015   Status as Surviving Spouse

The person receiving the decedent's property for which a marital deduction is claimed must qualify as a "surviving spouse" on the date of the decedent's death. A legal separation that has not terminated the marriage at the time of death does not change the status of the surviving spouse.[62] If an interest in property passes from the decedent to a person who was the decedent's spouse, but who was not married to the decedent at the time of death, the interest is not considered as passing to the surviving spouse. If a decedent's divorce from a prior spouse is declared invalid by a state court having jurisdiction, the IRS will not allow a marital deduction for the decedent's bequest of property to a subsequent spouse.[63]

---

[61] Rev. Rul. 58-66, 1958-1 CB 60.

[62] *M.S. Eccles*, 19 TC 1049, CCH Dec. 19,508, aff'd on other issues by CA-4, 54-1 USTC ¶ 9129, 208 F2d 769.

[63] Rev. Rul. 67-442, 1967-2 CB 65; *W.A. Steffke Est.*, CA-7, 76-2 USTC ¶ 13,145, 538 F2d 730, cert. denied; *L.J. Goldwater Est.*, CA-2, 76-2 USTC ¶ 13,146, 539 F2d 878, cert. denied.

A transfer by the decedent during his lifetime to an individual to whom he was not married at the time of the transfer but to whom he was married at the time of his death and who survives him is a transfer by the decedent to his surviving spouse with respect to gifts includible in a decedent's gross estate under Code Sec. 2035.[64]

Status as a surviving spouse cannot be established by a will provision that treated the first spouse to die as a surviving spouse for purposes of the marital deduction.[65] The Tax Court concluded that in order for a marital deduction to apply, Code Sec. 2056(a) required that "surviving spouse" be given its ordinary meaning, that is, the spouse for whom the deduction is claimed must have actually survived the decedent. The fact that a will provided that a decedent would be deemed to predecease his wife if she died within six months of his death did not operate to confer surviving spouse status on his wife, who died 46 days before her husband.

¶ 1020   Life Estate or Other Terminable Interest

Generally, no marital deduction is allowed for property interests that are terminable interests[66] (but see the exception for qualified terminable interest property, discussed at ¶ 1002). A terminable interest is an interest in property that will terminate or fail on the lapse of time or on the occurrence, or the failure to occur, of some event or contingency. The purpose of the rule is to require that if property is transferred to the surviving spouse, it will be includible in the surviving spouse's estate unless disposed of or dissipated during the surviving spouse's lifetime.

• Types of Terminable Interests

Terminable interests include life estates, terms for years, annuities, patents and copyrights. However, a bond, note, or similar contractual obligation that would not have the effect of an annuity or a term for years, is not a terminable interest.[67] Whether or not an interest is a terminable interest is determined by state law[68] at the death of the decedent.[69]

• Nondeductible Terminable Interests

A terminable interest is nondeductible if:

(1) an interest in the same property has passed (for less than adequate and full consideration in money or money's worth) from the decedent to any person other than the surviving spouse or other than the estate of the surviving spouse; and

(2) by reason of its passing, such person or his heirs or assigns may possess or enjoy any part of the property after such termination or failure of the interest passing to the surviving spouse.

It is not necessary that the contingency or event occur or fail to occur in order to make the interest terminable.[70]

Example: Tom Atwood dies leaving stocks in trust, the income to pass to his wife, Sandy, for life, with the corpus to be distributed to his son,

---

[64] Rev. Rul. 79-354, 1979-2 CB 334.

[65] *K. Lee Est.*, TC Memo. 2007-371, CCH Dec. 57,205(M), 94 TCM 604.

[66] Code Sec. 2056(b)(1).

[67] Reg. § 20.2056(b)-1(b).

[68] *H.P. Shedd Est.*, CA-9, 56-2 USTC ¶ 11,644, 237 F2d 345.

[69] *M. Kellmann, Transferee*, DC Mo., 68-1 USTC ¶ 12,518, 286 FSupp. 632.

[70] Reg. § 20.2056(b)-1.

Jason, free of the trust when he reaches maturity. If Jason predeceases Sandy, the corpus is to be turned over to Sandy, free of the trust. There is also a gift over in the event of Jason's death after the date of Sandy's death but before the date of Jason's maturity. The interest passing to Sandy on Tom's death is a nondeductible terminable interest.

An estate for the life of the surviving spouse is an interest that will terminate in all events. If conditions (1) and (2), described above, exist, it is immaterial whether the interest passing to the surviving spouse is considered a vested interest or a contingent interest. No marital deduction is allowed in any event if the life estate or terminable interest is to be acquired for the surviving spouse, pursuant to directions of the decedent, by his executor or by the trustee of a trust.[71]

If the decedent by will bequeaths a terminable interest for which a deduction is not allowed and the surviving spouse takes under the will, the marital deduction is not allowed. A deduction is denied, even though, under local law, the interest that the spouse could have taken against the will was a fee interest for which a deduction would be allowed.[72] Similarly, the marital deduction was disallowed for the interest passing to the surviving spouse as an income beneficiary or annuitant under a trust in which other persons had an interest if the surviving spouse had no power over the principal.[73]

The IRS has ruled that a cash bequest that a decedent's surviving spouse elected in lieu of a life income interest in a trust pursuant to a provision in the decedent's will qualified for an estate tax marital deduction because it was not a terminable interest. However, no such deduction was allowable for an additional amount that the spouse could demand from the trustee in order to assist the spouse in purchasing a new house. In the former situation, the spouse had an absolute right to the cash bequest as of the date of the decedent's death and the election in the will was a mere procedural requirement that did not constitute an event or contingency for marital deduction purposes. The additional amount that the spouse could demand from the trustee constituted a nondeductible terminable interest because it was conditioned on the spouse's purchase of a new house.[74]

The interest of the surviving spouse is not considered a terminable interest merely because the spouse's possession or enjoyment may be affected by events not provided for by the terms of the bequest. These events are the surviving spouse's death, or loss of the property by fire, earthquake, condemnation, or nonpayment of taxes, or the fact that the property may be used up in an indefinite period of time. However, interests in patents, copyrights, and annuity contracts that will be used up in a fixed length of time are terminable interests and are not deductible if an interest of a third person in the same property will outlast the termination of the interest of the surviving spouse.[75]

Although it formerly contested the matter, the IRS now agrees that the property passing to a decedent's spouse under an "equalization clause" governing a trust created for the spouse's benefit by the decedent is not a nondeductible terminable interest.[76] Under the clause, the trustee has the power to select as

---

[71] Reg. §20.2056(b)-1(c) and (f).

[72] *E.J. Allen, Exr.*, CA-2, 66-1 USTC ¶12,393, cert. denied. See also IRS Letter Ruling 8236004 (May 23, 1982).

[73] *C.H. Stockdick Est.*, DC Tex., 65-2 USTC ¶12,351.

[74] Rev. Rul. 82-184, 1982-2 CB 215.

[75] Reg. §20.2056(b)-1(g).

[76] Rev. Rul. 82-23, 1982-1 CB 139; *C.W. Smith Est.*, 66 TC 415, CCH Dec. 33,862 (Acq.), aff'd per curiam, CA-7, 77-2 USTC ¶13,215, 565 F2d 455; and *V.S. Laurin Est.*,

the valuation date the date of death or the alternate valuation date, whichever produces the greatest tax savings, in order to determine the percentage of trust assets to be placed in the marital portion so as to equalize the estates of both spouses.

¶ 1023   Widow's Allowance—Dower Interest

An allowance to a surviving spouse for support during the period of settlement of a decedent's estate will qualify for the marital deduction if it is not classified as a terminable interest. Although a widow's (or widower's) allowance may fall within the terminable interest rule, a marital deduction can be obtained for any portion thereof that would, in any event, pass to the surviving spouse by operation of law or of the decedent's will.[77]

State Law Alert: Whether a widow's allowance is a terminable interest is dependent upon the state statute that authorizes the support payments. If, under the authorizing state law, the widow's right to a support allowance is a vested one, her interest in the allowance will qualify for the estate tax marital deduction. If, however, the right would not survive her death or remarriage prior to the securing of an award by the court, her interest is considered a nondeductible terminable one.[78] The nature of the widow's interest in the allowance must be determined as of the date of the decedent's death.[79] The courts have ruled that widows' allowances in Illinois, Maine, Maryland, Michigan, Minnesota, Missouri, Ohio, and Oklahoma qualify for the marital deduction. (Some of these cases were decided before the *Jackson* case and may not be followed.) Widows' allowances or awards have been held to be nondeductible terminable interests in the states of California, Connecticut, Florida, Georgia, Iowa, Massachusetts, Montana, Nebraska, Oregon, Tennessee, Texas, and Wisconsin. (State laws should be consulted for possible changes that would permit a deduction.)

Dower and curtesy interests (or statutory estates in lieu thereof) may also qualify for a marital deduction, or they may not be deductible because of the terminable interest rule. The deductibility of such interests is also dependent upon state law. A deduction will be allowed if the surviving spouse has a fixed or vested right to the dower at the moment of the decedent's death and if the dower interest is an absolute interest.[80] A payment of the commuted value of a widow's dower, if requested and paid in accordance with applicable state law, also qualifies for the marital deduction if the right to it vests at the moment of the decedent-spouse's death, even though the payment is in lieu of a dower life estate in the decedent's property.[81]

State Law Alert: Dower interests (or amounts awarded in lieu of such interests) in the states of Arkansas, Colorado, Florida, Hawaii, Illinois, Iowa, Kentucky, Montana, New York, North Carolina, South Carolina, Tennessee, and Virginia have qualified for marital deductions. If the surviving spouse does not have such a vested interest under state law, the interest will not

---

(Footnote Continued)

CA-6, 81-1 USTC ¶ 13,398, 645 F2d 8, aff'g TC, 72 TC 73, CCH Dec. 35,987 (Acq.).

[77] Rev. Rul. 82-23, 1982-1 CB 139; *C.W. Smith Est.*, 66 TC 415, CCH Dec. 33,862 (Acq.), aff'd per curiam, CA-7, 77-2 USTC ¶ 13,215, 565 F2d 455; and *V.S. Laurin Est.*, CA-6, 81-1 USTC ¶ 13,398, 645 F2d 8, aff'g TC, 72 TC 73, CCH Dec. 35,987 (Acq.).

[78] Rev. Rul. 83, 1953-1 CB 395.

[79] *L.R. Jackson*, SCt, 64-1 USTC ¶ 12,221, 376 U.S. 503.

[80] Rev. Rul. 72-8, 1972-1 CB 309.

[81] Rev. Rul. 72-7, 1972-1 CB 308, modified by Rev. Rul. 83-107, 1983-2 CB 159.

qualify for the marital deduction. The U.S. Court of Appeals for the Fifth Circuit has held that dower interests in Alabama do not qualify for the marital deduction, but that money received in lieu of dower may qualify.[82] The Tax Court has stated, by way of dictum, that dower in New Jersey also does not qualify for the deduction.[83]

¶ 1027   Life Interest with Power of Appointment

The terminable interest rule is designed primarily to prevent the allowance of a marital deduction with respect to property that, by the terms of the transfer, is likely to escape inclusion in the gross estate of the surviving spouse. Although there is a limited elective exception to this rule for qualified terminable interest property with respect to estates of decedents dying after 1981 (see ¶ 1002), this property is includible in the surviving spouse's gross estate by specific statutory provision.[84]

When a decedent gives to his or her spouse an interest for life, together with a general power of appointment, the possibility of exclusion from the surviving spouse's gross estate is substantially removed. Therefore, such transfers (which are usually made in the form of a "marital deduction" trust), are permitted to qualify for the marital deduction as exceptions to the terminable interest rule, so long as they meet certain conditions.[85]

• *All of the Income Requirement*

The surviving spouse must be entitled for life to all income from the property interest and have a general power of appointment over the property. Without disqualifying the property interest from the marital deduction, a surviving spouse may be entitled to the income from a specific portion of the property interest.[86] In general, for decedents dying after October 24, 1992, a "specific portion" is a portion of a property interest determined on a fractional or percentage basis only.[87]

Prior to the enactment of Code Sec. 2056(b)(10), the U.S. Supreme Court had held that "specific portion" included a fixed dollar amount.[88] Under a transitional rule, a right to a specific amount of income will qualify for the marital deduction if the interest was created under a will or revocable trust executed before October 24, 1992, if either (1) the decedent dies within three years after October 24, 1992, or (2) on October 24, 1992, the decedent was under a mental disability to change the disposition of his or her property and did not regain competence to dispose of such property before death. The transitional rule, however, does not apply if the will or trust is amended after October 24, 1992, to increase the amount of the transfer qualifying for the marital deduction or to alter the terms by which the interest passes.[89] Under the transitional rule, a specific sum payable annually, or at more frequent intervals, out of property and its income that is not limited by the income of the property is treated as the right to receive the income from a specific portion of the property. The specific portion is the portion of the property that, assuming the interest rate generally applicable

---

[82] *F.A. Crosby, Admr.*, CA-5, 58-2 USTC ¶ 11,808, 257 F2d 515; *M.I. Hiles, Exr.*, CA-5, 63-1 USTC ¶ 12,146.

[83] *J. Nachimson Est.*, 50 TC 452, CCH Dec. 28,993.

[84] Code Sec. 2044.

[85] Code Sec. 2056(b)(5).

[86] Reg. § 20.2056(b)-5.

[87] Code Sec. 2056(b)(10).

[88] *Northeastern Pennsylvania National Bank & Trust Co., Exr.*, SCt, 67-1 USTC ¶ 12,470, 387 US 213.

[89] Reg. § 20.2056(b)-5(c)(3).

for the valuation of annuities at the time of the decedent's death, would produce income equal to such payments.

• *Annual Income Requirement*

The surviving spouse must be entitled to receive the income annually, or at more frequent intervals. Such spouse must have the power, exercisable in favor of herself or himself or of her or his estate, to appoint the property interest or specific portion from which he or she has a right to the income. Such power must be exercisable by the spouse alone and in all events. It is not necessary that the surviving spouse have the right to exercise the power during lifetime if he or she can exercise it by will and in favor of her or his estate as well as in favor of other persons. The property must not be subject to a power in any other person to appoint to anyone other than the surviving spouse any of the property for which the deduction is sought. Nor is it necessary that the property be in trust.

> *Comment:* In determining whether a transfer meets the above requirements, state law should be consulted. For example, if the transfer does not specify the frequency of income payments, the transfer may still qualify, if, under state law, income must be distributed at least annually.

• *Powers*

The IRS has issued rules that cover the power of a fiduciary to allocate income and expenses between income and principal and to provide depreciation reserves, without causing the loss or diminution of the marital deduction, where the spouse has a life estate and power of appointment.[90] A fiduciary may have these powers if state law or the governing instrument (1) prevents the fiduciary from favoring the other beneficiaries over the spouse, (2) gives the spouse enforceable rights to enjoy the trust, and (3) limits the fiduciary from making allocations, based on the composition of the assets, that would deprive the spouse of enjoyment. A fiduciary may also have discretionary powers to retain trust cash without investing it and to determine in what form distributions are to be made. These powers are permissible if the governing instrument or state law provides reasonable limitations.

A surviving spouse does not have a power of appointment exercisable by the survivor alone and in all events over that portion of a marital trust that an executor has the authority to use to pay death taxes to the federal or state government.[91] In one situation, the IRS denied a marital deduction for property that passed to a trust for the benefit of a decedent's spouse, even though the spouse received a life estate in the trust and the power to appoint the trust corpus for herself or her creditors. The spouse did not have the power to exercise the power "alone and in all events" because the trustee could prevent exercise of the power in his sole discretion if the remainder beneficiaries of the trust objected to a proposed exercise. However, because the trustee did not have a substantial interest in the trust corpus adverse to that of the spouse, the value of the trust corpus was includible in her gross estate as property subject to a general power of appointment.[92] A testamentary power of appointment over a trust was not exercisable by a surviving spouse alone and in all events where the trust agreement provided that the spouse's right to the income and principal of the trust and the testamentary general power of appointment terminated if the

---

[90] Rev. Rul. 69-56, 1969-1 CB 224.

[91] *M.S. Wycoff Est.*, CA-10, 74-2 USTC ¶ 13,037, 506 F2d 1144, cert. denied.

[92] Rev. Rul. 82-156, 1982-2 CB 216.

spouse became incompetent before either withdrawing the corpus or exercising the power of appointment.[93]

¶ 1028   Life Insurance and Annuities

The proceeds of life insurance, endowment, or annuity contracts over which a surviving spouse is given a power of appointment may qualify for a marital deduction.[94] (Also, note the treatment of certain joint and survivor annuities as discussed at ¶ 1002.) The proceeds must be payable in installments or held by the insurer subject to an agreement to pay interest. The surviving spouse alone must have the right to receive all or a specific portion of the payments to be made during his or her lifetime. If held at interest, the proceeds, following termination of the period during which interest is to be paid, may be distributed in a lump sum or in installments. The distributions of interest or installments must be made at least annually and the first payment must be made not later than 13 months after the decedent's death.

The surviving spouse must have the power to appoint the entire proceeds or the portion from which he or she is entitled to receive installments or interest distributions. The power must be in favor of that person or that person's estate, regardless of whether he or she may also exercise the power in favor of others. There must be no power in any other person to appoint to any person other than the surviving spouse.

The power must also be exercisable in all events. Formal administrative restrictions on the survivor's right of withdrawal of the proceeds are considered to be for the convenience of the insurer and do not disqualify the survivor's interest from meeting the exercisable-in-all-events test.

¶ 1029   Interest of Spouse Conditioned on Survival for Limited Period

An interest passing to a surviving spouse will qualify for the marital deduction, so long as it is not terminable on other grounds, if it is conditioned upon (1) the surviving spouse's survival for six months after the death of the decedent and the spouse does not, in fact, die within this period, (2) the surviving spouse's not dying in a common disaster taking the lives of both spouses, which does not, in fact, occur, or (3) both events, and neither of them occurs.[95] The above rule does not apply to an ordinary life estate, such as a devise to the wife for her life, with remainder over to another because her death at *any* time will cause such termination or failure.

Otherwise qualifying marital bequests that are conditioned on survival to the final distribution of the decedent's estate, or to administration or settlement of the estate, are nearly always held to be terminable, even though the surviving spouse lives beyond this period. The U.S. Court of Appeals for the Second Circuit, however, has ruled that this rule had no application where state law vested real property in the surviving spouse at the date of the decedent's death.[96]

Status as a surviving spouse cannot be established by a "reverse survivorship" will provision that treated the first spouse to die as a surviving spouse for purposes of the marital deduction.[97] The Tax Court concluded that in order for a

---

[93] *D. Walsh Est.*, 110 TC 393, CCH Dec. 52,733.

[94] Code Sec. 2056(b)(6).

[95] Reg. § 20.2056(b)-3.

[96] *S.W. Horton Est.*, CA-2, 68-1 USTC ¶ 12,503, 388 F2d 51.

[97] *K. Lee Est.*, TC Memo. 2007-371, CCH Dec. 57,205(M), 94 TCM 604.

marital deduction to apply, Code Sec. 2056(a) required that "surviving spouse" be given its ordinary meaning, that is, the spouse for whom the deduction is claimed must have actually survived the decedent. The fact that a will provided that a decedent would be deemed to predecease his wife if she died within six months of his death did not operate to confer surviving spouse status on his wife, who died 46 days before her husband.

¶ 1030   Simultaneous Deaths of Joint Property Owners

For federal estate tax purposes, upon the decedent's death, any property that the decedent owned jointly with someone other than the surviving spouse is includible in the decedent's gross estate to the extent that the decedent paid for it. However, to the extent that such property passes to the surviving spouse, it qualifies for the marital deduction. If the decedent and his or her spouse are joint owners of property and it is determined that they have died simultaneously, the rule for distribution of such property may differ from general property rules, since most of the states have adopted the Uniform Simultaneous Death Act.

Section 3 of that Act provides that "Where there is no sufficient evidence that two joint tenants or tenants by the entirety have died otherwise than simultaneously the property so held shall be distributed one-half as if one had survived and one-half as if the other had survived . . . ". Thus, one-half of the property will pass to one decedent's heirs and the other half will pass to the spouse's heirs.

> *Comment:* The general tax rule that property be included in the decedent's gross estate to the extent that the decedent furnished consideration for it does not apply in the case of "qualified joint interests" owned by husbands and wives. A "qualified joint interest" created and held by a husband and wife is divided equally between the spouses for estate tax purposes. A qualified joint interest is any property owned solely by spouses in joint tenancy or tenancy by the entirety (see ¶ 502).

¶ 1031   Interest Passing to Unidentified Persons

A marital deduction is not allowed for property interests that may pass to unidentified persons after the death of the spouse. If it is not possible to determine the particular person or persons to whom an interest may pass from the decedent, the interest is considered as having passed to a person other than the decedent's surviving spouse. This rule is inapplicable, however, to a spouse's life interest in connection with a qualifying power of appointment.[98]

> *Example:* Andrew Martin, by his will, devised the family real estate and home on Elm Street to his wife, Emily, for life and then to such of his grandchildren as survive Emily, but if none survive her, then to Emily's estate. His estate elected not to treat the bequest as qualified terminable interest property. No marital deduction is allowable for either the life estate or the contingent remainder to Emily's estate. An interest in the property is considered to pass to the grandchildren. Some of them may possess or enjoy the Elm Street property upon the death of Emily. It is immaterial that the grandchildren are not in being at the time of Andrew's death.

---

[98] Reg. § 20.2056(c)-3.

¶ 1032   Interest in Unidentified Assets

If the interest passing to a spouse can be satisfied out of assets for which no marital deduction would be allowed, the marital deduction is affected.[99] The value of the interest passing to the spouse, for the purpose of the marital deduction, is reduced by the aggregate value of such assets.[100]

The assets out of which the interest passing to the surviving spouse may be satisfied are determined prior to payment of any general claims, but without including named property specifically bequeathed or devised.

> *Example:* Arthur Britton bequeathed $200,000 to his surviving spouse, Jean. The general estate includes a term-for-years interest (valued at $225,000 in determining the value of Britton's gross estate) in his country home and acreage—an interest retained by Britton after a gift of the realty to his son. If the bequest to Jean may be satisfied out of the term-for-years interest, the marital deduction with respect to the bequest of $200,000 is reduced to zero. It is immaterial whether Jean actually receives the term-for-years interest.

¶ 1033   Fiduciary's Powers to Distribute in Kind

The IRS has prescribed conditions under which the marital deduction will be allowed in cases of a pecuniary bequest in a will, or of a transfer in trust of a pecuniary amount, if the will or trust instrument either requires or permits the executor or trustee to satisfy the bequest in noncash properties selected at their values as finally determined for federal estate tax purposes.[101] The rules set out in the revenue procedure do not apply to transfers of fractional shares of the estate or to transfers of specific assets.

The marital deduction will not be allowed if the executor or trustee is required to, or has an option to, satisfy the pecuniary transfer in kind at estate tax values (and the property available for distribution includes assets that could fluctuate in value) *unless* applicable state law or the provisions of the will or trust instrument require the fiduciary to distribute to the surviving spouse either:

> (1) assets having an aggregate fair market value, on the dates of distribution, of not less than the amount of the pecuniary bequest or transfer in trust as finally determined for federal estate tax purposes; or

> (2) assets fairly representative of appreciation or depreciation in the value of all property available for distribution in satisfaction of the pecuniary bequest or transfer.

When condition (1) or (2) is not met, the IRS will consider the property interest passing from the decedent to the surviving spouse as unascertainable at the date of death, if the property available for distribution includes assets that could fluctuate in value.

With respect to wills and trust instruments executed prior to October 1, 1964, fiduciaries and surviving spouses were given an opportunity to preserve the marital deduction otherwise lost to the estate under the above policy by executing a "side agreement."

---

[99] Code Sec. 2056(b)(2).
[100] Reg. § 20.2056(b)-2.

[101] Rev. Proc. 64-19, 1964-1 CB (Part 1) 682.

¶ 1035   "Interest" vs. "Property"

The terms "interest" and "property," as used in connection with the marital deduction, have separate and distinct meanings. The term "property" is the more comprehensive. It includes all objects or rights that are susceptible of ownership. The term "interest" refers to the extent of ownership of property, such as a life estate in a farm. The farm is the property; the life estate is the interest. A lease is an interest, and, if the lease is transferred from the decedent at death, an interest in property is so transferred.[102]

If a decedent devises acreage to his or her spouse for life with remainder to another, both devisees have an interest in the property. If the fee is devised to a son, subject to a charge of the rents to the surviving spouse for life, both the spouse and son have an interest in the same property.

¶ 1037   Joint and Mutual Wills

Joint and mutual wills of spouses fixing disposition of their respective estates rate a note of caution: The IRS contends that joint wills so restrict the survivor's right to dispose of the property as to create a terminable interest label for the survivor's otherwise nonterminable share, even if the property had been held in joint tenancy.[103] However, the courts have made state law a key factor in generally permitting the marital deduction under the reciprocal will arrangement. Generally, the deduction will be disallowed if the terms of the wills can be enforced under state law. An agreement between the spouses can also limit disposition and create a terminable interest.[104]

¶ 1040   Valuation of Deductible Property Interest

Only the net interest received is considered in determining the value of the interest passing to the surviving spouse for purposes of the marital deduction. Any burdens on the property passing, such as mortgages, liens, and death taxes, must be subtracted from the value of the property in determining the deductible amount.[105] Similarly, the marital deduction is allowable only to the extent that property bequeathed to the surviving spouse exceeds in value the property such spouse is required to relinquish. This principle has major application where, in community property states, the surviving spouse elects to take under the decedent's will and allows its terms to govern the disposition of the survivor's community interest.

Where death taxes are payable out of property bequeathed to the surviving spouse or passing to him or her under state intestate laws, the computation of the marital deduction may be dependent upon the computation of such taxes. In such event, an interdependent computation is involved, which is accomplished most easily by means of computer programs designed for such computations. These interrelated computations can also be made by way of algebraic procedures (see ¶ 1075).

If the decedent by will leaves the residue of his or her estate to his or her surviving spouse and the surviving spouse pays, or if the estate income is used to pay, claims against the estate so as to increase the residue, such increase in the

---

[102] Reg. § 20.2056(a)-2.

[103] See, e.g., IRS Technical Advice Memorandum 8105006 (Sept. 26, 1980), and IRS Technical Advice Memorandum 9023004 (Feb. 20, 1990).

[104] A.J. Batterton, Exr., CA-5, 69-1 USTC ¶ 12,584, 406 F2d 247, cert. denied.

[105] Reg. § 20.2056(b)-4. See also V.H. Chiles, Exrx., CA-9, 88-1 USTC ¶ 13,763.

residue is acquired by purchase and not by bequest. Accordingly, the value of any such additional part of the residue passing to the surviving spouse cannot be included in the amount of the marital deduction.

The value of the marital deduction must be reduced by death taxes that the executor is authorized by will to pay out of the marital trust even though the will does not require him to pay such expenses from the marital trust and, in fact, such payments are not made from the marital trust.[106] The U.S. Supreme Court has held, however, that the payment of administration expenses that, under state law (Georgia), could be allocated to principal or income and, in fact were allocated to income, did not affect the spousal share payable from principal at death. The Court concluded that the payment of the administrative expenses did not constitute, under the rules of Reg. § 20.2056(b)-4(a), a "material limitation" on the surviving spouse's right to receive the income from the trust. Therefore, the estate was not required to offset the marital deduction by the amount of expenses that could be, but were not, paid from marital deduction property.[107]

However, a different result was obtained where the administration expenses were to be paid from the *principal (corpus)*, rather than the income, from a marital trust. In *B. Brown*,[108] an estate incurred significantly larger administration expenses than it had initially claimed on the estate tax return. Upholding the decision of the lower court, the U.S. Court of Appeals for the Ninth Circuit concluded that any such increase in the estate's administration expense deduction claimed by the estate had to be offset by a corresponding decrease in the estate's marital deduction to the extent that the expenses were paid from funds otherwise earmarked for the corpus of the marital trust. Further, because the decedent's gross estate and the deductions claimed by the estate were required to be valued as of the same date, the estate was not permitted to deduct the amount of its actual administration expenses while calculating the marital deduction based on date-of-death estimated expenses.

In order to avoid the difficulty, both for taxpayers and the IRS, to determine what constitutes a "material limitation" on a surviving spouse's right to income from a marital bequest, the IRS has amended Reg. § 20.2056(b)-4, effective for estates of decedents dying on or after December 3, 1999.[109] The amended regulation eliminates the materiality requirement. Instead, the regulations bifurcate estate expenses into estate transmission expenses and estate management expenses. Estate transmission expenses, but not estate management expenses, reduce the value of property for marital deduction purposes. Estate transmission expenses are those expenses that would not have been incurred but for the decedent's death. Estate transmission expenses include any administration expense that is not a management expense. Management expenses are expenses that would be incurred in investing, maintaining, and preserving the estate property. Pursuant to Code Sec. 2056(b)(9), the allowable amount of the marital deduction is reduced by the amount of these management expenses if they are deducted as administration expenses on the estate tax return.

Where the decedent's will does not clearly indicate what sources are to be used to pay death taxes and administration expenses, courts apply state law in determining whether marital deduction property is to be charged with these

---

[106] *M.S. Wycoff Est.*, CA-10, 74-2 USTC ¶ 13,037, 506 F2d 1144; Rev. Rul. 79-14, 1979-1 CB 309.

[107] *O. Hubert Est.*, SCt, 97-1 USTC ¶ 60,261.

[108] *B. Brown*, CA-9, 2003-1 USTC ¶ 60,462, cert. denied, 10/6/2003.

[109] T.D. 8846, amending Reg. § 20.2056(b)-4, filed with the *Federal Register* on December 2, 1999.

costs.[110] The Tax Court has also applied state law to determine that interest payable on federal estate tax and state inheritance tax, and on deficiencies with respect to these taxes, did not reduce the value of property passing to a surviving spouse.[111] State law provided that the interest did not have to be charged specifically to either income or principal. Thus, because a reduction of the principal by interest payments was contrary to the decedent's intent to obtain the maximum marital deduction as demonstrated by his will, the interest due was chargeable against the income of the estate.

The U.S. Court of Claims has held that the value of property passing to a marital trust under a decedent's will was to be reduced by the amount of the decedent's liability for unpaid federal gift taxes in order to determine the allowable marital deduction. This reduction was required because the property passing to the marital trust was the only source for payment of the gift tax liability available to the decedent's executors who, under applicable state law (New York), were empowered to use the property passing to the trust to pay the gift tax liability.[112]

• *Special Use Valuation Property*

In two separate IRS Technical Advice Memoranda relating to the same estate, the IRS ruled that an estate could claim a marital deduction for the full fair market value of property distributed to a marital trust, even though a portion of this property consisted of farmland that was included in the decedent's gross estate at its special use value (see ¶280 through ¶296).[113] The IRS National Office rejected the contention of its District Office that the allowable marital deduction should be reduced by the difference between the special use value and the fair market value of the farmland. However, the IRS ruled that the marital deduction claimed by the estate was allowable because the full value of the decedent's entire interest in the farmland was includible in his gross estate. In the second ruling, the IRS clarified this statement by defining the full value of the farmland to mean its special use value. Moreover, the allowance of a marital deduction based on the fair market value of the farmland did not violate the integrity of the marital deduction statute because the farmland would be includible in the spouse's gross estate at its fair market value upon her death.

However, in another Technical Advice Memorandum,[114] the IRS National Office determined that a marital bequest was overfunded when the executors used the special use value of the farm, as opposed to its fair market value when transferring property to the surviving spouse. The decedent's will directed that the spouse was to receive one-half of the adjusted gross estate but required the executor to use fair market value for transferring assets to satisfy the marital bequest. The effect of this ruling is to allow the executor to transfer less value to the surviving spouse and leave more property in the nontaxable residuary. The Tax Court has also ruled that farmland included in the decedent's gross estate at its special use value retained that value for purposes of calculating the marital deduction.[115]

---

[110] *G.B. Phillips*, 90 TC 797, CCH Dec. 44,717. See *J.E. Reid Est.*, 90 TC 304, CCH Dec. 44,583.

[111] *W.E. Richardson Est.*, 89 TC 1193, CCH Dec. 44,388.

[112] *W.E. Murray, Exr.*, CtCls, 82-2 USTC ¶13,488, 687 F2d 386.

[113] IRS Technical Advice Memorandum 8314001 (Sept. 22, 1982), and IRS Technical Advice Memorandum 8314005 (Dec. 14, 1982). See also IRS Technical Advice Memorandum 8509001 (Nov. 13, 1984).

[114] Technical Advice Memorandum 8708001 (May 6, 1986).

[115] *H.M. Evers Est.*, 57 TCM 718, CCH Dec. 45,776(M), TC Memo. 1989-292.

¶ 1045   Passing of Interest in Property

For purposes of the marital deduction, an interest in property is considered as passing from the decedent to his or her spouse if:

(1) the interest is bequeathed or devised to the spouse by the decedent;

(2) the interest is inherited by the spouse from the decedent;

(3) the interest is the dower or curtesy interest (or statutory interest in lieu thereof) of the surviving spouse;

(4) the interest has been transferred to the spouse by the decedent at any time;

(5) the interest was, at the time of the decedent's death, held by the spouse and the decedent (or by them in conjunction with any other person) in joint ownership with right of survivorship, such joint ownership including joint tenancy, tenancy by the entirety, a joint bank account, or any other co-ownership with right of survivorship;

(6) the decedent had a power of appointment over such interest (either alone or in conjunction with another), which he exercised in favor of the spouse, or the spouse takes the interest in default upon release or nonexercise of the power; or

(7) the interest consists of proceeds of insurance on the life of the decedent, receivable by the spouse, regardless of whether the decedent had previously assigned the policy or paid the premiums by way of gift.[116]

• *Settlement Agreements*

Property interests that a surviving spouse assigns or surrenders pursuant to a compromise agreement in settlement of a will contest are not deductible as an interest passing to the spouse.[117] Any interest received by the surviving spouse under a settlement will be regarded as having passed from the decedent to his surviving spouse if the settlement was based on an enforceable right, under state law, as properly interpreted. The U.S. Court of Appeals for the Eighth Circuit interpreted this test to mean that, where the constitutionality of a state dower statute was uncertain at the time of settlement, the Tax Court was required to make an independent determination as to the enforceability of the surviving spouse's dower claim.[118] Consent decrees will not necessarily be accepted as a bona fide evaluation of the rights of the spouse. The key factor is whether an interest passes from the decedent to his or her surviving spouse, so that the above rules also apply in the case of an intestate decedent where there is a dispute over the statutory share of the spouse.[119]

If a surviving spouse elects to take his or her share of the decedent's estate under local law instead of taking an interest under the will, the interest the surviving spouse takes under local law is considered as passing from the decedent.[120] The failure of a surviving spouse to elect to take an interest under the local law is not considered to any extent as a purchase of the interest the surviving spouse takes under the will.

---

[116] Code Sec. 2056(c).

[117] Reg. § 20.2056(c)-2(d)(1).

[118] *G.M. Brandon Est.*, CA-8, 87-2 USTC ¶ 13,733, rev'g and rem'g TC, 86 TC 327, CCH Dec. 42,911.

[119] *V. Pastor, Admr.*, DC N.Y., 75-1 USTC ¶ 13,045, 386 FSupp. 106.

[120] Reg. § 20.2056(c)-2(c).

An interest transferred to a surviving spouse, pursuant to an antenuptial agreement, is property passing from a decedent to his or her surviving spouse. A marital deduction will be allowed for it if all other requirements are met.[121]

¶ 1050   Disclaimers

A "qualified disclaimer" of property, as defined at ¶ 2009, may be made by a third person so that the property may pass to the decedent's surviving spouse and qualify for the marital deduction.[122]

> *Example:* At his death, Herbert Miller's testamentary trust provided that all of the trust income be paid to Wilma, his surviving spouse, for life, with the remainder to their descendants. Wilma's interest in the trust would not qualify for the marital deduction since it is a nondeductible terminable interest (see ¶ 1020). However, the trust also authorized the trustee to distribute principal to the descendants as the trustee deemed advisable for their support and maintenance. Pursuant to powers granted by the instrument, Herbert's executor split the trust into a marital trust and a family trust, and the children disclaimed their right to principal distributions from the marital trust during Wilma's lifetime. As a result of this action, Wilma received a qualifying income interest in the marital trust, which was thereby eligible for a marital deduction under the qualified terminable interest property rules (see ¶ 1002).

If the requirements are satisfied, refusals to accept property are given effect for estate tax purposes, even if local law does not characterize such refusals as "disclaimers." For requirements of a qualified disclaimer, see ¶ 2009.

Qualified disclaimers may be made with respect to transfers that created an interest in the person disclaiming and were made after December 31, 1976.

¶ 1055   Extensions for Future Interests

A six-month extension of time is provided for payment of estate tax on reversionary or remainder interests in property that are included in the value of the gross estate.[123] The extension is granted only for the part of the tax attributable to such interests. In determining the part of the tax attributable to the reversionary or remainder interests, proper effect must be given to any marital deduction allowed.

¶ 1060   Alternate Valuation Method

If the executor elects the alternate valuation method of valuing the estate (see ¶ 105), the amount of the marital deduction is governed by the value at the date of death. It is adjusted, however, for any difference in value (not due to mere lapse of time or the occurrence or nonoccurrence of a contingency) of the property as of the date six months after the date of death.[124] If the property was distributed, sold, exchanged, or otherwise disposed of during the alternate valuation period, it is to be valued as of the date of its first distribution, sale, exchange, or other disposition.

The alternate valuation election pertains only to valuation. It does not extend the time for determining the character of the interest passing to the surviving spouse.

---

[121] Rev. Rul. 68-271, 1968-1 CB 409.

[122] Code Sec. 2046, Code Sec. 2056, and Code Sec. 2518.

[123] Code Sec. 6163.

[124] Reg. § 20.2056(b)-4.

Example (1): Under Robert Babcock's will, a life estate is given to his surviving spouse, Ann, with remainder to Ann and to their son, Tom. No deduction results, even though Tom dies within the six-month period after the decedent's death.

Example (2): Tess True's will directed the executor to sell certain described real estate and to purchase stock of X corporation with the proceeds. The executor was then to turn the stock over to True's widower. The value of the real estate at True's death was $100,000. It was sold for $120,000 by the executor prior to six months after True's death. The stock was purchased for $120,000, but had a fair market value of $80,000 at True's death.

If the gross estate is valued at the date of True's death, the marital deduction is $100,000 (the value of the real estate at the time of death). That value was the value of the interest included in determining the value of the gross estate. If the value of the gross estate is determined under the alternate valuation rule the marital deduction is $120,000, the value of the real estate at the time of sale within the six-month period.

¶ 1065   Execution of Schedule

The instructions to Form 706 (United States Estate (and Generation-Skipping Transfer) Tax Return) (Rev. August 2013) specify items that should not be included in the marital deduction schedule, as well as the manner of listing those that may be included. Certain property interests that passed from the decedent to his or her surviving spouse are to be wholly or partially excluded from Schedule M (Bequests etc., to Surviving Spouse) of Form 706, as indicated below:

(1) When interests in the same property passed from the decedent both to his or her surviving spouse and (for less than an adequate and full consideration in money or money's worth) to some other person under such conditions that the other person may possess or enjoy any part of the property following the termination or failure of the interest therein that passed to the surviving spouse, the interest passing to the spouse must be excluded from the schedule (unless a qualified terminable interest property election is made).

Example (1): Property transferred by the decedent Bill Green in the following manner is excludable from Schedule M:

(1) a bequest of property to his spouse for life, with remainder to his daughter; and

(2) a bequest of property to his mother for life, with remainder to his spouse, if surviving, and, if not, to his daughter and her heirs.

Under each bequest, the spouse's interest in the property may terminate or fail, and the daughter may, thereafter, possess or enjoy the property.

(2) If the decedent directs the executor or trustee to purchase for his or her surviving spouse an annuity, a life estate or estate for years in certain property, or any other property interest that may terminate or fail, the property to be used in the acquisition may not be included on the marital deduction schedule. The ownership of a bond, note, or other contractual obligation, the discharge of which would not have the effect of an annuity for life or for a term, is not considered to be a property interest that may terminate or fail.

(3) If any property passing from the decedent to his or her surviving spouse may be paid or otherwise satisfied out of a group of assets, the value of such property interest is, for the purpose of entry on the marital deduction schedule, to be reduced by the aggregate value of any assets that, if passing from the

decedent to his surviving spouse, would be nondeductible terminable interests. Property interests that may be paid or otherwise satisfied out of any of a group of assets include bequests of the residue of the decedent's estate, or of a share of the residue, and cash legacies payable out of the general estate.

> *Example (2):* Carl Banks bequeathed $100,000 to his wife. His general estate includes a term for years (value of $10,000 in determining the value of his gross estate) in an office building. This interest was retained by Banks under a deed of the building by gift to his son. The portion of the value of the specific bequest to be entered on Schedule M is $90,000.

(4) Property interests are to be excluded from the marital deduction schedule to the extent that a deduction is taken for them under other, preceding schedules (Schedule J (Funeral Expenses and Expenses Incurred in Administering Property Subject to Claims), Schedule K (Debts of the Decedent, and Mortgages and Liens), and Schedule L (Net Losses During Administration and Expenses Incurred in Administering Property Not Subject to Claims) of Form 706, inclusive). Examples of interests to be so excluded are fees or commissions and payments made in satisfaction of a claim of the surviving spouse against the estate. To the extent that a protective claim for refund is filed with respect to a claim against the estate or an expense that would have been deductible under Code Sec. 2053(a) or (b) (see ¶803) if such item already had been paid and that is payable out of a share that meets the requirements for a marital deduction under Code Sec. 2056 or Code Sec. 2056A, the marital deduction is not reduced by the amount of such claim until the amount is actually paid, becomes ascertainable in amount, or meets the deduction requirements of Reg. §20.2053-4.[125]

(5) When a property interest passing to the surviving spouse is subject to a mortgage or other encumbrance, or when an obligation is imposed on the surviving spouse in connection with the passing of a property interest, only the net value of the interest after reduction by the amount of the mortgage or other encumbrance, or obligation, should be included on the marital deduction schedule.

¶1067 Listings on Schedule M

Each property interest listed on Schedule M (Bequests etc., to Surviving Spouse) of Form 706 (United States Estate (and Generation-Skipping Transfer) Tax Return) (Rev. August 2013)[126] should be fully described. This includes otherwise nondeductible terminable interest property for which a qualified terminable interest property election is intended. The items should be numbered in sequence. The description must indicate the instrument (including the clause or paragraph number of the instrument, if possible) or provision of law under which each item passed to the surviving spouse. The schedule and item number of the property interest as it appears in the schedules for reporting property includible in the gross estate should also be shown where possible. The value of each item listed on the schedule should be the value determined before taking into account the effect of federal and other death taxes.

If a residuary bequest is listed on Schedule M, a copy of the computation showing how the value of such item was determined should be submitted. The computation should include a statement showing:

---

[125] Reg. §20.2053-1(d)(5)(ii), as amended by T.D. 9468, October 16, 2009.

[126] An example of a filled-in Form 706, Schedule M, for a decedent dying in 2013, is reproduced at ¶3080.

(1) The value of all property that is included in the decedent's gross estate but is not part of the decedent's probate estate. This includes property transferred during life but taxed under Code Sec. 2035 through Code Sec. 2038, such as lifetime transfers, jointly owned property passing to the survivor on the decedent's death, and insurance payable to specific beneficiaries.

(2) The values of all specific and general legacies or devises, with an appropriate reference in each instance to the applicable clause or paragraph of the decedent's will or codicil. (In any case where legacies are made to each member of a class—for example, $1,000 to each of the decedent's employees—only the number in each class and the aggregate value of property received by them need be furnished.)

(3) The date of birth and the gender of all persons, the duration of whose lives may affect the value of the residuary interest passing to the surviving spouse.

(4) Any other information that may appear material, such as facts relating to any claim, not arising under the will, to any part of the estate.

¶ 1068   Adjustment for Death Taxes

The total of the values listed on Schedule M (Bequests, etc., to Surviving Spouse), item 4, of Form 706 (United States Estate (and Generation-Skipping Transfer) Tax Return) (Rev. August 2013)[127] must be reduced by the amount of any federal estate, federal generation-skipping transfer (GST) tax and state or other death and GST taxes that are payable out of, or chargeable against, the property interests (see ¶ 1075). Such amounts of taxes should be entered in the designated spaces of Schedule M, (items (5a), (5b), and (5c)) of the schedule. Items (5b) and (5c) must be supported by an identification and computation of the amount of state or other death and GST taxes shown.[128]

¶ 1069   Supplemental Documents

If property interests passing by the decedent's will are listed on Schedule M (Bequests, etc., to Surviving Spouse) of Form 706 (United States Estate (and Generation-Skipping Transfer) Tax Return) (Rev. August 2013), a certified copy of the order admitting the will to probate must be submitted with the return. If, at the time the return is filed, the court of probate jurisdiction has entered any decree interpreting the will or any of its provisions affecting property interests listed on the schedule, a copy of the decree is also required. Additional evidence to support the deduction claim may be requested by the district director.

¶ 1075   Marital Deduction and Interrelated Death Taxes

The federal estate tax law contemplates that the marital deduction will be allowed only with respect to the net amount passing to the surviving spouse.[129] Any charges that reduce the amount actually passing to such spouse will reduce the deduction.

State death taxes payable out of residue, including those chargeable against the amounts passing to the surviving spouse, reduce the amount of the deduction. Because they are not deductible under the federal estate tax law, the

---

[127] An example of a filled-in Form 706, Schedule M, for a decedent dying in 2013, is reproduced at ¶ 3080.

[128] Reg. § 20.2056(b)-4.
[129] Reg. § 20.2056(b)-4.

amounts of these taxes are subject to federal estate taxes just as is any other property not passing to the surviving spouse.

Federal estate taxes payable out of the residue are also part of the taxable estate. Determination of the amount of the residue is dependent upon the marital deduction, which in turn is dependent upon the amounts of both the federal and state taxes. The computation problems may be minimized by making specific transfers to the surviving spouse and by shifting the burden of tax payment to other interests. Where it has not been feasible to prepare a will in a manner that will avoid the involved computation, special formulas must be used.

IRS Publication No. 904, "Interrelated Computations for Estate and Gift Taxes,"[130] illustrates how the allowable marital and charitable deductions may be computed in cases in which these deductions are interrelated with death taxes.

The IRS National Office will furnish taxpayers with actuarial factors and assistance in the solution of interrelated tax computation problems. Taxpayers who have difficulty with tax computations may request assistance by writing to the IRS. The request should include sufficient supporting data to enable the IRS to make the computation. For most estates, copies of the will and relevant trust instruments, a schedule of assets and deductions, and a tentative computation of state tax should accompany the request.

In the event the estate includes community property, everything passing to the surviving spouse in excess of the surviving spouse's share of such community property should be listed in this schedule, regardless of whether such excess comes from the decedent's share of the community or from his or her separate property.

> *Comment:* Practitioners who would like to avoid the time-consuming and tedious calculations involved with using the mathematical formulae set out in Publication 904 should consider using CCH's *ProSystem fx*® *Tax*, which contains computer programs for calculating interrelated marital and charitable deductions.

---

[130] IRS Publication No. 904, "Interrelated Computations for Estate and Gift Taxes" (Rev. May 1985). Although no longer availa- ble from the IRS, Publication 904 is reproduced in CCH FEDERAL ESTATE AND GIFT TAX REPORTS.

Chapter 22

CHARITABLE, PUBLIC, AND SIMILAR TRANSFERS

¶ 1100   Transfers

A charitable deduction is allowed for the value of property transferred by the decedent to or for the use of certain organizations.[1] The deduction is allowed, without limitation as to amount, for transfers of property (to the extent included in the gross estate) to or for the use of:

(1) any corporation organized and operated exclusively for (a) religious, (b) charitable, (c) scientific, (d) literary, or (e) educational purposes, including the encouragement of art and the prevention of cruelty to children or animals;

(2) the United States, or any state or political subdivision thereof or the District of Columbia, for exclusively public purposes;

(3) any veterans' organization incorporated by Act of Congress, or of its departments or local chapters or posts;

(4) a trustee or trustees, or a fraternal society, order, or association operating under the lodge system if the contributions are to be used exclusively for the purposes enumerated in (1), above; or

(5) an employee stock ownership plan if the transfer qualifies as a qualified gratuitous transfer (see ¶ 1122).

A transfer to an individual member of a religious order will not qualify as a charitable contribution, even if the member has taken a vow of poverty requiring renunciation of any inheritance in favor of the order.[2] Bequests for masses qualify only if made directly to the church and not to a priest.[3] The IRS has permitted a charitable deduction for a bequest made to a church to say masses for previously deceased members of a decedent's family. In that situation, however, the masses

---

[1] Code Sec. 2055; Reg. § 20.2055-1.
[2] Rev. Rul. 55-760, 1955-2 CB 607.

[3] Rev. Rul. 68-459, 1968-2 CB 411.

would have been said even if the bequest had not been made, and the bequest became part of the general funds of the church.[4] A decedent's bequest in trust for the benefit of a nonprofit cemetery association did not qualify for an estate tax charitable deduction because the trust funds were not used for an exclusively charitable purpose. This was true because, under the decedent's will, the bequest was to be used to maintain the decedent's cemetery plot before it was used to maintain the cemetery in general.[5]

An estate tax deduction is not allowed for a bequest to a charity if the bequest is conditioned on the approval of a third party.[6] Bequests to foreign governments and political subdivisions thereof that are used exclusively for charitable purposes are deductible.[7]

¶ 1101 Disqualifications

The transfer to any organization qualifying under category (1) or (3), listed at ¶1100, will not be allowed as a deduction if any part of the net earnings of the organization inures to the benefit of any private stockholder or individual. A deduction is also denied where a substantial part of the transferee's activities involves the carrying on of propaganda or some other method of influencing legislation. A deduction is denied if the transferee participates or intervenes in (including the publishing or distributing of statements) any political campaign on behalf of or in opposition to any candidate for public office.[8] In any event, the amount of the deduction cannot exceed the portion of the contributed property included in the gross estate[9] (see also ¶2305).

¶ 1102 Form of Transfer—Disclaimers

A charitable deduction is allowable only if the transfer is made by the decedent rather than by the decedent's estate or by the beneficiaries of the estate. The transfer may be made pursuant to a will or by means of a lifetime transfer.

However, a charitable deduction is available for property that is indirectly cast into a charitable transfer by means of a "qualified disclaimer."[10] If the qualified disclaimer requirements are satisfied, refusals to accept property are given effect for estate tax charitable deduction purposes even if local law does not characterize such refusals as "disclaimers." Qualified disclaimers may be made with respect to those transfers creating an interest in the person disclaiming. For requirements of a qualified disclaimer, see ¶2009.

The complete termination of a power to consume, invade, or appropriate property for the benefit of an individual can also create a charitable deduction.[11] In order to qualify, the termination must occur before the due date of the estate tax return and before the power has been exercised.

¶ 1105 Qualifying Transferees

Transfers to organizations, such as the Red Cross, the Boy Scouts, the American Heart Fund, the American Cancer Society, the Salvation Army, and other well-known charitable organizations clearly qualify for the deduction.

---

[4] Rev. Rul. 78-366, 1978-2 CB 241.

[5] *First National Bank of Omaha, Exr. (Est. of G. McIninch)*, CA-8, 82-2 USTC ¶13,474, cert. denied Jan. 10, 1983; see also *Mellon Bank N.A., Exr.*, CA-3, 85-1 USTC ¶13,615, cert. denied Feb. 24, 1986.

[6] Rev. Rul. 64-129, 1964-1 CB (Part 1) 329.

[7] Rev. Rul. 74-523, 1974-2 CB 304; IRS Technical Advice Memorandum 9842004 (Jul. 7, 1998).

[8] Code Sec. 2055(a).

[9] Code Sec. 2055(d).

[10] Code Sec. 2046 and Code Sec. 2518.

[11] Reg. § 20.2055-2(c).

Similarly, transfers made directly to a recognized school or church organization are deductible when the transfer is to be used for educational or religious purposes.

> *Comment:* It is advisable to consult IRS Publication No. 78 (Cumulative List of Organizations Described in Section 170(c) of the IRC of 1986) and its supplement before making charitable bequests or distributions. IRS Publication No. 78 is the official list of those organizations to which charitable contributions are deductible under Code Sec. 170 and Code Sec. 2055.[12] Failure to consult the list and contributing to a charity not listed may result in the denial of the charitable deduction. For example, a charitable deduction was denied for funds distributed to a private school that no longer had tax-exempt status.[13] According to the Tax Court, the trustees would have been aware of the revocation had they consulted IRS Publication No. 78.

Whether various types of indirect discretionary transfers are deductible is not so clear. The courts have indicated that even these transfers will qualify if the terms under which the discretionary powers may be exercised are sufficiently explicit to limit use of the funds to the purposes specified in the law. Thus, a transfer in trust can qualify, even if the trustee is given complete discretion in selecting the ultimate beneficiaries of the transferred property. In like manner, specific charitable bequests paid by a trustee of a testamentary trust can qualify for a deduction even if the trustee has complete discretion as to which assets will be used to pay the bequests.[14]

So long as it is clear that the trustee's or other third person's discretion is limited to choosing the charitable, religious, or educational organizations to receive the funds or so long as it is clear that he must expend the funds directly and only for the purposes specified in the estate tax law, the transfers may qualify. The IRS maintains that, where a trustee has the power to select the charitable beneficiaries, the deduction is available only if state law (1) upholds the validity of the charitable trust, and (2) restricts the distribution of property to an organization that qualifies for an estate tax charitable deduction.[15]

No deduction is allowed for a transfer to or for the use of certain private foundations and foreign organizations. This matter is discussed for gift tax purposes at ¶ 2305.

¶ 1110   State Law Effect

State law often plays a part in determining whether a particular transfer will qualify for the charitable deduction. If the transfer is one that is void under state law, the deduction will not be allowed.[16] No deduction will be allowed even if the heirs who would otherwise receive the property take action to permit it to go to the charitable transferees, unless they make a "qualified disclaimer" (see ¶ 1102). On the other hand, if the transfer is merely voidable under state law and the persons who have a right to have the transfer voided fail to act, the deduction will be allowed.[17]

---

[12] IRS Publication No. 78 is available for sale from the Superintendent of Documents, U.S. Government Printing Office, Washington, D.C. 20402, and is available on the Internet at *www.irs.gov.*

[13] *S.H. Clopton,* 93 TC 275, CCH Dec. 45,978.

[14] Rev. Rul. 81-20, 1981-1 CB 471, clarified by Rev. Rul. 90-3, 1990-1 CB 174.

[15] Rev. Rul. 69-285, 1969-1 CB 222; Rev. Rul. 71-441, 1971-2 CB 335.

[16] *H.V. Watkins, Sr., Exr.,* CA-5, 43-1 USTC ¶ 10,042, 136 F2d 578.

[17] *M. Varick Est.,* 10 TC 318, CCH Dec. 16,258 (Acq.).

Estates of decedents dying in 2010. Until the matter was resolved by the Tax Relief, Unemployment Insurance Reauthorization, and Job Creation Act of 2010 (P.L. 111-312), the year 2010, during which the estate and GST taxes did not apply, presented difficulty and uncertainty for estate planners and drafters of estate planning documents. Prior to passage of P.L. 111-312, the estate of a wealthy decedent dying in 2010 would have the advantage of not having an estate or GST tax at death. However, this might have been at the expense of unexpectedly excluding loved ones from receiving property under will and trust documents. Traditional estate planning has often employed mathematical formulas to determine the amount of marital and charitable bequests. These formulas often determined a bequest by reference to the amount of property that could be passed from the decedent without incurring an estate tax liability. Because no estate tax liability was to be generated with respect to decedents dying in 2010, depending on the type of formula bequests and how they were used, a spousal or credit shelter bequest (in a marital bequest situation) (or a bequest to charitable or noncharitable beneficiaries (in a charitable bequest situation)) could unexpectedly be computed as zero, completely "cutting out" persons or organizations that the decedent wanted to support.

Currently, the District of Columbia and several states (listed at ¶3), have enacted legislation to avoid unintended disinheritances for estates of decedents dying in 2010, as noted above.

¶ 1115   Property Passing Under Power of Appointment

Property that is includible in the gross estate under Code Sec. 2041 (relating to powers of appointment, see ¶650) and that passes to a charitable beneficiary is considered to be a bequest by the decedent and is deductible as a charitable transfer.[18]

¶ 1120   Transfers Not Exclusively for Charitable Purposes

Special rules are provided for transfers that are not exclusively for charitable purposes.[19] An estate tax charitable deduction is allowed for the value of the charitable interest transferred to the extent that such interest is presently ascertainable and, thus, severable from the noncharitable interest. Transfers subject to a power to divert such property to noncharitable purposes are nondeductible.

Interests transferred for other than exclusively charitable purposes that are deductible include:[20]

(1) remainder interests in a charitable remainder annuity trust, a charitable remainder unitrust, or a pooled income fund (see ¶1122);[21]

(2) remainder interests in a personal residence (this transfer does not have to be in trust and the Tax Court has held that the transfer to charity of proceeds from the sale of a residence after the life tenant's death qualifies for the deduction);[22]

(3) remainder interests in a farm (this transfer does not have to be in trust);

---

[18] Code Sec. 2055(b).

[19] Code Sec. 2055(e).

[20] Reg. § 20.2055-2.

[21] Code Sec. 2055(e)(2)(A).

[22] *E.W. Blackford Est.*, 77 TC 1246, CCH Dec. 38,477. The IRS acquiesced in the result

in *Blackford;* however, in the IRS's view, the remainder would be deductible only if the governing state law followed the doctrine of equitable reconversion, under which the remainderman could elect to take the property in its original form. See Rev. Rul. 83-158, 1983-2 CB 159.

(4) a transfer of an undivided portion, not in trust, of the decedent's entire interest for the entire term of his interest (see, also, ¶ 1125, for discussion of the estate and gift tax charitable deductions for transfers of fractional interests in tangible personal property);

Example: The decedent, Tom Sanders, transfers a life estate in an office building to his wife, Lisa, for her life, retains a reversionary interest in such building, and then transfers one-half of the reversionary interest to charity while Lisa is still alive. His estate is denied a charitable deduction because an interest in the same property has already passed from Tom for private purposes and the reversionary interest is not considered the decedent's entire interest in the property.

(5) guaranteed annuity interests (An interest, whether or not in trust, involving a right to receive a guaranteed annuity, that is defined as a determinable amount paid at least annually for a specified term or for the life or lives of an individual or individuals, each of whom is living at the date of the decedent's death and can be ascertained at such date. (A charitable annuity trust is a form of a charitable lead trust; see ¶ 1123.) If not a trust, such interest must be paid by an insurance company or by an organization regularly engaged in issuing annuity contracts in order to qualify as a deductible charitable guaranteed annuity interest.);

(6) unitrust income interests (An interest, whether in trust, involving the right to receive payment, not less often than annually, of a fixed percentage of the net fair market value, determined annually, of the property that funds the unitrust interest. Payments under a unitrust (a form of charitable lead trust; see ¶ 1123) interest may be paid for a specified term or for the life or lives of an individual or individuals, each of whom must be living at the date of the decedent's death and can be ascertained at such date. If not in trust, such interest must be paid by an insurance company, or by an organization regularly engaged in issuing interests otherwise meeting the requirements of a unitrust interest, in order to qualify as a deductible charitable unitrust interest.);

(7) "conservation purpose" transfers (A deduction is also allowed for a bequest to a charitable organization exclusively for "conservation purposes" of (a) a "restriction" in perpetuity on the use of real property, e.g., easements, leases, restrictive covenants, etc., (b) remainder interests in real property, or (c) a decedent's entire interest in real property other than certain mineral rights.[23] "Conservation purposes" include the preservation of land, areas for public recreation, education, or scenic enjoyment, the preservation of historically important land or structures, or the preservation of natural environmental systems.); and

(8) artworks with retained copyrights (a charitable deduction will be allowed for the transfer of an artwork to charity even if the copyright covering the work is not so transferred).[24]

¶ 1121   Split-Interest Transfers

Transfers involving property interests split between charitable and noncharitable beneficiaries may arise in a number of factual situations. The IRS has ruled that a decedent's estate was not entitled to an estate tax charitable deduction for

---

[23] Code Sec. 170(f)(3)(B); Reg. § 1.170A-14 and Reg. § 20.2055-2(e)(2)(iv).

[24] Code Sec. 2055(e)(4).

the decedent's bequest of stock to charity because, under the terms of the will, the executor was to pay dividends from the stock to a noncharitable beneficiary during the period of estate administration.[25] In the IRS's view, this gave rise to a split-interest transfer because the noncharitable beneficiary's right to the dividends constituted a property right in the stock. Accordingly, the transfer was a split-interest transfer and no deduction was allowable because it was not in one of the forms required for such transfers (i.e., a charitable remainder annuity trust, charitable remainder unitrust, or pooled income fund).

Notwithstanding the position taken in the above ruling, the IRS has ruled that a decedent's bequest of the residue of his estate to charity was not a split-interest transfer, even though, pursuant to a state court order, his surviving spouse was to receive a support allowance from the residue during the period of estate administration.[26] The IRS allowed the deduction because the support allowance would be payable for only five years; the possibility that estate administration would last beyond five years was so remote as to be negligible. Because the charity was certain to receive an amount in excess of the present value of the support allowance, the IRS determined that only the charity had an interest in this amount of the residue, and, to the extent of this amount, the residuary bequest was not a split-interest transfer.

The U.S. Court of Appeals for the Eighth Circuit relied in part on this ruling in holding that a decedent's estate was entitled to an estate tax charitable deduction for a portion of the decedent's bequest to a trust having both charitable and noncharitable beneficiaries because the estate obtained a judicial modification of the trust to provide for immediate distributions to the charitable remainder beneficiaries.[27] The estate executors had a motive for the reformation, arising from state fiduciary law, that was independent of tax considerations; however, the court focused on the fact that the abuses calling for application of the split-interest transfer provisions were not a concern in the case because the charitable interests passed directly to the charities under the state court order. Also relying in part on the ruling, the Eighth Circuit allowed a charitable deduction for a decedent's bequest to charity of a remainder interest in a testamentary trust that was funded with the residue of his estate because his wife elected to take against his will, under which she was entitled to a life income interest in the trust.[28] The split-interest trust requirements did not apply to bar the deduction because the wife received an interest only in that portion of the residue necessary to fund an agreement in settlement of her election, while the charity was certain to receive the rest of the residue.

• *Charitable Split-Dollar Insurance Transactions*

In recent years, the benefits of charitable split-dollar insurance transactions have been scaled back by Congress and the IRS. Such transactions typically involve a transfer of funds by a taxpayer to a charity, with the understanding that the charity will use the funds to pay premiums on a cash value life insurance policy that benefits both the charity and the taxpayer's family. The charity or an irrevocable life insurance trust formed by the taxpayer usually purchases the

---

[25] Rev. Rul. 83-45, 1983-1 CB 233.

[26] Rev. Rul. 83-20, 1983-1 CB 231.

[27] *W. Oetting, Exr.*, CA-8, 83-2 USTC ¶13,533, 712 F2d 358. Similarly, *M. Jackson, Est.*, DC W.Va, 2005-2 USTC ¶60,513, where the charitable remainder beneficiary and the noncharitable income beneficiaries agreed to

terminate a trust because the trustees were concerned about possible disputes arising from potential conflicts of interests with respect to estate fiduciaries who were related to the income and remainder beneficiaries.

[28] *First National Bank of Fayetteville, Ark., Exr.*, CA-8, 84-1 USTC ¶13,558, 727 F2d 741.

insurance policy, and members of the taxpayer's family (or the taxpayer) are beneficiaries of the trust. A split-dollar agreement between the charity and the trust specifies what portion of the insurance policy premiums is to be paid by each. Generally, over the life of the split-dollar arrangement, the trust has access to a disproportionately high percentage of the cash surrender value and death benefits of the policy, compared to the percentage of premiums paid by the trust.

Code Sec. 170(f)(10) eliminates the tax benefits of charitable split-dollar arrangements. Code Sec. 170(f)(10) provides that no charitable contribution deduction will be allowed for a transfer made after February 8, 1999, to or for the use of a Code Sec. 170(c) organization, if the organization pays a premium on any personal benefit contract with respect to the transferor. A personal benefit contract includes any life insurance, annuity or endowment contract if any beneficiary under the contract is or is related to the transferor. The limitation also applies to organizations that understand or expect that any person will pay a premium on any personal benefit contract with respect to the transferor. The provision includes cross references to other Code provisions dealing with charitable contributions, including Code Sec. 2055, Code Sec. 2106(a)(2), and Code Sec. 2522.

Limited exceptions are provided for annuity contracts purchased by a charity to fund charitable gift annuities and for charitable remainder trusts that hold life insurance, annuity, or endowment contracts to pay annuity or unitrust amounts.

Reporting and excise tax requirements are also imposed. Although the reporting requirement is effective for premiums paid after February 8, 1999, the excise tax is imposed on premiums paid after December 17, 1999. Any charitable organization that pays premiums on a personal benefit contract in connection with a transfer for which a deduction is not allowed is required to pay an excise tax and to report certain information related to the premium payments.[29] For purposes of this excise tax, Code Sec. 170(f)(10)(F)(ii) provides that premium payments made by any other person pursuant to an understanding or expectation described in Code Sec. 170(f)(10)(A) are treated as made by the charitable organization.

Reporting and excise tax requirements. Pursuant to IRS Notice 2000-24,[30] a charitable organization liable for excise taxes under Code Sec. 170(f)(10)(F), must file Form 4720 (Return of Certain Excise Taxes Under Chapters 41 and 42 of the Internal Revenue Code) to report and pay the taxes due. The charitable organization must include the amount of the Code Sec. 170(f)(10)(F) tax on line 8 of part I.

Code Sec. 170(f)(10)(F)(iii) requires charitable organizations to annually report the amount of premiums paid that are subject to tax under Code Sec. 170(f)(10)(F) along with the name and taxpayer identification number of each beneficiary of a related contract. Form 8870 (Information Return for Transfers Associated with Certain Personal Benefit Contracts) is to be used for reporting this required information.

Code Sec. 6033 requires most charitable organizations to file annual information returns. Generally, this means that a charitable organization is to file either Form 990 (Return of Organization Exempt From Income Tax), or Form 990-PF (Return of Private Foundation or Code Sec. 4947(a)(1) Nonexempt Charitable Trust Treated as a Private Foundation). Form 5227 (Split-Interest Trust

---

[29] Code Sec. 170(f)(10)(F).

[30] Notice 2000-24, 2000-1 CB 952.

Information Return) is used by a split-interest trust to report its financial activities and whether it is subject to excise taxes under Chapter 42 of the Code.

Code Sec. 170(f)(10) follows the IRS's administrative attack on charitable split-dollar arrangements in Notice 99-36, in which the IRS applied a substance-over-form approach to deny a deduction with respect to such transactions.[31] Besides denying a charitable deduction, the Notice described the IRS's intent to challenge the tax-exempt status of charities participating in split-dollar transactions.

¶ 1122   Charitable Remainder Trusts

A deductible charitable remainder interest must be in the form of an annuity trust, a unitrust, or a pooled income fund.[32]

A charitable remainder annuity trust (CRAT) is a trust from which a sum certain or a specified amount (which is not less than five percent or more than 50 percent of the initial net fair market value of all property placed in trust) is to be paid to the income beneficiary or beneficiaries. The specified amount must be paid at least annually to the income beneficiary.[33]

A charitable remainder unitrust (CRUT) is a trust that specifies that the income beneficiary or beneficiaries are to receive payments (at least annually) based on a fixed percentage (which is not less than five percent or more than 50 percent) of the net fair market value of the trust's assets as determined each year. In the alternative, a qualified charitable remainder unitrust can provide for the distribution each year of five percent of the net fair market value of its assets (valued annually) or the amount of the trust income (other than capital gains), whichever is lower.[34] This payment requirement may not be discretionary with the trustee.

In addition, deficiencies in income (i.e., where the trust income was less than the stated amount payable to the income beneficiary) can be made up in later years when a CRUT's income exceeds the amount otherwise payable to the income beneficiary for that year. This is commonly referred to as a net income makeup charitable remainder unitrust (NIMCRUT). The determination of which items are trust income is to be made under state law and, therefore, cannot include such items as capital gains, which must be allocated to the trust principal. (No comparable rules are provided for CRATs.)

The Taxpayer Relief Act of 1997 (P.L. 105-34) imposed additional maximum payout and minimum charitable benefit requirements on both CRATs and CRUTs. Under the maximum payout limitation, a trust will fail to qualify as a charitable remainder trust if the annual payout exceeds 50 percent. Thus, a CRAT cannot pay out in any year an amount in excess of 50 percent of the initial fair market value of the trust's assets. A CRUT may not make an annual payout in excess of 50 percent of the fair market value of the trust's assets determined annually. The 50-percent maximum payout limitation applies to transfers in trust made after June 18, 1997.[35]

A minimum 10-percent charitable remainder value rule applies to transfers in trust made after July 28, 1997. To satisfy the rule, the value of a remainder

---

[31] Notice 99-36, 1999-1 CB 1284.

[32] Code Sec. 2055(e)(2)(A); E. La Meres Est., 98 TC 294, CCH Dec. 48,085.

[33] Reg. § 1.664-1 and Reg. § 1.664-2, respectively.

[34] Reg. § 1.664-1 and Reg. § 1.664-3, respectively.

[35] Code Sec. 664(d)(1)(A) and Code Sec. 664(d)(2)(A).

interest in a CRAT must be at least 10 percent of the initial net fair market value of all property transferred to the trust. With respect to a CRUT, the 10-percent rule applies to each contribution of property to the trust. Under a grandfather provision, however, the 10-percent rule and the 50-percent limitation discussed above do not apply to transfers in trust under the terms of a will or other testamentary instrument executed on or before July 28, 1997, if the decedent (1) dies before January 1, 1999, without having republished the will or amended it by codicil or otherwise, or (2) was, on July 28, 1997, unable to change the disposition of the property due to a mental disability and did not regain competency before dying.[36]

Charitable remainder annuity trusts and unitrusts cannot have noncharitable remainder interests if a deduction is to be allowed. Furthermore, the remainder interest must pass to a charity on the termination of the last income interest. There may be more than one noncharitable income beneficiary, either concurrently or successively, and the income interest may be a life estate or for a term of years, but the term of years cannot be in excess of 20 years (see, however, the exception for contingency provisions in charitable remainder trusts, noted above). Under the regulations that were effective prior to July 7, 2003, no deduction was allowable if a charitable unitrust interest was preceded by a noncharitable unitrust interest; however, the Tax Court held the regulations were invalid to the extent that they prohibit a deduction in such a situation.[37] In response to this decision, Reg. § 20.2055-2 and Reg. § 20.2522(c)-3 have been amended, effective July 7, 2003, to permit a deduction for charitable guaranteed annuity and unitrust interests that are preceded by a noncharitable annuity or unitrust interest.[38] The amendments eliminate the former requirement that a charitable interest commence no later than the start of a noncharitable interest that is in the form of a guaranteed annuity or unitrust interest. The regulations continue to require that any amounts payable for a private purpose before the expiration of the charitable interest either must be in the form of a guaranteed annuity or unitrust interest, or be payable from a separate group of assets exclusively devoted to private purposes. A trust will not qualify as a charitable remainder trust and no charitable deduction will be allowed if it is possible that federal estate and state death taxes may be payable from the trust assets.[39]

In a series of revenue procedures, the IRS has provided sample language in order to help taxpayers in drafting governing instruments for:

- An inter vivos CRAT for one measuring life (Rev. Proc. 2003-53, 2003-2 CB 230);

- An inter vivos CRAT for a term of years (Rev. Proc. 2003-54, 2003-2 CB 236);

- An inter vivos CRAT with consecutive interests for two measuring lives (Rev. Proc. 2003-55, 2003-2 CB 242);

- An inter vivos CRAT with concurrent and consecutive interests for two measuring lives (Rev. Proc. 2003-56, 2003-2 CB 249);

---

[36] Code Sec. 664(d)(1) and Code Sec. 664(d)(2); Act Sec. 1089(b)(6)(B) of the Taxpayer Relief Act of 1997 (P.L. 105-34).

[37] Reg. § 20.2055-2(e), held partially invalid in *M.L. Boeshore Est.*, 78 TC 523, CCH Dec. 38,902, appeal dismissed CA-7, 2-10-83. The IRS has acquiesced in result only in this decision, Acquiescence Announcement, 1987-2 CB 1.

[38] T.D. 9068, filed with the *Federal Register* on July 3, 2003.

[39] Rev. Rul. 82-128, 1982-2 CB 71; *M. Atkinson Est.*, 115 TC 26, CCH Dec. 53,962, aff'd, CA-11, 2002-2 USTC ¶ 60,449, 309 F3d 1290.

- A testamentary CRAT for one measuring life (Rev. Proc. 2003-57, 2003-2 CB 257);

- A testamentary CRAT for a term of years (Rev. Proc. 2003-58, 2003-2 CB 262);

- A testamentary CRAT with consecutive interests for two measuring lives (Rev. Proc. 2003-59, 2003-2 CB 268);

- A testamentary CRAT with concurrent and consecutive interests for two measuring lives (Rev. Proc. 2003-60, 2003-2 CB 274);

- An inter vivos CRUT for one measuring life (Rev. Proc. 2005-52, 2005-2 CB 326);

- An inter vivos CRUT for a term of years (Rev. Proc. 2005-53, 2005-2 CB 339);

- An inter vivos CRUT with consecutive interests for two measuring lives (Rev. Proc. 2005-54, 2005-2 CB 353);

- An inter vivos CRUT with concurrent and consecutive interests for two measuring lives (Rev. Proc. 2005-55, 2005-2 CB 367);

- A testamentary CRUT for one measuring life (Rev. Proc. 2005-56, 2005-2 CB 383);

- A testamentary CRUT for a term of years (Rev. Proc. 2005-57, 2005-2 CB 392);

- A testamentary CRUT with consecutive interests for two measuring lives (Rev. Proc. 2005-58, 2005-2 CB 402);

- A testamentary CRUT with concurrent and consecutive interests for two measuring lives (Rev. Proc. 2005-59, 2005-2 CB 412).

• *Safe Harbor for Charitable Remainder Trusts Subject to Spouse's Elective Share*

The IRS has provided a safe harbor procedure under which it will disregard a surviving spouse's right of election for purposes of determining whether a charitable remainder annuity trust (CRAT) or a charitable remainder unitrust (CRUT) satisfies the requirements of Code Sec. 664(d)(1)(B) or Code Sec. 664(d)(2)(B) continuously since the trust's creation.[40]

The safe harbor procedure applies to CRATs or CRUTs created by a grantor whose surviving spouse, under applicable state law, has a right of election exercisable on the grantor's death to receive a statutory share of the grantor's estate, and the estate share could be satisfied from assets of the CRAT or CRUT. The existence of the right of election, where the share could include assets of the CRAT or CRUT, causes the trust to fail to qualify under Code Sec. 664(d) because an amount other than the annuity or unitrust payment can be paid to a person other than a charitable organization. To reduce taxpayer burden, the IRS has provided a safe harbor procedure that will cause the right of election to be disregarded for purposes of determining whether the CRAT or CRUT meets the requirements of Code Sec. 664(d) continuously from the date the trust is created.

Specifically, a surviving spouse must irrevocably waive the right of election to the extent necessary to ensure that no part of the trust (other than the annuity or unitrust interest of which the surviving spouse is the named recipient) can be

---

[40] Rev. Proc. 2005-24, 2005-1 CB 909; extended by Notice 2006-15, 2006-1 CB 501.

used to satisfy the elective share. To meet the safe harbor requirements, the surviving spouse must execute a waiver that is valid under applicable state law, in writing, and signed and dated by the surviving spouse. In addition, a copy of the signed waiver must be provided to the trustee of the CRAT or CRUT. For CRATs or CRUTs created on or after June 28, 2005, the waiver must be executed on or before the date that is six months after the due date of Form 5227, Split-Interest Trust Information Return, for the year in which the later of the following occurs: (1) the creation of the trust, (2) the date of the grantor's marriage to the surviving spouse; (3) the date the grantor first becomes domiciled or a resident in a jurisdiction whose law provides a right of election that could be satisfied from trust assets; or (4) the effective date of applicable state law creating a right of election.

For CRATs or CRUTs created on or after June 28, 2005, the surviving spouse's failure to waive the right of election in accordance with the revenue procedure will result in the trust failing to qualify under Code Sec. 664(d) continuously since it creation, regardless of whether the spouse exercised the right of election. For trusts created before June 28, 2005, a waiver of the right of election is not necessary to prevent the trust from failing the requirements of Code Sec. 664(d) as long as the surviving spouse does not actually exercise the right of election. The safe harbor procedure is not available, in any event, to a CRAT or CRUT if the surviving spouse exercises the right of election. The procedure is effective as of March 30, 2005.

Extension of June 28, 2005 grandfather date. The IRS has announced an extension of the grandfather date of June 28, 2005, provided in Rev. Proc. 2005-24, until further guidance is published regarding the effect of a spousal right of election on a trust's qualification as a CRAT or a CRUT.[41]

• *Life Payment to Trust for Financially Disabled Individual*

With respect to a CRUT, the IRS has allowed a limited exception to the rule that a noncharitable interest cannot exceed 20 years. That is, a CRUT will not be disqualified if unitrust amounts are paid to a separate trust for the life of an individual who is "financially disabled" for purposes of Code Sec. 6511(h)(2)(A). Under this Code section, an individual is financially disabled if the individual is unable to manage his or her financial affairs because of a medically determinable physical or mental impairment that can be expected to result in death, or which has lasted, or can be expected to last, for a continuous period of not less than 12 months. However, the IRS has indicated that a trust will qualify as a CRUT if (1) the separate trust's sole function is to receive and administer the unitrust amounts for the benefit of the financially disabled beneficiary, and (2) upon such beneficiary's death, the separate trust's remaining assets will be distributed to the beneficiary's estate or (after reimbursing the state for any Medicaid benefits provided to the beneficiary) are subject to the beneficiary's general power of appointment. In these circumstances, according to the IRS, the use of the separate trust's assets is consistent with the manner in which the beneficiary's own assets would be used. Consequently, the beneficiary is considered to have received the unitrust amounts directly from the CRUT for purposes of Code Sec. 664(d)(2)(A) and it is permissible for the CRUT's term to be for the life of the beneficiary, and not simply for a term of years. The same result applies in the case of a charitable remainder annuity trust.[42]

---

[41] IRS Notice 2006-15, 2006-1 CB 501.

[42] Rev. Rul. 2002-20, 2002-1 CB 794, amplifying and superseding Rev. Rul. 76-270, 1976-2 CB 194.

• *Certain Transfers to Employee Stock Ownership Plans*

If a charitable remainder trust holds qualified employer securities transferred from a decedent dying before January 1, 1999, the securities transferred to an employee stock ownership plan in a "qualified gratuitous transfer" will qualify for the estate tax charitable deduction. The deduction is limited to the extent of the present value of the remainder interest in the trust.[43]

A transfer of qualified securities is treated as a qualified gratuitous transfer if (1) the securities are transferred to the trust by a decedent dying before January 1, 1999, (2) the decedent and his or her family members owned no more than 10 percent of the value of the outstanding stock at the time of the transfer to the employee stock ownership plan (ESOP), (3) the ESOP owns at least 60 percent of the value of the stock after the transfer, (4) the ESOP was in existence on August 1, 1996, (5) the employer agrees to pay an excise tax on certain prohibited distributions and allocations of the securities, and (6) no income tax deduction is allowable for the transfer. Additionally, the ESOP must meet certain antidiscrimination, administrative and distribution and allocation requirements.[44]

¶ 1123   Charitable Lead (Income) Trusts

A charitable lead trust is basically the reverse of a charitable remainder trust (see ¶ 1122). With a charitable lead trust, a charity is given an income interest for a term of years, or for the life (or lives) of designated individuals. At the end of the measuring period or the life (or lives) of the designated individuals, the property reverts to the grantor or the grantor's estate. Such an arrangement is used where a grantor has no immediate need for the income from the property to be transferred into the charitable lead trust, but still wants the property to benefit his or her chosen beneficiaries at a later date.

To sustain an estate or gift tax deduction, the payments to the charity under a charitable lead trust must be in the form of annuity or unitrust interests.[45] But there is no minimum payout requirement.

An annuity interest requires payment, at least annually, of a fixed amount for a specified term of years or the life (or lives) of named individuals.[46] Generally, the annuity interest will be a specified percentage of the value of the property transferred to the trust at the time of the transfer. The charitable lead annuity trust (CLAT) can only receive the one initial transfer of assets to it.

A unitrust interest requires payments, at least annually, of a fixed percentage of the fair market value of the trust assets as determined each year. The amount of the charitable deduction is determined by subtracting the value of the non-charitable interests from the fair market value of the property transferred to the trust.[47]

> *Comment:* Neither the Code nor the legislative history delineates the permissible term for which a charitable guaranteed annuity interest or a unitrust interest in a lead trust must be paid. The permissible term for these interests is set forth in the regulations as either a specified term of years, or the life or lives of an individual or individuals, each of whom must be living at the date of the transfer and can be ascertained at such date.

---

[43] Code Sec. 2055(a)(5).

[44] Code Sec. 664(g).

[45] Code Sec. 2055(e)(2)(B) and Code Sec. 2522(c)(2)(B); Reg. § 20.2055-2 and Reg. § 25.2522(c)-3.

[46] Rev. Rul. 85-49, 1985-1 CB 330.

[47] See, for example, IRS Letter Ruling 9737023 (June 16, 1997).

In recent years, donors have attempted to take advantage of the existing regulations by using the life of an unrelated individual as the measuring life for the term of a charitable lead trust, to artificially inflate the charitable deduction. Sometimes referred to as "ghoul trusts," the methodology involves selection of an individual who is seriously ill, but not "terminally ill," as the measuring life. Under the regulations, the annuity factor for a terminally ill person must be computed specifically to take into account that person's actual life expectancy (Reg. § 20.7520-3(b)(4), Example 1). However, because the individuals used for the measuring lives of these trusts are not terminally ill as defined by the regulations, the charitable interest is valued based on the standard actuarial tables. When the seriously ill individual dies (prematurely in comparison to what would have been expected under the actuarial tables), the amount the charity actually receives will be significantly less than the amount on which the charitable deduction was based. On the other hand, the amount transferred to the noncharitable remainder beneficiaries will be significantly greater than that subject to gift or estate tax.

This possibility is illustrated below in Example (1).

Example (1): Assume that a CLAT is established using a 40-year-old as the measuring life. One million dollars is transferred to the CLAT. The Code Sec. 7520 rate is 1.2% and the annuity payout rate is set at 2.5% of the initial value of the trust, to produce an annuity of $25,000 per year. Under these assumptions, the results are as follows:

Annuity factor: 30.2994

Present value of annuity interest: $754,455

Present value of remainder (gift) interest: $245,545

If the 40-year-old actually dies three years later, the charity would have received a total of $75,000 (3 × $25,000) in annuity payments. Assuming a 2% net return over the three-year period the remainder beneficiaries would receive approximately $984,698.

In two recent revenue procedures, the IRS has provided sample language in order to help taxpayer in drafting governing instruments for:

- An inter vivos nongrantor charitable lead unitrust (CLUT) with a term of years unitrust period (Rev. Proc. 2008-45, IRB 2008-30, 224);

- An inter vivos grantor CLUT (Rev. Proc. 2008-45, IRB 2008-30, 224); and

- A testamentary CLUT (Rev. Proc. 2008-46, IRB 2008-30, 238).

• *Amended Regulations*

In response to these trusts, the IRS has adopted amendments to regulations[48] that limit the use of certain charitable lead trusts that use the life expectancy of a seriously ill, but not "terminally ill," person as the measuring life. Because the IRS considers such arrangements to be abusive, as well as contrary to the legislative intent of restricting a charitable deduction to specific types of split-interest transfers, the amended regulations limit the permissible term for guaranteed annuity and unitrust interests to either a specified term of years or the lives of certain individuals who are living at the date of the transfer. With respect to

---

[48] T.D. 8923, filed with the *Federal Register* on Jan. 5, 2001, adopting amendments to Reg. § 20.2055-2 and Reg. § 20.2055(c)(3).

the latter requirement, only one or more of the following individuals may be used as measuring lives: (1) the donor; (2) the donor's spouse; and (3) a lineal ancestor (or a spouse of a lineal ancestor) of all the remainder beneficiaries. Thus, noncharitable remainder beneficiaries can include step-children and step-grandchildren of the individual who is the measuring life. Additionally, a trust will be deemed to satisfy the requirement that the measuring life be a person in the above three categories if there is a less than 15 percent probability that individuals who are not lineal descendants will receive any trust corpus. This probability must be computed, based on the current applicable Life Table contained in Reg. § 20.2031-7, as of the date of the decedent's death taking into account the interests of all primary and contingent remainder beneficiaries who are living at that time.

The limitation regarding permissible measuring lives does not apply to a charitable guaranteed annuity interest or unitrust interest payable under a charitable remainder trust described in Code Sec. 664.

The regulations allow an interest payable for a specified term of years to qualify as a guaranteed annuity or unitrust interest even if the governing instrument contains a "savings clause" intended to ensure compliance with a state's rule against perpetuities. The savings clause must utilize a vesting period of 21 years after the deaths of measuring lives who are selected to maximize, rather than limit, the term of the trust.

The amended regulations apply to transfers pursuant to wills and trusts where the decedent dies on or after April 4, 2000. Exceptions would apply for a will or revocable trust executed on or before April 4, 2000, if (1) the decedent dies on or before July 5, 2001, without having republished the will or amended the trust, or (2) the decedent was under a mental disability on April 4, 2000, under a mental disability to change the disposition of the decedent's property, and either does not regain competence to dispose of such property before the date of death, or dies prior to the later of (a) 90 days after the date on which the decedent first regains competence, or (b) July 5, 2001, without having republished the will (or amended the trust) by codicil or otherwise. In addition, the charitable deduction would not be disallowed where the charitable interest is payable for the life of an individual, other than one permitted under the regulations, if the interest is reformed into a lead interest payable for a specified term of years.

> *Example (2):* Assume an annuity interest is payable for the life of an individual who is age 40 at the time of the transfer July 1, 2013. If the Code Sec. 7520 interest rate is 1.4%, the annuity factor from Column 1 of Table S (1.4%), contained in IRS Publication 1457, Actuarial Values, Book Aleph, for the life of an individual age 40 is 29.1473. Based on Table B (1.4%), contained in Publication 1457, the factor 29.1473 corresponds to a term of years between 37 and 38 years. Accordingly, under the proposed amendments, the annuity interest would have to be reformed into an interest payable for a term of 38 years.

In the case of testamentary transfers, a judicial reformation would have to be commenced prior to the later of (1) July 5, 2001, or (2) the date prescribed by Code Sec. 2055(e)(3)(C)(iii). Any judicial reformation must be completed within a reasonable time after it is commenced. A nonjudicial reformation would be permitted if effective under state law, provided it is completed by the date on which a judicial reformation must be commenced.

The IRS has provided sample language to help taxpayers draft governing instruments for charitable lead annuity trusts (CLATs). These instruments, including alternative provisions, relate to: (1) an inter vivos nongrantor CLAT for a term of years, and an inter vivos grantor CLAT for a term of years,[49] and (2) a testamentary CLAT for a term or years.[50]

¶ 1124   Trust Reformation Rules

A nondeductible charitable split-interest contribution can be reformed into a deductible split-interest contribution for purposes of the income, estate, and gift tax charitable deductions.[51] No reformation occurs, however, unless a "reformable interest" is transformed into a "qualified interest" by means of a "qualified reformation."

• Qualified Interest

A qualified interest is an interest for which a charitable deduction is allowed under Code Sec. 2055(a).[52] If a qualified reformation occurs, the allowable charitable deduction is equal to the lesser of (1) the actuarial value of the charitable interest after the reformation, or (2) the actuarial value of the charitable interest before the reformation for which a deduction would have been allowable but for the disallowance rules of Code Sec. 2055(e)(2).

• Qualified Reformation

A qualified reformation is a reformation, amendment, construction, or other action pertaining to the governing instrument that changes a reformable interest (defined below) into a qualified interest.[53] A qualified reformation can be accomplished by any means permitted under applicable local law, provided that the change is binding on all relevant parties under applicable local law.[54]

A reformation will constitute a qualified reformation only if certain requirements are met:

(1) The difference between the actuarial value of the reformed charitable interest and the unreformed charitable interest cannot exceed five percent of the value of the interest prior to reformation. For purposes of this requirement, values are to be determined as of the date of the decedent's death.

(2) Charitable and noncharitable interests in charitable lead (income) trusts must terminate at the same time before and after reformation. The same is generally true with respect to charitable and noncharitable interests under a charitable remainder trust instrument, with the exception that a noncharitable interest for a term of years in excess of 20 years may be reduced to 20 years.

(3) The changes are made effective as of the date of the decedent's death.[55]

• Reformable Interest

A qualified reformation cannot occur unless the interest is "reformable." In order to be considered reformable, the following requirements must be met:

---

[49] Rev. Proc. 2007-45, 2007-2 CB 89. Alternative provisions include an annuity period for the life of an individual.

[50] Rev. Proc. 2007-46, 2007-2 CB 102. Alternative provisions include an annuity period for the life of an individual.

[51] Code Sec. 2055(e)(3).
[52] Code Sec. 2055(e)(3)(D).
[53] Code Sec. 2055(e)(3)(B).
[54] Senate Finance Committee Report to the Tax Reform Act of 1984 (P.L. 98-369).
[55] Code Sec. 2055(e)(3)(B).

(1) The interest must be of a type that would have qualified for a charitable deduction except for the charitable split-interest rules of Code Sec. 2055(e)(2).

(2) The interest of the beneficiaries, before the remainder interest vests in possession, must be expressed as either a specified dollar amount or as a fixed percentage of the fair market value of the property, taking into account the rules of Code Sec. 664(d)(3).[56]

Requirement (2) does not apply if a judicial proceeding is commenced to change the remainder interest into a qualified interest no later than 90 days after:

(1) the last day for filing the estate tax return, including extensions; or

(2) if no estate tax return is required to be filed, the last date, including extensions, for the filing of the income tax return for the first tax year the trust is required to file a return.[57]

In deciding whether an action was commenced within the required 90-day period, the actual date that the judicial proceeding was instituted governs. Thus, a judicial proceeding instituted after this deadline will not be deemed to have a retroactive effect based on probate documents filed within the 90-day period that were not in the nature of pleadings sufficient to begin an action to amend the trust.[58]

The IRS has privately ruled that it would not grant an *extension of time* to commence a judicial reformation of a split-interest trust. According to the IRS, discretionary relief is available under Reg. § 301.9100-3 for regulatory elections, but not for statutory elections (such as the deadline for judicial reformations set by Code Sec. 2055(e)(3)(C)(iii).[59]

The requirement that the interests of the beneficiaries be expressed as a specified dollar amount or fixed percentage of the property's fair market value does not apply to interests passing under wills or trusts executed before 1979, or for interests for which a timely judicial reformation proceeding is instituted.[60]

Application to income and gift taxes. Rules similar to the estate tax deduction rules apply to the determination of the allowance of income and gift tax charitable deductions for split-interest contributions.

Statute of limitations on assessment. The period for assessment of any tax deficiency arising out of the application of the rules for reformation of charitable split-interest contributions will not expire before one year after the date on which the IRS is notified that the reformation has occurred.[61]

Death of noncharitable income beneficiary. If, before the due date (including extensions) for filing the estate tax return on which the charitable split-interest contribution is claimed, the reformable interest becomes a wholly charitable interest because of the death of all noncharitable income beneficiaries, or because of a termination or distribution of a trust in accordance with the terms of the trust instrument, a deduction for such interest is to be allowed as if it met the requirements of a split-interest trust on the date of the decedent's death.[62]

---

[56] Code Sec. 2055(e)(3)(C).
[57] Code Sec. 2055(e)(3)(C)(iii).
[58] *Z. Hall*, 93 TC 745, CCH Dec. 46,219.
[59] IRS Letter Ruling 200548019 (Aug. 11, 2005).

[60] Code Sec. 2055(e)(3)(C)(iv).
[61] Code Sec. 2055(e)(3)(G).
[62] Code Sec. 2055(e)(3)(F).

Remainder interest in personal residence or farm. A charitable (as well as a gift) deduction is available for the transfer of a remainder interest, not in trust, in a personal residence and farm.[63] The value of the deduction is the fair market value of the remainder interest, determined by the actuarial tables at the date of transfer, the date of death or the alternative valuation date.[64]

Contingency provisions in charitable remainder trusts. Generally, non-charitable interests in a charitable remainder trust (whether a charitable remainder annuity trust or a charitable remainder unitrust) must terminate at the end of specified lives in being or a term of years not to exceed 20 years. However, where a trust complies with the termination rule (i.e., the noncharitable interest must terminate at the end of lives in being or a term of years not exceeding 20 years), a contingency may be placed in the trust providing that the noncharitable interest is to terminate, and the charitable interest is to be accelerated, upon the happening of an event at an earlier time (e.g., the noncharitable interest may terminate on the remarriage of an individual). In such a case, the value of the charitable remainder interest is determined without regard to the contingency.[65]

• *Effective Dates*

Code Sec. 2055(e)(3) applies to all reformations occurring after 1981.

• *Reformation to Comply with the Minimum Charitable Benefit Rule*

A trust that fails to qualify as a charitable remainder trust by reason of the failure to satisfy the 10-percent minimum charitable benefit requirement (see ¶1122) may be reformed to increase the value of the remainder interest. Generally, the remainder interest can be increased by reducing the payout percentage and/or shortening the trust term. If not reformed, the trust may be declared void as of its inception.[66]

¶1125 Fractional Interests in Tangible Personal Property

Subject to the exceptions noted at ¶1120, a donation of less than a donor's entire interest in property to a charity does not qualify for an estate or gift tax charitable deduction (Code Sec. 2055(e)(2) and Code Sec. 2522(c)(2)). One of these exceptions provides that such a deduction is allowed if the donor transfers an undivided portion of his or her entire interest in property to the charity. For purposes of the charitable deduction, an undivided portion is a fraction or percentage of every substantial interest and right that the donor owns in the property for the entire time that the donor owns the property. A gift to a charity of the right, as a tenant in common with the donor, to the possession and control of the property for a portion of the year is treated as a gift an undivided portion of the property. Accordingly, a charitable deduction is allowable (Reg. § 1.170A-7(b)(1)).

As a general rule, a gift of tangible personal property, such as a work of art, will not qualify for an estate or gift tax charitable deduction if the charity's possession or use of the property begins at a future time. However, the donor of an undivided present interest in property may claim a deduction when the gift is made even though the donee's initial possession may not begin immediately (Reg. § 1.170A-5(a)(2)). For example, if a donor makes a gift of an undivided fractional one-quarter interest in a painting that entitles the charity to possession during three months of each year, the donor may claim a deduction upon the

---

[63] Reg. § 20.2055-2(e)(2).
[64] Code Sec. 7520.

[65] Code Sec. 664(f).
[66] Code Sec. 2055(e)(3)(J).

donee's receipt of the deed of gift, provided that the charitable donee's initial possession is not deferred for longer than one year.

Recapture of deduction for gift and income tax purposes. Any gift (or income) tax charitable deduction allowed for contributions of undivided interests in tangible personal property will be recaptured (with interest) if:

(1) the donor fails to contribute all of the remaining interests in the property to the donee (or another charitable organization if the donee is no longer in existence) before the earlier of the tenth anniversary of the initial fractional contribution, or the donor's date of death; or

(2) the donee fails to take substantial physical possession of the property or fails to use the property in a manner related to the donee's exempt purpose during the period beginning after the initial fractional contribution and ending on the earlier of the tenth anniversary of the initial contribution, or the donor's date of death.[67]

Additions to tax. If a gift or income tax charitable deduction is recaptured, an additional tax will be imposed, equal to 10 percent of the amount recaptured.[68]

¶ 1126   Valuation of Trust Interests

An estate can claim estate tax charitable deductions for the present value of income and remainder interests in property that is bequeathed or which otherwise passes to qualifying charities. A deduction is allowed for the fair market value of a partial interest at the appropriate valuation date for transfers not exclusively for charitable purposes. The fair market value of an annuity, life estate, term for years, remainder, reversion, or unitrust interest is its present value.

For transfers not exclusively for charitable purposes (involving guaranteed annuity trusts, unitrusts, and pooled income funds—transfers (1), (5), and (6) of ¶ 1120 above) made by decedents dying after July 31, 1969, the rules for computing the present values of such interests for deduction purposes are as follows:

(1) The present value of a remainder interest in a charitable remainder annuity trust is determined under income tax Reg. § 1.664-2(c).

(2) The present value of a remainder interest in a charitable remainder unitrust is determined under income tax Reg. § 1.664-4 or Reg. § 1.664-4A, depending on the valuation date.

(3) The present value of a remainder interest in a pooled income fund is determined under income tax Reg. § 1.642(c)-6.

(4) The present value of a guaranteed annuity interest is determined under either estate tax Reg. § 20.2031-7 or estate tax Reg. § 20.2031-7A, depending on the date of the decedent's death (see ¶ 530), unless the annuity is issued by a company regularly engaged in the sale of annuities, in which case Reg. § 20.2031-8 should be used.

(5) The present value of a unitrust interest is determined by subtracting the present value of all interests in the transferred property other than the unitrust interest from the fair market value of the transferred property.[69]

---

[67] Code Sec. 170(o)(3) and Code Sec. 2522(e)(3), as added by the Pension Act of 2006 (P.L. 109-280).

[68] Code Sec. 170(o)(3)(B) and Code Sec. 2522(e)(3)(B).

[69] Reg. § 20.2055-2(f)(2)(v).

The above regulations are applicable only where the interest is dependent upon one life.

With respect to pooled income funds in existence for less than three tax years preceding the tax year in which the transfer is made, Reg. §1.642(c)-6(e)(3) provides the method for determining the rate of return for purposes of valuing a remainder interest in the fund.

For purposes of valuing charitable remainder interests in annuity trusts, unitrusts, and pooled income funds that are dependent upon the death of the survivor of more than one life, the IRS has issued several publications providing special factors and tables (see ¶530 for a discussion of these publications).

Any claim for deduction in any return (income, estate, or gift tax) for the value of a remainder interest in a trust or pooled income fund must be supported by a statement showing the computation of the present value of such interest. The IRS, on request, may furnish a factor that can be used to value such interests.

¶1127   Contingent Gifts

If, as of the date of a decedent's death, a transfer to a charitable organization is dependent upon performance of an act or happening of an event (whether a condition precedent or subsequent) before it takes effect (or is divested), no charitable deduction will be allowed unless the possibility that the charity may not receive the property is so remote as to be considered negligible. The requirement of an "effective transfer"[70] makes it necessary that enjoyment of the benefits of the transfer accrue in fact to the charity, so it may be immaterial that the value of the contingent interest could have been computed actuarially.

Likewise, if a bequest to charities is wholly contingent, so that no present value is determinable from known data, no deduction can be taken.[71] However, the fact that the remainder to charity is conditioned on the life tenant's dying without issue does not make the remainder contingent if the possibility of issue is extinct,[72] as, for example, where the life tenant has reached an advanced age.[73]

¶1128   Transfers Out of Which Death Taxes Must Be Paid

Deductions for charitable bequests are limited to the amount actually received by the charitable organization.[74] For example, where taxes are to be paid from the residuary estate and the residuary estate is left to charity, the deduction for charitable bequests must be reduced by the amount of federal estate tax payable out of the residuary estate.[75] This computation may be accomplished algebraically or by application of the principle of the converging series, which is in general use by accountants in the determination of interdependent factors.

However, whether administration expenses *allocable to the income of an estate* reduce the amount of a marital or charitable deduction had been a matter of controversy among the U.S. Courts of Appeals for the Federal, Sixth and Eleventh Circuits and the Tax Court. The Federal and Sixth Circuits held that administration expenses reduce the marital deduction regardless of whether the

---

[70] Reg. §20.2055-2(b).
[71] *A.L. Humes, Exr. (D.R. Gates Est.)*, SCt, 1 USTC ¶298, 276 US 487.
[72] *Provident Trust Co., Exr. (G.T. Roberts Est.)*, SCt, 4 USTC ¶1229, 291 US 272.
[73] *City Bank Farmers Trust Co., Exr. (T.B. Allen Est.)*, CA-2, 35-1 USTC ¶9079, 74 F2d 692.
[74] Code Sec. 2055(c).
[75] Reg. §20.2055-3.

payment is allocated to income or to principal.[76] But the Tax Court and the Eleventh Circuit had declined to follow the reasoning of those appellate courts and had held that administration expenses allocable to the *income* of an estate do not reduce a decedent's estate's marital or charitable deduction provided that the decedent's will and applicable state law allow for the payment of administration expenses out of the estate's income.[77] Settling the split among the circuits, the U.S. Supreme Court held in *O. Hubert Est.*[78] that the executor's or trustee's discretion, under the governing instrument and local law, to pay administration expenses out of principal or income reduces the marital deduction only if such discretion constitutes a material limitation on the spouse's right to receive income. In this case, the Court found that such discretion did not constitute a material limitation.

In order to avoid the difficulty, both for taxpayers and the IRS to determine what constitutes a "material limitation" on a charity's right to income from a charitable bequest, the IRS amended Reg. § 20.2055-3, effective for estates of decedents dying on or after December 3, 1999.[79] The amended regulation eliminates the materiality requirement. Instead, the regulations bifurcate estate expenses into estate transmission expenses and estate management expenses. Estate transmission expenses, but not estate management expenses, reduce the value of property for charitable deduction purposes. Estate transmission expenses are those expenses that would not have been incurred but for the decedent's death. Estate transmission expenses include any administration expense that is not a management expense. Management expenses are expenses that would be incurred in investing, maintaining, and preserving the estate property. However, the allowable amount of the charitable deduction is reduced by the amount of these management expenses if they are deducted as administration expenses on the estate tax return.

The deduction for charitable transfers allowed for federal estate tax purposes does not always correspond with state and foreign death tax exemptions or deductions for such transfers. In instances where a transfer is deductible under federal law, but taxable under state or foreign law, the federal estate tax law authorizes a deduction for the state or foreign death taxes paid if the executor elects to take it.

> *Comment:* In some instances, where the charitable transfer is reduced on account of state taxes and where the charitable transfer is a remainder interest, the complicated problem of interdependent taxes and deductions arises. This problem is identical in principle to the marital deduction situation at ¶ 1075. As in the case of the marital deduction, the problem can be avoided by providing for the payment of taxes out of other funds in the estate.

IRS Publication 904, "Interrelated Computations for Estate and Gift Taxes" (Rev. May 1985), contains examples for computing the charitable and marital deductions when these deductions are interrelated with the federal estate tax. Although no longer available from the IRS, IRS Publication 904 is reproduced in the CCH FEDERAL ESTATE AND GIFT TAX REPORTER.

---

[76] *G. Street Est.*, CA-6, 92-2 USTC ¶ 60,112, 974 F2d 723, rev'g in part TC, 56 TCM 774, CCH Dec. 45,201(M), TC Memo. 1988-553; *J. Burke*, CA-FC, 93-2 USTC ¶ 60,146, 994 F2d 1576.

[77] *O. Hubert Est.*, 95-2 USTC ¶ 60,209, aff'g TC, 101 TC 314, CCH Dec. 49,342; *F. Allen Est.*, 101 TC 351, CCH Dec. 49,346.

[78] *O. Hubert Est.*, SCt, 97-1 USTC ¶ 60,261.

[79] T.D. 8846, amending Reg. § 20.2055-3, filed with the *Federal Register* on Dec. 2, 1999.

Practitioners who would like to avoid the time-consuming and tedious calculations involved with using the mathematical formulae set out in Publication 904 should consider using CCH's *ProSystem fx® Tax*, which contains computer programs for calculating interrelated marital and charitable deductions.

Protective claims for refund. To the extent that a protective claim for a refund is filed with respect to a claim against the estate or an expense that would have been deductible under Code Sec. 2053(a) or (b) (see ¶803) if such item already has been paid and that is payable out of a share that meets the requirements for a charitable deduction under Code Sec. 2055, the charitable deduction is not reduced by the amount of such claim until the amount is actually paid, becomes ascertainable in amount, or meets the deduction requirements of Reg. §20.2053-4.[80]

¶1130   Contributions to Donor Advised Funds

Contributions to charitable organizations that are exempt from income tax under Code Sec. 501(c)(3) generally are deductible for estate and gift tax purposes. However, if the taxpayer retains control over the assets transferred to charity, the transfer may not qualify as a completed gift for purposes of claiming an income, estate, or gift tax deduction. Deductible bequests for estate tax purposes can include those made to a post or organization of war veterans[81] and to a domestic fraternal organization.[82] Similar deductions are allowed for gift tax purposes.[83] Code Sec. 509(a)(3) supporting organizations are public charities that carry out their exempt purposes by supporting one or more other exempt organizations, usually other public charities. These supporting organizations must have one of three relationships with the supported organizations, all of which are intended to ensure that the supporting organization is responsive to the needs of the supported organization and intimately involved in its operations and that the public charity is motivated to be attentive to the operations of the supporting organization. Type III supporting organizations (discussed below), are "operated in connection with" the supported organization.

Pension Act changes. Contributions to a donor advised fund made after February 13, 2007, will not be eligible for a charitable deduction for estate or gift tax purposes if the fund's sponsoring organization (Code Sec. 4966(d)(1)) is a war veterans organization[84] or fraternal lodge,[85] or a Type III supporting organization (Code Sec. 4943(f)(5)) that is not a functionally integrated Type III supporting organization. A Type III supporting organization is considered to be functionally integrated where it performs the functions of, or carries out the purposes of the supported charity.

Substantiation. An otherwise allowable contribution to a donor advised fund will be allowed only if the taxpayer obtains written acknowledgment of the fund's control of the assets. Specifically, a donor must obtain a contemporaneous written acknowledgment from the sponsoring organization providing that the sponsoring organization has exclusive legal control over the assets contributed. The contemporaneous written acknowledgment is similar to the acknowledgment needed to substantiate gifts of $250 or more under Code Sec. 170(f)(8)(C).[86]

---

[80] §20.2053-1(d)(5)(ii), as amended by T.D. 9468, October 16, 2009.

[81] Code Sec. 2055(a)(4).

[82] Code Sec. 2055(c)(3).

[83] Code Sec. 2522(a)(3) and Code Sec. 2522(c)(4).

[84] Code Sec. 2055(a)(4) and Code Sec. 2522(a)(4).

[85] Code Sec. 2055(a)(3) and Code Sec. 2522(a)(3).

[86] Code Sec. 170(f)(18)(B), Code Sec. 2055(e)(5)(B), and Code Sec. 2522(c)(5)(B), as

The provisions relating to the limitations on the charitable deductions for donor advised funds apply to contributions made after the date which is 180 days after August 17, 2006 (that is, February 13, 2007).

¶ 1140   Execution of Schedule

Deductions authorized for charitable, public, and similar gifts and bequests should be claimed on Form 706 (United States Estate (and Generation-Skipping Transfer) Tax Return) (Rev. August 2012),[87] Schedule O (Charitable, Public, and Similar Gifts and Bequests). This schedule must be filed if the estate claims a charitable deduction on its Form 706. If the transfer was made by will, a certified copy of the order admitting the will to probate, in addition to the copy of the will, should be submitted with the return. If the transfer was made by any other written instrument, a copy of the instrument should be submitted with the return. If the instrument is of record, the copy should be certified. If not of record, the copy should be verified.[88]

If the transfer was made by will, the executor must answer questions 1a and 1b at the top of Schedule O, which deal with whether any action has been instituted to interpret or to contest the will or any provision affecting the charitable deduction and whether, according to his or her information and belief, any such action is designed or contemplated. If the executor answers "yes" to either of these questions, full details of the action or contemplated action must be submitted with the return.

If a charitable deduction is claimed for the value of a split interest in property (see ¶ 1121), a copy of the computation of the deduction must be attached to the return. The computation must include the dates of birth of the life tenants or annuitants whose lives may affect the value of the interest passing to charity, and, in the case of a pooled income fund, the applicable yearly rate of return. If property passes to a charitable beneficiary as a result of a "qualified disclaimer" (see ¶ 1102), the executor must answer "yes" to question 2, and a copy of the written disclaimer must be attached to Schedule O.

¶ 1141   Valuation of Residuary Transfer

If a claim is made for a deduction of the value of the residue of the estate or a portion of the residue passing to charity under the decedent's will, a copy of the computation determining the value should be submitted.[89] The computation, or supporting documents, should include:

(1) a statement showing the values of all specific and general legacies or devises, indicating whether they are for charitable or noncharitable uses (Appropriate reference must be made to the applicable paragraph or section of the decedent's will or codicil. In any case where legacies are made to each member of a class, only the number in each class and the aggregate value of property received by them need be furnished.);

(2) the dates of birth of all life tenants or annuitants, the duration of whose lives may affect the value of the interest passing to charity under the decedent's will;

(Footnote Continued)

added by the Pension Act of 2006 (P.L. 109-280).

[87] An example of a filled-in Form 706, Schedule O, for a decedent dying in 2013, is reproduced at ¶ 3100.

[88] Reg. § 20.2055-1(c).

[89] Instructions for Form 706 (Rev. August 2013), p. 38.

(3) a statement showing the value of all property that is included in the decedent's gross estate but does not pass under the will (This includes jointly owned property that passed to the survivor on decedent's death and insurance payable to specific beneficiaries.); and

(4) any other information that may appear material, such as that relating to any claim, not arising under the will, to any part of the estate. This would include a spouse's claim to dower, curtesy, or similar rights.

¶ 1142   Alternate Valuation

Even if the alternate valuation (see ¶ 105) is used, any charitable transfer deductible on Schedule O (Charitable, Public, and Similar Gifts and Bequests) of Form 706 (United States Estate (and Generation-Skipping Transfer) Tax Return) (Rev. August 2013) should be valued as of the date of the decedent's death. However, adjustment must be made for any difference in the value of the property six months after the decedent's death, or at the date of its sale or exchange within this period. No adjustment may take into account any difference in value due to mere lapse of time or to the occurrence or nonoccurrence of a contingency.[90] If a decedent gives a percentage of his or her adjusted gross estate to charity, and his or her executor elects to use the alternate valuation method, the amount of the allowable charitable deduction is determined by using the value of the decedent's adjusted gross estate as of the alternate valuation date.[91]

---

[90] Reg. § 20.2032-1(g).

[91] Rev. Rul. 70-527, 1970-2 CB 193.

Chapter 23

STATE DEATH TAXES

¶ 1144 Deduction for State Death Taxes after 2004

Effective for decedents dying after December 31, 2004, a deduction from the gross estate is allowed for any amount of estate, inheritance, legacy, or succession taxes actually paid to a state or to the District of Columbia with respect to property included in the decedent's gross estate.[1] Prior to January 1, 2005, a credit for estate taxes paid was available under Code Sec. 2013 (see ¶1145.)

The state death tax deduction (Code Sec. 2058) was scheduled to expire after December 31, 2012, under the sunset provision of the Economic Growth and Tax Relief Reconciliation Act of 2001 (EGTRRA) (P.L. 107-16), as extended by the Tax Relief, Unemployment Insurance Reauthorization, and Job Creation Act of 2010 (the Tax Relief Act of 2010) (P.L. 111-312).[2] However, the state death tax deduction was made permanent by the American Taxpayer Relief Act of 2012 (P.L. 112-240) (ATRA).

The deduction for state death taxes is subject to no dollar limits. However, if property other than cash is transferred to the state in payment of state death taxes, the amount of the state death tax deduction is limited to *the lesser of*: (1) the amount of the state tax liability discharged, or (2) the fair market value of the property on the date of transfer. The amount of the deduction is claimed on Form 706 (Rev. August 2013), Part 2, line 3b.

In connection with claiming the deduction, evidence of payment of the state tax should be provided to the IRS (with the Form 706, if possible). This should take the form of a certificate of tax payment issued by the proper officer of the taxing state (or the District of Columbia) that shows the:

(1) Total amount of tax imposed (before adding interest and penalties, and before allowing discount);

(2) Amount of discount allowed;

(3) Amount of penalties and interest imposed;

(4) Total amount actually paid in cash; and

(5) Date of payment of the tax.[3]

In addition to the above items, the estate should be provide any additional proof of payment that the IRS specifically requests.[4]

If the state death tax is not paid on the date that the estate files the federal estate tax return (Form 706), a deduction can be claimed for an anticipated

---

[1] Code Sec. 2058, as added by the Economic Growth and Tax Relief Reconciliation Act of 2001 (P.L. 107-16), extended by the Tax Relief, Unemployment Insurance Reauthorization, and Job Creation Act of 2010 (P.L. 111-312), and made permanent by the American Taxpayer Relief Act of 2012 (P.L. 12-240).

[2] Act Sec. 101(a)(1), P.L. 111-312.

[3] Instructions for Form 706 (Rev. August, 2013), p. 6.

[4] Instructions for Form 706 (Rev. August 2013), p. 6.

amount of state death tax that will be paid. However, the estate tax deduction will not be finally allowed unless the state death taxes are paid within four years after the Form 706 is filed. This payment deadline date may be extended if:

(1) a timely petition for redetermination has been filed with the Tax Court;

(2) an extension of time has been granted for payment of estate tax or an estate tax deficiency; or

(3) a timely refund claim has been filed.

If the first exception ((1), above) applies, the deadline for payment of state death taxes may be extended to the date that is 60 days after the Tax Court decision becomes final. If the second exception ((2), above) applies, the deadline will run until the date the extension expires. If the final exception ((3), above) applies, the deadline will be extended to *the latest of the expiration of* (a) 60 days from the mailing of a notice to the taxpayer of a disallowance of the refund claim; (b) 60 days after a court decision on the merits of the claim becomes final; or (c) two years after a notice of waiver of disallowance is filed under Code Sec. 6532(a)(3).

A refund based on the deduction may be made if the refund claim is filed within the four-year period following the filing of the Form 706 (as extended by the exceptions noted, if applicable). Any refunds made will be without interest.[5]

Comment: Prior to passage of the Economic Growth and Tax Relief Reconciliation Act of 2001 (P.L. 107-16) (EGTRRA), the majority of states levied an estate tax in the amount of the credit for state death taxes allowed under federal law. In states with such a "pick-up" tax, the total estate tax burden did not exceed the federal tax liability. However, EGTRRA brought about the eventual repeal of the federal credit for state death taxes available under Code Sec. 2011 (see ¶1145), and replaced it with the Code Sec. 2058 deduction for death taxes paid, for estates of decedents dying after 2004, However, for states that levied a pick-up tax only, this meant the loss of a significant source of revenue. Some states addressed this situation by gearing their pick-up taxes to the amount of the federal tax credit under Code Sec. 2011 before its repeal by EGTRRA. Other states impose standalone estate or inheritance taxes. For detailed descriptions of the various death and transfer tax laws of the 50 states and the District of Columbia, see CCH FINANCIAL AND ESTATE PLANNING, ¶60.101.

¶1145   State Death Tax Credit before 2005

For decedents dying before January 1, 2005, a credit was allowed against the federal estate tax for any estate, inheritance, legacy, or succession taxes actually paid to any state of the United States or to the District of Columbia with respect to any property included in the decedent's gross estate.[6] This credit did not include, however, any taxes paid with respect to the estate of a person other than the decedent. The credit for state death taxes was available only to the extent that it did not exceed the estate's tax liability after reduction by the applicable credit amount.

---

[5] Code Sec. 2058(b), as added by P.L. 107-16.

[6] Code Sec. 2011; Reg. §20.2011-1. *J.B. Owen Est.*, 104 TC 498, CCH Dec. 50,607 (estate denied credit for state inheritance taxes paid with respect to gifts made by a decedent within three years of his death in 1986, because the gifts were not includible in the decedent's gross estate under Code Sec. 2035(d)(1)).

The state death tax credit was allowed for estate, inheritance, legacy, or succession taxes actually paid to any state or the District of Columbia with respect to any property included in a decedent's gross estate (Code Sec. 2011). Although the credit was scheduled to be restored for the estates of decedents dying after December 31, 2012, under the sunset provision of the Economic Growth and Tax Relief Reconciliation Act of 2001 (EGTRRA)[7], as extended by the Tax Relief, Unemployment Insurance Reauthorization, and Job Creation Act of 2010 (the Tax Relief Act of 2010),[8] the state death tax credit was permanently repealed by the American Taxpayer Relief Act of 2012 (P.L. 112-240).

The amount of the credit was based on the decedent's "adjusted taxable estate," defined as the taxable estate less $60,000 (Code Sec. 2001(b), prior to amendment by P.L. 107-16). The maximum allowable credit was computed under the a rate table (see ¶2630). Pursuant to the table, the credit was allowed only for the portion of the adjusted taxable estate that exceeded $40,000.

• *Phaseout and Repeal of Credit: 2002-2004*

The Economic Growth and Tax Relief Reconciliation Act of 2001 (P.L. 107-16) (2001 Act) phased out the state death tax credit between 2002 and 2004, with the credit repealed for the estates of decedents dying after December 31, 2004. Prior to the full phase-out, the credit was reduced by 25 percent for the estates of decedents dying in 2002, 50 percent for the estates of decedents dying in 2003 and 75 percent for the estates of decedents dying in 2004. Effective for decedents dying after December 31, 2004, the state death tax credit was replaced by a deduction for state death taxes paid (see ¶1144).[9]

---

[7] Act Sec. 901, P.L. 107-16.
[8] Act Sec. 101(a)(1), P.L. 111-312.

[9] Code Sec. 2058, as added by P.L. 107-16.

Chapter 24

QUALIFIED FAMILY-OWNED BUSINESS INTEREST DEDUCTION

¶ 1150 Qualified Family-Owned Business Interest Deduction: Pre-2004

In order to alleviate the impact of the estate tax on family-owned businesses, the Taxpayer Relief Act of 1997 (P.L. 105-34) created an exclusion for a portion of qualified family-owned business interests (QFOBIs) from a decedent's gross estate. However, because it was not clear whether Code Sec. 2033A excluded property or value from the gross estate, the Internal Revenue Service Restructuring and Reform Act of 1998 (P.L. 105-206) converted the exclusion into a deduction and redesignated Code Sec. 2033A as Code Sec. 2057.[1] Effective for estates of decedents dying after December 31, 1997, and before January 1, 2004, the qualified family-owned business interest deduction, in combination with the applicable exclusion amount (unified credit), shielded up to $1.3 million of qualified family-owned business interests from the estate tax.

• *Permanent Repeal of the QFOBI Deduction*

The Economic Growth and Tax Relief Reconciliation Act of 2001 (EGTRRA) (P.L. 107-16) repealed the QFOBI deduction, effective for the estates of decedents dying after December 31, 2003.[2] Although, the QFOBI deduction was scheduled to again be available for estates of decedents dying after December 31, 2012, under the sunset provisions of EGTRRA, as extended by the Tax Relief Act of 2010 (P.L. 111-312)[3], the deduction was permanently repealed by the American Taxpayer Relief Act of 2010.[4]

If an estate qualified and elected to take the deduction, up to $675,000 of the adjusted value of qualified interests could be deducted from the value of a decedent's gross estate. If the maximum $675,000 deduction was elected, the applicable exclusion amount (unified credit) was limited to $625,000, regardless of the date of death. In order to coordinate the deduction with the unified credit, if less than the maximum deduction was elected, the $625,000 applicable exclusion amount was increased by the excess of $675,000 over the amount of the deduction allowed. However, the applicable exclusion amount could not be increased above the amount that would apply to the estate if no QFOBI deduction had been elected.

Example (1): Ruth Roth died in 2001 when the applicable exclusion amount was $675,000. Roth's estate included $600,000 of qualified family-

---

[1] Code Sec. 2057, prior to repeal by P.L. 111-312.

[2] Act Sec. 901(a)(2), P.L. 107-16.

[3] Act Sec. 101(a)(1), P.L. 111-312.

[4] Act Sec. 101(a)(1), P.L. 112-240, striking title IX of P.L. 107-16).

owned business interests and her estate qualified for and elected a $600,000 deduction. Roth's estate was entitled to a deduction of $600,000 and an applicable exclusion amount of $675,000. The estate was not entitled to a $700,000 applicable exclusion amount ($625,000 + ($675,000 – $600,000)) because the applicable exclusion amount cannot exceed the amount that would apply to the estate without regard to the deduction.

Example (2): Adam Brook died in 2003 when the applicable exclusion amount (under the 2001 Act) was $1 million. Brook's estate included $1 million of qualified family-owned business interests and his estate qualified for and elected to take a $600,000 deduction. Brook's estate was entitled to a Code Sec. 2057 deduction of $600,000 and an applicable exclusion amount of $700,000 ($625,000 + ($675,000 – $600,000)).

Comment: In general, to qualify for the deduction the aggregate value of the decedent's qualified family-owned business interests passing to qualified heirs must have exceeded 50 percent of the decedent's adjusted gross estate. In addition, the decedent was required to be a U.S. citizen or resident at the time of death, the executor must have elected to take the deduction and file a recapture agreement signed by each person in being having an interest in the property, and must have met certain other requirements. The deduction was in addition to the special use valuation provisions (see ¶ 280) and the provisions for the installment payment of estate taxes attributable to a closely held business (see ¶ 1672).

¶ 1155   Ownership Requirement

Prior to the permanent repeal of the qualified family-owned business interest (QFOBI) deduction for decedents dying after December 31, 2004,[5] the term "qualified family-owned business" was defined is any interest in a trade or business, regardless of form, with a principal place of business in the United States, the ownership of which is held at least (1) 50 percent by one family, (2) 70 percent by two families, or (3) 90 percent by three families. If held by more than one family, the decedent's family must have owned at least 30 percent of the trade or business.[6] A decedent was treated as engaged in a trade or business if any member of the decedent's family was engaged in the trade or business.

Members of the individual's family included (1) the individual's spouse, (2) the individual's ancestors, (3) lineal descendants of the individual, of the individual's spouse, or of the individual's parents, and (4) the spouses of any such lineal descendants.[7]

In the case of a corporation, the ownership test was met if the decedent and family members owned the requisite percentage of both the total combined voting power of all classes of voting stock and the total value of all shares of all classes of stock. In the case of a partnership, the decedent and family members were required to own the requisite percentage of the capital interest in the partnership.

An interest in a trade or business did not qualify if the business's or a related entity's stock or securities were publicly traded at any time within three years of the decedent's death. In addition, the interest did not qualify if more than 35

---

[5] Act Sec. 101(a)(1) of the American Taxpayer Relief Act of 2012 (P.L. 112-240), striking title IX of the Economic Growth and Tax Relief Reconciliation Act of 2001 (P.L. 107-16).

[6] Code Sec. 2057(e)(1), prior to repeal by P.L. 111-312.

[7] Code Sec. 2057(e)(2) and Code. Sec. 2057(i)(2), prior to repeal by P.L. 111-312.

percent of the adjusted ordinary gross income from the business for the year of the decedent's death was personal holding company income. The second restriction did not apply to banks and domestic building and loan associations.

¶ 1160   Valuation

Before the permanent repeal of the qualified family-owned business interest (QFOBI) deduction for decedents dying after December 31, 2004,[8] the value of a trade or business qualifying as a QFOBI was reduced to the extent that the business held certain passive assets or cash and marketable securities in excess of reasonably expected day-to-day working capital needed for the trade or business. In addition, accumulations for capital acquisitions were not considered "working capital." Further, certain other passive assets were not considered in valuing QFOBIs.

The following assets were considered passive assets and were not included in the value of a qualified family-owned business: (1) assets that produced dividends, interest, rents, royalties, annuities, and Code Sec. 543(a) personal holding company income; (2) assets that were interests in a trust, partnership, or real estate mortgage investment conduit (as described in Code Sec. 954(c)(1)(B)(ii)); (3) assets that produced no income (as described in Code Sec. 954(c)(1)(B)(iii)); (4) assets that gave rise to income from commodities transactions or foreign currency gains (as described in Code Sec. 954(c)(1)(C) and Code Sec. 954(c)(1)(D)); (5) assets that produced income equivalent to interest (as described in Code Sec. 954(c)(1)(E)); and (6) assets that produced income from notional principal contracts or payments in lieu of dividends (as described in Code Sec. 954(c)(1)(F) and Code Sec. 954(c)(1)(G)). However, with respect to regular dealers in property, such property was not considered to produce passive income and, therefore, was not considered a passive asset.[9]

¶ 1165   Qualifying Estates

In order to qualify for the qualified family-owned business interest (QFOBI) deduction (available only for estates of decedents dying before January 1, 2004)[10], the decedent must have been a U.S. citizen or resident at the time of death and the aggregate value of the decedent's qualified family-owned business interests passing to qualified heirs must have exceeded 50 percent of the decedent's adjusted gross estate. For this purpose, qualified heirs included any individuals who were actively employed by the trade or business for at least 10 years prior to the date of the decedent's death, as well as members of the decedent's family.

Property passing to a trust could be treated as having passed to a qualified heir if all of the beneficiaries of the trust were qualified heirs.[11] The decedent's QFOBIs passing to qualified heirs included lifetime gifts of such interests made by the decedent to members of the decedent's family to the extent that those interests were held by family members (other than the decedent's spouse) between the date of the gift and the date of the decedent's death.

---

[8] Act Sec. 101(a)(1) of the American Taxpayer Relief Act of 2012 (P.L. 112-240), striking title IX of the Economic Growth and Tax Relief Reconciliation Act of 2001 (P.L. 107-16).

[9] Code Sec. 2057(e)(2), prior to repeal by P.L. 111-312.

[10] Act Sec. 101(a)(1) of the American Taxpayer Relief Act of 2012 (P.L. 112-240), striking title IX of the Economic Growth and Tax Relief Reconciliation Act of 2001 (P.L. 107-16).

[11] Code Sec. 2057(i)(3), prior to repeal by P.L. 111-312.

¶ 1170   Participation Requirements

Before the permanent repeal of the qualified family-owned business interest (QFOBI) deduction for decedents dying after December 31, 2003,[12] the decedent, or members of the decedent's family, must have owned and materially participated in the trade or business for at least five of the eight years preceding the decedent's death in order to qualify for the qualified family-owned business interest deduction.[13] In addition, a qualified heir was subject to a recapture tax if the heir, or a member of the qualified heir's family, did not materially participate in the trade or business for at least five years of any eight-year period within 10 years following the decedent's death. The definition of "material participation" provided in Code Sec. 2032A and Reg. § 20.2032A-3 pertaining to special use valuation applied. The principal factors to be considered included physical work and participation in management decisions. A qualified heir would not be treated as disposing of an interest in a trade or business by reason of ceasing to be engaged in a trade or business if any member of the qualified heir's family continued in the trade or business.[14] The material participation requirement would be met with respect to a qualified heir if the heir rented qualified property to a member of the qualified heir's family on a net cash basis, and that family member materially participated in the business.[15]

¶ 1175   Election

For the qualified family-owned business interest (QFOBI) deduction to have applied to estates of decedents dying before January 1, 2004[16], the executor must have made a Code Sec. 2057 election and filed a written agreement signed by each person in being having an interest in the property consenting to the application of the additional tax.[17] The election was made by filing Schedule T (Qualified Family-Owned Business Interest Deduction) of Form 706 (United States Estate (and Generation-Skipping Transfer) Tax Return) (Rev. Aug. 2003), attaching all required statements, and deducting the value of the QFOBIs on Form 706, page 3, part 5, Recapitulation, line 22. Because the QFOBI deduction has been repealed with respect to estates of decedents dying after December 31, 2003, Form 706 (Rev. Aug. 2003) is the last revision of the estate tax return that contains Schedule T.

• *Recapture Tax*

An additional tax is imposed if any of the following recapture events occurs within 10 years of the decedent's death and before the qualified heir's death: (1) the qualified heir ceases to meet the material participation requirements; (2) the qualified heir disposes of any portion of his or her interest in the family-owned business, other than by a disposition to a member of the qualified heir's family or through a conservation contribution under Code Sec. 170(h); (3) the principal place of business of the trade or business ceases to be located in the United States; or (4) the qualified heir loses U.S. citizenship.

---

[12] Act Sec. 101(a)(1) of the American Taxpayer Relief Act of 2012 (P.L. 112-240), striking title IX of the Economic Growth and Tax Relief Reconciliation Act of 2001 (P.L. 107-16).

[13] Code Sec. 2057(b)(1)(D), prior to repeal by P.L. 111-312.

[14] Code Sec. 2057(f)(3), prior to repeal by P.L. 111-312.

[15] Code Sec. 2057(b)(1)(D), prior to repeal by P.L. 111-312.

[16] Act Sec. 101(a)(1) of the American Taxpayer Relief Act of 2012 (P.L. 112-240), striking title IX of the Economic Growth and Tax Relief Reconciliation Act of 2001 (P.L. 107-16).

[17] Code Sec. 2057(h), prior to repeal by P.L. 111-312.

The recapture tax may be avoided if a qualified heir loses U.S. citizenship, provided the trade or business assets are placed into a qualified trust meeting the requirement similar to that for a qualified domestic trust under Code Sec. 2056A(a) or certain other security arrangements are met. The recapture period may be extended up to two years if the qualified heir does not begin to use the property for a period of up to two years after a decedent's death.

The recapture tax is a personal liability of each qualified heir to the extent of the portion of the additional tax that is imposed with respect to his or her interest in the qualified family-owned business.[18]

Example: John, Beth, and Sue Milton inherit equal qualified family-owned business interests from their father, and the estate elects special tax treatment. Only Sue continues to materially participate in the family business. Such participation by a family member causes all three children to meet the participation requirements. However, during the fourth year following the decedent's death, Sue ceases to materially participate in the business and neither John nor Beth participates. As a result, each of the three children would be personally liable for the portion of the recapture tax attributable to his or her interest.

A qualified heir uses Form 706-D (United States Additional Estate Tax Return Under Code Sec. 2057) (Rev. December 2008), to report and pay the additional estate tax. Form 706-D is due within six months after the recapture event occurs. See the Appendix at ¶3210 for an example of a filled-in Form 706-D.

Comment: The Committee Reports to the Economic Growth and Tax Relief Reconciliation Act of 2001 (P.L. 107-16) (2001 Act) indicate that the recapture tax imposed under Code Sec. 2057(f) if property ceases to qualify for the QFOBI deduction will be retained after repeal of the QFOBI deduction in 2004. The provision is retained so that estates that claimed the benefit of the deduction before repeal will be subject to recapture if a disqualifying event occurs following repeal.

• Amount of Additional Estate Tax

The additional estate tax is based on when the recapture event occurs in relation to the decedent's death. If the recapture event occurs within the first six years of material participation, 100 percent of the reduction in estate tax attributable to the heir's interest plus interest is recaptured. Thereafter, the applicable percentage is 80 percent in the seventh year, 60 percent in the eighth year, 40 percent in the ninth year, and 20 percent in the 10th year.[19]

---

[18] Code Sec. 2057(f), prior to repeal by P.L. 111-312.

[19] Code Sec. 2057(f)(2)(B), prior to repeal by P.L. 111-312.

DETERMINATION AND PAYMENT OF TAX

Chapter 25

EXECUTOR ELECTIONS, DETERMINATION OF TAXABLE ESTATE

¶ 1190   Executor Elections

Various federal estate tax elections that are available to the executor of a decedent's estate are to be made by marking the appropriate boxes on part 3 of Form 706 (United States Estate (and Generation-Skipping Transfer) Tax Return) (Rev. August 2013).

Executor elections include elections with respect to:

(1) alternate valuation;

(2) special use valuation;

(3) installment payment of tax;

(4) deferred payment of tax attributable to certain remainder and reversionary interests;

(5) portability of deceased spousal unused exclusion (DSUE) amount; and

(6) carryover basis rules (available only for decedents dying in 2010).

Preparation Tip: Qualified terminable interest property (QTIP) elections are deemed to have been made by the executor if (1) QTIP property is listed on Schedule M (Bequests, etc., to Surviving Spouse) of Form 706, and (2) the value of the property is entered as a deduction on Schedule M.

Election out of estate tax for 2010 decedents. An executor of a decedent dying after December 31, 2009, and before January 1, 2011, could elect out of the estate tax, and into the carryover basis rules (see ¶ 121). The executor wishing to make this election (known as a "Section 1022 election") was to file Form 8939 (Allocation of Increase in Basis for Property Acquired From a Decedent) by January 17, 2012.[1]

¶ 1195   General Information

Part 4 of Form 706 (United States Estate (and Generation-Skipping Transfer) Tax Return) (Rev. August 2013) contains general information questions relating to the decedent's death certificate, the decedent's business or occupation, the decedent's marital status, the surviving spouse's name, and the identity of individuals (other than the surviving spouse), trusts, or other estates receiving benefits (and the amount of such benefits) from the decedent's estate.

---

[1] Instructions for Form 8939 (2010), p. 2.

Part 4 on pages 3 and 4 of Form 706 also contains questions concerning assets owned by the decedent during his or her life, such as whether the decedent received any qualified terminable interest property, owned any life insurance, possessed any retained powers, held an interest in a partnership or closely held business, etc. The purpose of this section is to alert the executor and the IRS to any assets that should be reported on the estate tax return or to remind the executor of possible elections to which the estate might be entitled.

¶ 1200   Recapitulation

The Recapitulation, located in part 5 on page 3 of Form 706 (United States Estate (and Generation-Skipping Transfer) Tax Return) (Rev. August 2013),[2] brings together in one place the information reported in the schedules. This results in the determination of the size of the gross estate and the total allowable deductions.

With regard to the gross estate, part 5 lists the value of the estate's interest in different assets, by way of the following Form 706 schedules: Schedule A (Real Estate); Schedule B (Stocks and Bonds); Schedule C (Mortgages, Notes, and Cash); Schedule D (Insurance on the Decedent's Life); Schedule E (Jointly Owned Property); Schedule F (Other Miscellaneous Property Not Reportable Under Any Other Schedule); Schedule G (Transfers During Decedent's Life); Schedule H (Powers of Appointment); and Schedule I (Annuities).

Line 10 relates to the computation of the Deceased Spousal Unused Exclusion (DSUE) amount where the value of the gross estate and the adjusted taxable gifts is less than the basic exclusion amount, and Form 706 is being filed only to elect portability of the DSUE amount. Under Reg. § 20.2010-2T(a)(7)(ii), the estate is not required to report the value of certain property eligible for the martial or charitable deduction. For this property being reported on Schedules A, B, C, D, E, F, G, H, and I, the executor must calculate his or her best estimate of the value. The estimated value is not to be entered on the line corresponding to the schedule on which the property was reported. Instead, the total of the estimated value of theses assets subject to the special rule is entered on line 10 (from the table of estimated values reproduced below) that corresponds to that total. The total of these assets is then entered on line 11 of part 5.

---

[2] Filled-in Form 706, Parts 4 and 5, for a decedent dying in 2013, are reproduced at ¶ 2930 and ¶ 2940.

Table of Estimated Values

If the total estimated value of the assets eligible for the special rule under Reg. section 20.2010-2T(a)(7)(ii) is more than	But less than or equal to	Include this amount on lines 10 and 23:
$0	$250,000	$250,000
$250,000	$500,000	$500,000
$500,000	$750,000	$750,000
$750,000	$1,000,000	$1,000,000
$1,000,000	$1,250,000	$1,250,000
$1,250,000	$1,500,000	$1,500,000
$1,500,000	$1,750,000	$1,750,000
$1,750,000	$2,000,000	$2,000,000
$2,000,000	$2,250,000	$2,250,000
$2,250,000	$2,500,000	$2,500,000
$2,500,000	$2,750,000	$2,750,000
$2,750,000	$3,000,000	$3,000,000
$3,000,000	$3,250,000	$3,250,000
$3,250,000	$3,500,000	$3,500,000
$3,500,000	$3,750,000	$3,750,000
$3,750,000	$4,000,000	$4,000,000
$4,000,000	$4,250,000	$4,250,000
$4,250,000	$4,500,000	$4,500,000
$4,500,000	$4,750,000	$4,750,000
$4,750,000	$5,000,000	$5,000,000
$5,000,000	$5,119,999	$5,119,999

The amount claimed for the qualified conservation easement exclusion on Schedule U (Qualified Conservation Easement Exclusion) is subtracted from the gross estate. The amount of the exclusion is shown on line 12 and the total gross estate less exclusion so determined is shown on line 13 of part 5 and entered on line 1 of part 2 (Tax Computation).

The second half of the Recapitulation lists deductions allowed the estate that are figured on the following schedules: Schedule J (Funeral Expenses and Expenses Incurred in Administering Property Subject to Claims); Schedule K (Debts of the Decedent, and Mortgages and Liens); Schedule L (Net Losses During Administration and Expenses Incurred in Administering Property Not Subject to Claims); Schedule M (Bequests, etc., to Surviving Spouse); and Schedule O (Charitable, Public, and Similar Gifts and Bequests). The amount from line 10 is also entered on line 23.

• Limitation on Deductions from Schedules J and K

The amounts from Schedule J and Schedule K can be limited for purposes of determining the allowable deduction. This is the case when the sum of the items listed on Schedules J and K is more than the value (at the time of the decedent's death) of the "property subject to claims," a term that the IRS interprets as synonymous with the decedent's probate estate. In such an instance, the amount deductible is limited to the value of the property that is subject to the claims.

¶1200

However, if the amount actually paid at the time the return is filed is more than the amount subject to the claims, the amount actually paid, rather than the amount subject to the claims, is deductible. One court has rejected the IRS position that the amount of a decedent's probate estate limits the amount that may be deducted as a claim against the estate (see ¶805).[3]

The total of the deductions allowable from Schedules J and K and the deductions from Schedules L, M, and O is entered on line 24 of part 5, and on line 2 of part 2.

¶ 1210   Portability Election

Part 6 of Form 706 (United States Estate (and Generation-Skipping Transfer) Tax Return) (Rev. August 2013) relates to the Portability of Deceased Spousal Unused Exclusion (DSUE). (A substantive discussion of the DSUE election rules appears at ¶16; a discussion of the layout of Form 706, Part 6, appears below.)[4]

Section A of Part 6, which relates to election of portability, is to be filled out by the estate of a decedent having a surviving spouse. The predeceased spouse's estate makes the portability election merely by completing and timely filing his or her estate tax return. If, however, the surviving spouse's estate is to be denied portability, the representative of the predeceased spouse marks the checkbox indicating that preference, and does not complete Sections B and C of Part 6.

Section B of Part 6, contains a Yes/No checkbox asking whether the estate of the predeceased spouse contains any assets that are being transferred to a qualified domestic trust (QDOT). If the answer to this question is "Yes," the DSUE amount portable to a surviving spouse (as calculated in Section C of Part 6), is preliminary, and will be redetermined at the time of final distribution or other taxable event that imposes estate tax under Code Sec. 2056A.

Section C of Part 6, also to be completed by the estate of the predeceased spouse making the portability election, computes the DSUE amount that can be transferred to the surviving spouse.

Section D of Part 6, is to be completed by the estate of a surviving spouse that receives a DSUE amount from a predeceased spouse or spouses. Part 1 relates to the DSUE amount received from the last predeceased spouse; Part 2 relates to the DSUE amount(s) used by the decedent that were from other predeceased spouses. The amounts from Parts 1 and 2 are totaled, and the result is to be entered on Form 706, page 1, Part 2, line 9b.

¶ 1250   Size of Taxable Estate

In the case of a U.S. resident or citizen, the computation of the taxable estate is accomplished on part 2, page 1 (Tax Computation), of Form 706 (United States Estate (and Generation-Skipping Transfer) Tax Return) (Rev. August 2013). Schedule B (Taxable Estate) of Form 706-NA (United States Estate (and Generation-Skipping Transfer) Tax Return, Estate of nonresident not a citizen of the United States) (Rev. August 2013)[5] is used for this purpose by the estates of nonresidents not citizens.

---

[3] *R. Snyder Est.*, FedCl, 99-2 USTC ¶60,357.

[4] A filled-in Form 706 (Rev. August 2013), Part 6, is reproduced at ¶2942.

[5] A filled-in Form 706-NA (United States Estate (and Generation-Skipping Transfer

Tax Return, Estate of nonresident not a citizen of the United States)) (Rev. August 2013) for a decedent dying in 2013, is reproduced at ¶3260.

¶ 1255   Residents and Citizens

If the decedent was a resident or a citizen of the United States, the taxable estate is determined by subtracting from the total gross estate (line 1 of part 2, Form 706 (United States Estate (and Generation-Skipping Transfer) Tax Return) (Rev. August 2013) the total allowable deductions (line 2).

¶ 1260   Nonresidents Not Citizens

As noted above, the taxable estate of a nonresident not a citizen of the United States is computed on Schedule B (Taxable Estate) of Form 706-NA (United States Estate (and Generation-Skipping Transfer) Tax Return, Estate of nonresident not a citizen of the United States) (Rev. August 2013). The gross estate situated in the United States is entered on line 1, the gross estate situated outside of the United States is listed on line 2, and the sum of lines 1 and 2 is listed on line 3.[6] The value of the gross estate outside of the United States must be supported by proof (see ¶85).[7]

The total funeral expenses, administration expenses, debts of the decedent, mortgages and liens, and losses during the administration of the estate are entered on line 4. The allowable deduction for these expenses and debts is entered on line 5 and is computed by multiplying the total amounts of these expenses by the ratio of the gross estate within the United States (line 1) to the entire gross estate wherever situated (line 3).[8]

The amount of deductible charitable and marital transfers (line 6) and state death taxes (line 7) are then added to the amount on line 5 to arrive at the total deductions shown on line 8. The total deductions are then subtracted from the gross estate within the United States (line 1) to arrive at the taxable estate shown on line 9.

Form 706-NA is used only for the estate of a nonresident not a citizen of the United States (see ¶1625).

---

[6] Code Sec. 2103; Reg. § 20.2103-1.
[7] Reg. § 20.6018-3(b).

[8] Code Sec. 2106; Reg. § 20.2106-1.

Chapter 26

CREDITS FOR TAX ON PRIOR TRANSFERS AND FEDERAL GIFT TAXES

¶ 1300 Effective Period of Credit

A credit is allowed against the estate tax for all or a part of the estate tax paid with respect to the transfer of property (including property passing as a result of the exercise or nonexercise of a power of appointment, see ¶ 650) to the present decedent by or from a person who died within 10 years before, or within two years after, the decedent.[1] The credit is computed on Schedule Q (Credit for Tax on Prior Transfers) of Form 706 (United States Estate (and Generation-Skipping Transfer) Tax Return) (Rev. August 2013)[2] after completing the Worksheet provided in the Instructions for Form 706 (page 41). This schedule does not have to be filed if a credit is not claimed.

This credit can never be larger than it would have been if the present decedent had not received the property. Because the purpose of Code Sec. 2013 is to prevent diminution of an estate by successive taxes on the same property within a brief period, no credit is available for any gift tax that may have been paid with respect to the transfer of property to the present decedent. If the prior decedent (called the "transferor") predeceased the present decedent by more than two years, the credit allowable is reduced by 20 percent for each full two years by which the death of the transferor preceded the death of the decedent.[3] See ¶ 1325 for a table of the percentage allowable.

¶ 1310 General Requirements

The term "transferee" as used in Schedule Q (Credit for Tax on Prior Transfers) of Form 706 (United States Estate (and Generation-Skipping Transfer) Tax Return) (Rev. August 2013) for computing the credit for tax on prior transfers refers to the decedent for whose estate the return is filed.[4] It is not necessary that the property transferred be identified in or traced through the estate of the transferee. Nor is it necessary that the transferred property be in existence on the date of the transferee's death. It is sufficient for allowance of the credit that the transfer of the property was subject to federal estate tax in the estate of the transferor and that the specified period of time has not elapsed.[5] However, the

---

[1] Code Sec. 2013; Reg. § 20.2013-1.
[2] An example of a filled-in Form 706, Schedule Q, for a decedent dying in 2013, is reproduced at ¶ 3120. A filled-in worksheet for Schedule Q is reproduced at ¶ 3110.

[3] Reg. § 20.2013-1.
[4] Instructions for Form 706 (Rev. August 2013), p. 39.
[5] Reg. § 20.2013-1.

credit cannot be waived, in whole or in part, and each transfer eligible for the credit must be taken into account in computing it.[6]

>   *Comment:* A credit may be allowed with respect to property received as the result of the exercise or nonexercise of a power of appointment. The credit is available if the property is included in the gross estate of the donee of the power. If the transferee was the transferor's surviving spouse, no credit is allowed with respect to property received to the extent that a marital deduction was allowed the transferor's estate in connection with such property.

¶ 1315   "Property" Defined

The term "property" includes, for purposes of the credit, any beneficial interest received by the transferee,[7] including Louisiana usufruct interests.[8] The transferee is considered to be the beneficial owner of the property over which the transferee received a general power of appointment. "Property" does not include interests to which the transferee received bare legal title only, such as that of a trustee. Nor does it include an interest in property over which the transferee received a power that is not a general power of appointment under Code Sec. 2041 (see ¶ 652).

In addition to property interests in which the transferee received complete ownership, credit may be allowed for tax on annuities, life estates, terms for years, remainder interests (whether contingent or vested), and other future interests to the extent that the transferee became the beneficial owner of the interest. The credit is not available when the decedent "purchases" the property, as by electing to take a life estate in a spouse's community property and thereby relinquishing property greater in value than the property the decedent obtained.[9]

Additionally, the U.S. Courts of Appeals for the Fourth and Fifth Circuits and the Tax Court have held that the credit is not available for a life estate where the transferor and the transferee die simultaneously in a common disaster.[10] The Tax Court also reached the same conclusion with respect to a Louisiana usufruct interest passing from a husband to a wife on their simultaneous deaths.[11]

¶ 1320   Maximum Amount of the Credit

The credit for tax on prior transfers is limited to the smaller of the following:

>   (1) the amount of the estate tax of the transferor's estate pertaining to the transfer; or

>   (2) the amount by which (a) an estate tax on the transferee's estate (after deducting the unified tax credit and the credits for state death taxes (prior to 2005), gift taxes, and foreign death taxes) determined without regard to the credit provided for in the schedule exceeds (b) an estate tax on the transferee's estate determined by excluding from the gross estate the net value of the transfer.[12]

---

[6] Rev. Rul. 73-47, 1973-1 CB 397.

[7] Reg. § 20.2013-5.

[8] Rev. Rul. 66-271, 1966-2 CB 430.

[9] *I.M. Sparling Est.*, CA-9, 77-1 USTC ¶ 13,194, 552 F2d 1340, rev'g and rem'g TC, 60 TC 330, CCH Dec. 31,996 (Acq.).

[10] *G.A. Lion Est.*, CA-4, 71-1 USTC ¶ 12,745, 438 F2d 56, aff'g TC, 52 TC 601, CCH Dec.

29,646, cert. denied; *A.P. Carter Est.*, CA-5, 91-1 USTC ¶ 60,054, rev'g DC La., 90-1 USTC ¶ 60,003, 929 F2d 699, cert. denied; *J. Harrison Est.*, 115 TC 161, CCH Dec. 54,015.

[11] *E.W. Marks, Jr., Est.*, 94 TC 720, CCH Dec. 46,594.

[12] Code Sec. 2013(c).

Where credit for a particular foreign death tax may be taken under either the statute or a death duty convention and the credit actually is taken under the convention, credit for that foreign death tax may not be taken into consideration in computing estate tax (a) or estate tax (b).

The amounts in (1) and (2) are computed on the Worksheet provided for Schedule Q (Credit for Tax on Prior Transfers) of Form 706 (United States Estate (and Generation-Skipping Transfer) Tax Return) (Rev. August 2013) (see ¶1345).

¶1325   Percentage Reduction

If the transferor died within two years before or within two years after the transferee's death, the credit allowed for the tax on the prior transfer is 100 percent of the maximum amount allowable. If the transferor predeceased the transferee by more than two years, the credit allowed is a reduced percentage of the maximum amount allowable. The percentage allowable may be determined by using the following table:

Period of Time Exceeding	Not Exceeding	Percent Allowable
	2 years	100
2 years	4 years	80
4 years	6 years	60
6 years	8 years	40
8 years	10 years	20
10 years		none

¶1330   Formula for Estimating Credit

The formula for estimating the credit is described below. For computation of the credit on the return, see ¶1345 and the Worksheet for Schedule Q (Credit for Tax on Prior Transfers) of Form 706 (United States Estate (and Generation-Skipping Transfer) Tax Return) (Rev. August 2013) and Schedule Q.

(1) Determine the portion of the estate tax in the preceding estate for which the property transferred to the transferee was responsible. This portion is determined as follows:

$$\left[\frac{\text{Value of property transferred to decedent} + \text{Taxable estate of prior decedent}}{} - \text{Death tax on prior estate} \right] \times \text{Estate tax on prior estate}$$

For purposes of the above formula, "Death tax" includes state, federal, and foreign taxes. "Estate tax" means the federal estate tax paid, increased by any credit allowed against such tax on account of gift taxes and any credit allowed on account of prior transfers to such prior decedent.

(2) Determine the estate tax (after deducting the unified credit and credits for state death taxes (prior to 2005), gift taxes, and foreign death taxes) on the transferee's estate first including, and then excluding, the value of the property. If the difference between the two taxes is less than the amount computed under (1), above, the credit cannot exceed such difference.

(3) If the property previously taxed was transferred to the transferee more than two years before his or her death, reduce the lesser of (1) or (2) by 20 percent for each full two years by which the original transfer preceded the transferee's death so that, if the prior transfer occurred more than 10 years before the death, no credit would be allowed.

¶ 1335   Valuation

The value of the property transferred for purposes of the formula noted above is the value at which the property was included in the transferor's estate.[13] The interest received must be able to be valued under recognized valuation principles in order to claim the credit.[14] This value must be reduced by (1) the amount of any lien or encumbrance thereon that was assumed by or imposed on the transferee at the time of acquisition, (2) the amount of death taxes that the transferee might have been required to pay, and (3) any marital deduction that might have been allowed on the transfer to the transferee.

In calculating the estate tax on the decedent's estate less the value of the transferred property, any charitable deduction is reduced in the proportion that the transferred property bears to the gross estate reduced by deductions allowed for expenses, debts, taxes, losses, and administration expenses under Code Sec. 2053 and Code Sec. 2054 (or Code Sec. 2106(a)(1) for estates of nonresident noncitizens).[15] Thus, the U.S. Court of Appeals for the Seventh Circuit held that in computing the credit for estate tax paid on prior transfers available to a deceased wife's estate, it was not necessary to reduce the value of the property she received from her predeceased husband by the amount of interest assessed and paid as a result of the husband's estate having elected to defer the payment of estate taxes under Code Sec. 6166.[16]

> **Comment:** Property that, although difficult to value, is still capable of valuation will not result in loss of the credit. Thus, a trust provision requiring the termination of a transferee's life income interest in the event the transferee remarried did not result in the disallowance of the credit for the estate tax paid by the estate of the transferor-spouse. The IRS ruled that, because the possibility of termination of the life income interest on the remarriage of the transferee could be taken into account as a valuation factor in determining the value of the annuity includible in the transferee's gross estate, the credit for tax on prior transfers should be allowed.[17]

See ¶ 530 for further rules that apply when a life estate or remainder interest is part of the property transferred.

¶ 1340   Treatment of Additional Tax on Recapture of Special Use Valuation Realty

If the gross estate of the transferor included farm or other closely held business realty for which the special use valuation election was made (see ¶ 280), and if the additional estate tax is imposed on the transferor's estate within two years of his or her death because of the termination of a qualified use (see ¶ 284), the additional tax on recapture of the special use valuation benefits is treated as a federal estate tax payable with respect to the estate of the transferor.[18]

Further, the value of such property and the amount of the transferor's taxable estate are determined as if the special use valuation had not been elected.

---

[13] Code Sec. 2013(d); *S. Pollock Est.*, 77 TC 1296, CCH Dec. 38,503.
[14] Rev. Rul. 67-53, 1967-1 CB 265.
[15] Code Sec. 2013(c)(1).

[16] *R.M. Whittle Est.*, CA-7, 93-1 USTC ¶ 60,141, 994 F2d 379, aff'g TC, 97 TC 362, CCH Dec. 47,623.
[17] Rev. Rul. 85-111, 1985-2 CB 196.
[18] Code Sec. 2013(f).

¶ 1345   Computation of the Credit

The credit for tax on prior transfers is computed in two steps. First, a Worksheet that is included in the Instructions for Form 706 (United States Estate (and Generation-Skipping Transfer) Tax Return) (Rev. August 2013) is used to determine the transferor's tax on prior transfers (part I of the Worksheet) and the transferee's tax on the prior transfers (part II of the Worksheet). Second, this information is transferred to Schedule Q (Credit for Tax on Prior Transfers) of Form 706, where the proper percentage (see ¶ 1325) is applied to the lesser of the transferor's tax or the transferee's tax on the transfers (see ¶ 1320) in order to compute the allowable credit.

Part I of the Worksheet and Schedule Q provide for computation of the credit in situations involving up to three transferors. If there are more than three transferors, more than one Worksheet and Schedule Q should be used and the totals for the appropriate lines should be combined.

¶ 1382   Credit for Gift Taxes on Pre-1977 Gifts

A credit is allowed for gift taxes paid on pre-1977 gifts includible in the donor's gross estate under any one of the estate tax provisions that make prior gifts includible in the estate of the donor.[19] These provisions include (1) Code Sec. 2036, which requires the inclusion of transfers in which the transferor retains a life interest (see ¶ 570), (2) Code Sec. 2037, which requires the inclusion of certain retained reversionary interests (see ¶ 565), and (3) Code Sec. 2038, which requires the inclusion of revocable transfers (see ¶ 585).

The credit is allowable, even though the gift tax is paid after the decedent's death and the amount of the gift tax is deducted from the gross estate as a debt of the decedent.[20] The credit is allowed only when the gift tax has been paid on the transfer of nonprobate assets and double taxation would result.

• *Limitation*

The credit is limited to the lesser of:

(1) the gift tax paid on the gift that is included in the gross estate; or

(2) the amount of estate tax attributable to the inclusion of the gift in the decedent's gross estate.

This second limitation is computed as follows:[21]

$$\frac{\text{Gross estate tax, less the unified credit}}{\begin{array}{c}\text{The value of the gross estate,}\\ \text{less all marital and}\\ \text{charitable deductions}\\ \text{allowable}\end{array}} \times \begin{array}{c}\text{The value of the gift (at the}\\ \text{time of the gift or at time of}\\ \text{death, whichever is lower)}\end{array}$$

Form 4808 (Computation of Credit for Gift Tax) can be used to compute the credit for tax paid on pre-1977 gifts. The completed Form 4808 (or other attachment showing the computation of the credit), as well as copies of all Forms 709 evidencing payment of gift tax for pre-1977 gifts, should be attached to the transferor's Form 706 (United States Estate (and Generation-Skipping Transfer) Tax Return).

---

[19] Code Sec. 2012; Reg. § 20.2012-1.
[20] Reg. § 20.2012-1(a).

[21] Code Sec. 2012(a), as amended by P.L. 107-16.

The computation of the two limitations on the amount of the credit appears below.

> *Example:* Clay Calhoun transferred his residence by gift to his daughter, Reba, in 1974. When she received the gift, Reba agreed to allow her father to live in the house, then valued at $125,000, for the remainder of his life. Clay filed a gift tax return with respect to this transfer, paying gift tax of $21,150. (He had previously completely used up his $30,000 specific exemption by a one-time gift of $33,000 in cash to Reba in 1970.) At his death in 2013, Clay had a federal gross estate of $6.0 million, including the $270,000 value of the transferred residence on the date of his death that was included in his estate as a transfer under Code Sec. 2036. No marital or charitable deductions were claimed on Clay'sForm 706. The transfer of the residence in 1974 was the last taxable gift made by Clay. Clay's state of domicile levied a death tax equal to the amount allowed for the state death tax credit on a decedent's federal estate tax return (Form 706). Because the state death tax credit was eliminated for the estates of decedents dying after 2005, it does not factor into the calculation of the credit allowable under Code Sec. 2012.

First limitation:

Amount of gift tax paid on gift included in his gross estate: $21,150

Second limitation:

Gross estate tax:	$2,345,800
Less:	
Unified credit amount......................	2,045,800
	$300,000

$$(\$300,000 \div \$6,000,000) \times \$125,000 \quad =$$
$$.05 \times \$125,000 \quad = \$6,250$$

The credit allowable under Code Sec. 2012 is $6,250, the lower of the two amounts computed under the first and second limitations.

¶ 1384   Gifts Made After 1976

No credit is allowed for any gift tax paid on gifts made after 1976 because the gift tax payable on post-1976 gifts (includible in the gross estate) is automatically reflected in determining the estate tax liability under the unified transfer tax structure (see ¶ 11 and ¶ 12).[22]

---

[22] Code Sec. 2012(e).

Chapter 27

CREDIT FOR FOREIGN DEATH TAXES

¶ 1400   Double Taxation

The federal estate tax applies to the entire estate, wherever situated, of any decedent who was either a domiciled resident or a citizen of the United States. Because many other countries levy death taxes on the transfer by nonresidents not citizens of property situated within their boundaries, the estates of many persons are subject to double taxation. The United States has entered into estate tax conventions with a number of foreign countries to provide relief from such double taxation (see ¶1420).

¶ 1401   Statutory Credit

To protect against double taxation, the law provides a foreign estate tax credit for U.S. citizens and residents.[1] The credit applies when double taxation arises from imposition by the United States of a tax on the entire estate and the imposition by a foreign country of an estate or other death tax on property situated within that country. For the purpose of this credit, U.S. possessions are classified as foreign countries.[2]

The foreign estate tax credit, in each case, is limited by apportionment. Only taxes attributable to property taxed in both countries may be allowed as a credit. In addition, the credit cannot exceed the portion of U.S. taxes attributable to the property taxed in both countries.

Although credits against the estate tax must be claimed within the later of four years after filing the estate tax return (Form 706, United States Estate (and Generation-Skipping Transfer) Tax Return), before the date of the expiration of any extension of time for paying the U.S. tax, or 60 days after a final Tax Court decision, an extended period within which to claim this credit is provided.[3] An extension is possible where payment of the estate tax attributable to a reversionary or remainder interest is postponed.

> *Comment:* An executor is required to notify the IRS of any recovery of state or foreign death taxes for which credit has been claimed.[4] A redetermination of the federal estate tax on the basis of such recovery is authorized without regard to any statutory time limits that might otherwise apply.

¶ 1402   Reciprocity Requirement for Resident Aliens

Generally, the estates of resident aliens may take a credit for foreign inheritance and death taxes paid. However, the President may, by proclamation, limit

---

[1] Code Sec. 2014; Reg. § 20.2014-1.   [3] Code Sec. 2015.
[2] Code Sec. 2014(g).   [4] Code Sec. 2016.

the availability of the credit if (1) the foreign country of which the resident aliens are citizens does not give U.S. citizens a reciprocal credit, (2) that country, when asked to do so, has not acted to provide such a credit, and (3) it is in the public interest to deny the credit. If a citizen or subject of such foreign country dies during the proclamation period, the credit will be allowed only if the foreign country allows a similar credit in the case of U.S. citizens who are residents of the foreign country at the time of their deaths.[5]

¶ 1405   Procedure for Claiming Credit

In the case of a citizen or resident of the United States, a credit is allowed for any estate, inheritance, legacy, or succession taxes paid to a foreign country or its possessions or political subdivisions with respect to property situated in that country and included in the gross estate. Credit is authorized by statute or by treaty. Unless otherwise provided by the treaty, a comparison is made to determine which of the following amounts is greater:

(1) the amount of the total credit authorized by the statute for all death taxes (national and local) imposed in the particular foreign country; or

(2) the amount of the total credit authorized by the treaty for death taxes imposed in such foreign country.[6]

• Political Subdivisions

When a credit for taxes imposed by a foreign country and one or more of its political subdivisions is involved, a third alternative to the credit allowed under the tax treaty or by statute is available. If it proves the most beneficial of the three, both a credit for the combined foreign death taxes allowable under the tax treaty *and* a credit under Code Sec. 2014 for death taxes paid to each political subdivision of the country (but only to the extent the taxes were not directly or indirectly creditable under the treaty) may be taken by the decedent's estate.

• Multiple Foreign Countries

If credit for death taxes paid in more than one foreign country is allowable, a separate computation of the credit must be made with respect to each foreign country. For purposes of the credit, each possession of the United States is considered as a foreign country. The copies of Schedule P (Credit for Foreign Death Taxes) of Form 706 (United States Estate (and Generation-Skipping Transfer) Tax Return) on which the additional computations are made should be attached to the copy of Schedule P provided in the return.[7]

• Limitations and Allowance

The total amount of the credit allowable with respect to any property, whether subjected to tax by one or more than one foreign country, is limited to the amount of the estate tax attributable to such property. The anticipated amount of the credit may be computed on the return. The credit cannot be allowed until the foreign tax has been paid and a certificate on Form 706-CE (Certificate of Payment of Foreign Death Tax) (Rev. October 2013) evidencing payment of the tax is furnished.[8] The Instructions for Form 706-CE contain procedures that should be followed in those cases where a foreign government refuses to certify Form 706-CE.

---

[5] Code Sec. 2014(h).
[6] Reg. § 20.2014-4.

[7] Reg. § 20.2014-5.
[8] Reg. § 20.2014-5.

¶ 1410   Situs of Property

For purposes of the foreign death tax credit, a determination must be made as to whether a particular property is situated in the United States or a foreign country. This is made according to the same principles applicable in determining whether similar property of a nonresident not a citizen is situated within the United States for the purpose of the federal estate tax[9] (see ¶ 1620).

¶ 1415   Execution of Schedule P for Statutory Credit

Schedule P (Credit for Foreign Death Taxes) of Form 706 (United States Estate (and Generation-Skipping Transfer) Tax Return) (Rev. August 2013)[10] must be completed if an estate claims a credit for foreign death taxes paid. In addition, estates must attach Form 706-CE (Certificate of Payment of Foreign Death Tax) to support any credit claimed.

At item 1 on Schedule P, the amount of the estate, inheritance, legacy, and succession taxes paid to the foreign country and its possessions or political subdivisions attributable to property that (1) is situated in that country, (2) is subject to such taxes, and (3) is included in the gross estate should be entered. The amount entered at item 1 should not include any tax paid to the foreign country with respect to property not situated in that country. Nor should it include any tax paid to the foreign country with respect to property not included in the gross estate.

If only a part of the property subject to such foreign taxes is both situated in the foreign country and included in the gross estate, it will be necessary to determine the portion of the taxes that is attributable to such part of the property. The Instructions for Schedule P indicate that an additional sheet showing the computation of the amount entered at item 1 must be attached.

The value of the gross estate less the total of the deductions shown on Form 706, Part 5, lines 21 and 22, Recapitulation (the marital and charitable deductions, respectively) should be entered at item 2 on Schedule P.

The value of the property situated in the foreign country that is subject to the foreign taxes and included in the gross estate, less those portions of the deductions on Schedule M (Bequests, etc., to Surviving Spouse) and Schedule O (Charitable, Public, and Similar Gifts and Bequests) that are attributable to such property, should be entered at item 3 on Schedule P.

Any credit shown at item 15, Part 2, Form 706, that is claimed for federal gift taxes on pre-1977 gifts should be subtracted from the amount shown at item 13, Part 2, Form 706, and the result entered on Schedule P at item 4.

The amount of the federal estate tax attributable to the value of the property specified at item 3 is calculated at item 5. This figure is computed by dividing the amount of item 3 by the amount of item 2, and multiplying the result by the amount of item 4. This figure should then be entered on line 13 of Part 2, Form 706.

The final entry on Schedule P at item 6—the smaller of item 1 or item 5—represents the credit that may be subtracted from the estate tax otherwise payable.

---

[9] Reg. § 20.2014-1(a)(3).

[10] An example of a filled-in Form 706, Schedule P, for a decedent dying in 2013, is reproduced at 3170.

Preparation Tip: Schedule P must be filed if the estate claims a foreign death tax credit, and Form 706-CE must be filed for every such credit claimed.

¶ 1420   Execution of Schedule P for Credit Under Treaties

Where the provisions of a treaty apply to the estate of a citizen or resident of the United States, a credit is allowed for the payment of the foreign death tax or taxes specified in the treaty. Death tax conventions are in effect with the following countries:

Country	Death Tax
Australia	Commonwealth estate duty*
Austria	Austrian inheritance and gift taxes
Canada	Canadian income tax on certain income, profits, and gains realized in the year of death and on certain gains deemed realized at death
Denmark	Duties on inheritance and gifts
Finland	Finnish inheritance tax, the communal tax on inheritances, bequests and devises, and the "poors percentage"
France	Duties on gifts and successions
Germany	German inheritance and gift taxes
Greece	Greek inheritance tax
Ireland	Irish estate tax duty
Italy	Italian estate and inheritance taxes
Japan	Japanese inheritance tax, including gift tax
Netherlands	Netherlands succession and transfer duties at death
Norway	Norwegian tax on inheritances, including death gifts
South Africa	Union estate duty
Switzerland	Estate and inheritance taxes imposed by the cantons and their political subdivisions
United Kingdom	Capital transfer tax

* The Commonwealth estate tax duty was abolished, effective for decedents dying after July 1, 1979.

Credit claimed under a treaty is, in general, computed on Schedule P (Credit for Foreign Death Taxes) of Form 706 (United States Estate (and Generation-Skipping Transfer) Tax Return) in the same manner that credit is computed under the statute. The following principal exceptions apply:

(1) the situs rules contained in the treaty apply in determining whether property was situated in the foreign country;

(2) credit may be allowed only for payment of the death tax or taxes specified in the treaty;

(3) where specifically provided, the credit is proportionately shared for the tax applicable to property situated outside both countries, or that was deemed in some instances to be situated within both countries; and

(4) the amount entered as item 4 of Schedule P is the amount shown at line 12 in "Tax Computation" on page 1 of Form 706 less the total of credits claimed for federal gift taxes on pre-1977 gifts (Code Sec. 2012) and for tax on prior transfers (line 15 of Part 2, Form 706).

If a credit is claimed for tax on prior transfers, it will be necessary to complete Schedule Q (Credit for Tax on Prior Transfers) of Form 706 before completing Schedule P.[11]

See CCH Tax Treaties Reports for specific rules concerning the application of the treaties.

---

[11] Instructions for Form 706 (Rev. August 2013), p. 39.

Chapter 28
COMPUTATION OF TAX

¶ 1425   Unified Transfer Tax

The estate and gift tax rates are combined in a single rate schedule effective for the estates of decedents dying, and gifts made, after December 31, 1976. Lifetime gifts made after 1976 and transfers made at death are cumulated for estate tax purposes. Estate tax liability is determined by applying the unified transfer tax rate schedule to cumulated transfers and subtracting the gift taxes payable. A unified credit, referred in Code Sec. 2010 as the "applicable credit amount" for decedents dying after 1997) is subtracted after determining the decedent's estate tax liability.

• *Impact of the 2010 and 2012 Acts*

. The Tax Relief, Unemployment Insurance Reauthorization, and Job Creation Act of 2010 (P.L. 111-312) (Tax Relief Act of 2010) made several changes that directly impact on the computation of the estate tax, most of which were made permanent by later legislation (the American Taxpayer Relief Act of 2012 (ATRA) discussed below):

• The estate tax was reinstated retroactively for estates of decedents dying after December 31, 2009 and before January 1, 2013;

• The applicable exclusion amount is increased to $5,000,000 for 2010 and 2011; $5,120,000 (indexed) for 2012; $5,20,000 (indexed) for 2013; and $5.340,000 (indexed) for 2014

• The maximum tax rate is lowered to 35 percent for 2010 through 2012 (a 40 percent rate applies after 2013)

• Estates of decedents dying in 2010 may opt out of the estate tax if they elect application of the carryover basis rules (see ¶ 121);

• The estate tax (as well as the gift tax) applicable exclusion amounts, and the generation-skipping transfer tax exemption, will be subject to indexing for inflation beginning in 2012; and

• An election to allow the unused portion of the applicable exclusion amount of a predeceased spouse is available to the estate of the surviving spouse (see ¶ 16).

As a result of the operation of the increased applicable exclusion amount and the maximum tax rate of 35 percent for 2010 through 2012, the effective minimum estate tax rate for 2010—2012 is also 35 percent (which is, thus, the *only* effective estate tax rate that applies for these years). Changes made by the American Taxpayer Relief Act of 2012 (P.L. 112-240) (ATRA), raised the minimum (and only) effective estate, gift, and generation-skipping transfer tax rate to 40 percent for 2013 and beyond.

Surtax not reinstated. The five-percent surtax that had been applied to estates and taxable gifts larger than $10 million and up to $17,184,000 prior to 2002 (Code Sec. 2001(c)(2)) was not reinstated by the Tax Relief Act of 2010 for estates of decedents and taxable gifts made after December 31, 2009 and before January 1, 2013. This repeal was made permanent by ATRA for estates of decedents and taxable gifts made after December 31, 2012.

Modifications necessary to reflect impact of differences in tax rates. The computation of both estate and gift taxes is clarified to reflect the changes in transfer tax rates made by the Tax Relief Act of 2010. According to the Joint Committee on Taxation,[1] for purposes of determining the amount of gift tax that would have been paid on one or more prior year gifts, the estate tax rates in effect under Code Sec. 2001(c) at the time of the decedent's death are used to compute both (1) the gift tax imposed by Chapter 12 of the Internal Revenue Code with respect to such gifts, and (2) the unified credit allowed against such gifts under Code Sec. 2505 (including the computation of the applicable credit amount under Code Sec. 2505(a)(1), and the sum of amounts allowed as a credit for all preceding periods under Code Sec. 2505(a)(2)). See ¶2008 for a discussion of the steps required to make this computation.

American Taxpayer Relief Act of 2012 (ATRA)

As a result of the elimination of the EGTRRA sunset provision by ATRA, the estates of decedents dying, gifts and GSTs made after December 31, 2012, will not be subject to a lower exclusion/exemption amount that had been scheduled to take effect in 2013 (Code Secs. 2010 and 2631). The applicable tax rates and exclusion amounts are discussed separately at ¶10 and ¶15, respectively.

> *Comment:* In addition to provisions relating to the transfer tax rates and exclusions (including annual inflation adjustments), ATRA made permanent most of the provisions that were effective under EGTRRA and the Tax Relief Act of 2010. Thus, the portability deceased spousal unused exclusion (DSUE) election; the stepped-up basis of inherited property rules; the deduction for state death taxes paid; liberalized rules relating to the GST rules, qualification for installment payment of estate taxes and the estate tax exclusion for conservation easements; were made permanent. The application of the carryover basis at death rules continued to apply to one year only (2010), and only if an estate made the carryover basis election (see ¶121). Further, the qualified family-owned business interest (QFOBI) deduction was permanently repealed, and the five percent surtax on certain large estates was not reinstituted.

EGTRRA Sunset Provision

Until it was eliminated by ATRA, the sunset provision of EGTRRA (Act Sec. 901) stated that, for estates of decedents dying, gifts made, or generation-skipping transfers, after December 31, 2010, all changes made by EGTRRA ". . . shall be applied and administered to years, estates, gifts, and transfers . . . as if the provisions and amendments [of EGTRRA] had never been enacted." Thus, the estate, gift and generation-skipping transfer tax provisions were slated to revert to what they were before enactment of EGTRRA. The Tax Relief Act of 2010 extended the application of the EGTRRA provisions through December 31, 2013, by delaying the sunset until January 1, 2013. ATRA made most of the

---

[1] Technical Explanation of the Revenue Provisions Contained in the "Tax Relief, Unemployment Insurance Reauthorization, and Job Creation Act of 2010" (JCX-55-10), December 10, 2010.

EGTRRA changes permanent by setting aside the EGTRRA sunset provision, effective January 1, 2013.

• Impact of the 2001 Act

The enactment of the Economic Growth and Tax Relief Reconciliation Act of 2001 (EGTRRA) (P.L. 107-16) brought significant changes to the transfer tax system, the most notable being the repeal of the estate and generation-skipping transfer taxes in 2010 (which was set aside by the Tax Relief, Unemployment Insurance Reauthorization, and Job Creation Act of 2010 (P.L. 111-312) (Tax Relief Act of 2010)). Additionally, EGTRRA made a number of modifications to the maximum estate tax rate and applicable exclusion amount (discussed below).

Under the 2001 Act, the top marginal rate was 45 percent for decedents dying, and gifts made, in 2009 and the applicable exclusion amount was $3,500,000 for 2009.

• Unified Credit: 1977–1997

The unified estate and gift tax credit and the exemption equivalent for the years 1977 through 1997 are as follows:

Year	Amount of Credit	Amount of Exemption Equivalent
1977	$30,000	$120,667
1978	34,000	134,000
1979	38,000	147,333
1980	42,500	161,563
1981	47,000	175,625
1982	62,800	225,000
1983	79,300	275,000
1984	96,300	325,000
1985	121,800	400,000
1986	155,800	500,000
1987-1997	192,800	600,000

• Unified Credit: 1998–2013

For the years 1998 through 2013, the unified credit is determined by reference to the "applicable credit amount" and the "applicable exclusion amount" (formerly the exemption equivalent). The increases are phased in as follows:

Year	Applicable Credit Amount	Applicable Exclusion Amount
1998	$202,050	$625,000
1999	211,300	650,000
2000 and 2001	220,550	675,000

As a result of changes made by the 2001 Act, different unified credit amounts apply to the estate tax and to the gift tax until years 2011 and 2012, when the two taxes again become "unified" (see ¶15).

The estate tax unified credit (applicable credit amount) and the applicable exclusion amount for the years 2002 through 2012 appear below:

Year	Applicable Credit Amount	Applicable Exclusion Amount
2002–2003	$345,800	$1,000,000
2004–2005	555,800	1,500,000
2006–2008	780,800	2,000,000
2009	1,455,800	3,500,000

Year	Applicable Credit Amount	Applicable Exclusion Amount
2010	1,730,800	5,000,000
2011	1,730,800	5,000,000
2012	1,772,800 (indexed)	5,120,000 (indexed)
2013	2,045,800 (indexed)	5,250,000 (indexed)
2014	2,081,800 (indexed)	5,340,000 (indexed)

The gift tax applicable exclusion amount for the years 2002 through 2010 was $1 million. For years 2011 and thereafter the gift tax exclusion amount was reunified with those of the estate and generation-skipping transfer taxes. Thus, for 2013, the gift tax applicable exclusion amount is $5,250,000, as adjusted for inflation.

¶ 1426   Computation of Tax

The basic steps in computing the tax on a post-1976 estate under the unified transfer tax system are as discussed below. All line references are to Part 2 of Form 706 (United States Estate (and Generation-Skipping Transfer) Tax Return) (Rev. August 2013).

(1) Compute the decedent's tentative taxable estate (before state death tax deduction). The tentative taxable estate of a U.S. citizen is determined by subtracting the total tentative allowable deductions reported on line 2, from the total gross estate less exclusion reported on line 1. From this amount (entered on line 3a), subtract any state death tax deduction (line 3b), to arrive at the taxable estate (line 3c).

(2) Compute the "adjusted taxable gifts" (line 4)—the aggregate post-1976 lifetime taxable gifts, other than post-1976 gifts that are includible in the decedent's gross estate. (In limited situations, the IRS may revalue post-1976 gifts for purposes of computing a decedent's estate tax; see the discussion under the heading "Revaluing Lifetime Gifts," below.) When computing gift tax liability for prior years, a change made by the Tax Relief Act of 2010 requires that any unified credit allocated to the prior years/periods must be redetermined using current gift tax rates, rather than the rates that were effective when the prior gifts were made.[2]

(3) Add the amounts on line 3c and line 4 (this is entered on line 5).

(4) Determine the tentative tax by applying the rates in the unified rate schedule for 2013 (see ¶ 1430) to the amount obtained on line 5. This amount is entered on line 6.

(5) Subtract the total gift tax paid or payable on gifts made after 1976 according to the rate schedule in effect in the year of the decedent's death (including the gift tax paid on transfers includible in the gross estate on line 7). The resulting amount is the gross estate tax (entered on line 8). (New rules, effective for gifts made after December 31, 2009, compute the amount of the unified credit utilized for prior gifts based on the current year tax rates; see the Line 7 Worksheet at ¶ 2948, and tables to be used in filling in the Worksheet, at

---

[2] A filled-in Worksheet for computing unified credit allocated to prior taxable gifts, from the Instructions for Form 706 (United States Estate (and Generation-Skipping) Transfer Tax Return) (2013), is reproduced at ¶ 2948.

¶2944.) Where the Line 7 Worksheet is required with respect to prior taxable gifts, the completed Worksheet must be filed with the decedent's Form 706.

See the example at ¶1428 for details of these basic steps, including how to compute gift tax on lifetime gifts.

(6) Enter the basic exclusion amount on line 9a. The Deceased Spousal Unused Exclusion (DSUE) amount, if any, from Part 6, Section D, is entered on line 9b. The total of line 9a and line 9b is entered on line 9c as the applicable exclusion amount. The applicable credit amount is determined by applying the Unified Rate Schedule (see ¶1430) to the amount on line 9c. An adjustment (not to exceed $6,000) is to be entered on line 10 for an amount of specific exemption claimed for gifts made after September 8, 1976 and before January 1, 1977. The amount on line 11 is subtracted from that on line 8, and the amount (but not below zero) is entered on line 12.

The net estate tax (line 16) is then computed by subtracting the following tax credits: (1) the credit for federal gift taxes on pre-1977 gifts that are includible in the decedent's gross estate (see ¶1382); (2) the credit for foreign death taxes (line 13) (see ¶1400); and (3) the credit for prior transfer taxes (line 14) (see ¶1300).

The generation-skipping transfer tax reported (line 17) is added to the net estate tax to arrive at the total amount of transfer taxes that are payable on a decedent's estate tax return (line 18). Only the net amount of the generation-skipping tax, as computed on Schedule R (Generation-Skipping Transfer Tax) of Form 706, is entered in the computation part.

• *Split Gifts*

If spouses have made split gifts, special rules apply for determining the amount of the adjusted taxable gifts includible in a decedent's estate and the amount of the gift tax offset that may be claimed on a decedent's estate tax return. These rules are dependent on whether the decedent was the donor or the consenting spouse. First, if the entire amount of the gift is includible in the donor spouse's gross estate, any gift tax paid by the consenting spouse on the gift can be claimed as part of the gift tax offset in determining the estate tax payable by the estate of the donor spouse.[3] Second, a gift is not included in the adjusted taxable gifts of a consenting spouse in those cases where the amount of the split gift was includible in the donor spouse's gross estate under Code Sec. 2035. Further, the gift tax paid by the consenting spouse is not included in the gift tax offset on the consenting spouse's estate tax return in computing the final estate tax to the extent that an offset had been used on the donor spouse's estate tax return.[4]

• *Revaluing Lifetime Gifts*

For lifetime gifts made after August 5, 1997, if the reporting of the gift meets the adequate disclosure requirements (discussed below), the IRS is not permitted to revalue a gift for purposes of computing an estate tax liability if the three-year statute of limitations on the gift has expired.[5] For post-1976 gifts made before January 1, 1997, the Tax Court held that the value of a decedent's gifts, as reported on his federal gift tax returns, could be revised even though the three-year statute of limitations period on the assessment of gift taxes had expired.[6] In

---

[3] Code Sec. 2001(d).
[4] Code Sec. 2001(e).

[5] Code Sec. 2001(f) and Code Sec. 6501(c)(9).
[6] *F. Smith Est.*, 94 TC 872, CCH Dec. 46,648 (Acq.).

so holding, the Tax Court concluded that, although Code Sec. 2504(c) would have prevented such a revaluation of prior taxable gifts for gift tax purposes, there was no corresponding provision in the estate tax area. Accordingly, the post-1976 lifetime gifts of the decedent could be revalued. However, the Taxpayer Relief Act of 1997 (P.L. 105-34) added Code Sec. 2001(f), effective with respect to gifts made after August 5, 1997, which prohibits the IRS from revaluing gifts made during life in computing adjusted taxable gifts for estate tax purposes if the gift tax statute of limitations has expired. As retroactively amended by the IRS Restructuring and Reform Act of 1998 (P.L. 105-206), in order for this provision to apply, the value of the gift in question must have been finally determined for purposes of the gift tax. The value of a gift is finally determined if the value is (1) reported on a gift tax return and is not challenged by the IRS prior to the expiration of the statute of limitations, (2) determined by the IRS and not challenged by the taxpayer in court, (3) determined by a court, or (4) agreed on by the taxpayer and the IRS in a settlement.

In order to gain the benefit of the provision that bars the IRS from an estate tax revaluation of a lifetime gift for which the statute of limitations period has expired on the gift, the gift must have been adequately disclosed.[7] According to the regulations, a transfer will be adequately disclosed on the return only if it is reported in a manner adequate to apprise the IRS of the nature of the gift and the basis for the value so reported. The IRS will consider this standard met if the gift tax return (or a statement attached to the return) provides the following information:

(1) a description of the transferred property and any consideration received by the transferor;

(2) the identify of, and the relationship between, the transferor and each transferee;

(3) if the property is transferred in trust, the trust's tax identification number and a brief description of the terms of the trust; in the alternative, a copy of the trust document;

(4) a detailed description of the method used to determine the fair market value of the property transferred, including any financial data utilized in determining the value of the interest, any restrictions on the transferred property, and a description of any discounts claimed in valuing the property; and

(5) a statement describing any position taken with respect to the gift tax return that is contrary to any proposed, temporary, or final IRS regulations or revenue ruling published at the time of the transfer.

The IRS has issued guidance[8] on how to adequately disclose a gift if the required information was not initially submitted with a gift tax return filed for the year the gift was made. In this situation, the donor must file an amended gift tax return for the calendar year in which the gift was made that includes all of the information required by the regulations (items (1)-(5), listed above). Effective for amended returns filed after August 21, 2000, the period of assessment will generally expire three years after the date the amended return is filed.

---

[7] Reg. §301.6501(c)-1, as amended Dec. 2, 1999, by T.D. 8835.

[8] Rev. Proc. 2000-34, 2000-2 CB 186.

• *Deaths in 2010*

The executor of a decedent who died in 2010 may elect to apply the Internal Revenue Code as if the reinstatement of the estate tax by the Tax Relief Act of 2010 had not occurred. If made, this election would mean that the estate tax would not apply to that decedent's estate, but that the carryover basis rules would apply to assets transferred by the estate to heirs. If an executor wishes to elect application of the carryover basis rules for an estate, the executor must file an information return (Form 8939 (Allocation of Increase in Basis for Property Acquired From a Decedent) (2010)), by January 17, 2012 (see ¶ 121).

¶ 1428 Example of Application of Unified Transfer Tax

The following Example illustrates application of the unified transfer tax for a decedent dying in 2013.

Example: Nora Brown made the following taxable gifts to her son, Carl.

1984	$400,000
1987	$200,000
1989	$600,000
1990	$700,000

In 2013, Nora died with a gross estate of $5,600,000. After subtracting $291,200 for state death taxes paid, Nora's taxable estate was equal to $5,308,800.

For purposes of computing the total taxes due on Nora's estate tax return (Form 706), the calculations, below, must be made. Under rules enacted by the Tax Relief, Unemployment Insurance Reauthorization, and Job Creation Act of 2010 (P.L. 111-312) (Tax Relief Act of 2010) (see ¶ 2008) the amount of unified credit against taxable gifts for each year is recomputed based on the tax rate in effect under Code Sec. 2505(a)(1), rather than the amount of unified credit against taxable gifts that was actually reported under gift tax returns previously filed with respect to those taxable gifts. Because of this, the amounts computed below for the unified credit against estate tax (and hence the tax payable) for years 1984, 1987, 1989, and 1990 would not match up in all cases with the amounts that were actually reported by Nora on gift tax returns (Forms 709) filed with respect to those tax years.

1984

1. Taxable gifts in current year	$400,000
2. Prior taxable gifts	$0
3. Total taxable gifts	$400,000
4. Tentative tax on line 3 amount	$121,800
5. Less: Tentative tax on prior gifts	$0
6. Balance	$121,800
7. Maximum unified credit*	$96,300
8. Less: Unified credit used in prior periods	$0
9. Available unified credit	$96,300
10. Unified credit used to reduce tax	($96,300)
11. Gift tax (computed by 2013 rates)	$25,500

1987

1. Taxable gifts in current year	$200,000
2. Prior taxable gifts	$400,000
3. Total taxable gifts	$600,000
4. Tentative tax on line 3	$192,800
5. Less: Tentative tax on prior taxable gifts	($121,800)

1987

6. Balance	$71,000
7. Maximum unified credit*	$192,800
8. Less: Unified credit used in prior periods . . .	$96,300
9. Available unified credit	$96,500
10. Unified credit used to reduce tax	$71,000
11. Gift tax (computed by 2013 rates)	$0

1989

1. Taxable gifts in current year	$600,000
2. Prior taxable gifts	$600,000
3. Total taxable gifts	$1,200,000
4. Tentative tax on line 3	$425,800
5. Less: Tentative tax on prior taxable gifts	($192,800)
6. Balance	$233,000
7. Maximum unified credit*	$192,800
8. Less: Unified credit used in prior periods . . .	($167,300)
9. Available unified credit	$25,500
10. Unified credit used to reduce tax	$25,500
11. Gift tax (computed by 2013 rates)	$207,500

1990

1. Taxable gifts in current year	$700,000
2. Prior taxable gifts	$1,200,000
3. Total taxable gifts	$1,900,000
4. Tentative tax on line 3	$705,800
5. Less: Tentative tax on prior taxable gifts	($425,800)
6. Balance	$280,000
7. Maximum unified credit*	$190,800
8. Less: Unified credit used in prior periods . . .	$190,800
9. Available unified credit	$ 0
10. Unified credit used to reduce tax	$ 0
11. Gift tax (computed by 2013 rates)	$ 280,000

Estate

1. Amount of tentative taxable estate	$5,600,000
2. Less: State death tax paid	($291,200)
3. Taxable estate	$5,308,800)
4. Plus adjusted taxable gifts	$1,900,000
5. Estate tax base	$7,208,800
6. Tentative tax on base	$2,829,320
7. Less: Gift tax (computed using 2013 rates) . .	($513,000)
8. Balance	$2,316,320
9. Less: Unified credit (applicable credit amt) . .	($2,045,800)
10. Estate tax payable	$270,520

* Enter amount (as recalculated for current year rates), computed using the Form 706 Line 7 Worksheet reproduced at ¶ 2948, and the accompanying tables at ¶ 2944.

¶ 1430   Rate Schedule Table for Unified Tax

Appearing below are unified rate schedules applicable to the estates of decedents dying, and gifts made, after 2001:

Transfer Tax Rate Schedule: After December 31, 2012

(A) Amount subject to tax more than—	(B) Amount subject to tax equal to or less than—	(C) Tax on amount in column (A)	(D) Rate of tax on excess over amount in column (A) Percent
. . .	$10,000	. . .	18
$10,000	20,000	$1,800	20
20,000	40,000	3,800	22
40,000	60,000	8,200	24
60,000	80,000	13,000	26
80,000	100,000	18,200	28
100,000	150,000	23,800	30
150,000	250,000	38,800	32
250,000	500,000	70,800	34
500,000	750,000	155,800	37
750,000	1,000,000	248,300	39
1,000,000		345,800	40

Unified Tax Rate Schedule 2010-2012 Under the Tax Relief Act of 2010

(A) Amount subject to tax equal to or more than—	(B) Amount subject to tax less than—	(C) Tax on amount in column (A)	(D) Rate of tax on excess over amount in column (A) Percent
. . . . .	$10,000	. . . . . .	18
$10,000	20,000	$1,800	20
20,000	40,000	3,800	22
40,000	60,000	8,200	24
60,000	80,000	13,000	26
80,000	100,000	18,200	28
100,000	150,000	23,800	30
150,000	250,000	38,800	32
250,000	500,000	70,800	34
500,000	. . . . . .	155,800	35

Transfer Tax Rate Schedule: 2002–2009*

(A) Amount subject to tax more than—	(B) Amount subject to tax equal to or less than—	(C) Tax on amount in column (A)	(D) Rate of tax on excess over amount in column (A) Percent
. . .	$10,000	. . .	18
$10,000	20,000	$1,800	20
20,000	40,000	3,800	22
40,000	60,000	8,200	24
60,000	80,000	13,000	26
80,000	100,000	18,200	28
100,000	150,000	23,800	30
150,000	250,000	38,800	32
250,000	500,000	70,800	34
500,000	750,000	155,800	37
750,000	1,000,000	248,300	39
1,000,000	1,250,000	345,800	41
1,250,000	1,500,000	448,300	43
1,500,000	2,000,000	555,800	45
2,000,000	2,500,000	780,800	49
2,500,000	. . . . . .	1,025,800	50

* A special tax rate table that applies for members of U.S. armed forces who died while on active duty in a combat zone, and for the victims of certain terrorist attacks, is reproduced in the Appendix at ¶2605.

EGTRRA Sunset Provision

Until it was eliminated by ATRA, the sunset provision of EGTRRA (Act Sec. 901) stated that, for estates of decedents dying, gifts made, or generation-skipping transfers, after December 31, 2010, all changes made by EGTRRA ". . . shall be applied and administered to years, estates, gifts, and transfers . . . as if the provisions and amendments [of EGTRRA] had never been enacted." Thus, the estate, gift and generation-skipping transfer tax provisions were slated to revert to what they were before enactment of EGTRRA. The Tax Relief Act of 2010 extended the application of the EGTRRA provisions through December 31, 2013, by delaying the sunset until January 1, 2013. ATRA made most of the EGTRRA changes permanent by setting aside the EGTRRA sunset provision, effective January 1, 2013.

• *Impact of the 2012 Act*

The American Taxpayer Relief Act of 2012 (P.L. 112-240) (ATRA) increased the top marginal rate on taxable estates exceeding $1,000,000 to 40 percent for years for the estates of decedents dying after December 31, 2012.

The five-percent surtax, which was repealed by EGTRRA (discussed below), and not reinstated by the Tax Relief Act of 2010, was permanently repealed by ATRA.

• *Impact of the 2010 Act*

The Tax Relief, Unemployment Reauthorization Insurance, and Job Creation Act of 2010 (Tax Relief Act of 2010) (P.L. 111-312) (Tax Relief Act of 2010) reduced the top marginal rate on taxable estates exceeding $500,000 to 35 percent for years after 2010 through 2012.

The five-percent surtax, which was repealed by EGTRRA (discussed below), was not reinstated by the Tax Relief Act of 2010.

¶1430

• *Impact of the 2001 Act*

The Economic Growth and Tax Relief Reconciliation Act of 2001 (P.L. 107-16) (EGTRRA) reduced the top marginal rate on taxable estates exceeding $2,000,000 for years after 2002, according to the following schedule:

- 49 percent for decedents dying, and gifts made, in 2003;

- 48 percent in 2004;

- 47 percent in 2005;

- 46 percent in 2006;

- 45 percent in 2007, 2008, and 2009.

For years 2003 through 2009, the tentative tax is to be determined by using a table prescribed by the IRS, which will be the same as the rate schedule shown above except for the adjustments necessary to reflect the reductions in the maximum rate.

Effective for estates of decedents dying, and gifts made, after December 31, 2001, the 2001 Act repeals the five-percent surtax.

• *Phaseout of Benefits*

The benefits of the graduated rates and the unified credit under the unified transfer tax system are phased out beginning with cumulative transfers rising above $10 million prior to 1998. This is accomplished by adding five percent of the excess of any transfer over $10 million to the tentative tax computed in determining the ultimate transfer tax liability. This five-percent surtax was repealed, effective for estates of decedents dying after December 31, 2001, by the Tax Relief Act of 2010. The repeal was made permanent by ATRA.

• *Decedents Dying, and Gifts Made, After 1997 and Before 2002*

Due to mistakes in the wording of the amendment to Code Sec. 2001(c)(2) by the Taxpayer Relief Act of 1997 (P.L. 105-34), the five-percent additional tax phases out the benefits of the graduated rates, but not the benefits of the unified credit (applicable credit amount), for estates of decedents dying, and gifts made, after 1997. Therefore, the additional tax is levied on amounts transferred in excess of $10 million, but not exceeding $17,184,000 for decedents dying after 1997, but before 2002. The applicable credit amount is not recaptured.[9]

• *Decedents Dying, and Gifts Made, After 1987 and Before 1998*

For estates of decedents dying, and gifts made, after 1987 and before 1998, the tax is levied on amounts transferred in excess of $10 million, but not exceeding $21,040,000, in order to recapture the benefit of any transfer tax rate below 55 percent, as well as the unified credit.

---

[9] Code Sec. 2001(c)(2).

Chapter 29

SPECIAL TAXPAYERS: MEMBERS OF ARMED FORCES, TERRORIST VICTIMS, AND ASTRONAUTS; NONRESIDENTS NOT CITIZENS

¶ 1550 Special Reduction for Members of Armed Forces, Terrorist Victims, and Astronauts

Special estate tax relief is granted to the estates of certain members of the U.S. Armed Forces who died as a result of active duty service in a combat zone, and of certain qualifying decedents who were the victims of specified terrorist attacks.

Qualified decedents. Decedents who qualify for this tax-favored treatment include:

(1) Citizens or residents of the United States dying while in active service of the Armed Forces, if such decedent was killed in action while serving in a combat zone, or died as a result of wounds, disease, or injury suffered while serving in a combat zone, and while in the line of duty, by reason of a hazard to which such decedent was subjected as an incident of such service; and

(2) Decedents dying as a result of wounds or injuries incurred as a result of the terrorist attacks against the United States on April 19, 1995 (the Oklahoma City bombing), or September 11, 2001, or dying as a result of an attack involving anthrax occurring on or after September 11, 2001, and before January 1, 2002.[1]

The definition of "combat zone" is controlled by Code Sec. 112(c). That section defines the term to mean "any area which the President of the United States by Executive Order designates . . . as an area in which the Armed Forces of the United States are or have (after June 24, 1950) engaged in combat." For example, in 1991, the Arabian Peninsula (including the total land area of Iraq, Kuwait, Saudi Arabia, Oman, Bahrain, Qatar, the United Arab Emirates, and bodies of water adjacent to these countries)[2] was designated as a combat zone for Operation Desert Storm.[3] No authority has terminated this designation, which

---

[1] Code Sec. 2201; Reg. § 20.2201-1.
[2] Notice 2003-21, 2003-1 CB 818.

[3] Executive Order 12744, 1991-1 CB 31.

remains in effect. Effective September 19, 2001, Afghanistan was declared a combat zone.[4] Separately, the Department of Defense has certified that military personnel in Uzbekistan, Kyrgystan, Pakistan, Tajikistan, and Jordan are eligible for all combat-related tax benefits due to their direct support of military operations in Afghanistan.

The Federal Republic of Yugoslavia (Serbia/Montenegro), Albania, the Adriatic Sea, and the Ionian Sea north of the 39th parallel (including all of their air spaces) were designated as a combat zone, effective March 24, 1999, for personnel serving in NATO Operation Allied Force.[5] This extension is in addition to any other extensions for which the troops qualify. Combat zone tax treatment was also extended to those members of the Armed Forces serving in a qualified hazardous duty area.[6] Under P.L. 104-117, Bosnia, Croatia, Herzegovina, and Macedonia were designated qualified hazardous duty areas, effective November 21, 1995.

Under the Victims of Terrorism Relief Act of 2001, the executor of an eligible estate can elect not to have the special provisions of P.L. 107-134 apply, in which case estate tax liability will be calculated pursuant to the generally applicable rules. The Act also amended Code Sec. 7508A to give the IRS the power to suspend certain tax-related acts (such as the filing of returns and the payment of tax) for up to one year in cases of terrorist or military actions (see ¶1650 for IRS relief actions taken to date). The IRS can exercise this authority regardless of whether the President has declared the terrorist or military action to be in a disaster area. (In addition to the estate tax relief, the Act extended to the victims of these terrorist attacks the income tax relief provided by Code Sec. 692(c), which exempts federal military and civilian employees from income taxes in the year of their death (and generally the prior taxable year) if they die as a result of military or terrorist activity outside of the United States.)

A decedent who committed suicide after her husband died in the September 11, 2001 terrorist attacks was not considered to be a "specified terrorist victim" for purposes of Code Sec. 2202(b)(2), a U.S. District Court has held.[7] In order for the reduced tax rates to apply to the decedent's estate, the court noted that the decedent must have been a "qualified decedent", which includes any specified terrorist victim, as defined in Code Sec. 692(d)(4). Although it was not disputed that the decedent's death was caused, either directly or indirectly, by emotional suffering arising out of the September 11, terrorist attacks, the court concluded that under a narrow interpretation of Code Sec. 692(d)(4), the statutory reference to "injury" was intended to be limited to physical injuries. Furthermore, the categories of victims identified by a relevant Congressional committee report[8] did not support the view that Congress contemplated providing tax benefits to those who suffered nonphysical injuries resulting in death as a consequence of the attacks.

Computation of estate tax for qualified decedent (post-September 10, 2001). Unless the executor elects not to have Code Sec. 2201 apply, the federal estate tax of a qualified decedent is determined using a special rate schedule contained in Code Sec. 2201(c) (see ¶2605).[9] Although, while the special rate

---

[4] Executive Order 13239, 2001-2 CB 632.

[5] Executive Order 13119, Apr. 13, 1999.

[6] P.L. 106-21, generally effective Mar. 24, 1999.

[7] *P. Kalahasthi Est.*, DC Cal., 2008-2 USTC ¶60,565.

[8] Joint Committee Technical Explanation of the Victims of Terrorism Tax Relief Act of 2001 (P.L. 107-143).

[9] Code Sec. 2201(a).

schedule applies in computing the estate tax under Code Sec. 2001(b) (for citizens and residents) or Code Sec. 2101(b) (for noncitizens nonresidents), the amount of the unified credit is determined as if Code Sec. 2201 did not apply.[10]

> *Example:* Gerry Stack, a citizen of the U.S., was killed in action while in active military service as a U.S. Marine in Afghanistan on June 1, 2013. Stack's gross estate is $15.5 million, reduced by a state death tax of $1,162,500, for a taxable estate of $14,337,500. The executor of the estate did not elect out of the application of Code Sec. 2201. Stack's estate tax liability is computed as follows:

Taxable estate	$14,337,500
Federal estate tax (computed under Code Sec. 2201)	2,201,000
Applicable credit	(2,045,800)
Tax due	$ 155,200

• Extension to Astronauts

Congress, by enactment of the Military Family Tax Relief Act of 2003,[11] extended the estate tax relief applicable to members of the Armed Forces and terrorist victims to astronauts who die in the line of duty. This relief applies to estates of decedents dying after December 31, 2002.[12]

¶ 1565   Execution of Return

The estate tax return form does not provide instructions concerning the Armed Forces exemption. The amount reflecting the Code Sec. 2201 computation of the gross estate should be entered on line 8 on the first page of Form 706 (United States Estate (and Generation-Skipping Transfer) Tax Return) (Rev. August 2013).[13] A notation of the reason for variation is necessary, such as—"Am. Vet. killed in action" (Code Sec. 2201).

In all other respects, the form would be filled out in the same manner as for any other decedent. The "General Information" portion of Form 706 (part 4) should be supplemented with a statement concerning the basis for claiming the Armed Forces exemption.

Military service personnel and certain individuals who are serving in support of military personnel are generally granted extended filing and payment deadlines with respect to their federal tax obligations. These provisions relate to military service personnel who are in a combat zone, contingency operation, or qualified hazardous duty area, are hospitalized as a result of injury received in a combat zone or contingency operation, or are missing in action.[14] See also ¶ 1650 for special rules applicable to the terrorist attacks against the United States and astronauts who die in the line of duty.

¶ 1600   Nonresidents Not Citizens: Special Rules

There are a number of special requirements in the estate tax law that apply only to estates of persons who are neither residents nor citizens of the United

---

[10] The IRS has published sample computations of the estate tax liability of post-September 10, 2001, qualified decedents under Code Sec. 2201 (Rev. Rul. 2002-86, 2002-2 CB 993; modifying and superseding Rev. Rul. 78-361, 1978-2 CB 246).

[11] P.L. 108-121.

[12] Code Sec. 2201, as amended by the Military Family Tax Relief Act of 2003, P.L. 108-121.

[13] A filled-in Form 706, page 1, for a decedent dying in 2012, is reproduced at ¶ 2920.

[14] Code Sec. 7508, as amended by P.L. 108-121; Reg. § 301.7508-1.

States. They affect the definition of property subject to tax, the exemption, return requirements and deductions. Some of the requirements stem from the estate tax provisions of the Internal Revenue Code and apply to estates of all such persons, except to the extent modified by treaty. Others are based on treaty provisions that limit their application to nonresidents not citizens who are residents of the country with which the treaty exists.

A number of these special requirements were discussed previously (see ¶ 85). Some are the subject of special instructions in the estate tax return form. The following material should be read in conjunction with specific requirements already covered.

¶ 1605   Residents of U.S. Possessions

Decedents who are citizens of the United States and residents of U.S. possessions at the time of their death are treated as "nonresidents not citizens of the United States," for estate tax purposes, if they acquired U.S. citizenship solely by reason of:

(1) being a citizen of the possession; or

(2) birth or residence within the possession.[15]

For such purposes, there is no distinction between possession citizens who were residents of the same possession at the time of their death as that under which they acquired their citizenship and possession citizens who reside in a U.S. possession other than the possession through which U.S. citizenship is acquired.[16]

¶ 1615   Death Tax Conventions

If a death tax convention is applicable to the estate of a decedent who is a nonresident not a citizen, both the treaty and the regulations issued pursuant to the treaty should be consulted.[17]

Death duty conventions are in effect with each of the countries listed below. The provisions of a convention apply in the case of a decedent dying on or after the effective date shown.

Country	Effective Date
Australia*	January 7, 1954
Austria	July 1, 1983
Canada (revised protocol to income and capital tax treaty, entered into force December 15, 2008)	November 10, 1995
Denmark	November 7, 1984
Finland	December 18, 1952
France (modified by protocol entering into force December 21, 2006)	October 1, 1980
Germany (modified by protocol entering into force on December 14, 2000)	January 1, 1979
Greece (modified by protocol (affecting situs of real property) entering into force October 27, 1967)	December 30, 1953
Ireland	December 20, 1951
Italy	October 26, 1956
Japan	April 1, 1955
Netherlands	February 3, 1971
Norway	December 11, 1951
South Africa	July 15, 1952

---

[15] Code Sec. 2209; Reg. § 20.2209-1.
[16] Rev. Rul. 74-25, 1974-1 CB 284.

[17] See CCH TAX TREATIES REPORTS.

Country	Effective Date
Switzerland	September 17, 1952
United Kingdom	November 11, 1979

* Note: The Commonwealth estate tax duty for Australia was abolished, effective for the estates of decedents dying after July 1, 1979.

The U.S.-Germany estate tax treaty did not preempt a state (Maryland) statute of limitations for filing a refund claim for estate inheritance taxes, the Maryland Court of Appeals held.[18] In denying the refund claim, the appellate court concluded that because the treaty was binding on the U.S. government, but not its political subdivisions, it did not apply to state inheritance taxes and related statutes of limitations.

If, with regard to a tax treaty, a U.S. taxpayer believes that the actions of the United States, the other country party to the treaty (called the "treaty country"), or both, have resulted in taxation that is inconsistent with treaty provisions, the tax treaty will generally permit the taxpayer to request competent authority assistance. The IRS Director, International, acts as the competent authority for the United States, and is charged with administering tax treaties. Under procedures set forth by the IRS, a request for assistance may be filed at any time after an action results in taxation that is not in accordance with the provisions of the applicable treaty. The request, which must be in letter form and addressed to the Director, International, must include (among other information) a brief description of the relevant activities or other circumstances involved in the issues being raised and an explanation of the relief being sought. Special simplified procedures are available in "small cases" where the proposed adjustment does not exceed $200,000 ($1 million in the case of a partnership or corporation).[19]

A $27,500 user fee applies to requests for U.S. competent authority determinations received after February 4, 2012 (a fee of $15,000 applies to such requests made after December 4, 2006, and before February 5, 2012). The fee will apply for an initial determination, a renewal of a previously issued determination, or a supplemental determination. The user fee will not be charged until the U.S. competent authority has formally accepted the request for consideration. When this has happened, the user fee should be sent, along with a copy of the written notice of acceptance, to: IRS/BFC, P.O. Box 9002, Beckley, WV 25802. Once the request for consideration is accepted and the user fee paid, the fee cannot be refunded, except in very limited circumstances. Requests for advance rulings regarding the interpretation or application of a tax treaty, as distinguished from requests for assistance from the U.S. competent authority, must be submitted to the Associate Chief Counsel (International) under the IRS general ruling request procedures detailed in Rev. Proc. 2012-1, IRB 2012-1, 1.[20]

¶ 1617   Gross Estate

The gross estate of a nonresident not a citizen of the United States is determined in the same manner as that of a U.S. citizen or resident. It includes not only all property beneficially owned by the decedent, but also joint estates with right of survivorship, tenancies by the entirety, community property, property transferred by the decedent during his or her lifetime, and property subject

---

[18] *J. Arrowsmith*, Md. Ct. App., 2001-2 USTC ¶ 60,421, 778 A2d 364.

[19] Rev. Proc. 2006-54, 2006-2 CB 1035, superseded in part by Rev. Proc. 2012-1, IRB 2012-1, 1.

[20] Rev. Proc. 2006-54, 2006-2 CB 1035, superseded in part by Rev. Proc. 2012-1, IRB 2012-1, 1.

to the decedent's general power of appointment (see Chapter 6 through Chapter 17). However, the taxable estate is the part of the gross estate situated in the United States, less the authorized deductions.[21]

Only the part of the gross estate situated in the United States should be listed on the appropriate schedules (see ¶85 and ¶1620). The term "United States," when used in a geographical sense, includes only the states and the District of Columbia. Property transferred during the decedent's lifetime, and includible in the gross estate under one of the transfer provisions (Code Sec. 2035 through Code Sec. 2038), is deemed situated in the United States if it was so situated at the time of the transfer or at the time of death.

¶ 1620   Property Situated in the United States

Although the situs rules controlling the inclusion of property in estates of nonresidents not citizens may be modified under the provisions of an applicable death tax treaty with the United States, in general, only property located in the United States is includible in the gross estate of a nonresident not a U.S. citizen. Property located within the United States is reported on Schedule A (Gross Estate in the United States) of Form 706-NA (United States Estate (and Generation-Skipping Transfer) Tax Return) (Rev. August 2013).[22] Schedule E (Jointly Owned Property), Schedule G (Transfers During Decedent's Life), and Schedule H (Powers of Appointment) of Form 706 (United States Estate (and Generation-Skipping Transfer) Tax Return) (Rev. August 2013) must be attached to the return if the decedent transferred certain property or if the decedent possessed, exercised, or released a general power of appointment in U.S. property (see ¶85 for further details).

• Stocks and Bonds

The notable exception to this general situs rule is the stock of domestic corporations. This stock is includible in the gross estate regardless of where located. Debt obligations (bonds, etc.) that are owned and held by a nonresident not a citizen are considered property located within the United States if the primary obligor is a domestic corporation or other U.S. person, the United States, a state, a political subdivision of a state, or the District of Columbia.[23]

> *Comment:* For this purpose, it is immaterial whether the written evidence of the debt obligation is treated as being the property itself. Currency, however, is not to be considered a debt obligation.

If the obligation is a debt of a resident alien individual or domestic corporation that meets the 80-percent-foreign-business requirement, it will be treated as having a foreign situs.[24]

• Deposits with U.S. Financial Institutions and Insurers

Funds deposited by or for a nonresident alien in a U.S. bank (including a domestic banking branch of a foreign corporation), a savings and loan, or similar association or held by a domestic insurance company under an agreement to pay interest are not includible in a decedent's gross estate if the monies are not effectively connected with the conduct of a trade or business within the United States by the decedent.[25] Deposits with a foreign branch of a domestic corpora-

---

[21] Code Sec. 2106; Reg. § 20.2106-1.
[22] An example of a filled-in Form 706-NA, for a decedent dying in 2013, is reproduced at 3260.

[23] Code Sec. 2104.
[24] Code Sec. 861(a)(1)(A).
[25] Code Sec. 2105(b).

tion or partnership, if such branch is engaged in the commercial banking business, are also excludable from the gross estate.[26]

A nonresident alien's U.S. bank deposits, chartered savings institution accounts, and amounts held by insurance companies will not be treated as property located within the United States for federal estate tax purposes, if the interest paid on these amounts would have been treated as nontaxable foreign-source income for federal income tax purposes. To be exempt from federal income tax as foreign-source income, the interest from these deposits must not be "effectively connected" with the conduct of a trade or business within the United States.[27]

• *Stock in Regulated Investment Companies (pre-2012 Decedents)*

Effective for estates of nonresident, non-U.S. citizens dying after December 31, 2004, and before January 1, 2012,[28] a portion of stock in a regulated investment company (such as a mutual fund) owned by such a decedent was treated as property without the United States.[29] Accordingly, such property was not includible in the gross estate of such shareholder for federal estate tax purposes. The portion that was exempt from taxation was determined at the end of the quarter of the tax year of the regulated investment company (RIC) immediately preceding the decedent's date or death, or other time prescribed by regulation. The exempt amount was the proportion of the RIC's assets that were qualifying assets with respect to the decedent in relation to the total assets of the RIC. Qualifying assets were those assets that, if owned by the decedent, would have been:

(1) bank deposits that are exempt from income tax;

(2) portfolio debt obligations;

(3) certain original issue discount obligations;

(4) debt obligations of a U.S. corporation that are treated as giving rise to foreign source income; and

(5) other property not within the United States.[30]

• *Certain Other Properties*

The following special rules exist for determining whether property is situated in the United States:

(1) Real property and tangible personal property are within the United States if physically located therein.

(2) Proceeds of insurance on the life of a nonresident not a citizen of the United States are not situated in the United States.[31]

(3) Works of art are not considered situated in the United States if they were (a) imported into the United States solely for exhibition purposes, (b) loaned for such purposes to a public gallery or museum, no part of the net earnings of which inures to the benefit of any private stockholder or individual, and (c) on exhibit (or en route to or from exhibition) in such public gallery or museum at the time of the owner's death.[32]

---

[26] Code Sec. 2105(b).

[27] Code Sec. 864(c).

[28] Code Sec. 2105(d)(3), as added by P.L. 108-357, and amended by P.L. 110-343 and P.L. 111-312.

[29] Code Sec. 2105(d)(1), as added by P.L. 108-357.

[30] Code Sec. 2105(d)(2), as added by P.L. 108-357.

[31] Code Sec. 2105(a).

[32] Code Sec. 2105(c).

• *Gift Tax Paid on Gifts Made Within Three Years of Death*

The IRS Chief Counsel's Office has determined that the gift tax paid on gifts made within three years of death under Code Code Sec. Sec. 2035(b) are not included in the gross estate of a nonresident alien, pursuant to Code Sec. 2104(b).

In accordance with Code Sec. 2103, the value of a nonresident alien's gross estate is the portion of his or her gross estate, as determined under Code Sec. 2031, which is situated in the United States at the time of the decedent's death. Code Sec. 2104(b), in turn, requires that any property which a nonresident alien has transferred pursuant to Code Secs. 2035 through 2038 shall be deemed to be situated in the United States at the time of the decedent's death.

The IRS Chief Counsel determined that the transfers referenced in Code Sec. 2104(b) must be gratuitous in nature in order to be included in a nonresident alien's gross estate. It was noted that, pursuant to applicable case law and Reg. § 25.2511-1, the gift tax is merely a tax on a gratuitious transfer and is not considered to be a portion of the gift itself. Because the payment of gift tax is not considered to be a gratuitious transfer, the Chief Counsel found that the Code Sec. 2035 transfers referenced in Code Sec. 2104(b) apply only to gifts made within three years of death under Code Sec. 2035(a) and not the gift taxes paid in accordance with Code Sec. 2035(b). Consequently, a payment of gift tax made within three years of death is not property situated within the United States under Code Sec. 2104(b). Thus, a nonresident alien's gross estate is not increased by such an amount.[33]

• *Canadian Registered Retirement Savings Plan*

The IRS Office of Chief Counsel has ruled that a Canadian decedent's Canadian registered retirement savings plan (RRSP) was not includible in his gross estate for federal estate tax purposes under Code Sec. 2104. The decedent, a Canadian resident, citizen and domiciliary, owned an RRSP, which is similar to an individual retirement account in the United States. The RRSP held shares of Canadian mutual funds that, in turn, owned shares of U.S. corporations. Under the terms of the RRSP, the decedent was able to make taxable withdrawals from the RRSP at will and designate the beneficiary of the RRSP upon his death.

The IRS ruled that at the time of the decedent's death, the RRSP would be includible pursuant to Code Sec. 2031 if the interest was deemed to be an outright ownership, similar to a brokerage account, or Code Sec. 2036 or 2038 if the RRSP was considered a trust or other entity. The RRSP could also be includible under Code Sec. 2039 if the interest was considered to be similar to that of a retirement annuity. However, in accordance with Rev. Rul. 82-193, 1982-2 CB 219, the RRSP would only be includible in the decedent's gross estate if the assets held by the RRSP had a U.S. situs at the time of the decedent's death, regardless of the characterization of the RRSP.

The IRS determined that situs of the assets held by the RRSP was dependent upon whether the Canadian mutual funds owned by the RRSP were treated for U.S. tax purposes as corporations or trusts. Although the mutual funds were organized as trusts under Canadian law, the mutual funds should be classified as corporations for U.S. tax purposes, according to the entity classification rules of Reg. §§ 301.7701-1 through 301.7701-4. Consequently, the shares of the mutual funds were not U.S. situs property within the meaning of Code Sec. 2104(a), and

---

[33] IRS Chief Counsel Advice 201020009, April 16, 2010.

A donor making gifts to his or her noncitizen spouse may also exclude gifts of up to $133,000 annually (indexed; for gifts in 2009).[50] This amount is $134,000 for gifts made in 2010,[51] $136,000 for gifts made in 2011,[52] $139,000 for gifts made in 2012,[53] $143,000 for gifts made in 2013, and $145,000 for gifts made in 2014.[54]

• *Transfers to Minors*

To facilitate the making of gifts to minors, however, Congress has specified certain types of gifts that will not be treated as gifts of future interests (see ¶ 2270).[55]

¶ 2015   Deductions

Before applying the unified transfer tax rates, the donor may deduct the following from the value of the gifts he or she is required to report: (1) the allowable marital deduction for gifts to a spouse (see ¶ 2311); (2) transfers for public, charitable and religious uses (see ¶ 2305); and (3) any items that reduce the net value of the gift, such as partial consideration, mortgages and other charges against the specific property transferred. The tests and rules for determining the amounts of these various deductions are similar to those applied in determining the deductibility of corresponding items for estate tax purposes.

¶ 2016   Specific Exemption for Pre-1977 Gifts

In addition to the annual exclusion of $3,000 for gifts to each donee, a donor was entitled to a specific exemption of $30,000 for gifts made prior to 1977. The specific exemption was repealed, starting with gifts made in 1977, and was replaced by the unified credit (see ¶ 2007).

---

[50] Rev. Proc. 2008-66, IRB 2008-45, 1107.
[51] Rev. Proc. 2009-50, IRB 2009-45, 617.
[52] Rev. Proc. 2010-40, IRB 2010-46, 663.
[53] Rev. Proc. 2011-52, IRB 2011-45, 701.

[54] Rev. Proc. 2012-41, IRB 2012-45, 539; Rev. Proc. 2012-35, IRB 2012-47, October 31, 2013.
[55] Code Sec. 2503(c).

Chapter 32
FORMS REQUIRED

¶ 2050   Filing by Donor

Donors are required to report gifts of present and future interests using Form 709 (United States Gift (and Generation-Skipping Transfer) Tax Return). This is the principal form that is used in the administration of the gift tax law. Other forms and documents may be necessary, depending on the circumstances (see ¶2120).

¶ 2052   Gift Tax Return Filing Requirements

Effective for gifts made after 1981, gift tax returns must be filed, and any gift tax must be paid, on an annual basis. Generally, the due date for filing the annual gift tax return will be April 15. However, for the calendar year in which the donor dies, the gift tax return will be due on the earlier of the due date (with extensions) for filing the donor's estate tax return, or the "normal" due date with respect to the gifts (April 15 following the calendar year in which the gifts were made).[1]

See ¶1650 for special tax provisions for victims of terrorist attacks against the United States.

• *Gifts in Excess of the Annual Exclusion*

Transfers of present interests in the amount of the gift tax annual exclusion was $12,000 for gifts made in 2006, 2007 and 2008;[2] $13,000 for gifts made in 2009 through 2012,[3] and $14,000 for gifts made in 2013 or 2014[4]) or less to any donee are exempt from the gift tax and do not require a gift tax return, unless gift-splitting is elected (see ¶2013). Donors making gifts that exceed $14,000 to a single donee are required to file an annual gift tax return in the year of such gifts. A return must be filed with respect to transfers in excess of $14,000 to a charitable organization if the gift is only partially deductible. However, a donor who makes a gift to charity in excess of the annual gift tax exclusion is not required to file a gift tax return if the *entire* value of the donated property qualifies for a gift tax charitable deduction.[5] A gift tax return must be filed for gifts of future interests, regardless of the amount of the gift.

A contributor making a contribution after August 5, 1997, to a qualified tuition program (QTP) that exceeds the annual exclusion limit may elect to have

---

[1] Code Sec. 6075(b).

[2] Rev. Proc. 2007-66, IRB 2007-45, 970; Rev. Proc. 2006-53, 2006-2 CB 996; Rev. Proc. 2005-70, 2005-2 CB 979. The annual exclusion was $11,000 for 2003 through 2005, and $10,000 for gifts made after 1981 and before 2002.

[3] Rev. Proc. 2011-52, IRB 2011-45, 701; Rev. Proc. 2010-40, IRB 2010-46, 617; Rev. Proc. 2009-50, IRB 2009-45, 663; Rev. Proc. 2008-66, IRB 2008-45, 1107.

[4] Rev. Proc. 2012-41, IRB 2012-45, 539; Rev. Proc. 2013-35, IRB 2013-47, October 31, 2013.

[5] Code Sec. 6019(a)(3).

the contribution treated as if it were made ratably over five years.[6] A gift tax return must be filed with respect to any contribution in excess of the annual gift tax exclusion limit.

> *Example:* In September 2013, Heinrich Neble contributes $70,000 to a QTP, the designated beneficiary of which is his daughter, Gretchen. At Heinrich's election, the program treats the $70,000 as being paid ratably over a five-year period at $14,000 per year. Heinrich must make the election for the five-year averaging on his gift tax return.

• Other Rules

Married individuals who elect to split gifts (see ¶2013) must file a gift tax return, regardless of the amount of the gift.[7]

Only individuals are required to file returns. Where gifts are made by trusts, estates, partnerships, or corporations, the trust beneficiaries, the partners, or the stockholders become the donors and may incur a gift tax liability.[8]

The death of the donor before filing a gift tax return imposes the duty to file the return on the donor's executor or administrator. If a donor becomes legally incompetent before filing a gift tax return, the donor's guardian or conservator must file the return.[9]

> *Comment:* Loans of qualified works of art (any archaeological, historic, or creative tangible personal property) to a public charity or a private operating foundation are not treated as transfers subject to federal gift tax.

¶ 2056   Place for Filing Returns

All gift tax returns filed for year 2006 and after are to be filed with the Department of the Treasury, Internal Revenue Service Center, Cincinnati, OH 45999.[10]

¶ 2057   Description of Property

All property that is required to be listed on the return must be described in such a manner that it may be readily identified.[11]

> *Comment:* Thus, for example, pertinent information with respect to real estate would include a legal description, along with the street number, name and area (if the property is located in a city), and a short statement of any improvements made to the property.

¶ 2058   Supplemental Documents

A donor must provide information to support the value attributable to the gifts being made. For stock of closely held corporations or inactive stock, balance sheets of the corporation should be attached (particularly the most recent one), as should statements of net earning or operating results and dividends paid for each of the five preceding years. For every policy of life insurance listed on the return, the donor must obtain a statement by the insurance company that issued it on Form 712 (Life Insurance Statement) (Rev. April 2006). This form must then be filed with the return. If a gift was made by means of a trust, a certified or verified copy of the trust instrument must be submitted and the trust's identify-

---

[6] Code Sec. 529(c)(2)(B).
[7] Instructions for Form 709 (2013), p. 1.
[8] Reg. § 25.6019-1(e).

[9] Reg. § 25.6019-1(g).
[10] Instructions for Form 709 (2013), p. 4.
[11] Reg. § 25.6019-4.

ing number must be entered on Schedule A (Computation of Taxable Gifts) of Form 709 (United States Gift (and Generation-Skipping Transfer) Tax Return). Other special documents may also be required to substantiate the value shown for the property listed on the return[12] (see ¶ 2120).

¶ 2065 Signatures and Declarations

By signing the return at the bottom of page 1 of Form 709 (United States Gift (and Generation-Skipping Transfer) Tax Return), the donor is deemed to make the declaration under penalty of perjury that the donor has examined the return (including all accompanying schedules and statements), and to the best or his or her knowledge and belief, the return is correct and complete. A paid preparer must sign on the space provided (below the donor's signature). The preparer's declaration applies to all information of which the preparer has any knowledge. A checkbox allows the donor to indicate that the IRS is authorized to discuss certain basic information concerning the return with the preparer. This authorization gives the preparer the donor's permission to: give the IRS any information that is missing from the return; call the IRS for information about the processing of the return or the status of return payments; receive copies of notices or transcripts related to the return, upon request; and respond to certain IRS notices about math errors, offsets, and return preparation. The checkbox does not authorize the preparer to receive a refund check, to bind the donor to anything (including any additional tax liability), or to represent the donor before the IRS.

New regulations require tax return preparers to obtain preparer tax identification numbers (PTINs) and furnish such numbers on all returns or refund claims filed after December 31, 2010 (see ¶ 70).

¶ 2080 Penalties

Interest and penalties similar to those applicable to the estate tax apply to the failure to file a gift tax return and pay the tax when due (see ¶ 1680). Accordingly, there are penalties for late filing of the gift tax return,[13] and the late payment of any tax due.[14] There are also accuracy-related penalties that may apply to that portion of any underpayment attributable to negligence or disregard of rules and regulations.[15] Penalties may also be applicable where there is a substantial understatement of the value of any property shown on a gift tax return.[16] A fraud penalty may be imposed on any portion of any underpayment that is attributable to fraud. Interest must be paid on any amount of tax that is unpaid when the return is due even if the time for filing the return has been extended. Also, effective for gift tax returns prepared after May 25, 2007, a penalty may be imposed against return preparers in certain circumstances (see ¶ 1680).

In addition to the civil penalties noted above, criminal penalties may apply.

The willful failure to pay any tax, make any return, or to keep any records or supply any information that is required under the gift tax laws or regulations constitutes a misdemeanor and may subject the donor to additional penalties.

Any person who willfully attempts in any manner to evade or defeat any gift tax is guilty of a felony. On conviction, such person may be fined not more

---

[12] Reg. § 25.6019-3 and Reg. § 25.6019-4.
[13] Code Sec. 6651(a)(1).
[14] Code Sec. 6651(a)(2).

[15] Code Sec. 6662.
[16] Code Sec. 6662(g); Reg. § 1.6662-7.

than $100,000, or imprisoned for not more than five years, or both, and may be required to pay the costs of prosecution. Other penalties may also apply.[17]

Any person who willfully aids or assists in the preparation or presentation of a false or fraudulent notice or return, or procures, counsels, or advises the preparation or presentation of such notice or return (whether such falsity or fraud is with or without the knowledge or consent of the person required to make the notice or return) is guilty of a felony.

---

[17] Code Sec. 7201.

Chapter 33
VALUATION

¶ 2100   Gift Date Controls

Like the estate tax, the gift tax is levied on the value of the property transferred by gift. There are, however, no alternate valuation dates. The value is determined as of the date of the gift. In doing so, all relevant facts and elements of value as of the time of gift are to be considered,[1] but post-gift events are not relevant.[2] Recently, a Tax Court decision was overturned by the Court of Appeals for the Fifth Circuit, which concluded that the lower court had impermissibly relied on events that occurred two months after the date of a gift to set its taxable value.[3]

¶ 2105   Method of Valuation

Generally, the method of determining value for gift tax purposes is the same as that employed for estate tax purposes. Consequently, the paragraphs cited below, which explain the methods of valuation for estate tax purposes, are pertinent:

Real estate (¶ 270)
Stocks and bonds (¶ 318)
Mortgages and notes (¶ 355)
Interests in business (¶ 527)
Annuities, life estates, remainders, and reversions (¶ 530)
Household and personal effects (¶ 535)
Other property (¶ 535)
Cash (¶ 365)

Certain types of property interests, however, must be specifically valued for gift tax purposes. Other types of property are frequently subject to problems in valuation for gift tax purposes and, thus, are discussed specifically from a gift tax standpoint. These include transfers conditioned on survivorship, tenancies by the entirety, and life insurance and annuity contracts. In addition, Code Sec. 2701 through Code Sec. 2704 provide special valuation rules with respect to gifts involving certain intrafamily transfers of corporate, partnership, and trust interests (see ¶ 2500 and following).

---

[1] Reg. § 25.2512-1.
[2] See *Ithaca Trust Co.*, SCt, 1 USTC ¶ 386, 49 SCt 291; *McMorris Est.*, CA-10, 2001-1 USTC ¶ 60,396, 243 F3d 1254; *A. Smith Est.*, CA-5, 2000-1 USTC ¶ 60,366.

[3] *C. McCord, Jr.*, CA-5, 2006-2 USTC ¶ 60,530, 461 F3d 614, rev'g TC, 120 TC 358, Dec. 55,149 (Reviewed by Court).

The IRS will not issue advance rulings or determination letters with respect to actuarial factors for valuing prospective or hypothetical gifts of a donor.[4]

¶ 2106   Transfers Conditioned on Survivorship

Occasionally, a donor makes a gift of property in trust and retains no power over the trust corpus, but may, under certain contingencies, regain the corpus by surviving the various beneficiaries. An amount less than the entire value of the property transferred is taxable. The value of the gift is reduced by the present value of the donor's right to regain the corpus in the event all of the contingencies should occur, or fail to occur, as the case may be.[5] The value of such rights is determined in accordance with the applicable actuarial tables (see ¶ 530).

¶ 2107   Joint Tenancies Between Spouses

For estate tax purposes, a spouse's interest in any property owned in joint tenancy with right of survivorship is a qualified joint interest (see ¶ 502). Due to the unlimited gift tax marital deduction available for gifts made after 1981 (see ¶ 2311), the creation of a joint tenancy between spouses after 1981 is not a taxable gift.

• *Pre-1982 Tenancies in Real Property*

For tenancies created before 1982, a donor spouse may or may not have elected to treat the creation of a tenancy by the entirety in real property between the spouses as a gift. If the donor spouse elected not to treat the creation as a gift, the transaction was treated as a gift only in the event the tenancy was terminated other than by the death of one of the tenants. If the tenancy was terminated by death, its value was involved only in determining estate tax liability.[6] The above election applied only to real property and not to personal property. This election created, for joint interests created after 1976 and before 1982, a "qualified joint interest" for estate tax purposes, and such property was treated as belonging one-half to each spouse for estate tax purposes.

If the donor spouse elected not to treat the creation of a tenancy by the entirety as a gift, and the property was subsequently sold during the lives of both spouses, or if the tenancy was otherwise terminated during their joint lives, a gift was deemed to occur at the time of termination, as long as this event occurred before 1982. The termination resulted in a gift to the extent that the proportion of the total consideration furnished by the donor spouse multiplied by the value of the proceeds of termination exceeded the value of that part of the proceeds of termination received by him or her. However, the IRS has ruled that, due to the repeal of the rules governing the creation of joint tenancies in real property by spouses, a post-1981 termination of a tenancy by the entirety created before 1982 did not result in a gift to the spouse who had not contributed any of the consideration for the property, where the spouse who had purchased the property had not elected to treat the creation of the tenancy as a gift.[7] (See, also, ¶ 502 for decedent's treatment of pre-1977 spousal joint interests.)

• *Pre-1982 Tenancies in Personal Property*

In the case of personal property, creation of the joint interest before 1982 had to be a complete gift for gift tax purposes in order to be a "qualified joint

---

[4] Rev. Proc. 2012-3, IRB 2012-1, 113.
[5] Reg. § 25.2511-1(e).

[6] Code Sec. 2515, prior to repeal by P.L. 97-34.
[7] Rev. Rul. 83-178, 1983-2 CB 171.

interest." Joint bank accounts did not qualify because either co-owner could withdraw the entire amount. Therefore, the gift was incomplete.

The creation of a joint tenancy in personal property constituted a gift to the extent that a spouse's contribution exceeded his or her retained interest in the property.[8] Thus, in determining the amount of a gift where a joint tenancy in personal property was created after 1976 and before 1982, the retained interest of each spouse was considered to be one-half of the value of the personal property.

¶ 2108   Joint Tenancies Between Nonspouses

The creation by one person of a joint tenancy between that person and another in certain property that the first person owned, or for which he or she provided the entire consideration, normally constitutes a gift of one-half of the value of the transferred property.[9] In instances where each party provides part of the property or consideration, the gift is equal to one-half of the value of the difference between the contributions (see ¶ 2162).

¶ 2109   Life Insurance Contracts

The value of a gift of life insurance is deemed to be equal to the cost of replacing the policy on the date of the gift. This cost may be obtained from the insurer.[10]

Sometimes, however, valuation through the sale value of a comparable contract is not readily ascertainable when the gift is of a policy that has been in force for some time and on which further premium payments are to be made. In these instances, the value may be approximated. The approximation is made by adding to the interpolated terminal reserve at the date of the gift the proportionate part of the last premium paid before the gift that covers the period extending beyond that date.

> *Comment:* In cases where, because of the peculiar nature of the contract, approximation by this method is not close enough to the full value, some other method must be used. In no instance, however, may either the cash surrender or the loan value be used. The value should never be based on the face value of the policy except, perhaps, in the case of certain endowment policies.

> **Split-dollar policies.** Where a donor makes a lifetime gift of a split-dollar life insurance policy (see ¶ 472), the value of the gift is the interpolated terminable reserve value (a figure obtainable from the insurance company that issued the policy), plus the proportionate part of the gross premium paid before the date of the gift, reduced by the amount of any funds provided by the employer.[11]

The IRS has issued an explanation of the standards it will use in valuing current life insurance protection under what it has termed abusive split-dollar arrangements. More specifically, the IRS is targeting arrangements where a party pays inappropriately high current term insurance premiums, prepays premiums, or uses other techniques in order to understate the value of the taxable policy benefits.[12] Under such a scenario, it appears that the IRS intends to disregard policy arrangements that use two different insurance rates (one for the amount of

---

[8] Code Sec. 2515A(a), prior to repeal by P.L. 97-34.

[9] Reg. § 25.2511-1(h)(5).

[10] Reg. § 25.2511-1(h)(8) and Reg. § 25.2512-6(a).

[11] Rev. Rul. 81-198, 1981-2 CB 188.

[12] Notice 2002-59, 2002-2 CB 481.

coverage, and another one for purposes of the gift tax).[13] Under IRS Notice 2002-59, a party participating in a split-dollar life insurance arrangement may use the premium rates in Table 2001 (see Notice 2002-8), or the insurer's lower published premium rates only for the purposes of valuing current life insurance protection and when such protection confers an economic benefit by one party on another party, disregarding the premiums actually paid by this other party. However, if one party has any right to current life insurance protection under the split-dollar arrangement, neither the premium rates in Table 2001 nor the insurer's lower published rates may be used to value such party's current life insurance protection for purposes of determining the value of any policy benefits to which another party may be entitled.

Amendments to the regulations under Code Sec. 61 and Code Sec. 7872 govern the income and gift taxation of split-dollar life insurance arrangements.

The regulations provide two mutually exclusive methods for taxing split-dollar life insurance arrangements: an "economic benefit" regime[14] (generally applicable to endorsement arrangements), and a "loan" regime[15] (generally applicable to collateral assignments). Under a split-dollar endorsement arrangement, one party owns the policy and endorses an interest in it to another. The first party pays the premiums, but the second party makes reimbursements for his or her share of the costs. With a collateral assignment arrangement, a donee (such as a life insurance trust) owns a life insurance policy, and pays all the premiums. The donor makes advances—which in effect are no-interest loans—to the trust in the amount of the yearly increases in the cash value. At the termination of the policy or the death of the donor, the donor is entitled to the policy's cash value.

The regulations generally provide substantially different tax consequences to the parties depending on which person owns the policy. In most cases, the person named as the policy owner is treated as the owner of the contract. However, a donor is treated as the owner of a contract under a split-dollar arrangement entered into between a donor and a donee (such as a life insurance trust) if the only economic benefit available to the donee is the value of the current life insurance protection. (This is known as a "non-equity" split-dollar arrangement.)

Under the regulations, if an irrevocable insurance trust is the owner of the life insurance contract underlying the split-dollar arrangement and there is a reasonable expectation that the donor (or the donor's estate) will recover an amount equal to the premium payments, the donor's premium payments will be treated as loans made to the trust. In such a case, the value of the gift would be the amount of the premium payment less the present value of the donor's right to receive repayment. A different set of rules apply under the regulations if the donor is treated as the owner of the contract and the donor is entitled to recover premium payments from the contract proceeds.

The regulations are effective for split-dollar arrangements entered into after September 17, 2003. In addition, the regulations apply to any split-dollar life insurance arrangement entered into on or before September 17, 2003, if the arrangement is materially modified after September 17, 2003.[16]

Comment: Notwithstanding who is treated as the owner of the life insurance contract for purposes of the regulations, the gift tax consequences

[13] Notice 2002-8, 2002-1 CB 398.
[14] Reg. § 1.61-22, amended by T.D. 9092.
[15] Reg. § 1.7872-15, amended by T.D. 9092.
[16] Reg. § 1.61-22, amended by T.D. 9092.

of a transfer of an interest in the contract to a third party continue to be determined by established gift tax principles.

¶ 2110 Annuity Contracts

The value of a gift of an annuity for the primary benefit of a donee is the cost of the contract, if the annuity is purchased at the time of the gift.[17] If the annuity benefits are not to commence until the death of the donor, who is the primary annuitant, and if the donor has actually made a taxable gift of such secondary benefits, the value of the gift is the difference between the value of the donor's interest at the time of the gift and the value of the entire contract or trust in which the interest is created.

If the gift is of an interest in an annuity contract that has been in force for some time, the value must be based on the cost of an annuity contract purchased at the time of the gift with the same provision for payment in the future.

Annuities not involving any formal contract with an insurance company are valued in the same manner as for estate tax purposes (see ¶ 530).

¶ 2112 Stock Options

The IRS has provided a safe-harbor methodology for the estate or gift tax valuation of certain stock options.[18] This revenue procedure applies only to the transfer tax valuation of nonpublicly traded compensatory stock options (that is, stock options that are granted in connection with the performance of services, including stock options that are subject to the provisions of Code Sec. 421), on stock that, as of the valuation date, is publicly traded on an established securities market. The options to which this revenue procedure applies are referred to as "compensatory stock options."

The procedure allows for use of an option pricing model that takes into account specific factors that are similar to those established by the Financial Accounting Standards Board in "Accounting for Stock-Based Compensation," Statement of Financial Accounting Standards No. 123 (Financial Accounting Standards Board 1995) (SFAS 123). Under SFAS 123, the fair value of a stock option granted by a public entity is estimated using an option pricing model (for example, the Black-Scholes model or a binomial model) that takes into account as of the option grant date (1) the exercise price of the option, (2) the expected life of the option, (3) the current price of the underlying stock, (4) the expected volatility of the underlying stock, (5) the expected dividends on the underlying stock, and (6) the risk-free interest rate for the expected term of the option.

¶ 2115 Transfers for Consideration

The gift tax not only applies to transfers without consideration, but it also applies to sales and exchanges for less than adequate and full consideration in money or money's worth.[19] In the case of a transfer of property for less than adequate and full consideration in money or money's worth, the amount by which the value of the property exceeds the value of the consideration is a gift. Consideration that is not reducible to a money value, such as love and affection or a promise of marriage, is disregarded.

---

[17] Reg. § 25.2512-6(a).
[18] Rev. Proc. 98-34, 1998-1 CB 983.

[19] Code Sec. 2512(b).

A bona fide sale, exchange, or other transfer of property in the ordinary course of business and free from any donative intent is considered to have been made for adequate and full consideration in money or money's worth.

The initial step in the creation of a family limited partnership (FLP) transaction typically includes a transfer of property to the newly created FLP, in exchange for partnership interests in the FLP. The IRS may challenge the setup of the FLP by assessing gift tax on the transfers on a determination that the FLP interests received did not constitute full and adequate consideration for the property transferred to the FLP (see ¶ 2545).

¶ 2116   Transfers in Settlement of Marital Rights

If a husband and wife enter into a written agreement concerning their marital and property rights, transfers made pursuant to such an agreement may, under certain circumstances, be deemed to have been made for full and adequate consideration in money or money's worth. Transfers made on or before July 18, 1984, qualify under this rule if the parties obtained a final decree of divorce from each other within two years after entering into the settlement agreement.[20] For transfers occurring after July 18, 1984, the exemption will apply if divorce occurs within the three-year period beginning one year before the property settlement is entered into.[21] Thus, the divorce may precede the settlement agreement by as much as one year under this rule.

It is not necessary that the agreement be approved by the divorce decree. It is necessary, however, that the transfers made be in settlement of the transferee spouse's marital or property rights, or that the transfers be made to provide a reasonable allowance for the support of minor children of the marriage.

¶ 2117   Payment of Gift Tax by Donee

Although a donor is primarily liable for the gift tax, many donors transfer property with the understanding that the donee will pay the tax or that the tax will be paid from the transferred property. Gifts of this type are commonly called "net gifts." The gift tax paid by the donee may be deducted from the value of the transferred property, to compute the donor's gift tax, where it is expressly shown or implied that the payment of the tax by the donee or from the property itself is a condition of the transfer.[22] However, the value of the gift is not reduced by the amount of the donor's available unified credit that is applied to the tentative gift tax liability.[23] Any state gift tax paid by the donee pursuant to such a condition may also be deducted from the value of the gift for federal gift tax purposes to the extent that the donor would have been liable for payment of the state gift tax.[24] Special formulas must be used to compute the donor's gift tax liability, and the donor's, rather than the donee's, unified credit must be applied.[25]

The U.S. Supreme Court has held that, to the extent that the gift tax paid by the donee in a net gift situation exceeds the donor's basis in the transferred property, the donor recognizes gain on the transaction for income tax purposes.[26] Prior to that decision, several courts had ruled that the transfer of property

[20] Code Sec. 2516, prior to amendment by P.L. 98-369.
[21] Code Sec. 2516, as amended by P.L. 98-369.
[22] Rev. Rul. 75-72, 1975-1 CB 310.
[23] Rev. Rul. 81-223, 1981-2 CB 189.
[24] Rev. Rul. 80-111, 1980-1 CB 208.
[25] IRS Letter Ruling 8035004 (Nov. 16, 1979).
[26] V.P. Diedrich, SCt, 82-1 USTC ¶ 9419, 457 US 191.

subject to the donee's paying any gift taxes did not result in any gain being realized by the donor.[27]

An agreement between a decedent and his children, whereby the children assumed the liability for any additional gift tax in the event that the value of stock transferred to the decedent's heirs exceeded the value reported on the decedent's gift tax return, had no effect for gift tax valuation purposes, a U.S. District Court in Virginia has held.[28] The potential gift tax liability assumed by the children was entirely speculative at the time of the transfers and was not subject to any reasonable calculable estimation. To the contrary, where the Court of Appeals for the Fifth Circuit held that it was proper for the value of gifted property interests to be actuarially reduced to account for the donees' contingent obligation to pay additional estate tax that would be due under Code Sec. 2035 if either of the donors died within three years of making the gift.[29]

The IRS ruled, in a Technical Advice Memorandum,[30] that a net gift occurred where a surviving spouse made a nonqualified disclaimer of her interest in a qualified terminable interest property trust. Upon making the disclaimer, a taxable gift to the trust remaindermen occurred pursuant to Code Sec. 2519. Moreover, because the trust was includible in the surviving spouse's estate under Code Sec. 2044 (see ¶773), Code Sec. 2207A(b) statutorily shifted the burden for paying the gift tax to the remaindermen. Nonetheless, the surviving spouse remained liable for the gift tax. Thus, a net gift occurred on payment of the gift tax by the remaindermen.

¶2120   Supplemental Documents Required

Any documents required for an adequate explanation of the value or the basis of valuation of each gift should be filed with the return. Otherwise, full information as to the basis of valuation used should be set out in Schedule A (Computation of Taxable Gifts) of Form 709 (United States Gift (and Generation-Skipping Transfer) Tax Return).

• Closely Held Stock

Stock of a closely held corporation and stock not listed on an exchange or actively traded should be valued in accordance with estate tax principles (see ¶326). Various supplemental documents are required to be filed in connection with valuation of such stock. The donor must submit (1) balance sheets of the corporation, particularly the most recent one, (2) profit and loss statements for each of the five years preceding the date of the gift, and (3) statements of dividends paid during the same five-year period.

• Life Insurance

For every life insurance policy listed on the return, the donor must file Form 712 (Life Insurance Statement) (Rev. April 2006) with the return.

---

[27] See, for example, *R.H. Turner*, CA-6, 69-1 USTC ¶9416, 410 F2d 752 (Nonacq.).

[28] *F. Armstrong, Jr. Trust*, CA-4, 2002-1 USTC ¶60,427, 277 F3d 490, aff'g DC Va., 2001-1 USTC ¶60,392.

[29] *C. McCord, Jr.*, CA-5, 2006-2 USTC ¶60,530, 461 F3d 614, rev'g TC, 120 TC 358,

CCH Dec. 55,149 (Reviewed by the Court). Similarly, *J. Steinburg*, 141 TC --, No. 8, CCH Dec. 59,654 (Reviewed by Court).

[30] IRS Technical Advice Memorandum 9736001 (May 21, 1997). See also IRS Technical Advice Memorandum 200116006 (Dec. 14, 2000) and IRS Technical Advice Memorandum 200122036 (Mar. 1, 2001).

• *Real Estate*

A copy of the appraisal, if available, should be submitted with the return where the gift consists of real estate.

• *Transfers in Trust*

If the gift was made by means of a trust, a certified or verified copy of the trust instrument must be submitted and the trust's identifying number must be entered on Schedule A of Form 709.

• *Valuation Discounts*

If the value of any gift reflects a discount for lack of marketability, minority interest, fractional interest in real estate, blockage, market absorption, or any other reason, Checkbox A of Schedule A, Form 709, should be marked "Yes", and an explanation of the discount must be attached to the Schedule A.[31]

The U.S. Court of Appeals for the Eighth Circuit[32] and the Tax Court[33] have held that in determining the fair market value of closely held stock for gift tax purposes, a donor was entitled to discount the net asset value of the stock to reflect the built-in capital gains the corporation would incur if it were to liquidate, distribute, or sell appreciated corporate assets. After the 1986 legislative abrogation of the *General Utilities* doctrine,[34] which allowed a corporation to liquidate and distribute appreciated or depreciated property to shareholders without recognizing built-in gain or loss, a hypothetical willing buyer would take some account of the tax consequences of contingent built-in gains on the sale of an appreciated asset owned by the corporation in valuing the corporate stock. The adjustment for potential capital gains tax liabilities was appropriate, even if no liquidation or sale of the corporation or its assets was planned at the time of the gift of the stock.

¶ 2125　　IRS Statement Explaining Gift Valuation

Upon written request by a donor, the IRS is required to furnish a written statement explaining any determination or proposed determination of the value of gift property.[35] The IRS valuation statement must be furnished within 45 days after the request or the date of determination or proposed determination of value. The method and computation used in arriving at the valuation is not binding on the IRS. A request for such a statement must be filed no later than the deadline for filing a claim for refund of the tax with regard to which the valuation was made.[36]

A taxpayer may also request a statement of value for art objects from the IRS.[37] The taxpayer may rely on the valuation of the art objects when filing an income, estate or gift tax return. Statements of value will be given for art objects that have been appraised at $50,000 or more. The IRS will issue a statement of value for items appraised at less than $50,000 if at least one item of the items submitted is appraised at $50,000 or more.

---

[31] Instructions for Form 709 (2013), p. 6.

[32] *I. Eisenberg*, CA-2, 98-2 USTC ¶ 60,322, 155 F3d 50, Acq., IRB 1999-4, 4, vac'g and rem'g 74 TCM 1046, CCH Dec. 52,321(M), TC Memo. 1997-483.

[33] *A. Davis Est.*, 110 TC 530, CCH Dec. 52,764.

[34] P.L. 99-515, Act Secs. 631–633.

[35] Code Sec. 7517.

[36] Reg. § 301.7517-1(a).

[37] Rev. Proc. 96-15, 1996-1 CB 627, as modified by Announcement 2001-22, 2001-1 CB 895.

¶ 2130   Declaratory Judgments Contesting IRS Gift Valuations

Taxpayers are allowed under Code Sec. 7477 to seek a declaratory judgment in the Tax Court contesting an IRS determination regarding the value of a gift. Final regulations[38] provide the provide the procedure for donors to contest the value of a gift when the IRS's proposed adjustment does not result in a gift tax deficiency or refund, which occurs in cases where the increased valuation of a gift is offset by a donor's applicable Code Sec. 2505(a) gift tax credit. Code Sec. 7477 requires that the donors first exhaust all administrative remedies available before petitioning the Tax Court. The IRS will not contest the donor's allegation that the administrative remedies have been exhausted if the donor timely requests an Appeals conference and participates fully in the process. The final regulations clarify that full participation necessitates the donor to timely produce all requested information and disclose all facts relevant to the disputed valuation. Furthermore, if the IRS Appeals office denies a taxpayer's request for a conference, all administrative remedies will be deemed to be exhausted, so long as the donor fully participates fully in any Appeals office consideration offered by the IRS after the donor has petitioned the Tax Court. These regulations apply to civil proceedings described in Code Sec. 7477 filed in the Tax Court after September 8, 2009.

---

[38] Reg. § 301.7477-1 and Reg. § 301.7477-2;
T.D. 9460, September 8, 2009.

Chapter 34

TAXABLE GIFTS

¶ 2150 Imposition of Tax

The gift tax is an excise tax that is imposed on lifetime transfers of property for less than full and adequate consideration in money or money's worth.[1]

The tax applies "whether the transfer is in trust or otherwise, whether the gift is direct or indirect, and whether the property is real or personal, tangible or intangible; but, in the case of a nonresident not a citizen of the United States, shall apply to a transfer only if the property is situated within the United States."[2]

Gifts by U.S. citizens who are residents of U.S. possessions and who acquired their U.S. citizenship completely independent of their connections with the possessions are treated in the same manner as gifts made by resident citizens of the United States.[3] Gifts made by other citizen-residents of U.S. possessions are treated as gifts made by nonresidents not citizens of the United States.

¶ 2155 Elements of a Gift

By property law definition, a gift is a voluntary *inter vivos* transfer (in any form or manner) of property (of any kind or nature) by one person to another without consideration or compensation therefor. It is a gratuity that requires the fulfillment of three essential elements: (1) intent on the part of the donor to make a gift; (2) delivery by the donor of the subject matter of the gift; and (3) acceptance of the gift by the donee.

The presence of these elements in connection with any given transaction is determined in light of property law requirements rather than by the application of gift tax requirements. If a transfer is a gift within the meaning of property law, it is a gift for gift tax purposes as well, unless it is specifically excluded.

Comment: The property law definition of a gift is somewhat extended for gift tax purposes. Even transfers which, under contract law, constitute transfers in fulfillment of a contractual obligation rather than gifts may be

---

[1] Code Sec. 2501; Reg. § 25.2512-8.
[2] Code Sec. 2511(a).
[3] Reg. § 25.2501-1(c).

treated as gifts, at least in part, for gift tax purposes. They are deemed to be gifts to the extent that the value of the property transferred exceeds the value of the consideration received. The value used in determining the adequacy of the consideration is monetary value. Exceptions are made, however, for arm's-length business transactions and certain settlements in connection with divorces.

Although Congress dispensed with the requirement of donative intent, the courts have required that the transfer be donative in nature. In fact, except for the matter of inadequacy of consideration, the courts have generally required the property law elements of a gift to be present before a transfer may be taxed as a gift.[4] Thus, if there has been no delivery, there is no taxable gift.[5] This is so, even though the taxpayer may have announced an intention to make a gift. Similarly, if the taxpayer is incompetent and, therefore, incapable of understanding the nature of the transaction or of possessing the intention to make a gift, a transfer by him does not constitute a taxable gift. Nor is there a taxable gift of corpus until the donor relinquishes dominion and control.

¶ 2160 Specific Types of Transfers

Most types of transfers clearly fall into gift or nongift categories. In addition to direct deliveries of specific property to a donee, gifts (in the absence of consideration) include:[6]

(1) the irrevocable transfer of property pursuant to a declaration of trust;

(2) the forgiveness of a debt;

(3) the assignment of a judgment;

(4) the assignment of benefits under an insurance contract or the transfer of ownership of a policy of insurance;

(5) the payment of insurance premiums on policies owned by others and in which the donor has no interest as a beneficiary; and

(6) the purchase of an annuity contract for the benefit of another, where no control over such annuity is retained by the donor. This may extend also to secondary rights in an annuity contract under which the donor is primary beneficiary.

• *Gifts to Political Organizations*

Transfers of money or other property to a qualified political organization are not subject to the gift tax.[7] A "qualified political organization" is a party, committee, association, fund, or other organization (whether or not incorporated) that is organized and operated primarily for the purpose of directly or indirectly accepting contributions or making expenditures, or both, in order to influence or to attempt to influence the selection, nomination, election, or appointment of any individual to any public office or to any office in a political organization.[8]

• *Disclaimers*

A person who is a beneficiary, heir, or next-of-kin may refuse to accept ownership of property that would otherwise pass to him or her without being

---

[4] See, e.g., *W.H. Wemyss*, SCt, 45-1 USTC ¶ 10,179, 324 US 303.

[5] Reg. § 25.2511-2.

[6] Reg. § 25.2511-1(a).

[7] Code Sec. 2501(a)(5).

[8] Code Sec. 527(e).

subject to the gift tax. However, the refusal to accept the property must be made in the form of a "qualified disclaimer" (see ¶2009).[9]

• *Interspousal Transfers*

The payment of income taxes due on a joint income tax return by one spouse is not a taxable gift. The same rule applies to the payment of gift taxes in the case of a husband and wife who have elected the gift-splitting provisions of Code Sec. 2513 (see ¶2200).

• *Transfers Subject to Adjustment*

The IRS and the courts have disregarded adjustment clauses included in instruments of transfer that were designed to prevent the imposition of gift tax on an IRS determination that gift taxes were due.

The U.S. Court of Appeals for the Fourth Circuit has held that a trust provision nullifying a transfer that would otherwise be subject to gift tax was void as against public policy.[10] A settlor provided in a trust instrument that if any portion of the transfer in trust were subject to gift tax as determined by "final judgment or order of a competent federal court of last resort" then the property subject to the tax was not to be included in the transfer and remained the property of the settlor. The court stated that the gift tax may not be avoided in such a manner and that the condition subsequent was contrary to public policy.

Similarly, the IRS has ruled that the value of a gift of real estate was to be determined without regard to an adjustment clause in the transfer deed that provided for a recharacterization of the transfer depending on the IRS's valuation of the transferred property.[11] The IRS disregarded both an adjustment clause reconveying to the donor a fractional share of real property sufficient to reduce its value to the amount of the gift tax exclusion and one providing that the donee would transfer to the donor consideration equal to the excess of the property's value over the amount of the annual gift tax exclusion.

The IRS noted that such provisions operated to defeat what would otherwise be a gift and, thus, interfered with its enforcement of the gift tax regulations. In both cases, the IRS reasoned that the purpose of the adjustment clause was not to preserve or implement the original, bona fide intent of the parties, but, rather, to recharacterize the nature of the transaction in the event of a future adjustment to the donor's gift tax return by the IRS. Therefore, the value of the gifts was determined without regard to the adjustment clauses.

• *Indirect Transfers*

The gift tax also applies to gifts made indirectly.[12] Any transaction in which an interest is passed to another person, regardless of the means employed, is subject to the gift tax. To avoid gift tax complications, shareholders of a closely held corporation should try to ensure that sales of corporate property to family trusts are at the property's fair market value. If property is sold at a bargain price to the trust, the shareholders risk incurring both income and gift tax liability. The difference between the fair market value of the property and the sale price is taxable to the shareholders as dividends, and they are also deemed to have made a taxable gift to the trust in the amount of the dividend. For example, in *J. C.*

---

[9] Code Sec. 2518.

[10] *F.W. Procter*, CA-4, 44-1 USTC ¶10,110, 142 F2d 824, reh'g denied, CA-4, 44-1 USTC ¶10,123, 142 F2d 828, cert. denied, 323 US 756.

[11] Rev. Rul. 86-41, 1986-1 CB 300.

[12] Reg. §25.2511-1(c)(1).

Shepherd,[13] a transfer to a family partnership was an indirect gift of undivided interests in land, while in *M. Senda*,[14] transfers of stock to family limited partnerships were indirect gifts of stock to a couple's children.

Citing current case law for support (see *J. C. Shepherd* and *M. Senda*, noted above), the IRS has taken the position that transfers of assets to a family limited partnership (FLP) after transfers of limited partnership interests were made to family members are indirect gifts subject to the gift tax (*Appeals Settlement Guidelines: Family Limited Partnerships and Family Limited Liability Corporations*, effective October 20, 2006. This guideline is available at www.irs.gov on the "Appeals Coordinated Issues (ACI)" page.)

Distinguishing its holding based on a different factual situation from those in *J.C. Shepherd* and *M. Senda*, the Tax Court in *T. Holman*,[15] declined to treat transfers of limited partnership (LP) units by a husband and wife to a trust and custodial account as indirect gifts. The Tax Court noted that in *Holman*, the taxpayers did not transfer the shares to the trust and custodial account before making the contributions to the LP. Moreover, the Tax court dismissed application of the step transaction doctrine because the taxpayers bore a real economic risk of a change of value of the LP for the time period between contribution of the assets to the LP and the later gifts of the LP units.

¶ 2161   Below-Market Interest Loans

The U.S. Supreme Court has held that an interest-free demand loan between family members constitutes a taxable gift because such loans represent the transfer of a property right consisting of the use of money.[16] The Court did not, however, address the question of how to value the gift, nor did it determine the income tax consequences, if any, arising from such a transfer. In 1985, Congress established a set of rules under which both income and gift tax liability may be imposed on loans that are either interest free or payable at a rate lower than the applicable federal interest rate established by statute.[17] This type of loan is known as a below-market interest loan.

Any transfer of money that provides the transferor with a right to repayment either on demand or over a period of time may be subject to the rules of Code Sec. 7872. A demand loan is considered to be a below-market interest loan and, thus, is subject to Code Sec. 7872 rules if the interest payable on it is at a rate less than the applicable federal interest rate. A term loan is considered to be below market if the amount loaned exceeds the present value of all payments due under the loan. Although Code Sec. 7872 enumerates five types of demand or term loans that come within its purview, the discussion here will be limited to the rules applicable to gift loans, i.e., those in which the lender's forgoing of interest is in the nature of a gift to the borrower.[18]

> *Comment:* Generally, interest-free and below-market interest loans are recharacterized as arm's-length transactions in which the lender is deemed to have made the loan to the borrower at a statutory interest rate and the borrower is deemed to have paid the interest to the lender. These transactions can have both income and gift tax consequences. Thus, in the gift loan

---

[13] 155 TC 376, CCH Dec. 54,098, aff'd CA-11, 2002-1 USTC ¶ 60,431, 283 F3d 1258.

[14] 88 TCM 8, CCH Dec. 55,685(M), TC Memo. 2004-160, aff'd CA-8, 2006-1 USTC ¶ 60,515, 433 F3d 1044.

[15] 130 TC 170, CCH Dec. 57,455; aff'd, CA-8, 2010 ustc ¶ 60,592, 601 F3d 763.

[16] *E.C. Dickman*, SCt, 84-1 USTC ¶ 13,560, 465 US 330, 104 SCt 1086.

[17] Code Sec. 7872.

[18] Code Sec. 7872(f)(3).

situation, the deemed interest is includible in the lender's income, may be deductible by the borrower if it would constitute home mortgage interest and the borrower itemizes nonbusiness deductions, and may be characterized as a gift to the borrower.

• Applicable Federal Rates

To determine whether a loan is a below-market interest loan subject to the rules of Code Sec. 7872, it is first necessary to compare the interest rate stated in the loan with a rate published by the IRS called "the applicable federal rate." The applicable federal rate is as follows:[19]

Term of loan	Applicable federal interest rate
Three years or less	Federal short-term rate
More than three but no more than nine years .	Federal mid-term rate
More than nine years	Federal long-term rate

Because a demand loan is treated as a series of one-day term loans, the applicable federal rate is the federal short-term rate in effect for the period during which the forgone interest on the loan is being computed.[20]

Through 1985, the IRS determined the applicable federal rates for six-month periods, beginning on January 1 and July 1. Beginning with January 1985, the IRS, acting under its regulatory authority, began issuing alternative applicable federal rates on a monthly basis. The 1985 Imputed Interest Simplification Act (99-121) made the monthly rates the sole factors to be used in imputing interest. The rates are based on the average market yields on outstanding marketable obligations of the United States during the one-month period ending on the 14th day of the preceding month. The applicable federal rate is the lower of the rates for the current or two preceding months.[21]

Once it has been determined that a loan is subject to the below-market interest loan rules, the amount of forgone interest that is treated as a gift must be computed by using the applicable federal rate. In some cases, a simplified rate, called the blended annual rate, applies. This rate is published annually, along with the applicable federal short-term, mid-term and long-term rates for the month of July, and applies in the case of a below-market demand loan of a fixed principal amount that remains outstanding for the entire calendar year. The blended annual rate established for 2013 is 0.22 percent (.0022).[22] Forgone interest on a below-market demand loan of a fixed principal amount that remains outstanding for the entire year of 2013, therefore, is equal to the excess of 0.22 percent of the principal amount over any interest payable on the loan that was properly allocable to 2013.

> *Example:* Harriet Sheldon makes a demand loan in the amount of $5 million to her son, Nick, on January 1, 2013. The interest rate on the loan is 0.15% (.0015). The amount of forgone interest on the loan, as of December 31, 2013, is $3,500 (the excess of $11,000 (0.22% of $5 million) over $7,500 (0.15% of $5 million, the amount of interest payable on December 31, 2013).

•Below-Market Gift Loans

A gift loan is any below-market loan in which the lender's forgoing of interest is in the nature of a gift. Generally, any below-market interest loan that is

---

[19] Code Sec. 1274(d).
[20] Code Sec. 7872(f)(2)(B).

[21] Reg. §1.1274-4.
[22] Rev. Rul. 2013-28, IRB 2013-28, July 8, 2013.

not made in the ordinary course of business (i.e., in a bona fide, arm's-length transaction that is free from donative intent) is considered made for less than full and adequate consideration and is treated as a gift loan. Although most of these loans are made between related parties, the Conference Committee Report to the Tax Reform Act of 1984 (98-369) clearly states that a below-market interest loan between unrelated parties may be considered a gift loan for purposes of Code Sec. 7872.

> *Comment:* A below-market gift loan may generate both income tax and gift tax liability. One set of rules governs the gift taxation of such loans, and another set covers the income tax consequences arising from such transactions. However, there are certain statutory provisions that limit or prevent the imposition of the gift and income tax on these loans, and these exceptions are noted below.

• Gift Tax Liability

The extent of a lender's federal gift tax liability on a below-market interest gift loan is dependent on whether the loan is a demand or a term loan. If a demand loan is involved, the lender is deemed to have made a gift to the borrower on the last day of each year the loan is outstanding.[23] Thus, there may be annual gift tax consequences if the demand loan continues beyond one calendar year. The amount of the gift is calculated on December 31, and is equal to the amount of interest forgone during the year.

With respect to any tax period, forgone interest is defined as an amount equal to the excess of (1) the amount of interest that would have been payable on the loan for the tax period if interest had accrued at the applicable federal rate and was payable annually on the last day of each calendar year, over (2) any interest payable on the loan properly allocable to that period.[24]

In the case of a term loan, the lender is deemed to have made a cash gift to the borrower on the date the loan was made. The amount of cash deemed transferred is equal to the excess of the amount loaned over the present value of all payments that are required to be made under the terms of the loan.[25] The present value of the payments is computed as of the date of the loan by using a discount rate equal to the applicable federal rate in effect on that date, compounded semiannually. Therefore, in this situation, there will be only one taxable gift, because the amount is determined as of the date of the loan.

• Income Tax Liability

For federal income tax purposes, the lender in a below-market gift loan (whether term or demand) is deemed to have transferred any interest forgone to the borrower, and the borrower is then deemed to have retransferred an identical amount as interest to the lender. The transfer and retransfer of any forgone interest attributable to periods during any calendar year are deemed to have taken place on the last day of such calendar year.[26]

• De Minimis Exception

In the case of a gift loan between individuals, no interest will be imputed to either the borrower or the lender for any day on which the aggregate outstanding amount of loans between such individuals does not exceed $10,000.[27] However, if

---

[23] Code Sec. 7872(a)(2).
[24] Code Sec. 7872(e)(2).
[25] Code Sec. 7872(b).

[26] Code Sec. 7872(a).
[27] Code Sec. 7872(c)(2).

the loan balance exceeds $10,000 on any given date, the rules of Code Sec. 7872 will apply to the entire amount of the loan, and not just the amount in excess of $10,000. This *de minimis* exception does not apply where the loan proceeds may be directly attributed to the purchase or carrying of income-producing assets. For purposes of this exception, as well as all other provisions of Code Sec. 7872, a husband and wife are treated as one person.[28]

• *Special Rules for Gift Loans*

If the balance of all outstanding gift loans between individuals exceeds $10,000 but is not more than $100,000, the interest imputed as paid by the borrower will be limited to the borrower's net investment income for the year, provided that the loan's interest arrangement does not have tax avoidance as one of its principal purposes.[29] In determining the borrower's net investment income for purposes of this rule, the borrower is deemed to have no investment income for any year in which his net investment income is $1,000 or less. If the borrower has two or more outstanding gift loans, he must allocate his net investment income among such loans in proportion to the respective amounts that would be treated as retransferred to the lender without regard to the net investment income limitation.

For purposes of this exception, net investment income has the same meaning as that given under Code Sec. 163(d). Thus, the borrower must take into account all investment income from any source after offsetting for investment expenses (except interest) that are attributable to such income. Investment income includes gross income from interest, dividends, rents and royalties, net short-term capital gains from investment property, and amounts recaptured as ordinary income from the sale of investment property. The above rules apply to term loans made, renegotiated, extended, or revised after June 6, 1984, and demand loans outstanding after June 6, 1984.

¶ 2162   Transfers Subject to Special Rules

Special rules apply with respect to certain types of transfers, including the following:[30]

(1) When a donor, with his or her own funds, creates a joint bank account in his or her name and in another's name and grants the other person the right to make withdrawals, each withdrawal by the other person constitutes a gift at the time it is made.

(2) When a joint tenancy with rights of survivorship is created in property, other than a joint bank account, the transaction constitutes a gift if the contributions of the joint tenants are unequal. The amount of the gift is a fractional share or shares of the amount by which the contribution of one joint tenant exceeds the contributions of each of the others. If there are to be two joint tenants, one-half of the excess is treated as a gift. If there are three joint tenants, two-thirds of the excess, or one-third of the excess of each, will be the subject of a gift.

(3) When community funds are used to purchase insurance on the life of one spouse and a third person is revocably named as beneficiary, the death of the insured spouse results in a taxable gift by the surviving spouse of one-half of the proceeds of such insurance.

---

[28] Code Sec. 7872(f)(7).
[29] Code Sec. 7872(d).

[30] Reg. § 25.2511-1(h).

¶ 2163　Powers of Appointment

Transferred property need not belong to the person deemed to be the donor in order for a taxable gift to occur. If the property was transferred by some other person and the taxpayer was given a general power of appointment over the property, a taxable gift occurs if the taxpayer exercises the power (in favor of anyone other than him- or herself) during his or her lifetime. Further, if the general power was created after October 21, 1942, the mere release of the power will constitute a taxable gift.[31]

The meaning of the term "general power of appointment" is the same for gift tax purposes and estate tax purposes. The rules for determining the date of creation of a power are also the same (see ¶ 652).

¶ 2164　Real Estate Jointly Held by Husband and Wife

The creation between husband and wife of a tenancy by the entirety or joint tenancy with right of survivorship in real property is not a taxable gift if the tenancy is created after 1981. However, in the case of a tenancy created before 1982, the donor spouse could have elected to treat the creation of the tenancy as a gift by filing a timely gift tax return for the period during which the tenancy was created.[32] Also see ¶ 502 for special rules involving the transfer tax treatment of joint tenancies created prior to 1977.

¶ 2165　Transfers Incident to Divorce or Separation

Transfers of property or property interests under a written agreement between spouses settling their marital and property rights are considered to be made for adequate and full consideration and are exempt from the gift tax provided divorce occurs within the three-year period beginning one year before the property settlement is entered into.[33] Thus, the divorce may precede the settlement agreement by as much as one year. The condition applies regardless of whether the divorce decree approves the written settlement agreement of the spouses.

> *Comment:* Transfers made under the settlement agreement to provide reasonable allowance for the support of minor children of the marriage will also be exempt from gift tax.

¶ 2166　Life Insurance

Gratuitous transfers of life insurance are generally subject to the same rules as other gifts. An insured who relinquishes rights under an insurance policy in favor of another for less than full and adequate consideration makes a gift. If, however, the insured relinquishes only some rights, there is no gift unless the rights that are retained give the insured no control over the policy or the proceeds thereof.

> *Example:* Betty Williams gratuitously transfers a policy of insurance on her life to her daughter, Barbara. In transferring ownership of the policy, Betty relinquishes all of her rights except the right to change the beneficiary under certain circumstances. There is no gift for gift tax purposes.

---

[31] Code Sec. 2514.　　　　　　　　　　　[33] Code Sec. 2516.
[32] Code Sec. 2515, prior to repeal by P.L. 97-34.

The mere naming of a person as a beneficiary under a policy of insurance on one's life does not, by itself, constitute a gift for gift tax purposes. An irrevocable naming of the beneficiary does not constitute a gift if the insured reserves the right to surrender the policy for cash or to borrow against its cash surrender value. On the other hand, one may make a gift for gift tax purposes without disposing of every "incident of ownership" in the policy, with the result that the proceeds will be included in the insured's gross estate (see ¶430).

A gift of life insurance is complete when the insured disposes of all control over the policy or its reserves.[34] If the insured retains a possibility of reverter, the gift may be complete, even though the value of the possibility exceeds five percent of the value of the policy, which would require the inclusion of the proceeds in the insured's gross estate for estate tax purposes. The value of that possibility of reverter, however, may be excludable from the value of the gift for gift tax purposes.

The payment of premiums on policies of life insurance owned by another constitutes a gift whether the policy is on the life of the donor or on the life of some other person. The value of the gift is the amount of the premiums paid in the calendar year, less any dividends received by the donor as a partial return of premiums. If the premiums are paid on policies under which the donor owns rights, the premiums will not constitute gifts.

Life insurance policies may be given in trust either before or after they are paid for, or at any intermediate stage. If the trust is irrevocable, and if no strings are attached to the transfer of insurance to the trust, there is a gift of the value of the insurance at the time of the transfer. Likewise, any premium payments by the donor after the insurance has been transferred to the trust constitute gifts. If the trustee pays the premiums out of income from other assets held in trust or reinvests some of the other assets in the insurance by selling them to pay the premiums, the payment of premiums does not amount to a gift.

See ¶2109 for a discussion of split-dollar life insurance arrangements.

¶2167   Annuities

A transferor who irrevocably creates an annuity for the benefit of another makes a gift to the extent that the transfer is not supported by full and adequate consideration in money or money's worth.[35] Therefore, the gratuitous purchase of an annuity contract for another constitutes a gift if the purchaser retains no rights in the contract. Similarly, the creation of an annuity in a trust or other property constitutes a taxable gift. A taxable gift is also made when a person establishes an annuity for his or her own benefit and irrevocably names another to receive certain benefits that may be payable after the annuitant's death.

• *Qualified Employee's Annuity Plans*

Effective for transfers made after October 22, 1986, there is no longer a blanket gift tax exclusion where an employee designates a survivor beneficiary in a qualified employee benefit plan.[36] For transfers made before October 23, 1986, an employee was allowed to designate a survivor beneficiary under a qualified pension plan, stock bonus plan, profit-sharing plan, or individual retirement account or annuity without incurring a gift tax as to any portion of the benefits

---

[34] Reg. §25.2511-1(h)(8).
[35] See, for example, Rev. Rul. 69-74, 1969-1 CB 43.
[36] Code Sec. 2517, repealed by P.L. 99-514.

attributable to contributions regarded as being made by the employer. However, this gift tax exclusion did not apply to the extent that designated benefits were attributable to contributions made by the employee.

• Waiver of Survivor Benefits

The waiver of a joint and survivor benefit or a qualified pre-retirement survivor benefit or the right to such a benefit by a nonparticipant spouse prior to the death of the participant does not result in the imposition of the gift tax.[37]

¶ 2168   U.S. Savings Bonds

The IRS has issued comprehensive rules for determining whether purchases of U.S. savings bonds are taxable transfers.[38] Bonds that are purchased with an individual's own funds and registered in the purchaser's name, but that are payable to another person on the purchaser's death, are not taxable gifts. A taxable gift is made when the purchaser has the bonds registered in another person's name. Bonds that are purchased with an individual's own funds and registered in the names of the purchaser and another person as co-owners are not taxable gifts at the date of purchase. A taxable gift will result if the other co-owner cashes them. A person who purchases bonds and names two other persons as co-owners makes a gift of one-half of the purchase price to each of the co-owners.

¶ 2170   Donor's Dominion and Control

Before the gift tax may be imposed on any transaction, the gift must be complete. If the intention to make a gift is expressed at one time, but the delivery of the property and acceptance of the gift take place at a later date, the later date governs. It is only at that time that the gift is completed. A promise to make a gift is not a gift. Even the execution of a trust instrument in itself will not constitute a gift. The property subject to such a trust must be transferred without retention of powers by the donor.[39]

A transfer in trust is not complete for gift tax purposes if the trustee is given such broad powers to invade income and corpus for the grantor's benefit that there is no assurance, at the time of the transfer, that anything of value will be paid to any other beneficiary. Such a transfer will not result in a taxable gift even though the value of the trust property is large in amount. Similarly, if creditors of the grantor can reach the trust assets under applicable state law, the transfer in trust is not a taxable gift.[40]

¶ 2171   Cessation of Dominion and Control

A gift is incomplete unless the donor has parted with dominion and control and, thus, is without power to change the disposition of the transferred property—whether for the donor's benefit or for the benefit of another. A gift is incomplete in every instance where a donor reserves the power to reassume the beneficial title to the property. It is also incomplete when a donor reserves the power to name new beneficiaries or to change the interests of the various beneficiaries.[41] The U.S. Court of Appeals for the Tenth Circuit has held that the

---

[37] Code Sec. 2503(f).
[38] Rev. Rul. 68-269, 1968-1 CB 399.
[39] Reg. § 25.2511-2.

[40] M.M. Outwin, 76 TC 153, CCH Dec. 37,645 (Acq.).
[41] Reg. § 25.2511-2.

question of whether a transfer is a completed gift for purposes of the federal gift tax is strictly a matter of federal law.[42]

A gift will not be incomplete merely because the donor reserves the power to change the manner or time of enjoyment thereof. Also, it will not be incomplete as to an intermediate vested interest, such as a life estate or an estate for years, merely because it will return to the donor at a later date.

A donor is considered to retain a power if the donor may exercise that power in conjunction with any person not having a substantial adverse interest in the disposition of the transferred property or the income therefrom. A trustee who has no other interest in the trust is not a person having an adverse interest in the disposition of the trust property or its income.

The relinquishment or termination of a power to change the disposition of the transferred property, occurring otherwise than by the death of the donor, is regarded as the event that completes the gift and causes the tax to apply. However, if a donor retains the power to change the amount of the beneficiaries' interests or to designate the beneficiary of the trust corpus, any income that is transferred to the beneficiaries before the donor designates a recipient of the corpus is not a part of the property disposed of by the designation. The income received by the beneficiaries is a taxable gift at the time the gift is completed.[43]

¶ 2175   Transfers by Nonresidents Not Citizens

Except for the estates of nonresidents not citizens who are subject to the expatriate alternative gift tax regime (discussed below), a blanket exemption from federal gift taxation is provided for all gifts by nonresidents who are not U.S. citizens of intangible property having a situs within the United States, e.g., stocks and bonds.[44]

Transfers by U.S. citizens who are residents of a U.S. possession but who acquired their U.S. citizenship solely by reason of being a citizen of the possession or by reason of birth or residence within the possession will be treated as transfers made by nonresidents who are not citizens of the United States.

• *Alternative Gift Tax Regime for Expatriates*

Gratuitous transfers of tangible or intangible property situated in the United States by a former citizen or long-term resident who is subject to the alternative tax regime of Code Sec. 877(b), and made during the 10-year period following relinquishment of citizenship or long-term residency, are subject to federal gift tax. This provision is effective for individuals who expatriate after June 3, 2004.[45] Additionally, if such a former citizen or long-term resident is present in the United States for a period of 30 days or more in any calendar year that ends during the 10-year period following relinquishment of citizenship or long-term residency, he or she is treated as a resident of the United States for federal gift tax purposes.[46] Thus, all gratuitous transfers, regardless of where the property is situated, made by such former citizen or long-term resident in the calendar year are subject to the federal gift tax. U.S. citizens and residents are subject to a special transfer tax upon receipt after June 16, 2008, of property by gift, devise, bequest, or inheritance from an expatriate (see ¶ 2593).

---

[42] *Wells Fargo Bank, N.A.*, CA-10, 2003-1 USTC ¶ 60,456, 319 F3d 1222, rev'g *First Security Bank*, DC N.M., 2001-1 USTC ¶ 60,406.

[43] Reg. § 25.2511-2(f).

[44] Code Sec. 2501(a)(2).

[45] Code Sec. 2501(a), as amended by P.L. 108-357.

[46] Code Sec. 877(g), as added by the American Jobs Creation Act of 2004 (P.L. 108-357).

• *Transfer of Stock in Certain Closely Held Foreign Corporations*

Gratuitous transfers of stock in certain closely held foreign corporations, regardless of where the stock is located, by a former citizen or long-term resident who is subject to the alternative tax regime of Code Sec. 877(b), are subject to the federal gift tax, if made during the 10-year period following relinquishment of citizenship to long-term residency. This provision is effective for individuals who expatriate after June 3, 2004.[47] A foreign corporation that is subject to this gift tax rule is one in which the former citizen or long-term resident: (1) owns 10 percent or more of the total combined voting power of all classes of stock, and (2) directly or indirectly owns over 50 percent of the total combined voting power of all classes of stock or total value of stock.[48] The value of the stock for gift tax purposes is the U.S.-asset value of the stock at the time of the transfer. The U.S. asset value is equal to the proportionate share of the fair market value, at the time of the transfer, of the foreign stock transferred which the fair market value of any assets owned by the foreign corporation that are situated in the United States bears to the total fair market value of all assets owned by such foreign corporation.[49]

> **Example:** Marco Ferraro, owner of 75 percent of the voting block in Black Inc., a Spanish closely held corporation, transfers his interest to his two children on October 15, 2013. Ferraro, who relinquished his U.S. citizenship five years before the transfer, recently spent 45 days in the United States visiting relatives and friends. At the time of transfer, Black Inc. owned $2 million in assets, $500,000 of which were situated in the United States. On October 15, 2013, the fair market value of the transferred stock was $1.5 million. For purposes of determining Ferraro's gift tax liability on the transfer, the value of the stock is computed by first determining the fraction or percentage that the fair market value of the U.S.-situated assets bears to the fair market value of all assets owned by Black Inc. ($500,000/$2,000,000, which is 25 percent). This 25 percent amount is then applied to the fair market value of the transferred stock to determine the U.S.-asset value of the stock ($1,500,000 × 25% = $375,000).

¶ 2180   Manner of Reporting Gifts on Return

Gifts that are subject only to the gift tax are reported in part 1 of Schedule A (Computation of Taxable Gifts) of Form 709 (United States Gift (and Generation-Skipping Transfer) Tax Return). These gifts include charitable, public, and similar gifts. Gifts that are direct skips and are subject to both the gift tax and the generation-skipping transfer tax are reported in chronological order on part 2 of Schedule A. Indirect skips from a trust that are currently subject to gift tax and may later be subject to generation-skipping transfer tax are reported on part 3 of Schedule A.

If the total annual gifts of present interests to any donee exceed the amount of the gift tax annual exclusion ($13,000 for gifts made in 2009,[50] 2010,[51] 2011,[52] and 2012;[53] and $14,000 for gifts made in 2013 and 2014[54]), the donor must enter

---

[47] Code Sec. 2501(a)(5)(A), as added by P.L. 108-357.

[48] Code Sec. 2501(a)(5)(B), as added by P.L. 108-357.

[49] Code Sec. 2501(c)(5)(B), as added by P.L. 108-357.

[50] Rev. Proc. 2008-66, IRB 2008-45, 1107.

[51] Rev. Proc. 2009-50, IRB 2009-45, 617.

[52] Rev. Proc. 2010-40, IRB 2010-46, 663.

[53] Rev. Proc. 2011-52, IRB 2011-45, 701.

[54] Rev. Proc. 2012-41, IRB 2012-45, 539; Rev. Proc. 2013-35, IRB 2013-47, October 31, 2013.

all such gifts that are made during that year to or on behalf of that donee, including those gifts that will be excluded under the annual exclusion.[55] Gifts of future interests made during a calendar year must be reported on Schedule A regardless of their value.[56] was

Where one transfer results in gifts to two individuals (such as a life estate to one person with the remainder to another person), the gift to each individual must be listed separately. Gifts made by a donor to his or her spouse should be reflected on Schedule A only if they are gifts of terminable interests. All terminable interests that pass to the spouse should be reported regardless of whether they qualify for the gift tax marital deduction (see ¶ 2313).

An annual Form 709 need not be filed if the donor's gifts consisted solely of:

(1) transfers of present interests not in excess of the annual gift tax exclusion (see ¶ 2250);

(2) transfers to political organizations;

(3) qualified transfers for educational or medical expenses (see ¶ 2250); or

(4) transfers to the donor's spouse that qualify for the unlimited marital deduction (see ¶ 2311).

¶ 2181   Description of Property on Return

The property comprising the gifts listed in Schedule A (Computation of Taxable Gifts) of Form 709 (United States Gift (and Generation-Skipping Transfer) Tax Return)[57] should be described in enough detail to be easily identified. For interests in property based on the duration of a person's life, the date of birth of that person should be included in the description.[58]

• Real Estate

A legal description should be given for each parcel of real estate. If the property is located within a city, the name of the street, the street number, and the area of the city should be given. A short statement of any improvements to the realty should also be furnished.

• Bonds

A description of bonds transferred should include (1) the number of bonds transferred, (2) the principal amount, (3) the name of the obligor, (4) the maturity date, (5) the rate of interest, (6) the date or dates when interest is payable, (7) the series number, if there is more than one issue, (8) the exchange on which the bond is listed, and (9) the CUSIP (Committee on Uniform Security Identification Procedure) number, (see ¶ 313). If the bond is not listed on an exchange, the address of the principal business office of the corporation should be given.

• Stocks

A description of a gift of stock should include (1) the number of shares transferred, (2) a designation of the shares as common or preferred stock, (3) if a listed security, the principal exchange on which it is sold, and (4) the CUSIP

---

[55] The gift tax annual exclusion was $12,000 for gifts made in 2006, 2007 and 2008; $11,000 for gifts made in 2002, 2003, 2004 and 2005; and $10,000 for gifts made after 1981 and before 2002.

[56] Reg. § 25.6019-1.

[57] A filled in Form 709 (2013) is reproduced in the Appendix at ¶ 3280.

[58] Instructions for Form 709 (2013), p. 9.

number, (see ¶313). If the stock is not listed on an exchange, the description should give the location of the corporation's principal business office, the state in which the corporation was incorporated, and the date of incorporation. If the gift is of preferred stock, the description should contain the issue, the par value of the stock, the quotation at which returned, and the exact name of the corporation.

• Insurance Policies

A description of life insurance policies should include the name of the insurer and the policy number.

Chapter 35

GIFT-SPLITTING

¶ 2200   Practical Effect

A gift made by a husband or wife to a third person may be treated as made one-half by each, if both spouses consent.[1] This right is an optional one that is effective only for the calendar year, or quarter for certain prior periods, for which the election is made. If the consent is effective, all gifts by the husband and wife to third persons during that calendar year or quarter must receive the same treatment. By signifying their consent, the donor and his or her spouse become jointly and severally liable for the entire gift tax for that calendar year or quarter. See ¶2205 for guidelines concerning the manner of reporting these gifts on Schedule A (Computation of Taxable Gifts) of Form 709 (United States Gift (and Generation-Skipping Transfer) Tax Return).

Although the Code does not limit gift-splitting treatment to separately owned property, such treatment has no significance except in the case of separate property. The purpose of gift-splitting, in fact, is to equalize the effect of the gift tax as between community and separate property.

> **Example (1):** On March 5, 2013, Tony Sheaffer made a gift to his son, Roger, of bonds worth $30,000, representing his separate property. Tony and his spouse signed the required consent form. The gift is treated as one of $15,000 by Tony and one of $15,000 by his spouse.

> **Example (2):** On February 6, 2013, Patricia Rey made a gift to her grandson, Louis, of stock worth $28,000, representing community property. Whether the consent was filed, the gift is one of $14,000 by Patricia and one of $14,000 by her spouse (see ¶2220).

The gift-splitting benefit is not available unless the donor is married at the time of the gift and does not become married to a different person before the close of the calendar year. In addition, each spouse must be a citizen or resident of the United States at the time of the gift. Finally, to qualify for the gift-splitting privilege, the spouse making the gift must not give the other spouse a general power of appointment over the property transferred.

> **Comment:** If the spouse of the donor is given a partial interest in the property transferred, the gift-splitting privilege is available only for the value of the property transferred to persons other than the spouse and only to the extent that these persons' interests are ascertainable at the time the gift is reported.

---

[1] Code Sec. 2513.

¶ 2205   Gift Tax Returns

When gift-splitting is elected, the donor spouse must file a return if annual gifts to any one donee exceed the amount of the gift tax exclusion. However, the consenting spouse must file a return only if he or she made gifts to any one donee in excess of the gift tax exclusion, including gifts attributable to the consenting spouse under the gift-splitting provisions, or if any gifts made were of future interests.[2] The following examples illustrate this rule.

Example (1): Gary Alto made gifts valued at $30,000 during 2013 to a third party, and his wife, Vicki, made no gifts during this time, but elects gift-splitting for this year. Each spouse is required to file a return for 2013. Gary is required to file a return because the amount of the gift exceeds the amount of the annual exclusion ($14,000) by $16,000. Vicki is required to file because she is considered as having made a gift of $15,000 to the third party, which exceeds the annual gift tax exclusion by $1,000.

Example (2): Mimi Bradley made gifts valued at $16,000 during 2013 to a third party, and her husband, John, made no gifts. Only Mimi is required to file a return because John is considered as having made a gift of $8,000, which does not exceed the annual gift tax exclusion.

To report gifts on Schedule A (Computation of Taxable Gifts) of Form 709 (United States Gift (and Generation-Skipping Transfer) Tax Return) whenever spouses elect to treat gifts to third parties as being made one-half by each of them, the following rules apply:[3]

(1) If only one spouse makes gifts for which a return is required, the full value of all gifts made by the spouse filing the return must be entered in column F of part 1, 2, or 3, of Schedule A, even if the gift's value will be less than the annual exclusion limit ($13,000 for 2009 through 2012; $14,000 for 2013 and 2014) after it is split in column G.

(2) If split-gift treatment is elected and both spouses made gifts, the gifts made by the donor's spouse are listed in the space provided for "Gifts made by spouse" in Schedule A, part 1, 2, or 3, as appropriate.

Gifts entered in part 1 of Schedule A should be grouped into the following categories: (1) gifts to spouse; (2) gifts to third parties that are to be split; (3) gifts for charitable uses if gift-splitting is not elected; and (4) all other gifts.[4] Gifts entered in parts 2 and 3 of Schedule A should be listed in chronological order. In all cases in which it is not apparent how the amounts entered for Schedule A were computed, additional sheets of the same size as the return should be attached and the computations set forth thereon in detail. To avoid correspondence from the IRS, where both spouses must file a gift tax return, both returns should be filed together in the same envelope.[5]

¶ 2210   Annual Exclusions

Annual exclusions that are available to each spouse under Code Sec. 2503(b) are applicable to a single gift when gift-splitting is elected, resulting in a doubling of the exemptions and exclusions applicable to the transfer. Gifts of present interests in the amount of $28,000 annually may be made to each donee without incurring tax, because each spouse may claim a $13,000 exclusion for 2013 and

---

[2] Reg. § 25.2513-1 and Reg. § 25.6019-2.
[3] Instructions for Form 709 (2013), p. 7.
[4] Instructions for Form 709 (2013), p. 9.
[5] Instructions for Form 709 (2013), p. 5.

2014.[6] For 2009,[7] 2010,[8] 2011,[9] and 2012,[10] the annual exclusion was $13,000, which allowed the spouses to gift a total of $26,000 annually to each donee gift tax free.

¶ 2215   Consent of Both Spouses

The privilege of dividing a gift between husband-and-wife donors is granted only if both signify their consent to such division. When one spouse consents to have gifts made by the other treated as having been made one-half by each of them, gifts made by the consenting spouse must also be treated as having been made one-half by each spouse.[11]

¶ 2220   Community Property

The gift-splitting privilege does not apply to gifts of community property. Gifts of community property are automatically treated as being made one-half from each spouse. There is, consequently, no need to obtain consents with respect to gifts of community property.

¶ 2225   Time of Consent

Consent to split gifts must be given on or before April 15 of the year following the year in which the gifts were made.[12]

Consent to split-gift treatment may not be given after a deficiency notice with respect to tax in that year has been sent to either spouse.[13] Similarly, spouses may not consent to the election after the donor spouse has filed a gift tax return reporting the gifts and after the due date for the return has passed.[14] A consent, once given, may be revoked before the last day for filing the consent by filing a duplicate written notice with the IRS officer with whom the return was filed.[15]

The executor or administrator of the estate of a deceased spouse may give consent to gift-splitting treatment. The guardian or committee of a legally incompetent person may also give such consent.

¶ 2230   Form of Consent

In order to be effective, the consent to taxation to each spouse of one-half of the gifts must be signified by both husband and wife. The consent should be signified, by the spouse filing the return, by answering "Yes" on line 12, part 1, on Page 1 of Form 709 (United States Gift (and Generation-Skipping Transfer) Tax Return) (2013) reproduced in the Appendix at ¶3280) and, by the other spouse, by executing the "Consent of Spouse" appearing in part 1, line 18, Page 1, of the same return.

---

[6] Rev. Proc. 2012-41, IRB 2012-45, 539; Rev. Proc. 2013-35, IRB 2013-47, October 31, 2013.

[7] Rev. Proc. 2008-66, IRB 2008-45, 1107.

[8] Rev. Proc. 2009-50, IRB 2009-45, 617.

[9] Rev. Proc. 2010-40, IRB 2010-46, 663

[10] Rev. Proc. 2011-52, IRB 2011-45, 701.

[11] Rev. Rul. 146, 1953-2 CB 292.

[12] Code Sec. 2513(b).

[13] Code Sec. 2513(b).

[14] Rev. Rul. 80-224, 1980-2 CB 281.

[15] Code Sec. 2513(c); Reg. § 25.2513-3.

Chapter 36
ANNUAL EXCLUSIONS

¶ 2250   Exclusions Available

The first $14,000 ($28,000 where gift-splitting is elected) of gifts of present interests made in 2013 and 2014 to any donee during the tax year is excluded in determining the amount of taxable gifts.[1] The annual exclusion is indexed for inflation after 1998. Under the indexing formula, indexed amounts are rounded to the next lowest multiple of $1,000. For gifts made in 2009 through 2012, the first $13,000 ($26,000 with gift-splitting), made to any donee was nontaxable.[2] Before 2009, the annual exclusion had been $12,000 (for gifts made in 2006 through 2008),[3] $11,000 (for gifts made in 2002 through 2005), and $10,000 for gifts made after 1982. Prior to 1982, the annual exclusion was $3,000.

The annual exclusion is not limited in the number of donees for whom it may be taken or for the number of years in which it may be taken. However, it is limited to gifts of present, rather than future, interests (see ¶ 2265).

In the case of gifts in trust, the trust beneficiaries, rather than the trust or trustees, are treated as the donees for the purpose of determining the number of annual exclusions allowable to the donor.

• Unlimited Educational and Medical Expense Exclusion

An unlimited gift tax exclusion is available for amounts paid on behalf of a donee directly to an educational organization, provided that such amounts constitute tuition payments.[4] In addition, amounts paid to health care providers for medical services on behalf of a donee qualify for an unlimited exclusion. The exclusions for qualifying educational expenses and medical expenses are available without regard to the relationship between the donor and donee and are available in addition to the annual exclusion. Transfers to educational organizations and for medical expenses do not have to be reported as gifts on Schedule A (Computation of Taxable Gifts) of Form 709 (United States Gift (and Generation-Skipping Transfer) Tax Return).

Qualifying medical expenses, for purposes of the exclusion, are defined by reference to Code Sec. 213(d) (relating to the deductibility of medical and dental

---

[1] Code Sec. 2503; Rev. Proc. 2012-41, IRB 2012-45, 539; Rev. Proc. 2013-35, IRB 2013-47, October 31, 2013.

[2] Rev. Proc. 2008-66, IRB 2008-45, 1107; Rev. Proc. 2009-50, IRB 2009-45, 617; Rev.

Proc. 2010-40, IRB 2010-46, 663; Rev. Proc. 2011-52, IRB 2011-45, 701.

[3] Rev. Proc. 2005-70, 2005-2 CB 979; Rev. Proc. 2006-53, 2006-2 CB 996; Rev. Proc. 2007-66, 2007-2 CB, 970.

[4] Code Sec. 2503(e).

expenses for income tax purposes). The exclusion is not available to the extent that the amounts paid are reimbursed by insurance.

The IRS has privately ruled[5] that prepaid tuition payments qualified for the gift tax exclusion under Code Sec. 2503(c), where the payments were made directly to the educational institution in payment of specific tuition costs for designated individuals. Under the facts of the ruling, a donor transferred money to a private school pursuant to an agreement under which the money would be used exclusively for his two grandchildren. The donor agreed to pay any additional money in later years to reflect the costs of any increases in tuition, and agreed that if the grandchildren failed to attend the school in the specified years, the money would be forfeited to the school, rather than returned to the donor. Similarly, where a grandparent prepaid tuition payments for each of six grandchildren for each grade level through grade 12.[6]

• Contributions to Qualified Tuition Programs

Effective for transfers made after August 5, 1997, any contribution to a qualified tuition program (QTP) is treated as a completed gift of a present interest from the contributor to the beneficiary at the time of the contribution.[7] Annual contributions are eligible for the gift tax exclusion (for 2013 through 2014, it is $14,000 for an individual and $28,000 for a married couple electing gift-splitting). These numbers were 13,000 and $26,000, respectively, for contributions to QTPs made in 2009 through 2012. The contribution amounts eligible for the exclusion was $12,000 and $24,000 for 2006 through 2008.

Contributions to a QTP are not considered qualifying transfers under the rules providing an unlimited annual exclusion with respect to payments for educational and medical expenses.[8] Effective for tax years beginning after December 31, 2001, a contribution made to a qualified private institution can also qualify for this treatment.

A contributor making a contribution in excess of the exclusion limit may elect to have the contribution treated as if it were made ratably over five years.[9] A gift tax return must be filed with respect to any contribution in excess of the annual gift tax exclusion limit (see ¶2052).

If a beneficiary's interest is rolled over to another beneficiary or there is a change in beneficiary, no gift tax consequences result, provided that the new beneficiary is assigned to the same generation as the old beneficiary.[10] Although the rollover of a beneficiary's interest to a family-member beneficiary in a lower generation (that is, a parent to a child, or an aunt to a niece) will be treated as a taxable gift, the five-year averaging rule may be applied to exempt up to $70,000 (in 2013 and 2014) of the transfer.[11] If gift-splitting is elected, these amounts are doubled.

• Completion of Gift; Transfer by Check

A gift tax annual exclusion is available only in the year that the gift is completed—that is, the year in which the donor effectively parts with dominion and control over the transferred property. Problems may arise when a donor

---

[5] Technical Advice Memorandum 199941013 (July 9, 1999).

[6] IRS Letter Ruling 200602002, Sept. 6, 2005.

[7] Code Sec. 529(c)(2)(A)(i).

[8] Code Sec. 529(c)(2)(A).

[9] Code Sec. 529(c)(2)(B).

[10] Code Sec. 529(c)(5).

[11] Code Sec. 529(c)(2)(B); Rev. Proc. 2012-41, IRB 2012-45, 539; Rev. Proc. 2013-35, IRB 2013-47, October 31, 2013.

makes a gift by check in one year, but the check is not paid by the donor's bank until the following year. The IRS has taken the position that completion of a gift of a check to a noncharitable donee will relate back to the earlier of the date on which the donor no longer has the power to change the disposition of the check or the date on which the donee deposited, cashed, or presented the check if (1) the drawee bank paid the check when it was first presented, (2) the donor was alive when the bank paid the check, (3) the donor intended to make a gift, (4) delivery was unconditional, and (5) the check was deposited, cashed, or presented by the donee in the year in which gift tax treatment is sought.[12]

¶ 2255   Gifts in Prior Years

The annual exclusion is available only for gifts made after 1981. From 1982 through 2001, the annual exclusion amount was $10,000. Although the annual exclusion was $3,000 for all years beginning with 1943 and ending with 1981, larger exclusions were allowed for 1942 and earlier years. These exclusions are sometimes important in determining the tax for a current year. Gifts in prior years play a part in determining the tax for the current years because of the cumulative nature of the tax. For annual exclusion amounts after 2001, see ¶ 2250.

¶ 2260   Gifts by Married Persons

When a husband and wife have agreed to treat gifts to third persons made by either of them as being made one-half by each, they double the number of annual exclusions available with respect to their gifts. Each may claim an exclusion for each third-party donee, provided, of course, that the gifts are of present interests (see ¶ 2200 through ¶ 2230).

¶ 2265   Future Interests

The annual exclusion is not allowed for gifts of future interests.[13] Denial of the exclusion results from difficulty in determining the number of eventual donees and the values of their respective shares. This difficulty is especially significant where contingent remainders are involved. Rather than attempt to set up many fine-line distinctions, Congress chose to deny the exclusion with respect to all gifts of future interests in property.

"Future interests" refers to the interest taken by the donee. They are interests, whether vested or contingent, "limited to commence in use, possession, or enjoyment at some future date or time."[14] Thus, all gifts of remainder interests, whether vested or contingent, are gifts of future interests. However, a gift in trust of a remainder interest in personal property to a donee who is an income beneficiary of the trust is a gift of a present interest. Such a gift qualifies for the exclusion in those states whose laws provide for the merger of the interests and the termination of the trust.[15]

Gifts of income that commence immediately are gifts of present interests. If, however, the income is to be accumulated and paid over at a later time, the gift of the income is a gift of a future interest. This is so even if, on some specified

---

[12] Rev. Rul. 96-56, 1996-2 CB 161, modifying Rev. Rul. 67-396, 1967-2 CB 351; *A. Metzger*, CA-4, 1994-2 USTC ¶ 60,179, aff'g 100 TC 204, CCH Dec. 48,910. However, see *S. Newman Est.*, CA-DC, 99-2 USTC ¶ 60,358, and *R. Rosano, Exr.*, CA-2, 2001-1 USTC ¶ 60,401, cert. denied Feb. 19, 2002, in which the relation-back doctrine was not applied to situations involving noncharitable donees where the decedent died before checks were presented.

[13] Reg. § 25.2503-3.

[14] *A. Pelzer*, SCt, 41-1 USTC ¶ 10,027, 312 US 399; Reg. § 25.2503-3.

[15] Rev. Rul. 78-168, 1978-1 CB 298.

contingency, some portion or all of the income may be paid over earlier.[16] The IRS will not allow an exclusion for a gift of property in trust that provides that all income must be paid to a beneficiary, but permits corpus to be invested in non-income producing property and life insurance.[17] However, a gift to a minor is not a future interest if the property and its income may be expended for the benefit of the minor before the minor attains age 21 and may be distributed to the minor at that time or to the minor's estate if the minor dies before reaching age 21.[18]

The IRS has ruled that transfers by a donor of specified portions of real property equal in value to the annual exclusion constituted gifts of present interests that were eligible for the annual exclusion.[19] According to the IRS, the donees received the present, unrestricted right to the immediate use, possession and enjoyment of an ascertainable interest in the real property.

A partner's gift to the partnership accounts of other partners has been held to qualify for the annual exclusion where the donee partners had the immediate and unrestricted right to possess and enjoy the transferred amounts.[20] Under the Uniform Partnership Act, as adopted in Indiana, each partner was entitled to receive amounts from his or her capital account on demand, since the underlying partnership agreement did not contain a provision to the contrary.

The IRS has also privately ruled[21] that gifts of limited partnership interests by parents to their children qualified for the annual exclusion. In concluding that the gifts constituted present interests, the IRS National Office noted that, under the terms of the partnership agreement and applicable state law, the limited partnership interests conferred the rights to receive distributions before withdrawal or dissolution of the partnership, the right to assign or sell the interest in whole or in part, and the right to bring a cause of action against the general partners personally for breach of fiduciary duty. These rights entitled the donee-children to any current economic benefits generated by the limited partnership interests and, accordingly, the interests qualified for the gift tax annual exclusion.

A husband and wife's annual exclusions were denied with respect to limited liability company (LLC) membership units transferred to their children, where the children did not derive a substantial economic benefit from the transfers. The Tax Court found a present economic benefit to be lacking because, under the terms of the LLC operating agreement, the donee-children could not (1) unilaterally withdraw their capital accounts, (2) sell or transfer their units without consent of the LLC manager, or (3) unilaterally effect a dissolution of the LLC.[22]

• Crummey Trusts

A gift of the right to demand a portion of a trust corpus is a gift of a present interest,[23] so long as the donee-beneficiary is aware of the right to make the demand.[24] The Tax Court has held that transfers of property to a trust constituted a present interest where the trust beneficiaries (the grantor's grandchildren) had the right to withdraw an amount equal to the annual gift tax exclusion within 15 days of the transfer, even though the only other interests the grandchildren had

---

[16] *E.F. Fondren*, SCt, 45-1 USTC ¶ 10,164, 324 US 18.

[17] Rev. Rul. 69-344, 1969-1 CB 225.

[18] Code Sec. 2503(c).

[19] Rev. Rul. 83-180, 1983-2 CB 169.

[20] *J.P. Wooley, Exr.*, DC Ind., 90-1 USTC ¶ 60,013.

[21] Technical Advice Memorandum 199944003 (July 2, 1999).

[22] *C. Hackl*, 118 TC 279, CCH Dec. 54,686, aff'd, CA-7, 2003-2 USTC ¶ 60,465, 335 F3d 664.

[23] Rev. Rul. 80-261, 1980-2 CB 279.

[24] Rev. Rul. 81-7, 1981-1 CB 474.

in the trust were contingent remainder interests.[25] In so holding, the Tax Court applied the present interest test enunciated by the U.S. Court of Appeals for the Ninth Circuit in *D.C. Crummey*,[26] concluding that the grandchildren's withdrawal rights, if exercised, could not be legally resisted by the trustees.

¶ 2270 Gifts for the Benefit of a Minor

A gift of property to a minor in trust may qualify for the annual exclusion if certain statutory requirements are met. No part of a transfer for the benefit of a minor will be considered to be a future interest (which would not qualify for the exclusion) if the transfer meets the conditions specified in Code Sec. 2503(c):

(1) Both the property and its income may be expended by, or for the benefit of, the minor donee prior to his or her attaining the age of 21. To the extent the property and income were not so expended, they will pass to the donee at that time.

(2) In the event of the donee's death prior to reaching 21 years of age, the property and income not expended will pass to the donee's estate or to persons appointed by him or her under the exercise of a general power of appointment.

Persons drafting trust provisions for minor beneficiaries should include both of the above conditions in the trust instrument. The absence of one of the above provisions will cause the loss of annual gift tax exclusions for the trusts, and the courts have not permitted the donors to change the trust provisions in a later year in order to obtain annual exclusions.[27] In addition, the right of the trustees to expend property and income for the benefit of the minor beneficiaries should not be limited to a specific purpose or subject to a substantial restriction.[28] For example, the courts have disallowed annual exclusions where the trustees could expend property or income for a minor beneficiary's medical care only. However, it would appear that a trust could limit categories of expenditure to those allowed guardians under the law of the state where the gift was made.

A gift of an income interest in a trust to a minor may qualify for the annual exclusion, even though the gift of the trust corpus does not qualify, or even though the minor does not have any interest in the corpus at all.[29] This is true because income interests payable to minor beneficiaries qualify as separate property interests apart from the corpus. An annual gift tax exclusion will be allowed for an income interest if (1) the income may be used for the beneficiary's benefit during minority, (2) the accumulated income will be distributed to him or her at age 21, and (3) the accumulated income is payable to the beneficiary's estate, or to persons designated in his or her will, if he or she dies before reaching age 21.[30] An annual exclusion for the income interest may be lost where the trustee has power to allocate income and expenses between corpus and income.

---

[25] *M. Cristofani Est.*, 97 TC 74, CCH Dec. 47,491 (Acq.), and *L. Kohlsaat Est.*, 73 TCM 2732, CCH Dec. 53,031(M), TC Memo. 1997-212. But see Technical Advice Memorandum 9628004 (Apr. 1, 1996) and Technical Advice Memorandum 9731004 (Apr. 21, 1997).

[26] *D.C. Crummey*, CA-9, 68-2 USTC ¶ 12,541, 397 F2d 82.

[27] *S.S. Davis*, 55 TC 416, CCH Dec. 30,455; *A. Van Den Wymelenberg*, CA-7, 68-2 USTC ¶ 12,537, 397 F2d 443, cert. denied; *E.D. Harris*, CA-5, 72-1 USTC ¶ 12,853, 461 F2d 554.

[28] *S.L. Faber*, CA-6, 71-1 USTC ¶ 12,760, 439 F2d 1189; *J.T. Pettus, Jr.*, 54 TC 112, CCH Dec. 29,926.

[29] *A.I. Herr*, 35 TC 732, CCH Dec. 24,652 (Acq.), aff'd by CA-3, 62-2 USTC ¶ 12,079, 303 F2d 780; Rev. Rul. 68-670, 1968-2 CB 413.

[30] Many states have lowered the age at which custodian property must be distributed to the minor from 21 to 18 years. The IRS has ruled that the annual exclusion still will be available in those states that have lowered the distribution age from 21 to 18 (Rev. Rul. 73-287, 1973-2 CB 321).

Example: Ron Kovak created a trust for his granddaughter, Cindy, who was to receive the income until she reached the age of 30, when she would receive the entire trust principal. The trustee was given discretion to use the principal for the benefit of the beneficiary and to accumulate income not used. The accumulated income was to be paid to Cindy when she reached majority or to her estate in the event of her death before that time. The gift property is separable into its several interests. In light of this division, the gift of a right to income until age 21 qualifies for the annual exclusion. The gifts of principal and income payable after majority to age 30 do not qualify.

The annual exclusion is available where a minor beneficiary has, on reaching age 21, either (1) a continuing right to compel immediate distribution of the trust corpus by giving written notice to the trustee, or to permit the trust to continue by its own terms, or (2) a right during a limited period to compel immediate distribution of the trust corpus by giving written notice to the trustee, a right which, if not exercised, will permit the trust to continue by its own terms.[31]

¶ 2272   Uniform Transfers to Minors Act: Custodianship

A transfer of property for the benefit of a minor pursuant to the Uniform Transfers to Minors Act or one of its predecessors, the Uniform Gifts to Minors Act or the Model Gifts of Securities to Minors Act, is considered to be a complete gift of the full fair market value of the property. No taxable gift occurs by reason of a subsequent resignation of the custodian or termination of the custodianship for federal gift tax purposes. Such a gift also qualifies for the annual gift tax exclusion.

The value of the property transferred under the "Uniform" or the "Model" Act may be includible in the gross estate of the donor (with a credit against estate tax for prior gift taxes paid) if the donor appoints him- or herself as custodian of the property and dies while serving in that capacity before the minor donee attains majority. The income from such property, to the extent it is used for the support of the minor donee, is includible in the gross income of any person who is legally obligated to support the minor donee.[32]

¶ 2274   Reciprocal Transfers

The IRS will disallow annual exclusions that are artificially generated by reciprocal (cross) transfers, as illustrated below.

Example: Brothers Allen, Brian, and Charlie Fox each have two children. The brothers agree that in 2013, each will give $14,000 to each of their two children, and each of their four nephews and nieces, for total transfers of $84,000 by each brother. If annual exclusions apply to all of the transfers, each of the brothers will, in effect, cause a transfer of $42,000 for each of their children, without incurring any gift tax.

Where the IRS applies the reciprocal transfer doctrine within the context of determining the allowance of gift tax annual exclusions, it will look beyond the form of the transfers, and attribute all monies coming to each donee to his or her respective donor.[33] Accordingly, in the above Example, Allen, Brian, and Charlie

---

[31] Rev. Rul. 74-43, 1974-1 CB 285.

[32] Rev. Rul. 59-357, 1959-2 CB 212.

[33] *J.A. Schultz,* CA-4, 74-1 USTC ¶ 12,997, 493 F2d 1225; Rev. Rul. 85-24, 1985-1 CB 329; *L. Sather,* CA-8, 2001-1 USTC ¶ 60,409, aff'g in part (this issue) and rev'g in part (on another issue), 78 TCM 456, CCH Dec. 53,548(M), TC Memo. 1999-309; *R. Schuler Est.,* CA-8, 2002-1 USTC ¶ 60,432, aff'g 80 TCM 934, CCH Dec. 54,171(M), TC Memo. 2000-392.

will each be limited to two $14,000 annual exclusions. The additional $28,000 that each brother will be deemed to transfer to his two children will be taxable gifts.

¶ 2275   Present Interest with Possibility of Reduction

If a donor makes a gift of a present interest in property, the possibility that the interest may be diminished by an exercise of a power is disregarded in determining whether the interest qualifies for the annual exclusion if no part of the interest will at any time pass to any other person.[34]

¶ 2280   Reporting Exclusions on Gift Tax Return

After reporting all gifts by the donor on the gift tax return form, subtracting the portion, if any, reported by the donor's spouse on a separate return, and adding the portion of the spouse's gifts being taxed to donor, the annual exclusions are subtracted from the resulting "Total value of gifts of donor," resulting in the "Total included amount of gifts" (lines 1, 2, and 3, part 4 of Schedule A (Computation of Taxable Gifts) of Form 709 (United States Gift (and Generation-Skipping Transfer) Tax Return) (2013) (see the filled in Form 709 in the Appendix at ¶3280).Qualified terminable interest property (QTIP) elections are deemed to have been made by the executor if (1) QTIP property is listed on Schedule M (Bequests, etc., to Surviving Spouse) of Form 706, and (2) the value of the property is entered as a deduction on Schedule M.

---

[34] Reg. § 25.2503-3(b).

Chapter 37

DEDUCTIONS AND EXEMPTIONS

¶ 2300 Reductions to Taxable Amount

In addition to the annual exclusion (see ¶ 2250) available to a donor for gifts of present interests made to each donee, the gift tax law provides for various deductions. Their total serves to reduce the "Total included amount of gifts" (line 3, part 4 of Schedule A (Computation of Taxable Gifts) of Form 709 (United States Gift (and Generation-Skipping Transfer) Tax Return)) to the ultimate amount of taxable gifts for the calendar year on which the tax is to be paid. Allowable deductions include the deduction for charitable, public and similar gifts and the marital deduction. See the filled-in Form 709 (2013) in the Appendix at ¶ 3280.

For gifts made prior to 1977, a specific exemption of $30,000 was allowed, in addition to the above-noted reductions.

¶ 2305 Charitable, Public, and Religious Transfers

Various gifts for charitable, public, and religious purposes are deductible in determining net gifts subject to tax. Specifically, there may be deducted the value of gifts to or for the use of the following:

(1) The United States, any state, territory, or any political subdivision thereof, or the District of Columbia, for exclusively public purposes.

(2) Any corporation, trust, community chest, fund, or foundation, organized and operated exclusively for religious, charitable, scientific, literary, or educational purposes, including the encouragement of art and the prevention of cruelty to children or animals. No part of the net earnings of such organization may inure to the benefit of any private shareholder or individual. Furthermore, the organization may not attempt to influence legislation or participate in, or intervene in (including the publishing or distributing of statements), any political campaign on behalf of (or in opposition to) any candidate for public office.

(3) A fraternal society, order, or association, operating under the lodge system, provided such gifts are to be used by such fraternal society, order, or association exclusively for one or more of the purposes enumerated in (2), above.

(4) Any organization of war veterans or auxiliary unit or society thereof if such organization, auxiliary unit, or society thereof is organized in the United States or any of its possessions. No part of its net earnings may inure to the benefit of any private shareholder or individual.[1]

The charitable deduction is not limited to gifts for use within the United States, or to gifts to or for the use of domestic corporations, trusts, community chests, funds, or foundations, or fraternal societies, orders, or associations operating under the lodge system. The exercise or release of a power of appointment that results in the passing of the property subject to the power to or for the use of any of the organizations listed above is a transfer by gift for purposes of the deduction.

Contributions to a political party or to a candidate for public office do not constitute a gift "to or for the use of the United States, any State, Territory, or any political subdivision thereof" for "exclusively public purposes" and, therefore, do not qualify as deductible charitable contributions. Contributions to political organizations are not subject to the gift tax.[2]

• Disallowance of Deduction in Certain Cases

Charitable deductions (both estate and gift tax) will be denied for otherwise deductible bequests and gifts to an organization on which the Code Sec. 507 private foundation termination tax has been imposed. General contributors will be denied deductions after the organization is notified of the loss of its private foundation status.[3] Substantial contributors (generally, persons contributing more than $5,000 and whose contributions exceed two percent of the fund's year-end total) will be denied deductions in the year when the IRS takes action to terminate the private foundation status of an organization. Deductions are also denied for bequests and gifts to any private foundation or split-interest trust if such an entity or organization fails to meet these requirements.

The governing instrument of a private foundation must require the organization to distribute income currently and prohibit it from engaging in self-dealing, from retaining any excess business holdings, from making any speculative investments and from making taxable expenditures to government officials (for propaganda purposes or to influence legislation). Violations of these requirements by a donor and the entity may also cause the disallowance of deductions.[4]

> *Comment:* Contributions to "donor advised funds" made after February 13, 2007, will not be eligible for a gift tax charitable deduction unless certain requirements are met (see ¶1130).

• Partial Interests in Property

The allowance of gift tax deductions for split-interest gifts (where there are charitable and noncharitable donees) is limited to remainder interests in annuity trusts and unitrusts, to remainder interests in pooled income funds, to charitable lead trust interests (see ¶1123) that are payable in the form of a guaranteed annuity or a fixed percentage of the fair market value of the property distributed yearly, to remainder interests in nontrust transfers of residences and farms, and to nontrust transfers of an undivided portion of a donor's entire interest in property.

---

[1] Reg. §25.2522(a)-1.
[2] Code Sec. 2501(a)(5).
[3] Reg. §25.2522(c)-2(a).
[4] Code Sec. 508(e).

If the donor gives his or her entire interest to recognized charities, even though the interest is split among different charities, the gifts are not subject to the above rules and a charitable deduction may be claimed for the entire value of the property transferred.[5]

Whether a transfer to a pooled income fund (Code Sec. 642(c)(5)) or to an *inter vivos* charitable remainder trust (Code Sec. 664) qualifies for a charitable deduction under Code Sec. 2522(c)(2)(A) are questions on which the IRS ordinarily will not issue an advance ruling or determination.[6]

Although the Pension Protection Act of 2006 (P.L. 109-280) enacted rules requiring consistent valuation of certain charitable donations of fractional interests in tangible personal property that applied to property contributed after August 17, 2006, these rules have been repealed retroactively (see ¶ 1125).

• Nonresidents Not Citizens

If the donor is a nonresident who is not a U.S. citizen, the basic rules for determining whether a transfer qualifies for the charitable deduction are the same as those for citizens or residents.[7] In addition, the following requirements apply:

(1) If the gift is to or for the use of a corporation, such corporation must be one that is created or organized under the laws of the United States or of any state or Territory thereof.

(2) If the gift is made to or for the use of a trust, or community chest, fund, or foundation, or a fraternal society, order, or association, operating within the lodge system, the gift must be for use within the United States exclusively for religious, charitable, scientific, literary, or educational purposes, including the encouragement of art and the prevention of cruelty to children or animals.

The above requirements are, of course, subject to any special arrangements that may be made with the country of which such a donor is a citizen or resident.

• Claiming Deduction on Gift Tax Return

The values of all charitable, public, and religious gifts listed in Schedule A (Computation of Taxable Gifts) of Form 709 (United States Gift (and Generation-Skipping Transfer) Tax Return) (2013) should be totaled and then reduced by the total exclusions claimed on Schedule A with respect to the gifts. The difference should then be entered on part 4, line 7 (see the filled-in Form 709 in the Appendix at ¶ 3280).

¶ 2311   Unlimited Marital Deduction

The monetary ceiling on the gift tax marital deduction was eliminated for gifts made after 1981.[8] Thus, unlimited amounts of property, except for certain terminable interests (see ¶ 2318), may be transferred between spouses free of gift taxes. In accord with this unlimited deduction, the limitations on the marital deduction with respect to community property (see ¶ 2322) that applied to gifts made before 1982 have also been repealed.

---

[5] Code Sec. 2522(c); Reg. § 25.2522(c)-3(c).
[6] Rev. Proc. 2013-3, IRB 2013-1, 113.

[7] Code Sec. 2522(b); Reg. § 25.2522(b)-1.
[8] Code Sec. 2523(a).

• *Alien Spouses*

The first $143,000 (for 2013) and $145,000 (for 2014)[9] of gifts per year to an alien spouse will not be taxed. This amount is $139,000 for gifts made in 2012,[10] $136,000 for gifts made in 2011,[11] and $134,000 for gifts made in 2010.[12] To the extent that gifts are made in excess of this amount, no marital deduction will apply to reduce the gift tax. However, the annual exclusion for transfers by gift to a noncitizen spouse is allowed only for transfers that would qualify for the marital deduction if the donee were a U.S. citizen. For example, a gift in trust would not qualify for the annual exclusion unless it fell within one of the exceptions to the terminable interest rule.

Effective for gifts made on or after July 14, 1988, it is no longer required that the donor spouse be a U.S. citizen or a resident in order for a gift to qualify for the marital deduction if the surviving spouse is a U.S. citizen. However, this does not change the rule stipulating that the gift tax marital deduction will apply only if the donee spouse is a U.S. citizen.[13] For further discussion of the availability of the marital deduction for property passing to non-U.S. citizen spouses, see ¶ 1000 and ¶ 1004.

¶ 2313   Qualified Terminable Interests

Generally, transfers of terminable interests (such as life estates, terms for years, annuities, etc.) do not qualify for the marital deduction (see ¶ 2318). However, there is a major exception to the terminable interest rule for qualified terminable interest property (QTIP).[14] This type of property is also eligible for the estate tax marital deduction. The definition of such property is discussed at ¶ 1002. Briefly, under these rules, a life interest granted to a spouse will not be treated as a terminable interest and the entire value of property in which the spouse is granted the interest will qualify for the marital deduction.

If a spouse disposes of all or part of a qualifying interest for life in QTIP property for which a marital deduction was allowed, that spouse is deemed to have made a transfer of all interest in the property, other than the qualifying income interest, that is subject to the gift tax.[15] Effective July 18, 2003, Reg. § 25.2519-1 has been amended to provide that the amount of the donee spouse's transfer under Code Sec. 2519 is reduced by the amount of the gift tax that the spouse is entitled to recover from the recipient of the transferred property under Code Sec. 2207A(b). The amount of the recoverable gift tax and the amount of the remainder interest transferred under Code Sec. 2519 are determined by using the same interrelated computation applicable to other transfers in which the transferee assumes the gift tax liability.[16]

The IRS has ruled that a surviving spouse's purchase of the remainder interest in QTIP property for cash constituted a disposition of the spouse's income interest for purposes of Code Sec. 2519, resulting in a taxable gift of the remainder interest.[17] In so ruling, the IRS concluded that the spouse's purchase of the remainder interest was analogous to a commutation, that is, a proportionate distribution of the QTIP property between the income beneficiary (the spouse) and the remaindermen. (Commutations have been held to be taxable dispositions

---

[9] Rev. Proc. 2013-35, 2013-47, October 31, 2013; Rev. Proc. 2012-41, IRB 2012-45, 539.

[10] Rev. Proc. 2011-52, IRB 2011-45, 701.

[11] Rev. Proc. 2010-40, IRB 2010-46, 663.

[12] Rev. Proc. 2009-50, IRB 2009-45, 617.

[13] Reg. § 25.2523(i)-1.

[14] Code Sec. 2523(f).

[15] Code Sec. 2519.

[16] Reg. § 25.2519-1, amended by T.D. 9077.

[17] Rev. Rul. 98-8, 1998-1 CB 541.

of the spouse's income interest in QTIP property.[18]) This similarity between a sale of the spouse's interest and a commutation is demonstrated by the fact that after paying cash for the value of the remainder interest, the spouse's income interest in the QTIP property is terminated, and the spouse receives outright ownership of the property having a net value equal to the value of the spouse's remainder interest. Thus, following the transaction, the spouse would be in essentially the same economic position as if a commutation of the interest had been effectuated.

In addition, the spouse making a transfer of QTIP property may recover the gift tax, including penalties and interest, on the remainder interest from the recipients of the property.[19] Reg. §25.2207A-1 has been amended to provide, effective July 18, 2003, that if the donee spouse fails to exercise the right to recover the gift tax, such failure constitutes a gift in the amount of the unrecovered gift tax to the person from whom recovery could have been made. Further, any delay in the exercise of the right of recovery is a below-market loan that may be subject to imputation under Code Sec. 7872 (see ¶2161). The donee spouse may waive the right of recovery in writing, thereby causing the spouse's gift of the unrecovered amounts to be complete upon the later of the date of the waiver or the date of the gift tax payment.[20]

If QTIP property received by the surviving spouse is not transferred during the surviving spouse's lifetime, the entire value of the property is included in his or her gross estate at death.

Further, it should be noted that, generally, the transfer to a spouse of an interest in a joint and survivor annuity in which only the spouses have the right to receive payments prior to the death of the surviving spouse qualifies for the marital deduction. However, such a transfer does not qualify for a gift tax marital deduction if either the donor or the executor irrevocably elects out of QTIP treatment.[21] The donee's subsequent transfer of an interest in the annuity is treated as a transfer of all interest in the annuity other than the donor's interest. If the donee dies before the donor, no amount with respect to the annuity is includible in the estate of the donee.

¶ 2314   Split Gifts to Spouse and Charity

A special rule is provided for transfers of interests in the same property made after 1981 to a spouse and a qualifying charitable organization. If an individual creates a qualified charitable remainder annuity or unitrust and if the donor and his or her spouse are the only noncharitable beneficiaries, the prohibition on deduction of terminable interests (see ¶2318) does not apply. The individual receives a charitable deduction for the value of the remainder interest and a marital deduction for the value of the annuity or unitrust income interest, and no transfer tax is imposed.[22]

If the individual transfers a qualified income interest (see ¶1002 and ¶2313) to a spouse with a remainder to charity, the entire value of the property will be considered as passing to the spouse and will qualify for a marital deduction.

---

[18] Reg. §25.2519-1(g), Example 2; *H. Novotny Est.*, 93 TC 12, CCH Dec. 45,822.

[19] Code Sec. 2207A(b).

[20] Reg. §25.2207A-1, as amended by T.D. 9077.

[21] Code Sec. 2523(f)(6).

[22] Code Sec. 2523(g) and Code Sec. 2056(b)(8).

¶ 2316 Pre-1982 Gift Tax Marital Deduction

For gifts made after 1976 and before 1982, a marital deduction was allowed for the first $100,000 of lifetime gifts to the donor's spouse.[23] The next $100,000 of lifetime gifts was fully taxable (that is, gifts ranging from $100,001 to $200,000). A 50-percent deduction applied to lifetime gifts to a spouse in excess of $200,000. The $100,000 lifetime marital deduction was in addition to the $3,000 annual exclusion. Thus, an annual gift of $3,000 to the donor's spouse did not count for purposes of the $100,000 lifetime exclusion for transfers between spouses.

For gifts made prior to 1977, the gift tax marital deduction was limited to 50 percent of the value of the property transferred to the spouse.

¶ 2317 Income to One Other Than Spouse

A gift of a vested remainder interest in property to a donor's spouse qualifies for the marital deduction.[24] It qualifies, even though the income from the property is made payable to the donor or a third person. The two interests in the one property are separate and distinct.

¶ 2318 Life Estate or Other Terminable Interest

Except as discussed at ¶ 2314 for certain interests transferred after 1981, the gift tax marital deduction is not allowed for transfers of "terminable interests."[25] If the transfer is of an interest that will terminate or fail on lapse of time or the occurrence of an event or contingency, or on the failure of an event or contingency to occur, a deduction is not allowed if (1) the reversionary or remainder interest is in the donor or any transferee, other than the spouse, who has acquired the interest for less than an adequate and full consideration in money or money's worth, or (2) the donor or transferee may thereby possess or enjoy any part of the property after such termination or failure of the interest transferred to the spouse.[26]

An exercise or release at any time by the donor (either alone or in conjunction with any person) of a power to appoint an interest in property is deemed to be a transfer by the donor. If the exercise or release is made in favor of a person other than the donor's spouse, a marital deduction will not be allowed.

¶ 2319 Interest in Unidentified Assets

The marital deduction is reduced by the value of assets transferred in trust from which a marital gift may be satisfied and for which a marital deduction would not be allowed if they were transferred by gift to the donor's spouse.[27] This provision has particular application to gifts in trust under which the donor's spouse has the remainder interest or the trust income and a power to appoint to himself or his estate.

> *Example:* David Strom gave his wife, Shirley, an interest valued at $500,000 in a group of assets, most of which qualify for the marital deduction, but one of which does not. The item that does not qualify (an interest in the residual value of an estate) is worth $100,000. For purposes of computing the marital deduction, the value of the interest passing to Shirley is reduced by $100,000.

---

[23] Code Sec. 2523(a), prior to amendment by P.L. 97-34.

[24] Rev. Rul. 54-470, 1954-2 CB 320.

[25] Code Sec. 2523(b).

[26] Code Sec. 2523(b).

[27] Code Sec. 2523(c).

¶ 2320   Joint Ownership

Gifts by the donor to his or her spouse as joint tenant with the donor or as tenant by the entirety are exempt from the terminable interest provisions (see ¶ 2318) and will qualify for the marital deduction.[28] The possibility of the reacquisition of the property through survivorship or severance of the tenancy will not defeat the deduction.

¶ 2321   Power of Appointment

Life estates accompanied by certain powers of appointment are also exempt from terminable interest status.[29] If the donee spouse receives a power of appointment over property held in trust or otherwise, in addition to other interests in the transferred property, a deduction may be allowable. The donee spouse must be able to exercise the power in favor of him- or herself or his or her estate in all events. No one else may have the power to appoint any portion of the interest to anyone other than a donee spouse.

It is not essential that the life estate or the power exist with respect to the entire property involved. It is necessary only that the income be from all or a specific portion of the property transferred and that the power be coextensive with the deductible amount. When the income and power relate only to a portion of the transferred property, only that portion qualifies for the deduction. These requirements are substantially the same as the estate tax requirements.

¶ 2322   Gifts of Community Property

A gift of a donor's interest in community property qualifies for the marital deduction in the case of gifts made after 1981. For gifts made before 1982, no marital deduction was allowable for gifts of such interests or of interests in certain separate property that was considered to be community property for marital deduction purposes.[30]

¶ 2323   Limits on Deductions

The gift tax charitable and marital deductions are allowable only to the extent that the gifts with respect to which those deductions are authorized are included in the total amount of gifts made during the calendar year.[31] This means that both deductions are determined after the annual exclusion is deducted.

> *Example:* In 2013, Lisa Lake makes a cash gift of $17,000 to charity. The entire $17,000 would qualify for the charitable deduction. However, the annual exclusion of $14,000 is deducted first, and, therefore, only $3,000 is included in the total amount of gifts. Lake is entitled to a charitable deduction of $3,000.

¶ 2330   Specific Exemption for Pre-1977 Gifts

In determining the amount of taxable gifts made before 1977 for the calendar quarter, donors who were U.S. citizens or residents at the time the gifts were made were entitled to a specific exemption of $30,000. This amount was reduced by the sum of the amounts claimed and allowed as an exemption in prior calendar years and quarters.[32]

---

[28] Code Sec. 2523(d).

[29] Code Sec. 2523(e).

[30] Code Sec. 2523(f), prior to repeal by P.L. 97-34.

[31] Code Sec. 2524.

[32] Code Sec. 2521, prior to repeal by P.L. 94-455.

The donor had the option of taking the exemption in its entirety in a single calendar quarter or spreading it over a period of calendar quarters in such amounts as he or she saw fit. However, after the limit had been reached, no further exemption was allowable.

¶ 2331   Reporting Deductions on Gift Tax Return

The marital and charitable deductions that are allowed to a donor are reported on lines 6 and 7, respectively of part 4, Schedule A (Computation of Taxable Gifts) of Form 709 (United States Gift (and Generation-Skipping Transfer) Tax Return) (2013). (See the filled-in Form 709 in the Appendix at ¶ 3280.)

Chapter 38
COMPUTATION AND PAYMENT OF TAX

¶ 2350   Cumulative Effect of Tax

The gift tax is cumulative in nature. As a result, prior years' and quarters' gifts push the current year's gifts into higher tax brackets.

The gift tax for each year (quarter for pre-1982 gifts) is determined by computing a tax on the taxable gifts made in that year (or quarter) plus taxable gifts made in all prior years beginning with June 6, 1932, and in all prior quarters beginning with the first quarter of calendar year 1971. In computing the tax on gifts made after 1981, gifts made in all years after 1981 and before the year for which the tax is being computed are also added. There is then subtracted from the resulting figure a tax computed only on the taxable gifts made in prior calendar periods (years and quarters). The unified transfer tax rate schedules (see ¶ 2600) are used in both of these computations for gifts made after 1976. The difference between the two amounts, as computed above, is the amount of gift tax payable for the year or quarter less the unified credit (see ¶ 2376) to the extent it has not been used in preceding calendar periods.

Taxable gifts made after 1981 are reported on an annual return that is due April 15 of the year following the year of the gift.

Because of the method used to compute gift taxes for a given year, it is necessary on the gift tax return not only to determine the amount of taxable gifts for the year covered by the return but also to report the amount of taxable gifts determined for all prior calendar periods, beginning with 1932.

¶ 2355   Gifts for Prior Periods

Before the gift tax for a particular calendar year may actually be computed, it is necessary to take into account the taxable gifts made in prior calendar quarters and years. These gifts for prior quarters and years are recorded on Schedule B (Gifts From Prior Periods) of Form 709 (United States Gift (and Generation-Skipping Transfer) Tax Return) (see the filled-in Form 709 (2013)) in the Appendix at ¶ 3280).

The donor's name as used in each return previously filed should be shown on the current Schedule B if there has been a change in name on the current return or any prior return. Any variation in name (for example, the use of the full given name instead of initials used previously) should be noted.

The amount of the specific exemption claimed for periods prior to 1977 must be entered in column D of Schedule B. The amount of unified credit claimed in prior quarters is entered in column C.

If a tax has been assessed and paid with respect to prior taxable gifts reported on a gift tax return, the IRS may not increase the valuation of such prior gifts once the statutory period of limitation for assessing a deficiency on the gifts has expired.[1] Although this rule does not apply when computing the amount of adjusted taxable gifts for estate tax purposes for gifts made after August 5, 1997, the IRS is not permitted to revalue a gift for estate tax purposes if the three-year statute of limitations has expired on an adequately disclosed gift[2] (see ¶ 1426).

> *Preparation Tip:* For taxable gifts made after December 31, 2009, any unified credit allocated to the prior years/periods must be redetermined using current gift tax rates, rather than the rates that were effective when the prior gifts were made[3] (see ¶ 2008).

¶ 2375   Unified Rate Schedule for Computing Gift Tax

The amount of gift tax payable on gifts made after 1976, but before January 1, 2010 (for any calendar quarter or year), is determined by applying the unified rate schedule to the cumulative lifetime taxable transfers and then subtracting the taxes payable on the lifetime transfers made for past tax periods (including pre-1977 taxable gifts). In computing the tax payable, the subtraction for taxes previously paid is based on the unified rate schedule. (See, however, the discussion at ¶ 2376, "Modifications Necessary to Reflect Impact of Differences in Tax Rates," applicable to taxable gifts made after December 31, 2009.)

For estates of decedents dying and taxable gifts made after December 31, 2009, the unified transfer tax rate schedule applies for both estate and gift tax purposes (see ¶ 1430).

¶ 2376   Unified Gift Tax Credit

For lifetime gifts and at-death transfers made after 1976, a single unified credit is subtracted after the determination of the taxpayer's gift or estate tax liability (see ¶ 1430 and ¶ 2375, above). The use of the unified credit against the tentative gift tax is mandatory.[4] In the case of gift taxes, the unified credit replaced the pre-1977 $30,000 specific exemption. A chart indicating the applicable credit and "exemption equivalent" for 1977 and later years follows.

Unified Credits and "Exemption Equivalents"

Year	Unified Credit	Exemption Equivalent
Jan. 1, 1977–June 30, 1977	$ 6,000	
July 1, 1977–Dec. 31, 1977	30,000	$120,666
1978	34,000	134,000
1979	38,000	147,333
1980	42,500	161,563
1981	47,000	175,225
1982	62,800	225,000
1983	79,300	275,000

---

[1] Code Sec. 2504(c).

[2] *F.R. Smith Est.*, 94 TC 872, CCH Dec. 46,648 (Acq.); Code Sec. 2001(f) and Code Sec. 2504(c).

[3] Tax Relief, Unemployment Reauthorization, and Job Creation Act of 2010 (P.L. 111-312), and American Taxpayer Relief Act of 2012 (P.L. 112-240).

[4] Rev. Rul. 79-398, 1979-2 CB 338.

Year	Unified Credit	Exemption Equivalent
1984	96,300	325,000
1985	121,800	400,000
1986	155,800	500,000
1987–1997	192,800	600,000

Beginning in 1998, the unified credit is determined by reference to the "applicable credit amount" and "the applicable exclusion amount" (formerly the exemption equivalent). The unified credit is as follows:

Year	Applicable Credit Amount	Applicable Exclusion Amount
1998	$202,050	$625,000
1999	211,300	650,000
2000 and 2001	220,550	675,000

• Impact of the 2001, 2010 and 2012 Acts

Appearing below are the applicable credit and applicable exclusion amounts, as revised by the Economic Growth and Tax Relief Reconciliation Act of 2001 (P.L. 107-16) (EGTRRA), the Tax Relief, Unemployment Insurance Reauthorization, and Job Creation Act of 2010 (P.L. 111-312) (Tax Relief Act of 2010), and the American Taxpayer Relief Act of 2012 (P.L. 112-240) (ATRA) for the years 2002 through 2014:

Applicable Credit and Exclusion Amounts

Year	Applicable Credit	Applicable Exclusion
2002 through 2009	$345,800	$1,000,000
2010	330,800*	1,000,000

* The applicable credit is reduced for 2010 because in that year the maximum gift tax rate was reduced to 35 percent (from 45 percent in 2009).

2011	$1,730,800	$5,000,000
2012	1,772,800	5,120,000**
2013	2,045,800	5,250,000**
2014	2,081,800	5,340,000**

** Beginning in 2012 the applicable exclusion (and the applicable credit, which is based thereon), is indexed for inflation.

A husband and wife may each claim separate unified gift tax credits in the amounts specified above for gifts made by each of them, even though these gifts may have resulted from the gift-splitting provisions of Code Sec. 2513 (see ¶ 2013). Thus, married couples may give away substantial amounts to their children or other donees without incurring any gift tax liability.

• Computation of Credit Following Prior Year Gifts

When computing amount of the applicable credit for purposes of determining a current year gift tax liability, the credit noted in the chart above must be reduced by sum of the amounts allowable as a credit under Code Sec. 2505 for all preceding calendar periods.

• Modifications Necessary to Reflect Impact of Differences in Tax Rates

The computation of both estate and gift taxes was clarified to reflect the changes in transfer tax rates made by the Tax Relief Act of 2010. Effective for gifts made after December 31, 2009, for purposes of determining the amount of gift tax that would have been paid on one or more prior year gifts, the estate tax rates in effect under Code Sec. 2001(c) at the time of the decedent's death are used to compute both (1) the gift tax imposed by Chapter 12 of the Internal Revenue Code with respect to such gifts, and (2) the unified credit allowed against such gifts under Code Sec. 2505 (including the computation of the applicable credit amount under Code Sec. 2505(a)(1) and the sum of amounts allowed as a credit for all preceding periods under Code Sec. 2505(a)(2)). See ¶ 2008 for a discussion of the steps necessary to compute the unified credit used against taxable gifts made in prior quarters/years, and how to reflect the amounts computed on Schedule B of Form 709.

• *Portability of Deceased Spouse's Unused Applicable Exclusion Amount*

The estate of a decedent who is survived by a spouse may make an election to permit the surviving spouse to apply the decedent's unused exclusion (the deceased spousal unused exclusion amount, or DSUE amount) to the surviving spouse's own transfers made during lifetime and at death. This portability election may be made only by the estates of decedents dying after December 31, 2010 (see ¶ 16). See, also, ¶ 2007 for a discussion of Form 709 (United States Gift (and Generation-Skipping Transfer) Tax Return (2013)), Schedule C, relating to the DSUE election.

• *Computation of Credit for Prior Gifts (Pre-2010 Law)*

As discussed above, when computing the allowable credit for taxable gifts made after December 31, 2009, the unified credit available for prior taxable gifts must be recomputed with reference to the unified credit and gift tax rates applicable to the *current tax year*. With respect to gifts made before January 1, 2010, the unified credit utilized against the actual payment of gift tax was used to determine the unified credit available for current year gifts. However, the amount of the credit allowed could not exceed the amount of the gift tax imposed on the donor for the particular calendar quarter or year. In addition, the amount of the credit that was available for gifts made in one of the above years had to be reduced by the sum of the amounts allowable as a credit to the donor for all preceding calendar quarters or years.

• *IRS Revaluation of Prior Taxable Gifts*

Under Code Sec. 2504(c), the IRS may not, for gift tax purposes, revalue a prior taxable gift that was properly reported on a gift tax return once the statute of limitations for assessing a deficiency has expired on that prior gift. For this rule to apply, a gift tax must have been paid on the prior gift. However, for gifts made after December 31, 1996, recently adopted amendments to the regulations[5] state that the IRS will be barred from revaluing prior gifts only if such gifts were adequately disclosed (see ¶ 1426 for a discussion of what constitutes adequate disclosure). For gift tax returns covered by the adequate disclosure regulations, it is no longer necessary that a gift tax liability have been paid in order to block IRS revaluation of a time-expired prior gift. Thus, a gift tax return adequately disclosing gifts of present interests, each of which was shielded by the $10,000 annual exclusion (which, because of an inflation adjustment, rose to $11,000 for gifts made in 2002 through 2005; $12,000 for gifts made in 2006, 2007 and 2008; $13,000 for gifts made in 2009 through 2012; and $14,000 for gifts made in 2013 and 2014 (see ¶ 2250)), could not be revalued by the IRS once the statute of limitations for assessing a deficiency on the gifts had expired.

---

[5] Reg. § 25.2504-2 and Reg. § 301.6501(c)-1, as amended by T.D. 8845, Dec. 2, 1999; Rev. Proc. 2000-34, 2000-2 CB 186.

See, also ¶1426 regarding revaluation of prior gifts for estate tax purposes where the period of limitations has expired.

• *Transitional Rule for Certain Gifts Made in 1976*

A special adjustment (transitional) rule applied with respect to gifts made during the period September 9, 1976, through December 31, 1976. To the extent that use was made of the $30,000 lifetime exemption during this period, the allowable unified gift tax credit is reduced by an amount equal to 20 percent of the exemption. Thus, if the full $30,000 exemption was used during this period, a maximum reduction of $6,000 would be made to the unified credit.

¶ 2378   Benefits of Graduated Rates and Unified Credit Phased Out for Pre-2002 Gifts

For gifts made before January 1, 2002, the benefits of the graduated rates and the unified credit under the unified transfer tax system are phased out beginning with cumulative transfers rising above $10 million. This was accomplished by adding a surtax of five percent of the excess of any transfer over $10 million to the tentative tax computed in determining the ultimate transfer tax liability. The Economic Growth and Tax Relief Reconciliation Act of 2001 (P.L. 107-16) (2001 Act) repealed the five-percent surtax for estates of decedents dying, and gifts made, after December 31, 2001. The five-percent surtax was not reinstated by the Tax Relief, Unemployment Insurance Reauthorization, and Job Creation Act of 2010 (P.L. 111-312).

For estates of decedents dying and gifts made after 1987 and before 1998, the tax is levied on amounts transferred in excess of $10 million but not exceeding $21,040,000, in order to recapture the benefit of any transfer tax rate below 55 percent as well as the unified credit.

Due to mistakes in the wording of the amendment to Code Sec. 2001(c)(2) by the Taxpayer Relief Act of 1997 (P.L. 105-34), the five-percent additional tax phases out the benefits of graduated rates, but not the benefits of the unified credit (applicable credit amount), for estates of decedents dying, and gifts made, after 1997. Therefore, the additional tax is levied on amounts transferred after 1997, but before January 1, 2002, in excess of $10 million, but not exceeding $17,184,000. The applicable credit amount is not recaptured.

Although the provision of the Revenue Act of 1987 (P.L. 100-203) that added the phaseout rules is effective with respect to transfers made after 1987, the Conference Committee Report to that Act states that pre-effective-date gifts are included in cumulative transfers for purposes of determining the adjustment for transfers made after the effective date; however, the tax rate on the earlier gifts remains unchanged. Thus, according to the Committee Report, if a person makes a $9 million gift before 1988, and an additional $4 million gift after 1987, $3 million of the latter transfer will be subject to the additional tax under the phaseout.

¶ 2380   Generation-Skipping Transfers

Generation-skipping transfers made during a calendar year are subject to the normal gift tax and to the generation-skipping transfer (GST) tax. The gift tax on such transfers is computed in the usual manner as described at ¶2350 through ¶2376, above.

However, the GST tax is computed separately from the gift tax and, if applicable, represents an additional tax that must be paid on Form 709 (United

States Gift (and Generation-Skipping Transfer) Tax Return). The GST tax is computed on Schedule D (Computation of Generation-Skipping Transfer Tax) of Form 709. Lifetime generation-skipping transfers occurring in 2013 are to be reported on Schedule D. A filled-in Form 709 (2013) is reproduced at ¶3280.

¶2382   Gift Tax Treaties

Gift tax treaties are in force between the United States and Australia, Austria, Denmark, France, Germany, Japan, Sweden (which is no longer effective as of January 1, 2008), and the United Kingdom. For specific information, the applicable treaty should be consulted. See CCH FEDERAL ESTATE AND GIFT TAX REPORTS for the text of such treaties.

¶2400   Due Date for Payment

The gift tax is generally paid at the same time the return is required to be filed.[6] The annual gift tax return is due by April 15 of the year following that in which the gifts were made. However, for the calendar year in which the donor dies, the gift tax return will be due on the earlier of the due date (with extensions) for filing the donor's estate tax return, or the "normal" due date with respect to gifts (April 15 following the calendar year in which the gifts were made). However, see ¶1650 for special extensions allowed to those affected by federally declared disasters, and by terrorist attacks against the United States.

> *Preparation Tip:* Payment of gift tax should be sent to the IRS Service Center, Cincinnati, OH 45999 (the same address where the gift tax return is to be filed).

An extension of time to file an income tax return made on Form 4868 (Application for Automatic Extension of Time to File U.S. Individual Income Tax Return) (2013) also is deemed to be an extension of time to file an annual gift tax return.[7] Payment in full of gift and generation-skipping taxes with the extension application avoids interest and penalties.

If a taxpayer does not request an income tax extension, Form 8892, Application for Automatic Extension of Time To File Form 709 and/or Payment of Gift/Generation-Skipping Transfer Tax (Rev. Dec. 2008), should be used to request an extension of time to file the taxpayer's gift tax return. This form must be used instead of writing a letter to the Cincinnati Service Center to request an extension of time to file Form 709. In addition to containing an extension request, Form 8892 also serves as a payment voucher for the gift tax balance due at the time of the extension.[8]

Under Temp. Reg. §25.6081-1T, a donor will be allowed an automatic six-month extension of time to file Form 709 if Form 8892 is properly submitted.[9]

A donor who fails to pay the tax is liable for a penalty of one-half of one percent of the amount of such tax for each month that the tax remains unpaid up to a maximum of 25 percent.[10] In addition, a lien attaches to the transferred property and the donee may be held personally liable.[11]

---

[6] Code Sec. 6151.
[7] General Instructions for Form 4868 (2013).
[8] Instructions for Form 709 (2013), p. 4.

[9] T.D. 9229, Nov. 4, 2005.
[10] Code Sec. 6651(a)(2).
[11] Code Sec. 6901 and Code Sec. 6902.

¶ 2405   Form of Payment

Money orders and checks drawn on any bank or trust company incorporated under the laws of the United States, a state, territory or possession of the United States may be accepted by the appropriate IRS officer in payment of gift taxes. The check or money order in payment of the tax should be made payable to the "United States Treasury." The donor's Social Security number, along with the number of the accompanying form and the applicable year, should be written on the check or money order. A donor may not use an overpayment of income taxes on Form 1040 to offset gift and generation-skipping transfer taxes owed on Form 709.[12]

Effective for tax payments made after December 31, 1998, the IRS is authorized to accept payment of taxes by credit or debit card. A payment by credit or debit card is deemed made when the card issuer authorizes the transaction, provided that the payment is actually received in the ordinary course of business. Although the IRS is prohibited from imposing a fee on individuals who pay their taxes by such methods, third-party service providers contracted to process the credit and debit card transactions are not prohibited from charging fees.[13]

• Partial Payments

If additional taxes, penalty, and interest have been assessed against a taxpayer and the taxpayer provides specific written directions as to how his or her partial payment is to be applied, the IRS will apply the payment in accordance with such directions. However, if the taxpayer does not provide such written directions, the IRS will apply the payment to periods in the order of priority that will serve the "best interest" of the IRS. The payment will be applied to satisfy the liability for successive periods, in descending order of priority, until the payment is fully absorbed. If the amount applied is less than the liability, the amount will be applied to tax, penalty, and interest, in that order. Similar rules will apply for payments made pursuant to the terms of offers in compromise and collateral agreements.[14]

¶ 2410   Discount and Interest

No discount is allowed for payment of the gift tax in advance of the last day for payment of the tax. If the tax is not paid when due, interest and various penalties may be assessed. If the tax required to be shown on the return is simply not paid when due, interest at the current rate (see ¶ 1680) is charged from the last date for payment to the date when paid.[15] Under other circumstances, more serious penalties can apply.[16]

Extensions of time for payment of up to six months may be granted.[17]

---

[12] Instructions for Form 709 (2013), p. 17.
[13] Reg. § 301.6311-2.
[14] Rev. Proc. 2002-26, 2002-1 CB 746, superseding Rev. Rul. 73-304, 1973-2 CB 42, Rev. Rul. 73-305, 1973-2 CB 43, and Rev. Rul. 79-284, 1979-2 CB 83.

[15] Code Sec. 6601(a) and Code Sec. 6601(b).
[16] Code Sec. 6651.
[17] Code Sec. 6161(a).

GENERATION-SKIPPING TRANSFER TAX
Chapter 39
GENERAL RULES

¶ 2430   Purpose and Nature of the Tax

Property that is transferred to an heir or donee and eventually transferred to such person's own heirs or donees is generally exposed twice to federal estate or gift taxes. To avoid the second round of taxation, grantors sometimes have created life interests, with remainder interests reserved for members of subsequent generations. Generally, a generation-skipping transfer (GST) tax is imposed on such trusts or trust equivalents (see ¶ 2431). The GST tax is designed to tax this means of transferring accumulated wealth to successive generations in much the same way that a gift or estate tax would have taxed the outright transfer of the property by gift or inheritance.

The GST tax[1] attempts to simplify compliance and administration by applying the tax to direct beneficial interests only (powers over trust property are not subject to taxation). Additionally, the tax is applied to direct skips, as well as to taxable terminations and distributions (see ¶ 2433).

Generation-skipping transfers (whether made during lifetime, or at death), occurring after December 31, 2012, are taxed at a 40 percent rate; a 35 percent rate applies to GSTs made in 2011 and 2012. A zero percent rate applied to GSTs occurring in 2010 (see ¶ 2459).

Like the estate tax, the tax on generation-skipping transfers was repealed by the Economic Growth and Tax Relief Reconciliation Act of 2001 (P.L. 107-16) (2001 Act), effective for generation-skipping transfers after December 31, 2009. Also like the estate tax, the GST tax was retroactively reinstated for GSTs occurring after December 31, 2009. However, a zero percent tax rate applied to GSTs made in 2010 (see ¶ 2459).

¶ 2431   What Is a Generation-Skipping Transfer?

The generation-skipping transfer (GST) tax applies to direct skips (for example, a transfer from a grandparent to a grandchild), as well as to taxable distributions and terminations (see ¶ 2433) of generation-skipping trust property.[2] The tax does not apply to any transfer (other than a direct skip) from a trust if the transfer was subject to estate or gift tax with respect to a person in the first generation below that of the grantor.

---

[1] Code Sec. 2601 through Code Sec. 2664.   [2] Code Sec. 2611.

Gifts reported on Schedule A (Computation of Taxable Gifts) of Form 709 (United States Gift (and Generation-Skipping Transfer) Tax Return)[3] that are also generation-skipping transfers may be subject to both gift and GST taxes. On the other hand, with one exception, if a transfer is excluded from the gift tax, then it is not subject to the GST tax. For example, an *inter vivos* transfer that is not subject to gift tax due to the exclusion from the gift tax of certain transfers for educational or medical expenses[4] is not a generation-skipping transfer. An exception exists where there is a nontaxable gift to a trust that is also a direct skip. In that situation, the transfer is subject to the GST tax unless no corpus or income may be distributed to anyone other than the beneficiary and the trust assets are includible in the beneficiary's estate if the beneficiary dies during the trust term.

• Property Subject to Tax Only Once

Also excluded from the category of a taxable transfer is any transfer to the extent that the property transferred was previously subject to the GST tax.[5] However, the transferee in the prior transfer must have been a member of the same or a lower generation than the transferee in the later transfer. Additionally, the effect of the transfer must not be to avoid the GST tax entirely.

• Distributions from Trust Income Taxed

Distributions from a trust that qualify as generation-skipping distributions are subject to tax whether the distributions are from the trust income or the trust corpus. However, where the distribution is from the trust income, the recipient is entitled to an income tax deduction[6] for the amount of the GST tax paid.

¶ 2433   Taxable Terminations and Distributions; Direct Skips

The terms "direct skip," "taxable distribution," and "taxable termination" have special meanings for generation-skipping transfer (GST) tax purposes. The occurrence of any of these three situations can result in the imposition of the GST tax. However, there was a $3,500,000 exemption for 2009; a $5,000,000 exemption for 2010, and 2011; a $5,120,000 exemption (indexed for inflation) for 2012; a $5,250,000 exemption (indexed) for 2013; and a $5,340,000 exemption (indexed) for 2014 (see ¶ 2455[7]).

• Direct Skip

Two types of transfers considered direct skips are (1) a transfer outright for the benefit of a "skip person," and (2) a transfer of property to a trust exclusively for one or more such beneficiaries.[8] The transfer may occur during the transferor's lifetime or at death. Generally, a "skip person" is any beneficiary assigned to a generation that is two or more generations below that of the grantor. The term is further defined at ¶ 2435.

An exemption amount is provided for each person making a generation-skipping transfer. The amount of this exemption was $3,500,000 for 2009, $5,000,000 for 2010 and 2011, a $5,120,000 exemption (indexed) for 2012, a

---

[3] A filled-in Form 709 (2013) is reproduced at ¶ 3280.

[4] Code Sec. 529(c)(2), Code Sec. 2503(e), and Code Sec. 2611(b).

[5] Code Sec. 2611(b).

[6] Code Sec. 164(a)(4).

[7] Code Sec. 2010(c)(2)(A), as amended by the Tax Relief, Unemployment Insurance Reauthorization, and Job Creation Act of 2010 (P.L. 111-312), and the American Taxpayer Relief Act of 2012 (P.L. 112-240).

[8] Code Sec. 2612(c) and Code Sec. 2613.

$5,250,000 exemption (indexed) for 2013, and a $5,340,000 exemption (indexed) in 2014(see ¶2455).

• *Taxable Distribution*

A "taxable distribution" occurs whenever there is a distribution from a generation-skipping trust to a skip person.[9]

> *Example:* Lorna Lane establishes a discretionary trust for the benefit of Lilly and Lorenzo, her daughter and grandson. Lorenzo is a "skip person" because he is two or more generations younger than Lorna. If the trustee makes a distribution of trust corpus to Lorenzo, it will be a taxable distribution.

• *Taxable Termination*

A "taxable termination" occurs on the termination of an interest in property held in trust. However, no taxable termination will occur if a nonskip person has an interest in the property immediately after such termination or if a distribution may not be made from the trust to a skip person at any time after the termination.[10] Such a termination usually occurs on the death of the person holding a life interest in the trust or on the lapse of time in a case where the grantor created an estate for years.

A partial termination of a trust is taxable if, on the termination of an interest in property held in a trust, a specified portion of the trust assets is distributed to skip persons who are lineal descendants of the holder of the interest (or to one or more trusts for the exclusive benefit of such persons).

¶ 2435   Skip Person and Nonskip Person Defined

A "skip person" is a natural person assigned to a generation that is two or more generations below the generation of the transferor.[11]

> *Example (1):* Jim Feldman's grandchild, Sam, is a "skip person" for purposes of the generation-skipping transfer tax, as is his great-grandchild, Sally. Sam is in a generation that is two generations below that of his grandfather, Jim. Sally's generation is three generations below that of Jim. (See ¶2437 for a discussion of assignment of generations.)

The term "skip person" refers to a trust if (1) all interests in the trust are held by skip persons, or (2) there is no nonskip person holding an interest in such trust, and at no time after the generation-skipping transfer may a distribution be made from the trust to a nonskip person.

> *Example (2):* Maria Jacobs creates a testamentary trust wherein income will be distributed to her husband for his life and, at his death, the remainder will be split between Maria's daughter and her grandson. The trust would not be a "skip person" because two "nonskip persons" hold an interest in the trust: Maria's husband and her daughter.

A direct skip (see ¶2433) transfer to a transferor's grandchild will not be taxable, however, if the child of the transferor who was that grandchild's parent is deceased at the time of the transfer (see ¶2437). In such a situation, the grandchild and all succeeding lineal descendants are "moved up" a generation.[12] A descendant who dies within 90 days after a transfer is treated as having

---

[9] Code Sec. 2612(b).
[10] Code Sec. 2612(a).

[11] Code Sec. 2613.
[12] Code Sec. 2612(c)(2).

predeceased the transferor, if state law or the governing instrument so provides.[13]

¶ 2437 Assignment of Generations

Generally, assignment of generations is determined along family lines. For example, a transferor, the transferor's spouse, and the transferor's brothers and sisters are one generation. Their children constitute the next generation, and the transferor's grandchildren are two generations below that of the transferor.

• Predeceased Parent Rule

A transfer to an individual who is a descendant of the parent of the transferor (or the transferor's spouse or former spouse) is moved up one generation if the individual's parent, who is a lineal descendant of the parent of the transferor (or the transferor's spouse or former spouse) is dead at the time of the transfer.[14] Thus, a transfer to a grandchild whose parent is dead is not considered a generation-skipping transfer. The Taxpayer Relief Act of 1997 (P.L. 105-34) extended the predeceased parent rule to collateral heirs of the transferor, such as grandnieces and grandnephews. However, in order for transfers to collateral heirs to qualify for the exception, the transferor must have no lineal descendants. The Act also extended the predeceased parent rule to taxable terminations and taxable distributions, provided that the parent of the relevant beneficiary was dead at the earliest time that the transfer (from which the beneficiary's interest in the property was established) was subject to the estate or gift tax. For transfers prior to 1998, the rule only applied to direct skips to the grandchildren of the transferor, or the transferor's spouse or former spouse. For purposes of the predeceased parent rule, a living descendant who dies within 90 days after a transfer is treated as having predeceased the transferor if applicable state law or the governing instrument so provides.[15]

Final regulations adopted. Final amendments to regulations have been adopted that provide rules and examples regarding the application of the predeceased parent rule of Code Sec. 2651(e).[16] There is an exception to the general rule that a transfer to a grandchild of the transferor is subject to generation-skipping transfer (GST) tax. Under the predeceased parent rule of Code Sec. 2651(e), if a parent of the transferor's grandchild is a lineal descendant of the transferor and that parent is deceased at the time of the transfer, the grandchild is treated as the child of the transferor for purposes of the GST tax. The final regulations provide that for purposes of determining if an individual's parent is deceased at the time of a testamentary transfer, an individual's parent who dies no later than ninety days after a transfer occurring by reason of the death of the transferor is treated as having predeceased the transferor.

In addition, the regulations specify that an individual will be treated as a member of the generation that is one generation below an adoptive parent for purposes of determining whether a transfer from the adoptive parent to the adopted individual is subject to the GST tax if the individual is: (1) legally adopted by the adoptive parent; (2) a descendant of a parent of the adoptive parent or the adoptive parent's spouse; (3) under the age of 18 at the time of the adoption; and (4) not adopted primarily for GST tax-avoidance purposes, based on all of the facts and circumstances. Moreover, under the regulations, the

---

[13] Reg. §26.2612-1(a)(2)(i).
[14] Code Sec. 2651(e).
[15] Reg. §26.2612-1(a)(2)(i).

[16] Reg. §26.2651-1, 26.2651-2, and 26.2651-3, as amended by T.D. 9214, July 15, 2005.

predeceased parent rule applies to transfers to collateral heirs when the transferor has no living lineal descendants. Furthermore, the regulations clarify that an adoption may create another generation assignment but will not substitute for the blood relationship.

The rules of Reg. § 26.2651-1 and Reg. § 26.2651-2 are effective for terminations, distributions and transfers occurring after July 18, 2005. However, taxpayers may rely on any reasonable interpretation of Code Sec. 2651(e) for transfers occurring after December 31, 1997, and before July 18, 2005.

• Persons Who Are Not Lineal Descendants

An individual who is not a lineal descendant is assigned to a generation on the basis of that individual's date of birth (subject, however, to the rules for treatment of legal adoptions, etc., discussed below).[17] An individual born within $12^1/2$ years of the date of the transferor's birth is assigned to the same generation as the transferor. An individual born more than $12^1/2$ years after but within $37^1/2$ years of the transferor's birth is assigned to the first generation younger than the transferor. Subsequent generation assignments are similarly made on the basis of 25-year periods.

• Marriage, Legal Adoptions, and Half-Blood Relationships

For purposes of the generation-skipping transfer (GST) tax, a relationship by legal adoption or half-blood is equivalent to a relationship by whole-blood.[18] An individual who is married at any time to a transferor is assigned to the transferor's generation. Similarly, an individual who is married at any time to a lineal descendant of the transferor is assigned to the same generation as the descendant.[19] However, where, because of the application of the generation-skipping transfer predeceased parent rule, a grandchild was not deemed to be a skip person, the later adoption of the grandchild by his aunt did not alter his relationship to his grandparents for purposes of the GST tax. Accordingly, the adoption did not cause the grandchild to be reclassified as a skip person.[20]

• Other Special Rules

Unless otherwise provided in regulations, an individual who could be assigned to more than one generation is assigned to the youngest such generation.[21]

If an estate, trust, partnership, corporation, or other entity has an interest in property, each individual having a beneficial interest in such entity is treated as having an interest in the property and is assigned to a generation as discussed above. A charitable organization or a charitable trust is assigned to the transferor's generation.[22]

¶ 2439   Other Definitions

The following definitions apply with respect to the generation-skipping transfer (GST) tax.

---

[17] Code Sec. 2651(d).
[18] Code Sec. 2651(b)(3).
[19] Code Sec. 2651(c).

[20] IRS Letter Ruling 199907015 (Nov. 20, 1998).
[21] Code Sec. 2651(f).
[22] Code Sec. 2651(f)(3).

- *"Interest"*

A person has an interest in property held in trust if (at the time the determination is made) that person is a mandatory or permissible recipient of distributions from the trust.[23] A beneficiary of a charitable remainder annuity trust, a charitable remainder unitrust,[24] or a pooled income fund[25] also has an interest in trust property. Certain "interests" used primarily to avoid the GST tax are disregarded.

Additionally, the fact that income or corpus of the trust may be used to satisfy an obligation of support arising under state law is disregarded in determining if a person has an interest in a trust, if (1) such use is discretionary, or (2) such use is pursuant to a state law substantially like the Uniform Gifts to Minors Act.[26]

- *"Transferor"*

A decedent is the "transferor," for purposes of the GST tax, when the transfer is of any property that would be subject to the estate tax. The donor is the transferor when the transfer is of any property that would be subject to the gift tax.[27] In addition, the Tax Court has held that the holder of a general power of appointment over property includible in the estate of the holder for estate tax purposes is a transferor for purposes of the GST tax.[28]

- *"Trust" and "Trustee"*

The term "trust" includes any arrangement (other than an estate) that has substantially the same effect as a trust.[29] In such a case, the "trustee" is the person in actual or constructive possession of the property subject to such an arrangement. Examples of arrangements to which these definitions apply include life estates and remainders, estates for years, and insurance and annuity contracts.[30]

- *Special Election Available*

If property qualifies for estate[31] or gift[32] tax qualified terminable interest property (QTIP) treatment, the estate of the decedent or the donor spouse may elect to treat such property as if the QTIP election had not been made, for purposes of the GST tax. Once made, however, this "reverse QTIP election" is irrevocable.[33] The effect of the reverse QTIP election is to permit the first spouse to die to be treated as the transferor of the GST tax-exempt QTIP trust. This election is necessary, because otherwise the surviving spouse would be deemed to be the transferor by reason of the inclusion of the QTIP trust in the survivor's estate under Code Sec. 2044.

> *Caution:* Partial reverse QTIP elections may not be made. However, it may be possible to divide the QTIP trust into separate exempt and nonexempt trusts before the election is made.

---

[23] Code Sec. 2652(c).
[24] Code Sec. 664.
[25] Code Sec. 642(c)(5).
[26] Code Sec. 2652(c)(3).
[27] Code Sec. 2652(a)(1).
[28] *E. Peterson Marital Trust*, CA-2, 96-1 USTC ¶60,225, aff'g TC, 102 TC 790, CCH Dec. 49,935; Followed: *E. Gerson Est.*, CA-6, 2007-2 USTC ¶60,551, aff'g TC (Reviewed by Court), CCH Dec. 56,654, 121 TC 139. However, on similar facts the U.S. Court of Appeals for the Eighth Circuit reached an opposite result: *J. Simpson*, CA-8, 99-2 USTC ¶60,351, Nonacq., IRB 2000-9. Followed: *R. Bachler*, CA-9, 2002-1 USTC ¶60,430, rev'g DC Cal., 2000-2 USTC ¶60,390.
[29] Code Sec. 2652(b)(1).
[30] Code Sec. 2652(b)(3).
[31] Code Sec. 2056(b)(7).
[32] Code Sec. 2523(f).
[33] Reg. §26.2652-2.

Pursuant to Reg. §301.9100-1 and Reg. §301.9100-3, the IRS may grant an extension to file a reverse QTIP election on a showing that the taxpayer acted reasonably and in good faith, and that the interests of the government are not jeopardized. An executor who wishes to make a reverse QTIP after the deadline for doing so has expired can request relief by way of a letter ruling request under the rules of Rev. Proc. 2012-1[34] or its successor.

• *Simplified Procedure for Making Late Reverse QTIP Elections*

The IRS has detailed a simplified alternative method that may be used, effective August 9, 2004, to request an extension of time to make a reverse QTIP election.[35] Generally, an executor or trustee is eligible to use the alternative method in lieu of the letter ruling process if the following requirements are met:

(1) a valid Code Sec. 2056(b)(7) QTIP election was made for the property or trust on the decedent's federal estate tax return;

(2) the reverse QTIP election was not made on the return as filed because the qualified tax professional relied on by the taxpayer failed to advise the taxpayer of the need for making the election;

(3) the decedent has a sufficient amount of unused GST exemption, after the automatic allocation,[36] to result in a zero inclusion ratio for the reverse QTIP trust or property;

(4) the estate is not eligible for the automatic six-month extension;[37]

(5) the surviving spouse has not made a lifetime disposition of any part of the qualifying income interest for life in the QTIP property;

(6) the surviving spouse is alive, or no more than six months have passed since the surviving spouse's death; and

(7) the procedural requirements set forth in section 4.03 of Rev. Proc. 2004-47 have been met.

This simplified alternative procedure may not be used where the permission to file a late reverse QTIP election is in connection with a late severance of a trust included in the decedent's gross estate, or in conjunction with an allocation of GST exemption. Such requests must be made through the letter ruling process.

¶ 2440 Applicable Provisions

All of the Internal Revenue Code provisions on procedure and administration, including penalties (Subtitle F), that apply to estate and gift taxation are applicable to the generation-skipping transfer tax.[38] Estate tax rules govern transfers occurring as a result of death; gift tax rules apply to *inter vivos* transfers.

¶ 2441 Effective Dates

The rules affecting generation-skipping transfers are generally applicable to transfers made after October 22, 1986. However, certain transfers from trusts that were irrevocable prior to that date are not subject to the generation-skipping transfer (GST) tax. Consequently, care must be taken when a transfer is contemplated from such a trust. In general, the following exceptions to the effective date rules apply:[39]

---

[34] IRB 2012-1, 1.
[35] Rev. Proc. 2004-47, 2004-2 CB 169.
[36] Code Sec. 2632(e); Reg. § 26.2632-1(d)(2).

[37] Reg. § 301.9100-2(b).
[38] Code Sec. 2661.
[39] Reg. § 26.2601-1(b).

(1) The GST tax does not apply to any generation-skipping transfer under a trust that was irrevocable on September 25, 1985, but only to the extent that such transfer was not made out of corpus added to the trust after that date. This exception was amended by the Technical and Miscellaneous Revenue Act of 1988 (P.L. 100-647) to clarify that the exception regarding irrevocable trusts applies without regard to whether income received from corpus contributions made before September 26, 1985, is distributed or accumulated.[40] The exercise of a limited power of appointment over a trust that was irrevocable on September 25, 1985, does not cause property subject to the power to lose its exemption from the GST tax if the power may not be exercised to postpone or suspend the vesting, absolute ownership, or power of alienation of an interest in the property for the longer of (1) 90 years as provided by the Uniform Rule Against Perpetuities, or (2) 21 years after the death of any life in being when the irrevocable trust was created.[41] However, assets that were transferred from a marital trust that was irrevocable prior to the effective date of the GST tax were subject to the GST tax because the transfer was treated as being made from property constructively added after the effective date of the GST tax, because of the lapse of a surviving spouse's testamentary general power of appointment over the property.[42]

(2) Any generation-skipping transfers occurring under wills or revocable trusts executed before October 22, 1986, are not subject to the tax, provided that the following conditions are met: (a) the document in existence on October 21, 1986, was not amended after that date in a manner that resulted in the creation of, or an increase in the amount of, a generation-skipping transfer; (b) in the case of a revocable trust, no addition was made to the trust after October 21, 1986, that resulted in the creation of, or increase in the amount of, a generation-skipping transfer; and (c) the decedent died before January 1, 1987.[43] Furthermore, revocable trusts that became irrevocable due to the transferor's death between September 25, 1985, and October 23, 1986, are also excluded from the category of taxable transfers.[44]

(3) Any generation-skipping transfer occurring under a trust (to the extent that such trust consists of property, or proceeds thereof, the value of which was included in a decedent's gross estate) or which is a direct skip occurring by reason of a decedent's death is not subject to the tax if the decedent was legally incompetent on October 22, 1986, and at all times thereafter until death. However, the exception does not apply to property transferred to such incompetent decedent (or to a trust) by gift or by reason of the death of another person, after August 3, 1990.[45]

The delays in effective dates were adopted to permit a reasonable period of time for individuals to re-execute their wills to reflect the extension of the GST tax to direct skips.

---

[40] Act Sec. 1014(h) of P.L. 100-647, amending Act Sec. 1433(b) of P.L. 99-514.

[41] Reg. § 26.2601-1(b)(1)(v)(B)(2).

[42] *E. Peterson Marital Trust*, CA-2, 96-1 USTC ¶ 60,225, aff'g TC, 102 TC 790, CCH Dec. 49,935; Followed, with respect to an exercised power held under an exempt trust: *E. Gerson Est.*, CA-6, 2007-2 USTC ¶ 60,551, aff'g TC (Review by Court), CCH Dec. 56,654, 121 TC 139. However, on similar facts the U.S.

Court of Appeals for the Eighth Circuit reached an opposite result: *J. Simpson*, CA-8, 99-2 USTC ¶ 60,351, Nonacq., IRB 2000-9. Followed: *R. Bachler*, CA-9, 2002-1 USTC ¶ 60,430, rev'g DC Cal., 2000-2 USTC ¶ 60,390.

[43] Reg. § 26.2601-1(b)(2).

[44] Reg. § 26.2601-1(a)(4).

[45] Act Sec. 11703(c) of P.L. 101-508; Reg. § 26.2601-1(b)(3).

• *Grandfathered Trusts*

In the following instances, the IRS has ruled that grandfathered status was not disturbed:

(1) the partition of a trust into two or more separate trusts, so long as the quality, value, or timing of the beneficial interests, rights, or expectancies provided in the original trust did not change;[46]

(2) the distribution of corpus to trust beneficiaries pursuant to a settlement agreement so long as each beneficiary received a terminating distribution that fairly reflected the value of the beneficiary's interest in the trust;[47]

(3) a settlement agreement among beneficiaries of a decedent's estate to transfer a portion of trust assets to a new trust where the settlement agreement was within the range of reasonable settlement agreements;[48]

(4) the merger of trusts with substantially identical terms;[49]

(5) the merger of two charitable annuity trusts and the loan back of some or all of the surviving trust's distributions to the surviving trust;[50]

(6) qualified disclaimers made after October 22, 1986, with respect to the estate of a decedent who died prior to that date;[51]

(7) the transfer of a beneficiary's contingent remainder interest in a trust created under the transferor's will, provided that the transfer did not (a) cause any change in the quality, value, or timing of any beneficiary's interest in the trust, (b) confer any additional powers or beneficial interests on any beneficiaries, (c) create any additional generation-skipping transfers or increase the amount of any generation-skipping transfer, or (d) change the number of younger generations provided for in the decedent's will;[52]

(8) the renunciation by the income beneficiary of an annuity interest in a trust and the purchase by the remainder beneficiaries of a commercial annuity of equal or greater value for the income beneficiary's benefit;[53]

(9) a spouse's power to appoint herself as trustee of a trust under which she was a beneficiary was not a general power of appointment because of a state statute limiting the exercise of this type of power. The state (Florida) statute prohibited the trustee from exercising discretionary powers in a manner other than for the trustee's health, support, maintenance, or education. The statute limiting the trustee's discretion in this manner was enacted after the spouse had already become a co-trustee. The IRS also found that the amendment did not constitute a lapse of a general power of appointment for gift tax purposes;[54]

(10) the division of a trust created for the settlor's seven grandchildren into seven separate trusts did not affect the trusts' GST tax-exempt status;[55]

---

[46] IRS Letter Ruling 199920004 (Feb. 4, 1999), IRS Letter Ruling 9620016 (Feb. 15, 1996), and IRS Letter Ruling 9122027 (Feb. 28, 1991).

[47] IRS Letter Ruling 9442018 (July 19, 1994).

[48] IRS Letter Ruling 9848009 (Aug. 4, 1998).

[49] IRS Letter Ruling 9348049 (Sept. 7, 1993) and IRS Letter Ruling 199912012 (Dec. 21, 1998).

[50] IRS Letter Ruling 9613014 (Dec. 27, 1995).

[51] IRS Letter Ruling 8725022 (Mar. 20, 1987).

[52] IRS Letter Ruling 9446024 (Aug. 17, 1994).

[53] IRS Letter Ruling 9221005 (Feb. 13, 1992).

[54] IRS Letter Ruling 199909016 (Nov. 30, 1998).

[55] IRS Letter Ruling 199909037 (Dec. 7, 1998).

(11) the division of a trust and the assets on a pro rata basis, those trusts being independently managed, and future division in the same format did not result in a material change in the kind or extent of the beneficiaries' entitlements;[56]

(12) judicial interpretation of the definition of the term "issue" in one trust to include adopted children and removal of a provision from another trust that was to equalize treatment between natural issue and adopted issue;[57]

(13) the exercise of a testamentary special power of appointment by the decedent's grandchildren to a trust for the benefit of such grandchildren's descendants;[58]

(14) the creation of a charitable subtrust funded with property from a grandfathered generation-skipping transfer trust and the subsequent revocation or termination of the subtrust, which would result in the assets being returned to the original grandfathered trust;[59]

(15) judicial reformation to correct a scrivener's error;[60]

(16) the consent of the trustee to allow the trust's primary asset, a corporation, to make a subchapter S election and an election to treat the trust as an electing small business trust;[61] and

(17) a change in the situs of the trust from the state where the former trustee conducted business to the state where the successor trustee conducted business.[62]

(18) a trust reimbursement to a beneficiary for the beneficiary's erroneous payment of income taxes was not a constructive addition to the trust under Reg. § 26.2601-1(b)(1)(v)(C) because the beneficiary timely asserted her right to recovery and the trustee agreed to the reimbursement.[63]

However, a trust lost its grandfathered status when a decedent's children renounced their rights of encroachment, during the surviving spouse's life, on the principal of a testamentary trust in order to satisfy the requirements for a qualified subchapter S trust. Because the renunciations were not made within a reasonable time (nine months) of the creation of the interests, the renunciations constituted a gift and the value of the gift was an addition to the trust for GST tax purposes. Accordingly, a proportionate amount of distributions from, and terminations of interests in property held in, the trust were subject to the provisions of the GST tax.[64]

• *Trust Modifications*

A modification of a generation-skipping trust that is otherwise exempt under the grandfather rules will generally cause a loss of exempt status only if the modification changes the quality, value, or timing of any powers, beneficial

---

[56] IRS Letter Ruling 199912034 (Dec. 28, 1998).

[57] IRS Letter Ruling 199915038 (Jan. 13, 1999).

[58] IRS Letter Ruling 199918006 (Nov. 28, 1998).

[59] IRS Letter Ruling 199939010 (June 24, 1999), IRS Letter Ruling 199939011 (June 24, 1999), and IRS Letter Ruling 199939012 (June 24, 1999).

[60] IRS Letter Ruling 199942016 (July 22, 1999).

[61] IRS Letter Rulings 200012003–200012044 (Nov. 15, 1999).

[62] IRS Letter Rulings 200012052-200012056 (Dec. 17, 1999).

[63] IRS Letter Ruling 200816008 (Dec. 14, 2007).

[64] IRS Letter Ruling 9308007 (Nov. 24, 1992).

interests, rights, or expectancies originally provided for under the terms of the trust.[65]

No Loss of GST Exemption. In IRS Letter Ruling 9218053, the IRS was asked to rule on whether a construction of a 1962 trust would affect the trust's grandfathered status. Although the trust's purpose was to provide for the "security" of the income beneficiary, the beneficiary was unable to maintain her standard of living or pay her medical bills, and the trust's principal had increased to over $1 million. The proposed construction would authorize the trustee to make discretionary payments to the beneficiary and pay the beneficiary's medical bills. The IRS ruled that the construction would not cause the trust to be subject to the GST tax because it was a reasonable interpretation of the settlors' intent and did not alter the intended quality, quantity, or timing of the interests created by the trust. See IRS Letter Ruling 199917022, in which the IRS determined that the clarification of a trust provision to avoid the premature termination of the income interests of the spouses of decedent's children was reflective of the decedent's intent and did not cause the trust to be subject to GST tax.

Similarly, court orders modifying an exempt trust were ruled (1) to resolve the ambiguities that resulted from the liquidation of the closely held corporation whose stock was the primary asset of the trust, and (2) to be consistent with the grantor's intent to provide his grandchild with sufficient funds to finance his educational expenses.[66] Additionally, a court order allowing proceeds to be distributed as permitted under the original trust and the modification of the trust to follow state trustee investment rules outside those permitted in the original trust did not alter the trust's exempt status.[67]

A GST trust that was not irrevocable on prior to September 25, 1985, but was exempt from GST tax liability because an allocation of sufficient GST exemption to the trust gave it a zero inclusion ratio, did not lose its GST exemption as a result of trust modifications. After creation of the trust, the trustee, in accordance with applicable state law, made several administrative changes, including: changing the trust situs; removing a percentage limitation on discretionary distributions; and increasing the number of trustees. The IRS noted that no current guidance existed with respect to the consequences of administrative changes made to trusts that were exempt by way of having an inclusion ratio of zero, rather than having a grandfathered GST tax-exempt status. Accordingly, the IRS concluded that an administrative change that would not affect the exempt status of a trust that was irrevocable on September 25, 1985, should similarly not affect the exempt status of a trust that was exempt by reason of an allocation of GST exemption. Citing Reg. § 26,2601-1(b)(4)(i)(e) as authority, the IRS ruled that the trust modifications did not cause it to lose its GST tax-exempt status.[68]

GST Exemption Lost. In contrast, a proposed reformation of a 1967 trust whose annual income had increased from $9,000 to $270,000 would subject the trust to GST tax. The IRS ruled that the proposed reformation to eliminate the accumulation of surplus income and require the distribution of such income to

---

[65] IRS Letter Ruling 9508025 (Nov. 24, 1994).

[66] IRS Letter Ruling 9602016 (Oct. 11, 1995).

[67] IRS Letter Ruling 199907008 (Nov. 13, 1998), IRS Letter Ruling 199911026 (Dec. 17, 1998), and IRS Letter Ruling 199911027 (Dec. 17, 1998).

[68] IRS Letter Ruling 200841007 (May 30, 2008).

the trust beneficiaries at least quarterly changed the quality, value, and timing of the beneficiaries' interests.[69]

Distribution of all trust income, at the trustee's discretion, among an incompetent beneficiary and his children and grandchildren was considered a reformation of a grandfathered trust that would cause the trust to lose its exemption from the GST tax.[70] Even if the applicable state (Minnesota) probate court were to construe the original trust instrument to allow such discretionary distributions, the IRS maintained that the instrument authorized distributions only to the extent necessary for the support and maintenance of the original beneficiary and his children. In IRS Letter Ruling 9544015, the IRS considered a proposed construction of a GST tax-exempt trust that gave each of the decedent's children the power to appoint trust income to family members, including the child's children, with unappointed income payable to the child's descendants. The IRS ruled that the proposed construction permitting the decedent's children to exercise their limited powers of appointment to create further limited powers of appointment and appoint income would not modify the terms of the trust. However, the proposed construction permitting distributions of principal and creating powers of appointment in succeeding income beneficiaries in the event a child does not exercise his limited power of appointment would modify the trust and cause it to lose its exempt status.

Trust modifications intended to qualify a trust as a shareholder of an S corporation were also ruled to cause loss of grandfathered status.[71] On the other hand, reorganization of a corporation in which two identical trusts held a controlling interest did not cause the combined trust to lose its grandfathered status.[72] Pursuant to the reorganization, shares of voting common stock were exchanged for virtually identical shares of a newly organized holding company. Moreover, a court decree provided that the exchange was not a sale or disposition and that the holding company shares were subject to the same rights and restrictions applicable, under the trust agreement, to the original stock.

• *Modification of Administrative Provisions*

Proposed modifications that relate exclusively to the administration of a trust will not cause that trust to lose its grandfathered status. However, in light of the numerous private letter rulings requested concerning the effect of proposed modifications or construction proceedings on the GST tax-exempt status of a trust, the IRS has promulgated amendments to Reg. §26.2600-1 and Reg. §26.2601-1. The amendments provide a more liberal standard with respect to changes that may be made to a trust without the trust losing its GST tax-exempt status. The amendments are intended to clarify the types of modifications allowable and are intended to reduce the need for private letter rulings in this area. Under the amended regulations, the exempt status of a trust would not be affected if the modification is pursuant to:

> (1) the trustee's discretionary power to distribute principal to a new trust for the benefit of succeeding generations, provided that the vesting is not postponed beyond the perpetuities period of the original trust;

[69] IRS Letter Ruling 9449019 (Sept. 13, 1994).

[70] IRS Letter Ruling 9448024 (Aug. 31, 1994), as modified by IRS Letter Ruling 9522032 (Mar. 3, 1995).

[71] IRS Letter Ruling 8927026 (Apr. 6, 1989).

[72] IRS Letter Ruling 9507016 (Nov. 15, 1994).

¶2441

(2) a court-approved settlement produced from an arm's-length negotiation of a bona fide controversy relating to the administration of the trust or the construction of terms governing the trust;

(3) a court order in a construction proceeding to resolve an ambiguity or correct a scrivener's error; and

(4) a manner that does not shift a beneficial interest in the trust to any beneficiary that occupies a lower generation than the person who held the interest prior to modification and the time for vesting is not extended beyond the perpetuities period of the original trust.[73]

- ## Powers of Appointment

If property remains in a grandfathered trust that was irrevocable on September 25, 1985, after the release, exercise, or lapse of a power of appointment that is a taxable transfer for gift or estate tax purposes, the U.S. Court of Appeals for the Second Circuit in *E. Norman Peterson Marital Trust* held that the value of such property is treated as an addition to the trust.[74] For example, a general power of appointment marital deduction trust (or any other trust over which an individual has a general power of appointment) that is in existence on September 25, 1985, is not grandfathered from GST tax after the death of the powerholder.

However, the above situation should be compared to that in *J. Simpson*,[75] in which the U.S. Court of Appeals for the Eighth Circuit held that an exercise of a general power of appointment was not subject to the GST tax because the power was created "under a trust" that was irrevocable prior to September 25, 1985. Although conceding that in both cases the transfer at issue would have been subject to the GST tax unless grandfathered by operation of the effective date provision of the tax, the Eighth Circuit noted that in *Peterson*, the generation-skipping transfer came about as the result of a lapse of a general power of appointment rather than its exercise. Accordingly, the issue in *Peterson* was not whether the transfer effected by Mrs. Peterson's failure to exercise her power was "under the trust," but rather whether the transfer had been made "out of corpus added to the trust after September 25, 1985." The *Peterson* court held that the effective date provision did not protect a transfer involving the portion remaining in the trust after Mrs. Peterson's power of appointment had lapsed. In contrast, the power of appointment in *Simpson* was exercised with respect to the entire corpus leaving no remaining property in the trust. The IRS, however, has issued a nonacquiescence notice in *Simpson* regarding whether the transfer to the decedent's grandchildren as a result of the decedent's exercise of a power of appointment was exempt from GST tax under the effective date provisions.

The IRS has promulgated amendments to Reg. § 26.2600-1 and Reg. § 26.2601-1 that would clarify the application of the effective date provisions to transfers of property pursuant to the exercise, release, or lapse of a power of appointment. In its explanation of the regulations, the IRS concludes that there is no substantive difference between the transfer of property pursuant to the

---

[73] Reg. § 26.2601-1(b)(4), as amended by T.D. 8912, Dec. 19, 2000.

[74] *E. Peterson Marital Trust*, CA-2, 96-1 USTC ¶ 60,225, aff'g 102 TC 790, CCH Dec. 49,935. Followed, with respect to an exercised power held under an exempt trust: *E. Gerson Est.*, CA-6, 2007-2 USTC ¶ 60,551, aff'g TC (Reviewed by Court), CCH Dec. 56,654, 121 TC 139. See also Reg. § 26.2601-1(b)(1)(v)(A).

However, on similar facts the U.S. Court of Appeals for the Eighth Circuit reached an opposite result: *J. Simpson*, CA-8, 99-2 USTC ¶ 60,351, Nonacq., IRB 2000-9. Followed: *R. Bachler*, CA-9, 2002-1 USTC ¶ 60,430, rev'g DC Cal., 2000-2 USTC ¶ 60,390.

[75] *J. Simpson*, CA-8, 99-2 USTC ¶ 60,351, Nonacq., IRB 2000-9.

exercise of the power of appointment in *Simpson* and the lapse of the power of appointment in *Peterson*. The IRS reasons that the holder of the power of appointment has the equivalent of outright ownership in the property subject to the power and the value of such property is includible in the powerholder's estate. In addition, the powerholder in either *Simpson* or *Peterson* could avoid the GST tax by appointing the property to nonskip persons. Thus, the IRS agrees with the holding of the court in *Peterson* that the effective date provisions do not protect such transfers from the GST tax. Under the amended regulations, the transfer of property pursuant to the exercise, release, or lapse of a general power of appointment is not a transfer by the trust, but is a transfer by the holder of the power that becomes effective on such exercise, release, or lapse.[76] In a Reviewed by the Court decision[77] analyzing the impact of the amended Reg. § 26.2601-1 rules, the Tax Court (later affirmed by CA-6) held that the amended regulation was a valid and reasonable interpretation of the GST transitional rule.[78] Accordingly, a decedent's transfers to her grandchildren from a trust that was irrevocable before September 25, 1985, made pursuant to the exercise of a testamentary general power of appointment, were subject to the GST tax under Reg. § 26.2601-1(b)(1)(i).

If the release, exercise, or lapse of a general power over trust assets is not treated as a taxable transfer under the estate or gift tax provisions of the Internal Revenue Code, there is no deemed addition to the trust and no loss of grandfathered status. For example, in IRS Letter Ruling 9510009, a taxpayer proposed to release her pre-October 22, 1942 general power of appointment over a trust fund. The IRS pointed out that property subject to a pre-October 22, 1942, general power of appointment is includible in the gross estate only if the power is exercised and the release of a power is not treated as an exercise for this purpose. Therefore, the proposed release of the power was not subject to the estate tax. Similarly, it noted that Code Sec. 2514(a) provides that the complete release of a power created before this date is not deemed to be an exercise of the power for gift tax purposes. Because the transfer was not taxable under either the estate or gift tax provisions of the Code, the IRS concluded that there would be no deemed addition to the trust and no loss of grandfathered status.

By contrast, the release, exercise, or lapse of a special power of appointment is not treated as an addition to a trust if such power of appointment is created in an irrevocable trust that is not subject to the GST tax under Reg. § 26.2601-1(b)(1) and, in the case of an exercise, the power is not exercised in a manner that may postpone or suspend the vesting, absolute ownership, or power of alienation of an interest in trust property for a period, measured from the date of creation of the trust, that extends beyond either (1) any life in being at the date of creation of the trust plus 21 years (the common law rule against perpetuities period), or (2) 90 years (the Uniform Statutory Rule Against Perpetuities period).[79] An exercise of a power of appointment that would exceed the applicable state law rule against perpetuities but is limited by the law is not a constructive addition.[80]

A power of appointment is a general power if it is exercisable in favor of the individual possessing the power, his estate, his creditors, or the creditors of his

---

[76] Reg. § 26.2601-1(b)(1)(i), as amended by T.D. 8912, Dec. 19, 2000.

[77] *E. Gerson Est.*, CA-6, 2007-2 USTC ¶60,551, aff'g TC, CCH Dec. 56,654, 121 TC 139; Followed: *L. Timkin Est.*, CA-6, 2010-1 USTC ¶60,591, aff'g DC Ohio, 2009-1 USTC ¶60,574, where a taxable transfer resulted

from a lapse, rather than an exercise, of a power over the corpus of a pre-Sept. 25, 1985 trust.

[78] Tax Reform Act of 1986 (P.L. 99-514), Sec. 1433(b)(2)(A).

[79] Reg. § 26.2601-1(b)(1)(v)(B)(2).

[80] Reg. § 26.2601-1(b)(1)(v)(D), Ex. 7.

estate.[81] In contrast, a special power is one that is either (1) exercisable only in favor of one or more designated persons or classes other than the decedent or his creditors, or the decedent's estate or the creditors of his estate, or (2) expressly not exercisable in favor of the decedent or his creditors, or the decedent's estate or the creditors of his estate.[82] In IRS Letter Ruling 9511039, for example, modification of a trust agreement to allow beneficiaries to appoint the corpus of a trust only to their widows or children was not an addition to the trust because the power was a special power and was not exercised to improperly postpone or suspend vesting.

---

[81] Code Sec. 2041(b). [82] Reg. § 20.2041-1(c)(1).

Chapter 40
COMPUTATION OF TAX

¶ 2450 Amount of Tax

In general, the generation-skipping transfer (GST) tax imposes a flat tax at the "applicable rate" (see ¶ 2459) on the taxable amount of a generation-skipping transfer. For purposes of determining the taxable amount of a direct skip, taxable distribution, or taxable termination, the following exemptions from the tax are provided: 1) a GST exemption amount ($5,250,000 (indexed) for 2013; $5,340,000 for 2014)), that may be allocated among several generation-skipping transfers (see ¶ 2455), and (2) an exemption that applies if the parent of the transferee is deceased at the time of the transfer (see ¶ 2437).

¶ 2451 Determination of Tax Base

In general, the method of computing the tax base or the taxable amount of a generation-skipping transfer depends on whether a taxable distribution, a taxable termination, or a direct skip is involved. Unless a trust instrument specifically referring to the generation-skipping transfer (GST) tax directs otherwise, the tax imposed on a generation-skipping transfer is charged to the property being transferred.[1]

• Taxable Distributions

In the case of taxable distributions, the amount subject to the GST tax is the amount received by the transferee.[2] This amount is reduced by any expenses incurred in connection with the determination, collection, or refund of the tax. As discussed at ¶ 2470, the transferee pays the tax on the taxable distribution. If the trustee pays any amount of the tax, the trustee is treated as having made an additional taxable distribution of that amount.[3]

• Taxable Terminations

In the case of a taxable termination, the amount subject to tax is the value of the property with respect to which the termination occurred.[4] A deduction is allowed for expenses, indebtedness, and taxes (similar to that discussed at ¶ 800 through ¶ 820) for amounts attributable to the property with respect to which the termination has occurred. The trustee pays any tax due on a taxable termination.

• No Double Deductions for Expenses, Indebtedness, and Taxes

Administration expenses, indebtedness, and taxes may be taken either as an income tax deduction on Form 1041 (U.S. Income Tax Return for Estates and Trusts) or as a deduction in determining taxable distributions and taxable termi-

[1] Code Sec. 2603(b).
[2] Code Sec. 2621.
[3] Code Sec. 2621(b).
[4] Code Sec. 2622.

nations for GST tax purposes. These amounts may not be deducted twice, however. To deduct them from an estate's taxable income, the fiduciary must file a waiver electing not to deduct the amounts for GST tax purposes.[5]

• Direct Skips

The taxable amount on a direct skip is the value of the property received by the transferee.[6] If the direct skip is made from a trust, the tax is paid by the trustee; otherwise, it is paid by the transferor. This means that the tax base is the amount actually received by the skip person after reduction for the amount of GST tax paid on the transfer. This means that a direct skip is tax-exclusive.

To calculate the amount of GST tax payable, an interrelated computation is necessary. For 2013, the tax is 40 percent of the amount left after the amount of GST tax payable is removed from the tax base.[7]

This tax-exclusive rate (TER) is calculated according to the following formula:

$$TER = \frac{TIR \text{ (tax-inclusive rate)}}{1 + TIR}$$

Thus, for a 40-percent tax-inclusive rate, the tax-exclusive rate would be .40/1.40 = .285714. This rate is then applied to the amount subject to the GST tax to arrive at the amount of GST tax due. Form 706 (United States Estate (and Generation-Skipping Transfer) Tax Return), Schedule R (Generation-Skipping Transfer Tax) (Rev. August 2013), part 2, line 8, accomplishes the same result by dividing the amount subject to the GST tax by 3.5, to arrive at the amount of GST tax due.

> **Example (1):** David Green died in 2013, leaving all his assets to his grandson, Nick. Assume that, after payment of the estate tax, the amount left is $6.2 million. The full $6.2 million is not subject to the GST tax, but only the amount that Nick will receive after payment by the estate of the GST tax.
>
> Accordingly, under the facts of this Example, the GST tax would be .285714 × $6.2 million, which equals $1,771,427.

The rules applicable to a lifetime direct skip are the same as those applicable to a testamentary direct skip. The GST tax is paid by the transferor, and the transfer is tax-exclusive. However, the treatment of a lifetime direct skip resembles that of a tax-inclusive transfer because of the "gross-up" rule of Code Sec. 2515. Under this rule, the amount of any taxable gift that is also a direct skip is increased by the amount of GST tax payable on the transaction.

> **Example (2):** Laura Green makes a gift of $3,500,000 to her grandson, Paul, in 2013. (Assume that the whole value of the gift is in the 40-percent marginal bracket and her unified credit and generation-skipping transfer exemption have been used up on $5,250,000 of prior taxable gifts.) The GST tax on the gift is .40 times $3,500,000, which equals $1,400,000. This amount is then added to the amount of the tax base for purposes of calculating the gift tax. Thus, the gift tax base is $4,900,000, and the gift tax payable is

---

[5] Code Sec. 642(g).

[6] Code Sec. 2623.

[7] Because the Tax Relief, Unemployment Insurance Reauthorization, and Job Creation Act of 2010 (P.L. 111-312) set the GST tax rate at zero percent for 2010, no GST tax liability arose with respect to lifetime or at-death GSTs occurring in 2010. The GST tax rate is 35 percent for 2011 and 2012 and 40 percent for 2013 and beyond.

$1,905,800. Thus, the total transfer tax on a gift of $3,500,000 is $3,305,800 ($1,400,000 plus $1,905,300).

> *Comment:* Note that in the case of lifetime direct skips, the GST tax payable because of the gift is not itself subject to GST tax, but is subject to the gift tax. This makes the taxation of such transfers similar to a tax-inclusive treatment of taxable distributions and taxable terminations.

¶ 2453 Valuation

Generally, property is valued at the time of the generation-skipping transfer.[8] If property is transferred as a result of the death of a transferor, the value of the property, for generation-skipping transfer (GST) tax purposes, is its value for estate tax purposes. If an estate elects either alternate or special use valuation for the property, that value will be used to compute GST tax liability. Additionally, if one or more taxable terminations with respect to the same trust occur at the same time as, and as the result of, the death of an individual, an election may be made to value all of the property included in such terminations at its alternate value as set forth in Code Sec. 2032.[9]

For purposes of the valuation rules for generation-skipping transfers, the value of transferred property is reduced by the amount of any consideration provided by the transferee.[10]

¶ 2455 GST Exemption; Allocation

An exemption of $5,000,000 for 2010 and 2011, $5,120,000 (indexed) for 2012, $5,250,000 (indexed) for 2013, and $5,340,000 (indexed) for 2014, is provided for each person making generation-skipping transfers. The exemption may be allocated by a transferor (or the transferor's executor) to property transferred at any time but, once made, is irrevocable. The exemption is not transferable between spouses; however, married couples may elect to split a transfer and treat it as made one-half by each spouse pursuant to the gift-splitting rules under Code Sec. 2513 (see ¶2013 and ¶2200).[11] The GST exemption was originally set at $1,000,000. For generation-skipping transfers made after 1998 and before January 1, 2004, the generation-skipping transfer (GST) tax exemption was indexed for inflation.[12] The Economic Growth and Tax Relief Reconciliation Act of 2001 (P.L. 107-16) (EGTRRA) increased the amount of the exemption, but repealed the inflation adjustment, effective for GSTs occurring after December 31, 2003. The Tax Relief, Unemployment Insurance Reauthorization, and Job Creation Act of 2010 (P.L. 111-312), further increased the exemption for GSTs occurring after December 31, 2009, and reinstated the inflation adjustment for GSTs occurring after December 31, 2011.

The generation-skipping transfer tax exemptions for 1999 through 2014 are listed below:

- $1,010,000 for 1999
- $1,030,000 for 2000
- $1,060,000 for 2001
- $1,100,000 for 2002
- $1,120,000 for 2003

---

[8] Code Sec. 2624.
[9] Code Sec. 2624(c).
[10] Code Sec. 2624(d).

[11] Code Sec. 2652(a)(2).
[12] Code Sec. 2631(c), as added by P.L. 105-34.

- $1,500,000 for 2004 and 2005
- $2,000,000 for 2006, 2007, and 2008[13]
- $3,500,000 for 2009
- $5,000,000 for 2010 and 2011
- $5,120,000 (indexed) for 2012[14]
- $5,250,000 (indexed) for 2013
- $5,340,000 (indexed) for 2014

• *Allocation of Exemption*

The GST tax exemption may be allocated by a transferor or the transferor's executor to property transferred at any time.[15] The election is irrevocable once made and must be made on or before the due date for filing an estate tax return (with extensions), regardless of whether a return is required to be filed.

If an allocation of GST tax exemption is made on a timely filed gift tax return or is deemed to have been made under the deemed allocation rules of Code Sec. 2632(b)(1), the value of the transferred property for purposes of determining the denominator of the applicable fraction is its value for gift tax purposes (and the allocation becomes effective on the date of the transfer).

Subject to relief provisions recently enacted (see below), if the transferor fails to make an election to allocate the GST tax exemption on a timely filed gift tax return, the transferor cannot use the value of the property as of the date of the transfer, but instead must use the value of the property as of the date of the allocation. Prior to enactment by the 2001 Act, there was no statutory provision that provided relief to taxpayers who inadvertently failed to make an election to allocate the GST tax exemption on a timely filed gift tax return. Under pre-2001 Act rules, the date the allocation was actually made had to be used for valuation purposes, rather than an earlier date.[16]

• *Direct Skips*

If an individual makes a direct skip (as defined at ¶2433) during the individual's lifetime, any unused portion of the individual's exemption is deemed allocated to the transferred property to the extent necessary to reduce the inclusion ratio (as defined at ¶2461) for such property to zero.[17] If the amount of the direct skip exceeds the unused portion of the exemption, the entire unused portion is allocated to the property transferred. However, a transferor may elect to have these allocation rules not apply to a transfer. Once the election is made, it is irrevocable and cannot be modified after the date on which a timely filed Form 709 (United States Gift (and Generation-Skipping Transfer) Tax Return) is due.[18]

Allocating GST exemption when carryover basis elected. Although an executor may opt out of the estate tax and elect to apply the carryover basis rules for the estate of a decedent who died in 2010 (see ¶121), the GST tax applies to such an estate. If the executor of the estate of a 2010 decedent makes the carryover basis election, the decedent's available GST exemption can be allocated on Schedule R of Form 8939, Allocation of Increase in Basis for Property Ac-

---

[13] Code Sec. 2010(c), as amended by P.L. 107-16.
[14] Code Sec. 2010(c), as amended by P.L. 111-312 and P.L. 112-240.
[15] Code Sec. 2631.

[16] Code Sec. 2642(b)(3), prior to amendment by P.L. 107-16.
[17] Code Sec. 2632(b).
[18] Reg. § 26.2632-1(b).

quired From a Decedent (Notice 2011-66, IRB 2011-35, 184). For *inter vivos* direct skips occurring in 2010, where the donor wishes to pay tax at the zero-percent rate, an election out of the automatic allocation rules (see below), can be made in two ways. The donor may affirmatively elect out of the automatic allocation on a timely filed Form 709, United States Gift (and Generation-Skipping Transfer) Tax Return, or pay the GST tax shown on the return. According to Notice 2011-66, because a donor would never want to allocate GST exemption to a direct skip not in trust, the IRS will interpret the reporting of an *inter vivos* direct skip not in trust occurring in 2010 on a timely filed Form 709 as payment of the tax, at zero percent, and an election out of the automatic allocation rules.

Notice 2011-66 is applicable to the executors of the estates of decedents who died in 2010 and to recipients of property acquired from a 2010 decedent where the carryover basis election was made. The notice also applies to donors who made a GST transfer or an indirect gift for GST purposes during 2010.

• *Late Elections*

Effective for requests pending on, or filed after, December 31, 2000, the IRS is directed to prescribe, by regulation, such circumstances and procedures under which extensions of time will be granted to make (1) allocations of GST tax exemption under Code Sec. 2642(b)(1) or Code Sec. 2642(b)(2), and (2) an election under Code Sec. 2632(b)(3) or Code Sec. 2632(c)(5).[19] Such regulations are to include procedures for requesting comparable relief with respect to transfers made before the enactment of the 2001 Act.

In determining whether to grant relief, the IRS is directed to take into account all relevant circumstances, including evidence of intent contained in the trust instrument or instrument of transfer.[20]

If relief is granted, thereby giving a taxpayer an extension of time to make an allocation of GST tax exemption with respect to a specific transfer, it would be possible for the taxpayer to use the date-of-transfer value for allocation purposes.

> *Example (1):* In 2013, Fred Miller transfers $5,250,000 of stock to a trust for the benefit of his grandchild, Marilyn Lee. If Miller's full GST tax exemption is allocated to the transfer on a timely filed gift tax return, then regardless of any future appreciation in the stock's value, no GST tax will be owed on a later trust distribution or termination. If, however, Miller does not allocate his GST tax exemption on a timely filed gift tax return and the value of the stock has grown to $5,760,000 by the time Miller makes the allocation, the allocation will fail to shelter the additional $510,000 (and any appreciation on that unsheltered amount) from future GST tax liability. If, instead, Miller were allowed to make a late election pursuant to Code Sec. 2642(g)(1), then Miller would be able to allocate his GST tax exemption based on the stock's value as of the transfer date ($5,250,000), as opposed to its later appreciated value.

The IRS has announced that taxpayers may seek an extension of time to make an election under Code Sec. 2632 or an allocation under Code Sec. 2642 under the rules of Reg. § 301.9100-3. Thus, relief will generally be granted if (1) the taxpayer has acted reasonably and in good faith, and (2) the relief will not prejudice the government's interests. These rules are effective with respect to

---

[19] Code Sec. 2642(g)(1)(A), as added by P.L. 107-16, extended through December 31, 2012 by P.L. 111-312, and made permanent by P.L. 112-240.

[20] Code Sec. 2642(g)(1)(B), as added by P.L. 107-16, extended through December 31, 2012 by P.L. 111-312, and made permanent by P.L. 112-240.

requests for relief pending on, or filed after, December 31, 2000.[21] Taxpayers requesting relief are directed to follow the procedures for requesting a private letter ruling contained in Section 5.02 of Rev. Proc. 2001-1,[22] or its successor revenue procedures.

Proposed regulations for late GST allocations. The IRS has proposed regulations under Code Sec. 2642[23] that would replace Reg. § 301.9100-3 as the regulation governing extensions of time to make late allocations of GST exemptions. The proposed regulations would be effective upon adoption.

• *Alternate Method for Obtaining Extension to Allocate GST Exemption*

The IRS has detailed a simplified alternate method that may be used, effective August 2, 2004, to request an extension of time to make an allocation of the GST exemption.[24]

A taxpayer is eligible to use the alternate method in lieu of the letter ruling process to request an extension of time to allocate GST exemption if the following requirements are met:

(1) prior to January 1, 2001, the taxpayer made a transfer by gift to a trust from which a GST could be made;

(2) at the time the taxpayer files the request for relief under the alternate method, no taxable distributions had been made and no taxable terminations had occurred;

(3) the transfer qualified for the Code Sec. 2503(b) gift tax annual exclusion and the amount of the transfer (when combined with the value of all other gifts to the donee in that year) did not exceed the amount of the annual exclusion then in effect;

(4) no GST exemption was allocated to the transfer, whether or not a gift tax return was filed;

(5) at the time the taxpayer files the request, the taxpayer had unused GST exemption available to allocate to the transfer; and

(6) the procedural requirements detailed in Rev. Proc. 2004-46 are satisfied.

With respect to the procedural requirements, the taxpayer must file a Form 709 for the year of the transfer to the trust, regardless of whether a Form 709 had been previously filed. The taxpayer is directed to write "FILED PURSUANT TO REV. PROC. 2004-46" on the top of the Form 709. In addition to reporting the value of the transferred property as of the date of the transfer, the taxpayer must attach a "Notice of Allocation" statement containing several items of information, including the inclusion ratio of the trust after the allocation. The Form 709 must be filed on or before the due date for filing the taxpayer's federal estate tax return. Upon receipt of a request for relief using the alternate method, the IRS will determine whether the applicable requirements have been satisfied and will notify the taxpayer of the result of its determination. If the taxpayer satisfies the requirements, the allocation of GST exemption will be effective as of the date of the transfer. No user fee is charged for requests filed under Rev. Proc. 2004-46.

---

[21] Notice 2001-50, 2001-2 CB 189, modified by Rev. Proc. 2004-46, 2004-2 CB 142.

[22] 2001-1 CB 1.

[23] Prop. Reg. § 26.2642-7, NPRM-REG-147775-06, April 17, 2008.

[24] Rev. Proc. 2004-46, 2004-2 CB 142.

• *Substantial Compliance*

An allocation of GST tax exemption under Code Sec. 2632 that demonstrates an intent to have the lowest possible inclusion ratio with respect to a transfer or a trust is deemed to be an allocation of so much of the transferor's unused GST tax exemption as produces the lowest possible inclusion ratio.[25]

In determining whether there has been substantial compliance, all relevant circumstances are to be taken into account, including evidence of intent contained in the trust instrument or instrument of transfer.[26] The automatic allocation of GST tax exemption or election to prevent the allocation is irrevocable after the gift tax return due date, except that elections filed before January 27, 1996, became irrevocable on July 24, 1996.[27]

• *Indirect Skips*

If an individual makes a lifetime indirect skip, any unused portion of the individual's GST tax exemption is allocated to the property transferred to the extent necessary to make the inclusion ratio for such property equal to zero.[28] If the amount of the indirect skip exceeds the unused portion, then the entire unused portion is allocated to the property transferred.

Unused portion of GST tax exemption. For purposes of deemed allocations to lifetime indirect skips, the unused portion of an individual's GST tax exemption is the portion of the exemption that has not previously been (1) allocated by such individual, (2) treated as allocated under Code Sec. 2632(b) with respect to a direct skip occurring during or before the calendar year in which the indirect skip is made, *or* (3) treated as allocated under Code Sec. 2632(c)(1) with respect to a prior indirect skip.

Indirect skip. An "indirect skip" is defined as any transfer of property (other than a direct skip) subject to the gift tax made to a GST trust.[29]

GST trust. A "GST trust" is defined as a trust that could have a GST with respect to the transferor *unless:*

(1) the trust instrument provides that more than 25 percent of the trust corpus must be distributed to, or may be withdrawn by, one or more individuals who are nonskip persons (a) before the date that such individual attains age 46, (b) on or before one or more dates specified in the trust instrument that will occur before the date that such individual attains age 46, *or* (c) on the occurrence of an event that is reasonably expected to occur before the date that such individual attains age 46;

(2) the trust instrument provides that more than 25 percent of the trust corpus must be distributed to, or may be withdrawn by, one or more individuals who are nonskip persons *and* who are living on the date of death of another person identified in the instrument (either by name or by class) who is more than 10 years older than such individuals;

(3) the trust instrument provides that, if one or more individuals who are nonskip persons die on or before a date or event described in (1) or (2)

---

[25] Code Sec. 2642(g)(2), as added by P.L. 107-16. Effective for transfers made after December 31, 2000.

[26] Code Sec. 2642(g)(2), as added by P.L. 107-16 and extended through December 31 2012 by P.L. 111-312.

[27] Reg. § 26.2632-1(b)(1).

[28] Code Sec. 2632(c)(1), as added by (P.L.107-16). Effective for transfers made after December 31, 2000.

[29] Code Sec. 2632(c)(3)(A), as added by P.L. 107-16 , extended through December 31, 2012 by P.L. 111-312, and made permanent by P.L. 112-240.

above, more than 25 percent of the trust corpus (a) must be distributed to the estate or estates of one or more of such individuals, *or* (b) is subject to a general power of appointment exercisable by one or more of such individuals;

(4) any portion of the trust would be included in the gross estate of a nonskip person (other than the transferor) if such person died immediately after the transfer;

(5) the trust is a charitable lead annuity trust (per Code Sec. 2642(e)(3)(A)), a charitable remainder annuity trust, or a charitable remainder unitrust (per Code Sec. 664(d)); *or*

(6) a gift tax charitable deduction was allowed under Code Sec. 2522 with respect to the trust for the amount of an interest in the form of the right to receive annual payments of a fixed percentage of the net fair market value of the trust property (determined yearly) *and* which trust is required to pay principal to a nonskip person if such person is alive when the yearly payments for which the deduction was allowed terminate.[30]

Example (2): George Stack creates an irrevocable trust for the benefit of his lineal descendants. George has one child, Alice, who is age 21. The trust instrument provides that (1) all trust income is to be paid to Alice during her lifetime, and (2) one-third of the trust corpus is to be distributed to Alice when she reaches age 25. At Alice's death, the remaining corpus is to be distributed to Alice's issue, *per stirpes*. The trust is not a generation-skipping transfer trust because more than 25 percent of the corpus must be distributed to a nonskip person, Alice, before she attains age 46.

Example (3): Gertrude Stack creates an irrevocable trust for the benefit of her lineal descendants. Gertrude has one child, Andrew, who is age 25. The trust instrument provides that (1) the trustee has discretion to distribute trust income to Andrew during his lifetime, and (2) one-fifth of the trust corpus is to be distributed to Andrew when he reaches age 45. At Andrew's death, the remaining corpus is to be distributed to Andrew's issue, *per stirpes*. The trust is a generation-skipping transfer trust because a generation-skipping transfer may occur with respect to Gertrude and the trust does not fall within any of the exceptions specified in (1)–(6) above.[31]

Right of withdrawal limited to annual exclusion amount. For purposes of determining whether a trust is a generation-skipping transfer trust, the value of transferred property is *not* considered to be includible in the gross estate of a nonskip person or subject to a right of withdrawal by reason of such person holding a right to withdraw an amount that does not exceed the Code Sec. 2503(b) gift tax annual exclusion amount ($14,000 per donee in 2013 and 2014,[32] $13,000 per donee in 2009 through 2012[33] and $12,000 per donee in 2006, 2007, and 2008) with respect to any transferor. In addition, it is assumed that powers of appointment held by nonskip persons will not be exercised.[34]

---

[30] Code Sec. 2632(c)(3)(B), as added by P.L. 107-16, extended through December 31, 2012 by P.L. 111-312, and made permanent by P.L. 112-240.

[31] Code Sec. 2632(c)(3)(B)(i)-(vi), as added by P.L. 107-16, extended through December 31, 2012 by P.L. 111-312, and made permanent by P.L. 112-240.

[32] Rev. Proc. 2012-41, IRB 2012-45, 539; Rev. Proc. 2013-35, IRB 2013-47, October 31, 2013.

[33] Rev. Proc. 2011-52, IRB 2011-45, 701; Rev. Proc. 2008-66, IRB 2008-45, 1107; Rev. Proc. 2009-50, IRB 2009-45, 617; Rev. Proc. 2010-40, IRB 2010-46, 663.

[34] Code Sec. 2632(c)(3)(B), as added by P.L. 107-16, extended through December 31, 2012

Estate tax inclusion period. An indirect skip to which Code Sec. 2642(f) applies is deemed to have been made only at the close of the estate tax inclusion period (ETIP). The value of such transfer is the fair market value of the trust property at the close of the ETIP.[35]

Election. An individual may opt out of the deemed allocation rule for lifetime indirect skips. An individual may elect to have Code Sec. 2632(c) *not* apply to (1) an indirect skip, or (2) any or all transfers made by the individual to a particular trust. In addition, an individual may elect to treat any trust as a generation-skipping transfer trust for purposes of Code Sec. 2632(c) with respect to any and all transfers made by the individual to the trust.[36]

An election to have Code Sec. 2632(c) not apply to an indirect skip is deemed to be timely if it is filed on a timely filed gift tax return for the calendar year in which the transfer was made or deemed to have been made under Code Sec. 2632(c)(4) (i.e., the close of the ETIP). For other categories of elections permitted by Code Sec. 2632(c)(5)(A), the election may be made on a timely filed gift tax return for the calendar year for which the election is to become effective.[37]

Amendments to Reg. § 26.2632-1 have been adopted that provide procedures for electing out of the automatic allocation for indirect skips and for electing to treat a trust as a GST trust.[38] Under the final regulations, a transferor who wishes to elect out of the automatic allocation rules would have the option of: (1) electing out for the specific transfer to the GST trust; (2) making a single election that applies to the current transfer and all subsequent transfers made to the trust by that transferor; (3) electing out with respect to only certain designated future transfers; or (4) electing out with respect to all future transfers made by the transferor to any trust, whether or not the trust exists at the time of the election out. The regulations provide that a transferor may elect out with respect to future transfers, even though the transferor has not made a current-year transfer and is not otherwise obligated to file a federal gift tax return. A citation to the specific regulation section authorizing an election is not required on the statement to elect out of the automatic GST allocation or to treat a trust as a GST trust.

In addition, the regulations clarify that an election out of the automatic allocations rules for future years is limited to the automatic allocation rules under Code Sec. 2632(c), relating to indirect skips made during the transferor's life, and has no effect on the automatic allocation rules under Code Sec. 2632(e), which apply after the transferor's death. The regulations explain that an automatic allocation with respect to an indirect skip is effective as of the date of the transfer and is irrevocable on the due date for filing the federal gift tax return for the calendar year in which the transfer is made, regardless of whether a gift tax return is filed. Furthermore, an affirmative partial allocation of the GST exemption will be treated as an election out of the automatic allocation rules with respect to the balance of that specific transfer. Pursuant to the regulations, an automatic allocation to a direct or an indirect skip is considered to be made at he close of the estate tax inclusion period (ETIP), in accordance with Code Sec.

(Footnote Continued)

by P.L. 111-312, and made permanent by P.L. 112-240.

[35] Code Sec. 2632(c)(4), as added by P.L. 107-16, extended through December 31, 2012 by P.L. 111-312, and made permanent by P.L. 112-240.

[36] Code Sec. 2632(c)(5)(A), as added by P.L. 107-16, extended through December 31,

2012 by P.L. 111-312, and made permanent by P.L. 112-240.

[37] Code Sec. 2632(c)(5)(B), as added by P.L. 107-16, extended through December 31, 2012 by P.L. 111-312, and made permanent by P.L. 112-240.

[38] Reg. § 26.2632-1, as amended by T.D. 9208, June 28, 2005.

2632(c)(4). Therefore, at any time before the due date of the gift tax return for the calendar year in which an ETIP closes, a transferor may elect out of the automatic allocation rules for indirect or direct skips subject to an ETIP. The final regulations are effective June 29, 2005.

• Retroactive Allocations of Unused GST Tax Exemption

Effective for deaths of nonskip persons occurring after December 31, 2000, an individual may allocate unused GST tax exemption to any previous transfer(s) made to a trust, on a chronological basis.[39] This rule is designed to protect taxpayers when there is an "unnatural order of death" (such as when the second generation predeceases the first generation transferor) by allowing a transferor to allocate GST tax exemption retroactively to the date of the respective transfer to the trust.

Availability of retroactive allocation. An individual may make a retroactive allocation of GST tax exemption if (1) a nonskip person has an interest or a future interest in a trust to which any transfer has been made, (2) such person is a lineal descendant of a grandparent of the transferor or of a grandparent of the transferor's spouse or former spouse and such person is assigned to a generation below the generation assignment of the transferor, *and* (3) such person predeceases the transferor.[40]

Future interest. A person has a "future interest" in a trust if the trust permits income or corpus to be paid to such person on a future date or dates.[41]

Retroactive allocation made in calendar year within which nonskip person's death occurs. If a transferor's retroactive allocation is made on a gift tax return that is filed on or before the date prescribed by Code Sec. 6075(b) for gifts made within the calendar year within which the nonskip person's death occurred, then:

(1) for purposes of Code Sec. 2642(a), the value of such transfer(s) is determined as if such allocation had been made on a timely filed gift tax return for each calendar year within which each transfer was made;

(2) such allocation is effective immediately before such death; *and*

(3) the amount of the transferor's unused GST tax exemption that is available for allocation is determined immediately before such death.[42]

Example (4): In 2000, Gary Stack creates an irrevocable trust for the primary benefit of his child, Anthony, who is age 18. The trust instrument provides that (1) the trustee has discretion to distribute trust income to Anthony during his lifetime, and (2) one-third of the trust corpus is to be distributed to Anthony at age 28, one-half of the remaining corpus at age 32, and the remainder of the corpus at age 35 (which will terminate the trust). If Anthony dies before reaching age 35, the corpus is to be distributed in equal shares to Anthony's children. Gary makes transfers to the trust in 2000, but does not allocate any of his GST tax exemption to the transfers on the gift tax return reporting the transfers. (Because of the effective date provisions,

---

[39] Code Sec. 2632(d), as added by P.L. 107-16, extended through December 31, 2012 by P.L. 111-312, and made permanent by P.L. 112-240.

[40] Code Sec. 2632(d)(1), as added by P.L. 107-16, extended through December 31, 2012 by P.L. 111-312, and made permanent by P.L. 112-240.

[41] Code Sec. 2632(d)(3), as added by P.L. 107-16, extended through December 31, 2012 by P.L. 111-312, and made permanent by P.L. 112-240.

[42] Code Sec. 2632(d)(2), as added by P.L. 107-16, extended through December 31, 2012 by P.L. 111-312, and made permanent by P.L. 112-240.

the deemed allocation rule of Code Sec. 2632(c), as added by the 2001 Act, does not apply to the 2000 transfers.) On September 1, 2012, before reaching age 28, Anthony dies, thus resulting in a taxable termination for GST tax purposes. Stack may retroactively allocate unused GST tax exemption to the transfers made in 2000 and thereby exempt the trust property transferred to Anthony's children from the application of the GST tax.

• *Separate GST Exempt and GST Nonexempt Trust*

Although not required by the GST tax provisions of the Internal Revenue Code, it is usually a good idea from a tax planning viewpoint to have separate trusts for generation-skipping transfer exempt and generation-skipping transfer nonexempt assets. Where this is done, the generation-skipping transfer exempt trust will receive assets equal to the decedent's (or donor's) unused generation-skipping transfer exemption (or as much of it as he or she wishes to use). Because this trust will house only exempt assets—and will be drafted so as to not accept the receipt of nonexempt assets at a later date—the trust's inclusion ratio will always be zero (see ¶2461 for a discussion of the inclusion ratio rules). This means that no matter how much the assets in the trust appreciate after the initial transfer, no GST tax liability will be generated.

The second generation-skipping transfer trust in the typical two-generation-skipping transfer-trust arrangement will be the nonexempt trust, which will receive only assets against which the decedent's (grantor's) generation-skipping transfer exemption will not be allocated. Because this trust will have an inclusion ratio of one at all times (which means that all assets in the trust are subject to the GST tax), a recomputation of the inclusion ratio will not be required if additional assets are transferred into the trust at a later date.

Segregating completely exempt and completely nonexempt generation-skipping transfer assets can offer possible tax and cost savings:

(1) Funding the generation-skipping transfer exempt trust with assets that are expected to appreciate sharply will shield any increases in value from GST tax liability.

(2) The nonexempt trust should be funded with those assets that are not expected to appreciate as quickly. Even this trust can be a tax savings vehicle if it is used to make gift tax and GST tax deductible educational and medical payments. Since qualifying educational and medical payments are deductible in their own right, they should not be paid from the generation-skipping transfer exempt trust; doing so would waste a portion of the generation-skipping transfer exemption.

(3) The generation-skipping transfer exempt/nonexempt trusts arrangement is administratively less cumbersome than dealing with a partially generation-skipping transfer exempt trust (that is, a trust with an inclusion ratio of greater than zero, and less than one). Particularly if a trust has multiple beneficiaries, makes frequent distributions, and will be accepting future contributions of trust property, the trustee of the trust will spend more time and effort computing tax liabilities of such a partially exempt trust, and recomputing the inclusion ratio whenever additional contributions into the trust are accepted.

¶2455

• *Severing of Trusts*

If a trust is severed in a "qualified severance," the resulting trusts will be treated as separate trusts thereafter for purposes of the GST tax.[43]

Qualified severance. A "qualified severance" is defined as the division of a single trust and the creation (by any means available under the governing instrument or local law) of two or more trusts if:

(1) the single trust was divided on a fractional basis; *and*

(2) the terms of the new trusts, in the aggregate, provide for the same succession of interests or beneficiaries as are provided for in the original trust.[44]

Final regulations. Regulations have been finalized that provide guidance on the qualified severance of a trust for GST tax purposes.[45] Under amendments to Reg. §26.2642-6, each new trust must receive assets with a value equal to a fraction or percentage of the total value of the trust assets to satisfy the first requirement (relating to the division of a trust on a fractional basis). A severance of a trust based on a pecuniary amount, however, will not satisfy this requirement. Each separate trust does not need to be funded with a pro rata portion of each asset held by the original trust. However, if funding is done on a non-pro rata basis, it must be based on the total fair market value of the assets on the date of funding.

The regulations provide that the second requirement (relating to the trust terms of the new trust) will be satisfied with respect to trusts from which discretionary, non-pro rata distributions may be made to beneficiaries if: (1) the terms of the separate trusts are the same as the terms of the original trust; (2) each beneficiary's interest in the severed trusts (collectively) equals the beneficiary's interest in the original trust, determined by the terms of the trust instrument, or, if none, on a per-capita basis; (3) the severance does not shift a beneficial interest in the trust to any beneficiary in a lower generation than the person(s) who held the beneficial interest in the original trust; and (4) the severance does not extend the time for vesting of any beneficial interest in the trust beyond the period provided in the original trust. The IRS states that this rule regarding discretionary trusts is intended to facilitate the severance of trusts along family lines.

The regulations are effective August 2, 2007. For severances occurring after December 31, 2000, and before August 2, 2007, taxpayers are permitted to rely on any reasonable interpretation of Code Sec. 2642(a)(3), as long as reasonable notice is given to the IRS.

Trusts with an inclusion ratio greater than zero. A severance of a trust with an inclusion ratio of between zero and one is a "qualified severance" only if the single trust is divided into two trusts, one of which receives a fractional share of the total value of all trust assets equal to the applicable fraction of the single trust immediately before the severance. In such a case, the trust receiving the fractional share will have an inclusion ratio of zero and the other trust will have an inclusion ratio of one.[46]

---

[43] Code Sec. 2642(a)(3), as added by P.L. 107-16. Effective for severances after December 31, 2000.

[44] Code Sec. 2642(a)(3)(B)(i), as added by P.L. 107-16.

[45] Reg. §26.2642-6, as amended by T.D. 9348, August 2, 2007.

[46] Code Sec. 2642(a)(3)(B)(ii), as added by P.L. 107-16, extended through December 31, 2012 by P.L. 111-312, and made permanent by P.L. 112-240.

Example (5): George Stack creates an irrevocable trust for the benefit of his grandson, Albert. The trust instrument provides that the trustee has discretion to distribute trust income and corpus to Albert during his lifetime. At Albert's death, the corpus is to be distributed in equal shares to Albert's children. The trust instrument also gives the trustee the discretion to sever the trust for GST tax purposes. Based on the amount of GST tax exemption allocated to the trust and the value of the trust property, the trust's applicable fraction is $1/4$, making the inclusion ratio equal to $3/4$ ($1 - 1/4 = 3/4$). The trustee divides the trust into two trusts, each having terms identical to that of the original trust. One of the trusts receives a $1/4$-fractional share of the total value of the trust assets. The severance is a "qualified severance," with the trust receiving the $1/4$-fractional share having an inclusion ratio of zero, and the other trust having an inclusion ratio of one.

Timing and manner of severances. A severance under Code Sec. 2642(a)(3) may be made at any time. The Secretary is to prescribe the manner in which the qualified severance is to be reported.[47] Under Reg. § 26.2642-6, effective August 2, 2007, a qualified severance is reported by filing Form 706-GS(T), Generation-Skipping Transfer Tax Return for Terminations (or such other form that may be published by the IRS), and attaching a "Notice of Qualified Severance" to the return.[48]

Qualified Severances Funded on Non-Pro Rata Basis. Effective July 31, 2008, Reg. § 26.2642-6[49] permits a trust resulting from a qualified severance to be funded on a non-pro rata basis. However, if the funding is done on a non-pro rata basis, each asset received by a resulting trust must be valued by multiplying the fair market value of the asset held in the original trust as of the date of the severance by the fraction or percentage of that asset received by that resulting trust. Accordingly, the assets are valued without taking into account any discount or premium arising from the severance.

The final regulations also permit a qualified severance of a trust with an inclusion ratio between zero and one into more than two resulting trusts, provided that certain requirements are satisfied. Trusts resulting from a severance that does not meet the requirements of a qualified severance will be treated as separate trusts for purposes of the GST tax, provided that the resulting trusts are recognized as separate trusts under applicable state law. However, each such resulting trust will have the same inclusion ratio as that of the original trust. In the case of a mandatory severance, Reg. § 26.2654-1[50] provides that each resulting trust is recognized as a separate trust for GST purposes if the resulting trust is recognized as a separate trust under applicable state law. Each trust resulting from such a mandatory severance will have the same inclusion ratio as that of the original trust.

• *Appreciation in Value of Exempt Property*

Once the GST tax exemption is applied to a transfer of property, and the property (or a portion of it) is designated as exempt, all subsequent appreciation on the property (or that portion of it) is also exempt from tax. If only a portion of

---

[47] Code Sec. 2642(a)(3)(C), as added by P.L. 107-16, extended through December 31, 2012 by P.L. 111-312, and made permanent by P.L. 112-240.

[48] Reg. § 26.2642-6, as amended by T.D. 9348, Aug. 2, 2007.

[49] Reg. § 26.2642-6, as amended by T.D. 9421, July 30, 2008.

[50] Reg. § 26.2654-1, as amended by T.D. 9421, July 31, 2008.

the property is initially exempt, any subsequent appreciation will be exempt in the same ratio as the initially exempt property bore to the total property.

Example (6): In 2013, Elizabeth Davis establishes a $5,250,000 trust fund for the benefit of her grandchildren and great-grandchildren. Davis allocates her entire GST tax exemption to the trust. The assets in the trust appreciate to $7,000,000. None of the appreciation is subject to tax because the initial transfer was fully exempt.

Example (7): Charles Duvall establishes a $5,000,000 trust for the benefit of his children and grandchildren. Duvall allocates $500,000 of his GST tax exemption to the trust. The value of the trust appreciates to $8,000,000. Only one-tenth of the appreciation will be exempt because at the time of the transfer only one-tenth of the property qualified as exempt.

• Allocation of Unused Exemption at Death

Any portion of a decedent's GST tax exemption (which is $5,000,000 for 2010 and 2011, $5,120,000 (indexed) for 2012, $5,250,000 (indexed) for 2013, and $5,340,000 for 2014) that has not been allocated at the decedent's death is allocated in the following order:

(1) to property that is the subject of a direct skip occurring at the decedent's death; and

(2) to trusts with respect to which the decedent is the transferor and from which a taxable distribution or termination may occur at or after the decedent's death.[51]

An allocation of the generation-skipping transfer exemption is ineffective with regard to a lifetime transfer of property that would be included in the transferor's estate (other than by virtue of Code Sec. 2035) if the transferor died immediately after the transfer until the end of the estate tax inclusion period (ETIP).[52] An allocation made during an ETIP is irrevocable, however.[53]

Example (8): Dale Ashwood sets up a 10-year grantor retained annuity trust for the benefit of his three grandchildren, reporting a taxable gift of $500,000 on his gift tax return and allocating $500,000 of his generation-skipping transfer exemption to the trust property. If Ashwood dies eight years later, the entire value of the trust property (then $800,000) will be included in his gross estate and will be subject to GST tax. Although Ashwood's allocation of the $500,000 generation-skipping transfer exemption was not effective when made on his gift tax return, it becomes effective at the end of the ETIP (here, his death) and will not shield the appreciation in the trust's value ($300,000) that will be subject to generation-skipping transfers. Although Ashwood's claimed generation-skipping transfer exemption was ineffective when made, it was, nonetheless, irrevocable, and his executor at death will not have the opportunity to undo the $500,000 generation-skipping transfer allocation and use it against other generation-skipping transfers.

An ETIP ends on the earlier of (1) the date on which the property would not be includible in the transferor's estate (other than under Code Sec. 2035), (2) the date on which there is a generation-skipping transfer with respect to the property, or (3) the transferor's death.[54] Transfers subject to an ETIP include transfers

---

[51] Code Sec. 2632(c).
[52] Reg. § 26.2632-1(c)(2).
[53] Reg. § 26.2632-1(c)(1).
[54] Reg. § 26.2632-1(c)(3).

to qualified personal residence trusts, grantor retained annuity trusts, and grantor retained income trusts.

An ETIP also arises if, immediately after a transfer, the property would be includible in the estate of the transferor's spouse (other than under Code Sec. 2035). A spousal ETIP ends on the earlier of (1) the date on which the property would not be includible in the spouse's estate (other than under Code Sec. 2035), or (2) the spouse's death. Spousal ETIPs apply to transfers for which the spouse is treated as a transferor because of a gift-splitting election, transfers to lifetime marital deduction trusts (other than trusts for which the reverse qualified terminable interest property election is made), and transfers to the extent the spouse has a withdrawal power.

There are two exceptions to application of the ETIP provisions. First, there is no ETIP when the possibility that the property will be included in the estate of the transferor or the transferor's spouse is so remote as to be negligible (less than five-percent probability determined by actuarial standards).[55] Second, there is no spousal ETIP if a power of withdrawal held by the transferor's spouse (1) is limited to the greater of $5,000 or five percent of trust principal, and (2) lapses within 60 days of the transfer to the trust.[56]

¶ 2457 GST Credit for State Taxes

If a pre-January 1, 2005 generation-skipping transfer (other than a direct skip) occurred at the same time as, and as a result of, the death of an individual, a credit in the amount of the generation-skipping transfer (GST) tax paid to any state was permitted against the federal GST tax.[57] The amount of this credit was limited to five percent of the amount of federal GST tax imposed on the transfer.

• *Impact of the 2001, 2010 and 2012 Acts*

The Economic Growth and Tax Relief Reconciliation Act of 2001 (P.L. 107-16) (2001 Act) repealed the credit for state GST taxes allowed for generation-skipping transfers occurring after December 31, 2004 and before January 1, 2011.[58] The Tax Relief, Unemployment Insurance Reauthorization, and Jobs Creation Act of 2010 (P.L. 111-312) extended the "sunset" of this repeal provision by two years. Thus, the credit for state GST taxes was scheduled to apply again for GSTs occurring after December 31, 2012. However, the American Taxpayer Relief Act of 2012 (P.L. 112-240) permanently repealed the credit (see ¶ 1144 and ¶ 1145).

¶ 2459 Applicable Rate

All generation-skipping transfers (GSTs) are subject to tax at a flat rate equal to the product of the maximum estate tax rate[59] (see the discussion under "Application of the GST tax in 2010) and the "inclusion ratio" (as defined at ¶ 2461) with respect to the transfer.[60] The "maximum estate tax rate" is the maximum rate imposed by Code Sec. 2001 on the estates of decedents dying at the time of the taxable distribution, taxable termination or direct skip. For GSTs occurring in 2011 and 2012, this rate is 35 percent; for GSTs occurring in 2013 and beyond, the rate is 40 percent.

---

[55] Reg. § 26.2632-1(c)(2)(ii)(A).

[56] Reg. § 26.2632-1(c)(2)(ii)(B).

[57] Code Sec. 2604.

[58] Code Sec. 2604(c), as added by P.L. 107-16.

[59] The maximum estate tax rate is 35 percent for 2011 and 2012, and 40 percent for 2013 and beyond. The GST tax rate was zero percent for 2010 (see the discussion under "Application of the GST tax in 2010"); and 45 percent for 2009.

[60] Code Sec. 2641.

It should be noted, however, that, in the case of a direct skip occurring at death, the effective generation-skipping transfer tax rate will be considerably lower than the maximum estate tax rate in effect at the time. For any given rate, the tax exclusive, effective rate is calculated according to the following formula:

$$\frac{\text{Maximum Estate Tax Rate}}{1 + \text{Maximum Estate Tax Rate}}$$

A maximum estate tax rate of 40 percent (which is effective for generation-skipping transfers occurring in 2013; see below) yields the following result:

$$\frac{.40}{1.40} = .285714$$

Example: Harry West dies in 2013 and his will leaves his entire estate of $7,330,000 to his grandson, Jake.

Tax Base	$7,330,000
Tentative Estate Tax on above	2,877,800
Less: Unified Credit	(2,045,800)
Estate Tax	$832,000
GST Tax Base ($7,330,000 – $832,000)	$6,498,000
Less: GST Tax Exemption	(5,250,000)
Net GST Tax Base	$1,248,000
GST Tax Payable ($1,248,000 × .285714)	356,571
Total Transfer Tax ($832,000 + $356,571)	$1,188,571 *

* Note that the net GST tax base less the amount of GST tax paid times 40% is equal to the GST tax payable ($1,248,000 - $356,571 = $891,429; $891,429 × .40 = $356,572). (Results off by $1 due to rounding.)

The Economic Growth and Tax Relief Reconciliation Act of 2001 (P.L. 107-16) (EGTRRA) reduced the maximum estate tax rate from 55 percent (for 2001) to 50 percent, effective for estates of decedents dying after December 31, 2001.[61] EGTRRA and the Tax Relief, Unemployment Insurance Reauthorization, and Jobs Creation Act of 2010 (P.L. 111-312) (Tax Relief Act of 2010) further reduced the maximum rate as follows:

- 49 percent for decedents dying in 2003;
- 48 percent in 2004;
- 47 percent in 2005;
- 46 percent in 2006; and
- 45 percent in 2007, 2008, and 2009;[62]
- 0 percent in 2010;[63]
- 35 percent in 2011 and 2012;[64]
- 40 percent in 2013 and beyond.[65]

Application of the GST tax in 2010. The Tax Relief, Unemployment Insurance Reauthorization, and Jobs Creation Act of 2010 (P.L. 111-312) (Tax Relief Act of 2010) repealed the one-year repeal of the GST tax that was enacted in subtitle

---

[61] Code Sec. 2001(c)(1), as amended by P.L. 107-16.

[62] Code Sec. 2001(c)(2)(B), as added by P. L. 107-16.

[63] Act Sec. 302(c), P.L. 111-312. This zero percent rate meant that no GST liabilities were generated for GSTs occurring in 2010.

[64] Code Sec. 2001(c), as amended by P.L. 111-312.

[65] Code Sec. 2001(c), as amended by P.L. 112-240.

A of title V of the Economic Growth and Tax Relief Reconciliation Act of 2001 (P.L. 107-16) (EGTRRA). The Tax Relief Act of 2010 further provides that the applicable rate under Code Sec. 2641(a) for generation-skipping transfers made in 2010 is zero. Because the GST tax is a product of the applicable rate and the taxable amount (Code Sec. 2602), no GST tax will be imposed on any generation-skipping transfers that occur during 2010, as any amount multiplied by zero is equal to zero.

¶ 2461   Inclusion Ratio

The inclusion ratio for any property transferred in a generation-skipping transfer is the excess (if any) of one over the "applicable fraction" determined for the trust from which a generation-skipping transfer is made or, in the case of a direct skip, the applicable fraction determined for such a skip.[66] Stated differently, 1 – (applicable fraction) = inclusion ratio.

• *Applicable Fraction*

The applicable fraction is determined as follows: The numerator is the amount of the generation-skipping transfer exemption allocated to the trust or the property transferred in the direct skip. Its denominator is the value of the property transferred to the trust (or involved in the direct skip) reduced by the sum of any federal estate or state death tax attributable to the property that was recovered from the trust and any estate or gift tax charitable deductions allowed.[67]

$$\text{applicable fraction} = \frac{\text{amount of GST exemption allocated to trust or property}}{\begin{array}{ccc}(\text{value of} & [\text{state and} & \text{charitable deductions} \\ \text{property} & - \text{ federal estate} & + \text{ allowed under Code Sec.} \\ \text{transferred}) & \text{taxes} & 2055 \text{ or } 2522]\end{array}}$$

Example (1): Upon James Anderson's death in 2013, $7,245,000 is transferred to a trust for the benefit of his grandchildren. At the time of the transfer, the full $5,250,000 generation-skipping transfer (GST) tax exemption is allocated to this trust. Assuming that there are no estate/death tax and charitable deductions, the calculation of the GST tax would be as follows:

> (1) Determination of the applicable fraction: $5,250,000 exemption divided by $7,245,000 in property equals applicable fraction of 0.725;

> (2) Determination of the inclusion ratio: Subtract the applicable fraction from 1. Thus, the inclusion ratio is 1 minus 0.725, or 0.275.

The GST tax rate is the product of the inclusion ratio—in this case, 0.275—and the maximum federal estate tax rate at the time of the transfer—40%. Thus, the rate of tax on this transfer is 11.00%.

• *Gift for Which Gift Tax Return Filed or Deemed Allocation Made*

For purposes of the GST tax, the value of property is generally determined at the time of a transfer to the trust or at the time of a direct skip. However, if an allocation of the GST tax exemption (see ¶ 2455) is made on a timely filed gift tax return[68] or is deemed to be made under Code Sec. 2632(b)(1), the value of the

---

[66] Code Sec. 2642(a).
[67] Code Sec. 2642(a)(2).

[68] Code Sec. 6075(b).

transferred property is its value for gift tax purposes (and the allocation becomes effective on the date of such transfer).[69]

If any allocation of the GST tax exemption to any property not transferred as a result of the death of the transferor is not made on a timely filed gift tax return and is not deemed to have been made under Code Sec. 2632(b)(1), the value of the property will be determined as of the time the allocation is filed with the IRS.[70] The Economic Growth and Tax Relief Reconciliation Act of 2001 (P.L. 107-16), the Tax Relief, Unemployment Insurance Reauthorization, and Job Creation Act of 2010 (P.L. 111-312), and the American Taxpayer Relief Act of 2012 (P.L. 112-240) provided relief from this rule for certain late elections made with respect to generation-skipping transfer allocations (see ¶ 2455).

• QTIP Trusts

If the value of the property is included in the gross estate of a spouse as qualified terminable interest property (QTIP) for which a marital deduction was previously allowed[71] and if the spouse was the transferor of the property, the value of the property (for GST tax purposes) will be the same as its value for estate tax purposes.[72]

• Treatment of Certain Nontaxable Gifts

The inclusion ratio of a direct skip that is a nontaxable gift is zero. A nontaxable gift is one excluded from gift tax because of the annual exclusion or because it is a transfer for educational or medical expenses.[73] However, this rule does not apply to any transfer to a trust for the benefit of an individual unless (1) during the lifetime of that individual, no portion of the corpus or income of the trust may be distributed to (or for the benefit of) any other person, and (2) if the trust does not terminate before the individual dies, the assets of the trust will be includible in that individual's gross estate.

• Special Rules Where More Than One Transfer Is Made to a Trust

If a transfer of property (other than a nontaxable gift) is made to a trust in existence before the transfer, the applicable fraction must be recomputed.[74] The numerator of this recomputed fraction is the sum of (1) the amount of the GST tax exemption allocated to the property involved in such a transfer, plus (2) the nontax portion of the trust (as defined below) immediately before such transfer. The denominator is the sum of (1) the value of the property involved in the transfer (reduced by the sum of (a) any federal estate or state death tax paid, and (b) any charitable deduction allowed), and (2) the value of all property in the trust immediately before the transfer.

For purposes of the special rule outlined above, the nontax portion of a trust is the product of the value of all of the property in the trust and the applicable fraction in effect for such trust.

> *Example (2):* In 1998, Joseph Grant established a generation-skipping trust for the benefit of his descendants, which he initially funded with $1,000,000. However, he chose to allocate only $500,000 (or one-half) of his GST tax exemption ($1,000,000 in 1998) to the trust. Assuming that there

---

[69] Reg. § 26.2632-1(b)(2)(ii)(A) and Reg. § 26.2642-2(a)(1).
[70] Code Sec. 2642(b)(3).
[71] Code Sec. 2044.

[72] Code Sec. 2642(b)(4).
[73] Code Sec. 2642(c).
[74] Code Sec. 2642(d).

were no allocable deductions, his initial applicable fraction was 0.5 and his inclusion ratio was also 0.5.

In 2013, Grant placed an additional $5,200,000 into the trust and allocated his remaining $4,750,000 GST tax exemption to it (the GST exemption is $5,250,000 for 2013). This necessitated the following recalculation. Assume that no deductions are allowable and that the initial trust corpus has not appreciated in value.

$$
\frac{
\left(\substack{\text{amount of GST tax exemption}\\ \text{allocated to property involved in}\\ \text{transfer}}\right) + \left[\left(\substack{\text{value of all}\\ \text{property in}\\ \text{trust before}\\ \text{transfer}}\right)\left(\substack{\text{applicable}\\ \text{fraction}}\right)\right]
}{
\left[\left(\substack{\text{value of}\\ \text{property}\\ \text{involved in}\\ \text{transfer}}\right) - \substack{\text{federal estate or state}\\ \text{death taxes recovered}\\ \text{from trust attributable}\\ \text{to such property and}\\ \text{any charitable}\\ \text{deductions}}\right] + \left(\substack{\text{value of property}\\ \text{in trust before}\\ \text{transfer}}\right)
} =
$$

$$
\frac{(4,750,000) + [(1,000,000) \times (.5)]}{(\$5,200,000 - 0) + \$1,000,000} =
$$

$$
\frac{\$5,250,000}{\$6,200,000} = .847
$$

Thus, the new applicable fraction is 0.847. The new inclusion ratio is 1 minus 0.847, which equals 0.153.

If any allocation of the GST tax exemption to property transferred to a trust is not made on a timely filed gift tax return and there was a previous allocation with respect to property transferred to the same trust, the applicable fraction for the trust must be recomputed at the time of the allocation.

¶ 2463 Taxation of Multiple Skips

If there is a generation-skipping transfer of any property and immediately after the transfer the property is held in trust, subsequent transfers from the portion of the trust attributable to that property are treated as if the transferor of the property were assigned to the first generation above the highest generation of any person who has an interest in such trust immediately after the transfer.[75] In general, the inclusion ratio of the trust will not be affected. However, Code Sec. 2653(b) specifically provides that, under regulations prescribed by the IRS, adjustments to the inclusion ratio are to be made to take into account any generation-skipping transfer (GST) tax borne by such a trust.

• Pour-Over Trusts

The inclusion ratio of a trust is affected if the generation-skipping transfer involves the transfer of property from one trust to another (i.e., a "pour-over" trust).[76] In such a case, the inclusion ratio for the pour-over trust is determined by treating the nontax portion of such distribution as if it were a part of a GST tax exemption allocated to such trust. The nontax portion of any distribution in this case is the amount of such distribution multiplied by the applicable fraction that applies to the distribution.

---

[75] Code Sec. 2653.   [76] Code Sec. 2653(b)(2).

¶ 2465   Special Rules

The following special rules apply to the generation-skipping transfer (GST) tax.

• Basis Adjustments

If property is transferred in a generation-skipping transfer, the basis of the property in the hands of the transferee is stepped up (but not above fair market value) to reflect GST taxes attributable to appreciation.[77] For this purpose, the amount of GST tax imposed is computed without regard to the credit for state death taxes. The GST tax basis adjustment is applied after the basis adjustment for gift tax paid.[78] Thus, the two adjustments combined must not increase the basis of the property transferred above its fair market value.[79]

• Certain Transfers at Death

If the property is transferred in a taxable termination that occurs at the same time as, and as a result of, the death of an individual, the basis of the property is adjusted in a manner similar to that provided for in Code Sec. 1014(a) (relating to basis of property received from a decedent). However, if the inclusion ratio of the property is less than one, any increase or decrease in basis is limited by multiplying the increase by the inclusion ratio.[80] The Tax Relief, Unemployment Insurance Reauthorization, and Job Creation Act of 2010 (P.L. 111-312) (Tax Relief Act of 2010) retroactively repealed the carryover basis rules that were effective for decedents dying after December 31, 2009, and before January 1, 2011.[81] However, if the estate of a decedent dying in 2010 opts out of the application of the estate tax, the carryover basis provision apply to assets received by estate beneficiaries (see ¶ 121).

> *Example (1):* Ilsa Kuhn created an *inter vivos* trust funded with property with a basis of $2,500,000. Kuhn was to receive the income from the trust for her life and, upon her death, the remainder was directed to her grandson. When Kuhn died in 2013, the trust property had a fair market value of $6,775,000. Kuhn's estate allocates all of the $5,250,000 GST tax exemption to this taxable termination. The inclusion ratio would be .225 (1 − ($5,250,000 ÷ $6,775,000)). Thus, the adjusted basis of the property transferred to Kuhn's grandson would be $3,461,875 ([($6,775,000 − $2,500,000) × .225]+ $2,500,000).

• Certain Trusts Treated as Separate Shares

For purposes of the GST tax, the portions of a trust attributable to transfers from different transferors are treated as separate trusts. Similarly, substantially separate and independent shares of different beneficiaries in a trust are treated as separate trusts.[82]

> *Example (2):* Tom Johnson and Julie Kelly created a trust for the benefit of Johnson's grandson and Kelly's son, Michael. Johnson contributed property worth $1.2 million and Kelly contributed property worth $2 million. For purposes of the GST tax, the trust would be treated as one trust containing $1.2 million with Johnson as the grantor and one trust containing $2 million with Kelly as the grantor.

---

[77] Code Sec. 2654(a)(1).
[78] Code Sec. 1015(d).
[79] Code Sec. 2654(a).

[80] Code Sec. 2654(a)(2).
[81] Code Sec. 1022, as added by P.L. 107-16, and repealed by Act Sec. 301(a), P.L. 111-312.
[82] Code Sec. 2654(b).

Example (3): Larissa Jenkins created a trust to benefit her son, Manuel, and her granddaughter, Natalie, equally. She contributed $800,000 to the trust. The trust will be treated as two separate trusts containing $400,000 for each of Manuel and Natalie for purposes of the GST tax.

• Disclaimers

For the effect of disclaimer, taxpayers are referred by statute[83] to Code Sec. 2518, which relates to gift tax disclaimers (see ¶2009). The triggering event for the nine-month disclaimer period is the direct skip, taxable termination, or taxable distribution.

• Limitation on Liability of Trustee

A trustee is not personally liable for any increase in the GST tax that is attributable to the fact that the exemption of certain nontaxable gifts[84] does not apply to a transfer to the trust that was made during the life of the transferor and for which a gift tax return was not filed.[85]

The trustee is also not personally liable when the inclusion ratio (see ¶2461) with respect to the trust is greater than the amount of the ratio as computed on the basis of the return on which an allocation of the GST tax exemption to the property transferred to the trust was made (or deemed made under Code Sec. 2632).[86] The above exception, however, will not apply if the trustee has knowledge of facts sufficient to reasonably conclude that a gift tax return was required to be filed or that the inclusion ratio was erroneous.

• Nonresidents Not Citizens

In the case of a generation-skipping transfer by a person who is neither a U.S. citizen nor a resident, the GST tax applies only to property that is subject to gift or estate tax at the time of a direct skip or transfer to a trust.[87] In other words, the GST tax applies only if the property is U.S. situs property (see ¶1620).

---

[83] Code Sec. 2654(c).
[84] Code Sec. 2642(c).
[85] Code Sec. 2654(d).

[86] Code Sec. 2654(d).
[87] Reg. §26.2663-2(b).

Chapter 41
RETURN REQUIREMENTS

¶ 2470   Liability for Tax

Which party is liable for generation-skipping transfer (GST) tax depends on the type of generation-skipping transfer.

The transferor is liable for GST tax resulting from a direct skip other than one from a trust, the trustee is liable for tax resulting from a direct skip from a trust or a taxable termination, and the transferee is liable for tax resulting from a taxable distribution.[1] If the trustee pays any amount of the tax on a taxable distribution, the trustee is treated as having made an additional taxable distribution of that amount (see ¶2451).

Generally, unless a trust instrument specifically directs otherwise, the GST tax is charged to the property constituting the transfer.[2] The estate and gift tax provisions with respect to transferee liability, liens, and related matters are applicable to the GST tax.[3] As a result, the donees of stock were liable as transferees for unpaid GST tax, even though no assessment of the tax had been asserted against the donor-transferor who was primarily liable for the tax.[4]

For an explanation of the limitations on the personal liability of a trustee, see ¶2465. See ¶2451 for an explanation of the amount of the transfer that is subject to tax.

Application of the GST tax in 2011—2014. A 40 percent tax rate and a $5,250,000 exemption applies to GSTs occurring in 2013 (this exemption will be $5,340,000 in 2014). A 35 percent tax rate and a $5,120,000 exemption applied to GSTs occurring in 2012. For GSTs in 2011, the 35 percent tax rate applied, but the exemption was $5,000,000.

Application of the GST tax in 2010. The Tax Relief, Unemployment Insurance Reauthorization, and Job Creation Act of 2010 (P.L. 111-312) (Tax Relief Act of 2010) repealed the one-year repeal of the GST tax that was enacted in subtitle A of title V of the Economic Growth and Tax Relief Reconciliation Act of 2001 (P.L. 107-16) (EGTRRA). The Tax Relief Act of 2010 further provided that the applicable rate under Code Sec. 2641(a) for generation-skipping transfers made in 2010 was zero percent. Because the GST tax is a product of the applicable rate and the taxable amount (Code Sec. 2602), no GST tax was be imposed on any generation-skipping transfers that occur during 2010, as any amount multiplied by zero is equal to zero. The GST exemption of $5,000,000 still applied for GSTs occurring in 2010, even if the executor of a decedent dying in 2010 elected application of the carryover basis rules (see ¶121).[5]

---

[1] Code Sec. 2603(a).
[2] Code Sec. 2603(b).
[3] Code Sec. 2661.

[4] K. O'Neal II, 102 TC 666, CCH Dec. 49,810.

[5] Joint Committee on Taxation, Technical Explanation of the Revenue Provisions Contained in the "Tax Relief, Unemployment In-

¶ 2471 Persons Required to File Return; Required Returns

Regulations detail who is required to file generation-skipping transfer (GST) tax returns and the time and manner for filing such returns.[6] Generally, the person liable for the tax must file the return. The form of return is governed by the generation-skipping transfer involved.

• *Direct Skips*

In the case of a lifetime direct skip, the donor is required to file Form 709 (United States Gift (and Generation-Skipping Transfer) Tax Return).

If the direct skip occurs at death, the executor must file the return unless the direct skip is from a trust or with respect to property that continues to be held in trust.[7] For direct skips at death occurring in 2013, the executor must file Form 706 (United States Estate (and Generation-Skipping Transfer) Tax Return) (Rev. August. 2013) or Form 706-NA (United States Estate (and Generation-Skipping Transfer) Tax Return) (Rev. August 2013).

If a Form 706 or Form 706-NA is filed for a decedent, the GST tax payable by the estate is computed on Schedule R (Generation-Skipping Transfer Tax) of Form 706.

If a direct skip occurring at death is payable from a trust, the trustee is liable for the GST tax.[8] The executor must use Schedule R-1 (Generation-Skipping Transfer Tax, Direct Skips From a Trust, Payment Voucher) of Form 706 to notify the trustee that such a tax is due. Instructions for completing these forms appear at ¶ 2473.

A special rule applies to direct skips occurring at death with respect to property held in a "trust arrangement."[9]

If the total value of the property involved in direct skips with respect to the trustee of that trust arrangement is less than $250,000, the executor is liable for the GST tax on the direct skip and is required to file Form 706 or Form 706-NA (and not Schedule R-1 of Form 706).[10] An executor who is subject to such liability may recover the tax attributable to the transfer from the trustee of the trust arrangement if the property continues in trust or from the recipient of the property if the property is distributed.[11] The limits on the personal liability of a trustee are described at ¶ 2465.

Direct skips in 2010. For direct skips at death occurring in 2010, the executor was required to file Form 706 (July, 2011) or Form 706-NA (July, 2011). Although the Form 706-NA (July, 2011) was used for filing for both 2010 and 2011 decedents, different Instructions applied to each: Instructions for Form 706-NA (Rev. August 2011) were used to prepare Forms 706-NA for 2011 decedents; Instructions for Form 706-NA (Rev. July 2011) were used to prepare Forms 706-NA for 2010 decedents.

(Footnote Continued)

surance Reauthorization, and Job Creation Act of 2010" (JCX-55-10), December 10, 2010, Footnote 53.

[6] Reg. § 26.2662-1.

[7] Reg. § 26.2662-1(c)(1)(iv) and Reg. § 26.2662-1(c)(1)(v).

[8] Reg. § 26.2662-1(c)(1)(iv).

[9] Reg. § 26.2662-1(c)(2)(ii) states that the term "trust arrangement" includes any arrangement (other than an estate) which, although not an explicit trust, has the same effect as an explicit trust.

[10] Reg. § 26.2662-1(c)(2)(iii).

[11] Reg. § 26.2662-1(c)(2)(v).

• *Taxable Distributions*

The distributee is liable for the GST tax in the case of a taxable distribution and must file Form 706-GS(D) (Generation-Skipping Transfer Tax Return for Distributions). The trustee of the trust involved in a taxable distribution must file Form 706-GS(D-1) (Notification of Distribution From a Generation-Skipping Trust). The trustee must send a copy of this form to each distributee. Instructions for completing each of these forms appear at ¶2479. A filled-in Form 706-GS(D) (Rev. August 2013) is reproduced in the Appendix at ¶3230; a filled-in Form 706-GS(D-1) (Rev. October 2008) is reproduced at ¶3240.

• *Taxable Terminations*

The trustee is liable for the GST tax in the case of a taxable termination and is required to file Form 706-GS(T) (Generation-Skipping Transfer Tax Return for Terminations). A filled-in Form 706-GS(T) (Rev. November 2013) is reproduced in the Appendix at ¶3250.

¶ 2473 Reporting Direct Skips Occurring at Death

Direct skips occurring at death are reported on Form 706 (United States Estate (and Generation-Skipping Transfer) Tax Return).

The entire generation-skipping transfer (GST) tax must be paid on the due date of the return (within nine months of the decedent's date of death).[12] However, estates of decedents dying in 2010 could have qualified for a special extension that would delay the due date until March, 2012 (see ¶66).

The estate tax is imposed on the value of the entire taxable estate regardless of who the distributees are. The GST tax is imposed on the value of property interests that actually pass to skip persons.

To report direct skips on Form 706, complete Schedules A through I in order to determine the property interests that are includible in the gross estate. Determine who the skip persons are. Then determine which skip persons are transferees of interests in property. Following these determinations, the direct skips to be reported must be divided between Schedule R (Generation-Skipping Transfer Tax) and Schedule R-1 (Generation-Skipping Transfer Tax), and these schedules must then be completed.[13]

Unless the Form 706 Instructions specifically provide that a generation-skipping transfer is to be reported on Schedule R-1, all GSTs are reported on Schedule R.[14] For a direct skip to be reportable on Schedule R-1, the trust must be includible in the decedent's gross estate. The trustee, not the estate, is liable for the tax on direct skips from a trust. Schedule R-1 is to be used by the executor to notify the trustee that such a tax is due.

The estate tax value of the property interests subject to the direct skips are entered on Schedules R and R-1. If alternate valuation or special use valuation has been elected, those values must be entered on Schedules R and R-1. The allocation of the GST tax exemption ($5,000,000 for 2010 and 2011; $5,120,000 (indexed) for 2012; $5,250,000 (indexed) for 2013; $5,340,000 (indexed)) is calcu-

---

[12] Instructions for Form 706 (Rev. August 2013), p. 3. However, an installment payment of tax under Code Sec. 6166 may be available if an interest in a qualifying closely held business is transferred in a direct skip (within the meaning of Code Sec. 2012(c))

occurring at the same time, and as a result of the decedent's death (Code Sec. 6166(i)).

[13] Instructions for Form 706 (Rev. August 2013), p. 42.

[14] Instructions for Form 706 (Rev. August 2013), p. 44.

lated for 2013 using lines 4, 5, and 6 in part 1 of Schedule R after completing parts 2 and 3 of Schedule R, and Schedule R-1.

Part 2 of Schedule R is used to compute the GST tax on direct skips in which the property interests transferred bear the GST tax on the transfers.[15] The tax on transfers in which the property interests transferred do not bear the GST tax on the transfers is reported on part 3.

¶ 2479   Reporting Distributions

Form 706-GS(D-1) (Notification of Distribution From a Generation-Skipping Trust) (Rev. October 2008) and Form 706-GS(D) (Generation-Skipping Transfer Tax Return for Distributions) (Rev. August 2013) must be filed for trust distributions that are subject to the generation-skipping transfer (GST) tax.

• *Form 706-GS(D-1)*

Form 706-GS(D-1) is used by the trustee of a generation-skipping trust to report taxable distributions and to provide skip person distributees (see ¶ 2435) with information needed to compute the GST tax on the distribution. The form has two copies: Copy A (to be filed with the IRS) and Copy B (to be sent to the skip person distributee).

When to file. Form 706-GS(D-1) must be filed with the IRS (Copy A), and sent to the distributee (Copy B) no later than April 15 of the year following the calendar year in which the distributions were made.[16]

The distributee is to report on part II (Distributions) of Form 706-GS(D) all taxable distributions occurring in the year having an inclusion ratio greater than zero.

Nonexplicit trusts. An arrangement that has substantially the same effect as a trust is treated as a trust for purposes of the GST tax even though it is not an explicit trust. Arrangements treated as nonexplicit trusts include insurance and annuity contracts, life estates, remainders, and estates for years. Decedents' estates are not classified as nonexplicit trusts for purposes of Form 706-GS(D-1) (Rev. Oct. 2008).

The person in actual or constructive possession of the property held in a nonexplicit trust is considered to be the trustee and is liable for filing Form 706-GS(D-1).[17]

Separate trusts. Portions of a single trust must be treated as separate trusts for purposes of Form 706-GS(D-1) where:

(1) there are portions of the trust that are attributable to transfers from different transferors; or

(2) there are substantially separate and independent shares of different trust beneficiaries.[18]

---

[15] Instructions for Form 706 (Rev. August 2013), p. 46.

[16] Reg. § 26.2662-1(d).

[17] Instructions for Form 706-GS(D-1) (Rev. November 2013), p. 1. (For use with Form 706-GS(D-1) (October 2008)).

[18] Instructions for Form 706-GS(D-1) (Rev. November 2013), p. 1. (For use with Form 706-GS(D-1) (October 2008).

Return Requirements   463

• *Form 706-GS(D-1)—Line-by-Line Instructions*[19]

Part I, General Instructions. The identifying number of the skip person distributee (whether an individual or a trust) is entered on line 1a of part I (General Information) of Form 706-GS(D-1) (Rev. Oct. 2008). Enter the social security number of the individual distributee on line 1a; if the skip person distributee is a trust, the trust's employer identification number (EIN) is entered on line 1a. Enter the skip person distributee's name, address, and ZIP code on line 1b.

The employer identification number of the trust from which the distribution was made is entered on line 2a, and the trust's name, address, and ZIP code are entered on line 2b.

Part II, Distributions. Report all distributions from any given trust to a single skip person distributee during the calendar year on part II. The following information is entered under the columns of line 3 for each distribution:

(Column a) Item number: Consecutive numbers should be assigned to each distribution made during the year. Properties having different inclusion ratios are listed separately. Properties having the same inclusion ratio may be included under a single item number, even if they were distributed at different times.

(Column b) Description of property: Each parcel of real estate should be described in enough detail so that it may be located for inspection and valuation. If the parcel is improved, the improvements should be described. Any personal property distributed must be described in enough detail that the IRS can ascertain its value.

Stocks: For stocks, the following information should be supplied:
— Number of shares
— Classification of stock: common or preferred
— Issue
— Par value (where needed for valuation)
— Price per share
— Exact name of corporation
— Principal exchange upon which the stock is sold
— CUSIP number

Bonds: For bonds, the following information should be supplied:
— Quantity and denomination
— Name of obligor
— Date of maturity
— Principal exchange upon which the bond is listed
— Interest rate
— Interest due date
— CUSIP number

If a stock or bond is not listed on an exchange, the company's principal business office should be listed.

---

[19] A filled-in Form 706-GS(D-1) (October 2008) is reproduced in the Appendix at ¶3240.

¶2479

(Column c) Date of distribution: The trustee must disclose the date of distribution.

(Column d) Inclusion ratio: The trustee must provide an inclusion ratio (see ¶ 2461) for every distribution.

(Column e) Value: The trustee's responsibility with respect to valuing the property depends on the type of the property distributed. The trustee is required to provide the value of property having an objectively identifiable value, such as cash, stocks, or bonds. For other property, the trustee may provide a value but is only required to give the distributee all the information the trustee has that will help the distributee to determine the value of the distribution.

(Column f) Tentative transfer: The amount of the tentative transfer is the value, entered in column e, multiplied by the inclusion ratio, entered in column d.

Part III, Trust Information. Only Copy A (which goes to the IRS) contains part III, Trust Information, which requires the trustee to answer the questions on lines 4 through 7.

If the trust for which the Form 706-GS(D-1) is filed is a nonexplicit trust, the trustee filing the form must check the box on line 4 and attach a statement describing the trust arrangement that is substantially similar to an explicit trust.

If property has been contributed to the trust since the last Form 706-GS(T) (Generation-Skipping Transfer Tax Return For Terminations) or 706-GS(D-1) was filed, a schedule must be attached showing how the inclusion ratio was calculated (line 5).

Line 6 questions whether any contributions were made to the trust since the last Form 706-GS(T) or 706-GS(D-1) was filed that were not included in calculating the trust's inclusion ratio. If the answer is "Yes," a statement explaining why the contribution was not included must be attached.

If any exemption has been allocated to the trust by reason of the deemed allocation rules, this is indicated on line 7.

Signature required. Copy A of Form 706-GS(D-1) must be signed by the trustee or an authorized representative.

Where to File. On Copy B of Form 706-GS(D-1), the copy sent to the skip person distributee, the trustee must enter the name and address of the IRS Service Center where the distributee should report the distribution on Form 706-GS(D). The trustee must file this return to: Department of the Treasury, Internal Revenue Service, Cincinnati, OH 45999, regardless of whether the trust settlor is (or was at death) a resident U.S. citizen, a resident alien, a nonresident citizen, or a nonresident alien.[20]

• *Form 706-GS(D)*

Form 706-GS(D) generally must be filed with respect to taxable trust distributions (see ¶ 2471).

The form is filed by the skip person (see ¶ 2435) recipients of the trust distributions. In preparing Form 706-GS(D), trust distributees will have to con-

---

[20] Instructions for Form 706-GS(D-1) (Rev. November 2013), p. 1. (For use with Form 706-GS(D-1) (Rev. October 2008)).

sult the applicable portions of the copy of the completed Form 706-GS(D-1) that the trustee of the generation-skipping trust is required to submit to them.

Deadline for filing. Form 706-GS(D) generally must be filed no later than April 15 of the year following the calendar year in which the distributions were made. Thus, for distributions made in 2013, Form 706-GS(D) must be filed by April 15, 2014.

Where to file. Form 706-GS(D) should be filed at the following address: Department of the Treasury, Internal Revenue Service Center at Cincinnati, Ohio 45999.[21] To request an automatic six-month extension of time to file Form 706-GS(D), the skip person distributee should file Form 7004 (Application for Automatic 6-Month Extension of Time to File Certain Business Income Tax, Information, and Other Returns).[22]

○ *Form 706-GS(D)—Line-by-Line Instructions*[23]

Part I, General Information. The name of the skip person distributee (whether an individual or a trust) is entered on line 1a of part I, General Information, Form 706-GS(D) (Generation-Skipping Transfer Tax Return). If the skip person distributee is an individual, that individual's Social Security number is entered on line 1b; if the skip person distributee is a trust, the trust's employer identification number (EIN) is entered on line 1c. In no case should numbers appear on both lines 1b and 1c.

The name and title of the person filing the return is entered on line 2a, but only if different from the name entered on line 1a. The trustee's name should be entered here if the skip person distributee is a trust. If the skip person distributee is a minor, or an adult under a disability that precludes the distributee from filing the return, the name of the person who is legally responsible for conducting the distributee's affairs, such as a parent or guardian, should be entered on line 2a. The parent's or guardian's title or relationship to the distributee should be included.

The address of the distributee or person filing the return is entered on line 2b.

Part II, Distributions. All taxable distributions with inclusion ratios greater than zero that the distributee received during the year are reported on part II of Form 706-GS(D). If additional space is required, the distributee should attach an additional sheet of the same size and use the same format that is used in part II to report any additional distributions.

(Column a) Trust EIN: The employer identification number of the distributing trust, from line 2a, Form 706-GS(D-1), is entered in column a of part II.

(Column b) Item number: The same item number that was used for the corresponding distribution on Form 706-GS(D-1), line 3, column a, should be entered in column b. If the distributee receives distributions from more than one trust, the same item number may have to be repeated.

(Column c) Amount of transfer: The amount of transfer will usually be entered from line 3, column f, of Form 706-GS(D-1), unless the trustee has not entered any amount there or the distributee disagrees with the amount that the trustee has entered. If the distributee and the trustee disagree about the amount

---

[21] Instructions for Form 706-GS(D) (Rev. August 2013), p. 1.
[22] Reg. § 26.6081-1T.

[23] A filled-in Form 706-GS(D) (Rev. August 2013) is reproduced in the Appendix at ¶3230.

of the tentative transfer, the distributee should attach a statement to Form 706-GS(D) showing what the distributee considers to be the correct amounts and how they were computed.

The total tentative transfers from part II and from any continuation sheet should be entered on line 3 of part II. The distributee should also attach to Form 706-GS(D) a copy of each Form 706-GS(D-1) received during the year.

Part III, Tax Computation. Enter the amount of total transfers on line 3 of part II. Adjusted allowable expenses (line 4) are deducted from the line 3 amount, and the resulting amount entered on line 5 (Taxable amount) which appears in part III. For purposes of this deduction, expenses incurred in connection with the preparation of Form 706-GS(D), or any other expenses incurred in connection with the determination, collection, or refund of the GST tax reported on the return are totalled and multiplied by the inclusion ratio. The resulting product is the amount of the "adjusted allowable expenses." A distributee who has more than one inclusion ratio to report on part II must prorate the total expense among them, based on the relative value of each distribution.

Returns for 2011, 2012, and 2013 distributions. The maximum estate tax rate (40 percent for 2013 and beyond; 35 percent for 2011 and 2012) is entered on line 6. Line 5 is multiplied by line 6, and the result (Generation-skipping transfer tax) is entered on line 7. If a payment was made with Form 7004, the amount on line 8 is deducted from the amount on line 7, to give the Total due, which is entered on line 9.

Signature required. Form 706-GS(D) must be signed by the distributee or by the distributee's authorized representative. A paid preparer must also include his or her PTIN.

¶ 2487   Reporting Terminations

Generation-skipping terminations are reported on Form 706-GS(T) (see ¶ 2471). The form is used by a trustee to compute and report the generation-skipping transfer (GST) tax due with respect to certain trust terminations (see ¶ 2433).

The trustee must file the form at the following address: Department of the Treasury, Internal Revenue Service, Cincinnati, Ohio 45999. This address is to be used regardless of whether the trust settlor is (or was at death) a resident U.S. citizen, a resident alien, a nonresident U.S. citizen, or a nonresident alien.

Deadline for filing. Generally, the return is to be filed by April 15th of the year following the calendar year in which the termination occurred. Thus, for GST terminations occurring in 2013, the filing date is April 15, 2014.[24]

To request an automatic six-month extension of time to file Form 706-GS(T), the trustee should file Form 7004 (Application for Automatic Extension of Time to File Certain Business Income Tax, Information, and Other Returns).[25]

• Nonexplicit Trust

An arrangement that has substantially the same effect as a trust is treated as a trust for purposes of the GST tax even though it is not an explicit trust. Arrangements treated as nonexplicit trusts include insurance and annuity contracts, life estates, remainders, and estates for years. Decedents' estates are not

---

[24] Instructions for Form 706-GS(T) (Rev. November 2013), p. 1.

[25] Reg. § 26.6081-1T.

classified as nonexplicit trusts for purposes of Form 706-GS(T) (see ¶2439). The person in actual or constructive possession of the property held in a nonexplicit trust is considered to be the trustee and is responsible for filing Form 706-GS(T).[26]

● *Separate Trusts*

Portions of a single trust must be treated as separate trusts for purposes of Form 706-GS(T) when:

> (1) portions of the trust are attributable to transfers from different transferors; or

> (2) substantially separate and independent shares are for different trust beneficiaries.

If a single trust is treated as separate trusts under the above rules, a single Form 706-GS(T) is filed, but a separate Schedule A (Taxable Terminations) must be filed with respect to each such separate trust.

● *Medical and Educational Exclusions*

Form 706-GS(T) need not be filed if the termination is not a generation-skipping transfer by reason of the gift tax exclusion for amounts paid for medical or educational expenses. This occurs if the property was distributed and used for medical or educational expenses of the transferee and would not have been subject to gift tax if the transfer had been made during an individual's lifetime.

● *Form 706-GS(T)—Line-by-Line Instructions*[27]

Page 3 of the Form 706-GS(T) Instructions (Rev. November 2013) indicates that the form is to be filled out in the following order: (1) parts I and II; (2) Schedule A (through line 4); (3) Schedule B; (4) Schedule A (lines 5 through 10); and (5) part III.

Part I, General Information. Enter the name of the trust and the trust's employer identification number (EIN) on lines 1a and 1b of part I, General Information, of Form 706-GS(T). Nonexplicit trusts, as well as explicit trusts, must have an EIN. The name and the address of the trustee (or the person who is considered to be the trustee under the nonexplicit trust rules) are entered on lines 2a and 2b.

Part II, Trust Information. The trustee is required to answer the questions on lines 3 through 8 of part II.

Line 3 questions whether any exemption has been allocated to the trust by reason of the deemed allocation rules of Code Sec. 2632 (see ¶2455). If the answer is "Yes," the allocation must be described on an attachment to Schedule A, line 7, showing how the inclusion ratio (see ¶2461) was calculated.

If property has been contributed to the trust since the last Form 706-GS(T) or 706-GS(D-1) was filed, a schedule showing how the inclusion ratio was calculated should be attached (line 4).

If terminations occurred that were not reported because of payments relating to medical and educational exclusions or prior payment of the GST tax, check the "Yes" box on line 5, and attach a statement describing the termination.

---

[26] Instructions for Form 706-GS(T) (Rev. November 2013), p. 1.

[27] A filled-in Form 706-GS(T) (Rev. November 2013) is reproduced in the Appendix at ¶3250.

Line 6 asks whether any contributions were made to the trust that were not included in calculating the trust's inclusion ratio. If the answer is "Yes," a statement explaining why the contribution was not included must be attached.

If the special qualified terminable interest property election (known as a "reverse QTIP" election) with respect to Code Sec. 2652(a)(3) has been made for the trust, this is indicated on line 7.

If the trust to which the Form 706-GS(T) is filed is a nonexplicit trust, check the box on line 8, and attach a statement describing the trust arrangement that makes it substantially similar to an explicit trust.

Schedule A. Separate copies of Schedule A will have to be filed for each terminating interest of a single trust that has a different inclusion ratio. Under line 1 are listed the names of the skip persons and their respective Social Security numbers, EINs, and the item number from line 4 of Schedule A in which the interest is held. The terminating power or interest is described in the space provided at line 2. If the trustee is reporting separate trusts, the reason for treating parts of the trust as separate trusts should be included here.

If the trustee wishes to elect alternate valuation, the election is made on line 3 of Schedule A.

The following information must be entered under the columns of line 4 for each taxable termination:

(Column a) Item number: All property having the same termination date, valuation date, and unit price may be combined under the same item number. Otherwise, a separate item number should be assigned to each article of property.

(Column b) Description of property subject to termination: Each parcel of real estate should be described in enough detail so that it may be located for inspection and valuation. If the parcel is improved, the improvements should be described. Personal property should be described in enough detail so that the IRS can ascertain its value.

Stocks: For stocks, the following information should be supplied:

— Number of shares
— Classification of stock: common or preferred
— Issue
— Par value (where needed for valuation)
— Price per share
— Exact name of corporation
— Principal exchange upon which stock is sold
— CUSIP number

Bonds: For bonds, the following information should be supplied:

— Quantity and denomination
— Name of obligor
— Date of maturity
— Principal exchange, if listed on an exchange
— Interest rate
— Interest due date

¶2487

— CUSIP number

If a stock or bond is not listed on an exchange, the company's principal business office should be listed.

(Column c) Date of termination: The trustee must disclose the date of termination.

(Column d) Valuation date: Unless the trustee elected the alternate valuation date, this date should be the same as the termination date.

(Column e) Value: The value of property to be reported on Schedule A should be entered, reduced by the amount of any consideration that was provided by the skip person. An explanation of how the values were determined should be included, along with copies of any appraisals.

Deductible expenses. In determining the taxable amount for a taxable termination, certain expenses (under rules generally similar to those discussed at ¶ 780) may be deducted from the value of the property subject to the termination. These expenses are deducted on Schedule B(1) or Schedule B(2).

Schedule B(1). Enter the item number, description and amount of expenses that are related to the entire trust in columns a, b, and c, respectively, of Schedule B(1). In addition to a description of the nature of the expenses listed in column b, the name and address of the persons to whom the expenses were paid should be included.

The percentage of the expenses allocable to the property involved in the termination is to be entered on line 2. This percentage is determined by way of a two-step computation, as follows:

(1) the value of the interest that was terminated is divided by the total value of the trust at the time of the termination; and

(2) the amount determined under (1), above, is to be multiplied by a fraction, the numerator of which is the number of days in the year through the date of the termination, and the denominator of which is the total number of days in the year, or, if the entire trust was terminated during the year, the total number of days the trust was in existence during the year.

Schedule B(2). The item number, description, and amount of expenses that are related solely to the interest that has terminated are entered in columns a, b, and c, respectively, of Schedule B(2). If the expense entered relates to more property than is involved in the termination, but less than the entire trust, only the amount attributable to the property involved in the termination is to be entered in column c. This amount is determined by multiplying the total expense by a fraction, the numerator of which is the value of the property involved in the termination and to which the expense pertains, and the denominator of which is the total value of the property to which the expense pertains.

Schedule A, lines 5–7. The amount of the total deductions applicable to the Schedule A (carried over from the corresponding Schedule B, line 5) is entered on line 5. The inclusion ratio (see ¶ 2461) must be calculated with respect to every termination, and entered on line 7. All terminations, or any parts of a single termination that have different inclusion ratios must be shown on a separate Schedule A. The product of the amount shown on line 7 (inclusion ratio).

Schedule A, Lines 8–10. The total maximum estate tax rate for 2013 (40 percent) is entered on line 8. The line 7 (Inclusion ratio) is multiplied by line 8, and the result (Applicable rate) is entered on line 9. The GST tax (line 10) is computed as the result of line 6 multiplied by line 9.

Signature required. Form 706-GS(T) must be signed by the trustee or by his or her authorized representative.

SPECIAL VALUATION RULES

Chapter 42

ESTATE FREEZES

¶ 2500   Special Valuation Rules for Estate Freezes

The special valuation rules of Code Sec. 2701 through Code Sec. 2704 were enacted to prevent the transfer tax avoidance achieved by certain transfers to younger generations. In such transfers, the value of the transferred interest was determined by subtracting the value of the retained interest from the total value of the property. The value of the retained interest was overstated in order to reduce the value of the transferred interest and, consequently, the amount of the taxable gift.

In general, the special valuation rules preclude the undervaluation of gifts by providing rules for valuing retained interests. Code Sec. 2701 provides special rules for determining the amount of a gift when an individual transfers an equity interest in a corporation or a partnership to a family member while retaining an interest in the entity (see ¶ 2505). Code Sec. 2702 provides rules for determining the amount of a gift when an individual makes a transfer in trust to or for the benefit of a family member while retaining an interest in the trust (see ¶ 2550). Code Sec. 2703 disregards certain rights and restrictions for transfer tax valuation purposes (see ¶ 2580). Code Sec. 2704 forestalls the use of lapsing rights and restrictions to reduce transfer taxes (see ¶ 2590).

¶ 2505   Function of Code Sec. 2701

The classic estate freeze of a closely held business transferred the business's future appreciation to a younger generation in a manner that reduced or eliminated the transferor's gift tax cost.

Example (1): Ben Thompson owns all of the common stock in Famco, which is valued at $50,000. As a result of a recapitalization, Ben receives common and preferred noncumulative voting stock. Because the preferred stock has a par value approximating the corporation's liquidation value and confers a right to put the stock at par value, Ben values the preferred stock at $50,000. He then gives the common stock to his son, Chuck, and assigns no value to the gift. At Ben's death, the value of the preferred stock included in his gross estate is $50,000, but the value of Chuck's common stock has appreciated to $200,000.

Code Sec. 2701 addresses estate freezes by revaluing the older generation's retained interests. By assigning zero value or a lower value to the retained interest and using the subtraction method to value the gift, a higher value is assigned to the gifted interest for gift tax purposes. When the transferor dies, a special valuation adjustment may apply to lower the transferor's estate tax. Post-transfer appreciation, however, is not includible in the transferor's estate.

Example (2): Assume the same facts as in Example (1), except that Code Sec. 2701 applies. Ben's retained preferred stock is valued at zero, and the gift of common stock to Chuck is valued at $50,000. The $50,000 value of the preferred stock included in Ben's gross estate may be offset by a special valuation adjustment.

¶ 2510   Application of Code Sec. 2701

The Code Sec. 2701 valuation rules apply when (1) an interest in a corporation or a partnership is "transferred" to a "member of the family" of the transferor, and (2) the transferor or an "applicable family member" retains an "applicable retained interest."[1]

Members of the transferor's family. Members of the family of the transferor are generally members of the younger generation and include:

(1) the transferor's spouse;

(2) a lineal descendant of the transferor or the transferor's spouse; and

(3) the spouse of any such descendant.[2]

Applicable family members. Applicable family members are generally members of the older generation and include:

(1) the transferor's spouse;

(2) any ancestor of the transferor or the transferor's spouse; and

(3) the spouse of any such ancestor.[3]

• *Code Sec. 2701 Transfers*

The following types of transactions are transfers for purposes of Code Sec. 2701:

(1) transactions in which full and adequate consideration is given, but such consideration is less than the value of the transferred interest as determined under Code Sec. 2701 (such transactions would not otherwise be treated as taxable gifts under the gift tax provisions);[4]

---

[1] Code Sec. 2701(a)(1); Reg. § 25.2701-1(a)(1).

[2] Code Sec. 2701(e)(1); Reg. § 25.2701-1(d)(1).

[3] Code Sec. 2701(e)(2); Reg. § 25.2701-1(d)(2).

[4] Reg. § 25.2701-1(b)(1).

(2) capital contributions to a new or existing entity;[5]

(3) changes in capital structure, including redemptions and recapitalizations, in which (a) the transferor or an applicable family member receives an applicable retained interest, (b) the transferor or applicable family member who holds an applicable retained interest before the transaction surrenders a junior equity interest and receives property other than an applicable retained interest, or (c) the transferor or applicable family member who holds an applicable retained interest before the transaction surrenders an equity interest other than a junior interest and the fair market value of the applicable retained interest is increased;[6] and

(4) terminations of an indirect holding in an entity through a grantor trust, or, if through another type of trust, then to the extent the value of the indirectly held interest would have been included in the indirect holder's gross estate if the indirect holder died immediately prior to the termination.[7]

The following transactions are not treated as Code Sec. 2701 transfers:

(1) capital structure transactions that do not substantially change the interests held by the transferor, applicable family members, and members of the transferor's family (for example, an exchange of nonvoting common stock for common stock with nonvoting lapsing rights);

(2) the shift of rights resulting from the execution of a qualified disclaimer; and

(3) the shift of rights resulting from the exercise, release, or lapse of a power of appointment (other than a general power under Code Sec. 2514) except to the extent that such exercise, release, or lapse would constitute a transfer under the gift tax provisions.[8]

• *Applicable Retained Interests*

An applicable retained interest is either an extraordinary payment right or a distribution right in a family-controlled entity.[9]

Extraordinary payment rights include any put, call, or conversion right, any right to compel liquidation, or any similar right, the exercise or nonexercise of which affects the value of the transferred interest.[10] Extraordinary payment rights do not include (1) mandatory payment rights, (2) liquidation participation rights, (3) rights to Code Sec. 707(c) guaranteed payments, or (4) nonlapsing conversion rights.[11]

A distribution right is the right to receive distributions with respect to an equity interest.[12] Distribution rights do not include (1) rights to receive distributions with respect to an interest that is of the same class as, or junior to, the transferred interest, (2) extraordinary payment rights, (3) mandatory payment rights, (4) liquidation participation rights, (5) rights to Code Sec. 707(c) guaranteed payments, or (6) nonlapsing conversion rights.[13]

For a distribution right to be considered an applicable retained interest, the entity must be family controlled.[14] Such control exists if at least 50 percent of the

---

[5] Reg. § 25.2701-1(b)(2)(i)(A).
[6] Reg. § 25.2701-1(b)(2)(i)(B).
[7] Reg. § 25.2701-1(b)(2)(i)(C).
[8] Reg. § 25.2701-1(b)(3).
[9] Code Sec. 2701(b)(1).

[10] Code Sec. 2701(c)(2)(A); Reg. § 25.2701-2(b)(2).
[11] Reg. § 25.2701-2(b)(4).
[12] Code Sec. 2701(c)(1)(A).
[13] Reg. § 25.2701-2(b)(3)-(4).
[14] Code Sec. 2701(b)(1)(A).

total voting power or fair market value of the equity interests in a corporation (or at least 50 percent of the capital or profits interests in a partnership) are owned by the transferor, applicable family members, or any lineal descendants of the transferor or the transferor's spouse. In the case of a limited partnership, control means the holding of any interest as a general partner.[15]

• *Exceptions to Application of Code Sec. 2701*

Code Sec. 2701 does not apply under the following circumstances:

(1) market quotations on an established securities market are readily available for the value of an applicable retained interest or for the transferred interest;

(2) the retained interest is of the same class as the transferred interest;

(3) the rights in the retained interest are proportionally the same as all the rights in the transferred interest, without regard to nonlapsing differences in voting power (or, for a partnership, nonlapsing differences with respect to management and limitations on liability);[16] or

(4) the transfer results in a proportionate reduction of each class of equity interest held by the transferor and all applicable family members in the aggregate immediately before the transfer.[17]

For purposes of (3), above, a right that lapses by reason of federal or state law is treated as a nonlapsing right unless the IRS issues a contrary regulation or ruling.[18] Thus, for example, the IRS has ruled that the interest of a general partner who made a gift of limited partnership interests while retaining an interest as a general partner was not treated as an applicable retained interest since the retained rights were identical to the rights of the interest transferred except for nonlapsing differences with respect to management and limitations on liability.[19]

¶ 2515   Valuation of Applicable Retained Interests

Extraordinary payment rights are valued at zero. Distribution rights are also valued at zero unless they are qualified payment rights. (See ¶ 2510, "Applicable Retained Interests", for definitions of extraordinary payment rights and distribution rights.) If a qualified payment right exists in conjunction with one or more extraordinary payment rights, it is presumed that each extraordinary payment right is exercised in a way that results in the lowest value for all such rights.[20] If an applicable retained interest does not contain rights that are valued at zero or under the "lower of" rule, the retained interest is valued at its fair market value.[21]

• *Qualified Payments*

Qualified payments include the following:

(1) dividends payable on a periodic basis (at least annually) with respect to any cumulative preferred stock to the extent such dividends are determined at a fixed rate;

---

[15] Code Sec. 2701(b)(2); Reg. § 25.2701-2(b)(5).

[16] Code Sec. 2701(a)(2); Reg. § 25.2701-1(c)(1)-(3).

[17] Reg. § 25.2701-1(c)(4).

[18] Reg. § 25.2701-1(c)(3).

[19] IRS Letter Ruling 9415007 (Jan. 12, 1994).

[20] Code Sec. 2701(a)(3).

[21] Reg. § 25.2701-2(a)(4).

(2) other cumulative distributions payable on a periodic basis (at least annually) with respect to an equity interest to the extent they are determined at a fixed rate or as a fixed amount; and

(3) any distribution rights that the transferor has elected (or partially elected) to treat as qualified payments, provided that the amounts and times of payment specified in the election do not exceed the distributions authorized under the instrument.[22]

The IRS concluded that prepayment of annual distribution payments in accordance with the operating agreement of a limited liability company (LLC) constituted a qualified payment for purposes of Code Sec. 2701.[23] Under the operating agreement, which contemplated compliance with the special valuation rules, preferred LLC members were entitled to receive a specified percentage of that member's initial value in the entity. The prepayment was deemed to be a cumulative distribution payable on a periodic basis.[24]

A payment rate is determined at a fixed rate if it bears a fixed relationship to a specified market interest rate.

A transferor holding a qualified payment right may elect (or partially elect) to treat all rights of the same class as not being qualified payment rights.[25]

Example: Betty Edson owns all of the common and preferred stock in Famco. Edson has the right to put all 200 shares of preferred stock having an annual cumulative dividend of $20 per share to Famco for $180,000. Assuming that the fair market value of Famco is $300,000 and the value of the cumulative dividend is $200,000, she transfers the common stock to her child and retains the preferred. Because Edson holds an extraordinary payment right (the put right) in conjunction with a qualified payment right (the right to cumulative dividends), the "lower of" rule applies and it is assumed that the put will be exercised immediately. The preferred stock is valued at $180,000 (lower of $180,000 or $200,000). Accordingly, the resulting gift is $120,000 ($300,000 minus $180,000). If Edson's put right did not exist, the applicable retained interest would consist only of a qualified payment right. Accordingly, the value of the preferred stock would be $200,000 and the resulting gift would be $100,000.

¶ 2520 Determination of Amount of Gift

After the amount of the retained interest has been determined, the subtraction method is used to determine the amount of the gift.[26] In general, the values of all family-held senior equity interests are subtracted from the fair market value of all family-held interests in the entity as determined immediately before the transfer. Although the values of senior equity interests are determined under the rules of Code Sec. 2701 if they are held by the transferor and applicable family members, other family-held senior equity interests are valued at their fair market value. The resulting balance is allocated among the transferred interests and other family-held junior interests. Certain discounts and other reductions are allowed under appropriate circumstances.[27] A 10-percent minimum value rule also applies to the valuation of gifts of junior equity interests.[28]

---

[22] Code Sec. 2701(c)(3); Reg. § 25.2701-2(b)(6).

[23] IRS Letter Ruling 200114004 (Nov. 30, 2000).

[24] Code Sec. 2701(c)(3); Reg. § 25.2701-2(b)(6)(9)(B).

[25] Code Sec. 2701(c)(3)(C)(i); Reg. § 25.2701-2(c).

[26] Reg. § 25.2701-3.

[27] Reg. § 25.2701-3(a)(1).

[28] Code Sec. 2701(a)(4); Reg. § 25.2701-3(c).

Family-held interests. Family-held interests are interests held directly or indirectly by the transferor, applicable family members, and any lineal descendants of the parents of the transferor or the transferor's spouse.[29]

Senior equity interests. Senior equity interests are interests that carry a right to distributions of income or capital that is preferred in comparison to the rights of the transferred interest.[30]

Junior (subordinate) equity interests. Junior equity interests are equity interests that are junior to the applicable retained interest.[31]

* *Four-Step Subtraction Method*

The amount of the gift is determined in the following four steps:

(1) **Value family-held interests.** In general, determine the value of all family-held equity interests in the entity immediately after the transfer (under the assumption that they are held by one individual). In the case of a contribution to capital, determine the fair market value of the contribution.

(2) **Subtract the value of senior equity interests.** Subtract from the amount determined in Step (1), (a) the sum of the fair market value of all family-held senior equity interests (other than applicable retained interests held by the transferor or applicable family members) *plus* the fair market value of any family-held interests of the same class or a junior class to transferred interests held by persons other than the transferor, applicable family members, and members of the transferor's family, and (b) the value of all applicable retained interests held by the transferor or applicable family members, as adjusted (see below).

If the value in Step (1) was determined under the special rule for contributions to capital, the value of any applicable retained interest received in exchange for the contribution must be subtracted from that value.

Adjustment. The percentage of any class of applicable retained interest held by the transferor and applicable family members that exceeds the "family interest percentage" is treated as a family-held interest that is not held by the transferor or an applicable family member. The family interest percentage is the highest ownership percentage (based on relative fair market values) of family-held interests in any class of junior equity interest or all junior equity interests, valued in the aggregate.

(3) **Allocate the remaining value.** The amount remaining after Step (2) is allocated among the transferred interests and the other junior equity interests held by the transferor, applicable family members, and members of the transferor's family. If there is more than one class of family-held junior equity interests, the allocation begins with the most senior class of junior equity interests in a manner that most fairly approximates their value if all the rights valued at zero did not exist. Any amount not appropriately allocated in this manner is allocated to the interests in proportion to their fair market values without regard to Code Sec. 2701.

(4) **Determine the amount of the gift.** The amount allocated to the transferred interests in Step (3) is reduced to make such of the following adjustments as are applicable:

---

[29] Reg. § 25.2701-3(a)(2)(i).
[30] Reg. § 25.2701-3(a)(2)(ii).

[31] Reg. § 25.2701-3(a)(2)(iii).

(a) *Reduction for minority or similar discounts.* The amount of the gift is reduced by the excess, if any, of (1) a pro rata portion of the fair market value of the family-held interests of the same class (determined as if all voting rights conferred by family-held equity interests were held by one person), over (2) the value of the transferred interest (determined without regard to Code Sec. 2701).

(b) *Reduction for transfers with retained interest.* The amount of the gift is reduced by the amount, if any, of the reduction required under Code Sec. 2702 to reflect the value of a retained interest (see ¶ 2550).

(c) *Reduction for consideration.* The amount of the gift is reduced up to the amount of the gift determined without regard to Code Sec. 2701 by the amount, if any, of consideration received by the transferor. Consideration in the form of an applicable retained interest is determined under Code Sec. 2701, except that in the case of a contribution to capital, the value of such an interest is zero.[32]

- *Minimum Value Rule*

In addition to the four-step subtraction method, Code Sec. 2701 applies a minimum value rule in determining the amount of a gift. Under this rule, the value of a junior equity interest cannot be less than its pro rata portion of 10 percent of the sum of:

(1) the total value of all equity interests in the entity; and

(2) the total amount of any indebtedness the entity owes to the transferor and applicable family members.[33]

Example: Famco has 1,000 shares of nonvoting common stock and 1,000 shares of $1,000 par value voting preferred stock outstanding. Each share of preferred stock carries a cumulative annual dividend of 8% and a right to put the stock to Famco for its par value at any time. Jim Warner owns 60% of the preferred stock and 75% of the common stock. The balance of the preferred and common stock is owned by Mike Brooks, who is unrelated to Warner. Warner transfers all of his common stock to his daughter. Because the preferred stock confers both a qualified payment right and an extraordinary payment right, Warner's rights are valued under the "lower of" rule at $800 per share, taking into account Warner's voting rights.

The amount of Warner's gift is computed as follows:

Step 1: Assume that the value of all family-held interests in Famco, taking account of Warner's control of Famco, is $1 million.

Step 2: Subtract the value of the preferred stock held by Warner (.60 × $800,000 = $480,000, computed under the "lower of" rule of Reg. § 25.2701-2(a)(3)).

Step 3: The balance of $520,000 is allocated to the 750 shares of family-held common stock.

Step 4: No adjustments are made because no minority or similar discount is appropriate and no consideration was furnished for the transfer. The amount of the gift is $520,000.[34]

---

[32] Reg. § 25.2701-3(b).
[33] Code Sec. 2701(a)(4); Reg. § 25.2701-3(c).

[34] Reg. § 25.2701-3(d), Example 1.

¶ 2525   Subsequent Valuations of Qualified Payment Rights

If a "taxable event" occurs with respect to any distribution right that was previously valued as a qualified payment interest (see ¶ 2515), the taxable estate or the taxable gifts of the individual holding the interest are increased.[35]

• *Taxable Event*

A taxable event occurs if a qualified payment interest is transferred by the individual in whose hands the interest was originally valued under Code Sec. 2701 (or by certain individuals treated in the same manner as the original interest holder).[36] The transfer could be made either during life or at death.

A taxable event also occurs on the termination of an individual's rights with respect to a qualified payment interest.[37] A taxpayer also may elect to treat a late payment of certain qualified payments as a taxable event.[38] A qualified payment is late if it is paid more than four years after it is due. Qualified payments made during the four-year grace period are treated as having been made on the actual due date.[39]

A transfer is not a taxable event to the extent that a marital deduction (see ¶ 1000 and ¶ 2311) is allowable for the transfer.[40] In such a case, the transferee or surviving spouse is treated as the holder of the interest from the time it is received.[41] In addition, if the interest holder transfers the qualified payment interest to an applicable family member in a taxable event, the transferee will be treated from that time on in the same manner as the transferor with respect to late or unpaid qualified payments that are first due after the taxable event.[42]

• *Amount of Increase*

The taxable estate or taxable gifts of the interest holder are increased by the excess, if any, of:

(1) the amount of the qualified payments payable during the period beginning on the date of the transfer to which Code Sec. 2701 applied and ending on the date of the taxable event; and

(2) the earnings on such payments determined as if each payment were paid on its due date and reinvested on that date at a yield equal to the appropriate discount rate;

over the sum of:

(1) the amount of the qualified payments actually paid during the same period;

(2) the earnings on those payments determined as if each payment were reinvested as of the date actually paid at a rate equal to the appropriate discount rate; and

(3) to the extent necessary to prevent double inclusion, an amount equal to the sum of (a) the portion of the fair market value of the qualified payment interest solely attributable to the right to receive unpaid qualified payments (determined as of the date of the taxable event), (b) the fair market value of any equity interest received in lieu of qualified payments,

---

[35] Code Sec. 2701(d).
[36] Code   Sec.   2701(d)(3);   Reg. § 25.2701-4(b)(3).
[37] Reg. § 25.2701-4(b)(1).
[38] Code Sec. 2701(d)(3)(A)(iii).

[39] Code Sec. 2701(d)(2)(C).
[40] Code Sec. 2701(d)(3)(B).
[41] Code Sec. 2701(d)(3)(B)(iii).
[42] Reg. § 25.2701-4(b)(3).

and (c) the amount of any increase in the individual's aggregate taxable gifts by reason of the failure to enforce the right to receive qualified payments.[43]

The appropriate discount rate is the discount rate that was applied in determining the value of the qualified payment at the time of the original Code Sec. 2701 transfer.[44]

Limitation. Except in the case of an election to treat nonpayment of qualified payments as a taxable event, the amount of the increase in the individual's taxable estate or taxable gifts is limited to the "applicable percentage" of the excess, if any, of:

(1) the sum of:

(a) the fair market value (determined as of the date of the taxable event) of all equity interests in the entity that are junior to any applicable retained interests; and

(b) any amounts expended by the entity to redeem or acquire any such junior interests; over

(2) the fair market value of such junior equity interests on the date of the original Code Sec. 2701 transfer.

The applicable percentage is equal to the number of shares of the applicable retained interest held by the interest holder on the date of the taxable event divided by the total number of shares of such interests in the business on the same date.[45]

¶ 2530 Attribution Rules

Under the attribution rules of Code Sec. 2701, an individual is treated as holding an equity interest to the extent that interest is held indirectly by that individual through ownership of a corporation, partnership, trust or other entity.[46] If an individual is deemed to hold an interest in more than one capacity, the interest is treated as held in a manner that attributes the largest ownership interest to the individual.[47]

Corporations. An individual is deemed to own any equity interest held by or for a corporation in the proportion that the fair market value of the stock held by the individual bears to the fair market value of all the stock of the corporation.[48]

Partnerships. An individual is deemed to own any equity interest held by or for a partnership in the proportion that the fair market value of the larger of the individual's profits interest or capital interest bears to the fair market value of the total profits interest or capital interest of the partnership.[49]

Trusts and estates. An individual is deemed to own any equity interest held by or for an estate or trust to the extent that the individual's beneficial interest may be satisfied by the equity interest or the income or proceeds from the equity interest. It is assumed that the fiduciary will exercise maximum discretion in favor of the individual. In the case of a grantor trust, the individual is deemed to hold 100 percent of any equity interest held by the trust. If the trust has multiple

---

[43] Reg. § 25.2701-4(c).
[44] Reg. § 25.2701-4(c)(3).
[45] Reg. § 25.2701-4(c)(6) and Reg. § 25.2701-4(d)(2).

[46] Code Sec. 2701(e)(3).
[47] Reg. § 25.2701-6(a)(1).
[48] Reg. § 25.2701-6(a)(2).
[49] Reg. § 25.2701-6(a)(3).

grantors, an individual grantor is deemed to own equity interests held by the trust to the extent of such individual's fractional share.[50]

¶ 2535   Mitigation of Double Taxation

If Code Sec. 2701 applies to reduce the value of a retained interest, double taxation would result if the retained interest were valued under generally applicable valuation rules when the transferor subsequently transfers the retained interest or the retained interest is included in the transferor's estate. Code Sec. 2701(e)(6) therefore provides that, if there is a subsequent transfer, or inclusion in the gross estate, of an applicable retained interest that was valued under Code Sec. 2701, appropriate adjustments are to be made for purposes of the transfer tax provisions to reflect the increase of amount of any prior taxable gift made by the transferor or decedent by reason of such valuation.

Regulations provide that, for purposes of determining the transferor's estate tax, the transferor's adjusted taxable gifts are reduced to reflect the increase of the transferor's taxable gifts under Code Sec. 2701.[51]

In general, the amount of the reduction is the lesser of (1) the amount by which the transferor's gifts are increased as a result of the application of Code Sec. 2701 to the transfer, or (2) the amount by which the individual's transfers are increased as a result of not applying the valuation rules to the later transfer of the applicable retained interest.

The regulations also provide an adjustment for split gifts that are generally consistent with the general principles of transfer taxation so that each spouse is treated as the transferor for one-half of the initial transfer and is entitled to mitigation under Code Sec. 2701(e)(6).

> **Example:** Ellen O'Brien owns 15,000 shares of $1,000 par value preferred stock of X Corp. and all of the 1,000 shares of common stock of X Corp. On January 15, 1999, when the fair market value of the common stock is $500,000 and the value of the preferred stock is $1.5 million, she transfers the common stock to her daughter, Sally. The fair market value of all of Ellen's interests prior to the transfer is $2 million. The Code Sec. 2701 value of the preferred interest is zero. The value of Ellen's taxable gift is $2.5 million (the Code Sec. 2701 transfer and Ellen's other taxable gifts). In 2010, when the preferred stock has a value of $1.4 million, Ellen transfers all of the preferred stock to Sally. She is entitled to reduce the amount on which her tax is computed by $1.4 million.

¶ 2540   Statute of Limitations

Although the statute of limitations on the assessment of gift tax is three years after the return was filed, special rules apply under the special valuation rules.

The statute of limitations for assessment of gift tax is modified so that it will not run on an undisclosed or inadequately disclosed transfer, regardless of whether a gift tax return was filed for other transfers in the year in which the Code Sec. 2701 transfer occurred.[52]

---

[50] Reg. § 25.2701-6(a)(4).
[51] Reg. § 25.2701-5.

[52] Code Sec. 6501(c)(9).

¶ 2545   Family Limited Partnerships

Family limited partnerships (FLPs) have become an extremely popular way to transfer assets to children and grandchildren. An FLP is typically created by transferring assets that are likely to appreciate rapidly to a newly created limited partnership under the limited partnership laws of the applicable state. In exchange for the assets, the transferor generally receives a very small general partnership interest (e.g., one or two percent) and a large limited partnership interest. The transferor retains the general partnership interest and transfers a portion of the limited partnership interest to the children. The interests received by the children are typically minority interests. The general partnership interest gives the transferor control over the operation of the business despite the fact that this interest represents only a small percentage of the value of the business.

• *Nontax Advantages of FLPs*

Although the tax advantages associated with FLPs (discussed below) are usually the reasons most transferors create FLPs, there are other significant nontax advantages, including retained control over transferred assets, ease of probate, ease of amendment, protection from creditors, and facilitation of annual exclusion gifts.

• *Tax Advantages*

Limited partnership interests transferred to children under an FLP are worth significantly less for transfer tax purposes than the same proportionate interest in the underlying assets would be worth. The holder of a minority limited partnership interest cannot make decisions about how the business is run, demand distributions, or force a liquidation of the partnership. In addition, an interest in an FLP may be far less marketable than an interest in the underlying assets of the business. As a result, minority interest and lack of marketability discounts are generally allowed on the transfer of interests in an FLP. The combined discount for a minority interest and lack of marketability is typically in the 20 percent to 40 percent range, but can be even higher.

Restricted management accounts (RMAs) have sometimes been advanced as offering the tax advantages of a FLP, with the possibility of lower cost and easier operation. However, the IRS has recently ruled that the fair market value of an RMA for estate and gift tax purposes is the actual value of the assets in the account, without any reduction or discount.[53] See ¶ 320 for a discussion of restricted management accounts.

• *IRS Attack on FLPs*

In addition to attacks on the tax advantages of FLPs based on application of the special valuation rules of the Code (discussed below), the IRS may well apply its "swing vote" theory to set aside valuation discounts claimed with respect to FLPs. Under this swing vote analysis, where family members can combine their voting power to create a collective swing vote, each member's interest must be considered to have a valuation premium.

Additionally, the IRS may invoke the investment company rule of Code Sec. 721(b) to require the recognition of gain upon contribution of appreciated securities to an FLP. Further, unless it can be shown that the children have a legitimate capital interest in the partnership, the IRS can disregard their partnership inter-

---

[53] Rev. Rul. 2008-35, 2008-2 CB 116.

ests for income tax purposes. Finally, even if the FLP arrangement is successful in lowering transfer taxes, it will be at the cost of a loss of a Code Sec. 1014 stepped-up basis, which could lead to devastating income tax consequences, if the sharply appreciated assets were used to fund the FLP.

• Application of Special Valuation Rules

If a person transfers an interest in an FLP to or for the benefit of a family member and the transferor or an "applicable family member" retains an interest in the same partnership, the value of any partnership assets retained by the transferor will be zero (see ¶2510). However, if the interest retained by the transferor is proportionate to the transferred interest, without regard to nonlapsing differences with respect to management and limitations on liability, the zero value rule does not apply. Thus, to avoid the zero value rule, the FLP agreement will normally give the same proportionate rights to the transferor and transferees with respect to income, gain, loss, and deductions.

Code Sec. 2703 and the sham transaction doctrine. In IRS Technical Advice Memorandum 9719006,[54] the IRS launched a major attack on FLPs. Under the facts of this ruling, assets were transferred from two trusts to an FLP that was created two days before a decedent's death. Immediately after the FLP received the assets, limited partnership interests were transferred to the transferor's children. The IRS ruled that valuation discounts claimed with respect to the FLP transaction should be disallowed under either of two theories. One theory was that, consistent with the sham transaction doctrine, the formation of the partnership interest should be treated as a single testamentary transaction and, therefore, the partnership should be disregarded for estate tax valuation purposes.

The IRS's alternative position was to apply Code Sec. 2703 (see ¶2580) to the transaction, with the result that, for transfer tax purposes, the value of the property is determined without regard to any option, agreement, or other restriction on the right to sell or use the property. The taxpayer argued that the property transferred was the partnership interests, and because there were no restrictions in the partnership agreement relating to the transferees' ability to sell, transfer, or use the interests, Code Sec. 2703 did not apply. The IRS disagreed, taking the position that what the children really received was the underlying assets subject to the partnership agreement. Thus, the partnership agreement was a restriction within the meaning of Code Sec. 2703, and any reduction in value caused by the partnership agreement was to be disregarded under Code Sec. 2703 unless the bona fide business arrangement exception of Code Sec. 2703(b) was applicable.

The IRS concluded that even if the steps of the transaction were not collapsed and the partnership interest, rather than the underlying assets, were treated as the subject of the transfers, Code Sec. 2703 would still apply, since under Reg. §25.2703-1(a)(3), a Code Sec. 2703 restriction can either be contained in a partnership agreement or implicit in the capital structure of the partnership.

A U.S. district court in Texas has concluded that a decedent's entering into an FLP agreement two days prior to her death was pursuant to a bona fide business arrangement, rather than an attempt to transfer property to members of her family for less than full and adequate consideration.[55] The court concluded that the transaction was a bona fide business transaction because (1) the primary

---

[54] IRS Technical Advice Memorandum 9719006 (Jan. 14, 1997).

[55] E. Church, DC Tex., 2000-1 USTC ¶60,369, aff'd, CA-5, in an unpublished opinion, 2001-2 USTC ¶60,415, 268 F3d 1063.

purpose in forming the FLP was a desire to centralize management and preserve the family ranching operation, (2) the partnership was formed with the possibility of actively engaging in raising cattle in the future, (3) the partnership was not formed solely to reduce the decedent's estate tax, and (4) the decedent had no reason to believe she would die in the near future. Accordingly, the decedent's partnership interest was taxed under Code Sec. 2033 and came within the bona fide business transaction exception to Code Sec. 2703.

In another case involving Texas law, the Tax Court, in a decision reviewed by the entire Tax Court, rejected the IRS's attack against an FLP created by a donor two months before his death. The FLP was recognized as having sufficient substance for federal estate tax purposes because the partnership (1) was valid under Texas law, (2) changed the relationships between the decedent and his heirs and creditors, and (3) would not have been disregarded by potential purchasers of the decedent's assets. The court rejected the IRS's argument that, under Code Sec. 2703(a), the property to be valued was the partnership's underlying assets and that the partnership form was the restriction to be disregarded. According to the court, neither the language of, nor the intent behind, Code Sec. 2703(a) suggested that partnership assets were to be treated as the assets of a decedent's estate where the legal interest owned by the decedent at the time of death was a limited partnership interest.[56]

Code Sec. 2704. Citing the underlying Code and regulations, the IRS has published several Technical Advice Memoranda denying FLP valuation discounts that were deemed to relate to "applicable restrictions" (see ¶2590). With respect to an FLP, an applicable restriction is one that effectively limits the ability of the partnership to liquidate and with respect to which the transferor or any member of the transferor's family has the right after the transfer to remove the restriction. Reg. § 25.2704-2(b) provides that a limitation on the ability to liquidate the partnership that is more restrictive than the limitations that would apply under state law in absence of the restriction will be deemed an applicable restriction for purposes of Code Sec. 2704. If an applicable restriction is disregarded, the transferred interest is valued as if the restriction did not exist and as if the rights of the transferor were determined under the state law that would apply in the absence of the restriction.

The Tax Court has analyzed the liquidation provisions of an FLP and found the provisions were no more restrictive than those imposed under applicable state law (Texas).[57] In so holding, the court rejected the IRS's argument that Texas law regarding the withdrawal from a partnership was germane to the analysis of the FLP liquidation provision.

¶ 2550 Function of Code Sec. 2702

Prior to the enactment of Code Sec. 2702, a transferor could transfer property and its future appreciation to younger family members at a fraction of the gift tax cost of an outright transfer by retaining various limited interests in the gifted property.

---

[56] *A. Strangi Est.*, TC 478, CCH Dec. 54,135, aff'd, CA-5, on the issue of the property subject to the restriction, rev'd with respect to another issue, 2002-2 USTC ¶60,441, 293 F3d 279.

[57] *B. Kerr*, 113 TC 450, Dec. 13, 2000, CCH Dec. 53,667, aff'd, CA-5, 2002-2 USTC ¶60,440, 292 F3d 490. See also, *I. Knight*, 115 TC 506, CCH Dec. 54,136, a reviewed-by-the-court decision interpreting FLP restrictions as being no more restrictive than Texas law, and *M. Harper Est.*, 79 TCM 2232, CCH Dec. 53,939(M), TC Memo. 2000-202, following *Kerr*, and interpreting California law.

A popular form of transfer with a retained interest was the grantor retained interest trust (GRIT). In a typical GRIT, a grantor retains an income interest for a certain number of years, after which the remainder passes to specified beneficiaries. If the grantor dies during the term of the trust, the grantor's retained income interest causes the entire value of the trust property to be includible in the grantor's taxable estate, just as if the GRIT had never been created.[58]

The grantor is deemed to have made a taxable gift at the time the GRIT is funded. The GRIT lowers the value of the gift to the beneficiaries because the grantor retains an income interest in the gift property. There is the possibility that the property will not pass to the beneficiaries if the grantor dies before the end of the specified term, and the beneficiaries do not have use of the trust property before the end of the specified term. The value of the gift is equal to the present value of the actuarial value of the remainder interest, as determined under Code Sec. 7520 (see ¶ 530).

> *Example (1):* Brian Foley, age 60, transfers $1 million to a 10-year GRIT. At the end of the 10 years, the trust will be distributed to his daughter, Jill. At the time of the transfer, the applicable interest rate under Code Sec. 7520 is 6.0%, which results in the retained interest being valued at $534,170 and the gift being valued at $465,830. If Brian survives the 10-year period, $1 million is removed from his estate at a gift tax cost of approximately four-tenths of the cost had $1 million been transferred outright.

Code Sec. 2702 limits the application of Code Sec. 7520 to the valuation of "qualified retained interests" and retained interests in personal residence trusts (see ¶ 2570).[59] All other retained interests are valued at zero.[60] The subtraction method is used to determine the value of the gift. If the value of the retained interest is zero, the value of the gift is increased to equal the value of the property transferred in trust.

> *Example (2):* Assume the same facts as in Example (1), except that Code Sec. 2702 applies. Because Brian's retained interest is not a qualified retained interest, it is valued at zero and the gift to his daughter, Jill, is valued at $1 million.

¶ 2555   Application of Code Sec. 2702

Code Sec. 2702 applies when (1) an interest in trust is transferred to a "member of the transferor's family" and (2) the transferor or "applicable family member" retains an interest in the trust.[61]

Members of the transferor's family. Members of the transferor's family include:

(1) the transferor's spouse;

(2) any ancestor or lineal descendant of the transferor or the transferor's spouse;

(3) any brother or sister of the transferor; and

(4) any spouse of the persons described in (2) and (3).[62]

---

[58] Code Sec. 2036(a)(1).

[59] Code Sec. 2702(a)(2)(B) and Code Sec. 2702(a)(3)(A)(ii).

[60] Code Sec. 2702(a)(2)(A).

[61] Code Sec. 2702(a)(1); Reg. § 25.2702-1(a).

[62] Code Sec. 2702(e) and Code Sec. 2704(c)(2); Reg. § 25.2702-2(a)(1).

Applicable family members. Applicable family members are generally members of the older generation and include:

(1) the transferor's spouse;

(2) any ancestor of the transferor or the transferor's spouse; and

(3) the spouse of any such ancestor.[63]

• *Transfers of an Interest in Trust*

Transfers in trust include transfers to a new or existing trust and assignments of an interest in an existing trust. They do not include the exercise, release, or lapse of a power of appointment that is not a transfer under the gift tax provisions or the execution of a qualified disclaimer.[64] A transfer of an interest in trust includes a transfer of an interest in property that results in the creation of one or more term interests.[65] A term interest is one of a series of successive interests, which includes a life interest or an interest for a term of years.[66]

The following interests are not treated as term interests:

(1) concurrent fee interests, such as those held by tenants in common, tenants by the entireties, or joint tenants with right of survivorship; and

(2) leasehold interests to the extent the lease was acquired for adequate consideration, provided a good faith effort was made to determine the fair rental value of the property.[67]

The joint purchase of interests in the same property by a taxpayer and a member of the taxpayer's family is a transfer in trust if the taxpayer acquires only a term interest in the property. The taxpayer will be treated as acquiring the entire property and transferring to the family members the interests they acquired. However, any consideration paid by the acquiring family members will be considered in determining the amount of any gifts deemed made by the taxpayer.[68]

Example: Arlene Ricci purchases a 15-year term interest in a commercial building, and her child, Carol, purchases the remainder interest. Arlene is treated as if she had acquired the entire property and then transferred the remainder interest to Carol.

• *Retained Interest*

A retained interest is an interest held by the same individual before and after a transfer in trust. If the transfer creates a term interest, the transferor is deemed to hold the interest both before and after the transfer[69] (see ¶ 2560).

• *Exceptions to Application*

Code Sec. 2702 does not apply to the following transfers:

(1) transfers treated as incomplete for gift tax purposes;

(2) transfers to a "personal residence trust" (see ¶ 2570);

(3) transfers to a charitable remainder trust;

(4) transfers to a charitable lead trust;

---

[63] Code Sec. 2701(e)(2); Reg. § 25.2701-1(d)(2).

[64] Reg. § 25.2702-2(a)(2).

[65] Code Sec. 2702(c)(1).

[66] Code Sec. 2702(c)(3).

[67] Reg. § 25.2702-4(a) and Reg. § 25.2702-4(b).

[68] Code Sec. 2702(c)(2); Reg. § 25.2702-4(c).

[69] Reg. § 25.2702-2(a)(3).

(5) transfers to a pooled income fund;

(6) transfers of a remainder interest if the only interest retained by the transferor or applicable family members is the right to income distributions in the sole discretion of an independent trustee; and

(7) transfers in trust incident to a divorce.[70]

¶ 2560   Valuation of Retained Interests

Retained interests are valued at zero unless:

(1) the interest is a "qualified retained interest" (see ¶ 2565);

(2) the interest is a retained interest in a personal residence trust or qualified personal residence trust (see ¶ 2570); or

(3) the interest is in certain nondepreciable tangible property.

• *Special Rule for Tangible Property*

A special valuation rule applies to interests in nondepreciable tangible property, such as land and works of art. The exception applies to transfers in trust of tangible property that would not be entitled to a depreciation or depletion deduction if the property were used in a trade or business or held for the production of income. In addition, the nonexercise of rights under a term interest must not increase the value of the remainder interest in the property. Depreciable improvements to property that would otherwise disqualify the property will be ignored if the fair market value of the improvements do not exceed five percent of the fair market value of the entire property.[71]

For such transfers, the value of the retained interest (other than a qualified interest) is the amount that the holder of the term interest establishes as the amount for which such interest could be sold to an unrelated party.[72] However, if the transferor cannot reasonably establish the value of the term interest, it will be valued at zero.[73] If tangible property is converted during the term of the interest into property that does not qualify for valuation under the special rule, for gift tax purposes, the conversion will be treated as a transfer of the value of the unexpired portion of the term interest for no consideration.[74]

• *Application to Flip Charitable Remainder Unitrusts*

Amendments to the regulations clarify the application of the zero value rule to flip charitable remainder unitrusts (CRUTs).[75] A flip CRUT is a CRUT that can be converted from one of the income exception methods of determining the unitrust amount to a fixed percentage method. The amended regulations allow the governing instrument of a CRUT to convert from one of the income exceptions to the fixed percentage method, provided that the date or event that triggers the conversion is outside the control of the trustees or any other person. Trustees had until June 30, 2000, to begin legal proceedings for special reformations of CRUTs to include a flip provision.[76]

The amended regulation clarifies that unitrust interests in an income-exception CRUT that are retained by the donor or any applicable family member will be valued at zero when a noncharitable beneficiary of the trust is someone other

---

[70] Reg. § 25.2702-1(c).
[71] Reg. § 25.2702-2(c)(2).
[72] Code Sec. 2702(c)(4)(B).
[73] Reg. § 25.2702-2(c)(1).

[74] Reg. § 25.2702-2(c)(4)(i).
[75] T.D. 8791, amending Reg. § 25.2702-1, Dec. 9, 1998.
[76] Notice 99-31, 1999-1 CB 1185.

than (1) the donor, (2) the donor's U.S. citizen spouse, or (3) both the donor and the donor's U.S. citizen spouse. The zero value rule also applies both to CRUTs that use only the net income method and to a flip unitrust if it does not fall within one of the exemptions. The amended regulation clarifies that Code Sec. 2702 will not apply when there are only two consecutive noncharitable beneficial interests and the transferor holds the second of the two interests.

¶ 2565   Qualified Retained Interests

There are three types of qualified retained interests that are not valued at zero under Code Sec. 2702. The trusts that correspond to these interests are:

(1) a grantor retained annuity trust (GRAT), which makes fixed payments to the grantor at least annually;

(2) a grantor retained unitrust (GRUT), which makes payments to the grantor at least annually, but the amount of the payments is a fixed percentage of the trust's assets determined annually; or

(3) a noncontingent remainder interest if all the other interests in the trust consist of interests described in (1) and (2).[77]

• Qualified Annuity Interest

A qualified annuity interest is an irrevocable right to receive a fixed amount payable to, or for the benefit of, the holder of the interest for each taxable year of the term. A fixed amount is either (1) a stated dollar amount, or (2) a fixed fraction or percentage of the initial fair market value of the property transferred to the trust. The amount must be payable at least annually. In valuing a qualified annuity interest, an amount will be considered only to the extent that it does not exceed 120 percent of the stated dollar amount or the fixed fraction or percentage payable in the preceding year.[78]

The governing instrument must:

(1) prohibit distributions to or for the benefit of any person other than the holder of the interest during the term of the interest;

(2) fix the term of the interest for the life of the holder, for a specific term of years, or for the shorter of those periods;

(3) prohibit prepayment of the income interest;[79]

(4) if the annuity is stated in terms of a fraction or percentage of the initial fair market value of the trust property, require payment adjustments or repayments as a result of any incorrect determination of the fair market value of the property;

(5) require the pro rata computation of the annuity amount in the case of a short taxable year and the last taxable year of the term; and

(6) prohibit additional contributions to the trust.[80]

The Court of Appeals for the Seventh Circuit has held that a husband's and wife's retained interests in four GRATs were not qualified interests and were valued as single-life annuities rather than dual-life annuities.[81] The interests

---

[77] Code Sec. 2702(b).

[78] Reg. § 25.2702-3(b)(1).

[79] Reg. § 25.2702-3(d)(2)-(4).

[80] Reg. § 25.2702-3(b)(2)-(4).

[81] W. Cook, CA-7, 2001-2 USTC ¶ 60,422, 269 F3d 854, aff'g 115 TC 15, CCH Dec. 53,960.

The appellate court in W. Cook cited Reg. § 25.2703-3(e), Example 6 for the proposition that the term of the annuity or unitrust interest must be fixed and ascertainable at the creation of the trust.

retained in favor of the surviving spouses were not qualified interests under Code Sec. 2702(b) because (1) the spousal interests in each GRAT were not fixed or ascertainable at the inception of the GRAT, and (2) the retained interests could have extended beyond the death of the grantor. Therefore, the remainder interest (that is, the amount of the taxable gift) was increased. The Court of Appeals for the Ninth Circuit, however, has reached the opposite result in a case involving similar facts.[82] There, the court concluded that a two-life annuity retained by a husband and wife in each of their GRATs was a qualified interest. In reaching this result, the court reasoned that there was no difference between the annuity contained in each of the spouse's GRAT and the one described in Reg. § 25.2702-2(d)(1), Example 7, which was treated as a qualified interest. According to the court, the value of each spouse's gifts to the GRAT was ascertainable through the use of the two-life annuity table. The court distinguished the result in *W. Cook,* on the ground that case involved the additional contingency that the grantor and the spouse be married at the time the annuity began. Because the spouses' retained annuities were qualified interests, the amount of the gifts to each GRAT was equal to the value of the property transferred to the GRAT, reduced by both the value of the grantor's qualified interest and the value of the qualified interest transferred to the grantor's spouse.

The Tax Court, relying on the *Cook*[83] decision, held that grantor retained annuity trusts (GRATs) created by a husband and wife were not qualified interests under Code Sec. 2702 (*C. Focardi Est.*[84]). This was so because (1) the spousal interests were contingent on the grantor's failing to survive an applicable two-year or four-year GRAT term, and (2) the spousal interests were not payable for the life of the term holder, for a term of years, or for the shorter of those periods. Applying the rationale of *Cook,* the court determined that the terms of the spousal interests were not fixed and ascertainable a the inception of the trusts. The Tax Court distinguished *Schott*[85] by noting that in *Focardi,* as in *Cook,* the spouse would receive the interest only if the spouse survived the grantor and the trust instruments contained an implicit understanding of a marriage contingency for any payment under the spousal interest. In addition, although the trust instruments provided that a determination that the spousal interests were not qualified interests essentially meant that the spousal gifts were revoked, the grantors were not entitled to treat each GRAT as one of a set term of years. The court noted that a "savings clause" like the one provided in the GRATs was ineffective for federal transfer tax purposes.

In response to the decision in *Schott,* the IRS has adopted amended regulations that clarify when a revocable spousal interest is a qualified interest. The exception treating a spouse's revocable successor interest as a retained qualified interest applies only if the spouse's annuity or unitrust interest, standing alone, constitutes a qualified interest that meets the requirements of Reg. § 25.2702-3(d)(3), but for the grantor's revocation power. In response to comments, the IRS notes that the "existing regulations make it clear that the ability to actuarially determine an interest is not sufficient to secure recognition of that interest as a qualified interest for purposes of Code Sec. 2702." New *Example 8* is added to the final regulations in Reg. § 25.2702-3(e) to clarify that the grantor makes a completed gift to the spouse when the revocation right lapses on the

---

[82] *P. Schott,* CA-9, 2003-1 USTC ¶ 60,457, 319 F3d 1203, rev'g TC, 81 TCM 1600, CCH Dec. 54,331(M), TC Memo. 2001-110.

[83] CA-7, 2001-2 USTC ¶ 60,422, 269 F3d 854.

[84] CCH Dec. 56,462(M) TC Memo. 2006-56, Mar. 7, 2006.

[85] CA-9, 2003-1 USTC ¶ 60,457, 319 F3d 1203.

expiration of the grantor's retained term. The amendments to the regulation are effective for trusts created on or after July 26, 2004.[86]

• Qualified Unitrust Interest

A qualified unitrust interest is an irrevocable right to receive payment, at least annually, of a fixed percentage of the net fair market value of the trust assets, determined annually. The unitrust amount must be payable to, or for the benefit of, the holder of the unitrust interest for each taxable year of the term. In valuing a qualified unitrust interest, a percentage will be considered a fixed percentage only to the extent that it does not exceed 120 percent of the fixed fraction or percentage payable in the preceding year.[87]

The governing instrument must meet requirements (1)–(5) enumerated above for instruments creating qualified annuity interests.[88]

• Payment of Annuity and Unitrust Amount

The IRS has adopted amended regulations that prohibit the use of notes, other debt instruments, options, or similar financial arrangements that effectively delay the receipt by the grantor of a GRAT or GRUT of the annual payment necessary to satisfy the annuity or unitrust amount.[89] In the case of trusts created on or after September 20, 1999, the trust instrument must prohibit the trustee from issuing any of these delayed-payment instruments in satisfaction of an annuity or unitrust payment obligation. A transition rule provides that if a trust created before September 20, 1999, does not prohibit the above techniques, the retained interest is treated as a qualified interest under Code Sec. 2702(b) if the notes, other debt instruments, etc., are not issued after September 20, 1999, to satisfy the annuity or unitrust payments. In addition, any notes or other debt instruments issued on or before September 20, 1999, to satisfy the annual payment obligation must have been paid in full by December 31, 1999, and any option or similar financial arrangement must be terminated by such date, so that the grantor actually receives cash or other trust assets in satisfaction of the payment obligation.

• Zeroed-Out GRATs

In order to "zero out" a GRAT, the annuity payout rate must be set high enough so as to result in no gift. Simply put, this involves dividing the original principal amount by the appropriate factor for the corresponding term of years and Code Sec. 7520 rate in order to compute an annual payment that results in an annuity having a present value equal to the original trust principal.

> *Example:* If we assume the Code Sec. 7520 rate is 1.2% and the initial value of the trust principal is $1 million, in order to zero out a 10-year GRAT under those assumptions would require an annuity payment of $106,718.
>
> *Table B (IRS Publication 1457) annuity factor (1.2% and 10 years):* 9.3705
>
> *$1,000,000 ÷ 9.3705 = $106,718*

The IRS has long taken the position that it is impossible to zero out a GRAT, stating "in a trust where the annuity amount will exhaust the funds of the trust precisely at the termination of the trust, the value of the retained interest cannot

---

[86] Reg. §25.2702-3, as amended by T.D. 9181, February 24, 2005.
[87] Reg. §25.2702-3(c)(1).
[88] Reg. §25.2702-3(c)(2)-(3) and Reg. §25.2702-3(d)(2)-(4).
[89] Reg. §25.2702-3, as amended by T.D. 8899, Sept. 1, 2000.

equal the amount transferred to the trust because of the possibility that the grantor may die before the expiration of the term of the trust."[90] Accordingly, under this analysis, an annuity stemming from a GRAT cannot be valued for a term certain, but must be valued for the shorter of a term certain or the prior death of the grantor.

The Tax Court has rejected the IRS's analysis in a unanimous reviewed-by-the-court opinion. In this case, a grantor's retained qualified interest in two GRATs was valued for gift tax purposes as an annuity for a specified term of years, rather than as an annuity for the shorter of a term certain or the period ending on the grantor's death.[91] In reaching its decision, the Tax Court also held that Reg. § 25.2702-3(e), Example 5, was an invalid interpretation of Code Sec. 2702.

Under the facts of *Walton*, the grantor established two substantially identical GRATs, each of which had a term of two years and was funded by a transfer of common stock in a publicly traded corporation. Each GRAT proved that the grantor was to receive an annuity amount equal to 49.35 percent of the GRAT's initial value in the first year and 59.99 percent of such initial value in the second year. In the event the grantor died prior to the expiration of the two-year term, the unpaid annuity amounts were payable to the grantor's estate. After the completion of the two-year term, the remaining balance in the GRATs was to be distributed to the grantor's two daughters.

The Tax Court concluded that, for purposes of Code Sec. 2702, even if it viewed the GRATs as creating separate interests in favor of the grantor and her estate, both such interests were retained by the grantor because she could not, as a matter of law, make a gift to herself or to her estate. The GRATs, according to the court, created a single, noncontingent annuity interest payable for a specified term of years to the undifferentiated unit of the grantor or her estate. Such a result was consistent with Congressional intent to allow individuals to retain qualified annuity interests for a specified term of years, and the proper method for doing so was to make the balance of payments due after the grantor death payable to the grantor's estate.

Arguing at the Tax Court, the IRS relied on Reg. § 25.2702-3(e), Example 5, in support of the position that only the value of annuity payable for the shorter of two years or the period ending on the grantor's death could be subtracted from the fair market value of the gifted stock in calculating the taxable gift made by the grantor upon the creation of the GRATs. In rejecting the IRS's position, the court held that Example 5 was an unreasonable interpretation and an invalid extension of Code Sec. 2702. The court determined that the annuities at issue were more akin to the fixed-term interests cited with approval in the legislative history of Code Sec. 2702 than to the reversionary interests identified as leading to undervaluation.

Subsequently, the IRS announced its acquiescence to the Tax Court's *Walton* decision. As a result, in the fact situation described in Reg. § 25.2702-3(e), Example 5, the IRS will treat the retained interest payable to the grantor or the grantor's estate as a qualified interest payable for a 10-year term.[92] Consistent with the position taken in Notice 2003-72, the IRS has adopted amendments to Reg. § 25.2702-3(e), *Example 5* and *Example 6*, to conform the regulation to the

---

[90] IRS Letter Ruling 9239015 (Jun. 25, 1992).

[91] *A. Walton*, 115 TC 589, CCH Dec. 54,165 (Acq.).

[92] Notice 2003-72, 2003-2 CB 964.

Walton decision. Under the final regulations, a unitrust or annuity interest payable for a specified term of years to the grantor, or to the grantor's estate if the grantor dies before the term expires, is a qualified interest for the specified term.[93] The amendments to the regulation apply to trusts created on or after July 26, 2004. However, the IRS will not challenge any prior application of the changes to *Examples 5* and *6* in Reg. § 25.2702-3(e).

• Qualified Remainder Interest

A remainder interest (which includes a reversion) is the right to receive all or a fractional share of trust property on the termination of all or a fractional share of the trust. Therefore, a right to receive an amount that is a stated or pecuniary amount would not be a remainder interest.[94] A remainder interest is a qualified remainder interest if (1) it is payable to the beneficiary or the beneficiary's estate in all events, and (2) all interests in the trust, other than noncontingent remainder interests, are qualified annuity or unitrust interests. Therefore, the governing instrument cannot permit payment of income in excess of the annuity or unitrust amount to the holder of a qualified annuity or unitrust interest.[95]

• Intentionally Defective Grantor Trusts

A planning technique that is increasingly being used as an alternative to a GRAT involves an installment sale to an intentionally defective grantor trust (hereinafter referred to as a "defective trust"). This technique offers possible tax advantages (discussed below), but it remains judicially untested.

Under the typical scenario, a grantor sets up an irrevocable trust (usually for the benefit of the grantor's children and/or grandchildren) and initially funds it with an amount of cash. The trust will be drafted so that sufficient trustee powers are retained so as to cause the property transfer to be deemed ineffective to shift ownership of trust assets for income tax purposes yet complete for transfer tax purposes. The grantor will thereafter enter into an installment sales agreement with the trust whereby the grantor will sell appreciated assets to the trust in exchange for the trust's installment note equal to the fair market value of the asset the trust receives. Interest will be paid by the trust to the grantor in an amount equal to the current AFR rate under Code Sec. 1274(d) for the term of the installment sale, with a balloon payment of principal due at the end of the installment term. If the trust document is properly structured and all the terms of the installment sale contract are carried out as if it were an arm's-length transaction between unrelated parties, there should be no income tax on the grantor's transfer of the property into the trust. This is so because, for income tax purposes, the trust will be a grantor trust, which has no independent tax standing apart from the grantor.[96] Although the initial cash transfer will be a completed gift, the installment sale between the grantor and the trust should have no gift tax consequences, since full and adequate consideration was exchanged.[97]

The installment sale to the defective trust effects an estate freeze by allowing the grantor to transfer appreciating assets in exchange for fixed assets in a transaction that will incur no gift tax consequences, yet shift future asset appreciation to the grantor's children/grandchildren estate tax free. Although the gran-

---

[93] Reg. § 25.2702-3, as amended by T.D. 9181, February 24, 2005.

[94] Reg. § 25.2702-3(f)(2).

[95] Reg. § 25.2702-3(f)(1).

[96] Code Sec. 671 through Code Sec. 677.

[97] See IRS Letter Ruling 9535026 (May 31, 1995), where the IRS ruled that stock sold to a grantor trust in exchange for a promissory note was a sale and therefore not subject to Code Sec. 2701 or Code Sec. 2702.

tor's initial cash transfer into the trust will generate gift/generation-skipping transfer tax liability (or at least use up some of the grantor's unified credit and/or generation-skipping transfer exemption), this step is suggested by several tax planning commentators to ensure that the trust's existence is independent of the installment sales transaction that garners the tax advantages. Commentators suggest that the initial cash contribution be at least 10 percent of the value of the assets that will be the subject of the installment sale.

The defective trust technique certainly carries more risk potential than a GRAT transaction, which has predictable tax results if all rules specified in the Code are followed. However, the defective trust approach offers the possibility of several advantages over a GRAT:

(1) The defective trust can utilize an interest rate equal to 100 percent of the AFR rate, rather than 120 percent of the federal midterm rate, as required by for a GRAT. Therefore, more wealth is being removed from the grantor's estate for transfer tax purposes, since any income earned on the transferred appreciative assets will be retained by the trust, free of taxation in the grantor's gross estate.

(2) With a defective trust, the generation-skipping transfer lifetime exemption ($5,000,000 for 2010 and 2011, $5,120,000 (indexed) for 2012,[98] $5,250,000 for 2013[99] and $5,340,000 for 2014[100]) can be allocated when the transfer to the trust is made, thereby shielding any future appreciation from generation-skipping transfers. However, because a GRAT is subject to an estate tax inclusion period, the generation-skipping transfer exemption cannot be allocated at the funding of the trust, and more of the generation-skipping transfer exemption later may have to be used.

(3) With a defective trust, if the grantor dies before the end of the installment period, only the value of the unpaid note will be included in the grantor's gross estate. With a GRAT, the entire value of the trust assets must be included in the grantor's gross estate.

¶ 2570   Personal Residence Trusts

The zero valuation rule (see ¶ 2560) does not apply to retained interests in personal residence trusts and qualified personal residence trusts. Instead, such interests are valued under Code Sec. 7520. Grantor retained interest trusts, therefore, play a continued role in yielding transfer tax savings if they are used to transfer the grantor's personal residence.

• Personal Residence Trust

The governing instrument of a personal residence trust must prohibit the trust from holding any asset other than the personal residence of the term holder and "qualified proceeds" for the entire term of the trust.[101] Qualified proceeds refer to insurance proceeds received if the residence is damaged, destroyed, or involuntarily converted during the term of the trust. The trust instrument must require that the proceeds and income thereon are reinvested in a personal residence within two years of receipt.[102]

---

[98] Rev. Proc. 2011-52, IRB 2011-45, 701.

[99] Rev. Proc. 2012-41, IRB 2012-45, 539.

[100] Rev. Proc. 2013-35, IRB 2013-47, October 31, 2013.

[101] Reg. § 25.2702-5(b)(1).

[102] Reg. § 25.2702-5(b)(3).

A personal residence is the principal residence or the second residence (within the meaning of Code Sec. 280A(d)(1)) of the term holder.[103] A personal residence may include appurtenant structures used by the term holder for residential purposes. It may also include adjacent land to the extent such land is reasonably appropriate for residential purposes, given the residence's size and location.[104] The amount of land that can be included under this provision can be substantial. For example, in one private letter ruling, the IRS allowed 10 acres of land surrounding a very large residence to be included,[105] and, in another, allowed the inclusion of two lots across the street from the personal residence that provided the term holder with access to a bay and a view of the bay.[106] The personal residence may not be used by anyone other than the term holder or the holder's spouse or dependent and may not be sold or transferred, directly or indirectly, to the grantor, the grantor's spouse, or an entity controlled by the grantor or the grantor's spouse.[107] A personal residence may not be used for purposes other than as a personal residence unless such use is secondary (such as a home office). Use as a hotel or as a bed and breakfast is not considered secondary.[108]

• *Qualified Personal Residence Trust*

Unlike a personal residence trust, a qualified personal residence trust (QPRT) may hold property other than a personal residence. In other respects, the rules governing the definition of a personal residence and the use thereof with respect to QPRTs are substantially similar to those governing personal residence trusts.[109] Cash may be added to or held by the trust for the following limited purposes:

    (1) to pay trust expenses (including mortgage payments) already incurred or expected to be incurred within the next six months;

    (2) to pay for improvements to the residence within the next six months;

    (3) to purchase the initial or replacement residence pursuant to a contract within the next three months.[110]

Governing instruments. The governing instrument of a qualified personal residence trust must require the following:

    (1) any trust income must be distributed to the term holder at least annually;

    (2) no principal may be distributed to a beneficiary other than the transferor during the term of the retained interest;

    (3) the term holder's interest may not be prepaid;

    (4) the trust may not hold any assets other than the personal residence of the term holder and the assets permitted by the regulations;

    (5) the trustee must determine the amount of cash holdings allowed by the regulations and distribute the excess to the term holder at least quarterly and within 30 days of the termination of the term holder's interest;

---

[103] Reg. § 25.2702-5(b)(2).

[104] Reg. § 25.2702-5(b)(2)(ii).

[105] IRS Letter Ruling 9442019 (Jul. 19, 1994).

[106] IRS Letter Ruling 9503025 (Oct. 27, 1994).

[107] Reg. § 25.2702-5(b)(1).

[108] Reg. § 25.2702-5(b)(2)(iii).

[109] Reg. § 25.2702-5(c)(1) and Reg. § 25.2702-5(c)(2).

[110] Reg. § 25.2702-5(c)(5)(ii)(A)(1).

(6) the trust will cease to be a qualified personal residence trust if the residence ceases to be used as a personal residence or if the residence is sold and the trust instrument prohibits the holding of sales proceeds;

(7) the trust will cease to be a QPRT if (a) the personal residence is sold, damaged or destroyed, and (b) a replacement residence is not acquired or the residence is not repaired within two years;

(8) if the trust ceases to be a qualified residence, the assets will be distributed to the term holder or converted into a qualified annuity interest for the benefit of the term holder within 30 days;[111] and

(9) the trust instrument must prohibit the trust from selling or transferring the residence, directly or indirectly, to the grantor, the grantor's spouse, or an entity controlled by either of them during the retained term interest or at any time thereafter in which the trust is a grantor trust.[112]

Sample forms. The IRS has provided in Rev. Proc. 2003-42[113] a sample declaration of trust and alternate provisions that meet the requirements for a QPRT. The sample declaration of trust is designed for a QPRT with one transferor for a term equal to the lesser of the term holder's life or a term of years. The alternate provisions relate to additions to the trust to purchase a personal residence and to the disposition of trust assets on cessation of its qualification as a QPRT. The IRS will recognize a trust as meeting all of the QPRT requirements if: (1) the trust instrument is substantially similar to the sample declaration or properly integrates one or more of the alternate provisions in a document that is substantially similar to the sample declaration, and (2) the trust operates in a manner consistent with the terms of the trust instrument and is a valid trust under applicable local law.

A trust instrument that contains substantive provisions in addition to those provided in the sample declaration, or that omits any of the provisions contained in the sample declaration, will not be assured of QPRT qualification, but will not necessarily be disqualified from satisfying the QPRT requirements. The IRS generally will not issue a letter ruling on whether a trust with one term holder qualifies as a QPRT. However, the IRS will generally issue a letter ruling regarding the effect of substantive trust provisions on the qualification of a trust as a QPRT.[114]

¶ 2575 Mitigation of Double Taxation

If the value of a retained interest is reduced to zero under Code Sec. 2702, double taxation results if the retained interest is subsequently transferred by gift or at death. To mitigate double taxation, the transferor's taxable gifts are reduced at the time of the subsequent lifetime transfer or in determining the transferor's estate tax.[115]

The amount of the reduction is the lesser of:

(1) the increase in taxable gifts on the original transfer due to the application of Code Sec. 2702; or

(2) the increase in taxable gifts or gross estate on the subsequent transfer of the retained interest.[116]

---

[111] Reg. § 25.2702-5(c)(5)(ii)(A)(2).
[112] Reg. § 25.2702-5(c)(9).
[113] 2003-1 CB 993.

[114] Rev. Proc. 2003-42, 2003-1 CB 993.
[115] Reg. § 25.2702-6(a).
[116] Reg. § 25.2702-6(b)(1).

¶ 2580 Rights and Restrictions Disregarded Under Code Sec. 2703

The purpose of Code Sec. 2703 is to prevent possible distortions in value that might result if a transferor retained certain rights or imposed certain restrictions with respect to the transferred property without intending to exercise the rights or restrictions. Unless the taxpayer establishes that the right or restriction qualifies for an exception to Code Sec. 2703, options, restrictive sale agreements and buy-sell agreements will be disregarded for transfer tax valuation purposes.

• *Rights and Restrictions*

A right or restriction includes any option, agreement, or other right to acquire or use property at a price that is less than fair market value, or any restriction on the right to sell or use the property. For example, a lease entered into between a parent and child, the terms of which are not comparable to leases relating to similar property between unrelated parties, would be disregarded in valuing the leased property.

The right or restriction may be part of a partnership agreement, corporate bylaws, or articles of incorporation, or may be implicit in the capital structure of an entity. However, Code Sec. 2703 will not apply to a qualified easement under Code Sec. 2522(d) or Code Sec. 2055(f).[117]

• *Exceptions*

A right or restriction will not be disregarded for valuation purposes if the taxpayer can establish that it is:

(1) a bona fide arrangement;

(2) not a device to transfer property to family members for less than full and adequate consideration; and

(3) comparable to similar arrangements entered into by persons in arm's-length transactions.[118]

For purposes of the second requirement, family members include applicable family members, lineal descendants of the parents of the transferor or the transferor's spouse, and any other individual who is a natural object of the transferor's bounty.[119] Each of the above requirements must be satisfied independently.[120]

Considering these exceptions, the Court of Appeals for the Eleventh Circuit in *G. Blount Est.*[121] held that a redemption price in a modified buy-sell agreement did not control the value of a decedent's closely held stock for purposes of Code Sec. 2703(a). Because the only parties to the contract were the decedent and a company that the decedent controlled, the agreement filed to satisfy the Reg. § 20.2031-2(h) requirement that, in order to govern for valuation purposes, the restrictive agreement must be binding on the decedent during his life. Moreover, because the estate failed to show that the modified agreement was comparable to an arm's-length bargain, the agreement failed to satisfy the requirements of Code Sec. 2703(b)(3), and was therefore disregarded in valuing the decedent's closely held company stock.

---

[117] Reg. § 25.2703-1(a).
[118] Code Sec. 2703(b); Reg. § 25.2703-1(b)(1).

[119] Reg. § 25.2703-1(b)(3) and Reg. § 25.2701-2(b)(5).
[120] Reg. § 25.2703-1(b)(2).
[121] 2005-2 USTC ¶ 60,509, 428 F3d 1338.

A result contrary to *Blount,* above, was reached by the Tax Court in *P. Amlie Est.,*[122] where a buy-sell agreement was not disregarded under Code Sec. 2703 with respect to valuing a decedent's closely held bank stock. In 1991, the decedent's conservator, a holding company formed by the controlling share-holder of the bank, and the controlling shareholder agreed that the controlling shareholder would be prohibited from selling his interests to a third party unless the decedent could offer to sell her interests to such third party for the same per share price. The controlling shareholder later agreed to sell his interests to another bank. Because of an acrimonious relationship among the decedent's prospective heirs, the conservator negotiated an agreement in 1995 between the heirs, other than the decedent's son, that set the stock's purchase price at $118 per share. In 1997, the son negotiated an agreement with the bank that estab-lished the price that the son would receive for the bank stock that he purchased or received by bequest at $218 per share.

The court in *Amlie* determined that the agreement would not be disregarded under Code Sec. 2703(a) because the requirements of Code Sec. 2703(b) were met. Specifically, the court ruled that the buy-sell agreement: (1) furthered a business purpose by securing a guaranteed price for the decedent's minority interest in the bank; (2) was not a testamentary device to transfer property to the decedent's family members for less than full and adequate consideration because the dece-dent received a fixed price for a minority interest; and (3) was comparable to similar arm's-length arrangements because the price was originally reached in the 1994 agreement that was based on a survey of comparable transactions.

• *Application*

Code Sec. 2703 applies to rights or restrictions that are created or substan-tially modified after October 8, 1990. A substantial modification includes any discretionary modification of a right or restriction, whether or not authorized by the terms of an agreement, that results in anything more than a *de minimis* change in the quality, value, or timing of the rights of any party with respect to the property that is subject to the right or restriction. The addition of a family member as a party to a right or restriction is treated as a substantial modification unless the addition is required under the terms of the right or restriction or the person is assigned to a generation no lower than the lowest generation of individuals who already are parties to the right or restriction.[123]

The following items are not treated as substantial modifications:

(1) modifications required by the terms of a right or restriction;

(2) discretionary modifications that do not change the right or restriction;

(3) modifications of a capitalization rate with respect to a right or restriction, if done in such a way that the rate bears a fixed relationship to a specified market rate; and

(4) modifications that result in an option price that more closely ap-proximates fair market value.[124]

A recent case illustrates an analysis of whether changed terms under a restrictive buy-sell agreement will be considered to be a substantial modifica-tion.[125] In 1996, about one year before the decedent's death, the decedent unilat-

---

[122] CCH Dec. 56,482(M), TC Memo. 2006-76, April 17, 2006.
[123] Reg. § 25.2703-1(c)(1).

[124] Reg. § 25.2703-1(c)(2).
[125] *G. Blount Est.,* CA-11, 2005-2 USTC ¶ 60,509, 428 F3d 1338.

erally modified a buy-sell agreement, and set a $4 million redemption price for his shares in a closely held business. The modification was substantial because the valuation under the 1996 agreement limited the value of the company with respect to the decedent's stock to $4.8 million, which was calculated by dividing $4 million by the decedent's 83-percent interest in the company. Before the modification, the earlier agreement would have used the 1997 book value of $8.5 million to establish the value of the company. In addition, after the modification, the parties' rights to the contract were substantially different because the company could no longer pay the buyout in installments and both parties lost the ability to adjust the price according to book value or an annually agreed-upon figure. Accordingly, the modification was substantial within the meaning of Reg. § 25.2703-1(c)(1).

The IRS has ruled[126] that restrictions on the sale and use of property held in a restricted management account (RMA) (see ¶ 320) were disregarded under Code Sec. 2703(a)(2) for estate and gift tax purposes, with the result that claimed reduction or discount from the actual value of the assets in the RMA were disallowed.

¶ 2590   Treatment of Lapsing Rights and Restrictions

Code Sec. 2704 was enacted to reduce or eliminate the use of lapsing rights and restrictions as a way of reducing transfer taxes.

> *Example (1):* During her life, Betty Smith owned 80% of the voting stock of Famco, and her children owned the remaining 20%. The bylaws of Famco provided that a shareholder's voting rights lapsed at death. Smith's will provided that, upon her death, all of her Famco stock would pass to her children. The value of Smith's stock with the voting rights is $750,000. However, the value of the same stock without the voting rights is $500,000. Prior to the enactment of Code Sec. 2704, Smith's estate would have been worth $250,000 less than it was when she was alive.

Under Code Sec. 2704(a), the lapse of a voting or liquidation right created after October 8, 1990, is treated as a transfer for transfer tax purposes if the holder of the lapsing right and members of the holder's family control the entity both before and after the lapse. The amount of the transfer is the excess, if any, of the value of the holder's interests in the entity immediately before the lapse over the value of such interests after the lapse.[127] Code Sec. 2704(b) covers the other side of lapsing rights—the restrictions placed on the transferor. Under Code Sec. 2704(b), if an interest in a corporation or partnership is transferred to, or for the benefit of, a member of the transferor's family, and the transferor and members of the transferor's family control the entity before the transfer, any "applicable restrictions" are disregarded in valuing the transferred interest.

> *Example (2):* Assume the same facts as in Example (1), except that Code Sec. 2704(a) applies. Smith is deemed to have made a transfer of $250,000, the difference between the value of the stock with voting rights and the value of the stock without the voting rights. The amount of the transfer plus the $500,000 value of the stock in Smith's estate equals the value of Smith's stock before she died.

---

[126] Rev. Rul. 2008-35, 2008-2 CB 116.   [127] Code Sec. 2704(a).

• *Lapse of Voting and Liquidation Rights*

For purposes of Code Sec. 2704(a), a voting right is the right to vote with respect to any matter of the entity. The right of a general partner to participate in partnership management is a voting right.[128] A liquidation right is the right to compel the entity to acquire all or a portion of the holder's interest in the entity. It is not necessary that the exercise of the right result in the complete liquidation of the entity.[129]

A voting or liquidation right lapses when a currently exercisable right is restricted or ceases to exist. The transfer of an interest conferring a right generally is not a lapse. However, a transfer that eliminates the transferor's right to compel the entity to acquire an interest retained by the transferor that is junior to the transferred interest is a lapse of a liquidation right with respect to the junior interest.[130]

A lapse of a liquidation right is not treated as a transfer (1) to the extent that the holder and members of the holder's family cannot, immediately after the lapse, liquidate an interest the holder could have liquidated before the lapse, (2) if the lapse was previously valued under Code Sec. 2701, or (3) if the lapse occurred by reason of a change in state law.[131]

A recent U.S. Court of Federal Claims decision[132] dealt with application of Reg. § 25.2704-1 to a situation involving lapsed voting rights. Therein, the decedent's corporation, which was formed in order to operate an NFL franchise, was converted from a C corporation to an S Corporation in 1986. At that time, the decedent's shares of preferred stock were converted into Class A stock, which had voting rights of exceeding 11 votes per share. According to the articles of incorporation, which were amended in 1991, upon the death of the decedent, his Class A stock would be converted into Class B shares, which had one vote per share. The court held that Code Sec. 2704 applied to the conversion of the Class A stock into Class B stock at the decedent's death. In so ruling, the court rejected the estate's argument that Code Sec. 2704 should not apply because the decedent and his family did not have the power to restore the lapsed voting rights. The court concluded that pursuant to Reg. § 25.2704-1(a), because the decedent and his family controlled the corporation both before and after the lapse of voting rights, the transfer was subject to Code Sec. 2704.

Furthermore, because the decedent had the unrestricted ability to take advantage of his enhanced voting rights until his death, the lapse of voting rights was deemed to have occurred on the date of the decedent's death in 1997, not at the time that the articles of incorporation were amended in 1991, in accordance with Reg. § 25.2704-1(b) and Code Sec. 25.2704(f), Examples 1 and 3. Finally, the court determined that the exception under Code Sec. 2703 did not apply. Code Sec. 2703 applies generally to any restrictions on the right to transfer property, whereas Code Sec. 2704 contains specific provisions regarding the lapse of voting rights. Thus, the fair market value of the Class A shares, and not the converted Class B shares, was includible in the decedent's gross estate.

---

[128] Reg. § 25.2704-1(a)(2)(iv).
[129] Reg. § 25.2704-1(a)(2)(v).
[130] Reg. § 25.2704-1(b) and Reg. § 25.2704-1(c)(1).

[131] Reg. § 25.2704-1(c)(2).
[132] *R. Smth, Sr. Est.*, FedCl, 2012-1 USTC ¶ 60,640.

• Disregard of Applicable Restrictions

An applicable restriction is a limitation on the ability to liquidate the entity that is more restrictive than the limitations that would apply under state law. Thus, a provision on liquidation that is no more restrictive than the corresponding state law should not be deemed to be an applicable restriction. To date, taxpayers have found this to be a winning argument in the Tax Court with respect to liquidation restrictions under Texas[133] and California[134] law.

A restriction is an applicable restriction only to the extent that (1) the restriction lapses after the transfer, or (2) the transferor or a member of the transferor's family has the right to remove the restriction immediately after the transfer.

Applicable restrictions do not include restrictions imposed by state or federal law or commercially reasonable restrictions on liquidation imposed by an unrelated person providing financing to the entity for trade of business operations. An unrelated person is any person who is not related to the transferor, the transferee, or any member of the family of either in a way specified by Code Sec. 267.[135] An option, right or agreement subject to Code Sec. 2703 is not an applicable restriction.[136]

• Control Requirement

Control has the same definition for purposes of Code Sec. 2704 as for purposes of Code Sec. 2701 (see ¶ 2510).[137] In the case of a corporation, it means at least 50 percent of the stock of the corporation, measured by vote or value. In the case of a partnership, it means at least 50 percent of the capital or profits interest and, in the case of a limited partnership, the holding of any interest as a general partner.[138]

Family member. For purposes of Code Sec. 2704, the following are family members with respect to any individual:

(1) the individual's spouse;

(2) an ancestor or lineal descendant of the individual or the individual's spouse;

(3) a brother or sister of the individual; and

(4) a spouse of any individual described in (2) or (3) above.[139]

The attribution rules of Code Sec. 2701(e)(3) apply in determining the interest held by any individual (see ¶ 2510).[140]

---

[133] *I. Knight,* 115 TC 506, CCH Dec. 54,136. *B. Kerr,* 113 TC 450, CCH Dec. 53,667, aff'd CA-5, 2002-1 USTC ¶ 60,440, 292 F3d 490. Although affirming the Tax Court's holding, the U.S. Court of Appeals for the Fifth Circuit did so on the ground that the partnership agreement was not an applicable restriction because it did not allow family members, after the transfer, to remove the right to liquidate the partnership.

[134] *M. Harper Est.,* 79 TCM 2232, CCH Dec. 53,939(M), TC Memo. 2000-202.

[135] An individual's family, under Code Sec. 267, includes brothers, sisters (whether by whole or half-blood), spouse, ancestors, and lineal descendants.

[136] Reg. § 25.2704-2(b).

[137] Code Sec. 2704(c)(1).

[138] Code Sec. 2701(b)(2).

[139] Code Sec. 2704(c)(2).

[140] Code Sec. 2704(c)(3).

EXPATRIATE TRANSFERS

Chapter 43

GIFTS AND BEQUESTS FROM EXPATRIATES

Transfers from expatriates
taxed . . . . ¶ 2593

¶ 2593   Transfers from Expatriates Taxed

Beginning on June 17, 2008, a U.S. citizen or resident is subject to a special transfer tax upon receipt of property by gift, devise, bequest, or inheritance from an expatriate.[1] More specifically, the recipient of such a transfer from a covered expatriate (a "covered gift or bequest") after the date of expatriation must pay a tax equal to the value of the covered gift or bequest multiplied by: (1) the highest rate in effect under Code Sec. 2001(c) (40 percent for 2013 and beyond; 35 percent for 2010—2012; 45 percent for 2007—2009), or, if greater, (2) the highest rate in effect under Code Sec. 2502(a) (also 40 percent for 2013 and beyond; 35 percent for 2010—2012; 45 percent for 2007—2009).[2] This special transfer tax applies to indirect, as well as direct transfers, but only to the extent that the value of the covered gifts and bequests received by any person during the calendar year exceeds the annual gift tax exclusion amount in effect under Code Sec. 2503(b) for the calendar year ($13,000 for 2009 through 2012;[3] rising to $14,000 for 2013 and 2014[4]). The tax is reduced by the amount of any estate tax paid to a foreign country with respect to such covered gift or bequest.

Exceptions to definition of covered gift or bequest. A covered gift or bequest does not include property that:

- is a taxable gift by a covered expatriate that is reported on a timely filed gift tax return;

- is included in the gross estate of a covered expatriate and reported on a timely filed estate tax return;[5] or

- would be eligible for an estate or gift tax charitable deduction or marital deduction if the transfer were a U.S. person.[6]

Example 1: Todd Pennington, a nonresident expatriate, died in 2013 with a gross estate of $20,000,000, $5,000,000 of which was situated in the United States as of the date of his death. Todd bequeathed his U.S.-situs property to his U.S. citizen cousin, Jill Pennington. Todd's executor timely filed a federal estate tax return reporting the property situated in the United States. As a result, Jill does not have to pay the special transfer tax under Code Sec. 2801 upon receipt of the bequest.

---

[1] Code Sec. 2801, as enacted by the Heroes Earnings Assistance and Relief Tax Act of 2008 (HEART Act) (P.L. 110-245).
[2] Code Sec. 2801(a) and (b).
[3] Rev. Proc. 2008-66, IRB 2008-45, 1107; Rev. Proc. 2009-50, IRB 2009-45, 617; Rev. Proc. 2010-40, IRB 2010-46, 663; Rev. Proc. 2011-52, IRB 2011-45, 701. The annual exclu-

sion was $12,000 for 2007 and 2008; Rev. Proc. 2006-53, 2006-2 CB 996; Rev. Proc. 2007-66, 2007-2 CB 970.
[4] Rev. Proc. 2012-41, IRB 2012-45, 539; Rev. Proc. 2013-35, IRB 2013-47, October 31, 2013.
[5] Code Sec. 2801(e)(2).
[6] Code Sec. 2801(e)(3).

Covered expatriate. For purposes of the Code Sec. 2801 rules, a "covered expatriate" is defined as an individual who has either relinquished U.S. citizenship or ceased to be a lawful permanent long-term resident of the United States and who would meet the requirements needed to be subject to the alternative tax regime under Code Sec. 877(a)(2). A covered expatriate does not include: (1) a former dual citizen who continues to be taxed as a resident of the other country of citizenship and who was a U.S. resident for not more than 10 years during the 15-year period prior to expatriation; or (2) an individual who relinquished citizenship or long-term residency prior to reaching the age of eighteen and one-half years and was a resident of he U.S. for not more than 10 years prior to the date of expatriation.[7]

Transfers in trust. A covered gift or bequest made to a domestic trust is subject to tax in the same manner as a U.S. citizen or resident described above and, as the recipient, the trust is required to pay the tax imposed.[8] A covered gift or bequest made to a foreign trust is also subject to tax, but only at the time a distribution (whether from income or principal) is made to a U.S. citizen or resident from the trust that is attributable to the covered gift of bequest.[9] The recipient is allowed an income tax deduction under Code Sec. 164 for the amount of tax paid or accrued under Code Sec. 2801 by reason of a distribution from a foreign trust, but only to the extent the tax is imposed on the portion of the distribution included in the recipient's gross income.[10] For purposes of Code Sec. 2801 only, a foreign trust may elect to be treated as a domestic trust. This election may be revoked with the IRS's consent.[11]

> *Example 2:* If in Example 1, above, Todd Pennington bequeathed the $5,000,000 of U.S.-situs property to a foreign trust created for the benefit of his cousin, Jill, the trust would not be subject to tax on receipt of the covered bequest. Rather, Jill must pay a tax upon receipt of each distribution that is attributable to the bequest and is allowed to take a corresponding income tax deduction to the extent that the taxed portion of the distribution is included in her gross income. However, if the foreign trust elects to be treated as a domestic trust, the tax is paid at the trust level.

Effective date. The provision applies to gifts and bequests received on or after June 17, 2008, from transferors (or the estates of transferors) whose expatriation date is on or after June 17, 2008.[12]

---

[7] Code Sec. 2801(f) and Code Sec. 877A(g)(1)(B).

[8] Code Sec. 2801(e)(4)(A).

[9] Code Sec. 2801(e)(4)(B)(i).

[10] Code Sec. 2801(e)(4)(B)(ii).

[11] Code Sec. 2801(e)(4)(B)(iii).

[12] Heroes Earnings Assistance and Relief Tax Act of 2008 (P.L. 110-245), Act Sec. 301(g)(2).

APPENDIX

RATES AND TABLES

¶ 2597   Transfer Tax Timeline

The Economic Growth and Tax Relief Reconciliation Act of 2001 (P.L. 107-16) (EGTRRA) included a one-year repeal of the federal estate and generation-skipping transfer (GST) taxes for decedents dying after December 31, 2009 and before January 31, 2011, and also made numerous changes to the transfer tax system for decedents dying, and gifts made, during the years preceding repeal. The Tax Relief, Unemployment Insurance Reauthorization, and Job Creation Act of 2010 (P.L. 111-312) (Tax Relief Act of 2010) retroactively reinstated the estate and GST taxes, as well as extending many of the changes made by the 2001 Act. The American Taxpayer Relief Act of 2012 (P.L. 112-240) (ATRA) made permanent most of the provisions of the Tax Relief Act of 2010. The major provisions of EGTRRA, the Tax Relief Act of 2010, and ATRA are depicted in the following timeline:

2001

- Distance requirement for conservation easement exclusion lifted

- Deemed and retroactive allocations of GST tax exemption allowed

- Qualified severance of GST trusts available

- Valuation rules concerning date when allocation of GST tax exemption becomes final modified

- Relief provided for late elections to allocate GST tax exemption and for substantial compliance with regulations

2002

- Maximum estate, gift, and GST tax rate: 50 percent

- Surtax on large estates repealed

- Applicable exclusion amount for estate, gift, and GST tax: $1 million

- State death tax credit reduced to 75 percent of prior law amount

- Rules on installment payment of estate taxes liberalized

2003

- Maximum estate, gift, and GST tax rate: 49 percent

- Applicable exclusion amount for estate, gift, and GST tax: $1 million

• State death tax credit reduced to 50 percent of prior law amount

2004

• Maximum estate, gift, and GST tax rate: 48 percent

• Applicable exclusion amount for estate and GST tax: $1.5 million

• Inflation adjustment for GST tax exemption ends

• Exclusion amount for gift tax: $1 million

• State death tax credit reduced to 25 percent of prior law amount

• Deduction for qualified family-owned business interests (Code Sec. 2057) repealed

2005

• Maximum estate, gift, and GST tax rate: 47 percent

• Applicable exclusion amount for estate and GST tax: $1.5 million

• Exclusion amount for gift tax: $1 million

• State death tax credit becomes a deduction

2006

• Maximum estate, gift, and GST tax rate: 46 percent

• Applicable exclusion amount for estate and GST tax: $2 million

• Exclusion amount for gift tax: $1 million

2007–2008

• Maximum estate, gift, and GST tax rate: 45 percent

• Applicable exclusion amount for estate and GST tax: $2 million

• Exclusion amount for gift tax: $1 million

2009

• Maximum estate, gift, and GST tax rate: 45 percent

• Applicable exclusion amount for estate and GST tax: $3.5 million

• Exclusion amount for gift tax: $1 million

2010

• Estate tax reinstated

• Estate tax maximum rate: 35 percent

• Estate tax applicable exclusion: $5 million

• Gift tax remains in force with maximum rate of 35 percent and exclusion amount of $1 million

• "Modified" carryover basis rules repealed; replaced with stepped-up basis rules

• Special executor election (available only for decedents dying in 2010) to apply pre-Relief Act estate tax and carryover basis law (no estate tax, but carryover basis applies)

• GST tax restored

• GST tax maximum rate: zero percent

¶2597

- GST exemption: $5 million

2011

- Estate tax maximum rate: 35 percent
- Estate tax applicable exclusion: $5 million
- Gift tax maximum rate: of 35 percent
- Gift tax applicable exclusion: $5 million
- Stepped-up basis rules apply
- GST tax maximum rate: 35 percent
- GST exemption: $5 million

2012

- Estate tax maximum rate: 35 percent
- Estate tax applicable exclusion: $5,120,000 (as indexed for inflation)
- Gift tax maximum rate: of 35 percent
- Gift tax applicable exclusion: $5,120,000 (as indexed for inflation)
- Stepped-up basis rules apply
- GST tax maximum rate: 35 percent
- GST exemption: $5,120,000 (as indexed for inflation)

2013

- Estate tax maximum rate: 40 percent
- Estate tax applicable exclusion: $5,250,000 (as indexed for inflation)
- Gift tax maximum rate: of 40 percent
- Gift tax applicable exclusion: $5,250,000 (as indexed for inflation)
- Stepped-up basis rules apply
- GST tax maximum rate: 40 percent
- GST exemption: $5,250,000 (as indexed for inflation)

2014

- Estate tax maximum rate: 40 percent
- Estate tax applicable exclusion: $5,340,000 (as indexed for inflation)
- Gift tax maximum rate: of 40 percent
- Gift tax applicable exclusion: $5,340,000 (as indexed for inflation)
- Stepped-up basis rules apply
- GST tax maximum rate: 40 percent
- GST exemption: $5,340,000 (as indexed for inflation)

¶ 2600   Unified Rates and Credit

I. Estates of U.S. Citizens and Residents Dying, and Gifts Made, After 1976

Estate and gift tax rates are combined in a single rate schedule effective for the estates of decedents dying, and for gifts made, after December 31, 1976. For years prior to 2002, the rates are graduated from 37 percent for transfers in excess of $500,000 to 55 percent for transfers in excess of $3 million. Lifetime transfers and transfers made at death are cumulated for gift and estate tax purposes.

- *Law Following the 2001, 2010 and 2012 Acts*

The enactment of the Economic Growth and Tax Relief Reconciliation Act of 2001 (P.L. 107-16) (EGTRRA) brought significant change to the transfer tax system, the most notable being the one-year repeal of the estate and generation-skipping transfer (GST) taxes for decedents dying after December 31, 2009 and before January 1, 2011. Prior to repeal, a number of modifications were made to the maximum estate tax rate and the estate tax applicable exclusion amount (discussed below). The 2001 Act reduced the top marginal rate to 50 percent for decedents dying, and gifts made, in 2002, with further reductions in later years, according to the following schedule: 49 percent for decedents dying (and gifts made) in 2003; 48 percent in 2004; 47 percent in 2005; 46 percent in 2006; and 45 percent in 2007, 2008, and 2009.

The Tax Relief, Unemployment Insurance Reauthorization, and Job Creation Act of 2010 (P.L. 111-312) (Tax Relief Act of 2010) retroactively reinstated the estate and GST tax for estates of decedents dying after December 31, 2009. The 2010 Act also made other substantial changes to the transfer tax system, including reducing the maximum unified tax rate to 35 percent, and increasing estate and gift tax applicable exclusions, and the GST exemption (although the gift tax applicable exclusion remained at $1 million for 2010 only).

The changes made to the estate, gift and generation-skipping transfer (GST) taxes made by EGTRRA (and extended through 2012 by the Tax Relief Act of 2010), have been made permanent by ATRA, effective for estates of decedents dying, gifts, and GSTs made after December 31, 2012. ATRA accomplished this by striking title IX (the sunset provision) of EGTRRA. Additionally, ATRA raised the maximum transfer tax rate to 40 percent (from 35 percent), and also made permanent the portability (Deceased Spousal Unused Exclusion (DSUE) amount election), which had been enacted by the Tax Relief Act of 2010, but was scheduled to expire after December 31, 2012. The DSUE election is discussed at ¶16.

Prior to 1998, the benefits of the graduated rates and the unified credit under the unified transfer tax system were phased out beginning with cumulative transfers above $10 million. This was accomplished by adding five percent of the excess of any transfer over $10 million to the tentative tax computed in determining the ultimate transfer tax liability. For estates of decedents dying, and gifts made, after 1987 and before 1998, the additional tax was levied on transfers above $10 million, but not exceeding $21,040,000. Beginning in 1998, the five-percent additional tax phased out the benefits of the graduated rates, but not the benefits of the unified credit. Therefore, for years after 1997 and before 2002, the additional tax is levied on amounts transferred in excess of $10 million, but not exceeding $17,184,000.

- *Law Following the 2001, 2010 and 2012 Acts*

The Economic Growth and Tax Relief Reconciliation Act of 2001 (EGTRRA) repealed the five-percent surtax for estates of decedents dying, and gifts made, after December 31, 2001. The surtax was not reinstated by the Tax Relief Act of 2010, or by the American Taxpayer Relief Act of 2012 (ATRA).

The estate tax liability is determined by applying the unified rate schedule to the cumulated transfers and subtracting the gift taxes payable. The cumulated transfers to which the tentative tax applies is the sum of (1) the amount of the taxable estate, and (2) the amount of the taxable gifts made by the decedent after 1976, other than gifts includible in the gross estate. Gift taxes to be subtracted in computing the estate tax include the aggregate gift tax payable on gifts made after December 31, 1976. For this purpose, the amount of gift taxes paid by a decedent after 1976 is to be determined as if the rate schedule in effect in the year of death was in effect the year of the gift. However, with respect to certain gifts subsequently included in a decedent's gross estate, a credit is allowed (Code Sec. 2012) for gift taxes paid on pre-1977 gifts.

Gift tax liability for any calendar quarter (for gifts made after 1970 and before 1982) or year (for gifts made before 1971 and after 1981) is determined by applying the unified rate schedule to cumulative lifetime taxable transfers and subtracting the taxes payable for prior taxable periods. Preceding calendar periods are: (1) calendar year 1932 (after June 6) and 1970 and all intervening calendar years; (2) the first calendar quarter of 1971 and all quarters between that quarter and the first quarter of 1982; and (3) all calendar years after 1981 and before the year for which the tax is being computed. In computing cumulative taxable gifts for prior taxable periods, the donor's pre-1977 taxable gifts are to be taken into account, with the reduction for taxes previously paid to be based on the unified rate schedule.

• *Law Following the 2001, 2010 and 2012 Acts*

Unlike the one-year repeal of the estate and GST taxes (which was retroactively set aside by the Tax Relief Act of 2010), EGTRRA retained the gift tax following estate tax repeal in 2010. Gift tax liability for years after 2009 was determined using a rate schedule created by the EGTRRA, which contains graduated rates ranging from 18 percent to 35 percent (for transfers in excess of $500,000). By amendment of the 2001 Act's "sunset" provision, the 2010 Act provided that this rate schedule will remain effective for gifts made before January 1, 2013. ATRA raised this maximum rate to 40 percent for decedents dying, and gifts and GSTs made after December 31, 2012.

The GST tax is applied at a flat rate derived from the maximum estate tax rate to direct skips, taxable distributions, and taxable terminations. The method for computing the taxable amount depends on whether a taxable distribution, a taxable termination, or a direct skip is involved. For a taxable distribution, as well as a direct skip, the amount received by the transferee is subject to the tax. In the case of a taxable termination, the tax is applied to the value of the property in which the interest terminates. Each transferor is provided with a $1 million exemption (adjusted for inflation occurring after 1997 and before 2004) that may be allocated among several generation-skipping transfers. (This exemption is $2 million for the years 2006 through 2008, $3.5 million for 2009, and $5.0 million for 2010, $5,120,000 (as indexed for inflation) for 2012, $5,250,000 (indexed) for 2013, $5,340,000 (indexed) for 2014.)

A special $2 million per grandchild exemption was allowed for direct skips made prior to 1990. In addition, the GST tax does not apply to direct skips to a transferor's grandchildren (or the grandchildren of the transferor's spouse or former spouse) if the grandchild's parent, who is a lineal descendant of the transferor (or the transferor's spouse or former spouse), is deceased. Beginning in 1998, this deceased parent exception was expanded to include direct skips, taxable terminations, and distributions made to collateral heirs if the deceased parent was a descendant of the parent of the transferor (or of the transferor's spouse or former spouse). However, the deceased parent exception only applies

¶2600

to collateral heirs if the transferor has no living lineal descendants at the time of the transfer.

• Rate Schedule (2010–2013)

Prior to its retroactive reinstatement by the Tax Relief Act of 2010, the 2001 Act repealed the GST tax with respect to generation-skipping transfers made after December 31, 2009 and before January 1, 2011. The reductions in the maximum estate tax rate under the 2001 Act (discussed above) caused corresponding reductions in the rate used to determine the GST tax for the years leading up to repeal. In addition, the 2001 Act provided that the amount of the GST tax exemption for any calendar year will be equal to the estate tax applicable exclusion amount in effect for such calendar year. The 2010 Act set the GST tax rate at zero percent for GSTs made in 2010. For GSTs made in 2011 and 2012, the GST tax was subject to 35 percent rate; the GST tax rate for 2013 and beyond is 40 percent.

The basic rate structure that applied to decedents dying and gifts made during 2010 through 2012, will continue to apply to the estates of decedents dying and gifts made after December 31, 2012, with the exception of the rates applied to taxable estates in excess of $500,000. Accordingly, the maximum tax rate after December 31, 2012 will be 40 percent (Code Sec. 2001(c), as amended by the American Taxpayer Relief Act of 2012 (P.L. 112-240)).

The estate and gift tax rate schedule applicable to the estates of decedents dying and gifts made after December 31, 2012 is as follows:

Transfer Tax Rate Schedule: After December 31, 2012

(A) Amount subject to tax more than—	(B) Amount subject to tax equal to or less than—	(C) Tax on amount in column (A)	(D) Rate of tax on excess over amount in column (A) Percent
. . .	$10,000	. . .	18
$10,000	20,000	$1,800	20
20,000	40,000	3,800	22
40,000	60,000	8,200	24
60,000	80,000	13,000	26
80,000	100,000	18,200	28
100,000	150,000	23,800	30
150,000	250,000	38,800	32
250,000	500,000	70,800	34
500,000	750,000	155,800	37
750,000	1,000,000	248,300	39
1,000,000		345,800	40

The following unified transfer tax rate schedule generally applies to estates of decedents dying, and gifts and GSTs made in 2010 through 2012. However, a special zero percent tax rate applied to GSTs made in 2010. Also, although the rate schedule below applies to compute the estate tax of decedents dying in 2010, executors for such decedents could elect to opt out of the estate tax (see ¶ 121).

Transfer Tax Rate Schedule: 2010–2012

(A) Amount subject to tax more than— $	(B) Amount subject to tax equal to or less than— $	(C) Tax on amount in column (A) $	(D) Rate of tax on excess over amount in column (A) Percent
. . . .	10,000	. . . . . .	18
10,000	20,000	1,800	20
20,000	40,000	3,800	22

Transfer Tax Rate Schedule: 2010–2012

(A) Amount subject to tax more than— $	(B) Amount subject to tax equal to or less than— $	(C) Tax on amount in column (A) $	(D) Rate of tax on excess over amount in column (A) Percent
40,000	60,000	8,200	24
60,000	80,000	13,000	26
80,000	100,000	18,200	28
100,000	150,000	23,800	30
150,000	250,000	38,800	32
250,000	500,000	70,800	34
500,000	. . . .	155,800	35

• Rate Schedule (2002–2009)

The estate and gift tax rate schedule applicable to the estates of decedents dying, and gifts made, in 2002 through 2009 is as follows:

Transfer Tax Rate Schedule: 2002–2009*

(A) Amount subject to tax more than— $	(B) Amount subject to tax equal to or less than— $	(C) Tax on amount in column (A) $	(D) Rate of tax on excess over amount in column (A) Percent
. . . .	10,000	. . . .	18
10,000	20,000	1,800	20
20,000	40,000	3,800	22
40,000	60,000	8,200	24
60,000	80,000	13,000	26
80,000	100,000	18,200	28
100,000	150,000	23,800	30
150,000	250,000	38,800	32
250,000	500,000	70,800	34
500,000	750,000	155,800	37
750,000	1,000,000	248,300	39
1,000,000	1,250,000	345,800	41
1,250,000	1,500,000	448,300	43
1,500,000	2,000,000	555,800	45
2,000,000	2,500,000	780,800	49
2,500,000	. . . .	1,025,800	50*

* The 2001 Act reduces the top marginal rate for years after 2002, according to the following schedule:
  • 49 percent for decedents dying, and gifts made, in 2003;
  • 48 percent in 2004;
  • 47 percent in 2005;
  • 46 percent in 2006;
  • 45 percent in 2007, 2008, and 2009.

For years 2003 through 2009, the tentative tax is to be determined by using a table prescribed by the IRS, which will be the same as the rate schedule shown above except for the adjustments necessary to reflect the reductions in the maximum rate.

• Rate Schedule (1984–2001)

The unified rate schedule applying to estates of decedents dying, and gifts made, after 1983 and before 2002 appears below.

¶2600

Unified Tax Rate Schedule

Column A Taxable amount over $	Column B Taxable amount not over $	Column C Tax on amount in column A $	Column D Rate of tax on excess over amount in column A Percent
0	10,000	0	18
10,000	20,000	1,800	20
20,000	40,000	3,800	22
40,000	60,000	8,200	24
60,000	80,000	13,000	26
80,000	100,000	18,200	28
100,000	150,000	23,800	30
150,000	250,000	38,800	32
250,000	500,000	70,800	34
500,000	750,000	155,800	37
750,000	1,000,000	248,300	39
1,000,000	1,250,000	345,800	41
1,250,000	1,500,000	448,300	43
1,500,000	2,000,000	555,800	45
2,000,000	2,500,000	780,800	49
2,500,000	3,000,000	1,025,800	53
3,000,000	. . . .	1,290,800	55

Prior to 1984, different tax rates applied to cumulative lifetime and at-death transfers exceeding $3 million.

• **1983.** A 57-percent tax rate applied to transfers in the $3 to $3.5 million range and a 60-percent rate applied to amounts in excess of $3.5 million.

• **1982.** A 57-percent tax rate applied to transfers in the $3 to $3.5 million range; a 61-percent rate applied to transfers in the $3.5 to $4 million range; and a 65-percent rate applied to transfers in excess of $4 million.

• **1977–1981.** A 57-percent tax rate applied to transfers in the $3 to $3.5 million range; a 61-percent rate applied to transfers in the $3.5 to $4 million range; a 65-percent rate applied to transfers in the $4 to $4.5 million range; a 69-percent rate applied to transfers in the $4.5 to $5 million range; and a 70-percent rate applied to transfers in excess of $5 million.

In general, the amount of estate tax payable under the unified tax rate schedule is determined by applying the applicable rate to the aggregate of lifetime and at-death transfers, and then subtracting the gift taxes payable on gifts made after 1976. For this purpose, the amount of gift taxes paid by a decedent is to be determined as if the rate schedule in effect in the year of death was in effect in the year of the gift. See specific details at ¶1426 for computing the tax.

• *Benefits of Graduated Rates and Unified Credit Phased Out (Pre-2002)*

The benefits of the graduated rates and the unified credit under the unified transfer tax system are phased out for the estates of decedents dying before 1998 beginning with cumulative transfers above $10 million. This is accomplished by adding five percent of the excess of any transfer over $10 million to the tentative tax computed in determining the ultimate transfer tax liability. For estates of decedents dying, and gifts made, after 1987 and before 1998, the tax is levied on amounts transferred in excess of $10 million, but not exceeding $21,040,000, in order to recapture the benefit of any transfer tax rate below 55 percent, as well as the unified credit.

Due to mistakes in the wording of the amendment to Code Sec. 2001(c)(2) by the Taxpayer Relief Act of 1997 (P.L. 105-34), the five-percent additional tax phases out the benefits of the graduated rates, but not the benefits of the unified credit (applicable credit amount), for estates of decedents dying, and gifts made, after 1997 and before 2002. A provision in the Senate Committee Report on the IRS Restructuring and Reform Act of 1998 (P.L. 105-206) clarifying the phaseout range for the five-percent surtax to phase out the benefits of the unified credit was not included in the Conference Committee Report. Therefore, the additional tax is levied on amounts transferred after 1997 and before 2002 in excess of $10 million, but not exceeding $17,184,000. The applicable credit amount is not recaptured.

Although Code Sec. 2001(c)(2) was effective with respect to transfers made after 1987 under the Revenue Act of 1987 (P.L. 100-203), the Conference Committee Report for that Act states that pre-effective date gifts are included in cumulative transfers for purposes of determining the adjustment for transfers made after the effective date; however, the tax rate on the earlier gifts remains unchanged. Thus, according to the Committee Report, if a person makes a $9 million gift before 1988, and an additional $4 million gift after 1987, $3 million of the latter transfer will be subject to the additional tax under the phase-out.

• *Repeal of Five-Percent Surtax*

The 2001 Act repealed the five-percent surtax for the estates of decedents dying, and gifts made, after December 31, 2001. This surtax was not reinstated by the Tax Relief Act of 2010; ATRA made the repeal permanent.

• *Unified Credit*

For estates of decedents dying after 1976 and gifts made after 1976, both the $60,000 estate tax exemption and the $30,000 lifetime gift tax exemption were replaced by a single unified credit. The amount of this credit is subtracted from the amount of the decedent's gross estate tax. In effect, the amount of the unified credit available at death will be reduced to the extent that any portion of the credit is used to offset gift taxes on lifetime transfers.

Amounts allowed as lifetime exemptions on gifts made after September 8, 1976, but before January 1, 1977, reduce the unified credit allowable by 20 percent of the exemption used, to a maximum of $6,000.

For estates of decedents dying in 1977 and thereafter, the credit was phased in as follows:

Year	Amount of Credit	Amount of Exemption Equivalent
1977	$ 30,000	$120,667
1978	34,000	134,000
1979	38,000	147,333
1980	42,500	161,563
1981	47,000	175,625
1982	62,800	225,000
1983	79,300	275,000
1984	96,300	325,000
1985	121,800	400,000
1986	155,800	500,000
1987–1997	192,800	600,000

The Taxpayer Relief Act of 1997 replaced the unified credit amount with an applicable credit amount, effective for the estates of decedents dying, and gifts made, after December 31, 1997. The applicable credit amount is defined as the amount of the tentative tax that would be determined under the Code Sec. 2001(c) rate schedule if the amount with respect to which the tentative tax is computed were the applicable exclusion amount. However, the amount of the credit cannot exceed the amount of estate tax imposed. The table below provides the applicable credit amount and the applicable exclusion amount for the period between 1998 and 2001.

Year	Applicable Credit Amount	Applicable Exclusion Amount
1998	$202,050	$625,000
1999	211,300	650,000
2000 and 2001	220,550	675,000

• Impact of the 2001, 2010, and 2012 Acts

The enactment of the Economic Growth and Tax Relief Reconciliation Act of 2001 (EGTRRA) brought significant change to the transfer tax system, the most notable being the one-year repeal of the estate and GST taxes in 2010 (which was retroactively set aside by the Tax Relief Act of 2010). Additionally, EGTRRA made a number of modifications to the maximum estate tax rate and the estate and gift tax applicable exclusion amounts. EGTRRA increased the *estate tax* applicable exclusion amount according to the following schedule:

- $1 million for decedents dying in 2002 and 2003;
- $1.5 million in 2004 and 2005;
- $2 million in 2006, 2007, and 2008; and
- $3.5 million in 2009.

EGTRRA also increased the *gift tax* applicable exclusion amount to $1 million, beginning with gifts made in 2002. However, unlike the gradual increase in the estate tax applicable exclusion amount for the years 2002 through 2009, the gift tax applicable exclusion amount remained at $1 million and was not indexed for inflation. For years 2002 through 2009, the amount of the gift tax unified credit is equal to (1) the applicable credit amount in effect under Code Sec. 2010(c) for such calendar year, determined as if the applicable exclusion amount were $1 million, reduced by (2) the sum of the amounts allowable as a credit under Code Sec. 2505 for all preceding calendar periods.[1]

The Tax Relief Act of 2010 made the following changes with respect to the estate tax and gift tax applicable exclusion amounts and the GST exemption amounts:

- $1 million for *gifts* made in 2010;
- $5 million for *estates of decedents of dying, and GSTs made* in 2010;
- $5 million for *estates of decedents dying, and gifts and GSTs made* in 2011;
- $5,120,000 (as adjusted for inflation) for *estates of decedents dying, and gifts and GSTs made* in 2012;

The American Taxpayer Relief Act of 2012 (ATRA) made the following changes to the estate and gift tax applicable exclusion amounts and to the GST exemption:

- $5,250,000 (as adjusted for inflation) for *estates of decedents dying, and gifts and GSTs made* in 2013;
- $5,340,000 (as adjusted for inflation) for *estates of decedents dying, and gifts and GSTs made* in 2014.

---

[1] Code Sec. 2505(a), as amended by P.L. 107-16.

II. Estates of Nonresidents Not Citizens

Effective for the estates of decedents dying after November 10, 1988, estate and gift tax rates applicable to U.S. citizens are also applicable to the estates of nonresident aliens.

The gift tax applies to transfers made by nonresidents not U.S. citizens only with respect to transfers of tangible property situated within the United States.

A separate estate tax rate schedule applies in the case of nonresidents not U.S. citizens dying after December 31, 1976, and before November 11, 1988. The amount of estate tax is determined by applying the unified rate schedule below to the cumulative lifetime and deathtime transfers subject to United States transfer taxes and then subtracting gift taxes payable on the lifetime transfers made after December 31, 1976, but before January 1, 2010.

If the amount is:	The tentative tax is:
Not over $100,000	6% of the taxable estate.
Over $100,000 but not over $500,000	$6,000, plus 12% of excess over $100,000.
Over $500,000 but not over $1,000,000	$54,000, plus 18% of excess over $500,000.
Over $1,000,000 but not over $2,000,000	$144,000, plus 24% of excess over $1,000,000.
Over $2,000,000	$348,000, plus 30% of excess over $2,000,000.

• Scheduled Repeal of Estate and GST Taxes in 2010

The Tax Relief Act of 2010 retroactively set aside the 2001 Act's repeal the estate and GST taxes, which was to apply to the estates of decedents dying after December 31, 2009 and before January 1, 2011 (Code Sec. 2210, see ¶2595).

• Credit

Effective for the estates of decedents dying after November 10, 1988, where permitted by treaty, the estate of a nonresident alien is allowed the same unified credit as a U.S. citizen multiplied by the percentage of the decedent's total gross estate situated in the United States. In other cases, the estate of a nonresident alien is allowed a unified credit of $13,000 (which exempts the first $60,000 of the estate from estate tax). The estate of a resident of a U.S. possession, dying after November 10, 1988, is entitled to a unified credit equal to the greater of (1) $13,000, or (2) $46,800 multiplied by the percentage of the decedent's gross estate situated in the United States.

A $30,000 estate tax exemption was available to the estates of nonresident aliens dying before January 1, 1977. Applicable for the estates of nonresident aliens dying after December 31, 1976, and before November 11, 1988, that exemption was eliminated and replaced by a credit of $3,600 that is allowed against the estate tax. In the case of residents of a possession of the United States (who are not considered citizens) dying after December 31, 1976, and before November 11, 1988, the credit allowable is the greater of $3,600 or that proportion of $15,075 that the value of that part of the decedent's property situated in the United States bears to the value of the entire gross estate wherever situated. The $15,075 figure was phased in over a five-year period.

III. Gifts and Bequests from Expatriates

A U.S. citizen or resident is subject to a special transfer tax upon receipt of property by gift or bequest from an expatriate (see ¶2593). Under Code Sec. 2801, as enacted by the Heroes Earnings Assistance and Relief Tax Act of 2008 (HEART Act) (P.L. 110-245), this tax is effective for property received on or after June 17, 2008.

¶2600

The tax assessed under Code Sec. 2801 is equal to the value of the "covered gift or bequest" (see ¶2593), multiplied by: (1) the highest rate in effect under Code Sec. 2001(c) (40 percent for 2013 and beyond; 35 percent for 2010–2012) or, if higher; (2) the highest rate in effect under Code Sec. 2502(a) (also 40 percent for 2013 and beyond; 35 percent for 2010–2012).

¶ 2605   Rate Schedule Under Victims of Terrorism Tax Relief Act and Military Family Tax Relief Act

The following estate tax table applies only to members of the U.S. military who died in a combat zone (see ¶1560), to civilians who died as a result of certain terrorist attacks (see ¶1650), and to astronauts who died in the line of duty after December 31, 2002.[2]

(A) Amount subject to tax more than—	(B) Amount subject to tax equal to or less than—	(C) Tax on amount in column (A)	(D) Rate of tax on excess over amount in column (A) Percent
0	$100,000	0	0
$100,000	150,000	0	1
150,000	200,000	$500	2
200,000	300,000	1,500	3
300,000	500,000	4,500	4
500,000	700,000	12,500	5
700,000	900,000	22,500	6
900,000	1,100,000	34,500	7
1,100,000	1,600,000	48,500	8
1,600,000	2,100,000	88,500	9
2,100,000	2,600,000	133,500	10
2,600,000	3,100,000	183,500	11
3,100,000	3,600,000	238,500	12
3,600,000	4,100,000	298,500	13
4,100,000	5,100,000	363,500	14
5,100,000	6,100,000	503,500	15
6,100,000	7,100,000	653,500	16
7,100,000	8,100,000	813,500	17
8,100,000	9,100,000	983,500	18
9,100,000	10,100,000	1,163,500	19
10,100,000	. . . .	1,353,500	20

¶ 2610   Postponement of Time-Sensitive Tax Acts

The IRS has issued[3] a list of time-sensitive acts, the performance of which may be postponed under Code Sec. 7508 (relating to individuals serving in the Armed Forces) and Code Sec. 7508A (relating to taxpayers affected by a Presidentially declared disaster). This IRS action does not, by itself, provide any postponements under Code Sec. 7508 and Code Sec. 7508A. In order for taxpayers to be entitled to a postponement of any act listed below, the IRS generally will publish a Notice or other guidance providing relief with respect to a specific combat zone or Presidentially declared disaster.

This revenue procedure is effective for acts that may be performed on or after August 20, 2007. It does not list acts specified in Code Sec. 7508, Code Sec. 7508A, or the regulations thereunder, such as the filing of tax returns or payment of taxes. Material not relevant to estate, gift, or generation-skipping transfer taxes has not been reproduced.

---

[2] Code Sec. 2201, as amended by the Military Family Tax Relief Act of 2003.

[3] Rev. Proc. 2007-56, 2007-2 CB 388.

¶2605

| *Statute or Regulation* | *Act Postponed* |

* * *

13. Sec. 529(c)(3)(C)(i)

A rollover contribution to another qualified tuition program must be made no later than the 60th day after the date of a distribution from a qualified tuition program.

* * *

28. Treas. Reg. § 7701-3(c)

The effective date of an entity classification election (Form 8832, Entity Classification Election) cannot be more than 75 days prior to the date on which the election is filed.

* * *

29. Treas. Reg. § 301.9100-2(a)(1)

An automatic extension of 12 months from the due date for making a regulatory election is granted to make certain elections described in § 301.9100-2(a)(2), including the election to use other than the required taxable year under section 444, and the election to use LIFO under section 472.

30. Treas. Reg. § 301.9100-2(b)-(d)

An automatic extension of 6 months from the due date of a return, excluding extensions, is granted to make the regulatory or statutory elections whose due dates are the due date of the return or the due date of the return including extension (for example, a taxpayer has an automatic 6-month extension to file an application to change a method of accounting under Rev. Proc. 2002-9), provided the taxpayer (a) timely filed its return for the year of election, (b) within that 6-month extension period, takes the required corrective action to file the election in accordance with the statute, regulations, revenue procedure, revenue ruling, notice or announcement permitting the election, and (c) writes at the top of the return, statement of election or other form "FILED PURSUANT TO § 301.9100-2."

Section 7. Corporate Issues

| *Statute or Regulation* | *Act Postponed* |

* * *

2. Sec. 303 and Treas. Reg. § 1.303-2

A corporation must complete the distribution of property to a shareholder in redemption of all or part of the stock of the corporation which (for Federal estate tax purposes) is included in determining the estate of a decedent. Section 303 and Treas. Reg. § 1.303-2 require, among other things, that the distribution occur within the specified period.

* * *

Section 9. Estate, Gift and Trust Issues

	Statute or Regulation	*Act Postponed*
1.	Sec. 643(g)	The trustee may elect to treat certain payments of estimated tax as paid by the beneficiary. The election shall be made on or before the 65th day after the close of the taxable year of the trust.
2.	Sec. 645 and Treas. Reg. § 1.645-1(c)	An election to treat a qualified revocable trust as part of the decedent's estate must be made by filing Form 8855, Election To Treat a Qualified Revocable Trust as Part of an Estate, by the due date (including extensions) of the estate's Federal income tax return for the estate's first taxable year, if there is an executor, or by the due date (including extensions) of the trust's Federal income tax return for the trust's first taxable year (treating the trust as an estate), if there is no executor.
3.	Sec. 663(b) and Treas. Reg. § 1.663(b)-2	The fiduciary of a trust or estate may elect to treat any amount properly paid or credited to a beneficiary within the first 65 days following the close of the taxable year as an amount that was properly paid or credited on the last day of such taxable year. If a return is required to be filed for the taxable year for which the election is made, the election shall be made on such return no later than the time for making such return (including extensions). If no return is required to be filed, the election shall be made in a separate statement filed with the internal revenue office with which a return would have been filed, no later than the time for making a return (including extensions).
4.	Sec. 2011(c)	The executor of a decedent's estate must file a claim for a credit for state estate, inheritance, legacy or succession taxes by filing a claim within 4 years of filing Form 706, United States Estate (and Generation Skipping Transfer) Tax Return. (Section 2011 is amended effective for estates of decedents dying after 12/31/04; see section 2058).
5.	Sec. 2014(e)	The executor of a decedent's estate must file a claim for foreign death taxes within 4 years of filing Form 706.
6.	Sec. 2016 and Treas. Reg. § 20.2016-1	If an executor of a decedent's estate (or any other person) receives a refund of any state or foreign death taxes claimed as a credit on Form 706, the IRS must be notified within 30 days of receipt. (Section 2016 is amended effective for estates of decedents dying after 12/31/04; see section 2058).
7.	Sec. 2031(c)	If an executor of a decedent's estate elects on Form 706 to exclude a portion of the value of land that is subject to a qualified conservation easement, agreements relating to development rights must be implemented within 2 years after the date of the decedent's death.

Section 9. Estate, Gift and Trust Issues

Statute or Regulation	*Act Postponed*

8.   Sec. 2032(d)

The executor of a decedent's estate may elect an alternate valuation on a late filed Form 706 if the Form 706 is not filed later than 1 year after the due date.

9.   Sec. 2032A(c)(7)

A qualified heir, with respect to specially valued property, is provided a two-year grace period immediately following the date of the decedent's death in which the failure by the qualified heir to begin using the property in a qualified use will not be considered a cessation of qualified use and therefore will not trigger additional estate tax.

10.   Sec. 2032A(d)(3)

The executor of a decedent's estate has 90 days after notification of incomplete information/ signatures to provide the information/ signatures to the IRS regarding an election on Form 706 with respect to specially valued property.

11.   Sec. 2046

A taxpayer may make a qualified disclaimer no later than 9 months after the date on which the transfer creating the interest is made, or the date the person attains age 21.

12.   Sec. 2053(d) and Treas. Reg. §§ 20.2053-9(c) and 10(c)

If the executor of a decedent's estate elects to take a deduction for state and foreign death tax imposed upon a transfer for charitable or other uses, the executor must file a written notification to that effect with the IRS before expiration of the period of limitations on assessments (generally 3 years). (Section 2053 is amended effective for estates of decedents dying after December 31, 2004, to apply only with respect to foreign death taxes).

13.   Sec. 2055(e)(3)

A party in interest must commence a judicial proceeding to change an interest into a qualified interest no later than the 90th day after the estate tax return (Form 706) is required to be filed or, if no return is required, the last date for filing the income tax return for the first taxable year of the trust.

14.   Sec. 2056(d)

A qualified domestic trust (QDOT) election must be made on Form 706, Schedule M, and the property must be transferred to the trust before the date on which the return is made. Any reformation to determine if a trust is a QDOT requires that the judicial proceeding be commenced on or before the due date for filing the return.

15.   Sec. 2056A(b)(2)

The trustee of a QDOT must file a claim for refund of excess tax no later than 1 year after the date of final determination of the decedent's estate tax liability.

Section 9. Estate, Gift and Trust Issues

Statute or Regulation	Act Postponed
16. Sec. 2057(i)(3)(G)	A qualified heir, with respect to qualified family owned business, has a two-year grace period immediately following the date of the decedent's death in which the failure by the qualified heir to begin using the property in a qualified use will not be considered a cessation of qualified use and therefore will not trigger additional estate tax. (The section 2057 election is not available to estates of decedents dying after December 31, 2004).
17. Sec. 2057(i)(3)(H)	The executor of a decedent's estate has 90 days after notification of incomplete information/ signatures to provide the information/ signatures to the IRS regarding an election on Form 706 with respect to specially valued property.
18. Sec. 2058(d)	The executor of a decedent's estate may deduct estate, inheritance, legacy, or succession taxes actually paid to any state or the District of Columbia from the decedent's gross estate. With certain exceptions, the deduction is only allowed provided the taxes are actually paid and the deduction claimed within 4 years of filing Form 706.
19. Sec. 2516	The IRS will treat certain transfers as made for full and adequate consideration in money or money's worth where husband and wife enter into a written agreement relative to their marital and property rights and divorce actually occurs within the 3-year period beginning on the date 1 year before such agreement is entered into.
20. Sec. 2518(b)	A taxpayer may make a qualified disclaimer no later than 9 months after the date on which the transfer creating the interest is made, or the date the person attains age 21.

* * *

Section 14. Procedure and Administration Issues

Statute or Regulation	Act Postponed
1. Treas. Reg. § 301.6036-1(a)(2) and (3)	A court-appointed receiver or fiduciary in a non-bankruptcy receivership, a fiduciary in aid of foreclosure who takes possession of substantially all of the debtor's assets, or an assignee for benefit of creditors, must give written notice within ten days of his appointment to the IRS as to where the debtor will file his tax return.

* * *

4. Sec. 6331(k)(1) and Treas. Reg. § 301.7122-1(g)(2)	If a taxpayer submits a good-faith revision of a rejected offer in compromise within 30 days after the rejection, the Service will not levy to collect the liability before deciding whether to accept the revised offer.

¶2610

Section 14. Procedure and Administration Issues
Statute or Regulation   *Act Postponed*

5.	Sec. 6331(k)(2) and Treas. Reg. § 301.6331-4(a)(1)	If, within 30 days following the rejection or termination of an installment agreement, the taxpayer files an appeal with the IRS Office of Appeals, no levy may be made while the rejection or termination is being considered by Appeals.

* * *

7.	Sec. 7122(d)(2) and Treas. Reg. § 301.7122-1(f)(5)(i)	A taxpayer must request administrative review of a rejected offer in compromise within 30 days after the date on the letter of rejection.

¶ 2630   Pre-2005 State Death Tax Credit Table

Prior to January 1, 2005, a credit was allowed against the federal estate tax for any estate, inheritance, legacy, or succession taxes actually paid to any state of the United States or the District of Columbia with respect to any property included in the decedent's gross estate. The credit was applied against the adjusted taxable estate, which for this purpose was the taxable estate reduced by $60,000. The credit was available only if it did not exceed the estate's tax liability after reduction by the unified credit. (The following table may not be used in computing taxes on estates of certain members of the Armed Forces.)

Estates of Decedents Dying After 1976

Adjusted Taxable Estate ("Adjusted Taxable Estate" is the decedent's taxable estate less $60,000) From	To	Credit =	+	%	Of Excess Over
0	$40,000	0		0.0	0
$40,000	90,000	0		0.8	$40,000
90,000	140,000	$400		1.6	90,000
140,000	240,000	1,200		2.4	140,000
240,000	440,000	3,600		3.2	240,000
440,000	640,000	10,000		4.0	440,000
640,000	840,000	18,000		4.8	640,000
840,000	1,040,000	27,600		5.6	840,000
1,040,000	1,540,000	38,800		6.4	1,040,000
1,540,000	2,040,000	70,800		7.2	1,540,000
2,040,000	2,540,000	106,800		8.0	2,040,000
2,540,000	3,040,000	146,800		8.8	2,540,000
3,040,000	3,540,000	190,800		9.6	3,040,000
3,540,000	4,040,000	238,800		10.4	3,540,000
4,040,000	5,040,000	290,800		11.2	4,040,000
5,040,000	6,040,000	402,800		12.0	5,040,000
6,040,000	7,040,000	522,800		12.8	6,040,000
7,040,000	8,040,000	650,800		13.6	7,040,000
8,040,000	9,040,000	786,800		14.4	8,040,000
9,040,000	10,040,000	930,800		15.2	9,040,000
10,040,000	. . . .	1,082,800		16.0	10,040,000

• *Phaseout and Repeal of Credit*

The 2001 Act gradually phased out the state death tax credit between 2002 and 2004, with the credit repealed for the estates of decedents dying after December 31, 2004. Beginning in 2005, the state death tax credit is replaced by a deduction for state death taxes paid.[4] (see ¶1144). The credit is reduced by 25 percent for the estates of decedents dying in 2002, 50 percent for the estates of decedents dying in 2003, and 75 percent for the estates of decedents dying in 2004.

¶ 2640   Pre-1977 Estate Tax Rates

I. Effective for Estates of U.S. Citizens and Residents Dying Before 1977

The federal estate tax on estates of U.S. citizens and residents is computed on a "taxable estate," after deduction of a $60,000 exemption, at the rates below. This amount is further reduced by a state death tax credit computed under the table at "III. State Death Tax Credit" below, or by the actual amount of state death taxes, whichever is less. Credits are also available for foreign death taxes, certain gift taxes, and federal estate taxes on prior transfers. (The following table may not be used in computing taxes on estates of certain members of the Armed Forces.[5])

Taxable Estate (After deducting the $60,000 exemption) From	To	Tax =	+	%	Of Excess Over
0	$5,000	0		3	0
$5,000	10,000	$150		7	$5,000
10,000	20,000	500		11	10,000
20,000	30,000	1,600		14	20,000
30,000	40,000	3,000		18	30,000
40,000	50,000	4,800		22	40,000
50,000	60,000	7,000		25	50,000
60,000	100,000	9,500		28	60,000
100,000	250,000	20,700		30	100,000
250,000	500,000	65,700		32	250,000
500,000	750,000	145,700		35	500,000
750,000	1,000,000	233,200		37	750,000
1,000,000	1,250,000	325,700		39	1,000,000
1,250,000	1,500,000	423,200		42	1,250,000
1,500,000	2,000,000	528,200		45	1,500,000
2,000,000	2,500,000	753,200		49	2,000,000
2,500,000	3,000,000	998,200		53	2,500,000
3,000,000	3,500,000	1,263,200		56	3,000,000
3,500,000	4,000,000	1,543,200		59	3,500,000
4,000,000	5,000,000	1,838,200		63	4,000,000
5,000,000	6,000,000	2,468,200		67	5,000,000
6,000,000	7,000,000	3,138,200		70	6,000,000
7,000,000	8,000,000	3,838,200		73	7,000,000
8,000,000	10,000,000	4,568,200		76	8,000,000
10,000,000	. . . .	6,088,200		77	10,000,000

II. Estates of Nonresidents Not Citizens Dying After November 13, 1966 and Before January 1, 1977

The federal estate tax on estates of nonresidents not citizens dying after November 13, 1966 and before January 1, 1977, after deduction of the $30,000 exemption, but prior to any credit for state death taxes, gift taxes or taxes on prior transfers, is computed at the rates below.

[4] Code Sec. 2058, as added by P.L. 107-16 and amended by P.L. 111-312, and P.L. 112-240.

[5] See Code Sec. 2011(d) and Code Sec. 2201.

Taxable Estate (After deducting the $30,000 exemption) From	To	Tax =	+	%	Of Excess Over
0	$100,000	0		5	0
$100,000	500,000	$5,000		10	$100,000
500,000	1,000,000	45,000		15	500,000
1,000,000	2,000,000	120,000		20	1,000,000
2,000,000	. . . .	320,000		25	2,000,000

III. State Death Tax Credit

Taxable Estate (After deducting the applicable exemption) From	To	Credit =	+	%	Of Excess Over
0	$40,000	0		0.0	0
$40,000	90,000	0		0.8	$40,000
90,000	140,000	$400		1.6	90,000
140,000	240,000	1,200		2.4	140,000
240,000	440,000	3,600		3.2	240,000
440,000	640,000	10,000		4.0	440,000
640,000	840,000	18,000		4.8	640,000
840,000	1,040,000	27,600		5.6	840,000
1,040,000	1,540,000	38,800		6.4	1,040,000
1,540,000	2,040,000	70,800		7.2	1,540,000
2,040,000	2,540,000	106,800		8.0	2,040,000
2,540,000	3,040,000	146,800		8.8	2,540,000
3,040,000	3,540,000	190,800		9.6	3,040,000
3,540,000	4,040,000	238,800		10.4	3,540,000
4,040,000	5,040,000	290,800		11.2	4,040,000
5,040,000	6,040,000	402,800		12.0	5,040,000
6,040,000	7,040,000	522,800		12.8	6,040,000
7,040,000	8,040,000	650,800		13.6	7,040,000
8,040,000	9,040,000	786,800		14.4	8,040,000
9,040,000	10,040,000	930,800		15.2	9,040,000
10,040,000	. . . .	1,082,800		16.0	10,040,000

¶ 2650   Pre-1977 Gift Tax Rates

The rate table below is applicable for gifts made in 1976 and prior years. See ¶ 2600 for unified rate table for gifts made after 1976. Gifts made prior to 1977 will be taken into account in the computation of the unified transfer tax generated by post-1976 gifts. In computing the tax payable on post-1976 gifts, the reduction for taxes paid previously is to be based on the unified rate schedule. See the illustration at ¶ 2008.

"Taxable gifts," as noted in the table below, are determined by deducting the $30,000 specific exemption (allowed only once, but cumulative until used up) and by deducting an annual exclusion of $3,000 per donee of gifts of present interests. The $30,000 specific exemption is eliminated for post-1976 gifts.

Taxable Gifts From	To	Tax =	+	%	Of Excess Over
. . . .	$5,000	0.00		$2^1/4\%$	. . . .
$5,000	10,000	$112.50		$5^1/4\%$	$5,000
10,000	20,000	375.00		$8^1/4\%$	10,000
20,000	30,000	1,200.00		$10^1/2\%$	20,000
30,000	40,000	2,250.00		$13^1/2\%$	30,000

| Taxable Gifts | | | | | Of Excess |
From	To	Tax =	+	%	Over
40,000	50,000	3,600.00		$16^1/2$%	40,000
50,000	60,000	5,250.00		$18^3/4$%	50,000
60,000	100,000	7,125.00		21%	60,000
100,000	250,000	15,525.00		$22^1/2$%	100,000
250,000	500,000	49,275.00		24%	250,000
500,000	750,000	109,275.00		$26^1/4$%	500,000
750,000	1,000,000	174,900.00		$27^3/4$%	750,000
1,000,000	1,250,000	244,275.00		$29^1/4$%	1,000,000
1,250,000	1,500,000	317,400.00		$31^1/2$%	1,250,000
1,500,000	2,000,000	396,150.00		$33^3/4$%	1,500,000
2,000,000	2,500,000	564,900.00		$36^3/4$%	2,000,000
2,500,000	3,000,000	748,650.00		$39^3/4$%	2,500,000
3,000,000	3,500,000	947,400.00		42%	3,000,000
3,500,000	4,000,000	1,157,400.00		$44^1/4$%	3,500,000
4,000,000	5,000,000	1,378,650.00		$47^1/4$%	4,000,000
5,000,000	6,000,000	1,851,150.00		$50^1/4$%	5,000,000
6,000,000	7,000,000	2,353,650.00		$52^1/2$%	6,000,000
7,000,000	8,000,000	2,878,650.00		$54^3/4$%	7,000,000
8,000,000	10,000,000	3,426,150.00		57%	8,000,000
10,000,000	. . . .	4,566,150.00		$57^3/4$%	10,000,000

¶ 2800   Applicable Federal Rates

The present value of an annuity, interest for life or for a term of years, or a remainder or reversionary interest is generally determined by using the IRS valuation tables if the valuation date is after April 30, 1989. The interest rate component of the valuation tables is based on the applicable federal rate (AFR) as described under Code Sec. 7520. This rate is equal to 120 percent of the federal mid-term rate issued monthly by the Secretary of the Treasury, rounded to the nearest even tenth of a percent (see ¶ 530).

The following interest rate table provides the Code Sec. 7520 120-percent AFR mid-term valuation interest rate factors, beginning with January 2007.

Month	Interest factor	Month	Interest factor
December 2013	2.0%	June 2010	3.2%
November 2013	2.0%	May 2010	3.4%
October 2013	2.4%	April 2010	3.2%
September 2013	2.0%	March 2010	3.2%
August 2013	2.0%	February 2010	3.4%
July 2013	1.4%	January 2010	3.0%
June 2013	1.2%	December 2009	3.2%
May 2013	1.2%	November 2009	3.2%
April 2013	1.4%	October 2009	3.2%
March 2013	1.4%	September 2009	3.4%
February 2013	1.2%	August 2009	3.4%
January 2013	1.0%	July 2009	3.4%
December 2012	1.2%	June 2009	2.8%
November 2012	1.0%	May 2009	2.4%
October 2012	1.2%	April 2009	2.6%
September 2012	1.0%	March 2009	2.4%
August 2012	1.0%	February 2009	2.0%
July 2012	1.2%	January 2009	2.4%
June 2012	1.2%	December 2008	3.4%
May 2012	1.6%	November 2008	3.6%
April 2012	1.4%	October 2008	3.8%
March 2012	1.4%	September 2008	4.2%
February 2012	1.4%	August 2008	4.2%
January 2012	1.4%	July 2008	4.2%
December 2011	1.6%	June 2008	3.8%
November 2011	1.4%	May 2008	3.2%
October 2011	1.4%	April 2008	3.4%
September 2011	2.0%	March 2008	3.6%
August 2011	2.2%	February 2008	4.2%
July 2011	2.4%	January 2008	4.4%
June 2011	2.8%	December 2007	5.0%
May 2011	3.0%	November 2007	5.2%
April 2011	3.0%	October 2007	5.2%
March 2011	3.0%	September 2007	5.8%
February 2011	2.8%	August 2007	6.2%
January 2011	2.4%	July 2007	6.0%
December 2010	1.8%	June 2007	5.6%
November 2010	2.0%	May 2007	5.6%
October 2010	2.0%	April 2007	5.6%
September 2010	2.4%	March 2007	5.8%
August 2010	2.6%	February 2007	5.6%
July 2010	2.8%	January 2007	5.6%

¶ 2900

FILLED-IN FORMS
TABLE OF CONTENTS

¶ 2910   Fact Situation for Form 706

The following example illustrates a timely filed federal estate tax return for the estate of James X. Diversey, who died on January 1, 2013, while a resident of Cook County, Illinois. James, a retired CEO of a publishing company, was survived by his wife, Carrie, two sons (Robert and Richard Diversey), two sisters (Martha Diversey and Ann Fagan), and a granddaughter (Katherine Diversey, the daughter of Robert). The executors of the estate are Carrie and National Bank. Carrie and National Bank also serve as trustees of the James X. Diversey Revocable Trust, which was created on January 1, 2008.

In January 2008, each son received a $60,000 loan from James to assist them with the start-up costs of business ventures. The loans were evidenced by identical promissory notes that called for repayment in 10 years. See Schedule C, items 5 and 6.

In early 2009, James and Carrie created the Diversey Family Limited Partnership (DFLP). Each spouse contributed $1,500,000 to DFLP in exchange for a one-percent general partnership (GP) interest and a 49-percent limited partnership (LP) interest. In December 2009, each spouse made a gift of a 19-percent LP interest to each son. Following the gifts, the LP interests were owned as follows: Robert: 38-percent interest; Richard: 38-percent interest; James: 11-percent interest; and Carrie: 11-percent interest. In valuing the LP interests for gift tax purposes, a combined minority interest and marketability discount of 31 percent was applied. The total value of the gifts made by James to his sons in 2009 was reported at $750,000. See Part 2, line 4 of page one.

Article III of James' will made several specific bequests: (1) 2009 Lincoln Town Car to Carrie; (2) all household goods and personal effects to Carrie; (3) the GP and LP interests in DFLP to Carrie; (4) 1,000 shares of Diversco, Inc. (a closely held company) to Katherine; (5) his art collection to Gessner Art Museum; (6) $50,000 in cash to the American Heart Association; and (7) an amount equal to the difference between $3,000,000 and the value of all other property passing to Carrie as a result of James's death, to fund the Carrie M. Diversey Marital Trust, which met the requirements for qualified terminable interest property (QTIP) under Code Sec. 2056(b)(7). The amount passing to the QTIP trust was $1,358,600. See Schedule M. In addition, each son received one-third (1/3) of the residue, and each sister received one-sixth (1/6) of the residue.

Because Carrie had significant wealth apart from the assets that she held with James, James' estate plan limited the total amount passing to Carrie to roughly one-third of his gross estate. See Schedule M. This generated an estate tax liability. The sons were named as the beneficiaries of James' individual retirement account. See Schedule I. James exercised his testamentary general power of appointment over a trust created under his father's will in favor of the estate. The trust held 300 shares of Diversco, Inc. See Schedule H, item 1.

James' lifelong friend, Albert Smith, bequeathed $750,000 in securities to James. Albert died on July 1, 2012. The transfer of the securities to James generated a credit for tax on prior transfers, computed using the worksheet for Schedule Q in the instructions for Form 706. See Schedule Q, Part 2.

After James's death, his sister Martha sued the estate, claiming that she had an ownership interest in the lake home in Olive Branch, Illinois. See Schedule A, item 1. At the time that the estate tax return was filed, the claim had not yet been resolved. Schedule PC was completed in order to preserve the right to deduct expenses related to the unresolved litigation.

The estate is assumed to have paid $434,982 in state (Illinois) estate taxes.

¶ 2920   Form 706 (Page One)

The filled-in page one of Form 706 relates to the James X. Diversey estate. See the fact situation at ¶2910.

Form **706** (Rev. August 2013) Department of the Treasury Internal Revenue Service	United States Estate (and Generation-Skipping Transfer) Tax Return		OMB No. 1545-0015

▶ Estate of a citizen or resident of the United States (see instructions). To be filed for decedents dying after December 31, 2012.
▶ Information about Form 706 and its separate instructions is at *www.irs.gov/form706.*

1a Decedent's first name and middle initial (and maiden name, if any) James X.	**1b** Decedent's last name Diversey		**2** Decedent's social security no. 987-65-4321
3a City, town, or post office; county; state or province; country; and ZIP or foreign postal code. Wheeling, Cook, il. usa. 60090	**3b** Year domicile established 1966	**4** Date of birth 10/31/1935	**5** Date of death 1/1/2013
6a Name of executor (see instructions) Carrie M. Diversey	**6b** Executor's address (number and street including apartment or suite no.; city, town, or post office; state or province; country; and ZIP or foreign postal code) and phone no. 123 Cory St. Wheeling, IL 60090		
6c Executor's social security number (see instructions)		Phone no. (847) 123-4567	

6d If there are multiple executors, check here [X] and attach a list showing the names, addresses, telephone numbers, and SSNs of the additional executors.

7a Name and location of court where will was probated or estate administered Probate Division, Cook County Circuit Court, 50 W. Washington, Chicago, IL 60602	**7b** Case number ABC-123

8 If decedent died testate, check here ▶ [X] and attach a certified copy of the will.   **9** If you extended the time to file this Form 706, check here ▶ [X]

10 If Schedule R-1 is attached, check here ▶ [ ]   **11** If you are estimating the value of assets included in the gross estate on line 1 pursuant to the special rule of Reg. section 20.2010-27(a) (7)(ii), check here ▶ [ ]

Part 2-Tax Computation

1	Total gross estate less exclusion (from Part 5—Recapitulation, item 13)	**1**	9,344,810
2	Tentative total allowable deductions (from Part 5—Recapitulation, item 24)	**2**	3,541,648
3 a	Tentative taxable estate (subtract line 2 from line 1)	**3a**	5,803,162
b	State death tax deduction	**3b**	434,982
c	Taxable estate (subtract line 3b from line 3a)	**3c**	5,368,180
4	Adjusted taxable gifts (see instructions)	**4**	750,000
5	Add lines 3c and 4	**5**	6,118,180
6	Tentative tax on the amount on line 5 from Table A in the instructions	**6**	2,393,072
7	Total gift tax paid or payable (see instructions)	**7**	0
8	Gross estate tax (subtract line 7 from line 6)	**8**	2,393,072
9 a	Basic exclusion amount **9a**	5,250,000	
9 b	Deceased spousal unused exclusion (DSUE) amount from predeceased spouse(s), if any (from Section D, Part 6-Portability of Deceased Spousal Unused Exclusion) **9b**	0	
9 c	Applicable exclusion amount (add lines 9a and 9b) **9c**	5,250,000	
9 d	Applicable credit amount (tentative tax on the amount in 9c from Table A in the instructions) **9d**	2,045,800	
10	Adjustment to applicable credit amount (May not exceed $6,000. See instructions.) **10**		
11	Allowable applicable credit amount (subtract line 10 from line 9d)	**11**	2,045,800
12	Subtract line 11 from line 8 (but do not enter less than zero)	**12**	347,272
13	Credit for foreign death taxes (from Schedule P). (Attach Form(s) 706-CE.) . **13**		
14	Credit for tax on prior transfers (from Schedule Q) . . . **14**	93,557	
15	Total credits (add lines 13 and 14)	**15**	93,557
16	Net estate tax (subtract line 15 from line 12)	**16**	253,715
17	Generation-skipping transfer (GST) taxes payable (from Schedule R, Part 2, line 10)	**17**	0
18	Total transfer taxes (add lines 16 and 17)	**18**	253,715
19	Prior payments (explain in an attached statement)	**19**	0
20	Balance due (or overpayment) (subtract line 19 from line 18)	**20**	253,715

Under penalties of perjury, I declare that I have examined this return, including accompanying schedules and statements, and to the best of my knowledge and belief, it is true, correct, and complete. Declaration of preparer other than the executor is based on all information of which preparer has any knowledge.

Sign Here	▶ *Carrie M. Diversey* Signature of executor	▶	Date 12/1/2013
	▶ *Robert Dupdale, VP National Bank* Signature of executor	▶	Date 12/1/2013

Paid Preparer Use Only	Print/Type preparer's name William S. Oak	Preparer's signature *William S. Oak*	Date 12/1/2013	Check [ ] if self-employed	PTIN
	Firm's name ▶ Oak Tax Services			Firm's EIN ▶	55-0357911
	Firm's address ▶ 987 Racine Blvd., Wheeling, IL 60090			Phone no.	(847)-444-1111

For Privacy Act and Paperwork Reduction Act Notice, see instructions.   Form **706** (Rev. 8-2013)

HTA

¶ 2930   Form 706 (Page Two)

The filled-in page two of Form 706 relates to the James X. Diversey estate. See the fact situation at ¶2910.

Form 706 (Rev. 8-2013)

Estate of: James X. Diversey	Decedent's social security number
	987-65-4321

Part 3—Elections by the Executor

Note. For information on electing portability of the decedent's DSUE amount, including how to opt out of the election, see Part 6—Portability of Deceased Spousal Unused Exclusion.

Note. Some of the following elections may require the posting of bonds or liens.

Please check "Yes" or "No" box for each question (see instructions).

			Yes	No
1	Do you elect alternate valuation?	1		X
2	Do you elect special-use valuation? If "Yes," you must complete and attach Schedule A-1	2		X
3	Do you elect to pay the taxes in installments as described in section 6166?			X
	If "Yes," you must attach the additional information described in the instructions.			
	Note. By electing section 6166 installment payments, you may be required to provide security for estate tax deferred under section 6166 and interest in the form of a surety bond or a section 6324A lien.	3		
4	Do you elect to postpone the part of the taxes due to a reversionary or remainder interest as described in section 6163?	4		X

Part 4—General Information

Note. Please attach the necessary supplemental documents. **You must attach the death certificate.** (See instructions)

Authorization to receive confidential tax information under Reg. section 601.504(b)(2)(i); to act as the estate's representative before the IRS; and to make written or oral presentations on behalf of the estate:

Name of representative (print or type)	State	Address (number, street, and room or suite no., city, state, and ZIP code)
William S. Oak	IL	987 Racine Blvd., Wheeling, IL 60090

I declare that I am the ☐ attorney/ ☐ certified public accountant/ ☐ enrolled agent (check the applicable box) for the executor. I am not under suspension or disbarment from practice before the Internal Revenue Service and am qualified to practice in the state shown above.

Signature	CAF number	Date	Telephone number
William S. Oak	123456789R	12/1/2013	(847) 444-1111

1 Death certificate number and issuing authority (attach a copy of the death certificate to this return).
CX-12345   Cook County, IL

2 Decedent's business or occupation. If retired, check here ► ☒ and state decedent's former business or occupation.
Executive XYZ Publishing Co., Linconshire, IL 60069

3a Marital status of the decedent at time of death:
☒ Married   ☐ Widow/widower   ☐ Single   ☐ Legally separated   ☐ Divorced

3b For all prior marriages, list the name and SSN of the former spouse, the date the marriage ended, and whether the marriage ended by annulment, divorce, or death. Attach additional statements of the same size if necessary.

4a Surviving spouse's name	4b Social security number	4c Amount received (see instructions)
Carrie M. Diversey	123-45-6789	3,000,000

5 Individuals (other than the surviving spouse), trusts, or other estates who receive benefits from the estate (do not include charitable beneficiaries shown in Schedule O) (see instructions).

Name of individual, trust, or estate receiving $5,000 or more	Identifying number	Relationship to decedent	Amount (see instructions)
Robert Diversey	999-88-7777	Son	1,690,616
Richard Diversey	999-77-5555	Son	1,690,616
Ann Fagan	555-44-3333	Sister	421,559
Martha Diversey	555-33-1111	Sister	781,558
Katherine Diversey	888-66-4444	Granddaughter	450,000
All unascertainable beneficiaries and those who receive less than $5,000 ►			
Total			5,034,349

If you answer "Yes" to any of the following questions, you must attach additional information as described.

		Yes	No
6	Is the estate filing a protective claim for refund?	X	
	If "Yes," complete and attach two copies of Schedule PC for each claim.		
7	Does the gross estate contain any section 2044 property (qualified terminable interest property (QTIP) from a prior gift or estate)? (see instructions)		X
8a	Have federal gift tax returns ever been filed?	X	
	If "Yes," attach copies of the returns, if available, and furnish the following information:		
b	Period(s) covered c Internal Revenue office(s) where filed		
	2009 Cincinnati, OH		
9a	Was there any insurance on the decedent's life that is not included on the return as part of the gross estate?		X
b	Did the decedent own any insurance on the life of another that is not included in the gross estate?		X

Page 2

¶ 2940   Form 706 (Recapitulation)

The filled-in page three of Form 706, containing the Recapitulation, relates to the James X. Diversey estate. See the fact situation at ¶2910.

Form 706 (Rev. 8-2013)

	Decedent's social security number
Estate of: James X. Diversey	987-65-4321

Part 4—General Information *(continued)*

	If you answer "Yes" to any of the following questions, you must attach additional information as described.	Yes	No
10	Did the decedent at the time of death own any property as a joint tenant with right of survivorship in which **(a)** one or more of the other joint tenants was someone other than the decedent's spouse, and **(b)** less than the full value of the property is included on the return as part of the gross estate? If "Yes," you must complete and attach Schedule E	X	
11 a	Did the decedent, at the time of death, own any interest in a partnership (for example, a family limited partnership), an unincorporated business, or a limited liability company; or own any stock in an inactive or closely held corporation?	X	
b	If "Yes," was the value of **any** interest owned (from above) discounted on this estate tax return? If "Yes," see the instructions on reporting the total accumulated or effective discounts taken on Schedule F or G	X	
12	Did the decedent make any transfer described in sections 2035, 2036, 2037, or 2038? (see instructions) If "Yes," you must complete and attach Schedule G	X	
13 a	Were there in existence at the time of the decedent's death any trusts created by the decedent during his or her lifetime? . . .	X	
b	Were there in existence at the time of the decedent's death any trusts not created by the decedent under which the decedent possessed any power, beneficial interest, or trusteeship?	X	
c	Was the decedent receiving income from a trust created after October 22, 1986, by a parent or grandparent? . . . . If "Yes," was there a GST taxable termination (under section 2612) on the death of the decedent?		X
d	If there was a GST taxable termination (under section 2612), attach a statement to explain. Provide a copy of the trust or will creating the trust, and give the name, address, and phone number of the current trustee(s).		
e	Did the decedent at any time during his or her lifetime transfer or sell an interest in a partnership, limited liability company, or closely held corporation to a trust described in lines 13a or 13b? . . . . If "Yes," provide the EIN for this transferred/sold item. ▶		X
14	Did the decedent ever possess, exercise, or release any general power of appointment? If "Yes," you must complete and attach Schedule H	X	
15	Did the decedent have an interest in or a signature or other authority over a financial account in a foreign country, such as a bank account, securities account, or other financial account?		X
16	Was the decedent, immediately before death, receiving an annuity described in the "General" paragraph of the instructions for Schedule I or a private annuity? If "Yes," you must complete and attach Schedule I	X	
17	Was the decedent ever the beneficiary of a trust for which a deduction was claimed by the estate of a predeceased spouse under section 2056(b)(7) and which is not reported on this return? If "Yes," attach an explanation		X

Part 5—Recapitulation. Note. If estimating the value of one or more assets pursuant to the special rule of Reg. section 20.2010-2T(a)(7)(ii), enter on both lines 10 and 23 the amount noted in the instructions for the corresponding range of values. (See instructions for details.)

Item no.	Gross estate		Alternate value	Value at date of death
1	Schedule A—Real Estate	1	0	1,600,000
2	Schedule B—Stocks and Bonds	2	0	2,842,500
3	Schedule C—Mortgages, Notes, and Cash	3	0	344,430
4	Schedule D—Insurance on the Decedent's Life (attach Form(s) 712)	4	0	825,000
5	Schedule E—Jointly Owned Property (attach Form(s) 712 for life insurance) . . .	5	0	795,500
6	Schedule F—Other Miscellaneous Property (attach Form(s) 712 for life insurance)	6	0	542,900
7	Schedule G—Transfers During Decedent's Life (att. Form(s) 712 for life insurance)	7	0	564,480
8	Schedule H—Powers of Appointment	8	0	135,000
9	Schedule I—Annuities	9	0	1,695,000
10	Estimated value of assets subject to the special rule of Reg. section 20.2010-2T(a)(7)(ii)	10		
11	Total gross estate (add items 1 through 10)	11	0	9,344,810
12	Schedule U—Qualified Conservation Easement Exclusion	12		0
13	Total gross estate less exclusion (subtract item 12 from item 11). Enter here and on line 1 of Part 2—Tax Computation	13	0	9,344,810

Item no.	Deductions		Amount
14	Schedule J—Funeral Expenses and Expenses Incurred in Administering Property Subject to Claims	14	151,400
15	Schedule K—Debts of the Decedent	15	37,170
16	Schedule K—Mortgages and Liens	16	134,700
17	Total of items 14 through 16	17	323,270
18	Allowable amount of deductions from item 17 (see the instructions for item 18 of the Recapitulation)	18	323,270
19	Schedule L—Net Losses During Administration	19	4,878
20	Schedule L—Expenses Incurred in Administering Property Not Subject to Claims	20	1,500
21	Schedule M—Bequests, etc., to Surviving Spouse	21	3,000,000
22	Schedule O—Charitable, Public, and Similar Gifts and Bequests	22	212,000
23	Estimated value of assets subject to the special rule of Reg. section 20.2010-2T(a)(7)(ii)	23	
24	Tentative total allowable deductions (add items 18 through 23). Enter here and on line 2 of the Tax Computation . .	24	3,541,648

Page 3

¶ 2942   Form 706 (Page Four)

The filled-in page four of Form 706, relates to the James X. Diversey estate. See the fact situation at ¶2910.

Form 706 (Rev. 8-2013)

Estate of: James X. Diversey	Decedent's social security number
	987-65-4321

Part 6—Portability of Deceased Spousal Unused Exclusion (DSUE)

Portability Election

A decedent with a surviving spouse elects portability of the deceased spousal unused exclusion (DSUE) amount, if any, by completing and timely-filing this return. No further action is required to elect portability of the DSUE amount to allow the surviving spouse to use the decedent's DSUE amount.

Section A. Opting Out of Portability

The estate of a decedent with a surviving spouse may opt out of electing portability of the DSUE amount. Check here and do not complete Sections B and C of Part 6 only if the estate opts NOT to elect portability of the DSUE amount. ☐

Section B. QDOT

	Yes	No
Are any assets of the estate being transferred to a qualified domestic trust (QDOT)?		X

If "Yes," the DSUE amount portable to a surviving spouse (calculated in Section C, below) is preliminary and shall be redetermined at the time of the final distribution or other taxable event imposing estate tax under section 2056A. See instructions for more details.

Section C. DSUE Amount Portable to the Surviving Spouse (To be completed by the estate of a decedent making a portability election.)

Complete the following calculation to determine the DSUE amount that can be transferred to the surviving spouse.

1	Enter the amount from line 9c, Part 2—Tax Computation	1	5,250,000
2	Reserved	2	
3	Enter the value of the cumulative lifetime gifts on which tax was paid or payable (see instructions) . . .	3	0
4	Add lines 1 and 3	4	5,250,000
5	Enter amount from line 10, Part 2—Tax Computation	5	0
6	Divide amount on line 5 by 40% (0.40) (do not enter less than zero) . . .	6	0
7	Subtract line 6 from line 4	7	5,250,000
8	Enter the amount from line 5, Part 2– Tax Computation	8	6,118,180
9	Subtract line 8 from line 7 (do not enter less than zero)	9	0
10	DSUE amount portable to surviving spouse (Enter lesser of line 9 or line 9a, Part 2 – Tax Computation) . .	10	0

Section D. DSUE Amount Received from Predeceased Spouse(s) (To be completed by the estate of a deceased surviving spouse with DSUE amount from predeceased spouse(s))

Provide the following information to determine the DSUE amount received from deceased spouses.

A Name of Deceased Spouse (dates of death after December 31, 2010, only)	B Date of Death (enter as mm/dd/yy)	C Portability Election Made?		D If "Yes," DSUE Amount Received from Spouse	E DSUE Amount Applied by Decedent to Lifetime Gifts	F Year of Form 709 Reporting Use of DSUE Amount Listed in col E	G Remaining DSUE Amount, if any (subtract col. E from col. D)
		Yes	No				
Part 1 — DSUE RECEIVED FROM LAST DECEASED SPOUSE							
							0
Part 2 — DSUE RECEIVED FROM OTHER PREDECEASED SPOUSE(S) AND USED BY DECEDENT							

Total (for all DSUE amounts from predeceased spouse(s) applied) . . . . . . | 0 |

Add the amount from Part 1, column D and the total from Part 2, column E. Enter the result on line 9b, Part 2—Tax Computation . . . . ▶ _____ 0

¶ 2944   Form 706 (Taxable Gifts Reconciliation Worksheet)

The filled-in Taxable Gifts Reconciliation worksheet and Line 4 worksheet, from page six of Form 706 Instructions, relates to the James X. Diversey estate. See the fact situation at ¶2910. Basic Exclusion Amounts and Taxable Gift Amount Tables, from page eight of Form 706 Instructions are provided for reference.

Part 2, Line 4 (706) - Taxable Gifts Reconciliation

Worksheet TG - Taxable Gifts Reconciliation

Gifts made after June 6, 1932, and before 1977	a. Calendar year or calendar quarter	b. Total taxable gifts for period (see Note)	Note. For the definition of a taxable gift, see section 2503. Follow Form 709. That is, include only the decedent's one-half of split gifts, whether the gifts were made by the decedent or the decedent's spouse. In addition to gifts reported on Form 709, you must include any taxable gifts in excess of the annual exclusion that were not reported on Form 709.			
			c. Taxable amount included in col. b for gifts included in the gross estate	d. Taxable amount included in col. b for gifts that qualify for "special treatment of split gifts" described in instructions	e. Gift tax paid by decedent on gifts in col. d	f. Gift tax paid by decedent's spouse on gifts in col. c
	1. Total taxable gifts made before 1977	0				
Gifts made after 1976	2009	750,000				
2. Totals for gifts made after 1976		750,000	0	0	0	0

Line 4 Worksheet - Adjusted Taxable Gifts Made After 1976

1. Taxable gifts made after 1976. Enter the amount from Worksheet TG, line 2, column b	1	750,000
2. Taxable gifts made after 1976 reportable on Schedule G. Enter the amount from Worksheet TG, line 2, column c 2	0	
3. Taxable gifts made after 1976 that qualify for "special treatment." Enter the amount from Worksheet TG, line 2, column d 3	0	
4. Add lines 2 and 3	4	0
5. Adjusted taxable gifts. Subtract line 4 from line 1. Enter here and on Part 2 - Tax Computation, line 4.	5	750,000

Table of Basic Exclusion Amounts

Period	Basic Exclusion Amount	Credit Equivalent at 2013 rates
1977 (Quarters 1 and 2)	$30,000	$6,000
1977 (Quarters 3 and 4)	$120,667	$30,000
1978	$134,000	$34,000
1979	$147,333	$38,000
1980	$161,563	$42,500
1981	$175,625	$47,000
1982	$225,000	$62,800
1983	$275,000	$79,300
1984	$325,000	$96,300
1985	$400,000	$121,800
1986	$500,000	$155,800
1987 through 1997	$600,000	$192,800
1998	$625,000	$202,050
1999	$650,000	$211,300
2000 and 2001	$675,000	$220,550
2002 through 2010	$1,000,000	$345,800
2011	$5,000,000	$1,945,800
2012	$5,120,000	$1,993,800
2013	$5,250,000	$2,045,800

Taxable Gift Amount Table

Column A Amount in Row (p) Line 7 Worksheet over...	Column B Amount in Row (p) Line 7 Worksheet not over...	Column C Property Value on Amount in Column A	Column D Rate (Divisor) on excess of amount in Column A
0	1,800	0	18%
1,800	3,800	10,000	20%
3,800	8,200	20,000	22%
8,200	13,000	40,000	24%
13,000	18,200	60,000	26%
18,200	23,800	80,000	28%
23,800	38,800	100,000	30%
38,800	70,800	150,000	32%
70,800	155,800	250,000	34%
155,800	248,300	500,000	37%
248,300	345,800	750,000	39%
345,800	------	1,000,000	40%

¶ 2948 Form 706 (Tax on Gifts Made After 1976 Worksheet)

The filled-in Line 7 worksheet, from page seven of Form 706 Instructions, relates to the James X. Diversey estate. See the fact situation at ¶ 2910.

Line 7 Worksheet – Submit a copy with Form 706

	Line 7 Worksheet Part A- Used to determine Applicable Credit Allowable for Prior Periods after 1976				
(a)	Tax Period[1]	Pre-1977	2009		
(b)	Taxable Gifts for Applicable Period		750,000		
(c)	Taxable Gifts for Prior Periods [2]				
(d)	Cumulative Taxable Gifts Including Applicable Period (add Row (b) and Row (c))		750,000		
(e)	Tax at Date of Death Rates for Prior Gifts (from Row (c))[3]				
(f)	Tax at Date of Death Rates for Cumulative Gifts including Applicable Period (from Row (d))		248,300		
(g)	Tax at Date of Death Rates for Gifts in Applicable Period (subtract Row (e) from Row (f))		248,300		
(h)	Total DSUE applied from Prior Periods and Applicable Period (from Line 2 of Schedule C of Applicable Period Form 709)				
(i)	Basic Exclusion for Applicable Period (Enter the amount from the Table of Basic Exclusion Amounts)		1,000,000		
(j)	Basic Exclusion amount plus Total DSUE applied in prior periods and applicable period (add Row (h) and Row (i))		1,000.000		
(k)	Maximum Applicable Credit amount based on Row (j) (Using Table A—Unified Rate Schedule)[4]		345,800		
(l)	Applicable Credit amount used in Prior Periods (add Row (l) and Row (n) from prior period)				
(m)	Available Credit in Applicable Period (subtract Row (l) from Row (k))		345,800		
(n)	Credit Allowable (lesser of Row (g) or Row (m))		248,300		
(o)	Tax paid or payable at Date of Death rates for Applicable Period (subtract Row (n) from Row (g))				
(p)	Tax on Cumulative Gifts less tax paid or payable for Applicable Period (subtract Row (o) from Row (f))		248,300		
(q)	Cumulative Taxable Gifts less Gifts in the Applicable Period on which tax was paid or payable based on Row (p) (Using the Taxable Gift Amount Table)		750,000		
(r)	Gifts in the Applicable Period on which tax was payable (subtract Row (g) from Row (d))				

	Line 7 Worksheet Part B	
1	Total gift taxes payable on gifts after 1976 (sum of amounts in Row (o)).	
2	Gift taxes paid by the decedent on gifts that qualify for "special treatment." Enter the amount from Worksheet TG, line 2, col. (e).	
3	Subtract line 2 from line 1.	
4	Gift tax paid by decedent's spouse on split gifts included on Schedule G. Enter amount from Worksheet TG, line 2, col. (f).	
5	Add lines 3 and 4. Enter here and on Part 2—Tax Computation, line 7.	
6	Cumulative lifetime gifts on which tax was paid or payable. Enter this amount on line 3, Section C, Part 6 of Form 706 (sum of amounts in Row (r)).	

Footnotes:
[1]Row (a): For annual returns, enter the tax period as (YYYY). For quarterly returns enter tax period as (YYYY-Q).
[2]Row (c): Enter amount from Row (d) of the previous column.
[3]Row (e): Enter amount from Row (f) of the previous column.
[4]Row (k): Calculate the applicable credit on the amount in column (j), using Table A — Unified Rate Schedule, and enter here. (For each row in column (k), subtract 20 percent of any amount allowed as a specific exemption for gifts made after September 8, 1976, and before January 1, 1977.)

¶ 2950　Filled-In Schedule A

Example Where Alternate Valuation Was Not Elected

The filled-in Schedule A of Form 706 relates to the James X. Diversey estate. See the fact situation at ¶ 2910.

Form 706 (Rev. 8-2013)

	Decedent's social security number
Estate of: James X. Diversey	987-65-4321

SCHEDULE A—Real Estate

- For jointly owned property that must be disclosed on Schedule E, see instructions.
- Real estate that is part of a sole proprietorship should be shown on Schedule F.
- Real estate that is included in the gross estate under sections 2035, 2036, 2037, or 2038 should be shown on Schedule G.
- Real estate that is included in the gross estate under section 2041 should be shown on Schedule H.
- If you elect section 2032A valuation, you must complete Schedule A and Schedule A-1.

Note. If the value of the gross estate, together with the amount of adjusted taxable gifts, is less than the basic exclusion amount and the Form 706 is being filed solely to elect portability of the DSUE amount, consideration should be given as to whether you are required to report the value of assets eligible for the marital or charitable deduction on this schedule. See the instructions and Reg. section 20.2010-2T (a)(7)(ii) for more information. If you are not required to report the value of an asset, identify the property but make no entries in the last three columns.

Item number	Description	Alternate valuation date	Alternate value	Value at date of death
1	House and lot, 987 Shoreline Rd., Olive Branch, IL 62969 (lot 9, square 000). Value based on appraisal, a copy of which is attached.			850,000
2	House and lot, 1455 Prescott Dr., Bartlett, IL 60103 (lot 4, square 000). Value based on appraisal, a copy of which is attached.			750,000
	Total from continuation schedules or additional statements attached to this schedule		0	0
	TOTAL. (Also enter on Part 5—Recapitulation, page 3, at item 1.)		0	1,600,000

(If more space is needed, attach the continuation schedule from the end of this package or additional statements of the same size.)

Schedule A

HTA

Example Illustrating Alternate Valuation

The amounts shown in the following Schedule are not entered in the example of the Recapitulation at ¶ 2940, because the alternate valuation method was not elected by the estate of the hypothetical decedent, James X. Diversey. This schedule is provided for illustrative purposes only.

Form 706 (Rev. 8-2013)

Estate of: James X. Diversey			Decedent's social security number 987-65-4321	

SCHEDULE A—Real Estate

- For jointly owned property that must be disclosed on Schedule E, see instructions.
- Real estate that is part of a sole proprietorship should be shown on Schedule F.
- Real estate that is included in the gross estate under sections 2035, 2036, 2037, or 2038 should be shown on Schedule G.
- Real estate that is included in the gross estate under section 2041 should be shown on Schedule H.
- If you elect section 2032A valuation, you must complete Schedule A and Schedule A-1.

Note. If the value of the gross estate, together with the amount of adjusted taxable gifts, is less than the basic exclusion amount and the Form 706 is being filed solely to elect portability of the DSUE amount, consideration should be given as to whether you are required to report the value of assets eligible for the marital or charitable deduction on this schedule. See the instructions and Reg. section 20.2010-2T (a)(7)(ii) for more information. If you are not required to report the value of an asset, identify the property but make no entries in the last three columns.

Item number	Description	Alternate valuation date	Alternate value	Value at date of death
1	House and lot, 987 Shoreline Rd., Olive Branch, IL 62969 (lot 9, square 000). Value based on appraisal, a copy of which is attached.	7/1/2013	795,000	850,000
2	House and lot, 1455 Prescott Dr., Bartlett, IL 60103 (lot 4, square 000). Value based on appraisal, a copy of which is attached.	7/1/2013	680,000	750,000
	Total from continuation schedules or additional statements attached to this schedule		0	0
	TOTAL. (Also enter on Part 5—Recapitulation, page 3, at item 1.)		1,475,000	1,600,000

(If more space is needed, attach the continuation schedule from the end of this package or additional statements of the same size.)

HTA

Schedule A

¶2950

¶ 2960   Filled-In Schedule B

Example Where Alternate Valuation Was Not Elected

The filled-in Schedule B of Form 706 relates to the James X. Diversey estate. See the fact situation at ¶2910.

Form 706 (Rev. 8-2013)

Estate of: James X. Diversey

	Decedent's social security number
	987-65-4321

SCHEDULE B—Stocks and Bonds
(For jointly owned property that must be disclosed on Schedule E, see instructions.)

Note. If the value of the gross estate, together with the amount of adjusted taxable gifts, is less than the basic exclusion amount and the Form 706 is being filed solely to elect portability of the DSUE amount, consideration should be given as to whether you are required to report the value of assets eligible for the marital or charitable deduction on this schedule. See the instructions and Reg. section 20.2010-2T (a)(7)(ii) for more information. If you are not required to report the value of an asset, identify the property but make no entries in the last four columns.

Item number	Description, including face amount of bonds or number of shares and par value for identification. Give CUSIP number. If trust, partnership, or closely held entity, give EIN.		Unit value	Alternate valuation date	Alternate value	Value at date of death
		CUSIP number or EIN, where applicable				
1	4,000 shs. Neron Corp., common, NYSE	010101010	135.			540,000
	Dividend on item 1 of $3 per share declared on Dec. 14, 2012, payable on Jan. 16, 2013, to shareholders of record on Dec. 31, 2012.					12,000
2	2,500 shs. GloboCom Corp., common, NYSE	101010101	105.			262,500
	Dividend on item 2 of $5 per share declared on Dec. 5, 2012, payable on Jan. 5, 2013, to shareholders of record on Dec. 31, 2012.					12,500
3	2,800 shs. KWHCC Corp., common, NYSE	110011001	85.			238,000
4	2,000 shs. Pleaptech Corp., common, NASDAQ	001100110	145.			290,000
5	8,000 shs. Big Value mutual fund, NASDAQ	011011011	75.			600,000
6	17,500 shs. Max Return mutual fund, NASDAQ	100100100	25.			437,500
7	1,000 shs. Diversco, Inc., closely held company. Value based on appraisal, a copy of which is attached.		450.			450,000
	Total from continuation schedules (or additional statements) attached to this schedule				0	0
	TOTAL. (Also enter on Part 5—Recapitulation, page 3, at item 2.)				0	2,842,500

(If more space is needed, attach the continuation schedule from the end of this package or additional statements of the same size.)

HTA   **Schedule B**

Example Illustrating Alternate Valuation

The amounts shown in the following Schedule are not entered in the example of the Recapitulation at ¶2940, because the alternate valuation method was not elected by the estate of the hypothetical decedent, James X. Diversey. This schedule is provided for illustrative purposes only.

Form 706 (Rev. 8-2013)

Estate of: James X. Diversey		Decedent's social security number 987-65-4321		

SCHEDULE B—Stocks and Bonds
(For jointly owned property that must be disclosed on Schedule E, see instructions.)

Note. If the value of the gross estate, together with the amount of adjusted taxable gifts, is less than the basic exclusion amount and the Form 706 is being filed solely to elect portability of the DSUE amount, consideration should be given as to whether you are required to report the value of assets eligible for the marital or charitable deduction on this schedule. See the instructions and Reg. section 20.2010-2T (a)(7)(ii) for more information. If you are not required to report the value of an asset, identify the property but make no entries in the last four columns.

Item number	Description, including face amount of bonds or number of shares and par value for identification. Give CUSIP number. If trust, partnership, or closely held entity, give EIN.		Unit value	Alternate valuation date	Alternate value	Value at date of death
		CUSIP number or EIN, where applicable				
1	4,000 shs. Neron Corp., common, NYSE	010101010	135.			540,000
	1,500 shs. distributed to legatee on June 1, 2013,		125.	6/1/2013	187,500	
	2,500 shs. not disposed of within 6 months of death.		128.	7/1/2013	320,000	
	Dividend on item 1 of $3 per share declared on Dec. 14. 2012. payable on Jan. 15. 2013.				12,000	12,000
2	2,500 shs. GloboCom Corp., common, NYSE	101010101	105.			262,500
	2,500 shs. sold by executor on April 15, 2013.		100.	4/15/2013	250,000	
	Dividend on item 2 of $5 per share declared on Dec. 5, 2012, payable on Jan. 4, 2013, to shareholders of record on Dec. 31, 2012.				12,500	12,500
3	2,800 shs. KWHCC Corp., common, NYSE	110011001	85.			238,000
	Not disposed of within 6 months of death		81.	7/1/2013	226,800	
4	2,000 shs. Pleaptech Corp., common, NASDAQ	001100110	145.			290,000
	Not disposed of within 6 months of death		130.	7/1/2013	260,000	
5	8,000 shs. Big Value mutual fund, NASDAQ	011011011	75.			600,000
	Not disposed of within 6 months of death		72.	7/1/2013	576,000	
6	17,500 shs. Max Return mutual fund, NASDAQ	100100100	25.			437,500
	Not disposed of within 6 months of death		28.	4/1/2013	490,000	
7	1,000 shs. Diversco, Inc., closely held company. Value based on appraisal, a copy of which is attached.		450.			450,000
	1,000 shs. distributed to legatee on April 1, 2013		440.	4/1/2013	440,000	
	Total from continuation schedules (or additional statements) attached to this schedule				0	0
	TOTAL. (Also enter on Part 5—Recapitulation, page 3, at item 2.)				2,774,800	2,842,500

(If more space is needed, attach the continuation schedule from the end of this package or additional statements of the same size.)

HTA

Schedule B

¶ 2970 Filled-In Schedule C

The filled-in Schedule C of Form 706 relates to the James X. Diversey estate. See the fact situation at ¶2910.

Form 706 (Rev. 8-2013)

	Decedent's social security number
Estate of: James X Diversey	987-65-4321

SCHEDULE C—Mortgages, Notes, and Cash

(For jointly owned property that must be disclosed on Schedule E, see instructions.)

Note. If the value of the gross estate, together with the amount of adjusted taxable gifts, is less than the basic exclusion amount and the Form 706 is being filed solely to elect portability of the DSUE amount, consideration should be given as to whether you are required to report the value of assets eligible for the marital or charitable deduction on this schedule. See the instructions and Reg. section 20.2010-2T (a)(7)(ii) for more information. If you are not required to report the value of an asset, identify the property but make no entries in the last three columns.

Item number	Description	Alternate valuation date	Alternate value	Value at date of death
1	Money market account #123-987, National Bank, Wheeling, IL 60090.			90,000
	Unpaid interest accrued at date of death.			85
2	$85,000 certificate of deposit, National Bank, Wheeling, IL; 12-mo. Term; 2.5% interest; maturity October 1, 2013.			85,000
	Unpaid interest accrued at date of death.			500
3	$95,000 certificate of deposit, National Bank, Wheeling, IL; 18-mo. Term; 3% interest; maturity July 2, 2013.			95,000
	Unpaid interest accrued at date of death.			2,750
4	Cash on decedent's person.			95
5	Promissory note of $60,000, unpaid balance of $35,500; dated Jan. 1, 2008; Robert Diversey to decedent; due Jan. 1, 2018; interest payable at 7.5% per annum.			35,500
6	Promissory note of $60,000, unpaid balance of $35,500; dated Jan. 1, 2008; Richard Diversey to decedent; due Jan. 1, 2018; interest payable at 7.5% per annum.			35,500
	Total from continuation schedules (or additional statements) attached to this schedule		0	0
	TOTAL. (Also enter on Part 5—Recapitulation, page 3, at item 3.)		0	344,430

(If more space is needed, attach the continuation schedule from the end of this package or additional statements of the same size.)

Schedule C

HTA

¶ 2980   Filled-In Schedule D

The filled-in Schedule D of Form 706 relates to the James X. Diversey estate. See the fact situation at ¶2910.

Form 706 (Rev. 8-2013)

Estate of: James X. Diversey	Decedent's social security number
	987-65-4321

SCHEDULE D—Insurance on the Decedent's Life
You must list all policies on the life of the decedent and attach a Form 712 for each policy.

Note. If the value of the gross estate, together with the amount of adjusted taxable gifts, is less than the basic exclusion amount and the Form 706 is being filed solely to elect portability of the DSUE amount, consideration should be given as to whether you are required to report the value of assets eligible for the marital or charitable deduction on this schedule. See the instructions and Reg. section 20.2010-2T (a)(7)(ii) for more information. If you are not required to report the value of an asset, identify the property but make no entries in the last three columns.

Item number	Description	Alternate valuation date	Alternate value	Value at date of death
1	$825,000 Provisional Life Insurance Co. policy #13579-86420, proceeds payable to Carrie M. Diversey in lump sum. Form 712 attached.			825,000
	Total from continuation schedules (or additional statements) attached to this schedule		0	0
	TOTAL. (Also enter on Part 5—Recapitulation, page 3, at item 4.)		0	825,000

(If more space is needed, attach the continuation schedule from the end of this package or additional statements of the same size.)

HTA   **Schedule D**

¶ 2990   **Filled-In Schedule E**

The filled-in Schedule E of Form 706 relates to the James X. Diversey estate. See the fact situation at ¶2910.

Form 706 (Rev. 8-2013)

Estate of: James X. Diversey	Decedent's social security number 987-65-4321

SCHEDULE E—Jointly Owned Property

(If you elect section 2032A valuation, you must complete Schedule E and Schedule A-1.)

PART 1. Qualified Joint Interests—Interests Held by the Decedent and His or Her Spouse as the Only Joint Tenants (Section 2040(b)(2))

Note. If the value of the gross estate, together with the amount of adjusted taxable gifts, is less than the basic exclusion amount and the Form 706 is being filed solely to elect portability of the DSUE amount, consideration should be given as to whether you are required to report the value of assets eligible for the marital or charitable deduction on this schedule. See the instructions and Reg. section 20.2010-2T (a)(7)(ii) for more information. If you are not required to report the value of an asset, identify the property but make no entries in the last three columns.

Item number	Description. For securities, give CUSIP number. If trust, partnership, or closely held entity, give EIN	Alternate valuation date	Alternate value	Value at date of death
		CUSIP number or EIN, where applicable		
1	House and lot, 123 Cory St., Wheeling, IL (lot 0, square 999). Value based on an appraisal, a copy of which is attached.			750,000
2	Checking acct. #987, National Bank, Wheeling, IL 60090.			25,000
3	Savings acct. #123, National Bank, Wheeling, IL 60090.			96,000
	Total from continuation schedules (or additional statements) attached to this schedule		0	0
1a	Totals 1a		0	871,000
1b	Amounts included in gross estate (one-half of line 1a) 1b		0	435,500

PART 2. All Other Joint Interests

2a State the name and address of each surviving co-tenant. If there are more than three surviving co-tenants, list the additional co-tenants on an attached statement.

	Name	Address (number and street, city, state, and ZIP code)
A.	Martha Diversey	417 Euclaire Ln. Wausau, WI 54403
B.		
C.		

Item number	Enter letter for co-tenant	Description (including alternate valuation date if any). For securities, give CUSIP number. If trust, partnership, or closely held entity, give EIN	Percentage includible	Includible alternate value	Includible value at date of death
		CUSIP number or EIN, where applicable			
A		Brokerage account No. 000-111, Investors Bank, Wheeling, IL. Decedent and co-tenant each contributed 50% of funds used to purchase securities held in account. See attached list.	50.00%		360,000
		Total from continuation schedules (or additional statements) attached to this schedule		0	0
2b	Total other joint interests 2b		0	360,000
3	Total includible joint interests (add lines 1b and 2b). Also enter on Part 5—Recapitulation, page 3, at item 5 3		0	795,500

(If more space is needed, attach the continuation schedule from the end of this package or additional statements of the same size.)

HTA   **Schedule E**

¶ 3000   Filled-In Schedule F

The filled-in Schedule F of Form 706 relates to the James X. Diversey estate. See the fact situation at ¶2910.

Form 706 (Rev. 8-2013)

Estate of: James X. Diversey	Decedent's social security number
	987-65-4321

SCHEDULE F—Other Miscellaneous Property Not Reportable Under Any Other Schedule

(For jointly owned property that must be disclosed on Schedule E, see instructions.)

(If you elect section 2032A valuation, you must complete Schedule F and Schedule A-1.)

Note. If the value of the gross estate, together with the amount of adjusted taxable gifts, is less than the basic exclusion amount and the Form 706 is being filed solely to elect portability of the DSUE amount, consideration should be given as to whether you are required to report the value of assets eligible for the marital or charitable deduction on this schedule. See the instructions and Reg. section 20.2010-2T (a)(7)(ii) for more information. If you are not required to report the value of an asset, identify the property but make no entries in the last three columns.

		Yes	No
1	Did the decedent own any works of art, items, or any collections whose artistic or collectible value at date of death exceeded $3,000?	X	
	If "Yes," submit full details on this schedule and attach appraisals.		
2	Has the decedent's estate, spouse, or any other person received (or will receive) any bonus or award as a result of the decedent's employment or death?		X
	If "Yes," submit full details on this schedule.		
3	Did the decedent at the time of death have, or have access to, a safe deposit box?	X	
	If "Yes," state location, and if held jointly by decedent and another, state name and relationship of joint depositor. National Bank, Wheeling, IL		
	If any of the contents of the safe deposit box are omitted from the schedules in this return, explain fully why omitted.		

Item number	Description. For securities, give CUSIP number. If trust, partnership, or closely held entity, give EIN	CUSIP number or EIN, where applicable	Alternate valuation date	Alternate value	Value at date of death
1	11% limited partnership interest in Diversey Family Limited Partnership. Value based on appraisal, a copy of which is attached.				285,000
2	1% general partnership interest in Diversey Family Limited Partnership. Value based on appraisal, a copy of which is attached.				45,000
3	2009 Lincoln Town Car Signature 4-dr. sedan, 25,000 miles, VIN 1GJD5YZYU807991.				19,500
4	Household goods and personal effects.				31,400
5	Art collection. Value based on appraisal, a copy of which is attached.				162,000

Total from continuation schedules (or additional statements) attached to this schedule . . .		0	0
TOTAL. (Also enter on Part 5—Recapitulation, page 3, at item 6.)		0	542,900

(If more space is needed, attach the continuation schedule from the end of this package or additional statements of the same size.)

HTA   Schedule F

¶ 3010   Filled-In Schedule G

The filled-in Schedule G of Form 706 relates to the James X. Diversey estate. See the fact situation at ¶2910.

Form 706 (Rev. 8-2013)

		Decedent's social security number
		987-65-4321

Estate of: James X Diversey

SCHEDULE G—Transfers During Decedent's Life
(If you elect section 2032A valuation, you must complete Schedule G and Schedule A-1.)

Note. If the value of the gross estate, together with the amount of adjusted taxable gifts, is less than the basic exclusion amount and the Form 706 is being filed solely to elect portability of the DSUE amount, consideration should be given as to whether you are required to report the value of assets eligible for the marital or charitable deduction on this schedule. See the instructions and Reg. section 20.2010-2T (a)(7)(ii) for more information. If you are not required to report the value of an asset, identify the property but make no entries in the last three columns.

Item number	Description. For securities, give CUSIP number. If trust, partnership, or closely held entity, give EIN	Alternate valuation date	Alternate value	Value at date of death
A.	Gift tax paid or payable by the decedent or the estate for all gifts made by the decedent or his or her spouse within 3 years before the decedent's death (section 2035(b))	X X X X X		
B.	Transfers includible under sections 2035(a), 2036, 2037, or 2038:			
	Assets held in James X. Diversey Revocable Trust, dated January 1, 2008:			
	a. Cash held by trust.			1,200
	b. $125,000 Illinois General Development 30-year bond, due 2018; 5.25% interest, payable quarterly on January 1, April 1, July 1, and October 1.			129,000
	Interest accrued to the date of death.			1,580
	c. $250,000 Illinois Public Improvement 20-year bond, due 2014; 4.75% interest, payable quarterly on February 1, May 1, August 1, and November 1.			252,000
	Interest accrued to the date of death.			1,350
	d. $125,000 Illinois State Projects 25-year bond, due 2016; 5% interest, payable quarterly on March 1, June 1, September 1, and December 1.			178,500
	Interest accrued to the date of death.			850
	Total from continuation schedules (or additional statements) attached to this schedule . . .		0	0
	TOTAL. (Also enter on Part 5—Recapitulation, page 3, at item 7.)		0	564,480

¶ 3030 Filled-In Schedule H

The filled-in Schedule H of Form 706 relates to the James X. Diversey estate. See the fact situation at ¶2910.

SCHEDULE H—Powers of Appointment

(Include "5 and 5 lapsing" powers (section 2041(b)(2)) held by the decedent.)

(If you elect section 2032A valuation, you must complete Schedule H and Schedule A-1.)

Note. If the value of the gross estate, together with the amount of adjusted taxable gifts, is less than the basic exclusion amount and the Form 706 is being filed solely to elect portability of the DSUE amount, consideration should be given as to whether you are required to report the value of assets eligible for the marital or charitable deduction on this schedule. See the instructions and Reg. section 20.2010-2T (a)(7)(ii) for more information. If you are not required to report the value of an asset, identify the property but make no entries in the last three columns.

Item number	Description	Alternate valuation date	Alternate value	Value at date of death
1	Decedent held testamentary general power of appointment over trust created under the will of the decedent's father, Joseph X. Diversey. Power exercised pursuant to Article XIII of the decedent's will. Property subject to power: 300 shares Diversco Inc., closely held company. Value based on appraisal (see Sch. B, item 7)			135,000
	Total from continuation schedules (or additional statements) attached to this schedule		0	0
	TOTAL. (Also enter on Part 5—Recapitulation, page 3, at item 8.)		0	135,000

(If more space is needed, attach the continuation schedule from the end of this package or additional statements of the same size.)

HTA

¶ 3040　　**Filled-In Schedule I**

The filled-in Schedule I of Form 706 relates to the James X. Diversey estate. See the fact situation at ¶ 2910.

Form 706 (Rev. 8-2013)		Decedent's social security number
Estate of:　James X. Diversey		987-65-4321

SCHEDULE I—Annuities

Note. Generally, no exclusion is allowed for the estates of decedents dying after December 31, 1984 (see instructions).

Note. If the value of the gross estate, together with the amount of adjusted taxable gifts, is less than the basic exclusion amount and the Form 706 is being filed solely to elect portability of the DSUE amount, consideration should be given as to whether you are required to report the value of assets eligible for the marital or charitable deduction on this schedule. See the instructions and Reg. section 20.2010-2T (a)(7)(ii) for more information. If you are not required to report the value of an asset, identify the property but make no entries in the last three columns.

		Yes	No
A	Are you excluding from the decedent's gross estate the value of a lump-sum distribution described in section 2039(f)(2) (as in effect before its repeal by the Deficit Reduction Act of 1984)?		X

If "Yes," you must attach the information required by the instructions.

Item number	Description. Show the entire value of the annuity before any exclusions	Alternate valuation date	Includible alternate value	Includible value at date of death
1	Individual Retirement Account, No. 999-666, Investors Bank, Wheeling, IL . See attached list of marketable securities held in IRA.			1,695,000
	Total from continuation schedules (or additional statements) attached to this schedule		0	0
	TOTAL. (Also enter on Part 5—Recapitulation, page 3, at item 9.)		0	1,695,000

(If more space is needed, attach the continuation schedule from the end of this package or additional statements of the same size.)

Schedule I

HTA

¶3040

¶ 3050   Filled-In Schedule J

The filled-in Schedule J of Form 706 relates to the James X. Diversey estate. See the fact situation at ¶2910.

Form 706 (Rev. 8-2013)

Estate of: James X. Diversey	Decedent's social security number
	987-65-4321

SCHEDULE J—Funeral Expenses and Expenses Incurred in Administering Property Subject to Claims

▶ Use Schedule PC to make a protective claim for refund due to an expense not currently deductible.

For such a claim, report the expense on Schedule J but without a value in the last column.

Note. Do not list expenses of administering property not subject to claims on this schedule. To report those expenses, see instructions.

If executors' commissions, attorney fees, etc., are claimed and allowed as a deduction for estate tax purposes, they are not allowable as a deduction in computing the taxable income of the estate for federal income tax purposes. They are allowable as an income tax deduction on Form 1041, U.S. Income Tax Return for Estates and Trusts, if a waiver is filed to forgo the deduction on Form 706 (see Instructions for Form 1041).

Are you aware of any actual or potential reimbursement to the estate for any expense claimed as a deduction on this schedule?			Yes	No
If "Yes," attach a statement describing the expense(s) subject to potential reimbursement. (see instructions)				X

Item number	Description	Expense amount	Total amount
	A. Funeral expenses:		
1	Heelwing Funeral Home, Wheeling, IL 60090, Funeral and related expenses	8,000	
		0	
	Total funeral expenses . . . . ▶		8,000
	B. Administration expenses:		
	1 Executors' commissions—amount estimated/~~agreed upon~~/~~paid~~. (Strike out the words that do not apply.)		70,000
	2 Attorney fees—amount estimated/~~agreed upon~~/~~paid~~. (Strike out the words that do not apply.)		40,000
	3 Accountant fees—amount estimated/~~agreed upon~~/~~paid~~. (Strike out the words that do not apply.)		5,000
	4 Miscellaneous expenses:	Expense amount	
a.	Landgrab Realty Appraisers, Wheeling, IL. Appraisals of real estate and household items (Sch. A, item 1, Sch. E, part 1, item 1, and Sch. F, item 4)	6,000	
b.	Work of Art Appraisals, Wheeling, IL. Appraisal of collection (Sch. F, item 5)	950	
c.	MGS Business Valuation Services, Chicago, IL. Appraisal of closely held stock (Sch. B, item 7 and Sch. H, item 1)	6,500	
d.	MGS Business Valuation Services, Chicago, IL. Appraisal of Diversey FLP (Sch. F, items 1 and 2)	7,500	
e.	Probate court, Cook County, IL. Fees relating to administration of estate	650	
f.	Upkeep and maintenance of real estate (Sch. A, items 1 and 2)	6,800	
	Total miscellaneous expenses from continuation schedules (or additional statements) attached to this schedule	0	
	Total miscellaneous expenses . . . . ▶		28,400
	TOTAL. (Also enter on Part 5—Recapitulation, page 3, at item 14.). . . . . ▶		151,400

(If more space is needed, attach the continuation schedule from the end of this package or additional statements of the same size.)

HTA

Schedule J

¶ 3060   Filled-In Schedule K

The filled-in Schedule K of Form 706 relates to the James X. Diversey estate. See the fact situation at ¶2910.

Form 706 (Rev. 8-2013)

	Decedent's social security number
Estate of: James X. Diversey	987-65-4321

SCHEDULE K—Debts of the Decedent, and Mortgages and Liens

▶Use Schedule PC to make a protective claim for refund due to a claim not currently deductible.
For such a claim, report the expense on Schedule K but without a value in the last column.

	Yes	No
Are you aware of any actual or potential reimbursement to the estate for any debt of the decedent, mortgage, or lien claimed as a deduction on this schedule? . . .		X
If "Yes," attach a statement describing the items subject to potential reimbursement. (see instructions)		
Are any of the items on this schedule deductible under Reg. section 20.2053-4(b) and Reg. section 20.2053-4(c)? . . .		X
If "Yes," attach a statement indicating the applicable provision and documenting the value of the claim.		

Item number	Debts of the Decedent—Creditor and nature of debt, and allowable death taxes	Amount
1	Internal Revenue Service, federal income tax for 2012	29,470
2	Illinois Department of Revenue, state income taxes for 2012	4,700
3	Investors Bank, Wheeling, IL, credit card purchases from November 22 to December 21, 2012	750
4	Roberts and Oaks, Wheeling, IL legal services rendered from October 1 to December 31, 2012	2,250
5	Unresolved claim filed against the estate by Martha Diversey, claiming a 50% ownership interest in the Olive Branch property (Sch. A, item 1)	
	Total from continuation schedules (or additional statements) attached to this schedule . . .	0
	TOTAL. (Also enter on Part 5—Recapitulation, page 3, at item 15.) . . .	37,170

Item number	Mortgages and Liens—Description	Amount
1	Mortgage on house and lot, 1455 Prescott Dr., Bartlett, IL (Sch. A, item 2), for which the decedent was personally liable. Mortgagee is Homeland Mortgage Co., Wheeling, IL. 20-year mortgage, dated January 1, 1999. Purchase amount $325,000; unpaid balance $115,000; interest at 6.5% per annum. Interest paid through December 1, 2012, prior to decedent's death.	115,000
2	Property taxes with respect to Sch. A, item 1. Taxes are lien on property.	8,000
3	Property taxes with respect to Sch. A, item 2. Taxes are lien on property.	7,200
4	Property taxes with respect to Sch. E, Part 1, item 1. Taxes are lien on property.	4,500
	Total from continuation schedules (or additional statements) attached to this schedule . . .	0
	TOTAL. (Also enter on Part 5—Recapitulation, page 3, at item 15.) . . .	134,700

(If more space is needed, attach the continuation schedule from the end of this package or additional statements of the same size.)

Schedule K

HTA

¶3060

¶ 3070   Filled-In Schedule L

The filled-in Schedule L of Form 706 relates to the James X. Diversey estate. See the fact situation at ¶2910.

Form 706 (Rev. 8-2013)

Estate of: James X. Diversey	Decedent's social security number 987-65-4321

SCHEDULE L—Net Losses During Administration and Expenses Incurred in Administering Property Not Subject to Claims

▶ Use Schedule PC to make a protective claim for refund due to an expense not currently deductible.
For such expenses, report the expense on Schedule L but without a value in the last column.

Item number	Net losses during administration (Note. Do not deduct losses claimed on a federal income tax return.)	Amount
1	Damages sustained to residence (Sch. E, item 1) resulting from high winds on Aug. 30, 2013. Loss was not covered by insurance.	4,878
	Total from continuation schedules (or additional statements) attached to this schedule	0
	TOTAL. (Also enter on Part 5—Recapitulation, page 3, at item 19.)	4,878

Item number	Expenses incurred in administering property not subject to claims. (Indicate whether estimated, agreed upon, or paid.)	Amount
1	National Bank, Wheeling, IL, trustees fees for James X. Diversey Revocable Trust (see Sch. G, item B.1)	1,500
	Total from continuation schedules (or additional statements) attached to this schedule	0
	TOTAL. (Also enter on Part 5—Recapitulation, page 3, at item 20.)	1,500

(If more space is needed, attach the continuation schedule from the end of this package or additional statements of the same size.)

HTA

Schedule L

¶3070

¶ 3080   Filled-In Schedule M

The filled-in Schedule M of Form 706 relates to the James X. Diversey estate. See the fact situation at ¶2910.

Form 706 (Rev. 8-2013)

	Decedent's social security number
Estate of: James X. Diversey	987-65-4321

SCHEDULE M—Bequests, etc., to Surviving Spouse

Note. If the value of the gross estate, together with the amount of adjusted taxable gifts, is less than the basic exclusion amount and the Form 706 is being filed solely to elect portability of the DSUE amount, consideration should be given as to whether you are required to report the value of assets eligible for the marital or charitable deduction on this schedule. See the instructions and Reg. section 20.2010-2T (a)(7)(ii) for more information. If you are not required to report the value of an asset, identify the property but make no entry in the last column.

		Yes	No
1	Did any property pass to the surviving spouse as a result of a qualified disclaimer? **1**		X
	If "Yes," attach a copy of the written disclaimer required by section 2518(b).		
2 a	In what country was the surviving spouse born? United States		
b	What is the surviving spouse's date of birth? 2/22/1938		
c	Is the surviving spouse a U.S. citizen? . . . . **2c** X		
d	If the surviving spouse is a naturalized citizen, when did the surviving spouse acquire citizenship?		
e	If the surviving spouse is not a U.S. citizen, of what country is the surviving spouse a citizen?		
3	**Election Out of QTIP Treatment of Annuities.** Do you elect under section 2056(b)(7)(C)(ii) not to treat as qualified terminable interest property any joint and survivor annuities that are included in the gross estate and would otherwise be treated as qualified terminable interest property under section 2056(b)(7)(C)? (see instructions) . . . **3**		X

Item number	Description of property interests passing to surviving spouse. For securities, give CUSIP number. If trust, partnership, or closely held entity, give EIN	Amount
	QTIP property:	
A1	Property passing to Carrie M. Diversey Marital Trust under will of James X. Diversey. Under terms of will, an amount equal to $3 million less the value of all other property passing to Carrie M. Diveresy passes to the marital trust. See attached list of assets.	1,358,600
	All other property:	
B1	Proceeds of Provisional Life Insurance Co. policy (Sch. D, item 1)	825,000
2	One half of the value of the home and lot, held in tenancy by entirety (Sch. E, part 1, item 1)	375,000
3	One-half of the value of the checking account (Sch. E, part 1, item 2)	12,500
4	One-half of the value of the savings account (Sch. E, part 1, item 3)	48,000
5	2009 Lincoln Town Car, bequest under Art III of will (Sch. F, item 3)	19,500
6	Household goods, bequest under Art. III of will (Sch. F, item 4)	31,400
7	11% limited partnership interest in Diversey FLP, bequest under Art. III of will (Sch. F, item 1)	285,000
8	1% general partnership interest in Diversey FLP, bequest under Art. III of will (Sch. F, item 2)	45,000

	Total from continuation schedules (or additional statements) attached to this schedule		0
4	Total amount of property interests listed on Schedule M **4**		3,000,000
5 a	Federal estate taxes payable out of property interests listed on Schedule M . . . **5a**		
b	Other death taxes payable out of property interests listed on Schedule M **5b**		
c	Federal and state GST taxes payable out of property interests listed on Schedule M . . . **5c**		
d	Add items 5a, 5b, and 5c **5d**		0
6	Net amount of property interests listed on Schedule M (subtract 5d from 4). Also enter on Part 5— Recapitulation, page 3, at item 21 . . . . **6**		3,000,000

(If more space is needed, attach the continuation schedule from the end of this package or additional statements of the same size.)

Schedule M

HTA

¶ 3100   Filled-In Schedule O

The filled-in Schedule O of Form 706 relates to the James X. Diversey estate. See the fact situation at ¶2910.

Form 706 (Rev. 8-2013)

Estate of: James X. Diversey	Decedent's social security number
	987-65-4321

SCHEDULE O—Charitable, Public, and Similar Gifts and Bequests

Note. If the value of the gross estate, together with the amount of adjusted taxable gifts, is less than the basic exclusion amount and the Form 706 is being filed solely to elect portability of the DSUE amount, consideration should be given as to whether you are required to report the value of assets eligible for the marital or charitable deduction on this schedule. See the instructions and Reg. section 20.2010-2T (a)(7)(ii) for more information. If you are not required to report the value of an asset, identify the property but make no entry in the last column.

		Yes	No
1 a	If the transfer was made by will, has any action been instituted to contest or have interpreted any of its provisions affecting the charitable deductions claimed in this schedule?		X
	If "Yes," full details must be submitted with this schedule.		
b	According to the information and belief of the person or persons filing this return, is any such action planned?		X
	If "Yes," full details must be submitted with this schedule.		
2	Did any property pass to charity as the result of a qualified disclaimer?		X
	If "Yes," attach a copy of the written disclaimer required by section 2518(b).		

Item number	Name and address of beneficiary	Character of institution	Amount
1	Gessner Art Museum, Chicago, IL. Bequest of art collection under decedent's will (Sch. F, item 5)	Museum	162,000
2	American Heart Association, Chicago, IL. Cash bequest under Art. III of decedent's will.	Medical research	50,000

Total from continuation schedules (or additional statements) attached to this schedule		0
3	Total **3**	212,000

4 a	Federal estate tax payable out of property interests listed above	**4a**	
b	Other death taxes payable out of property interests listed above	**4b**	
c	Federal and state GST taxes payable out of property interests listed above . . .	**4c**	
d	Add items 4a, 4b, and 4c	**4d**	0
5	Net value of property interests listed above (subtract 4d from 3). Also enter on Part 5—Recapitulation, page 3, at item 22	**5**	212,000

(If more space is needed, attach the continuation schedule from the end of this package or additional statements of the same size.)

HTA

Schedule O

¶ 3110   Filled-In Worksheet for Schedule Q

The filled-in Worksheet for Schedule Q of Form 706 relates to the James X. Diversey estate. See the fact situation at ¶2910.

Worksheet for Schedule Q - Credit for Tax on Prior Transfers

Part I   Transferor's tax on prior transfers

Item	A	B	C	D	E	F	G	H	I	Total for all transfers (line 8 only)
1. Gross value of prior transfer to this transferee	750,000									
2. Death taxes payable from prior transfer										
3. Encumbrances allocable to prior transfer										
4. Obligations allocable to prior transfer										
5. Marital deduction applicable to line 1 above, as shown on transferor's Form 706										
6. TOTAL (Add lines 2, 3, 4, and 5)	0	0	0	0	0	0	0	0	0	
7. NET VALUE OF TRANSFERS (Subtract line 6 from line 1)	750,000	0	0	0	0	0	0	0	0	
8. NET VALUE OF TRANSFER (Add columns A, B, and C of line 7)										750,000
9. Transferor's taxable estate	6,000,000									
10. Federal estate tax paid	811,778									
11. State death taxes paid	680,634									
12. Foreign death taxes paid										
13. Other death taxes paid										
14. TOTAL TAXES PAID (Add lines 10, 11, 12, and 13)	1,492,412	0	0	0	0	0	0	0	0	
15. VALUE OF TRANSFEROR'S ESTATE (Subtract line 14 from line 9)	6,507,588	0	0	0	0	0	0	0	0	
16. Net Federal estate tax paid on transferor's estate	811,778									
17. Credit for gift tax paid on transferor's estate with respect to pre-1977 gifts (section 2012)										
18. Credit allowed transferor's estate for tax on prior transfers from prior transferor(s) who died within 10 years before death of decedent										
19. TAX ON TRANSFEROR'S ESTATE (Add lines 16, 17, and 18)	811,778	0	0	0	0	0	0	0	0	
20. Transferor's tax on prior transfers ((Line 7/ line 15) x line 19 of respective estates)	93,557	0	0	0	0	0	0	0	0	

Part II   Transferee's tax on prior transfers

Item		Amount
21. Transferee's actual tax before allowance of credit for prior transfers (see instructions)	21	377,272
22. Total gross estate of transferee (from line 1 of the Tax Computation, page 1, Form 706)	22	9,344,810
23. Net value of all transfers (from line 8 of this worksheet)	23	750,000
24. Transferee's reduced gross estate. Subtract line 23 from line 22	24	8,594,810
25. Total debts and deductions (not including marital and charitable deductions) (line 3b of Part 2 - Tax Computation, page 1 and items 18, 19, and 20 of the Recapitulation, page 3, Form 706)	25 764,630	
26. Marital deduction from item 21, Recapitulation, page 3, Form 706 (see instructions)	26 3,000,000	
27. Charitable bequests from item 22, Recapitulation, page 3, Form 706	27 212,000	
28. Charitable deduction proportion ([line 23 / (line 22 - line 25)] x line 27)	28 18,531	
29. Reduced charitable deduction. Subtract line 28 from line 27	29 193,469	
30. Transferee's deduction as adjusted. Add lines 25, 26, and 29	30	3,958,099
31. (a) Transferee's reduced taxable estate. Subtract line 30 from line 24	31(a)	4,636,711
(b) Adjusted taxable gifts	31(b)	750,000
(c) Total reduced taxable estate. Add lines 31(a) and 31 (b)	31(c)	5,386,711
32. Tentative tax on reduced taxable estate	32 2,100,484	
33. (a) Post-1976 gift taxes paid	33(a) 0	
(b) Unified credit (applicable credit amount)	33(b) 2,045,800	
(c) Section 2012 gift tax credit	33(c)	
(d) Section 2014 foreign death tax credit	33(d)	
(e) Total credits. Add lines 33(a) through 33(d)	33(e) 2,045,800	
34. Net tax on reduced taxable estate. Subtract line 33(e) from line 32	34	54,684
35. Transferee's tax on prior transfers. Subtract line 34 from line 21	35	322,588

Instructions for Schedules; Sch. Q Worksheet; Index

¶ 3120   Filled-In Schedule Q

The filled-in Schedule Q of Form 706 relates to the James X. Diversey estate. See the fact situation at ¶2910.

SCHEDULE Q—Credit for Tax on Prior Transfers

Part 1. Transferor Information

	Name of transferor	Social security number	IRS office where estate tax return was filed	Date of death
A	Albert Smith	333-33-3333	Cincinnati, OH	7/1/2012
B				
C				

Check here ▶ ☐ if section 2013(f) (special valuation of farm, etc., real property) adjustments to the computation of the credit were made (see instructions).

Part 2. Computation of Credit (see instructions)

Item	A	B	C	Total A, B, & C
		Transferor		
1 Transferee's tax as apportioned (from worksheet, (line 7 ÷ line 8) × line 35 for each column)	322,588			
2 Transferor's tax (from each column of worksheet, line 20)	93,557			
3 Maximum amount before percentage requirement (for each column, enter amount from line 1 or 2, whichever is smaller)	93,557	0	0	
4 Percentage allowed (each column) (see instructions)	100.00%			
5 Credit allowable (line 3 × line 4 for each column)	93,557	0	0	
6 TOTAL credit allowable (add columns A, B, and C of line 5. Enter here and on line 14 of Part 2—Tax Computation				93,557

HTA

¶ 3130   Filled-In Schedule R

The filled-in Schedule R of Form 706 relates to the James X. Diversey estate. See the fact situation at ¶2910.

Form 706 (Rev. 8-2013)

SCHEDULE R—Generation-Skipping Transfer Tax

Note. To avoid application of the deemed allocation rules, Form 706 and Schedule R should be filed to allocate the GST exemption to trusts that may later have taxable terminations or distributions under section 2612 even if the form is not required to be filed to report estate or GST tax.

The GST tax is imposed on taxable transfers of interests in property located outside the United States as well as property located inside the United States. (see instructions)

Part 1. GST Exemption Reconciliation (Section 2631) and Special QTIP Election (Section 2652(a)(3))

You no longer need to check a box to make a section 2652(a)(3) (special QTIP) election. If you list qualifying property in Part 1, line 9 below, you will be considered to have made this election. See instructions for details.

1	Maximum allowable GST exemption **1**	5,250,000
2	Total GST exemption allocated by the decedent against decedent's lifetime transfers **2**	
3	Total GST exemption allocated by the executor, using Form 709, against decedent's lifetime transfers **3**	
4	GST exemption allocated on line 6 of Schedule R, Part 2 . . . . **4**	
5	GST exemption allocated on line 6 of Schedule R, Part 3 . . . . **5**	450,000
6	Total GST exemption allocated on line 4 of Schedule(s) R-1 . . . . **6**	
7	Total GST exemption allocated to *inter vivos* transfers and direct skips (add lines 2–6) **7**	450,000
8	GST exemption available to allocate to trusts and section 2032A interests (subtract line 7 from line 1) **8**	4,800,000

9   Allocation of GST exemption to trusts (as defined for GST tax purposes):

A Name of trust	B Trust's EIN (if any)	C GST exemption allocated on lines 2–6, above (see instructions)	D Additional GST exemption allocated (see instructions)	E Trust's inclusion ratio (optional—see instructions)

9 D Total. May not exceed line 8, above **9D**		0
10 GST exemption available to allocate to section 2032A interests received by individual beneficiaries (subtract line 9D from line 8). You must attach special-use allocation statement (see instructions) . . **10**		0

Schedule R

HTA

Form 706 (Rev. 8-2013)

| Estate of: | James X Diversey | Decedent's social security number 987-65-4321 |

Part 2. Direct Skips Where the Property Interests Transferred Bear the GST Tax on the Direct Skips

Name of skip person	Description of property interest transferred	Estate tax value

Total from continuation schedules (or additional sheets) attached to this schedule . 0

1	Total estate tax values of all property interests listed above	1	0
2	Estate taxes, state death taxes, and other charges borne by the property interests listed above . . .	2	
3	GST taxes borne by the property interests listed above but imposed on direct skips other than those shown on this Part 2 (see instructions)	3	
4	Total fixed taxes and other charges (add lines 2 and 3)	4	0
5	Total tentative maximum direct skips (subtract line 4 from line 1)	5	0
6	GST exemption allocated	6	
7	Subtract line 6 from line 5	7	0
8	GST tax due (divide line 7 by 3.5)	8	0
9	Enter the amount from line 8 of Schedule R, Part 3	9	
10	Total GST taxes payable by the estate (add lines 8 and 9). Enter here and on line 17 of Part 2—Tax Computation	10	0

Schedule R

¶3130

Filled-In Forms

Form 706 (Rev. 8-2013)

	Decedent's social security number
Estate of: James X. Diversey	987-65-4321

Part 3. Direct Skips Where the Property Interests Transferred Do Not Bear the GST Tax on the Direct Skips

Name of skip person	Description of property interest transferred	Estate tax value
Katherine Diversey	1,000 shs. Diversco, Inc. (Sch. B, item 7). Under Art. II of decedent's will, all federal estate and generation-skipping transfer taxes are payable from the residuary estate	450,000

	Total from continuation schedules (or additional sheets) attached to this schedule .		0
1	Total estate tax values of all property interests listed above	1	450,000
2	Estate taxes, state death taxes, and other charges borne by the property interests listed above . .	2	
3	GST taxes borne by the property interests listed above but imposed on direct skips other than those shown on this Part 3 (see instructions)	3	
4	Total fixed taxes and other charges (add lines 2 and 3)	4	0
5	Total tentative maximum direct skips (subtract line 4 from line 1)	5	450,000
6	GST exemption allocated	6	450,000
7	Subtract line 6 from line 5	7	0
8	GST tax due (multiply line 7 by .40). Enter here and on Schedule R, Part 2, line 9	8	0

Schedule R

¶ 3135   Filled-In Schedule PC

The filled-in Schedule PC of Form 706 relates to the James X. Diversey estate. See the fact situation at ¶ 2910.

Schedule **PC** Rev. August 2013) Department of the Treasury Internal Revenue Service	**Protective Claim for Refund**	OMB No. 1545-0015
	▶ To be used for decedents dying after December 31, 2011. File 2 copies of this schedule with Form 706 for each pending claim or expense under section 2053.	

- Timely filing a protective claim for refund preserves the estate's right to claim a refund based on the amount of an unresolved claim or expense that may not become deductible under section 2053 until after the limitation period ends.

- Schedule PC can be used to file a protective claim for refund and, once the claim or expense becomes deductible, Schedule PC can be used to notify the IRS that a refund is being claimed.

- Schedule PC can be used by the estate of a decedent dying after 2011.

- Schedule PC must be filed with Form 706 and cannot be filed separately. (To file a protective claim for refund or notify the IRS that a refund is being claimed in a form separate from the Form 706, instead use Form 843, Claim for Refund and Request for Abatement.)

- Each separate claim or expense requires a separate Schedule PC (or Form 843, if not filed with Form 706).

- Schedule PC must be filed in duplicate (two copies) for each separate claim or expense.

Part 1. General Information

1. Name of decedent James X. Diversey	2. Decedent's social security number 987-65-4321
3. Name of fiduciary Carrie M. Divsery	4. Date of death 1/1/2013
5a. Address (number, street, and room or suite no.) 123 Cory St.	5b. Room or suite no.
5c. City or town, state, and ZIP or postal code Wheeling, IL 60090	6. Daytime telephone number (847) 123-4567

7. Number of Claims. Enter number of Schedules PC being filed with Form 706. _____ 1

If the number is greater than one OR if another Schedule PC or Form 843 was previously filed by or on behalf of the estate, complete Part 3 of this Schedule PC.

8. Fiduciary [X] Check here if this Schedule PC is being filed with the original Form 706 or is being filed by the same fiduciary who filed the original Form 706 for decedent's estate. If a different fiduciary is filing this Schedule PC, see instructions for establishing the legal authority to pursue the claim for refund on behalf of the estate.

Part 2. Claim Information

Check the box that applies to this claim for refund.

a. [X] Protective claim for refund made for unresolved claim or expense.

   Amount in contest: _____ 425,000

b. [ ] Partial refund claimed: partial resolution and/or satisfaction of claim or expense for which a protective claim for refund has been filed previously.

   Date protective claim for refund filed for this claim or expense: _____

   Amount of claim or expense partially resolved and/or satisfied and presently claimed as a deduction under section 2053 (do not include amounts previously deducted): _____

c. [ ] Full and final refund claimed for this claim or expense: resolution and/or satisfaction of claim or expense for which a protective claim for refund has been filed previously.

   Date protective claim for refund filed for this claim or expense: _____

   Amount of claim or expense finally resolved and/or satisfied and presently claimed as a deduction under section 2053 (do not include amounts previously deducted): _____

HTA

Schedule PC

Form 706 (Rev. 8-2013)

Estate of: James X. Diversey

		Decedent's social security number
		987-65-4321

A Form 706 Schedule and Item number	B Identification of the claim • Name or names of the claimant(s) • Basis of the claim or other description of the pending claim or expense • Reasons and contingencies delaying resolution • Status of contested matters • Attach copies of relevant pleadings or other documents	C Amount, if any, deducted under Treas. Reg. sections 20.2053-1(d)(4) or 20.2053-4 (b) or (c) for the identified claim or expense	D Amount presently claimed as a deduction under section 2053 for the identified claim	E Ancillary expenses estimated/ agreed upon/paid (Please indicate)	F Amount of tax to be refunded
Sch. K, item 5	Claim filed against the estate by Martha Diversey claiming a 50% interest in the Olive Branch property (Sch. A, item 1). Litigation is still pending at the time of filing. Pleadings attached.				

Part 3. Other Schedules PC and Forms 843 Filed by Estate

If a Schedule PC or Form 843 was previously filed by the estate, complete Part 3 to identify each claim for refund reported.

A Date of death 1/1/2013	B Internal Revenue office where filed	C Date filed	D Indicate whether (1) Protective Claim for Refund; (2) Partial Claim for Refund; or (3) Full and Final Claim for Refund	E Amount in Contest
1				

To inquire about the receipt and/or processing of the protective claim for refund, please call (866) 699-4083.

(Rev. 8-2013)

Schedule PC

¶ 3140   Portability Example

James X. Diversey, the hypothetical decedent in the main Form 706 example (see ¶2910), did not have any Deceased Spousal Unused Exclusion (DSUE) amount. The following filled-in forms (Form 706) (Rev. August 2013), relate to the fact pattern below.

Dean and Ann Elmer married in 1962. On March 13, 2013, Dean died. At the time of his death, he had made no lifetime gifts and had a gross estate valued at $5 million. Pursuant to his will, $500,000 was bequeathed to his church, Orchard Park Presbyterian Church, with the remainder of his estate passing to his wife outright.

On August 28, 2013, Ann died. At the time of her death, Ann had made no lifetime gifts. Her gross estate, including the $4.5 million received from Dean, was valued at $14.8 million. Her will directed that $500,000 was to be given to Orchard Park Presbyterian Church. After deductions for funeral and administration expenses, Ann's taxable estate was approximately $14.25 million. The amount remaining after payment of taxes was bequeathed to trusts benefitting the couple's children, Miranda Cole and Paul Elmer.

Paul was appointed the executor of both estates. Paul filed a Form 706 for Dean's estate, making the portability election, even though his father's estate owed no federal estate tax as a result of the marital and charitable deductions. Pursuant to Reg. § 20.2010-2T(a)(7), Paul was not required to report the value of the property subject to the marital and charitable deductions. Paul certified on the estate return that the estate's value was his best estimate, determined by exercising due diligence, of the fair market value of the gross estate in accordance with Reg. § 20.2010-2T(a)(7)(ii)(B). On the Form 706 filed for Ann's estate, Dean's DSUE amount was applied to result in a combined applicable exclusion amount of $10.5 million.

The filled-in Form 706 relates to the Dean Elmer estate.

Form **706** (Rev. August 2013)	United States Estate (and Generation-Skipping Transfer) Tax Return		OMB No. 1545-0015

Department of the Treasury
Internal Revenue Service

▶ Estate of a citizen or resident of the United States (see instructions). To be filed for decedents dying after December 31, 2012.
▶ Information about Form 706 and its separate instructions is at *www.irs.gov/form706.*

Part 1—Decedent and Executor

1a Decedent's first name and middle initial (and maiden name, if any)	**1b** Decedent's last name	**2** Decedent's social security no.
Dean J.	Elmer	121-21-2121

3a City, town, or post office; county; state or province; country; and ZIP or foreign postal code.	**3b** Year domicile established	**4** Date of birth	**5** Date of death
Marion, IN 46202	1973	10/15/1938	3/13/2013

6b Executor's address (number and street including apartment or suite no.; city, town, or post office; state or province; country; and ZIP or foreign postal code) and phone no.

6a Name of executor (see instructions)
Paul D. Elmer

1830 W. Prospect St.
Bartlett, IL 60103

6c Executor's social security number (see instructions)
444-55-6677

Phone no. (630) 555-5555

6d If there are multiple executors, check here ☐ and attach a list showing the names, addresses, telephone numbers, and SSNs of the additional executors.

7a Name and location of court where will was probated or estate administered
Marion Superior Court, 200 E. Washington St., Indianapolis, IN 46204

7b Case number
CV: 12-4652

8 If decedent died testate, check here ▶ ☒ and attach a certified copy of the will. **9** If you extended the time to file this Form 706, check here ▶ ☐

10 If Schedule R-1 is attached, check here ▶ ☐ **11** If you are estimating the value of assets included in the gross estate on line 1 pursuant to the special rule of Reg. section 20.2010-2T(a) (7)(ii), check here ▶ ☒

Part 2—Tax Computation

1	Total gross estate less exclusion (from Part 5—Recapitulation, item 13)	**1**	5,000,000
2	Tentative total allowable deductions (from Part 5—Recapitulation, item 24)	**2**	5,000,000
3 a	Tentative taxable estate (subtract line 2 from line 1)	**3a**	0
b	State death tax deduction	**3b**	
c	Taxable estate (subtract line 3b from line 3a)	**3c**	0
4	Adjusted taxable gifts (see instructions)	**4**	
5	Add lines 3c and 4	**5**	0
6	Tentative tax on the amount on line 5 from Table A in the instructions	**6**	0
7	Total gift tax paid or payable (see instructions)	**7**	0
8	Gross estate tax (subtract line 7 from line 6)	**8**	0
9 a	Basic exclusion amount	**9a** 5,250,000	
b	Deceased spousal unused exclusion (DSUE) amount from predeceased spouse(s), if any (from Section D, Part 6-Portability of Deceased Spousal Unused Exclusion)	**9b** 0	
c	Applicable exclusion amount (add lines 9a and 9b)	**9c** 5,250,000	
d	Applicable credit amount (tentative tax on the amount in 9c from Table A in the instructions)	**9d** 2,045,800	
10	Adjustment to applicable credit amount (May not exceed $6,000. See instructions.)	**10**	
11	Allowable applicable credit amount (subtract line 10 from line 9d)	**11**	2,045,800
12	Subtract line 11 from line 8 (but do not enter less than zero)	**12**	0
13	Credit for foreign death taxes (from Schedule P). (Attach Form(s) 706-CE.)	**13**	
14	Credit for tax on prior transfers (from Schedule Q)	**14**	
15	Total credits (add lines 13 and 14)	**15**	0
16	Net estate tax (subtract line 15 from line 12)	**16**	0
17	Generation-skipping transfer (GST) taxes payable (from Schedule R, Part 2, line 10)	**17**	0
18	Total transfer taxes (add lines 16 and 17)	**18**	0
19	Prior payments (explain in an attached statement)	**19**	0
20	Balance due (or overpayment) (subtract line 19 from line 18)	**20**	0

Under penalties of perjury, I declare that I have examined this return, including accompanying schedules and statements, and to the best of my knowledge and belief, it is true, correct, and complete. Declaration of preparer other than the executor is based on all information of which preparer has any knowledge.

Sign Here

Signature of executor   *Paul D. Elmer*   Date 12/13/2013

Signature of executor   Date

Paid Preparer Use Only

Print/Type preparer's name	Preparer's signature	Date	Check ☐ if self-employed	PTIN
Firm's name ▶			Firm's EIN ▶	
Firm's address ▶			Phone no.	

For Privacy Act and Paperwork Reduction Act Notice, see instructions.   Form **706** (Rev. 8-2013)

HTA

Filled-In Forms 557

Form 706 (Rev. 8-2013)

Estate of: Dean J. Elmer

	Decedent's social security number
	121-21-2121

Part 3—Elections by the Executor

Note. For information on electing portability of the decedent's DSUE amount, including how to opt out of the election, see Part 6—Portability of Deceased Spousal Unused Exclusion.

Note. Some of the following elections may require the posting of bonds or liens.

Please check "Yes" or "No" box for each question (see instructions).

			Yes	No
1	Do you elect alternate valuation?	1		X
2	Do you elect special-use valuation? If "Yes," you must complete and attach Schedule A-1	2		X
3	Do you elect to pay the taxes in installments as described in section 6166?			X
	If "Yes," you must attach the additional information described in the instructions.			
	Note. By electing section 6166 installment payments, you may be required to provide security for estate tax deferred under section 6166 and interest in the form of a surety bond or a section 6324A lien.	3		
4	Do you elect to postpone the part of the taxes due to a reversionary or remainder interest as described in section 6163?	4		X

Part 4—General Information

Note. Please attach the necessary supplemental documents. **You must attach the death certificate.** (See instructions)

Authorization to receive confidential tax information under Reg. section 601.504(b)(2)(i); to act as the estate's representative before the IRS; and to make written or oral presentations on behalf of the estate:

Name of representative (print or type)	State	Address (number, street, and room or suite no., city, state, and ZIP code)

I declare that I am the ☐ attorney/ ☐ certified public accountant/ ☐ enrolled agent (check the applicable box) for the executor. I am not under suspension or disbarment from practice before the Internal Revenue Service and am qualified to practice in the state shown above.

Signature		CAF number	Date	Telephone number

1 Death certificate number and issuing authority (attach a copy of the death certificate to this return).
MA-12-4590x   Indiana State Department of Health

2 Decedent's business or occupation. If retired, check here ▶ [X] and state decedent's former business or occupation.
Doctor

3a Marital status of the decedent at time of death:
[X] Married   ☐ Widow/widower   ☐ Single   ☐ Legally separated   ☐ Divorced

3b For all prior marriages, list the name and SSN of the former spouse, the date the marriage ended, and whether the marriage ended by annulment, divorce, or death. Attach additional statements of the same size if necessary.

4a Surviving spouse's name	4b Social security number	4c Amount received (see instructions)
Ann E. Elmer	212-12-1212	4,500,000

5 Individuals (other than the surviving spouse), trusts, or other estates who receive benefits from the estate (do not include charitable beneficiaries shown in Schedule O) (see instructions).

Name of individual, trust, or estate receiving $5,000 or more	Identifying number	Relationship to decedent	Amount (see instructions)

All unascertainable beneficiaries and those who receive less than $5,000 ▶

Total	0

If you answer "Yes" to any of the following questions, you must attach additional information as described.

		Yes	No
6	Is the estate filing a protective claim for refund?		X
	If "Yes," complete and attach two copies of Schedule PC for each claim.		
7	Does the gross estate contain any section 2044 property (qualified terminable interest property (QTIP) from a prior gift or estate)? (see instructions)		X
8a	Have federal gift tax returns ever been filed?		X
	If "Yes," attach copies of the returns, if available, and furnish the following information:		
b	Period(s) covered	c Internal Revenue office(s) where filed	
9a	Was there any insurance on the decedent's life that is not included on the return as part of the gross estate?		X
b	Did the decedent own any insurance on the life of another that is not included in the gross estate?		X

Page 2

¶3140

Form 706 (Rev. 8-2013)

	Decedent's social security number
Estate of: Dean J. Elmer	121-21-2121

Part 4—General Information *(continued)*

If you answer "Yes" to any of the following questions, you must attach additional information as described.

		Yes	No
10	Did the decedent at the time of death own any property as a joint tenant with right of survivorship in which (a) one or more of the other joint tenants was someone other than the decedent's spouse, and (b) less than the full value of the property is included on the return as part of the gross estate? If "Yes," you must complete and attach Schedule E		X
11 a	Did the decedent, at the time of death, own any interest in a partnership (for example, a family limited partnership), an unincorporated business, or a limited liability company; or own any stock in an inactive or closely held corporation?		X
b	If "Yes," was the value of **any** interest owned (from above) discounted on this estate tax return? If "Yes," see the instructions on reporting the total accumulated or effective discounts taken on Schedule F or G		X
12	Did the decedent make any transfer described in sections 2035, 2036, 2037, or 2038? (see instructions) If "Yes," you must complete and attach Schedule G		X
13 a	Were there in existence at the time of the decedent's death any trusts created by the decedent during his or her lifetime?		X
b	Were there in existence at the time of the decedent's death any trusts not created by the decedent under which the decedent possessed any power, beneficial interest, or trusteeship?		X
c	Was the decedent receiving income from a trust created after October 22, 1986, by a parent or grandparent?		X
	If "Yes," was there a GST taxable termination (under section 2612) on the death of the decedent?		X
d	If there was a GST taxable termination (under section 2612), attach a statement to explain. Provide a copy of the trust or will creating the trust, and give the name, address, and phone number of the current trustee(s).		
e	Did the decedent at any time during his or her lifetime transfer or sell an interest in a partnership, limited liability company, or closely held corporation to a trust described in lines 13a or 13b?		X
	If "Yes," provide the EIN for this transferred/sold item. ▶		
14	Did the decedent ever possess, exercise, or release any general power of appointment? If "Yes," you must complete and attach Schedule H		X
15	Did the decedent have an interest in or a signature or other authority over a financial account in a foreign country, such as a bank account, securities account, or other financial account?		X
16	Was the decedent, immediately before death, receiving an annuity described in the "General" paragraph of the instructions for Schedule I or a private annuity? If "Yes," you must complete and attach Schedule I		X
17	Was the decedent ever the beneficiary of a trust for which a deduction was claimed by the estate of a predeceased spouse under section 2056(b)(7) and which is not reported on this return? If "Yes," attach an explanation		X

Part 5—Recapitulation.

Note. If estimating the value of one or more assets pursuant to the special rule of Reg. section 20.2010-2T(a)(7)(ii), enter on both lines 10 and 23 the amount noted in the instructions for the corresponding range of values. (See instructions for details.)

Item no.	Gross estate		Alternate value	Value at date of death
1	Schedule A—Real Estate	1	0	0
2	Schedule B—Stocks and Bonds	2	0	0
3	Schedule C—Mortgages, Notes, and Cash	3	0	0
4	Schedule D—Insurance on the Decedent's Life (attach Form(s) 712)	4	0	0
5	Schedule E—Jointly Owned Property (attach Form(s) 712 for life insurance)	5	0	0
6	Schedule F—Other Miscellaneous Property (attach Form(s) 712 for life insurance)	6	0	0
7	Schedule G—Transfers During Decedent's Life (att. Form(s) 712 for life insurance)	7	0	0
8	Schedule H—Powers of Appointment	8	0	0
9	Schedule I—Annuities	9	0	0
10	Estimated value of assets subject to the special rule of Reg. section 20.2010-2T(a)(7)(ii)	10		5,000,000
11	Total gross estate (add items 1 through 10)	11	0	5,000,000
12	Schedule U—Qualified Conservation Easement Exclusion	12		0
13	Total gross estate less exclusion (subtract item 12 from item 11). Enter here and on line 1 of Part 2—Tax Computation	13	0	5,000,000

Item no.	Deductions		Amount
14	Schedule J—Funeral Expenses and Expenses Incurred in Administering Property Subject to Claims	14	0
15	Schedule K—Debts of the Decedent	15	0
16	Schedule K—Mortgages and Liens	16	0
17	Total of items 14 through 16	17	0
18	Allowable amount of deductions from item 17 (see the instructions for item 18 of the Recapitulation)	18	0
19	Schedule L—Net Losses During Administration	19	0
20	Schedule L—Expenses Incurred in Administering Property Not Subject to Claims	20	0
21	Schedule M—Bequests, etc., to Surviving Spouse	21	0
22	Schedule O—Charitable, Public, and Similar Gifts and Bequests	22	0
23	Estimated value of assets subject to the special rule of Reg. section 20.2010-2T(a)(7)(ii)	23	5,000,000
24	Tentative total allowable deductions (add items 18 through 23). Enter here and on line 2 of the Tax Computation	24	5,000,000

Page 3

Form 706 (Rev. 8-2013)

Estate of: Dean J. Elmer	Decedent's social security number
	121-21-2121

Part 6—Portability of Deceased Spousal Unused Exclusion (DSUE)

Portability Election

A decedent with a surviving spouse elects portability of the deceased spousal unused exclusion (DSUE) amount, if any, by completing and timely-filing this return. No further action is required to elect portability of the DSUE amount to allow the surviving spouse to use the decedent's DSUE amount.

Section A. Opting Out of Portability

The estate of a decedent with a surviving spouse may opt out of electing portability of the DSUE amount. Check here and do not complete Sections B and C of Part 6 only if the estate opts NOT to elect portability of the DSUE amount. ☐

Section B. QDOT

	Yes	No
Are any assets of the estate being transferred to a qualified domestic trust (QDOT)?		X

If "Yes," the DSUE amount portable to a surviving spouse (calculated in Section C, below) is preliminary and shall be redetermined at the time of the final distribution or other taxable event imposing estate tax under section 2056A. See instructions for more details.

Section C. DSUE Amount Portable to the Surviving Spouse (To be completed by the estate of a decedent making a portability election.)

Complete the following calculation to determine the DSUE amount that can be transferred to the surviving spouse.

1	Enter the amount from line 9c, Part 2—Tax Computation	1	5,250,000
2	Reserved	2	
3	Enter the value of the cumulative lifetime gifts on which tax was paid or payable (see instructions)	3	0
4	Add lines 1 and 3	4	5,250,000
5	Enter amount from line 10, Part 2—Tax Computation	5	0
6	Divide amount on line 5 by 40% (0.40) (do not enter less than zero)	6	0
7	Subtract line 6 from line 4	7	5,250,000
8	Enter the amount from line 5, Part 2—Tax Computation	8	0
9	Subtract line 8 from line 7 (do not enter less than zero)	9	5,250,000
10	DSUE amount portable to surviving spouse (Enter lesser of line 9 or line 9a, Part 2 – Tax Computation) . .	10	5,250,000

Section D. DSUE Amount Received from Predeceased Spouse(s) (To be completed by the estate of a deceased surviving spouse with DSUE amount from predeceased spouse(s))

Provide the following information to determine the DSUE amount received from deceased spouses.

A Name of Deceased Spouse (dates of death after December 31, 2010, only)	B Date of Death (enter as mm/dd/yy)	C Portability Election Made?		D If "Yes," DSUE Amount Received from Spouse	E DSUE Amount Applied by Decedent to Lifetime Gifts	F Year of Form 709 Reporting Use of DSUE Amount Listed in col E	G Remaining DSUE Amount, if any (subtract col. E from col. D)
		Yes	No				
Part 1 — DSUE RECEIVED FROM LAST DECEASED SPOUSE							
Part 2 — DSUE RECEIVED FROM OTHER PREDECEASED SPOUSE(S) AND USED BY DECEDENT							0

Total (for all DSUE amounts from predeceased spouse(s) applied) . . . . . . | 0 |

Add the amount from Part 1, column D and the total from Part 2, column E. Enter the result on line 9b, Part 2—Tax Computation . . . . ▶ _____ 0

¶3140

Filled-In Forms

The filled-in Form 706 relates to the Ann Elmer estate.

Form **706** (Rev. August 2013)	United States Estate (and Generation-Skipping Transfer) Tax Return	OMB No. 1545-0015

Department of the Treasury
Internal Revenue Service

▶ Estate of a citizen or resident of the United States (see instructions). To be filed for decedents dying after December 31, 2012.
▶ Information about Form 706 and its separate instructions is at *www.irs.gov/form706*.

Part 1—Decedent and Executor

1a Decedent's first name and middle initial (and maiden name, if any)	1b Decedent's last name	2 Decedent's social security no.
Ann E. Carson	Elmer	212-12-1212

3a City, town, or post office; county; state or province; country; and ZIP or foreign postal code.	3b Year domicile established	4 Date of birth	5 Date of death
Marion, IN 46202	1973	5/13/1940	8/28/2013

6b Executor's address (number and street including apartment or suite no.; city, town, or post office; state or province; country; and ZIP or foreign postal code) and phone no.

6a Name of executor (see instructions)	
Paul D. Elmer	1830 W. Prospect St.
6c Executor's social security number (see instructions)	Bartlett, IL 60103
444-55-6677	Phone no. (630) 555-5555

6d If there are multiple executors, check here ☐ and attach a list showing the names, addresses, telephone numbers, and SSNs of the additional executors.

7a Name and location of court where will was probated or estate administered	7b Case number
Marion Superior Court, 200 E. Washington St., Indianapolis, IN 46204	CV: 12-4652

8 If decedent died testate, check here ▶ [X] and attach a certified copy of the will. 9 If you extended the time to file this Form 706, check here ▶ [X]

10 If Schedule R-1 is attached, check here ▶ ☐ 11 If you are estimating the value of assets included in the gross estate on line 1 pursuant to the special rule of Reg. section 20.2010-2T(a)(7)(ii), check here ▶ ☐

Part 2—Tax Computation

1	Total gross estate less exclusion (from Part 5—Recapitulation, item 13)	1	14,810,700
2	Tentative total allowable deductions (from Part 5—Recapitulation, item 24)	2	551,950
3 a	Tentative taxable estate (subtract line 2 from line 1)	3a	14,258,750
b	State death tax deduction	3b	
c	Taxable estate (subtract line 3b from line 3a)	3c	14,258,750
4	Adjusted taxable gifts (see instructions)	4	
5	Add lines 3c and 4	5	14,258,750
6	Tentative tax on the amount on line 5 from Table A in the instructions	6	5,649,300
7	Total gift tax paid or payable (see instructions)	7	0
8	Gross estate tax (subtract line 7 from line 6)	8	5,649,300
9 a	Basic exclusion amount	9a	5,250,000
9 b	Deceased spousal unused exclusion (DSUE) amount from predeceased spouse(s), if any (from Section D, Part 6-Portability of Deceased Spousal Unused Exclusion)	9b	5,250,000
9 c	Applicable exclusion amount (add lines 9a and 9b)	9c	10,500,000
9 d	Applicable credit amount (tentative tax on the amount in 9c from Table A in the instructions)	9d	4,145,800
10	Adjustment to applicable credit amount (May not exceed $6,000. See instructions.)	10	
11	Allowable applicable credit amount (subtract line 10 from line 9d)	11	4,145,800
12	Subtract line 11 from line 8 (but do not enter less than zero)	12	1,503,500
13	Credit for foreign death taxes (from Schedule P). (Attach Form(s) 706-CE.)	13	
14	Credit for tax on prior transfers (from Schedule Q)	14	
15	Total credits (add lines 13 and 14)	15	0
16	Net estate tax (subtract line 15 from line 12)	16	1,503,500
17	Generation-skipping transfer (GST) taxes payable (from Schedule R, Part 2, line 10)	17	0
18	Total transfer taxes (add lines 16 and 17)	18	1,503,500
19	Prior payments (explain in an attached statement)	19	0
20	Balance due (or overpayment) (subtract line 19 from line 18)	20	1,503,500

Under penalties of perjury, I declare that I have examined this return, including accompanying schedules and statements, and to the best of my knowledge and belief, it is true, correct, and complete. Declaration of preparer other than the executor is based on all information of which preparer has any knowledge.

Sign Here

▶ *Paul D. Elmer*	▶ Date 12/13/2013
Signature of executor	
Signature of executor	Date

Paid Preparer Use Only

Print/Type preparer's name	Preparer's signature	Date	Check ☐ if self-employed	PTIN
Firm's name ▶			Firm's EIN ▶	
Firm's address ▶			Phone no.	

For Privacy Act and Paperwork Reduction Act Notice, see instructions. Form **706** (Rev. 8-2013)

HTA

Form 706 (Rev. 8-2013)

Estate of: Ann E. Carson Elmer	Decedent's social security number
	212-12-1212

Part 3—Elections by the Executor

Note. For information on electing portability of the decedent's DSUE amount, including how to opt out of the election, see Part 6—Portability of Deceased Spousal Unused Exclusion.

Note. Some of the following elections may require the posting of bonds or liens.

Please check "Yes" or "No" box for each question (see instructions).

			Yes	No
1	Do you elect alternate valuation?	1		X
2	Do you elect special-use valuation? If "Yes," you must complete and attach Schedule A-1	2		X
3	Do you elect to pay the taxes in installments as described in section 6166?			X
	If "Yes," you must attach the additional information described in the instructions.			
	Note. By electing section 6166 installment payments, you may be required to provide security for estate tax deferred under section 6166 and interest in the form of a surety bond or a section 6324A lien.	3		
4	Do you elect to postpone the part of the taxes due to a reversionary or remainder interest as described in section 6163?	4		X

Part 4—General Information

Note. Please attach the necessary supplemental documents. **You must attach the death certificate.** (See instructions)

Authorization to receive confidential tax information under Reg. section 601.504(b)(2)(i); to act as the estate's representative before the IRS; and to make written or oral presentations on behalf of the estate:

Name of representative (print or type)	State	Address (number, street, and room or suite no., city, state, and ZIP code)

I declare that I am the ☐ attorney/ ☐ certified public accountant/ ☐ enrolled agent (check the applicable box) for the executor. I am not under suspension or disbarment from practice before the Internal Revenue Service and am qualified to practice in the state shown above.

Signature	CAF number	Date	Telephone number

1 Death certificate number and issuing authority (attach a copy of the death certificate to this return).

MA-12-6267x   Indiana State Department of Health

2 Decedent's business or occupation. If retired, check here ▶ ☒ and state decedent's former business or occupation.

Homemaker

3a Marital status of the decedent at time of death:

☐ Married   ☒ Widow/widower   ☐ Single   ☐ Legally separated   ☐ Divorced

3b For all prior marriages, list the name and SSN of the former spouse, the date the marriage ended, and whether the marriage ended by annulment, divorce, or death. Attach additional statements of the same size if necessary.

Dean J Elmer 121-21-2121, 3/13/2013. Ended due to death.

4a Surviving spouse's name	**4b** Social security number	**4c** Amount received (see instructions)
None		

5 Individuals (other than the surviving spouse), trusts, or other estates who receive benefits from the estate (do not include charitable beneficiaries shown in Schedule O) (see instructions).

Name of individual, trust, or estate receiving $5,000 or more	Identifying number	Relationship to decedent	Amount (see instructions)
Paul Elmer Family Trust	44-5566777	Trust	6,377,625
Miranda Cole Family Trust	44-5577888	Trust	6,377,625
All unascertainable beneficiaries and those who receive less than $5,000 ▶			
Total			12,755,250

If you answer "Yes" to any of the following questions, you must attach additional information as described.

			Yes	No
6	Is the estate filing a protective claim for refund?			X
	If "Yes," complete and attach two copies of Schedule PC for each claim.			
7	Does the gross estate contain any section 2044 property (qualified terminable interest property (QTIP) from a prior gift or estate)? (see instructions)			X
8a	Have federal gift tax returns ever been filed?			X
	If "Yes," attach copies of the returns, if available, and furnish the following information:			
b	Period(s) covered	c Internal Revenue office(s) where filed		
9a	Was there any insurance on the decedent's life that is not included on the return as part of the gross estate?			X
b	Did the decedent own any insurance on the life of another that is not included in the gross estate?			X

Page 2

Form 706 (Rev. 8-2013)

	Decedent's social security number
Estate of: Ann E. Carson Elmer	212-12-1212

Part 4—General Information *(continued)*

If you answer "Yes" to any of the following questions, you must attach additional information as described.		Yes	No
10	Did the decedent at the time of death own any property as a joint tenant with right of survivorship in which **(a)** one or more of the other joint tenants was someone other than the decedent's spouse, and **(b)** less than the full value of the property is included on the return as part of the gross estate? If "Yes," you must complete and attach Schedule E		X
11 a	Did the decedent, at the time of death, own any interest in a partnership (for example, a family limited partnership), an unincorporated business, or a limited liability company; or own any stock in an inactive or closely held corporation?		X
b	If "Yes," was the value of **any** interest owned (from above) discounted on this estate tax return? If "Yes," see the instructions on reporting the total accumulated or effective discounts taken on Schedule F or G		X
12	Did the decedent make any transfer described in sections 2035, 2036, 2037, or 2038? (see instructions) If "Yes," you must complete and attach Schedule G		X
13 a	Were there in existence at the time of the decedent's death any trusts created by the decedent during his or her lifetime?		X
b	Were there in existence at the time of the decedent's death any trusts not created by the decedent under which the decedent possessed any power, beneficial interest, or trusteeship?		X
c	Was the decedent receiving income from a trust created after October 22, 1986, by a parent or grandparent?		X
	If "Yes," was there a GST taxable termination (under section 2612) on the death of the decedent?		X
d	If there was a GST taxable termination (under section 2612), attach a statement to explain. Provide a copy of the trust or will creating the trust, and give the name, address, and phone number of the current trustee(s).		
e	Did the decedent at any time during his or her lifetime transfer or sell an interest in a partnership, limited liability company, or closely held corporation to a trust described in lines 13a or 13b?		X
	If "Yes," provide the EIN for this transferred/sold item. ▶		
14	Did the decedent ever possess, exercise, or release any general power of appointment? If "Yes," you must complete and attach Schedule H		X
15	Did the decedent have an interest in or a signature or other authority over a financial account in a foreign country, such as a bank account, securities account, or other financial account?		X
16	Was the decedent, immediately before death, receiving an annuity described in the "General" paragraph of the instructions for Schedule I or a private annuity? If "Yes," you must complete and attach Schedule I		X
17	Was the decedent ever the beneficiary of a trust for which a deduction was claimed by the estate of a predeceased spouse under section 2056(b)(7) and which is not reported on this return? If "Yes," attach an explanation		X

Part 5—Recapitulation. Note. If estimating the value of one or more assets pursuant to the special rule of Reg. section 20.2010-2T(a)(7)(ii), enter on both lines 10 and 23 the amount noted in the instructions for the corresponding range of values. (See instructions for details.)

Item no.	Gross estate		Alternate value	Value at date of death
1	Schedule A—Real Estate	1	0	2,170,000
2	Schedule B—Stocks and Bonds	2	0	2,664,500
3	Schedule C—Mortgages, Notes, and Cash	3	0	191,200
4	Schedule D—Insurance on the Decedent's Life (attach Form(s) 712)	4	0	5,000,000
5	Schedule E—Jointly Owned Property (attach Form(s) 712 for life insurance)	5	0	0
6	Schedule F—Other Miscellaneous Property (attach Form(s) 712 for life insurance)	6	0	4,785,000
7	Schedule G—Transfers During Decedent's Life (att. Form(s) 712 for life insurance)	7	0	0
8	Schedule H—Powers of Appointment	8	0	0
9	Schedule I—Annuities	9	0	0
10	Estimated value of assets subject to the special rule of Reg. section 20.2010-2T(a)(7)(ii)	10		
11	Total gross estate (add items 1 through 10)	11	0	14,810,700
12	Schedule U—Qualified Conservation Easement Exclusion	12		0
13	Total gross estate less exclusion (subtract item 12 from item 11). Enter here and on line 1 of Part 2—Tax Computation	13	0	14,810,700

Item no.	Deductions		Amount
14	Schedule J—Funeral Expenses and Expenses Incurred in Administering Property Subject to Claims	14	51,950
15	Schedule K—Debts of the Decedent	15	0
16	Schedule K—Mortgages and Liens	16	0
17	Total of items 14 through 16	17	51,950
18	Allowable amount of deductions from item 17 (see the instructions for item 18 of the Recapitulation)	18	51,950
19	Schedule L—Net Losses During Administration	19	0
20	Schedule L—Expenses Incurred in Administering Property Not Subject to Claims	20	0
21	Schedule M—Bequests, etc., to Surviving Spouse	21	0
22	Schedule O—Charitable, Public, and Similar Gifts and Bequests	22	500,000
23	Estimated value of assets subject to the special rule of Reg. section 20.2010-2T(a)(7)(ii)	23	
24	Tentative total allowable deductions (add items 18 through 23). Enter here and on line 2 of the Tax Computation	24	551,950

Page 3

Form 706 (Rev. 8-2013)

Estate of: Ann E. Carson Elmer	Decedent's social security number 212-12-1212

Part 6—Portability of Deceased Spousal Unused Exclusion (DSUE)

Portability Election

A decedent with a surviving spouse elects portability of the deceased spousal unused exclusion (DSUE) amount, if any, by completing and timely-filing this return. No further action is required to elect portability of the DSUE amount to allow the surviving spouse to use the decedent's DSUE amount.

Section A. Opting Out of Portability

The estate of a decedent with a surviving spouse may opt out of electing portability of the DSUE amount. Check here and do not complete Sections B and C of Part 6 only if the estate opts NOT to elect portability of the DSUE amount. ☐

Section B. QDOT

	Yes	No
Are any assets of the estate being transferred to a qualified domestic trust (QDOT)?		X

If "Yes," the DSUE amount portable to a surviving spouse (calculated in Section C, below) is preliminary and shall be redetermined at the time of the final distribution or other taxable event imposing estate tax under section 2056A. See instructions for more details.

Section C. DSUE Amount Portable to the Surviving Spouse (To be completed by the estate of a decedent making a portability election.)

Complete the following calculation to determine the DSUE amount that can be transferred to the surviving spouse.

1	Enter the amount from line 9c, Part 2—Tax Computation	1	
2	Reserved	2	
3	Enter the value of the cumulative lifetime gifts on which tax was paid or payable (see instructions)	3	0
4	Add lines 1 and 3	4	0
5	Enter amount from line 10, Part 2—Tax Computation	5	0
6	Divide amount on line 5 by 40% (0.40) (do not enter less than zero)	6	0
7	Subtract line 6 from line 4	7	0
8	Enter the amount from line 5, Part 2– Tax Computation	8	0
9	Subtract line 8 from line 7 (do not enter less than zero)	9	0
10	DSUE amount portable to surviving spouse (Enter lesser of line 9 or line 9a, Part 2 – Tax Computation) . .	10	0

Section D. DSUE Amount Received from Predeceased Spouse(s) (To be completed by the estate of a deceased surviving spouse with DSUE amount from predeceased spouse(s))

Provide the following information to determine the DSUE amount received from deceased spouses.

A Name of Deceased Spouse (dates of death after December 31, 2010, only)	B Date of Death (enter as mm/dd/yy)	C Portability Election Made?		D If "Yes," DSUE Amount Received from Spouse	E DSUE Amount Applied by Decedent to Lifetime Gifts	F Year of Form 709 Reporting Use of DSUE Amount Listed in col E	G Remaining DSUE Amount, if any (subtract col. E from col. D)
		Yes	No				
Part 1 — DSUE RECEIVED FROM LAST DECEASED SPOUSE							
Dean Elmer	03/13/13	X		5,250,000			5,250,000
Part 2 — DSUE RECEIVED FROM OTHER PREDECEASED SPOUSE(S) AND USED BY DECEDENT							
Total (for all DSUE amounts from predeceased spouse(s) applied)					0		

Add the amount from Part 1, column D and the total from Part 2, column E. Enter the result on line 9b, Part 2—Tax Computation . . . . ▶ 5,250,000

Form 706 (Rev. 8-2013)

Estate of: Ann E. Carson Elmer

Decedent's social security number
212-12-1212

SCHEDULE A—Real Estate

- For jointly owned property that must be disclosed on Schedule E, see instructions.
- Real estate that is part of a sole proprietorship should be shown on Schedule F.
- Real estate that is included in the gross estate under sections 2035, 2036, 2037, or 2038 should be shown on Schedule G.
- Real estate that is included in the gross estate under section 2041 should be shown on Schedule H.
- If you elect section 2032A valuation, you must complete Schedule A and Schedule A-1.

Note. If the value of the gross estate, together with the amount of adjusted taxable gifts, is less than the basic exclusion amount and the Form 706 is being filed solely to elect portability of the DSUE amount, consideration should be given as to whether you are required to report the value of assets eligible for the marital or charitable deduction on this schedule. See the instructions and Reg. section 20.2010-2T (a)(7)(ii) for more information. If you are not required to report the value of an asset, identify the property but make no entries in the last three columns.

Item number	Description	Alternate valuation date	Alternate value	Value at date of death
1	House and lot, 1475 E. Walnut Ave., Indianapolis, IN (lot 3, square 000). Value based on appraisal, a copy of which is attached.			820,000
2	House and lot, 456 Ocean Way, Naples, FL (lot 8, square 000). Value based on appraisal, a copy of which is attached.			1,350,000
	Total from continuation schedules or additional statements attached to this schedule . . .		0	0
	TOTAL. (Also enter on Part 5—Recapitulation, page 3, at item 1.)		0	2,170,000

(If more space is needed, attach the continuation schedule from the end of this package or additional statements of the same size.)

Schedule A

HTA

¶3140

Form 706 (Rev. 8-2013)

| **Estate of:** Ann E. Carson Elmer | | | | | Decedent's social security number
212-12-1212 |

SCHEDULE B—Stocks and Bonds

(For jointly owned property that must be disclosed on Schedule E, see instructions.)

Note. If the value of the gross estate, together with the amount of adjusted taxable gifts, is less than the basic exclusion amount and the Form 706 is being filed solely to elect portability of the DSUE amount, consideration should be given as to whether you are required to report the value of assets eligible for the marital or charitable deduction on this schedule. See the instructions and Reg. section 20.2010-2T (a)(7)(ii) for more information. If you are not required to report the value of an asset, identify the property but make no entries in the last four columns.

Item number	Description, including face amount of bonds or number of shares and par value for identification. Give CUSIP number. If trust, partnership, or closely held entity, give EIN.	CUSIP number or EIN, where applicable	Unit value	Alternate valuation date	Alternate value	Value at date of death
1	3,500 shs., Big Power Co., common, NYSE	101101101	30.			105,000
2	400 shs., Green Tech Industries, common, NYSE	202202202	200.			80,000
3	19,000 shs. KHC Corp., common NYSE	303303303	85.5			1,624,500
4	9,000 shs. Premium mutual fund, NASDAQ	404404404	95.			855,000
	Total from continuation schedules (or additional statements) attached to this schedule				0	0
	TOTAL. (Also enter on Part 5—Recapitulation, page 3, at item 2.)				0	2,664,500

(If more space is needed, attach the continuation schedule from the end of this package or additional statements of the same size.)

HTA

Schedule B

¶3140

Form 706 (Rev. 8-2013)

	Decedent's social security number
Estate of: Ann E. Carson Elmer	212-12-1212

SCHEDULE C—Mortgages, Notes, and Cash

(For jointly owned property that must be disclosed on Schedule E, see instructions.)

Note. If the value of the gross estate, together with the amount of adjusted taxable gifts, is less than the basic exclusion amount and the Form 706 is being filed solely to elect portability of the DSUE amount, consideration should be given as to whether you are required to report the value of assets eligible for the marital or charitable deduction on this schedule. See the instructions and Reg. section 20.2010-2T (a)(7)(ii) for more information. If you are not required to report the value of an asset, identify the property but make no entries in the last three columns.

Item number	Description	Alternate valuation date	Alternate value	Value at date of death
1	Money market account #465A-32-876, First State Bank of Indiana			102,000
	Interest accrued at date of death.			100
2	$86,000 certificate of deposit, First State Bank of Indiana, Indianapolis, IN; 12-mo. term; 2.5% interest; maturity March 3, 2013.			85,000
	Interest accrued at date of death.			500
3	Cash on decedent's person			3,600
	Total from continuation schedules (or additional statements) attached to this schedule		0	0
	TOTAL. (Also enter on Part 5—Recapitulation, page 3, at item 3.)		0	191,200

(If more space is needed, attach the continuation schedule from the end of this package or additional statements of the same size.)

Schedule C

HTA

¶3140

Form 706 (Rev. 8-2013)

Estate of: Ann E. Carson Elmer	Decedent's social security number
	212-12-1212

SCHEDULE D—Insurance on the Decedent's Life

You must list all policies on the life of the decedent and attach a Form 712 for each policy.

Note. If the value of the gross estate, together with the amount of adjusted taxable gifts, is less than the basic exclusion amount and the Form 706 is being filed solely to elect portability of the DSUE amount, consideration should be given as to whether you are required to report the value of assets eligible for the marital or charitable deduction on this schedule. See the instructions and Reg. section 20.2010-2T (a)(7)(ii) for more information. If you are not required to report the value of an asset, identify the property but make no entries in the last three columns.

Item number	Description	Alternate valuation date	Alternate value	Value at date of death
1	$2,500,000 Provisional Life Insurance Co. policy #56823-87135, proceeds payable to Paul Elmer Family Trust in lump sum. Form 712 attached.			2,500,000
2	$2,500,000 Provisional Life Insurance Co. policy #56823-87140, proceeds payable to Miranda Cole Family Trust in lump sum. Form 712 attached.			2,500,000
	Total from continuation schedules (or additional statements) attached to this schedule		0	0
	TOTAL. (Also enter on Part 5—Recapitulation, page 3, at item 4.)		0	5,000,000

(If more space is needed, attach the continuation schedule from the end of this package or additional statements of the same size.)

HTA

Schedule D

Form 706 (Rev. 8-2013)

	Decedent's social security number
Estate of: Ann E. Carson Elmer	212-12-1212

SCHEDULE F—Other Miscellaneous Property Not Reportable Under Any Other Schedule

(For jointly owned property that must be disclosed on Schedule E, see instructions.)

(If you elect section 2032A valuation, you must complete Schedule F and Schedule A-1.)

Note. If the value of the gross estate, together with the amount of adjusted taxable gifts, is less than the basic exclusion amount and the Form 706 is being filed solely to elect portability of the DSUE amount, consideration should be given as to whether you are required to report the value of assets eligible for the marital or charitable deduction on this schedule. See the instructions and Reg. section 20.2010-2T (a)(7)(ii) for more information. If you are not required to report the value of an asset, identify the property but make no entries in the last three columns.

		Yes	No
1	Did the decedent own any works of art, items, or any collections whose artistic or collectible value at date of death exceeded $3,000?	X	
	If "Yes," submit full details on this schedule and attach appraisals.		
2	Has the decedent's estate, spouse, or any other person received (or will receive) any bonus or award as a result of the decedent's employment or death?		X
	If "Yes," submit full details on this schedule.		
3	Did the decedent at the time of death have, or have access to, a safe deposit box?	X	

If "Yes," state location, and if held jointly by decedent and another, state name and relationship of joint depositor.

Safe deposit box, First National Bank of Indiana, Indianapolis, IN

If any of the contents of the safe deposit box are omitted from the schedules in this return, explain fully why omitted.

Item number	Description. For securities, give CUSIP number. If trust, partnership, or closely held entity, give EIN	CUSIP number or EIN, where applicable	Alternate valuation date	Alternate value	Value at date of death
1	15% interest in Elmer Family Enterprises. Value based on appraisal, a copy of which is attached.				4,500,000
2	Household goods and personal effects.				55,000
3	Art collection. Value based on appraisal, a copy of which is attached.				230,000
	Total from continuation schedules (or additional statements) attached to this schedule . . .			0	0
	TOTAL. (Also enter on Part 5—Recapitulation, page 3, at item 6.)			0	4,785,000

(If more space is needed, attach the continuation schedule from the end of this package or additional statements of the same size.)

HTA

Schedule F

¶3140

Form 706 (Rev. 8-2013)

Estate of: Ann E. Carson Elmer	Decedent's social security number
	212-12-1212

SCHEDULE J—Funeral Expenses and Expenses Incurred in Administering Property Subject to Claims

▶ Use Schedule PC to make a protective claim for refund due to an expense not currently deductible.
For such a claim, report the expense on Schedule J but without a value in the last column.

Note. Do not list expenses of administering property not subject to claims on this schedule. To report those expenses, see instructions.

If executors' commissions, attorney fees, etc., are claimed and allowed as a deduction for estate tax purposes, they are not allowable as a deduction in computing the taxable income of the estate for federal income tax purposes. They are allowable as an income tax deduction on Form 1041, U.S. Income Tax Return for Estates and Trusts, if a waiver is filed to forgo the deduction on Form 706 (see Instructions for Form 1041).

		Yes	No
Are you aware of any actual or potential reimbursement to the estate for any expense claimed as a deduction on this schedule?			X
If "Yes," attach a statement describing the expense(s) subject to potential reimbursement. (see instructions)			

Item number	Description	Expense amount	Total amount
	A. Funeral expenses:		
1	Family Funeral Home, Indianapolis, IN	7,500	
		0	
	Total funeral expenses . . . . ▶		7,500

B. Administration expenses:

1	Executors' commissions—amount ~~estimated/agreed upon/~~paid. (Strike out the words that do not apply.)		14,000
2	Attorney fees—amount ~~estimated/agreed upon/~~paid. (Strike out the words that do not apply.)		12,000
3	Accountant fees—amount ~~estimated/agreed upon/~~paid. (Strike out the words that do not apply.)		8,000

Item number	4 Miscellaneous expenses:	Expense amount
1	Real Deal Realty Appraisers, Indianapolis, IN. Appraisals of real estate and household items (Sch. A, item 1; Sch. F, item 2)	3,300
2	Orange State Realty Appraisers, Naples, FL. Appraisal of real estate (Sch. A, item 2)	2,100
3	Fine Art Appraisals, Indianapolis, IN. Appraisals of of art collection (Sch. F, item 3)	1,000
4	ACE Business Valuation Services, Indianapolis, IN. Appraisals of Elmer Family Enterprises (Sch. F, item 1)	3,600
5	Marion Superior Court. Fees related to administration of estate.	450

Total miscellaneous expenses from continuation schedules (or additional statements) attached to this schedule		0
Total miscellaneous expenses . . . . ▶		10,450
TOTAL. (Also enter on Part 5—Recapitulation, page 3, at item 14.). . . . . ▶		51,950

(If more space is needed, attach the continuation schedule from the end of this package or additional statements of the same size.)

HTA

Schedule J

Form 706 (Rev. 8-2013)

Estate of: Ann E. Carson Elmer	Decedent's social security number
	212-12-1212

SCHEDULE O—Charitable, Public, and Similar Gifts and Bequests

Note. If the value of the gross estate, together with the amount of adjusted taxable gifts, is less than the basic exclusion amount and the Form 706 is being filed solely to elect portability of the DSUE amount, consideration should be given as to whether you are required to report the value of assets eligible for the marital or charitable deduction on this schedule. See the instructions and Reg. section 20.2010-2T (a)(7)(ii) for more information. If you are not required to report the value of an asset, identify the property but make no entry in the last column.

		Yes	No
1 a	If the transfer was made by will, has any action been instituted to contest or have interpreted any of its provisions affecting the charitable deductions claimed in this schedule?		X
	If "Yes," full details must be submitted with this schedule.		
b	According to the information and belief of the person or persons filing this return, is any such action planned?		X
	If "Yes," full details must be submitted with this schedule.		
2	Did any property pass to charity as the result of a qualified disclaimer?		X
	If "Yes," attach a copy of the written disclaimer required by section 2518(b).		

Item number	Name and address of beneficiary	Character of institution	Amount
1	Orchard Park Presbyterian Church, 1605 E. 106th St., Indianapolis, IN	Religious	500,000

Total from continuation schedules (or additional statements) attached to this schedule			0
3	Total	3	500,000
4 a	Federal estate tax payable out of property interests listed above 4a		
b	Other death taxes payable out of property interests listed above 4b		
c	Federal and state GST taxes payable out of property interests listed above . . 4c		
d	Add items 4a, 4b, and 4c	4d	0
5	Net value of property interests listed above (subtract 4d from 3). Also enter on Part 5—Recapitulation, page 3, at item 22	5	500,000

(If more space is needed, attach the continuation schedule from the end of this package or additional statements of the same size.)

HTA   **Schedule O**

¶ 3150   Filled-In Schedule A-1

James X. Diversey, the hypothetical decedent in the main Form 706 example (see ¶ 2910), did not own property that would have qualified his estate for special use valuation (reported on Schedule A-1). The following filled-in Schedule A-1, Form 706 (Rev. August 2013), relates to the fact pattern below.

Donald Whitecliffe owned and operated a farm in Antioch, Illinois, until his death on March 15, 2013. The farm has been in the Whitecliffe family since 1954. Whitecliffe, a widower, is survived by his son, Brad, and two grandchildren, John and Randy (Brad's sons). Because Brad had no interest in continuing to operate the farm, Whitecliffe's will devised the farm to the grandchildren, who will jointly run the farm.

The value of Whitecliffe's gross estate, without regard to special use valuation, is $6,500,000. The fair market value of the Antioch property is $3,540,000. However, the property has a value of $2,240,000 as a farm. Because the estate meets all of the requirements under Code Sec. 2032A, and the heirs consent to the imposition of the recapture tax, the estate has elected special use valuation for the Antioch farm (see ¶ 280 and following). In 2013, the aggregate decrease in the farm's value for special valuation purposes may not exceed $1,070,000. Consequently, the heirs are limited to a special use valuation of $2,470,000.

The $2,470,000 value of the farm transferred to the two grandchildren is a generation-skipping transfer (GST) that the decedent's executor would report on Form 706, Schedule R. In order to avoid GST tax liability, a portion of Donald's $5,250,000 GST exemption would have to be allocated to the transfer.

Form 706 (Rev. 8-2013)

Estate of:	Donald Whitecliffe	Decedent's social security number
		020-30-4050

SCHEDULE A-1—Section 2032A Valuation

Part 1. Type of election (Before making an election, see the checklist in the instructions.):

☐ **Protective election (Regulations section 20.2032A-8(b)).** Complete Part 2, line 1, and column A of lines 3 and 4. (see instructions)

☒ **Regular election.** Complete all of Part 2 (including line 11, if applicable) and Part 3. (see instructions)

Before completing Schedule A-1, see the instructions for the information and documents that must be included to make a valid election.

The election is not valid unless the agreement (that is , *Part 3. Agreement to Special Valuation Under Section 2032A):*
* Is signed by each qualified heir with an interest in the specially valued property and
* Is attached to this return when it is filed.

Part 2. Notice of election (Regulations section 20.2032A-8(a)(3))

Note. All real property entered on lines 2 and 3 must also be entered on Schedules A, E, F, G, or H, as applicable.

1   Qualified use—check one ▶ ☒ Farm used for farming, or

                                  ☐ Trade or business other than farming

2   Real property used in a qualified use, passing to qualified heirs, and to be specially valued on this Form 706.

A Schedule and item number from Form 706	B Full value (without section 2032A(b)(3)(B) adjustment)	C Adjusted value (with section 2032A (b)(3)(B) adjustment)	D Value based on qualified use (without section 2032A(b)(3)(B) adjustment)
Schedule , Item 1	3,540,000	3,540,000	2,470,000
	0	0	0
Totals	3,540,000	3,540,000	2,470,000

Attach a legal description of all property listed on line 2.

Attach copies of appraisals showing the column B values for all property listed on line 2.

3   Real property used in a qualified use, passing to qualified heirs, but not specially valued on this Form 706.

A Schedule and item number from Form 706	B Full value (without section 2032A(b)(3)(B) adjustment)	C Adjusted value (with section 2032A (b)(3)(B) adjustment)	D Value based on qualified use (without section 2032A(b)(3)(B) adjustment)
	0	0	0
Totals	0	0	0

If you checked "Regular election," you must attach copies of appraisals showing the column B values for all property listed on line 3.

(continued on next page)

Schedule A-1

HTA

Form 706 (Rev. 8-2013)   Donald Whitecliffe   020-30-4050

4   Personal property used in a qualified use and passing to qualified heirs.

A Schedule and item number from Form 706	B Adjusted value (with section 2032A(b)(3)(B) adjustment)	A (continued) Schedule and item number from Form 706	B (continued) Adjusted value (with section 2032A(b)(3)(B) adjustment)
		"Subtotal" from Col. B, below left	
Subtotal	0	Total adjusted value	0 0

5   Enter the value of the total gross estate as adjusted under section 2032A(b)(3)(A). ▶

6   **Attach a description of the method used to determine the special value based on qualified use.**

7   Did the decedent and/or a member of his or her family own all property listed on line 2 for at least 5 of the 8 years immediately preceding the date of the decedent's death? . . . .   [X] Yes   [ ] No

8   Were there any periods during the 8-year period preceding the date of the decedent's death during which the decedent or a member of his or her family:

		Yes	No
a	Did not own the property listed on line 2?		X
b	Did not use the property listed on line 2 in a qualified use?		X
c	Did not materially participate in the operation of the farm or other business within the meaning of section 2032A(e)(6)?		X

If you answered "Yes" to any of the above, attach a statement listing the periods. If applicable, describe whether the exceptions of sections 2032A(b)(4) or (5) are met.

9   **Attach affidavits describing the activities constituting material participation and the identity and relationship to the decedent of the material participants.**

10   Persons holding interests. Enter the requested information for each party who received any interest in the specially valued **property. (Each of the qualified heirs receiving an interest in the property must sign the agreement, to be found on Part 3 of this Schedule A-1, and the agreement must be filed with this return.)**

	Name	Address
A	John Whitecliffe	104 Basswood Way, Fox Lake, IL 60020
B	Randy Whitecliffe	18150 Gaither Road, Volo, IL 60030
C		
D		
E		
F		
G		
H		

	Identifying number	Relationship to decedent	Fair market value	Special-use value
A	341-34-1341	Grandson	1,770,000	1,235,000
B	341-41-3413	Grandson	1,770,000	1,235,000
C				
D				
E				
F				
G				
H				

You must attach a computation of the GST tax savings attributable to direct skips for each person listed above who is a skip person. (see instructions)

11   **Woodlands election.** Check here ▶ [ ] if you wish to make a Woodlands election as described in section 2032A(e)(13). Enter the schedule and item numbers from Form 706 of the property for which you are making this election ▶ - - - - - - - - - - - - - - -

Attach a statement explaining why you are entitled to make this election. The IRS may issue regulations that require more information to substantiate this election. You will be notified by the IRS if you must supply further information.

Schedule A-1

¶3150

Form 706 (Rev. 8-2013)

Part 3. Agreement to Special Valuation Under Section 2032A

	Decedent's social security number
Estate of: Donald Whitecliffe	020-30-4050

There cannot be a valid election unless:
- The agreement is executed by each one of the qualified heirs and
- The agreement is included with the estate tax return when the estate tax return is filed.

We (list all qualified heirs)

John Whitecliffe

Randy Whitecliffe

being all the qualified heirs and (list all other persons having an interest in the property required to sign this agreement)

being all other parties having interests in the property which is qualified real property and which is valued under section 2032A of the Internal Revenue Code, do hereby approve of the election made by   Flournoy Lombard

Executor/Administrator of the estate of   Donald Whitecliffe

pursuant to section 2032A to value said property on the basis of the qualified use to which the property is devoted and do hereby enter into this agreement pursuant to section 2032A(d).

The undersigned agree and consent to the application of subsection (c) of section 2032A with respect to all the property described on Form 706, Schedule A-1, Part 2, line 2, attached to this agreement. More specifically, the undersigned heirs expressly agree and consent to personal liability under subsection (c) of 2032A for the additional estate and GST taxes imposed by that subsection with respect to their respective interests in the above-described property in the event of certain early dispositions of the property or early cessation of the qualified use of the property. It is understood that if a qualified heir disposes of any interest in qualified real property to any member of his or her family, such member may thereafter be treated as the qualified heir with respect to such interest upon filing a Form 706-A, United States Additional Estate Tax Return, and a new agreement.

The undersigned interested parties who are not qualified heirs consent to the collection of any additional estate and GST taxes imposed under section 2032A(c) from the specially valued property.

If there is a disposition of any interest which passes, or has passed to him or her, or if there is a cessation of the qualified use of any specially valued property which passes or passed to him or her, each of the undersigned heirs agrees to file a Form 706-A, and pay any additional estate and GST taxes due within 6 months of the disposition or cessation.

It is understood by all interested parties that this agreement is a condition precedent to the election of special-use valuation under section 2032A and must be executed by every interested party even though that person may not have received the estate (or GST) tax benefits or be in possession of such property.

Each of the undersigned understands that by making this election, a lien will be created and recorded pursuant to section 6324B of the Code on the property referred to in this agreement for the adjusted tax differences with respect to the estate as defined in section 2032A(c)(2)(C).

As the interested parties, the undersigned designate the following individual as their agent for all dealings with the Internal Revenue Service concerning the continued qualification of the specially valued property under section 2032A and on all issues regarding the special lien under section 6324B. The agent is authorized to act for the parties with respect to all dealings with the Internal Revenue Service on matters affecting the qualified real property described earlier. This includes the authorization:

- To receive confidential information on all matters relating to continued qualification under section 2032A of the specially valued real property and on all matters relating to the special lien arising under section 6324B;

- To furnish the Internal Revenue Service with any requested information concerning the property;

- To notify the Internal Revenue Service of any disposition or cessation of qualified use of any part of the property;

- To receive, but not to endorse and collect, checks in payment of any refund of Internal Revenue taxes, penalties, or interest;

- To execute waivers (including offers of waivers) of restrictions on assessment or collection of deficiencies in tax and waivers of notice of disallowance of a claim for credit or refund; and

- To execute closing agreements under section 7121.

(continued on next page)

Schedule A-1

Form 706 (Rev. 8-2013)

Part 3. Agreement to Special Valuation Under Section 2032A *(continued)*

Estate of: Donald Whitecliffe	Decedent's social security number
	020-30-4050

• Other acts (specify) ▶ _____

By signing this agreement, the agent agrees to provide the Internal Revenue Service with any requested information concerning this property and to notify the Internal Revenue Service of any disposition or cessation of the qualified use of any part of this property.

Flournoy Lombard   *Flournoy Lombard*   990 S. Ridgeland, Oak Park, IL 60304
Name of Agent   Signature   Address

The property to which this agreement relates is listed in Form 706, United States Estate (and Generation-Skipping Transfer) Tax Return, and in the Notice of Election, along with its fair market value according to section 2031 of the Code and its special-use value according to section 2032A. The name, address, social security number, and interest (including the value) of each of the undersigned in this property are as set forth in the attached Notice of Election.

IN WITNESS WHEREOF, the undersigned have hereunto set their hands at _____

this _____ day of _____

SIGNATURES OF EACH OF THE QUALIFIED HEIRS:

Randy Whitecliffe   *John Whitecliffe*
Signature of qualified heir   Signature of qualified heir

_____   _____
Signature of qualified heir   Signature of qualified heir

_____   _____
Signature of qualified heir   Signature of qualified heir

_____   _____
Signature of qualified heir   Signature of qualified heir

_____   _____
Signature of qualified heir   Signature of qualified heir

_____   _____
Signature of qualified heir   Signature of qualified heir

_____
Signatures of other interested parties

_____
Signatures of other interested parties

Schedule A-1

¶3150

¶ 3170   Filled-In Schedule P

James X. Diversey, the hypothetical decedent in the main Form 706 example (see ¶ 2910), did not own property that would have generated a credit for foreign death taxes paid. The following filled-in Schedule P, Form 706 (Rev. August 2013), relates to the fact situation below.

Tom Wilson was a citizen of, and domiciled in, the United States at the time of his death in 2013. For purposes of illustrating the foreign death tax credit, the following will be assumed: Tom's gross estate consisted of real property in Finland valued at $125,000; real property in the United States valued at $1,500,000; stocks of U.S. corporations, $4,250,000; bonds of corporations organized under the laws of Finland, $70,000; stocks of corporations organized under the laws of Finland where more than 50 percent of the corporate assets consisted of Finnish real property, $150,000.

The Finnish real property, which is valued at $125,000, and $540,000 of the U.S. stock were the only items that passed to Wilson's surviving spouse (also a U.S. citizen and resident) and qualified for the marital deduction. The amount of the federal estate tax, less the unified credit, was $72,000. Assume the amount of Finnish inheritance tax imposed on the surviving spouse's inheritance of $125,000 was $1,310. The stock in Finnish corporations, valued at $150,000, passed to Wilson's daughter, who resided in Finland at the time of her father's death. Assume, further, that the amount of Finnish inheritance tax imposed on the stock was $14,993 and that Finland does not impose an inheritance tax on bonds issued by Finnish corporations.

Form 706 (Rev. 8-2013)

Estate of: Tom Wilson	Decedent's social security number		
	900	80	7060

SCHEDULE P—Credit for Foreign Death Taxes

List all foreign countries to which death taxes have been paid and for which a credit is claimed on this return.

Finland

If a credit is claimed for death taxes paid to more than one foreign country, compute the credit for taxes paid to one country on this sheet and attach a separate copy of Schedule P for each of the other countries.

The credit computed on this sheet is for the **Finish Inheritance Tax**
(Name of death tax or taxes)

imposed in **Finland**
(Name of country)

Credit is computed under the **US--Finland Death Tax Convention**
(Insert title of treaty or statute)

Citizenship (nationality) of decedent at time of death **United States**

(All amounts and values must be entered in United States money.)

1 Total of estate, inheritance, legacy, and succession taxes imposed in the country named above attributable to property situated in that country, subjected to these taxes, and included in the gross estate (as defined by statute) .	1	14,993
2 Value of the gross estate (adjusted, if necessary, according to the instructions)	2	5,430,000
3 Value of property situated in that country, subjected to death taxes imposed in that country, and included in the gross estate (adjusted, if necessary, according to the instructions)	3	150,000
4 Tax imposed by section 2001 reduced by the total credits claimed under sections 2010 and 2012 (see instructions)	4	72,000
5 Amount of federal estate tax attributable to property specified at item 3. (Divide item 3 by item 2 and multiply the result by item 4.)	5	1,989
6 Credit for death taxes imposed in the country named above (the smaller of item 1 or item 5). Also enter on line 13 of Part 2—Tax Computation	6	1,989

¶ 3180   Filled-In Schedule R-1

James X. Diversey, the hypothetical decedent in the main Form 706 example (see ¶ 2910), did not make a generation-skipping transfer reportable on Schedule R-1. The following filled-in Schedule R-1, Form 706 (Rev. August 2013), relates to the fact pattern below.

Howard Buckner died in June 2013, the owner of a $500,000 life insurance policy on his own life, with his granddaughter, Melissa Buckner, as sole beneficiary. At Buckner's election, the insurer would pay out the proceeds as an annuity for the life of the beneficiary with the remainder payable to the beneficiary's estate. Because this payout method is deemed to be a "trust arrangement" under Reg. § 26.2662-1(c)(2)(ii), with a value exceeding $250,000, the direct skip to the grandchild is reported on Schedule R-1, rather than Schedule R (see Reg. § 26.2662-1(c)(2)(vi), Ex. 3). No GST exemption was allocated to the policy.

SCHEDULE R-1
(Form 706)
(Rev. August 2013)
Department of the Treasury
Internal Revenue Service

Generation-Skipping Transfer Tax

Direct Skips From a Trust
Payment Voucher

OMB No. 1545-0015

Executor: File one copy with Form 706 and send two copies to the fiduciary. Do not pay the tax shown. See instructions for details.
Fiduciary: See instructions for details. Pay the tax shown on line 6.

Name of trust	Trust's EIN
Insurance trust (non-explicit trust)	5 6 1 2 3 4 5 6 7

Name and title of fiduciary	Name of decedent
Total Life Co. of Louisiana	**Howard Buckner**

Address of fiduciary (number and street)	Decedent's SSN	Service Center where Form 706 was filed
4500 Rue Rivage	1 2 0 0 1 1 2 1 2	Cincinnati, OH

City, state, and ZIP or postal code	Name of executor
New Orleans, LA 70130	**First National Bank of Atlanta, N.A.**

Address of executor (number and street)	City, state, and ZIP or postal code
101 First Street	**Atlanta, GA 30328**

Date of decedent's death	Filing due date of Schedule R, Form 706 (with extensions)
6/15/2013	**3/15/2014**

Part 1. Computation of the GST Tax on the Direct Skip

Description of property interests subject to the direct skip	Estate tax value
Total Life Co. of Louisiana, Universal Variable Life Insurance, Policy No. 412399-UV. Value as listed on Schedule D, item 1. Proceeds payable under settlement option no. 4 as an annuity for the life of the beneficiary, Melissa Buckner, the decedent's granddaughter.	500,000

1	Total estate tax value of all property interests listed above	1	500,000
2	Estate taxes, state death taxes, and other charges borne by the property interests listed above	2	
3	Tentative maximum direct skip from trust (subtract line 2 from line 1)	3	500,000
4	GST exemption allocated	4	
5	Subtract line 4 from line 3	5	500,000
6	**GST tax due from fiduciary** (divide line 5 by 3.5). **(See instructions if property will not bear the GST tax.)**	6	142,857

Under penalties of perjury, I declare that I have examined this document, including accompanying schedules and statements, and to the best of my knowledge and belief, it is true, correct, and complete.

Virginia M. Buckner   3/15/2014
Signature(s) of executor(s)   Date

_____   _____
                                                     Date

_____   _____
Signature of fiduciary or officer representing fiduciary   Date

Schedule R-1—Page 26

¶ 3190   Filled-in Schedule U

James X. Diversey, the hypothetical decedent in the main Form 706 example (see ¶ 2910), did not own property that would have generated a qualified conservation easement exclusion. The following filled-in Schedule U, Form 706 (Rev. August 2013), relates to the fact situation below.

Pursuant to her will, Dee Jones conveyed a qualified conservation easement for open space with respect to 160 acres of land proximate to the Everglades National Park, Collier County, Florida. The fair market value of the property on the date of Jones' death on May 16, 2013, was $400,000. The value of the conservation easement is $150,000. The decedent's children, who will receive the property, will retain no development rights in the property.

Form 706 (Rev. 8-2013)

	Decedent's social security number

Estate of: Dee Jones

109	87	6543

SCHEDULE U—Qualified Conservation Easement Exclusion

Part 1. Election

Note. The executor is deemed to have made the election under section 2031(c)(6) if he or she files Schedule U and excludes any qualifying conservation easements from the gross estate.

Part 2. General Qualifications

1. Describe the land subject to the qualified conservation easement (see instructions) <u>160 acres of undeveloped pasture and</u> <u>marshland in Collier County, Florida</u>

2. Did the decedent or a member of the decedent's family own the land described above during the 3-year period ending on the date of the decedent's death? . . . . ☑ Yes ☐ No

3. Describe the conservation easement with regard to which the exclusion is being claimed (see instructions). <u>Perpetual easement for open space to Everglades Preservation Fund Inc.</u>

Part 3. Computation of Exclusion

4	Estate tax value of the land subject to the qualified conservation easement (see instructions)		**4**	400,000
5	Date of death value of any easements granted prior to decedent's death and included on line 10 below (see instructions)	**5**		
6	Add lines 4 and 5	**6**	400,000	
7	Value of retained development rights on the land (see instructions)	**7**		
8	Subtract line 7 from line 6	**8**	400,000	
9	Multiply line 8 by 30% (.30)	**9**	120,000	
10	Value of qualified conservation easement for which the exclusion is being claimed (see instructions)	**10**	150,000	
	Note. If line 10 is less than line 9, continue with line 11. If line 10 is equal to or more than line 9, skip lines 11 through 13, enter ".40" on line 14, and complete the schedule.			
11	Divide line 10 by line 8. Figure to 3 decimal places (for example, ".123")	**11**		
	Note. If line 11 is equal to or less than .100, stop here; the estate does not qualify for the conservation easement exclusion.			
12	Subtract line 11 from .300. Enter the answer in hundredths by rounding any thousandths up to the next higher hundredth (that is, .030 = .03, but .031 = .04)	**12**		
13	Multiply line 12 by 2	**13**		
14	Subtract line 13 from .40	**14**	.40	
15	Deduction under section 2055(f) for the conservation easement (see instructions)	**15**	0	
16	Amount of indebtedness on the land (see instructions)	**16**	0	
17	Total reductions in value (add lines 7, 15, and 16)	**17**	0	
18	Net value of land (subtract line 17 from line 4)	**18**	400,000	
19	Multiply line 18 by line 14	**19**	160,000	
20	Enter the smaller of line 19 or the exclusion limitation (see instructions). Also enter this amount on item 12, Part 5—Recapitulation, page 3	**20**	160.000	

¶ 3200   Filled-In Form 706-A

James X. Diversey, the hypothetical decedent in the main Form 706 example (see ¶ 2910), did not have special use valuation property. The following filled-in Form 706-A, (Rev. September. 2013) relates to the fact situation below.

Helen Gower, daughter and qualified heir of Henry Gower, who died on May 1, 2005, continued the qualified use of the family farm until it was acquired by eminent domain by the county airport authority on February 22, 2013. At the date of Henry Gower's death, the farm property, valued at its highest and best use, was worth $1,600,000. Operating as a farm, the farm property had a fair market value of $600,000. However, in the year of Henry's death (2005), the special use valuation election could reduce the value of special use valuation property by a maximum of $870,000. Accordingly, the value of the farm property entered on Henry's Form 706 (which is not reproduced herein) was $730,000 ($1,600,000 – $870,000), rather than $600,000.

Electing special use valuation, the estate of Henry Gower computed its federal estate tax liability as follows:

Tentative taxable estate of $2,200,000 less state death tax deduction ($91,567)	$ 2,108,433
Tentative tax on above	$ 831,764
Less: Applicable credit amount	$ 555,800
Estate tax reported on Form 706	$ 275,964

As required by Form 706-A, Part II, Line 3b, Helen Gower recomputed the federal estate tax on Henry Gower's estate, without the benefit of the reduced value of the farm based on its special use value:

Tentative taxable estate of $3,070,000 less state death tax deduction ($172,941)	$ 2,897,059
Tentative tax on above	$1,202,418
Less: Applicable credit amount	$ 555,800
Recomputed federal estate tax.	$ 646,618

Gower received compensation in the amount of $2,200,000 from the airport authority; she reinvested $1,100,000 in the acquisition of a replacement farm property on July 9, 2013.

Form **706-A**		**United States Additional Estate Tax Return**			
(Rev. September 2013)		To report dispositions or cessations of qualified use under section 2032A of the Internal Revenue Code.			OMB No. 1545-0016
Department of the Treasury Internal Revenue Service		▶ Information about Form 706A and its instructions is at *www.irs.gov/form706*.			

Part I   General Information

1a Name of qualified heir	2 Heir's social security number
Helen Gower	279-33-1234
1b Address of qualified heir (number and street, including apt. no., or P.O. box)	3 Commencement date (see instructions)
124 South Elmwood	5/24/2006
1c City, town or post office, state, and ZIP code	
Twin Lakes, WI, 51534	

4 Decedent's name reported on Form 706	5 Decedent's social security number	6 Date of death
Henry Gower	315-71-4711	5/1/2005

7 Check here if you are making an election under section 1016(c) to increase the basis of specially valued property. Attach the statement described on page 2 of the instructions . . . . ▶ ☐

Part II   Tax Computation (First complete Schedules A and B. See instructions.)

1	Value at date of death (or alternate valuation date) of all specially valued property that passed from decedent to qualified heir:			
a	Without section 2032A election	1a	1,600,000	
b	With section 2032A election .	1b	730,000	
c	Balance. Subtract line 1b from line 1a		1c	870,000
2	Value at date of death (or alternate valuation date) of all specially valued property in decedent's estate:			
a	Without section 2032A election	2a	1,600,000	
b	With section 2032A election .	2b	730,000	
c	Balance. Subtract line 2b from line 2a		2c	870,000
3	Decedent's estate tax:			
a	Recomputed without section 2032A election (attach computation) . .	3a	646,618	
b	Reported on Form 706 with section 2032A election	3b	275,964	
c	Balance. Subtract line 3b from line 3a		3c	370,654
4	Divide line 1c by line 2c and enter the result as a percentage		4	100 %
5	Total estate tax saved. Multiply line 3c by percentage on line 4		5	370,654
6	Value, without section 2032A election, at date of death (or alternate valuation date) of specially valued property shown on Schedule A of this Form 706-A	6	1,600,000	
7	Divide line 6 by line 1a and enter the result as a percentage		7	100 %
8	Multiply line 5 by percentage on line 7		8	370,654
9	Total estate tax recaptured on previous Form(s) 706-A (attach copies of 706-A) . . .		9	
10	Remaining estate tax savings. Subtract line 9 from line 5. (do not enter less than zero)		10	370,654
11	Enter the lesser of line 8 or line 10		11	370,654
12	Enter the total of column D, Schedule A, page 2	12	2,200,000	
13	Enter the total of column E, Schedule A, page 2	13	730,000	
14	Balance. Subtract line 13 from line 12 (But enter the line 12 amount in the case of a disposition of standing timber on qualified woodland)		14	1,470,000
15	Enter the lesser of line 11 or line 14		15	370,654

If you completed Schedule B, complete lines 16–19. If you did not complete Schedule B, skip lines 16–18 and enter the amount from line 15 on line 19.

16	Enter the total cost (or fair market value (FMV)) from Schedule B		16	1,100,000
17	Divide line 16 by line 12 and enter the result as a percentage. (do not enter more than 100%) . .		17	50 %
18	Multiply line 15 by percentage on line 17		18	185,327
19	**Additional estate tax.** Subtract line 18 from line 15. (do not enter less than zero)		19	185,327
20	Enter section 1016(c) interest (where applicable)		20	

Under penalties of perjury, I declare that I have examined this return, and to the best of my knowledge and belief, it is true, correct, and complete. Declaration of preparer (other than taxpayer) is based on all information of which preparer has any knowledge.

Sign Here	Signature of executor *Helen Gower*	Date 8/20/2013	
	Signature of executor	May the IRS discuss this return with the preparer shown below (see instructions)? Yes ☐ No ☐	

Paid Preparer Use Only	Print/Type preparer's name Frederick Paulson	Preparer's signature *Frederick Paulsen*	Date 8/20/2013	Check ☐ if self-employed	PTIN 550-97-8653
	Firm's name ▶ Howard and Paulson LLC			Firm's EIN ▶	11-567901
	Firm's address ▶ 418 Barry Rd. Twin Lakes, WI			Phone no.	261-444-8999

For Privacy Act and Paperwork Reduction Act Notice, see the separate instructions.   Cat. No. 10141S   Form **706-A** (Rev. 9-2013)

Form 706-A (Rev. 9-2013)

Schedule A. Disposition of Specially Valued Property or Cessation of Qualified Use
Note. List property in chronological order of disposition or cessation.

A Item number	B Description of specially valued property and schedule and item number where reported on the decedent's Form 706	C Date of disposition (or date qualified use ceased)	D Amount received (or fair market value if applicable) (see instructions)	E Special use value (see instructions)
1	Form 706, Schedule ___A___, Item ___1___ Description—**Farm, Kenosha County, WI**	2/22/2013	2,200,000	730,000
	Totals: Enter total of column D on page 1, Part II, Tax Computation, line 12, and total of column E on page 1, Part II, Tax Computation, line 13		2,200,000	730,000

Form **706-A** (Rev. 9-2013)

Schedule B. Involuntary Conversions or Exchanges		Check if for: ☑ Involuntary Conversion ☐ Exchange
Qualified replacement (or exchange) property		
A Item	**B** Description of qualified replacement (or exchange) property	**C** Cost (or FMV)
1	Farm R.R. 6, Box 15, Kenosha Corners, WI (Northeast quarter, Section 12, Kenosha County, WI). This farm was acquired on July 9, 2013 as a replacemnt property for the involuntarily converted property listed in Schedule A, item 1.	1,100,000
Total cost (or FMV). Enter here and on line 16 of Part II, Tax Computation, page 1		1,100,000

Form **706-A** (Rev. 9-2013)

Schedule C. Dispositions to Family Members of the Qualified Heir

Each transferee must enter into an agreement to be personally liable for any additional taxes imposed by section 2032A(c) and the agreement must be attached to this Form 706-A. (see instructions)

	Last name	First name	Middle initial
Transferee #1:	N/A		
	Social security number	Relationship to the qualified heir	

Description of property transferred

A Item number	B Description of specially valued property and schedule and item number where reported on the decedent's Form 706	C Date of disposition
1	Form 706, Schedule _____, Item _____ Description:	

	Last name	First name	Middle initial
Transferee #2:			
	Social security number	Relationship to the qualified heir	

Description of property transferred

A Item number	B Description of specially valued property and schedule and item number where reported on the decedent's Form 706	C Date of disposition
1	Form 706, Schedule _____, Item _____ Description:	

If there are more than two transferees, attach additional sheets using the same format.

Form **706-A** (Rev. 9-2013)

¶ 3210   Filled-In Form 706-D

The filled-in Form 706-D, United States Additional Estate Tax Return Under Code Section 2057 (Rev. Dec. 2008), illustrates a disposition of a qualified family-owned business interest (QFOBI) for which a deduction under Code Sec. 2057 was taken.

Fred Willins, a farmer, died on February 1, 2003. Willins died with a federal gross estate of $1,875,000, which included the farm business valued at $950,000. Willins' farm was bequeathed to his son, Bob (also a farmer), who intended to continue to operate the business after his father's death. Willins' executor had two categories of deductions that he claimed on the Form 706: $50,000 for administration expenses, and $675,000 as the maximum qualified family-owned business interest deduction. After credit for $21,000 in state death taxes paid, the Willins estate paid federal estate taxes of $184,250.

On June 1, 2013, the State of Illinois acquired the farm by eminent domain under a plan to develop a state park. Bob Willins received compensation in the amount of $985,000 for his farm. Three months later, Bob acquired a replacement farm for $600,000 in McHenry County, Illinois.

As required by Form 706-D, part II, line 3a, Bob Willins recomputed the federal estate tax on his father's estate, without the deduction for the qualified family-owned business interest:

Federal gross estate:	$1,875,000
Less: Administrative expenses	50,000
Taxable estate	$1,825,000
Tentative tax on above	$ 702,050
Less: Applicable credit amount	345,800
Less: Credit for state death taxes	43,500
Recomputed federal estate tax	$312,750

Using Form 706-D, Bob figured that he owed additional estate tax of $10,046. Because he did not want to incur additional interest assessments, he paid interest that he estimated would be due for the period beginning on the date that the original estate tax liability under Code Sec. 2001 was due (from November 1, 2003, the due date of Fred Willins' estate tax return) until the filing date, when he submitted with the return a check for $13,630 (a total of $10,046 tax and $3,584 interest). Note that, in conformance to the Form 706-D Instructions (page 2), the amount of the estimated interest due was entered on the dotted line to the left of the entry space for line 15, and was not included in the amount of tax entered on line 15.

Form **706-D**	United States Additional Estate Tax Return	

Form **706-D**
(Rev. December 2008)
Department of the Treasury
Internal Revenue Service

United States Additional Estate Tax Return
Under Code Section 2057

OMB No. 1545-1680

Part I — General Information

1a Name of qualified heir
Bob Willins

2 Qualified heir's social security number
098 : 12 : 4567

1b Address of qualified heir (number and street, including apt. no. or P.O. box)
1800 Gilmore Road

3 Commencement date (see instructions)
7/1/2003

1c City, town or post office, state, and ZIP code
Richmond, IL 60071

4 Decedent's name reported on Form 706
Fred Willins

5 Decedent's social security number
098 : 12 : 5678

6 Date of death
2/1/2003

Part II — Tax Computation (First complete Schedules A and B. See instructions.)

1	Qualified heir's share of the total qualified family-owned business interests (from line 4, Schedule T (Form 706), of the decedent's estate tax return)	**1**	950,000
2	Total reported value of qualified family-owned business interests (from line 6, Schedule T (Form 706), of the decedent's estate tax return)	**2**	950,000
3	Decedent's estate tax:		
a	Recomputed without the qualified family-owned business interest deduction (attach computation) . . . **3a** 312,750		
b	Reported on Form 706 (or as finally agreed to) . . . **3b** 184,250		
c	Gross additional estate tax (subtract line 3b from line 3a)	**3c**	128,500
4	Qualified heir's percentage of qualified family-owned business interests. Divide line 1 by line 2. Enter result as a percentage (carry out your answer to at least the nearest tenth of a percent)	**4**	100 . %
5	Qualified heir's share of total reduction in estate tax. Multiply line 3c by line 4 .	**5**	128,500
6	Enter the **Total** from column (E), Schedule A, page 2 .	**6**	950,000
7	Divide line 6 by line 1. Enter the result as a percentage (carry out your answer to at least the nearest tenth of a percent)	**7**	100 . %
8	Multiply line 5 by the percentage on line 7 .	**8**	128,500
9	Applicable percentage (see instructions) .	**9**	20 %
10	**Total additional estate tax.** Multiply line 8 by the percentage on line 9 .	**10**	25,700

If you completed Schedule B on page 2, complete lines 11 through 15. If you did not complete Schedule B, skip lines 11 through 14 and enter the amount from line 10 on line 15.

11	Enter the total cost or fair market value (FMV) from column (C), Schedule B, page 2 .	**11**	600,000
12	Enter the total of column (D), Schedule A, page 2 .	**12**	985,000
13	Divide line 11 by line 12. Enter the result as a percentage (carry out your answer to at least the nearest tenth of a percent) (do not enter more than 100%) .	**13**	60.91 %
14	Multiply line 10 by the percentage on line 13 .	**14**	15,654
15	**Additional estate tax due.** Subtract line 14 from line 10 (do not enter less than zero) .	**15**	10,046

Interest included in payment $3,584

Under penalties of perjury, I declare that I have examined this return, including accompanying schedules and statements, and to the best of my knowledge and belief, it is true, correct, and complete. Declaration of preparer (other than taxpayer) is based on all information of which preparer has any knowledge.

Sign Here

Bob Willins
Signature of taxpayer or person filing on behalf of taxpayer

Date 1/1/2014

Paid Preparer's Use Only

Preparer's signature	Franklin Burns	Date 1/1/2014	Check if self-employed ☑	Preparer's SSN or PTIN 765-32-1987
Firm's name (or yours if self-employed), address, and ZIP code	Franklin Burns 800 Main Street Antioch, IL	60002	EIN 80	2467913
			Phone no. (847)	833-3333

For Privacy Act and Paperwork Reduction Act Notice, see instructions.   Cat. No. 26107A   Form **706-D** (Rev. 12-2008)

Form 706-D (Rev. 12-2008)   Page **2**

Schedule A. Disposition of Qualified Family-Owned Business Interest, Failure to Materially Participate, or Disqualifying Act (Taxable Under Section 2057(f)(1))

(A) Item number	(B) Description of property and explanation of disqualifying act	(C) Date of disposition, failure to materially participate, or disqualifying act (see instructions)	(D) Amount realized or fair market value (FMV) if applicable (see instructions)	(E) Date of death value (see instructions)
1	Form 706, Schedule F, Item 1 Description — 250-acre farm, Kane County, IL	6/1/2013	985,000	950,000
	Total. Enter the total of column (D) on page 1, Part II, Tax Computation, line 12, and the total of column (E) on page 1, Part II, Tax Computation, line 6.		985,000	950,000

Schedule B. Involuntary Conversions or Exchanges

Check if for: ☑ Involuntary Conversion ☐ Exchange

(A) Item	(B) Description of qualified replacement (or exchange) property	(C) Cost or fair market value (FMV)
1	200-acre farm, 1800 Gilmore Road, Richmond, McHenry County, IL	600,000
	Total. Enter the total of column (C) on page 1, Part II, Tax Computation, line 11.	600,000

Schedule C. Nontaxable Transfers

Transferee	Last name	First name	Middle initial
	Social security number	Relationship to the qualified heir	

Check if for: ☐ Disposition to Family Member ☐ Qualified Conservation Contribution ☐ Loss of U.S. Citizenship

(A) Item	(B) Description of property and explanation of nontaxable transfers	(C) Date of disposition, contribution, trust agreement, or bond
1	Form 706, Schedule ___, Item ___ Description —	

Form **706-D** (Rev. 12-2008)

¶ 3220   Fact Situation for Forms 706-GS(D) and 706-GS(D-1)

For purposes of the filled-in Forms 706-GS(D), Generation-Skipping Transfer Tax Return for Distributions (Rev. August 2013), and 706-GS(D-1), Notification of Distribution From a Generation-Skipping Trust (Rev. October 2008), the following facts are assumed:

On his death in February 2013, Able Smith's will established the Able Smith GST Trust for the benefit of his son, Brian, his grandson, Charles, and his granddaughter, Donna. The trust provides that the income from the $5.7 million trust corpus is to go to Brian for life, with the remainder to go to Charles and Donna at Brian's death. In addition, the trustee is given the power to invade trust corpus for the benefit of Charles and/or Donna. Ten months after the trust is created, the trustee exercises the power, transferring $100,000 in cash to Charles.

No Schedule R or R-1 was filed with Able Smith's Form 706 because the transfer was to a trust having at least one nonskip person beneficiary, thus making the trust a nonskip person. $2,558,200 of Able Smith's GST exemption was allocated to the $5.7 million GST Trust, resulting in an inclusion ratio of .551. Charles Smith paid his accountant $250 to prepare Form 706-GS(D), resulting in $138 of adjusted allowable expenses.

¶ 3230   Filled-In Form 706-GS(D)

Form **706-GS(D)**	**Generation-Skipping Transfer Tax Return For Distributions**	
(Rev. August 2013) Department of the Treasury Internal Revenue Service	▶ Use for distributions made after December 31, 2010. For calendar year 2013 . ▶ Information about Form 706-GS(D) and its separate instructions is at *www.irs.gov/form706gsd*.	OMB No. 1545-1144

Attach a copy of all Forms 706-GS(D-1) to this return.

Part I   General Information

1a Name of skip person distributee	**1b** Social security number of individual distributee (see instructions)
Charles Smith	123-40-6789
2a Name and title of person filing return (if different from 1a, see instructions)	**1c** Employer identification number of trust distributee (see instructions)
Charles Smith	

2b Address of distributee or person filing return (see instructions) (number and street or P.O. box; city, town, or post office; state; and ZIP code) If you have a foreign address, also complete the spaces below.

1310 South Harvey Avenue
Oak Park, IL. 6034

Foreign country name	Foreign province/county	Foreign postal code

Part II   Distributions

a Trust EIN (from Form 706-GS(D-1), line 2a)	b Item no. (from Form 706-GS(D-1), line 3, column a)	c Amount of transfer (from Form 706-GS(D-1), line 3, column f (Tentative transfer))
77-6654321	1	55,100

3	Total transfers (add amounts in column **c**)	**3**	55,100

Part III   Tax Computation

4	Adjusted allowable expenses (see instructions)	**4**	138
5	Taxable amount (subtract line 4 from line 3)	**5**	54,962
6	Maximum federal estate tax rate (see instructions)	**6**	40%
7	Generation-skipping transfer tax (Multiply line 5 by line 6)	**7**	21,985
8	Payment, if any, made with Form 7004	**8**	
9	**Tax due** . . . . ▶	**9**	21,985
10	**Overpayment.** If line 8 is larger than line 7, enter amount to be refunded . . . . . . ▶	**10**	

Under penalties of perjury, I declare that I have examined this return, including accompanying schedules and statements, and to the best of my knowledge and belief, it is true, correct, and complete. Declaration of preparer other than taxpayer is based on all information of which preparer has any knowledge.

Sign Here	▶ *Charles Smith*		4/15/2014
	Signature of taxpayer or person filing on behalf of taxpayer		Date

Paid Preparer Use Only	Print/Type preparer's name	Preparer's signature	Date	Check ☑ if self-employed	PTIN
	Gunderson Guyler III	*Gunderson Guyler*	4/15/2014		654332109
	Firm's name ▶ Gunderson Guyler III			Firm's EIN ▶	90-1245678
	Firm's address ▶ 1419 Granger Ave, Elk Grove, IL 60007			Phone no.	847-555-1212

For Privacy Act and Paperwork Reduction Act Notice, see instructions.   Cat. No. 10327Q   Form **706-GS(D)** (Rev. 8-2013)

¶ 3240   Filled-In Form 706-GS(D-1)

Form **706-GS(D-1)** (Rev. October 2008) Department of The Treasury Internal Revenue Service	**Notification of Distribution From a** **Generation-Skipping Trust** Complete for each skip person distributee. See separate instructions. For calendar year .. 2013.	OMB No. 1545-1143 **Copy A: Send to IRS**

Part I   **General Information**

1a Skip person distributee's identifying number (see instructions)
      123-40-6789
	2a Trust's employer identification number (see instructions)
	    77 ⋮ 6654321

1b Skip person distributee's name, address, and ZIP code Charles Smith 1310 South Harvey Avenue Oak Park, IL 60304	**2b** Trust's name, address, and ZIP code Able Smith GST Trust 100 South Lake Street Oak Park, IL 60302

Part II   **Distributions**

3   Describe each distribution below. (see instructions)

a Item no.	b Description of property	c Date of distribution	d Inclusion ratio	e Value (see instructions)	f Tentative transfer (multiply col. e by col. d)
1	Cash distributions from corpus of Able Smith GST Trust	12/31/2013	0.551	100,000	55,100

Part III   **Trust Information** (see instructions)

		Yes	No
4	If this is not an explicit trust, check here and attach a statement describing the arrangement that makes its effect substantially similar to an explicit trust . . . . ▶ ☐		
5	Has any property been contributed to this trust since the last Form 706-GS(T) or (D-1) was filed? If "Yes," attach a schedule showing how the trust's inclusion ratio has been refigured		✓
6	Have any contributions been made to this trust since the last Form 706-GS(T) or (D-1) was filed that were not included in calculating the trust's inclusion ratio? If "Yes," attach a statement explaining why the contributions were not included		✓
7	Has any exemption been allocated to this trust by reason of the deemed allocation rules?		✓

Under penalties of perjury, I declare that I have examined this return, including accompanying schedules and statements, and to the best of my knowledge and belief, it is true, correct, and complete. Declaration of preparer other than trustee is based on all information of which preparer has any knowledge.

Signature of trustee ▶ ....   Date ▶ ....

Signature of preparer other than trustee ▶ ....   Date ▶ ....

Address ▶ 1419 Granger Ave., Elk Grove, IL 60007

For Paperwork Reduction Act Notice, see page 5 of the separate trustee's instructions.   Cat. No. 10328B   Form **706-GS(D-1)** (Rev. 10-2008)

¶3240

Form **706-GS(D-1)**		Notification of Distribution From a	OMB No. 1545-1143
(Rev. October 2008)		**Generation-Skipping Trust**	
Department of The Treasury Internal Revenue Service		Complete for each skip person distributee. See separate instructions. For calendar year ..2013.	**Copy B: For Distributee**

Part I   General Information

1a Skip person distributee's identifying number (see instructions) 123-40-6789	**2a** Trust's employer identification number (see instructions) 77 ┊ 6654321
1b Skip person distributee's name, address, and ZIP code Charles Smith 1310 South Harvey Avenue Oak Park, IL 60304	**2b** Trust's name, address, and ZIP code Able Smith GST Trust 100 South Lake Street Oak Park, IL 60302

Part II   Distributions

3   Describe each distribution below (see instructions).

a Item no.	b Description of property	c Date of distribution	d Inclusion ratio	e Value (see instructions)	f Tentative transfer (multiply col. e by col. d)
1	Cash distributions from corpus of Able Smith GST Trust	12/31/2013	0.551	100,000	55,100

Skip person distributee. To report this distribution, you must file Form 706-GS(D), Generation-Skipping Transfer Tax Return for Distributions, at the following address: Department of the Treasury, Internal Revenue Service Center, Cincinnati, OH 45999.

For Paperwork Reduction Act Notice, see page 5 of the separate trustee's instructions.   Form **706-GS(D-1)** (Rev. 10-2008)

¶ 3250   Filled-in Form 706-GS(T)

For purposes of the filled-in Form 706-GS(T), Generation-Skipping Transfer Tax Return for Terminations (November 2013), below, the following facts are assumed:

Frank Wood established the Frank Wood Trust on January 1, 2000, funded with $4 million. The trust was irrevocable, and the grantor retained no interest in or powers to alter or amend the trust. Frank's son, Sanford, was to receive the trust income for life, with THE trust remainder to go to Glenn (Frank's grandson) at Sanford's death. Upon Sanford's death on November 7, 2013, the trust corpus, then having a value of $7,735,950, was distributed to Glenn.

At the time that Frank Wood set up the trust, he filed a gift tax return (Form 709) upon which he properly and timely elected to apply the full amount of his then-available $1 million generation-skipping transfer (GST) tax exemption to the $4 million transferred into the trust. Although the amount of the GST exemption had increased to $5.25 million by 2013, Frank Wood elected not to allocate any of this additional $4.25 million to the Frank Wood Trust. Instead, this $4.25 million was allocated to other generation-skipping transfers (the tax returns for which are not reproduced). Accordingly, the inclusion ratio reported on Form 706-GS(T) is computed as:

$$1 - \frac{1,000,000}{4,000,000} = 1 - 1/4 = 3/4, \text{ or } .75$$

Form **706-GS(T)**	Generation-Skipping Transfer Tax Return For Terminations	

(Rev. November 2013)
▶ Use for terminations made after December 31, 2012.

Department of the Treasury
Internal Revenue Service

▶ For calendar year   2013   .

▶ Information about Form 706-GS(T) and its separate instructions is at *www.irs.gov/form706gst*.

OMB No. 1545-1145

Part I   General Information

1a Name of trust

Frank Wood Trust

1b Trust's employer identification number (see instructions)

58-4343434

2a Name of trustee

Aldridge State Bank

2b Trustee's address (number and street or P.O. box; apt. or suite no.; city, town or post office; state and ZIP code) If you have a foreign address, also complete the spaces below (see instructions).

1234 Ridgeview, Oak Park, IL 60304

Foreign country name	Foreign province/county	Foreign postal code

Part II   Trust Information (see the instructions)

		Yes	No	Sch. A number(s)
3	Has any exemption been allocated to this trust by reason of the deemed allocation rules of section 2632? If "Yes," describe the allocation on the line 7, Schedule A, attachment showing how the inclusion ratio was calculated		✓	
4	Has property been contributed to this trust since the last Form 706-GS(T) or 706-GS(D-1) was filed? If "Yes," attach a schedule showing how the inclusion ratio was calculated		✓	
5	Have any terminations occurred that are not reported on this return because of the exceptions in section 2611(b)(1) or (2) relating to medical and educational exclusions and prior payment of Generation-Skipping Transfer (GST) tax? If "Yes," attach a statement describing the termination .		✓	
6	Have any contributions been made to this trust that were not included in calculating the trust's inclusion ratio? If "Yes," attach a statement explaining why the contribution was not included . .		✓	
7	Has the special QTIP election in section 2652(a)(3) been made for this trust?		✓	
8	If this is not an explicit trust (see the instructions under *Who Must File*), check here and attach a statement describing the trust arrangement that makes its effect substantially similar to an explicit trust . . . . ▶ ☐			

Part III   Tax Computation

9a Summary of attached Schedules A (see instructions for line 9b)

Schedule A No.

GST tax
(from Sch. A, line 10)

1	. . . .	**9a1**	2,297,580
2	. . . .	**9a2**	
3	. . . .	**9a3**	
4	. . . .	**9a4**	
5	. . . .	**9a5**	
6	. . . .	**9a6**	
9b	Total from all additional Schedules A, in excess of six, attached to this form . . . . ▶	**9b**	
10	**Total** GST tax (add lines 9a1 through 9b)	**10**	2,297,580
11	Payment, if any, made with Form 7004	**11**	
12	**Tax due.** If line 10 is larger than line 11, enter the amount owed	**12**	2,297,580
13	**Overpayment.** If line 11 is larger than line 10, enter amount to be refunded	**13**	0

Sign Here

Under penalties of perjury, I declare that I have examined this return, including accompanying schedules and statements, and to the best of my knowledge and belief, it is true, correct, and complete. Declaration of preparer other than fiduciary is based on all information of which preparer has any knowledge.

▶ *Amy Wolcott*

Signature of fiduciary or officer representing fiduciary

Date 4/15/2014

Paid Preparer Use Only	Print/Type preparer's name	Preparer's signature	Date	Check ☐ if self-employed	PTIN
	Michael N. Clifton	*Michael N. Clifton*	4/15/2014		888654321
	Firm's name ▶ Clifton and Lee LLP			Firm's EIN ▶	78-9122345
	Firm's address ▶ 2143 Roselle Road, Schaumburg, IL 60195			Phone no.	847-551-2322

For Paperwork Reduction Act Notice, see separate instructions.   Cat. No. 10329M   Form **706-GS(T)** (Rev. 11-2013)

Form 706-GS(T) (Rev. 11-2013)

Page **2**

Name of trust	EIN of trust

Schedule A No.	**Note.** Make copies of this schedule before completing it if you will need more than one Schedule A.

Schedule A—Taxable Terminations
(See the instructions before completing this schedule.)

a Name of skip persons	b SSN or EIN of skip person	c Item no. from line 4 below in which interest held
1 Glenn Wood	321-45-9876	1

2 Describe the terminating power or interest. If you need more space, attach an additional sheet.

Glenn Wood has the sole remainder interest in the Frank Wood Trust, created on January 1, 2000, by Frank Wood, Glenn's grandfather. Upon the death of the income beneficiary (Sanford Wood, Glenn's father) on November 7, 2013, all trust assets ($7,735,950) were distributed to Glenn.

3 If you elect alternate valuation, check here (see the instructions) . . . . ▶ ☐

4 Describe each taxable termination below (see the instructions)

a Item no.	b Description of property subject to termination	c Date of termination	d Valuation date	e Value
1	Cash from Frank Wood Trust	11/7/2013	11/7/2013	7,735,950

Total . . . . ▶	**4**	7,735,950
5 Total deductions applicable to this Schedule A (from attached Schedule B, line 5)	**5**	77,350
6 Taxable amount (subtract line 5 from line 4)	**6**	7,658,600
7 Inclusion ratio (attach separate schedule showing computation)	**7**	.75
8 Maximum federal estate tax rate (see Table in the instructions)	**8**	40 %
9 Applicable rate (multiply line 7 by line 8)	**9**	30%
10 GST tax (multiply line 6 by line 9) (enter here and on page 1, Part III, line 9)	**10**	2,297,580

Schedule A (Form 706-GS(T)) (Rev. 11-2013)

Form 706-GS(T) (Rev. 11-2013)

Name of trust	Schedule A No. ▶ 1
	EIN of trust
Frank Wood Trust	58-4343434

Note. Make copies of this schedule before completing it if you will need more than one Schedule B.

Schedule B(1) — General Trust Debts, Expenses, and Taxes
(Section 2622(b)) (Enter only items related to the entire trust; see the instructions.)

a Item no.	b Description	c Amount
1	Trustee fee paid to Aldridge State Bank, Oak Park	77,350

1	Total of Schedule B(1)	1	77,350
2	Percentage allocated to corresponding Schedule A	2	100 %
3	Net deduction (multiply line 1 by line 2)	3	77,350

Schedule B(2) — Specific Termination-Related Debts, Expenses, and Taxes
(Section 2622(b)) (Enter only items related solely to terminations appearing on corresponding Schedule A; see the instructions.)

a Item no.	b Description	c Amount
1		

4	Total of Schedule B(2)	4	
5	**Total.** Add lines 3 and 4 (enter here and on line 5 of the corresponding Schedule A)	5	77,350

Schedules B(1) and B(2) (Form 706-GS(T)) (Rev. 11-2013)

¶ 3260   Filled-In Form 706-NA

The following filled-in Form 706-NA, United States Estate (and Generation-Skipping Transfer) Tax Return—Estate of nonresident not a citizen of the United States (Rev. August 2013), is based on the hypothetical fact situation of Rodney M. Lodge, a Canadian citizen. Lodge died in 2013 owning a U.S. gross estate of $2,211,774 and a gross estate outside the United States of $3,538,870. In accordance with the 1995 Protocol, which is one of several protocols amending the applicable treaty between the United States and Canada, Lodge is entitled to a unified credit amount of $786,842, computed as follows:

$$\frac{\$2,211,774}{5,750,644} \quad \begin{array}{l}\text{(Gross estate in United States)}\\\text{(Entire gross estate, wherever located)}\end{array}$$

= 0.38461327 × $2,045,800 (Applicable credit amount for U.S. citizens in 2013)

= $786,842

Form **706-NA**	United States Estate (and Generation-Skipping Transfer) Tax Return	OMB No. 1545-0531

(Rev. August 2013)
Department of the Treasury
Internal Revenue Service

Estate of nonresident not a citizen of the United States
To be filed for decedents dying after December 31, 2011.
► Information about Form 706-NA and its separate instructions is at *www.irs.gov/form706na*.

Attach supplemental documents and translations. Show amounts in U.S. dollars.

Part I — Decedent, Executor, and Attorney

1a Decedent's first (given) name and middle initial	b Decedent's last (family) name	2 U.S. taxpayer ID number (if any)
Rodney M.	Lodge	493-22-8876

3 Place of death	4 Domicile at time of death	5 Citizenship (nationality)	6 Date of death
Washington, DC, USA	Ontario, Canada	Canadian	2/4/2013

7a Date of birth	b Place of birth	8 Business or occupation
1/4/50	Ontario, Canada	Television Reporter

In United States

9a Name of executor: Martin Lodge
b Address: 44 West Elm Street, Albany, NY 12207

10a Name of attorney for estate: Michelle K. Murphy
b Address: 120 Ohio Ave., Washington, DC 20036

Outside United States

11a Name of executor: Phillip Lodge
b Address: 224 Foxmoor Dr., Ontario, Canada

12a Name of attorney for estate: Rutherford Harvey
b Address: 422 Covington Road, Ontario, Canada

Part II — Tax Computation

1	Taxable estate from Schedule B, line 9	1	2,160,474
2	Total taxable gifts of tangible or intangible property located in the U.S., transferred (directly or indirectly) by the decedent after December 31, 1976, and not included in the gross estate (see section 2511)	2	0
3	Total. Add lines 1 and 2	3	2,160,474
4	Tentative tax on the amount on line 3 (see instructions)	4	809,990
5	Tentative tax on the amount on line 2 (see instructions)	5	0
6	Gross estate tax. Subtract line 5 from line 4	6	809,990
7	Unified credit. Enter smaller of line 6 amount or maximum allowed (see instructions)	7	786,842
8	Balance. Subtract line 7 from line 6	8	23,148
9	Other credits (see instructions) — 9		
10	Credit for tax on prior transfers. Attach Schedule Q, Form 706 — 10		
11	Total. Add lines 9 and 10	11	0
12	Net estate tax. Subtract line 11 from line 8	12	23,148
13	Total generation-skipping transfer tax. Attach Schedule R, Form 706	13	0
14	**Total transfer taxes.** Add lines 12 and 13	14	23,148
15	Earlier payments. See instructions and attach explanation	15	0
16	Balance due. Subtract line 15 from line 14 (see instructions)	16	23,148

Under penalties of perjury, I declare that I have examined this return, including accompanying schedules and statements, and to the best of my knowledge and belief, it is true, correct, and complete. I understand that a complete return requires listing all property constituting the part of the decedent's gross estate (as defined by the statute) situated in the United States. Declaration of preparer other than the executor is based on all information of which preparer has any knowledge.

Sign Here
Signature of executor: *Martin Lodge* — Date 11/4/2013
Signature of executor: *Phillip Lodge* — Date 11/4/2013

Paid Preparer Use Only

Print/Type preparer's name	Preparer's signature	Date	Check ☐ if self-employed	PTIN
Michelle K. Murphy	*Michelle K. Murphy*	11/4/2013		135-79-1357

Firm's name ► Murphy and Lyons LLC — Firm's EIN ► 55-0246813
Firm's address ► 120 Ohio Ave., Washington DC 20036 — Phone no. 202-555-4252

For Privacy Act and Paperwork Reduction Act Notice, see the separate instructions.   Cat. No. 10145K   Form **706-NA** (Rev. 8-2013)

Form 706-NA (Rev. 8-2013)

| Part III | General Information | | | | | | | | | Page **2** |

		Yes	No				Yes	No
1a	Did the decedent die testate?	✓		**7**	Did the decedent make any transfer (of property that was located in the United States at either the time of the transfer or the time of death) described in sections 2035, 2036, 2037, or 2038 (see the instructions for Form 706, Schedule G)?			
b	Were letters testamentary or of administration granted for the estate?	✓						
	If granted to persons other than those filing the return, include names and addresses on page 1.							✓
					If "Yes," attach Schedule G, Form 706.			
2	Did the decedent, at the time of death, own any:			**8**	At the date of death, were there any trusts in existence that were created by the decedent and that included property located in the United States either when the trust was created or when the decedent died?			
a	Real property located in the United States?	✓						
b	U.S. corporate stock?	✓						
c	Debt obligations of (1) a U.S. person, or (2) the United States, a state or any political subdivision, or the District of Columbia?		✓					✓
d	Other property located in the United States?		✓		*If "Yes," attach Schedule G, Form 706.*			
3	Was the decedent engaged in business in the United States at the date of death?		✓	**9**	At the date of death, did the decedent:			
				a	Have a general power of appointment over any property located in the United States?			✓
4	At the date of death, did the decedent have access, personally or through an agent, to a safe deposit box located in the United States?		✓	**b**	Or, at any time, exercise or release the power?			✓
					If "Yes" to either a or b, attach Schedule H, Form 706.			
5	At the date of death, did the decedent own any property located in the United States as a joint tenant with right of survivorship; as a tenant by the entirety; or, with surviving spouse, as community property?		✓	**10a**	Have federal gift tax returns ever been filed?			✓
				b	Periods covered ▶			
	If "Yes," attach Schedule E, Form 706.			**c**	IRS offices where filed ▶			
6a	Had the decedent ever been a citizen or resident of the United States (see instructions)?		✓	**11**	Does the gross estate in the United States include any interests in property transferred to a "skip person" as defined in the instructions to Schedule R of Form 706?			
b	If "Yes," did the decedent lose U.S. citizenship or residency within 10 years of death? (see instructions)							✓
					If "Yes," attach Schedules R and/or R-1, Form 706.			

Schedule A. Gross Estate in the United States (see instructions)

Do you elect to value the decedent's gross estate at a date or dates after the decedent's death (as authorized by section 2032)? ▶

	Yes	No
		✓

*To make the election, you must check this box "Yes." If you check "Yes," complete **all** columns. If you check "No," complete columns (a), (b), and (e); you may leave columns (c) and (d) blank or you may use them to expand your column (b) description.*

(a) Item no.	(b) Description of property and securities For securities, give CUSIP number	(c) Alternate valuation date	(d) Alternate value in U.S. dollars	(e) Value at date of death in U.S. dollars
1	Condominium, 82 8th Street, Washington, DC			1,347,774
	9600 shares Power Co., Richmond, VA, common stock,			
	$90 per share on date of death. Traded on NYSE;			
	CUSIP No. 020202020			
				864,000

(If you need more space, attach additional sheets of same size.)

| **Total** | | | | | | 2,211,774 |

Schedule B. Taxable Estate

Caution. You must document lines 2 and 4 for the deduction on line 5 to be allowed.

1	Gross estate in the United States (Schedule A total)	1	2,211,774
2	Gross estate outside the United States (see instructions)	2	3,538,870
3	Entire gross estate wherever located. Add amounts on lines 1 and 2	3	5,750,644
4	Amount of funeral expenses, administration expenses, decedent's debts, mortgages and liens, and losses during administration. Attach itemized schedule. (see instructions)	4	26,539
5	Deduction for expenses, claims, etc. Divide line 1 by line 3 and multiply the result by line 4	5	10,207
6	Charitable deduction (attach Schedule O, Form 706) and marital deduction (attach Schedule M, Form 706, and computation)	6	8,500
7	State death tax deduction (see instructions)	7	32,593
8	Total deductions. Add lines 5, 6, and 7	8	51,300
9	Taxable estate. Subtract line 8 from line 1. Enter here and on line 1 of Part II	9	2,160,474

Form **706-NA** (Rev. 8-2013)

¶ 3270   Filled-In Form 706-QDT

The filled-in Form 706-QDT, U.S. Estate Tax Return for Qualified Domestic Trusts (Rev. August 2013), illustrates a taxable distribution made from a qualified domestic trust (See ¶ 1004 for a discussion of qualified domestic trusts.)

Corazon M. Costa, a nonresident alien, is the widow of Jose D. Costa, who died on July 18, 2003. The decedent left his entire estate to his surviving spouse, payable from a qualified domestic trust (QDOT). In September 2013, pursuant to her general power of appointment over the trust, Costa appointed to herself 500 shares of X Corporation stock. The stock was worth $64.50 per share, for a total value of $32,250. This withdrawal was not made as a result of a hardship situation.

Schedule A was left blank because this fact pattern only concerns a single QDOT. Form 706-QDT requires that the amounts entered on lines 10 and 11 be supported by attached computations. These computations are reproduced below:

Computation for Line 10:

Tentative tax on $1,110,918:	$391,276
Less: Unified credit	345,800
Less: State death tax credit	$19,749
Recomputed estate tax on amount on line 9 . . .	$25,727

Computation for Line 11:

Tentative tax on $1,078,668	$378,054
Less: Unified credit	345,800
Less: State death tax credit	$18,803
Recomputed estate tax on amount on line 8 . .	$13,451

Form **706-QDT**	**U.S. Estate Tax Return for**	
(Rev. August 2013)	**Qualified Domestic Trusts**	
Department of the Treasury Internal Revenue Service	Calendar Year ----------	OMB No. 1545-1212

▶ **Information about Form 706-QDT and its separate instructions is at *www.irs.gov/form706qdt*.**

Part I   General Information

1a Name of surviving spouse (see *Definitions* in the instructions)	1b TIN of surviving spouse
Corazon M. Costa	491-23-8463
2a Name of trustee/designated filer (see instructions)	2b SSN or EIN of trustee/designated filer
Toni L. Costa	484-26-1943

2c   Address of trustee/designated filer

1428 Forest View Drive, Northbrook, IL 60062

3a Surviving spouse's date of death (if applicable)		3b Surviving spouse's current marital status
		Widow
4a Name of decedent	4b SSN of decedent	4c Decedent's date of death
Jose Costa	480-29-1830	7/18/2003

Part II   Elections by the Trustee/Designated Filer (see instructions)

Please check the "Yes" or "No" box for each question.

		Yes	No
1	Do you elect alternate valuation?		✓
2	Do you elect special use valuation?		✓
	If "Yes," you must complete and attach Schedule A-1 of Form 706.		
3	Do you elect to pay the taxes in installments as described in section 6166?		✓
	If "Yes," you must attach the additional information described in the instructions.		
	Note. By electing section 6166, you may be required to provide security for estate tax deferred under section 6166 and interest in the form of a surety bond or a section 6324A lien.		
4	If the surviving spouse has become a U.S. citizen, does he or she elect under Code section 2056A(b)(12)(C) to treat all prior taxable distributions as taxable gifts and to treat any of the decedent's unified credit applied to the QDOT tax on those distributions as the surviving spouse's unified credit used under section 2505? (If not a U.S. citizen, enter "N/A")		

Part III   Tax Computation

1	Current taxable trust distributions (total from Part II of Schedule A)	1	32,250
2	Value of taxable trust property at date of death (if applicable) (total from Part III of Schedule A) .	2	
3	Add lines 1 and 2	3	32,250
4	Charitable and marital deductions. See Schedule B instructions (total from col. d, Part IV of Sch. A)	4	
5	Net tentative taxable amount. Subtract line 4 from line 3	5	32,250
6	Prior taxable events (total from Part I of Schedule A)	6	
7	Taxable estate of the decedent. See instructions	7	1,078,668
8	Add lines 6 and 7	8	1,078,668
9	Add lines 5 and 8	9	1,110,918
10	Recomputation of decedent's estate tax based on the amount on line 9. See instructions. Attach computation	10	25,727
11	Recomputation of decedent's estate tax based on the amount on line 8. See instructions. Attach computation	11	13,451
12	Net estate tax. Subtract line 11 from line 10	12	12,276
13	Payment made with request for extension, if any, and credit under section 2056A(b)(2)(B)(ii) . .	13	
14	**Tax due.** (If the amount on line 12 exceeds the amount on line 13, enter the difference here.) ▶	14	12,276
15	**Overpayment.** (If the amount on line 13 exceeds the amount on line 12, enter the difference here.)	15	0

Under penalties of perjury, I declare that I have examined this return, along with accompanying schedules and statements, and to the best of my knowledge and belief, it is true, correct, and complete. Declaration of preparer (other than trustee or designated filer) is based on all information of which preparer has any knowledge.

Sign Here	▶ *Tony L. Costa*		▶		4/15/2014
					Date

Paid Preparer's Use Only	Preparer's signature ▶	*Robert Ryan*	Date 4/15/2014	Check if self-employed ▶ ✓	Preparer's PTIN 234-89-0123
	Firm's name (or yours if self-employed), address, and ZIP code	Robert Ryan 2017 N. California Ave., Chicago, 60647		EIN ▶ 88-4152637	
				Phone no. 773-278-9792	

For Paperwork Reduction Act Notice, see the separate instructions for this form.   Cat. No. 12292E   Form **706-QDT** (Rev. 8-2013)

Form 706-QDT (Rev. 8-2013)   Page **2**

Schedule A	Complete Schedule A only if you are a designated filer filing this return for multiple trusts.

Part I   **Summary of Prior Taxable Distributions**

a Year	b Amount	c Year	d Amount
	$		$
	$		$
	$		$
	$		$
	$		$
	$		$
	$		$
	$		$

Total. Combine columns **b** and **d** . . . . ▶

Part II   **Summary of Current Taxable Distributions**

a EIN of QDOT	b Total Taxable Distributions for the Year	c EIN of QDOT	d Total Taxable Distributions for the Year
	$		$
	$		$
	$		$
	$		$
	$		$
	$		$
	$		$
	$		$

Total. Combine columns **b** and **d** . . . . ▶

Part III   **Summary of Property Remaining in QDOTs at Death of Surviving Spouse**

a EIN of QDOT	b Alternate Valuation Date (if applicable)	c Value	d EIN of QDOT	e Alternate Valuation Date (if applicable)	f Value
21-3683414		$ 32,250			$
		$			$
		$			$
		$			$
		$			$
		$			$
		$			$
		$			$

Total. Combine columns **c** and **f** . . . . ▶ | 32,250

Part IV   **Summary of Marital and Charitable Deductions**

a EIN of QDOT	b Total Marital Deduction	c Total Charitable Deduction	d Total Deductions (add cols. **b** and **c**)
	$	$	$
	$	$	$
	$	$	$
	$	$	$
	$	$	$
	$	$	$
	$	$	$
	$	$	$

Total . . . . ▶

Form **706-QDT** (Rev. 8-2013)

Form 706-QDT (Rev. 8-2013)

Page **3**

Schedule B	To be completed by trustee.

Part I General Information (see instructions)

1a Name of trust	1b EIN of trust
Jose D. Costa Trust	21-3683414
2a Name of trustee	2b SSN or EIN of trustee
Toni L. Costa (Trustee)	484-26-1943
2c Address of trustee	
1428 Forest View Drive, Northbrook, IL 60062	
3 Name of designated filer, if applicable	
Toni L. Costa	
4a Name of surviving spouse	4b TIN of surviving spouse
Corazon M. Costa	491-23-8463
4c Surviving spouse's date of death (if applicable)	4d Surviving spouse's current marital status (or at death, if applicable)
	Widow
5a Name of decedent	5b SSN of decedent	5c Decedent's date of death
Jose D. Costa	480-29-1830	7/18/2003

Part II Taxable Distributions From Prior Years

a Year	b Amount	c Year	d Amount
	$		$
	$		$
	$		$
	$		$
	$		$
	$		$
	$		$
	$		$
	$		$

Total. Combine columns **b** and **d** . . . . ▶

Part III Current Taxable Distributions

a Date of Distribution	b Description	c Value	d Amount of Hardship Exemption Claimed (see instructions)	e Net Transfer (col. c minus col. d)
9/15/2013	500 shares of X Corp., common stock (traded on NYSE), $64.50 per share. CUSIP No. 109438765.	32,250		32,250

Total . . . . ▶ | | | | 32,250

Form **706-QDT** (Rev. 8-2013)

Form 706-QDT (Rev. 8-2013)

Schedule B   To be completed by trustee. *(continued)*

Part IV   Taxable Property in Trust at Death of Surviving Spouse

a Item No.	b Description	c Alternate Valuation Date	d Value
1			
Total . . . . ▶			

Part V   Marital Deductions

a Item No.	b Description of Property Interests Passing to Spouse	c Value
1		
Total . . . . ▶		

Part VI   Charitable Deductions

a Item No.	b Description	c Name and Address of Beneficiary	d Character of Institution	e Amount
1				
Total . . . . ▶				

Form **706-QDT** (Rev. 8-2013)

¶ 3280   Filled-In Form 709

The filled-in Form 709, United States Gift Tax Return (2013), that follows illustrates the gift tax computations with respect to several transfers made by Robert A. Simon. Robert filed a Form 709 with respect to a taxable gift of $500,000 made to his sister in 1987. He made no further taxable gifts until 2013, when he gave $514,000 in cash to his daughter, Deborah Miller, and 20,000 shares of Wayne Corp. common stock to each of his two grandchildren, Dan Miller and Eve Miller. Robert's basis in the 40,000 shares transferred to his grandchildren was $1,242,000. On the date of the gift, the Wayne Corp. stock (which was publicly traded on the New York Stock Exchange) had a value of $150.70 per share.

The Worksheet for Form 709 Schedule B, Column C (reproduced from page 13 of the Instructions), and the Table of Unified Credits (as recalculated for 2013 Rates) (reproduced from page 15 of the Instructions), are included at the end of the filled-in Form 709, even though they would not be used for computing the gift tax liability of Robert A. Simon for 2013.

Form **709**	United States Gift (and Generation-Skipping Transfer) Tax Return	OMB No. 1545-0020
Department of the Treasury Internal Revenue Service	▶ Information about Form 709 and its separate instructions is at *www.irs.gov/form709.* (For gifts made during calendar year 2013) ▶ See instructions.	20**13**

Part 1—General Information

1 Donor's first name and middle initial Robert A.	2 Donor's last name Simon	3 Donor's social security number 362-54-7878		
4 Address (number, street, and apartment number) 4700 S. Michigan Ave.		5 Legal residence (domicile) Cook County, IL		
6 City or town, state or province, country, and ZIP or foreign postal code Chicago, IL 60615		7 Citizenship (see instructions) United States		

			Yes	No
8	If the donor died during the year, check here ▶ ☐ and enter date of death _____ , _____			
9	If you extended the time to file this Form 709, check here ▶ ☐			
10	Enter the total number of donees listed on Schedule A. Count each person only once. ▶ 3			
11a	Have you (the donor) previously filed a Form 709 (or 709-A) for any other year? If "No," skip line 11b		✓	
b	Has your address changed since you last filed Form 709 (or 709-A)?			✓
12	**Gifts by husband or wife to third parties.** Do you consent to have the gifts (including generation-skipping transfers) made by you and by your spouse to third parties during the calendar year considered as made one-half by each of you? (see instructions.) (If the answer is "Yes," the following information must be furnished and your spouse must sign the consent shown below. **If the answer is "No," skip lines 13–18.**)			✓
13	Name of consenting spouse **14** SSN			
15	Were you married to one another during the entire calendar year? (see instructions)			
16	If 15 is "No," check whether ☐ married ☐ divorced or ☐ widowed/deceased, and give date (see instructions) ▶			
17	Will a gift tax return for this year be filed by your spouse? (If "Yes," mail both returns in the same envelope.)			
18	**Consent of Spouse.** I consent to have the gifts (and generation-skipping transfers) made by me and by my spouse to third parties during the calendar year considered as made one-half by each of us. We are both aware of the joint and several liability for tax created by the execution of this consent.			

Consenting spouse's signature ▶   Date ▶

Part 2—Tax Computation

					Yes	No
19	Have you applied a DSUE amount received from a predeceased spouse to a gift or gifts reported on this or a previous Form 709? If "Yes," complete Schedule C					✓
1	Enter the amount from Schedule A, Part 4, line 11	1	6,800,000			
2	Enter the amount from Schedule B, line 3	2	500,000			
3	Total taxable gifts. Add lines 1 and 2	3	7,300,000			
4	Tax computed on amount on line 3 (see *Table for Computing Gift Tax* in instructions)	4	2,865,800			
5	Tax computed on amount on line 2 (see *Table for Computing Gift Tax* in instructions)	5	155,800			
6	Balance. Subtract line 5 from line 4	6	2,710,000			
7	Applicable credit amount. If donor has DSUE amount from predeceased spouse(s), enter amount from Schedule C, line 4; otherwise, see instructions	7	2,045,800			
8	Enter the applicable credit against tax allowable for all prior periods (from Sch. B, line 1, col. C)	8	155,800			
9	Balance. Subtract line 8 from line 7. Do not enter less than zero	9	1,890,000			
10	Enter 20% (.20) of the amount allowed as a specific exemption for gifts made after September 8, 1976, and before January 1, 1977 (see instructions)	10				
11	Balance. Subtract line 10 from line 9. Do not enter less than zero	11	1,890,000			
12	Applicable credit. Enter the smaller of line 6 or line 11	12	1,890,000			
13	Credit for foreign gift taxes (see instructions)	13				
14	Total credits. Add lines 12 and 13	14	1,890,000			
15	Balance. Subtract line 14 from line 6. Do not enter less than zero	15	820,000			
16	Generation-skipping transfer taxes (from Schedule D, Part 3, col. H, Total)	16	300,000			
17	Total tax. Add lines 15 and 16	17	1,120,000			
18	Gift and generation-skipping transfer taxes prepaid with extension of time to file	18				
19	If line 18 is less than line 17, enter **balance due** (see instructions)	19	1,120,000			
20	If line 18 is greater than line 17, enter **amount to be refunded**	20				

Sign Here

Under penalties of perjury, I declare that I have examined this return, including any accompanying schedules and statements, and to the best of my knowledge and belief, it is true, correct, and complete. Declaration of preparer (other than donor) is based on all information of which preparer has any knowledge.

May the IRS discuss this return with the preparer shown below (see instructions)? ☑ Yes ☐ No

▶ *Robert A. Simon*   4/15/2014
Signature of donor   Date

Paid Preparer Use Only	Print/Type preparer's name Wayne Farwell	Preparer's signature *Wayne Farwell*	Date 4/15/2014	Check ☐ if self-employed	PTIN 765-55-4321
	Firm's name ▶ Bracken & Farwell, LLC			Firm's EIN ▶	22-9876543
	Firm's address ▶ 2805 N. Sheridan Rd., Chicago, IL 60657			Phone no.	773-424-2424

Attach check or money order here.

For Disclosure, Privacy Act, and Paperwork Reduction Act Notice, see the instructions for this form.   Cat. No. 16783M   Form **709** (2013)

Form 709 (2013)

Page **2**

SCHEDULE A	Computation of Taxable Gifts (Including transfers in trust) (see instructions)

A   Does the value of any item listed on Schedule A reflect any valuation discount? If "Yes," attach explanation . . . . Yes ☐   No ☑

B   ☐ ◄ Check here if you elect under section 529(c)(2)(B) to treat any transfers made this year to a qualified tuition program as made ratably over a 5-year period beginning this year. See instructions. Attach explanation.

Part 1—Gifts Subject Only to Gift Tax. Gifts less political organization, medical, and educational exclusions. (see instructions)

A Item number	B • Donee's name and address • Relationship to donor (if any) • Description of gift • If the gift was of securities, give CUSIP no. • If closely held entity, give EIN	C	D Donor's adjusted basis of gift	E Date of gift	F Value at date of gift	G For split gifts, enter 1/2 of column F	H Net transfer (subtract col. G from col. F)
1	Cash to daughter, Deborah Miller 2566 N. Sacramento Ave. Chicago, IL 60647		514,000	3/15/13	514,000		514,000

Gifts made by spouse —complete **only** if you are splitting gifts with your spouse and he/she also made gifts.

Total of Part 1. Add amounts from Part 1, column H . . . . ► | 514,000

Part 2—Direct Skips. Gifts that are direct skips and are subject to both gift tax and generation-skipping transfer tax. You must list the gifts in chronological order.

A Item number	B • Donee's name and address • Relationship to donor (if any) • Description of gift • If the gift was of securities, give CUSIP no. • If closely held entity, give EIN	C 2632(b) election out	D Donor's adjusted basis of gift	E Date of gift	F Value at date of gift	G For split gifts, enter 1/2 of column F	H Net transfer (subtract col. G from col. F)
1	20,000 shs. Wayne Corp. stock, CUSIP #009000AA to grandson, Dan Miller, 18 W. Ash St., Erie, PA		621,000	3/15/13	3,014,000		3,014,000
2	20,000 shs. Wayne Corp. stock, CUSIP #009000AA to granddaughter, Eve Miller, 32 E. Oak Ln., Dallas, TX		621,000	3/15/15	3,014,000		3,014,000

Gifts made by spouse —complete **only** if you are splitting gifts with your spouse and he/she also made gifts.

Total of Part 2. Add amounts from Part 2, column H . . . . ► | 6,028,000

Part 3—Indirect Skips. Gifts to trusts that are currently subject to gift tax and may later be subject to generation-skipping transfer tax. You must list these gifts in chronological order.

A Item number	B • Donee's name and address • Relationship to donor (if any) • Description of gift • If the gift was of securities, give CUSIP no. • If closely held entity, give EIN	C 2632(c) election	D Donor's adjusted basis of gift	E Date of gift	F Value at date of gift	G For split gifts, enter 1/2 of column F	H Net transfer (subtract col. G from col. F)
1							

Gifts made by spouse —complete **only** if you are splitting gifts with your spouse and he/she also made gifts.

Total of Part 3. Add amounts from Part 3, column H . . . . ► |

(If more space is needed, attach additional statements.)

Form **709** (2013)

Part 4—Taxable Gift Reconciliation

1	Total value of gifts of donor. Add totals from column H of Parts 1, 2, and 3	1	6,542,000
2	Total annual exclusions for gifts listed on line 1 (see instructions)	2	42,000
3	Total included amount of gifts. Subtract line 2 from line 1	3	6,500,000

Deductions (see instructions)

4	Gifts of interests to spouse for which a marital deduction will be claimed, based on item numbers _____ of Schedule A . .	4			
5	Exclusions attributable to gifts on line 4	5			
6	Marital deduction. Subtract line 5 from line 4	6			
7	Charitable deduction, based on item nos. _____ less exclusions	7			
8	Total deductions. Add lines 6 and 7			8	0
9	Subtract line 8 from line 3			9	6,500,000
10	Generation-skipping transfer taxes payable with this Form 709 (from Schedule D, Part 3, col. H, Total) . .			10	300,000
11	**Taxable gifts.** Add lines 9 and 10. Enter here and on page 1, Part 2—Tax Computation, line 1			11	6,800,000

Terminable Interest (QTIP) Marital Deduction. (see instructions for Schedule A, Part 4, line 4)

If a trust (or other property) meets the requirements of qualified terminable interest property under section 2523(f), and:

   a. The trust (or other property) is listed on Schedule A, and

   b. The value of the trust (or other property) is entered in whole or in part as a deduction on Schedule A, Part 4, line 4,

then the donor shall be deemed to have made an election to have such trust (or other property) treated as qualified terminable interest property under section 2523(f).

If less than the entire value of the trust (or other property) that the donor has included in Parts 1 and 3 of Schedule A is entered as a deduction on line 4, the donor shall be considered to have made an election only as to a fraction of the trust (or other property). The numerator of this fraction is equal to the amount of the trust (or other property) deducted on Schedule A, Part 4, line 6. The denominator is equal to the total value of the trust (or other property) listed in Parts 1 and 3 of Schedule A.

If you make the QTIP election, the terminable interest property involved will be included in your spouse's gross estate upon his or her death (section 2044). See instructions for line 4 of Schedule A. If your spouse disposes (by gift or otherwise) of all or part of the qualifying life income interest, he or she will be considered to have made a transfer of the entire property that is subject to the gift tax. See *Transfer of Certain Life Estates Received From Spouse* in the instructions.

12 Election Out of QTIP Treatment of Annuities

  ☐ ◀Check here if you elect under section 2523(f)(6) **not** to treat as qualified terminable interest property any joint and survivor annuities that are reported on Schedule A and would otherwise be treated as qualified terminable interest property under section 2523(f). See instructions. Enter the item numbers from Schedule A for the annuities for which you are making this election ▶ _____

SCHEDULE B   Gifts From Prior Periods

If you answered "Yes," on line 11a of page 1, Part 1, see the instructions for completing Schedule B. If you answered "No," skip to the Tax Computation on page 1 (or Schedules C or D, if applicable). Complete Schedule A before beginning Schedule B. See instructions for recalculation of the column C amounts. Attach calculations.

A Calendar year or calendar quarter (see instructions)	B Internal Revenue office where prior return was filed	C Amount of applicable credit (unified credit) against gift tax for periods after December 31, 1976	D Amount of specific exemption for prior periods ending before January 1, 1977	E Amount of taxable gifts
1987	IRS Service Center, Kansas City, MO	155,800		500,000

1	Totals for prior periods	1	155,800		500,000
2	Amount, if any, by which total specific exemption, line 1, column D is more than $30,000			2	
3	Total amount of taxable gifts for prior periods. Add amount on line 1, column E and amount, if any, on line 2. Enter here and on page 1, Part 2—Tax Computation, line 2			3	500,000

(If more space is needed, attach additional statements.)

Form **709** (2013)

Form 709 (2013)

Page **4**

SCHEDULE C — Deceased Spousal Unused Exclusion (DSUE) Amount

Provide the following information to determine the DSUE amount and applicable credit received from prior spouses. Complete Schedule A before beginning Schedule C.

A Name of Deceased Spouse (dates of death after December 31, 2010 only)	B Date of Death	C Portability Election Made?		D If "Yes," DSUE Amount Received from Spouse	E DSUE Amount Applied by Donor to Lifetime Gifts (list current and prior gifts)	F Date of Gift(s) (enter as mm/dd/yy for Part 1 and as yyyy for Part 2)
		Yes	No			
Part 1—DSUE RECEIVED FROM LAST DECEASED SPOUSE						
Part 2—DSUE RECEIVED FROM PREDECEASED SPOUSE(S)						
TOTAL (for all DSUE amounts applied for Part 1 and Part 2)						

1	Donor's basic exclusion amount (see instructions)	**1**
2	Total from column E, Parts 1 and 2	**2**
3	Add lines 1 and 2	**3**
4	Applicable credit on amount in line 4 (See *Table for Computing Gift Tax* in the instructions). Enter here and on line 7, Part 2—Tax Computation	**4**

SCHEDULE D — Computation of Generation-Skipping Transfer Tax

Note. Inter vivos direct skips that are completely excluded by the GST exemption must still be fully reported (including value and exemptions claimed) on Schedule D.

Part 1—Generation-Skipping Transfers

A Item No. (from Schedule A, Part 2, col. A)	B Value (from Schedule A, Part 2, col. H)	C Nontaxable Portion of Transfer	D Net Transfer (subtract col. C from col. B)
1	3,014,000	14,000	3,000,000
2	3,014,000	14,000	3,000,000
Gifts made by spouse (for gift splitting only)			

(If more space is needed, attach additional statements.)

Form **709** (2013)

Part 2—GST Exemption Reconciliation (Section 2631) and Section 2652(a)(3) Election

Check here ▶ ☐ if you are making a section 2652(a)(3) (special QTIP) election (see instructions)

Enter the item numbers from Schedule A of the gifts for which you are making this election ▶ _____

1	Maximum allowable exemption (see instructions)	1	5,250,000
2	Total exemption used for periods before filing this return	2	
3	Exemption available for this return. Subtract line 2 from line 1	3	5,250,000
4	Exemption claimed on this return from Part 3, column C total, below	4	5,250,000
5	Automatic allocation of exemption to transfers reported on Schedule A, Part 3 (see instructions)	5	
6	Exemption allocated to transfers not shown on line 4 or 5, above. **You must attach a "Notice of Allocation."** (see instructions)	6	
7	Add lines 4, 5, and 6	7	5,250,000
8	Exemption available for future transfers. Subtract line 7 from line 3	8	0

Part 3—Tax Computation

A Item No. (from Schedule D, Part 1)	B Net Transfer (from Schedule D, Part 1, col. D)	C GST Exemption Allocated	D Divide col. C by col. B	E Inclusion Ratio (Subtract col. D from 1.000)	F Maximum Estate Tax Rate	G Applicable Rate (multiply col. E by col. F)	H Generation-Skipping Transfer Tax (multiply col. B by col. G)
1	3,000,000	2,625,000	.875	.125	40% (.40)	.05	150,000
2	3,000,000	2,625,000	.875	.125	40% (.40)	.05	150,000
					40% (.40)		
					40% (.40)		
					40% (.40)		
					40% (.40)		
Gifts made by spouse (for gift splitting only)							
					40% (.40)		
					40% (.40)		
					40% (.40)		
					40% (.40)		
					40% (.40)		

Total exemption claimed. Enter here and on Part 2, line 4, above. May not exceed Part 2, line 3, above 5,250,000	**Total generation-skipping transfer tax.** Enter here; on page 3, Schedule A, Part 4, line 10; and on page 1, Part 2—Tax Computation, line 16	300,000

(If more space is needed, attach additional statements.)   Form **709** (2013)

¶ 3290 Table of Basic Exclusion and Credit Amounts and Credit Allowable for Prior Periods Worksheet

Table of Basic Exclusion and Credit Amounts (as Recalculated for 2013 Rates)

Period	Exclusion Amounts	Credit Amounts
1977 (Quarters 1 & 2)	$30,000	$6,000
1977 (Quarters 3 & 4)	$120,667	$30,000
1978	$134,000	$34,000
1979	$147,333	$38,000
1980	$161,563	$42,500
1981	$175,625	$47,000
1982	$225,000	$62,800
1983	$275,000	$79,300
1984	$325,000	$96,300
1985	$400,000	$121,800
1986	$500,000	$155,800
1987 through 1997	$600,000	$192,800
1998	$625,000	$202,050
1999	$650,000	$211,300
2000 and 2001	$675,000	$220,550
2002 through 2010	$1,000,000	$345,800
2011	$5,000,000	$1,945,800
2012	$5,120,000	$1,993,800
2013	$5,250,000	$2,045,800

Worksheet for Schedule B, Column C (Credit Allowable for Prior Periods).

Prior Years Credit Recalculation (for Form 709 Schedule B, Column C) (Keep for your records.)

A	B	C	D	E	F	G	H	I	J	K	L	M	N
Period	Taxable Gifts for Current Period	Taxable Gifts for Prior Periods[1]	Cumulative Taxable Gifts Including Current Period (Col. B + Col. C)	Tax on Gifts for Prior Periods (Col. C)[2] [3]	Tax on Cumulative Gifts Including Current Period (Col. D)[3]	Tax on Gifts for Current Period (Col. F - Col. E)	DSUE from Predeceased Spouse	Basic Exclusion for Year of Gift[4]	Applicable Exclusion Amount (Col. H + Col. I)	Applicable Credit Amount based on Column J[3, 5]	Applicable Credit Amount Used in Prior Periods[3, 6]	Available Credit in Current Period (Col. K - Col. L)	Credit Allowable (lesser of Col. G or Col. M)
Pre-1977													
YYYY													
YYYY													
YYYY													

Total Applicable Credit Used in Prior Periods (Enter the Total of Column N on line 8, Part 2—Tax Computation):

1. Column C: Enter amount from column D of the *previous* row.
2. Column E: Compute the tax on the amount in Column C or enter amount from column F of the *previous* row.
3. To compute tax or credit amount, see *Table for Computing Gift Tax*, later.
4. For years prior to 2010, the basic exclusion amount equals the applicable exclusion amount.
5. For each row in Column K, subtract 20 percent of any amount allowed as a specific exemption for gifts made after September 8, 1976, and before January 1, 1977.
6. Enter the total of Columns L and N of the *previous* row.

¶ 4000
CODE FINDING LIST

This table lists the Internal Revenue Code Sections that are cited as authority in the *2014 U.S. Master™ Estate and Gift Tax Guide*.

The citations appear at the paragraphs indicated.

Code Sec.	Par. (¶)	Code Sec.	Par. (¶)
61	2109	671	477, 570, 2011, 2565
79	460		
112(c)	1550	672	477, 570, 2011, 2565
163(d)	2161		
163(h)	1165	673	477, 570, 2011, 2565
164(a)	2431		
165(h)(3)(C)	1650	674	477, 570, 2011, 2565
170	1105		
170(c)	1105, 1121	675	477, 570, 2011, 2565
170(f)	1120, 1121		
170(h)	253, 1175	676	477, 570, 2011, 2565
213(c)	813		
213(d)	2250	677	477, 570, 2011, 2565
219	770		
267	2590	678	2011
267(c)	1672	679	2011
280A(d)	2570	691	797
303	555, 1165, 1672, 2610	691(c)	737
		692(c)	1550, 1650
318	570	692(d)	1650
368(a)	326	707(c)	2510
421	2112	721(b)	2545
444	2610	861(a)	1620
469	292	864(c)	1620
472	2610	954(c)	1160
507	2305	1014	121, 2545, 2465
508(e)	2305	1014(a)	296, 2465
527(e)	2160	1014(e)	121
529(b)	2250	1014(f)	121
529(c)	2052, 2250, 2431, 2610	1014(g)	2465
		1015(d)	2465
543(a)	1160	1016(c)	296
642(c)	1705, 2305, 2439	1022	121, 2465
		1022(b)	121
642(g)	780, 797, 2451	1022(c)	121
643(g)	2610	1031	286
664	1123, 1705, 2305, 2439	1033	286
		1040(a)	285
664(d)	1122, 1124, 2455	1040(c)	296
		1223(12)	285
664(f)	1124	1274(d)	2161, 2565
664(g)	1122	1504	1672
		1504(b)	1672

Code Sec.	Par. (¶)
2001	11,15, 820, 2005, 2007, 2459, 3210
2001(a)	28
2001(b)	12, 15, 29, 36, 1550
2001(c)	10, 11, 16, 20, 35, 1430, 2378, 2459, 2600
2001(d)	1426
2001(e)	1426
2001(f)	1426, 2355
2010	15, 29
2010(b)	15
2010(c)	15, 16, 22, 2007, 2376, 2455, 2600
2011	2457, 2610
2011(c)	2610
2011(d)	2640
2012	1382, 2600
2012(e)	1384
2013	1300
2013(c)	1320, 1335
2013(d)	1335
2013(f)	1340
2014	1401, 1405
2014(e)	2610
2014(g)	1401
2014(h)	1402
2015	1401
2016	1401, 2610
2031	1002
2031(b)	325
2031(c)	253, 2610
2032	105, 107, 605, 2453
2032(a)	107
2032(c)	105
2032(d)	105, 2610
2032A	50, 66, 73, 80, 109, 253, 285, 289, 292, 1170
2032A(a)	280, 281
2032A(b)	281, 284, 291, 292, 293
2032A(c)	284, 288, 290, 2610
2032A(d)	289, 2610
2032A(e)	253, 282, 283, 285, 288, 290, 292, 293, 295
2032A(f)	284

Code Sec.	Par. (¶)
2032A(g)	294
2032A(h)	286
2032A(i)	286
2033	150, 155, 156, 250, 262, 310, 326, 350, 400, 410, 435, 500, 525, 526, 700, 725, 733, 1002, 2545
2033A	1150
2034	175
2035	403, 430, 477, 535, 555, 595, 610, 655, 1015, 1067, 1426, 1617, 2117, 2455
2035(a)	555
2035(b)	555
2035(c)	555
2035(d)	281, 750, 1145
2035(e)	555, 595
2036	535, 555, 570, 580, 585, 605, 610, 655, 733, 1067, 1382, 1617
2036(a)	570, 2550
2036(b)	570
2036(c)	326, 570
2037	535, 555, 565, 610, 655, 733, 1067, 1382, 1617
2038	326, 535, 555, 585, 590, 605, 610, 655, 700, 733, 1067, 1382, 1617
2039	415, 420, 535, 715, 720, 725, 733, 1002
2039(a)	700
2039(c)	730, 735, 739
2039(e)	737
2039(f)	73, 739
2040	2009
2040(b)	502
2041	555, 610, 650, 652, 655, 725, 1115, 1315
2041(a)	655, 665
2041(b)	655, 2441

Index

References are to (¶) numbers.

TRA